D0607010

HOUSTON PUBLIC LIBRARY

Gift of
Foley's

ANNALS OF COMMUNISM

Each volume in the series Annals of Communism will publish selected and previously inaccessible documents from former Soviet state and party archives in a narrative that develops a particular topic in the history of Soviet and international communism. Separate English and Russian editions will be prepared. Russian and American scholars work together to prepare the documents for each volume. Documents are chosen not for their support of any single interpretation but for their particular historical importance or their general value in deepening understanding and facilitating discussion. The volumes are designed to be useful to students, scholars, and interested general readers.

EXECUTIVE EDITOR OF THE ANNALS OF COMMUNISM SERIES
Jonathan Brent, Yale University Press

ADMINISTRATOR
Vadim A. Staklo

AMERICAN EDITORIAL COMMITTEE

Ivo Banac, Yale University
Jeffrey Burds, Northeastern University, Boston
William Chase, University of Pittsburgh
Victor Erlich, Yale University
F. I. Firsov, former head of the Comintern research group at RGASPI
Sheila Fitzpatrick, University of Chicago
Gregory Freeze, Brandeis University
John L. Gaddis, Yale University
J. Arch Getty, University of California, Los Angeles
Jonathan Haslam, Cambridge University

Robert L. Jackson, Yale University
Czeslaw Milosz, University of California, Berkeley
Norman Naimark, Stanford University
Gen. William Odom, Hudson Institute and Yale University
Daniel Orlovsky, Southern Methodist University
Mark Steinberg, University of Illinois, Urbana-Champaign
Mark Von Hagen, Columbia University
Piotr Wandycz, Yale University

RUSSIAN EDITORIAL COMMITTEE

K. M. Anderson, director, Russian State Archive of Social and Political History (RGASPI)
N. N. Bolkhovitinov, Russian Academy of Sciences
A. O. Chubaryan, Russian Academy of Sciences
V. P. Danilov, Russian Academy of Sciences
A. A. Fursenko, secretary, Department of History, Russian Academy of Sciences (head of the Russian Editorial Committee)

V. P. Kozlov, director, Rosarkhiv
N. S. Lebedeva, Russian Academy of Sciences
S. V. Mironenko, director, State Archive of the Russian Federation (GARF)
O. V. Naumov, assistant director, RGASPI
E. O. Pivovar, Moscow State University
V. V. Shelokhaev, president, Association ROSSPEN
Ye. A. Tyurina, director, Russian State Archive of the Economy (RGAE)

SERIES COORDINATOR, MOSCOW
N. P. Yakovlev

Enemies Within the Gates?

The Comintern and the Stalinist Repression, 1934–1939

William J. Chase

Russian documents translated by Vadim A. Staklo

Yale University Press

New Haven and London

HOUSTON PUBLIC LIBRARY

R01259 86828

IN MEMORIAM

Nikolai Petrovich Yakovlev

1948-2001

This volume has been prepared with the cooperation of the Russian State Archive of Social and Political History (RGASPI) of the State Archival Service of Russia in the framework of an agreement concluded between RGASPI and Yale University Press.

Published with assistance from the foundation established in memory of Philip Hamilton McMillan of the Class of 1894, Yale College.

Copyright © 2001 by Yale University.
All rights reserved.

The documents and photographs held by RGASPI are used by permission. The two photographs not held by RGASPI, of the Comintern leaders and of Dimitrov with a pipe, are from a private collection and are also used by permission.

This book may not be reproduced, in whole or in part, including illustrations, in any form (beyond that copying permitted by Sections 107 and 108 of the U.S. Copyright Law and except by reviewers for the public press), without written permission from the publishers.

Designed by James J. Johnson and set in Sabon Roman types by The Composing Room of Michigan, Inc., Grand Rapids, Michigan. Printed in the United States of America by Vail-Ballou Press, Binghamton, New York.

Library of Congress Cataloging-in-Publication Data

Chase, William J., 1947–
    Enemies within the gates? : the Comintern and the Stalinist repression, 1934–1939 / William J. Chase ; Russian documents translated by Vadim A. Staklo.
        p.   cm. — (Annals of Communism)
    Includes bibliographical references and index.
    ISBN 0-300-08242-8
    1. Communist International—History.
    2. Soviet Union—Politics and government—1936–1953.   3. Political persecution—Soviet Union—History.   I. Title.   II. Series.
    HX11.I5 C484   2002
    947.084′2—dc21   2001039023

A catalogue record for this book is available from the British Library.

The paper in this book meets the guidelines for permanence and durability of the Committee on Production Guidelines for Book Longevity of the Council on Library Resources.

10   9   8   7   6   5   4   3   2   1

Yale University Press gratefully acknowledges the financial support given for this publication by the John M. Olin Foundation, the Lynde and Harry Bradley Foundation, Lloyd H. Smith, the William H. Donner Foundation, Joseph W. Donner, the David Woods Kemper Memorial Foundation, the Daphne Seybolt Culpeper Foundation, and the Milton V. Brown Foundation.

For
Matthew, Alex, and Donna
May they be spared the self-righteous

Contents

Illustrations follow page 216

Acknowledgments

This volume would not have been possible without the assistance, advice, and suggestions of many people. Much of the initial collection of documents in RGASPI and the compilation of biographical materials was performed by the following very dedicated scholars and researchers: Dr. Fridrikh I. Firsov, Dr. Mansur M. Mukhamedzharov, Dr. Elena A. Nechaeva, and Dr. Mikhail M. Panteleev. They worked diligently and professionally despite the hardships that defined their daily and working lives, and were extremely helpful in many ways. Mere acknowledgment does not adequately convey the depth of my gratitude. Special thanks go to Mikhail Panteleev, whose research support and insights have enriched my understanding of Comintern affairs, and to Vadim Staklo, whose superb translations and cogent advice greatly enhance this volume. Other friends and colleagues—Nikolai P. Yakovlev, Andrei K. Sokolov, Alexei Ovsiannikov, Lena Waintraub—helped me in innumerable ways during my stays in Moscow. I owe them a special thanks. Many colleagues— Jeffrey Burds, Fridrikh I. Firsov, Arch Getty, Jonathan Harris, Evelyn Rawski, Gábor Rittersporn, Blair Ruble, Carmine Storella, Bob Supansic, and Lynne Viola, as well as the anonymous readers for the Press—have read the manuscript in one of its forms and have offered valuable criticisms and suggestions, for which I am extremely grateful.

This volume has benefited most of all from the knowledge, comments, and advice of Fridrikh I. Firsov. His counsel and comments, his sharing of his published and unpublished works and of documents in his possession, and his insights have greatly enhanced my understanding of the Comintern during this period. In the notes I acknowledge specific contributions that he has made, but such acknowledgments cannot convey the full measure of his influence and impact on me and this volume. To him I owe a special and profound debt of gratitude. Of course, I am responsible for any mistakes and other problems that may afflict this volume.

Acknowledgments usually have a celebratory tone. Sadly, this is not always the case. In May 2001, Nikolai Petrovich Yakovlev died unexpectedly. Not only did Petrovich provide me with considerable help, he was also a dear friend. He was a wise and gentle man and a bit of a rascal. In his capacity as coordinator for the Annals of Communism series as well as for the Russian Archive Series and other projects he has enabled many scholars to pursue successful careers. Thank you, Petrovich, for your friendship and labors. We will miss you.

Finally, my wife, Donna, and our sons, Matthew and Alex, tolerated my long absences while researching this work and my presence while writing it. For their patience and support, I dedicate this book to them.

A Note on the Documents

This book has two integrated elements: (1) translations of original documents that illuminate the dynamics and consequences of the repression within the Comintern and (2) a narrative text that provides the political and historical contexts for the documents and an analytical framework for interpreting them. The book is therefore neither a traditional monograph nor a traditional document collection, but a combination of both. The documents come from the Comintern collection in the Russian State Archive of Social and Political History (Rossiiskii gosudarstvennyi arkhiv sotsialnoi i politicheskoi issledovanii, RGASPI). Commonly known throughout most of its history as the Central Party Archive, from 1992 to mid-1999 it was the Russian Center for the Preservation and Study of Documents of Contemporary History (Rossiiskii gosudarstvennyi arkhiv sotsialnoi i politicheskoi issledovanii, RTsKhIDNI). The Comintern collection there is massive. For a survey of the Comintern holdings in this archive, see J. Arch Getty and V. P. Kozlov, *Kratkii putevoditel fondov i kollektsii, sobrannye Tsentral'nym partiinyi arkhivom* (Moscow, 1993), 70–103. In selecting the documents presented here, every effort was made to strike a balance between those that illuminate the Comintern's roles as agent, instrument, and victim of repression and those that convey the administrative, political, and cognitive processes that helped to set the stage for and drive the repression. Of necessity, many intriguing documents were excluded. Many of those selected are reproduced here in full; where excerpts of very long documents are used, every effort has been made to preserve the essential elements. The selection of documents for this volume occurred over four years, from 1992 to 1996. During this time, many files that had been open in 1992 were reclassified. In August 1996, RTsKhIDNI (now RGASPI) closed a considerable portion of the Comintern collection to the public.

Most of this book is organized chronologically so that readers can appreciate not only the way the repression unfolded but also the synergy and dialectical relationships of the Comintern's multiple roles. Chapter 1 presents a survey of aspects of the Comintern's history and a discussion of its bureaucratic structure, the relationships among its many sections, and its relationships to the Communist Party and the security organs. Chapters 2–6 conform to notable political subperiods of the years 1934–1939. Chapter 7 consists of case studies of selected victims of the repression. The case studies are of two different groups: people who worked in the Comintern apparatus and political émigrés. As rich as the Comintern collection is, it is not complete. Readers should bear this in mind. The Executive Committee of the Comintern, its Cadres Department, and its party committee sent many materials to security and judicial organs that those bodies did not return. Those and other materials that would fill in gaps in the volume and in our knowledge reside in other archives that are closed.

The documents in this volume, very few of which have been published previously, were selected from the collections of the leading organs of the Comintern, various branches of the apparatus of its Executive Committee, and the party committee and organization of the All-Union Communist Party. Unless otherwise noted, the documents published in this volume are located in the Comintern collection at RGASPI. The records there are organized by *fond* (collection), *opis* (inventory), *delo* (file), and *list* (page) or *listy* (pages). Source references are abbreviated as f., op., d., and l. or ll.

The vast majority of the documents published here are translated into English from the original Russian. In a few cases, Comintern translators had already translated a document from Russian into English, in which case the English version is used. Other documents were originally written in other languages (Hungarian, German) and were translated into Russian by Comintern translators; the English translations here generally come from the Russian translations. In translating these documents into English, Vadim Staklo, the translator, and I adhered to one rule: be faithful to the original document. Some documents contain the written or transcribed language of non-native Russian speakers and consequently contain turgid formulations. Although it was tempting to render these passages more fluid, we avoided the temptation so that readers could appreciate what a person said or wrote and what people heard or read. In the same spirit, we have attempted to preserve a visual sense of the original—headings, underlinings, and the like. We have, however, corrected obvious misspellings and some mistakes and turned some abbreviations into whole words. We have also standardized certain items, such as typed dates (by replacing roman and arabic numerals with the names of months), and standardized the classifications of documents.

For ease of use, each document has been assigned a number and a title indicating its contents. The numbers do not appear in the original documents, nor in many cases do the titles. Typed documents appear here in regular roman type. Handwritten comments, notations, and documents appear here in **_boldface italic_**. Typed underlining is indicated here with a <u>single underscore</u>. Underlining by hand is indicated with a <u>double underscore</u>. When we know who underlined the text, we give the name. Ellipses in brackets [. . .] indicate editorial omissions. Ellipses in angle brackets < . . . > indicate illegible words or signatures. Ellipses without brackets are in the original document.

In transliterating from Russian to English, we have used a modified version of the standard Library of Congress system. Hard and soft signs are omitted. For familiar names, the common English spelling is used (e.g., Leon Trotsky, not Lev Trotskii; Joseph Stalin, not Iosif Stalin). Certain changes have been made in initial letters (e.g., _E_ is _Ye_, as in Yezhov; _Iu_ is _Yu_, as in Yudin; _Ia_ is _Ya_, as in Yagoda). Many foreign personal names appear in this volume. In the original documents, these names appear in their Russified form. In the English translations published here, every effort has been made to present those names in their original spelling. The Asian names posed a particular problem, and mistakes may well have occurred. We apologize for any errors.

Abbreviations and Acronyms

agitprop	agitation and propaganda
BSDWP	Bulgarian Social Democratic Workers' Party
BSDWP(T)	Bulgarian Social Democratic Workers' Party (Tesniak)
C., c.	comrade
C.c., c.c.	comrades
CC	Central Committee
CCC	Central Control Commission
CEC	Central Executive Committee
Cheka	Extraordinary Commission to Combat Counterrevolution, Sabotage, and Speculation (state security)
CI	Communist International
Com., com.	comrade
Comintern	Communist International
CP, CPs	Communist Party or Parties
CPA	Communist Party of Austria
CPBel	Communist Party of Belgium
CPBul	Communist Party of Bulgaria
CPC	Communist Party of China
CPCan	Communist Party of Canada
CPCz	Communist Party of Czechoslovakia
CPFin	Communist Party of Finland

CPFr	Communist Party of France
CPG	Communist Party of Germany
CPGB	Communist Party of Great Britain
CPI	Communist Party of Italy
CPLat	Communist Party of Latvia
CPLith	Communist Party of Lithuania
CPM	Communist Party of Mexico
CPP	Communist Party of Poland
CPR	Communist Party of Romania
CPSp	Communist Party of Spain
CPSU	Communist Party of the Soviet Union
CPSwed	Communist Party of Sweden
CPSwit	Communist Party of Switzerland
CPT	Communist Party of Turkey
CPUSA	Communist Party of the United States of America
CPWB	Communist Party of Western Belorussia
CPWU	Communist Party of Western Ukraine
CPYu	Communist Party of Yugoslavia
EC	Executive Committee
ECCI	Executive Committee of the Communist International
FEC	Far Eastern Committee
Glavlit	Main Administration for Literature
gorkom	city party committee
GPU	Main Political Administration (state security)
GUGB	Main Administration for State Security
ICC	International Control Commission
IMEL	Institute of Marx, Engels, and Lenin
KGB	Committee for State Security
KIM	Communist International of Youth
Komsomol	Communist Union of Youth
kraikom	regional party committee
KUNMZ	Communist University for National Minorities of the West
KUTV	Communist University for Toilers of the East
MAI	International Agrarian Institute
MCC	Moscow Control Commission
MiUD	International Youth Day
MGB	Ministry for State Security, 1946–1953

MLSh	International Lenin School (Communist school adminis- tered by the ECCI for foreign and Soviet Communists)
MOPR	International Organization for Aid to Revolutionary Fighters
MVD	Ministry for Internal Affairs, 1953–1954
MVO	Moscow Military District
NKID	People's Commissariat of Foreign Affairs
NKTP	People's Commissariat of Heavy Industry
NKVD	People's Commissariat of Internal Affairs
obkom	*oblast* (provincial) party committee
OC	*oblast* committee
OGIZ	Association of State Publishing Houses for Books and Periodicals
OGPU	Unified Main Political Administration (state security)
okhranka	contraction of Okhrannoe Otdelenie, the police in tsarist Russia. The term was used in the 1930s to refer to police abroad, especially in Poland.
OMS	Department of International Relations (in the ECCI apparatus; later it was renamed the Communication Department)
Orgburo	Organizational Bureau (of the CC VKP)
ORPO	Department of Leading Party Organs (of the CC VKP)
OSO	Special Council of NKVD
partkom	party committee
PCC	Party Control Commission
Politburo	Political Bureau
POUM	Partido Obrero de Unificación Marxists (Spain)
POW	Polish Military Organization
PPS	Polish Socialist Party
Profintern	Trade Union International
Rabkrin	Workers and Peasants Inspectorate
raikom or RK	district (*raion*) party committee
Razvedupr	Military Intelligence
RGASPI	Russian State Archive of Social and Political History
RK	See *raikom*
RKI	Workers and Peasants Inspectorate
RKKA	Workers and Peasants Red Army
RKP(b)	Russian Communist Party (Bolshevik)
ROSTA	Russian Telegraph Agency

RSDRP	Russian Social Democratic Workers' Party
RSDRP(b)	Russian Social Democratic Workers' Party (Bolshevik)
RSFSR	Russian Soviet Federated Socialist Republic
RUNAG	Rundshau, the information agency of the Comintern
SD, S.D.	Social Democrat
SDP	Social Democratic Party
SDPKPiL	Social Democratic Party of the Kingdom of Poland and Lithuania
SFIO	French Socialist Party
SNK	Council of People's Commissars
SPD	Socialist Party of Germany
SR, S.R.	Socialist Revolutionary
SSR	soviet socialist republic
TASS	Soviet news information service
TsIK	Central Executive Committee
USPD	United Socialist Party of Germany
USSR	Union of Soviet Socialist Republics
UVO	Ukrainian Military Organization
VKLSM	Komsomol (All-Union Leninist Youth League)
VKP	All-Union Communist Party
VKP(b)	All-Union Communist Party (Bolshevik)
VSNKh	Supreme Council of the National Economy
VTsIK	All-Union Central Executive Committee
VTsSPS	All-Union Central Council of Trade Unions
YCL	Young Communist League
YCLP	Young Communist League of Poland

Chronology

2–9 March 1919	First Comintern Congress
19 July–7 August 1920	Second Comintern Congress; passage of the Twenty-One Points
22 June–12 July 1921	Third Comintern Congress
24 February–4 March 1922	First Enlarged Plenum of the Executive Committee of the Comintern (ECCI)
7–11 June 1922	Second Enlarged ECCI Plenum
5 November–5 December 1922	Fourth Comintern Congress
1923	Left Opposition (Trotsky et al.) censured for factional political activities
12–23 June 1923	Third Enlarged ECCI Plenum
1924	New Opposition (Zinoviev, Kamenev, and others) censured for factional political activities
17 June–8 July 1924	Fifth Comintern Congress
12–13 July 1924	Fourth Enlarged ECCI Plenum
21 March–6 April 1925	Fifth Enlarged ECCI Plenum
17 February–15 March 1926	Sixth Enlarged ECCI Plenum
October 1926	Zinoviev removed as chairman of the Comintern
22 November–16 December 1926	Seventh Enlarged ECCI Plenum
18–30 May 1927	Eighth ECCI Plenum
November 1927–early 1928	United (Left) Opposition condemned for factional political activities; many expelled from the All-Union Communist Party (Bolshevik), or VKP(b)
9–25 February 1928	Ninth ECCI Plenum
17 July–1 September 1928	Sixth Comintern Congress ("Third Period" begins)
1929	Trotsky exiled from the USSR

3–19 July 1929	Tenth ECCI Plenum
26 March–11 April 1931	Eleventh ECCI Plenum
27 August–15 September 1932	Twelfth ECCI Plenum
January 1933	Hitler comes to power in Germany
January 1933–December 1934	Purge (*chistka*) of the VKP
28 November–12 December 1933	Thirteenth ECCI Plenum
1 December 1934	Assassination of Sergei Kirov
16 December 1934	Arrest of Zinoviev, Safarov, and others in connection with Kirov's murder
28 December 1934	Meeting of the ECCI party organization regarding the case of Magyar (see Document 4)
January–December 1935	Verification of party documents (*proverka*)
20 February 1935	Closed meeting of the ECCI party organization, dedicated to the lessons flowing from Kirov's murder (see Document 5)
25 July–20 August 1935	Seventh Comintern Congress; adoption of the Popular Front; Georgi Dimitrov elected general secretary of the Comintern
21–25 December 1935	Plenary meeting of the Central Committee
2 January 1936	Manuilsky's letter to Yezhov regarding the closing of special routes ("green passages") into the USSR and measures against "spies and saboteurs disguised as political émigrés" (see Document 6)
February 1936	Special commission formed to oversee verification of émigrés
3 March 1936	Resolution of the ECCI Secretariat on the obligations of the Cadres Department regarding émigrés (see Document 10)
March 1936–late 1936	Exchange of party documents
July 1936	Spanish Civil War begins
29 July 1936	Secret Central Committee letter "concerning the terroristic activity of the Trotskyist-Zinovievite counterrevolutionary bloc"
11 August 1936	Memorandum from Kotelnikov to Dimitrov, Manuilsky, and Moskvin about the work of exposing "the wreckers in the ECCI" (see Document 11)
19–24 August 1936	Trial of the "Anti-Soviet United Trotskyist-Zinovievite Center"
4 September 1936	Cadres Department memorandum "On Trotskyist and other hostile elements in the émigré community of the German CP [Communist Party]" (see Document 17)
	A list of VKP members "formerly in other parties, having Trotskyist and Rightist tendencies," sent by Kotelnikov to the NKVD (see Document 18)
26 September 1936	Yezhov appointed head of the NKVD
3 January 1937	Trotsky arrives in Mexico from Norway

23–30 January 1937	Trial of the "Anti-Soviet Trotskyist Center"
5 February 1937	Memorandum "On the results of the work of the ECCI Secretariat's commission to verify the qualifications of the ECCI apparatus" (see Document 29)
23 February–4 March 1937	Plenary meeting of the Central Committee
22 June 1937	Closed meeting of VKP members and candidate members in the ECCI Secretariat (see Document 32)
30 July 1937	NKVD issues Decree No. 00447 targeting "former kulaks, criminals, and other anti-Soviet elements"
	Arrests per NKVD Order No. 00439 ("German operation") begin
5 August 1937	Arrests per NKVD Order No. 00447 begin
9 August 1937	Politburo confirms NKVD Decree No. 00485, "On the liquidation of the Polish sabotage-espionage group and the POW organization"
11 August 1937	Yezhov issues NKVD Order No. 00485
15 August 1937	Arrests per NKVD Order No. 00485 ("Polish operation") begin
28 November 1937	ECCI resolution on the dissolution of the Polish CP (see Document 38)
2–13 March 1938	Trial of the "Right-Trotskyist Bloc"
17 May 1938	ECCI directives on carrying out a campaign of enlightenment in connection with the trial of the "Bloc of Rights and Trotskyites" (see Document 39)
15 September 1938	Politburo orders creation of commissions in each region to review national operations and resolves to create special troikas to review "remaining unconsidered cases of those arrested" under national operations
17 November 1938	Politburo resolution suspends all national operations
25 November 1938	Yezhov removed as head of NKVD

Enemies Within the Gates?

Introduction

> Nothing appears more surprising to those who consider human affairs with a philosophical eye than the easiness with which the many are governed by the few, and the implicit submission with which men resign their own sentiments and passions to those of their rulers. When we inquire by what means this wonder is effected, we shall find that, as Force is always on the side of the governed, the governors have nothing to support them but opinion. It is, therefore, on opinion only that government is founded, and this maxim extends to the most despotic and most military governments as well as to the most free and most popular.
>
> — DAVID HUME

THIS IS A STORY of idealism twisted into carnage, of comradeship betrayed, of hopes deformed by fear, of conspiracies perceived. It is another of those many stories that detail human brutality in the name of a higher good: a story told and retold until it almost numbs us to people's capacity for rationalized fear and wasteful violence. We give such phenomena labels—Stalinism, Nazism, Maoism, McCarthyism, nationalism, racism—but all labels mask the complex realities. This is not a story easily told, for it defies anyone's skill to recapture the anxieties and fears, to express the coherence underlying seeming contradictions, to trace the logic, to penetrate the rhetoric, to separate personal from political motives, to comprehend people's simultaneous capacity for idealism, obedience, and betrayal. This is a story about how the Stalinist repression affected the Communist International, the Comintern, a revolutionary organization born of sectarian idealism in 1919 and decimated by an implosion of fear and suspicion in 1937–1938.

At the founding congress in 1919, the Comintern set as its goals the destruction of a world ravaged by war, poverty, greed, and exploitation and the construction of a new world of collective abundance, enlightenment, and equality. It demanded that those parties that wished to join it adhere to a strict set of organizational and behavioral rules, which mirrored those that governed the Bolshevik Party.[1] Although its headquarters were in Moscow, and although the Bolshevik Party was the preeminent party within it, the Comintern was not the Bolshevik Party. Precisely because it was the headquarters of the world revolutionary movement, because many of its leaders were not Soviet citizens, because it attracted political refugees from countries that had outlawed or repressed communist and radical activities, the Comintern was distinct—not independent, not autonomous, but nonetheless distinct in small ways that by their accretion became notable. These distinctions were subtle and were often hidden by the membership rules and by the Bolshevization of the Comintern, which began in the mid-1920s and was well advanced by the time our story begins in 1934.

This is not a history of the Comintern but rather a study of what happened in its headquarters during the mass repression that swept the Soviet Union in the late 1930s. Known by various names—the Great Terror, the Great Purges, the Stalinist Terror, the *Yezhovshchina*—the mass repression destroyed the lives of many residents of the USSR, native-born and foreign-born, and profoundly altered, even deformed, the Bolshevik Party and Soviet society. It mortally wounded the Comintern.

Although the historiography of the mass repression and its consequences is substantial, there remain many questions about the reasons it occurred, Stalin's role, the role played by other party leaders and institutions, the attitudes and behaviors of rank-and-file party members and Soviet citizens, and its dimensions.[2] Prior to the opening of Soviet archives in 1991–1992, the lack of access to internal party and state documents constrained scholars' efforts to answer certain questions essential to understanding it.[3] The opening of many formerly closed archives has yielded a veritable treasure trove of materials through which scholars are still sifting. How the newly available materials will affect the historiography and our understanding of the Stalin era remains to be seen. But the evidence presented in this volume challenges all of us to reconsider the forces and concerns that fueled the repression, the role of popular participation, and the attitudes of persecutors and victims alike.

This book originated in my belief that to understand the repression, we must ascertain how it unfolded in a variety of contexts. To base overarching interpretations on the existing literature is presumptuous. Only when the repression has been examined from various angles will it be possible to grasp and appreciate its dimensions and dynamics. This volume, like others in the Annals of Communism series, is an attempt to illuminate this historical period and provide readers with insights into how people devoted to constructing a world free of the cruelties that had defined the previous social order participated in new cruelties in the name of another.

Examining how the mass repression unfolded within and affected the Comintern headquarters in particular offers numerous advantages.[4] The most obvious is that it enables us to understand the ways a specific organization and its members interpreted and acted on party policies that contributed to the repression. It thereby allows us to examine individual and group behaviors as well as the relationship over time between the leaders of the organization and the rank and file. For much of the period discussed here, late 1934 to 1939, Comintern headquarters was a relatively stable institution. Although the Seventh Congress of the Comintern, held in July–August 1935, occasioned the removal of certain members of its Executive Committee (ECCI), most ECCI members were reelected. The organizational reforms approved by that Congress affected the ECCI's administrative structure more than its personnel. The reviews of party members from 1933 to 1936 resulted in some people being relieved of work. Yet from late 1934 to spring 1937, when the mass repression erupted, the composition of the ECCI apparatus (bureaucracy) and its party organization and committee changed relatively little. The mass arrests in 1937–1938 dramatically affected the composition of these bodies. But as we shall see, the political values and campaigns that were preconditions for the mass repression had by that time become accepted frames of reference and social norms within the ECCI apparatus.

Using the Comintern headquarters as a case study has several other advantages. It was home to both a central political organization and a local party organization. The Comintern directed the international communist movement from Moscow. The presence on the ECCI of Stalin, members of the Central Committee (CC) of the All-Union Communist Party (VKP), and leaders of the fraternal parties abroad attests to the importance of this mission, as does the fact that the Central Committee of the VKP assigned one of its members to be its representative in the ECCI.[5] Although the ECCI Secretariat, ECCI Presidium, and ECCI apparatus ran the Comintern's day-to-day operations, the presence of powerful VKP members on the ECCI tightly linked the Comintern headquarters to high-level VKP politics. That Georgi Dimitrov, the Comintern's General Secretary from mid-1935 until 1943, socialized with Stalin and other Politburo members reinforced the political ties between the Comintern and the party leadership. These ties significantly influenced the political dynamics within the ECCI and its apparatus.

The Comintern headquarters also hosted a local party organization. The vast majority of workers in the ECCI apparatus, who numbered about six hundred in early 1937, were Communist Party members—either VKP members or members of fraternal Communist Parties—who belonged to the ECCI party organization. Like all local party organizations, the ECCI party organization applied VKP policies to local realities and dealt with a myriad of internal issues. Precisely because the membership of the ECCI party organization was relatively stable, its local character allows us to observe behaviors over time and thereby identify both specifically Soviet or Stalinist behaviors and universal human behaviors.[6]

One distinctive feature of the Comintern headquarters makes it especially valuable as a case study: its international composition. Among the members and staff of the ECCI were Soviet citizens and foreigners, native-born VKP members, foreign-born VKP members, and members of fraternal parties. It had the most diverse ethnic composition of any institution on Soviet soil; more than half the members of its party organization were foreign-born. Its ethnic composition made that organization different from all others in the USSR and meant that the mass repression unfolded in somewhat different ways than it did in other party organizations. Still, it housed a sizable VKP party organization, so VKP policies that contributed to the repression profoundly affected it.

Not only were many who staffed the ECCI apparatus foreign-born, but most of them came from countries where the Communist Party was illegal and operated underground. Many Communists who resided in the USSR in the 1930s had been arrested and interrogated by police back home; many had been convicted and served prison time there. Their experiences were analogous to the Bolsheviks' with the Okhrana (the tsarist political police) in prerevolutionary Russia. The suspicions engendered among one's comrades by being arrested and interrogated remained latent but, at times, powerful reasons for suspecting someone's loyalty to the party. Divisions often ran deep among the members of fraternal parties who resided in the USSR. Away from home those parties were quite fractious. Removed from the daily underground struggles that provided a common sense of purpose (or at least persecution), foreign-born Communists in the USSR commonly split into groups of trusted friends who feuded with others over political and personal issues and who jockeyed for favor with their Soviet hosts. Native-born Soviet comrades viewed foreign comrades and their squabbles with attitudes that ranged from annoyance to suspicion.

As the international situation deteriorated in the 1930s, suspicion of foreigners, especially those from the western borderlands, intensified, weakening the bonds of comradeship and strengthening the importance of ethnicity. The 1930s in the USSR were a decade of mounting suspicion of foreigners, spy mania, and xenophobia, which reached their peak in 1937–1938 with the mass arrests of foreigners and Soviet citizens accused of participating in hostile conspiracies, often allegedly directed from abroad. Precisely because the Comintern was a central and local party organization staffed by native-born and foreign-born comrades who had pledged their allegiance to the VKP, we can use it as a case study to chart the emergence, evolution, and consequences of political campaigns and xenophobia, as well as the dynamics of the mass repression, in ways that no other case study permits.

The mass repression evolved in a sequence of steps between 1934 and 1939, although at no point before 1937 was it apparent that the repression would take the violent form and scale that it did. The assassination of Leningrad party leader Sergei Kirov in December 1934 was followed by the assertion that a secret faction within the VKP was engaged in treasonous activities directed at the VKP and its leaders—the first time such an assertion was made. The Politburo of the VKP demanded that party members heighten their political vigilance to expose any and all threats. Under this charge, from early 1935 to mid-1936 the vigilance campaign against "Trotskyists" unfolded. From late 1935, as VKP leaders' suspicions of foreigners mounted, the vigilance campaign focused increasingly on foreign comrades. During 1936 all foreigners in the USSR were subjected to political review. Arrests ensued. In August 1936 the first of the Moscow show trials occurred; several of the defendants were foreigners. The defendants' confessions, convictions, and executions intensified the vigilance campaign and skewed other policies that antedated the trial.

From the August 1936 trial until spring 1937, when members of the military high command were arrested, party leaders and members pressed the vigilance campaign with increasing stridency. The appointment of Nikolai Yezhov to head the NKVD, the state security organ, in September 1936, together with the January 1937 show trial contributed to the shift in tone, but so, too, did the revelations from various personnel review boards that "suspicious" and "hostile elements" existed within the VKP and émigré communities.[7] In June 1937, Stalin unleashed the NKVD and the search for "enemies" took on hysterical dimensions. Yezhov and his minions conducted that search with brutal enthusiasm until December 1938, when he was removed. Only then did the hysteria begin to subside.

This is the larger context within which the decimation of the ECCI apparatus took place. Some historians see in these events a conscious long-term plan directed by Stalin to rid himself of potential enemies. True or not, those who lived through the events did not see it that way. The authors and subjects of the documents found in this volume had no such privileged perspective on the events unfolding around them. Their words and actions are often incomprehensible unless we appreciate that the events of 1934–1938 often came as a shock (or, as some of them put it, revealed their "lack of vigilance"), that they had no reason to doubt—on the contrary, they often believed they had good reason to believe—that "enemies" threatened the VKP and the USSR. None knew where these events were tending; many vigilant denouncers were, in the fullness of time, themselves denounced and arrested. Even in prison they clung to the values and perspectives that had earlier led them to demand vigilance and denounce others. The roles played by those who appear in this volume were multiple.

The Comintern itself was an agent, instrument, and victim of repression. It had always been a sectarian organization, but in the aftermath of Kirov's assassination and in conformity with VKP directives, it implemented a political vigilance campaign against critics of the party line, in particular Leon Trotsky and international Trotskyists. From then until late 1938 the ECCI's leaders demanded increasingly heightened vigilance from their staff and comrades worldwide. The conspiratorial logic that underpinned the campaign returned to haunt the Comintern. Many members of its apparatus and many political émigrés living in the USSR fell victim to that campaign. This was the most obvious way in which the Comintern was the agent of repression. But it was not the only way.

Besides being the headquarters of the world Communist movement, the Comintern was responsible for political émigrés who, having fled persecution in their native countries, had taken up residence in the USSR. The largest European émigré groups came from Germany, Poland, Hungary, Bulgaria, Finland, Yugoslavia, Latvia, Estonia, and Lithuania. Not without cause, increasingly from 1933 the Soviet government viewed the governments of those nations as threats.[8] During 1935 the VKP's and ECCI's leaders had become convinced that spies, saboteurs, and enemy agents existed among the political émigrés, and at year's end they ordered VKP and ECCI commissions to review every political émigré in the country. The ensuing reviews resulted in the accumulation of considerable information on people, some of whom were ordered to leave the country, some of whom were further investigated, and others of whom were arrested. These commissions sent their materials and conveyed their conclusions to the ECCI's Cadres Department, which maintained careful files and, when it deemed it appropriate or when the security organs requested it, forwarded information in the files to the NKVD. Because Yezhov, head of the NKVD, considered the Comintern to be a "nest of spies," the NKVD frequently requested and received such information.[9]

As the orchestrator of the international vigilance campaign and a key actor in the domestic campaigns to identify "hostile" and "suspicious" elements among its members and political émigrés, the Comintern had a substantial role as an agent of repression. Those campaigns, which came before the mass repression, affected the attitudes and beliefs of ECCI's leaders and staff. Convinced as they were of the dangers posed by Trotskyists and spies, "real" Bolsheviks in the Comintern became the instruments of repression. At ECCI party organization meetings, party members, native-born and foreign-born alike, demanded vigilance against "enemies," closely scrutinized some comrades' political pasts and behaviors, denounced others, and recommended the expulsion (and on occasion the arrest) of still others. The Cadres Department continually investigated party members' pasts and augmented its lists of alleged oppositionists and suspicious people that later provided the "evidence" that the NKVD used to arrest people.

Even fraternal party members who resided in the USSR acted on occasion as the instruments of repression. Many members of the Communist Parties of Poland, Hungary, Germany, and elsewhere lived in the USSR. Political differences and schisms in the parties, as well as personal frictions among members, led some to denounce others of Trotskyism or other political "crimes." When fraternal party members denounced their comrades to the ECCI, the Cadres Department, VKP authorities, or the NKVD, they put all party members at risk.

In acting as an agent and an instrument of repression, the ECCI and its apparatus contributed to legitimizing a process initiated by VKP leaders that was a precondition for the mass repression—the dehumanization of selected groups. Labeling a person a Trotskyist or Zinovievite, a spy or an enemy agent, transformed him or her from a comrade into someone outside the group, into a threat to the group. Denouncing people as possible enemy agents, hostile elements, or Trotskyists transformed them into the "Other." If former comrades were Others, it was easier to accept and explain when they became victims of repression.

The Comintern was also a victim of repression. The ECCI and its apparatus, as well as the ranks of fraternal parties, suffered greatly during the mass repression of 1937–1938. Exact figures are unavailable, but many Comintern members residing in the USSR became victims.[10] Because NKVD materials remain closed to the public, the specifics on each case are not always clear. Whatever the precise figures may be, what unfolded within the Comintern in 1937–1938 was primarily a repression of Communists by Communists in the name of protecting Soviet Communism.

In examining the Comintern as an agent, instrument, and victim of repression, we can glimpse the mindset, the *mentalité* of the period. It is not surprising that dedicated VKP members and foreign Communists adopted the VKP's rhetoric and political line. Yet it may surprise some to learn that many foreign Communists shared the belief of VKP leaders that spies and enemy agents had penetrated the party and state bureaucracies. It seems paradoxical that some foreign Communists believed in what Gábor Rittersporn has called the "omnipresent conspiracy," because foreigners were obviously at risk to be accused.[11] But they did believe in it.

What enhanced the widely shared belief among Comintern members that the enemy was within the gates was that the VKP's leaders, the Comintern, and its member parties followed with alarm and horror the spread of fascism, right-wing dictatorships, and military imperialism throughout the world in the 1930s. Although the brief successes of the Comintern's anti-fascist Popular Front in France and Spain offered occasional glimmers of hope, the realities of the 1930s were grim for Communists and the USSR. From 1933 the USSR was a country besieged, facing the prospect of a two-front war. The fear of war permeated a society that in 1914–1921 had experienced a world war and one of Europe's most brutal civil wars and had repulsed many foreign armies. Two decades of "capitalist encirclement" and foreign hostility, of periodic public trials of alleged foreign agents, and of harsh economic conditions created fertile soil in which the seeds of suspicion, spy mania, and xenophobia could sprout, mature, and spread.

There were no doubt spies in the USSR in the 1930s. What modern state has ever been free of them? The USSR had enormous and somewhat porous borders. It was a haven for political émigrés fleeing oppression and the object of antipathy of many governments. Soviet security officials were convinced that German, Polish, Japanese, and other intelligence agencies engaged in disinformation and other activities designed to destabilize the USSR.[12] To believe that there were no spies is naive. To believe, as Stalin, Yezhov, and others did in 1937–1938, that the country was awash with spies bespeaks the conspiratorial worldview that propelled the mass repression. Who the real spies were and whether NKVD agents ever arrested them is unknown, perhaps unknowable. What is clear is that, in the effort to ferret out spies and enemy agents, the NKVD repressed many innocent people, many dedicated Communists, many noble idealists. No spy network could have inflicted the damage that the NKVD did.

The perceived political and military threats to the USSR contributed to what one historian has dubbed political and social "psychoses" that gripped many VKP and Comintern leaders, Soviet citizens, and even political émigrés in the 1930s.[13] These psychoses produced and made credible the fears and accusations that fueled the mass repression. It is indeed a tragic story.

Precisely because the Comintern was a many-tentacled organization that oversaw its own bureaucracy, political émigrés, and the activities of its fraternal parties within the USSR and abroad and that was linked in many ways to the VKP and Soviet state bureaucracies, this book cannot be and is not an exhaustive study. The organs of the Comintern and the ECCI, as well as some fraternal parties, particularly the Polish and Hungarian parties, receive considerable attention here; others receive less attention, not least because of the unavailability of materials and the work being done by other scholars.

Let me note what this volume does *not* do. It is not an exhaustive study of the Great Terror, the Yezhovshchina. No case study could be. Nor does it explain how and why the mass repression of 1937–1938 began, although it offers some insights into the constellation of political, administrative, and psychological factors that contributed to it. Nor does it fully explain Stalin's, the Politburo's, or Yezhov's direct role in the repression. The available Comintern materials do not allow that. Rather, this is a case study of how the mass repression unfolded within and affected one key Soviet organization. The story is well worth telling.

CHAPTER ONE

The Comintern

The psychological mechanism whereby each single militant becomes progressively identified with the collective organization is the same as that used in certain religious orders and military colleges, with identical results. . . . The links which bound us to the Party grew steadily firmer, not in spite of the dangers and sacrifices involved, but because of them. . . . The history of the Comintern was therefore a history of schisms, a history of intrigues and arrogance on the part of the directing Russian group toward every independent expression of opinion by the other affiliated parties.

— IGNAZIO SILONE

A GROUP OF Bolsheviks and representatives of a few Communist trends and groups who happened to be in Moscow in March 1919 constituted the founding Congress of the Comintern. During World War I, Lenin had condemned the Second International, a loose coalition of socialist parties, because most of its leaders had voted for war credits and supported participation in the war. To Lenin, socialists who supported the imperialist war were traitors to Marxism and the proletariat. During the war years, he and other socialists who opposed the war convened conferences in Switzerland and Sweden to condemn the war and the behavior of the Second International. Before and after the Bolsheviks' victory in 1917, Lenin repeatedly called for the creation of a new international, a Communist international, that would lead the workers of the world to socialism.[1]

The Comintern's founding Congress was the first step toward the realization of Lenin's dream. The first Congress accomplished little other than to announce the birth of the Comintern, to promulgate its basic principles, and to make plans for a future Congress. But the hopes expressed at the Congress remained those of the Comintern until its dissolution in 1943. The delegates to the 1919 Congress fervently believed that the hoped-for world socialist revolution was imminent, and not without good cause. Revolutionary unrest was widespread in Europe and beyond, and a socialist state existed in Soviet Russia. Yet there was also much cause for concern. Embroiled in a vicious civil war, the new Soviet government struggled to fend off its domestic enemies and armed intervention by France, England, the United States, Japan, and other nations. To Lenin and the delegates, these realities instilled a sense of urgency into creating the Comintern—"a unified world Communist Party, specific sections of which were parties active in each country," which Soviet leaders hoped would exploit the postwar political instability and increase domestic pressures on the interventionists.[2]

In that perilous but optimistic year, when revolution seemed both imminent and endangered, solidarity with the Soviet state became the bedrock of the Comintern's adherents as well as a criterion for Comintern membership. A sectarianism born of conviction and disdain proved to be the major legacy of the first Congress. Member parties gave their unswerving allegiance to the VKP and the Soviet government and set as their goal the political destruction of both the imperialist world and the Social Democratic parties that Communists deemed hopelessly reformist and incapable of igniting, let alone leading, a socialist revolution.

In 1920 the Second Comintern Congress convened in Moscow. The elected delegates represented newly formed Communist Parties. The adoption of the Twenty-One Points, written by Lenin and Grigori Zinoviev, which defined the criteria for and rules of membership, proved crucial to the Comintern's development.[3] For our purposes, certain of the Twenty-One Points deserve special note.

To guard against the "danger of dilution by unstable and irresolute elements which have not completely discarded the ideology of the Second International," the Comintern demanded that "every organization which wishes to join . . . must, in an orderly and planned fashion, remove reformists and supporters of the center from all responsible positions . . . and replace them with tried Communists" (point 5). Such a purge was essential to creating a militant, revolutionary party. To further enhance that goal, the Comintern insisted that member parties "be based on the principles of democratic centralism" because a party could "fulfill its duty only if its organization is as centralized as possible, [and] if iron discipline prevails" (point 12). To ensure that "unstable and irresolute elements" would not corrode a party's revolutionary élan, it demanded in point 13 that "Communist Parties . . . must from time to time undertake a cleansing [re-registration] of the membership of the party in order to get rid of any petty-bourgeois elements which have crept in." The principles of democratic centralism applied not only within member parties but also to the member parties in relation to the Comintern: "The programme of every party belonging to the Communist International must be ratified by the regular congress of the Communist International or by the Executive Committee" (point 15); "All decisions of the congresses of the Communist International, as well as the decisions of its Executive Committee, are binding on all parties belonging to the Communist International" (point 16).[4]

Adherence to these conditions was intended to ensure that all member parties would "subordinate so-called national interests to the interests of the international revolution" in order to avoid what happened in August 1914, when the elected representatives of some socialist parties placed national interests above those of international revolution by voting for war credits.[5] The Twenty-One Points accomplished that goal to some degree, but they also accomplished something much more immediate—they provided the mechanism for centralization.

The Second Congress also approved the Comintern's organizational structure.[6] Henceforth, the Comintern was not only the leader of the world Communist movement but also a bureaucracy in its own right, a bureaucracy headquartered in Moscow and therefore inevitably influenced by the Bolshevik Party and Soviet state. In 1920 the Comintern was already becoming a complex institution that played many roles. It was the leader of the world Communist movement and a collective organization of fraternal parties; it was also a bureaucracy that had many obvious and subtle ties to the VKP and the Soviet state.

Comintern Policies for World Revolution

The primary function of the Comintern was to identify and enact the proper strategies and tactics to hasten international socialist revolution. During its existence the Comintern elaborated several policies to achieve that goal. Until 1921 it urged Communist Parties to pursue the policy of the united front from below, the goals of which were to win workers away from Social Democratic and radical parties, to reject any cooperation with Social Democratic leaders, to use all appropriate revolutionary methods to win workers' allegiance, and to seize power in their respective countries. An unshakable belief in the inevitability of revolution drove this policy. But by 1921 the prospects for revolution had ebbed dramatically, and the Comintern adopted a more flexible set of united front tactics, which did not exclude cooperation with Social Democratic parties if it served the Comintern's strategic goals. In 1924 the Fifth Comintern Congress stressed that it was essential "always and everywhere" to pursue the united-front-from-below tactic, but allowed for the possibility of discussions with Social Democratic leaders. The Congress characterized this tactic as the "method of agitation and revolutionary mobilization for the entire period."[7] The tactic required member parties to concentrate their energies on extending and strengthening Communist Party influence among rank-and-file workers and trade unionists. In this way, Communists hoped to win workers to their cause, to turn workers against moderate socialist and reformist union leaders, and thereby to radicalize both the working class and trade unions. Success would transform the unions into instruments of the Communist Party.

At its Sixth Congress in 1928, the Comintern adopted a far more strident policy toward Social Democrats. From then until the Seventh Comintern Congress in 1935, Social Democrats and reform socialists became the main enemy; they were dubbed "social fascists." Any collaboration with social fascists became unthinkable. Henceforth the goal was to work from below to turn workers, unions, and other mass organizations against the Social Democrats and destroy them. The Congress resolved that the "center of gravity of the united front from below is to carry out decisively the intensification of the struggle against Social Democrats, but it does not replace, but on the contrary strengthens, the duty of Communists to make distinctions between sincerely mistaken Social Democratic workers on the one hand and Social Democratic leaders, the lackeys of imperialism, on the other." Many delegates disagreed with this formulation. Acceptance came only after the Tenth ECCI Plenum in June 1929, which removed Nikolai Bukharin, then the chairman of the ECCI and one of Stalin's political rivals, and only with the formulation "a special form of fascism in countries with strong Social Democratic parties is social-fascism."[8]

During what is known in Comintern history as the Third Period, this policy proved to be a disaster. Despite the hardships inflicted on workers and working people by the Great Depression—objective conditions that might otherwise have enhanced the possibility of socialist revolution—the gains made by Communist Parties were minor and ephemeral. Only in Germany, where animosity between Communists and Social Democrats ran deep, did the policy produce even short-lived success, and even then at great cost. Both parties' sectarian behaviors divided the discontented population, reduced their electoral influence, and thereby promoted the Nazis' electoral success and rise to power in 1933.

Social Democrats were not the only recipient of the Comintern's vitriol. Throughout its history, the Comintern was embroiled in the political struggles within the VKP. In accordance with the rules of democratic centralism, it sided with the party majority, although many members of the fraternal parties expressed public support for the various opposition groups within the VKP. Following the VKP's lead, from 1923 it condemned Leon Trotsky and his followers for their leftist opposition to the party line. Expelled from the VKP in November 1927 and exiled from the USSR in 1929, Trotsky remained a staunch critic of Soviet domestic and foreign policies—and those of the Comintern. In 1926–1927 the Comintern took up the VKP leadership's struggle against Grigori Zinoviev, chairman of the Comintern until 1926, and his supporters, who at first constituted the New Opposition and who later joined with Trotsky's Left Opposition. In 1928–1929 the Comintern helped to carry out the party leadership's campaign against Bukharin and the so-called right deviation. From the mid-1920s, first Trotskyists, then Zinovievites, and later Bukharinists (real or alleged) were expelled from the Comintern and its fraternal parties, expulsions that sharply split many of those parties.[9] Strident opposition to cooperation with tendencies, movements, and parties to the VKP's right and left defined the Third Period, which marked the height of Comintern sectarianism and, outside Germany, the nadir of its influence abroad.

Although the policy of the Third Period remained the Comintern's official policy until 1935, doubts about it and demands for a change of policy appeared as early as 1933. The Spanish revolution of 1931, the Nazis' coming to power in Germany in 1933, and the abortive fascist coup in France in February 1934 sharply altered the dynamics of European politics and created demands within some fraternal parties for a change of Comintern tactics.[10] Among those who advocated a change was Georgi Dimitrov, the Bulgarian Communist. Dimitrov was one of the defendants at the Reichstag fire trial in Leipzig in 1933, a show trial orchestrated by the Nazis to justify the outlawing of the German Communist Party, which, alleged the Nazis, had organized the burning of the German Reichstag. Dimitrov used the trial to turn the evidence against his accusers and emerged the moral victor in the eyes of antifascists around the world. In 1934, Dimitrov took up political exile in the USSR, where he advocated a change in Comintern policy to Stalin and the VKP leadership, as well as within the Comintern.[11]

In a May 1934 conversation with Maurice Thorez, the French Communist Party leader, Dimitrov said: "The wall between Communist workers and Social Democrats should be destroyed. It is necessary to use all means that hasten that goal. It follows to free the policy of the united front from the old dogmatic ideas [*shkemy*] of Zinoviev's time: 'from above,' 'in the middle,' 'from below.' We should prove that the Communist Party wants to conduct an active and concrete cooperative struggle and is able to fight. The experience of February [1934 in France] and after prove just how successful this is."[12]

The Seventh Comintern Congress (July–August 1935) approved a dramatic change in Comintern policy. Henceforth fascism was the primary enemy. Member parties were required to drop their attacks on Social Democrats and other reformists and to forge broad antifascist coalitions. Known as the Popular (or United) Front, this new policy brought a stunning reversal in the Comintern's fortunes. Its call for a broad-based antifascist struggle won many supporters and catapulted the Comintern to the forefront of the international antifascist movement. In 1936, Popular Front coalition governments came to power in France and Spain. The ascendancy of a Popular Front government in Spain triggered the onset of the Spanish Civil War in July 1936. During that war, which proved to be a dress rehearsal for World War II, the USSR and the Comintern took the lead in organizing international support for the democratically elected Spanish Republic and the International Brigades, a ragtag army of international volunteers who flocked to Spain to defend a progressive government besieged by the armies and air forces of the Spanish, German, and Italian fascists. The Comintern's popularity reached a hitherto unknown peak in 1937. Ironically, at that very time many Cominternists fell victim to the mass repression in the USSR.

After the signing of the Nazi-Soviet nonaggression pact in August 1939, the Comintern abandoned its antifascist policy. From then until the Axis invasion of the USSR on 22 June 1941, its policy, like that of the Soviet government, was that the war in Europe was an imperialist war that deserved no support from Communists, whose primary purpose now was to fight imperialism. Following the invasion of the USSR, Comintern policy changed again, calling on supporters to oppose fascism and defend the USSR. In 1943, on orders from Stalin, the Comintern disbanded, a symbolic gesture of friendship toward Moscow's British and American allies, which ratified its de facto death in 1938.

Throughout its existence, with one brief but notable exception, Comintern policies reflected the domestic and foreign policy needs of the USSR. This is hardly surprising given that defense of the USSR was one of the Twenty-One Points. There were times when Comintern activities created problems for Soviet foreign policy toward a given country, but such incidents were short-lived. The notable exception occurred during 1933–1935, when, in the aftermath of Hitler's rise to power, Soviet foreign policymakers sought to forge an international coalition to stem the spread and influence of fascism while the Comintern pursued its campaign against "social fascists." This policy of collective security placed the USSR in the forefront of international antifascist efforts. But it was not until mid-1935 that the Comintern officially dropped its Third Period policies. The seeming discrepancy between Soviet foreign policy and Comintern policy should not be construed to mean that the Comintern operated independently of the Kremlin. On the contrary, Stalin was actively involved in Comintern policy. The Comintern's leaders in 1933–1935, Osip Pyatnitsky, Dmitri Manuilsky, and Wilhelm Knorin, regularly sought Stalin's approval for an array of policy documents. Stalin and the Politburo also exercised control of Comintern policies and activities through Molotov, formal leader of the Comintern. Stalin himself was a member of the Executive Committee of the Comintern. What remains less well understood is the logic behind maintaining the policy of social fascism while simultaneously pursuing collective security. This seeming anomaly stands as but one example of those distinctive features of the unique dependent relationship of the Comintern to the Soviet government and the VKP.

The twists and turns of Comintern policies and the Comintern's active political struggle against groups that opposed the VKP's and Comintern's lines created considerable confusion, disorientation, and discontent within the fraternal parties. Foreign Communists and VKP members who supported the various criticisms of VKP policies were reprimanded or expelled from their parties; those who criticized Comintern policies, such as the Third Period policies, experienced similar fates. Such periodic purges of "errant" party members served the long-standing Bolshevik tradition of ensuring party unity, but it also produced other effects. One of these was that sincere Communists, true believers, who were committed to the Communist vision and had no desire to leave the movement, endorsed the political line of the moment and gave at least rhetorical support to it. Such was the price one paid for belonging to a movement that promised to create a socialist world; such was the price that committed revolutionaries had to pay to fulfill their dreams. It seemed a modest price. But the true costs of compliance and party discipline ultimately proved to be much higher.

The Comintern and the VKP

The Comintern was a collective body composed of fraternal Communist Parties from around the world. Any party that agreed to subscribe to the Twenty-One Points was welcome to join. In reality, the VKP was the most influential party within the Comintern. There were reasons for its primacy. The most important was that it was the only party within the Comintern to have seized power and established a socialist government. Who could argue with success? Certainly not the smaller Communist Parties, such as those in the Baltic states, Finland, England, or South America, where the prospects for revolution were remote; and most certainly not those parties that were illegal in their own countries. Other factors were also at work. The VKP took the lead in organizing the Comintern and provided it and its member parties with ideological, political, organizational, and financial assistance—and a home. Such largess guaranteed the VKP decisive influence within the Comintern. The delegates to the founding Congress agreed that all member parties must "subordinate so-called national interests to the interests of the international revolution."[13] Because of the VKP's success and its support for the Comintern, its views determined what constituted those interests.

The VKP's role within the Comintern is hard to exaggerate. The principles enunciated in the Twenty-One Points and other Comintern directives reflected the organizational and operative principles of the VKP. VKP leaders prepared and decided many of the Comintern's major decisions. Until 1935 the VKP delegation constituted a plurality within the Executive Committee of the Comintern and its Presidium; as a rule, fraternal parties had one representative in the ECCI, although the more important parties (e.g., the German, French, Chinese) had more.[14] From 1935 five members of the ECCI—Stalin, Dmitri Manuilsky, Meer Moskvin (Trilisser), Nikolai Yezhov, and Andrei Zhdanov—were members of the VKP Central Committee (CC). Stalin, Manuilsky, and Moskvin sat on the ECCI Presidium; Manuilsky was a member and Moskvin a candidate member of the ECCI Secretariat.

The presence of five Central Committee members, together with Dimitrov's social ties to Stalin and other Politburo members, ensured that the ECCI and hence its apparatus were aware of the details and nuances of VKP policies. There was no Central Committee secretary assigned formal responsibility for the Comintern. The presence of three Central Committee secretaries—Stalin, Zhdanov, and Yezhov—on the ECCI obviated the need for any. Stalin, however, seems to have been the Comintern's de facto overseer on the Central

Committee. Otherwise, the ECCI worked with the Central Committee along functional lines; for example, on membership matters the ECCI dealt with ORPO (the Central Committee Department of Leading Party Organs); on finances, with its financial department, and so on.

So predominant was the VKP's power and influence within the Comintern that its delegation often decided among themselves not only which tactics and strategies the Comintern would pursue but who to remove from and appoint to the Central Committees of fraternal parties.[15] They also determined who would attend Comintern Congresses and which VKP members would serve on various Comintern leadership bodies. One ECCI member was the representative of the Central Committee of the VKP. Throughout the late 1920s and the early 1930s, that person was Osip Pyatnitsky. In 1935, after Pyatnitsky's transfer to work in the Central Committee offices, Manuilsky assumed that role. On certain occasions Dimitrov attended Central Committee meetings and plenums. He was also among a small group of individuals who regularly met and socialized with Stalin and other Politburo members.[16]

Many political émigrés in the USSR became VKP members, which augmented the party's predominance because the émigrés espoused VKP policies, values, and perceptions among their fellow citizens. The effective political results were that the principles by which the Comintern and its member parties operated, as well as their organizational structure, principles, and rules, reflected those of the VKP.

Within the ECCI apparatus, there were VKP committees (*partkom*) as well as Komsomol (Communist Union of Youth) cells. They performed the roles and functions of any other party organization in the USSR. They issued directives from the party's central organs, discussed issues relating to policy implementation, collected party dues, attended to personnel issues, conducted verifications of party members, and so forth. The secretary of the ECCI party committee from 1935 was Fyodor Kotelnikov. In February 1935 the membership of the ECCI party organization totaled 468.[17] This organization provided a strong institutional link between the workers in the ECCI apparatus and the VKP and played an important role in the unfolding of the mass repression within the Comintern's headquarters.[18]

By the 1930s the ethos of the VKP had saturated the Comintern, the ECCI, and its apparatus. Historians date the Bolshevization of the Comintern from the mid-1920s, by which they mean that the VKP's values and behaviors became those of the Comintern and its fraternal parties.[19] A variety of factors enhanced this process, the most notable being the removal of people who opposed the VKP line or the Comintern line or who supported people who did so. In the 1920s, on direct orders from the VKP leadership, the ECCI first removed the followers of Grigori Zinoviev, chairman of the Comintern from 1919 to fall 1926, for joining the Trotskyists, and later the followers of Nikolai Bukharin, Zinoviev's successor, for their opposition to the party line in 1928–1929.

The Bolshevization of the Comintern disheartened some Communists outside the USSR, some of whom quit their parties or were removed, others of whom endured the Bolshevization in silence. Among the latter was the German Communist Clara Zetkin, who wrote to Jules Humbert-Droz, a Swiss Communist and an adherent to the Bukharin line, that the Comintern had become "a dead mechanism that swallows orders in Russian and issues them in different languages."[20] Those who supported the party and Comintern viewed things very differently and justified the oppositionists' removal as a necessary action to guarantee the Comintern's political identity, health, and unity. By the 1930s the Bolshevization of the Comintern was well advanced. And as it advanced, the virulent campaigns against the deviant isms (Trotskyism, Zinovievism, Bukharinism, etc.) became defining realities and normal practices within the Comintern.[21]

In spite of its Bolshevization, the Comintern possessed some distinctive characteristics—in part because it was an international political institution. Most members of the ECCI and of the Comintern's apparatus were foreigners, who resided in the USSR for varying lengths of time. Delegations and representatives from abroad frequently came to participate in Comintern activities, to attend Comintern Congresses, or to report to the ECCI on their parties' activities. The ECCI was responsible for fraternal parties, each of which was assigned to a national or regional section (*sektsiia*) in the ECCI and had an official representative (*predstavitel'*) who reported to a designated ECCI Secretary. The ECCI was also responsible for thousands of Communist émigrés from countries where Communist Parties had been outlawed or from which individuals had fled to avoid persecution. These foreigners had had very different political, social, and cultural experiences than their Soviet comrades— experiences that Bolshevization could not entirely eradicate or replace. In short, the Comintern staff and those for whom they were responsible differed dramatically in composition from the staff and clients of all other Soviet institutions, including the VKP. That the Comintern was a polyglot organization symbolized its distinctive nature. German was its official language, although Russian effectively displaced it in the 1930s. But on any given day, Polish,

Hungarian, Bulgarian, Italian, French, Chinese, or other languages could be heard in its offices. Comintern documents, reports, and directives routinely appeared in a variety of languages, as did the books, pamphlets, and brochures that it published.

The Comintern, therefore, existed in two worlds: in the USSR, the socialist world; and in the international arena, the capitalist world. Within the USSR, its roles were to elaborate policies to hasten world Communist revolution abroad and to strengthen the international Communist movement, to defend Soviet foreign and domestic policies, and to cooperate with the appropriate party and Soviet offices (e.g., intelligence and security organs). In the capitalist world, the Comintern's role was multifaceted: it guided and directed Communist Parties, helped to build their organizational structures, worked to ensure party discipline, educated fraternal party members in Marxism-Leninism, and demanded that its followers defend USSR's policies and leaders.

Members of fraternal parties who lived in the USSR had grown up and become acculturated in societies very different from Russia. Although they had made conscious choices to destroy the social and economic orders of their native lands, their personal, social, cultural, and political experiences there had been formative. However much members of fraternal parties may have dedicated themselves to the USSR and to revolution, they carried within them the experiences and identities of their native lands. Although they may have been VKP members, they retained other identities—they were Poles, Germans, Bulgarians, Hungarians; they were members of other political parties or movements; they had been persecuted and arrested abroad; they were workers, intellectuals, teachers, employees; they were the sons and daughters, brothers and sisters, of workers, policemen, peasants, military officers, clerks, and factory owners. Although these foreigners may have believed that they had shed their pasts and become "real Bolsheviks" and, in some cases, loyal Soviet citizens, these identities became an increasing cause for concern to VKP leaders from 1934 on.

The Comintern Bureaucracy

To manage and coordinate its various activities, the Comintern had a large bureaucracy.[22] Formally, Comintern Congresses determined its policies. In reality, the policies and nominees put forth by the VKP delegation were those approved by the Congresses. The Congresses were held in 1919, 1920, 1921, 1922, 1924, 1928, and 1935. Before each Congress, plenary meetings were held at which the various representatives hammered out a wide array of issues and policies to present to the Congress for approval—which was always granted, though not without debate. The Congresses also elected the members of the Executive Committee (ECCI), which administered and interpreted policies between Congresses.[23]

The ECCI was the Comintern's counterpart to the Central Committee of the VKP and, like that body, had both full and candidate members. The ECCI's members were among the most important and powerful members of the international Communist movement and the VKP. Some ECCI members resided in the USSR, others in their native countries. The number of ECCI members varied somewhat over time; from 1935, there were 46 full members and 33 candidate members. Within the ECCI was a Presidium, a smaller and more powerful body.[24] Between 1926 and 1935 the Presidium elected a Political Secretariat, and the latter elected from its ranks the Political Commission of the ECCI Political Secretariat.[25] The Seventh Comintern Congress in 1935 approved a reorganization plan that simplified this layered leadership bureaucracy. From 1935 there existed only the ECCI, the ECCI Presidium, and the ECCI Secretariat, which was the key leadership body.[26] Georgi Dimitrov was the General Secretary of the ECCI.

Between 1926 and 1935, within the ECCI, there also existed Lendersecretariats, which were "obliged to keep up with developments and situations in the appropriate countries and appropriate Communist Parties, to support these parties in their current work, and to keep up with these parties' fulfillment of [Comintern] resolutions." Leading ECCI members headed the Lendersecretariats, which provided the ECCI's leaders with information about the parties for which they were responsible and transmitted to those parties ECCI resolutions and policies. After the Seventh Congress, the Lendersecretariats were renamed Secretariats, but their functions did not change.[27]

Each fraternal party had a representative in the ECCI who was the de facto head of that party on Soviet territory and who was expected to monitor and report on its activities, performance, successes, and weaknesses to the appropriate ECCI office and Secretariat. According to a February 1936 ECCI directive, the representatives in the ECCI were to be members of the Politburo or Central Committee of their party and were responsible to both the ECCI and their party. Each member party also belonged to a section within the ECCI.[28] Among those subordinate to each Secretary were analysts (*referenty*), whose primary responsibility was to monitor the political, economic, and social conditions in an assigned country or region.

Finally, there existed an International Control Commission (ICC). Its primary role was to act as an appeals board for those expelled or reprimanded by the fraternal parties. The ICC was also empowered to investigate and pass judgment on Comintern members accused of inappropriate political or personal conduct. Like its VKP counterpart, the Central Control Commission, ICC members could not serve on the ECCI, the ECCI Presidium, or the ECCI Secretariat.

The ECCI had functional departments to attend to routine operations. From 1935 they included the Cadres Department, the Department of Propaganda and Mass Organizations, the Administration of Affairs Department, the Translation Department, the Archive, and the Communications Department (formerly known as the International Relations [OMS] Department). For our purposes, the most important was the Cadres Department.[29] Like any other personnel department, the Cadres Department maintained files on its members, not only on persons living in the USSR for which the ECCI was responsible but also on many Communists who lived abroad.[30] Such files included routine information like name, date of birth, class background, occupational history, date of joining the party, and other parties to which one had belonged. Some people's files contained records of deviations from the party line; associations with people dubbed "Trotskyists," "provocateurs," or "renegades," or with others deemed "suspicious"; formal and sometimes informal complaints lodged against a member; and other types of political information, including denunciations.

A Cadres Department table compiled no later than 1934 and based on a review of the files of fraternal party members shows that, in the department's opinion, there were quite a few "Trotskyists and renegades" and other allegedly "suspicious" elements within each fraternal party. According to the report, the French Communist Party (CP) had 482 "suspicious" members; another 70 people had already been expelled for being "Trotskyists or renegades" or "provocateurs," or for other reasons.[31] By what criteria the Cadres Department or its party representatives judged a member to be "suspicious" or a "Trotskyist" is unclear. Nor is it clear how many of these people resided in the USSR or later suffered during the mass repression. What *is* clear is that the Cadres Department kept careful and extensive files on Communists. Those files played a crucial role during the repression.

The ECCI periodically created commissions to deal with important but unusual activities and problems that inevitably arose in an organization as complex as the Comintern. The Secretariat or Presidium usually created these commissions, defined their responsibility and mandate, and appointed their personnel. During the years after 1934 the ECCI created commissions to review the credentials of its apparatus, to investigate problems within fraternal parties, and to investigate charges against individuals. Each of these commissions played a significant role in the unfolding of the repression, although none was created with that role in mind.

During the 1920s and 1930s, the governments of many European states (Poland, Hungary, Italy, Bulgaria, Germany, Yugoslavia, Lithuania, Finland, Romania) outlawed the Communist Party. Nonetheless, these local parties maintained underground organizations, and the governments used a variety of tactics to infiltrate them. Many people who fled persecutions in those countries emigrated to the USSR, where they were originally welcomed as political refugees. Several of these outlawed parties (e.g., the German, Hungarian, Bulgarian, and Yugoslav parties) established headquarters in Moscow; others (e.g., the Italian and Polish parties) established their headquarters in Paris. The ability of the ECCI to directly influence the parties in Moscow was considerable. Overall responsibility for the affairs of political émigrés and refugees in the USSR was the responsibility of MOPR (International Organization for Aid to Revolutionary Fighters), which was responsible to the ECCI. Although some of these refugees were Communist Party members, many were not. MOPR's responsibilities included locating housing, work, schooling, and other types of aid for these refugees.[32]

Every worker in the ECCI apparatus underwent a verification procedure (*proverka*) conducted by the Cadres Department as a condition of employment. The verification of foreigners for employment or a visa consisted of two steps: the Cadres Department verified the person's political credentials, and then it sought approval from Soviet security organs. Issues regarding foreigners required that the Cadres Department routinely cooperate with the Third Department of the Main Administration for State Security (GUGB), a department of the NKVD.[33] The GUGB had responsibility for personnel issues relating to the Comintern, such as issuing visas to visiting foreign Communists and giving clearance for personnel to work in secret activities or to travel abroad. Such security clearances were necessary before foreign Communists received a Soviet visa, were promoted to a leading or sensitive post, or were granted asylum. For example, in January 1937 the ECCI wanted to invite fraternal party leaders, radicals, and journalists from abroad to attend the show trial of Yuri Pyatakov, Karl Radek, and others. Before it could issue invitations, it had to submit the names and a brief biographical sketch of those it wanted to invite.[34]

Likewise, the Cadres Department forwarded to the security organs information that it believed warranted their attention. In February 1933, for example, the Cadres Department passed on to Sosnovskii, a NKVD official, the following denunciation: "Paul Hengst lives in N[izhnyi] Novgorod, USSR. During [his] vacation, he was in Germany. He slandered the USSR—about the famine, about shadowing, [and stated] that, as a soldier, the Russian proletariat is rotten to the core."[35] Who sent the denunciation to the Cadres Department and whether or not it had any basis in fact are unknown. As we shall see, in many cases the author of a denunciation was known. Quite often the author was a comrade in a fraternal party (the denunciation was often transmitted to the department via MOPR), a fellow party member in emigration, a member of a local VKP committee, an informant, or simply a coworker or acquaintance. That the Cadres Department forwarded the denunciation of Hengst to the security organ illustrates an anxiety that increasingly defined Soviet life as the 1930s progressed—that foreigners who emigrated to the USSR posed potential security threats.

In short, the Cadres Department had regular dealings with the security organs. Given that neither security clearances for foreigners nor the sharing of intelligence information was an unreasonable bureaucratic activity, cooperation was hardly auspicious, although in hindsight it appears portentous.[36] In fact, in the Soviet context it would have been highly unusual for the Cadres Department not to have shared information with the security organs. More significantly, the long-standing relationship between the security organs and Comintern created a routine of compliance and cooperation that abetted the mass repression.

From 1933 the VKP, the ECCI apparatus, and the fraternal parties conducted political purges (*chistka*) and verifications of their members. These involved reviewing each member's credentials and, if the situation warranted it, either reprimanding the member or recommending the member's expulsion. Students from abroad who attended one of the educational institutions administered by the ECCI were also required to undergo periodic political verifications, the results of which were forwarded to the Cadres Department. An 8 May 1934 list of former students in the Communist University of Peoples of the East, entitled "Characteristics of Some Individuals Rejected During the Verification," contained the following information: "Wang, Sen Min, Korea. Suspected of espionage in the service of the Japanese. Kim, Fyodor, Korea, Neighbors [*sosedy*; i.e., NKVD] categorically object to his trip to the country [Korea]. . . . Li Wang, China. Leader of the right oppositionists, actively struggled against the CPC [Chinese CP]. . . . Sokol, Romania, Neighbors categorically object to [his being] dispatched to the country [Romania]."[37] The recording of the "neighbors'" opinion underscores the working relationship between the security organs and the Cadres Department on issues relating to foreigners.

These purges and verifications did not, however, portend the dramatic expansion of police powers in 1937–1938.[38] Purges and verifications of members of the VKP and some fraternal parties had occurred regularly since 1921, and none had led to mass police repression.[39] There is no evidence to suggest that the Comintern and party officials who recommended and conducted the verifications of different groups had any idea that the materials thus generated would later be used as the basis for the 1937–1938 mass repression.

Given the Comintern's activities abroad and its responsibilities for foreign Communists and political émigrés, it, not surprisingly, also routinely cooperated with the Commissariat of Foreign Affairs (NKID), as well as with military intelligence and security organs. The nature of the Comintern's relationships with these bodies evolved over time. During its early years, relations between it and Soviet security and intelligence services were defined with some measure of administrative precision. In August 1921 leading representatives of the Comintern, the Cheka—the state security service—and the military intelligence service established precise limits on the use of personnel and committed the Comintern to "close cooperation" with the intelligence services. Henceforth, a "representative of the Comintern is not able to simultaneously be a plenipotentiary of the Cheka and Razvedupr [military intelligence] and, conversely, representatives of the Razvedupr and the VChK [Cheka] may not function as representatives of the Comintern or its departments." Representatives of the Cheka and military intelligence were forbidden to finance foreign parties or groups. Only the ECCI could do so, although it could delegate to the People's Commissariats of Foreign Affairs and Foreign Trade the right to finance foreign parties. Even though "representatives of the VChK and Razvedupra cannot appeal to foreign parties or groups with suggestions for cooperation . . . representatives of the Comintern [are] obliged to offer those agencies and their representatives close cooperation."[40]

Over time mutual relations between Comintern organizations and Soviet intelligence and diplomatic organizations became more regularized. On 14 August 1925, Aralov, a member of the Collegium of the Commissariat of Foreign Affairs, wrote to Chicherin, the People's commissar of foreign affairs, that the ECCI had agreed that the "ambassador should be the only contact point for passing information between the local country and Moscow. All work should be done within our official institutions."[41] Thereafter, cooperation between the Comintern and the NKID, security organs, and the military intelligence service increased. The ECCI's Communications Department (before 1935, the OMS) often cooperated with these agencies to gather and convey information, political documents, and other materials in a given country. ECCI personnel and fraternal party leaders routinely sent information of intelligence value to high-ranking Soviet state officials.[42]

One of the Comintern's major functions was to gather and analyze information about the political, economic, and social conditions in various countries. Although such information served the needs of intelligence organizations, it also served the ECCI's needs by providing information that allowed it to adapt legal and illegal political activities abroad, to adapt political tactics in a given country, to keep an eye on fraternal parties and their members, and to acquire organizational skills.[43] It is hardly surprising, therefore, that VKP leaders often assigned people with experience in intelligence operations to the Comintern and Comintern officials with such experience to Soviet state agencies. Several examples will illustrate the practice.

From 1935 until his arrest in November 1938, Meer Trilisser, known in the Comintern as M. A. Moskvin, was a member of the ECCI Presidium and a candidate member of the ECCI Secretariat and worked closely with the Communications Department of the ECCI. He chaired the 1936 and 1937 commissions to verify the workers of the ECCI apparatus. As ECCI Secretary, Moskvin also played an active role in the verification of members of the Communist Party of Poland (CPP) living in Soviet emigration. Before joining the ECCI in 1935, Moskvin's experience had been in intelligence and investigation. From 1921 to 1929 he headed the Foreign Department of the Cheka and the Cheka's successor, the OGPU, and for a while was the deputy head of the OGPU. In the late 1920s, Moskvin was a leading official in the Workers and Peasants Inspectorate (Rabkrin).[44]

Bronislav Bortnovskii (aka Bronkowski) joined the ECCI apparatus in 1929 and became the CPP representative in the ECCI. In December 1933 he became a candidate member of both the ECCI Presidium and the Political Commission of the ECCI's Polish Secretariat; a year later he became the Secretary of the Polish-Pribaltic Lendersecretariat. At the Comintern's 1935 Congress, Bronkowski was elected an ECCI member and a candidate member of its Presidium as well. Bronkowski's work experience, like Moskvin's, was in intelligence. After serving in the Cheka and OGPU from 1918 to 1924, he worked for five years in the Red Army staff's Fourth Department, which specialized in intelligence. In fact, several ECCI officials at one time or another had worked in the Red Army's Fourth Department. Among them was Boris Melnikov (aka Müller), the head of the Communications Department from 1935 until his arrest in May 1937; Müller had worked in the Fourth Department from 1931 to 1933, before moving on to intelligence work in the NKID.[45]

The presence within the ECCI apparatus of people with close ties and experience in the security and intelligence services made sense from an organizational standpoint. The ECCI needed experienced and talented intelligence experts in order to properly assess political conditions abroad. But it also served those services' interests. The presence of so many foreigners in the ECCI apparatus and the close ties between the ECCI and the fraternal parties meant that the Comintern headquarters needed to be monitored. These people brought with them not only experience but also attitudes fashioned in the Cheka, OGPU, Rabkrin, or Red Army, as well as close professional ties to those staffs. Precisely what those attitudes were is today difficult to discern, but many appear to have shared Stalin's and the NKVD's belief that "enemy agents" disguised as émigrés operated within the VKP and the USSR. Ironically, all of those ECCI officials who had security or intelligence experience fell victim to the repression. Precisely why each did cannot be ascertained until the appropriate archives are open.

The Comintern not only had members with ties to various intelligence and security organs but members who engaged in clandestine activities abroad, which often required that they travel under assumed identities and with false passports. Usually the Communications Department (or its predecessor) directed and coordinated their operations. These people were multilingual, and many were not Soviet citizens. Their activities abroad included acting as couriers for the ECCI, intervening in the affairs of fraternal parties, and engaging in clandestine operations and intelligence work. The suppleness of their identity was an asset to the ECCI, but during the repression it attracted the suspicions of NKVD investigators. The Communications Department and its operatives were especially hard hit during the repression.

Penetrating Party Discipline and Political Rhetoric

The ECCI and its apparatus were complex political and bureaucratic institutions. The ECCI was the directing body of the worldwide Communist movement, but the bureaucracy that administered that movement was politically and financially dependent upon the VKP. It operated under the watchful eyes of the VKP and security organs in the Soviet bureaucratic and cultural context. There is little doubt that Comintern organizations had been Bolshevized, or perhaps more precisely Sovietized, by the mid-1930s.

Yet it would be a mistake to view all who served the Comintern as political or bureaucratic automatons. Although Clara Zetkin privately condemned the Comintern as a "dead mechanism," she nonetheless remained a party member until her death, as did Humbert-Droz, to whom she confided her opinion. They stayed in the party for many reasons, not least because, for all its shortcomings and failures, the Communist movement was to them the best hope for the realization of the political dreams to which they had dedicated their lives. Others in the ECCI apparatus and among the political émigrés living in the USSR must have shared Zetkin's opinion. But some people wholeheartedly embraced the VKP's values and perspectives; for them the rhetoric had meaning. Others fell somewhere between Zetkin, with her cynicism, and those who hung on Stalin's every word. Comintern members were, after all, human beings. Like all members of the species, they were capable of a bewildering variety of beliefs and behaviors.

Although the Comintern and fraternal parties were politically and financially dependent on the VKP, many of their members did not view themselves as subservient. Rather than sharing Zetkin's cynicism, they proudly viewed themselves as partners in the struggle to create a socialist world; and Soviet socialism, was, they were convinced by the mid-1930s, besieged from within and without by recent and long-standing enemies. They struggled against what they perceived as ultra-leftism, as well as reformism, against reaction and fascism, so that their dreams would one day be realized.[46] They were, in short, true believers who shared and proselytized the VKP's policies and values, not to mention its fears and anxieties, and who risked everything for the cause.

The ECCI and its apparatus were more than political appendages of the VKP and Soviet bureaucracies. They were also complex social institutions. The Comintern was a collective movement of international Communist Parties, a movement that drew together people of different nationalities, races, class backgrounds, cultures, and languages, a movement of people who shared a common political ideology but whose personal, political, social, and cultural experiences differed significantly, a movement that used a common political language but whose members interpreted it in terms of their own, often foreign experiences. It was, in short, a collective whose members shared certain identities but differed in other ways. Complex identities were as typical of those who staffed the ECCI's sprawling administrative offices as they were of those who pledged fealty to the Comintern. The differences could not help but affect the Comintern and its apparatus and contribute in some measure to the distinctive perceptions and behaviors of its members. For those who lived outside the USSR, the differences proved to be of less consequence than for those who lived there in the late 1930s, when the demands of party discipline meant that differences aroused suspicions and often led to tragic consequences.

The ECCI oversaw and administered the Comintern's fraternal parties. The important and petty internal debates, factional struggles, and personal squabbles of the parties also affected the Comintern, its policies, and its behavior, sometimes as much as did the domestic and foreign policies of the governments from which its members had fled. Within the USSR, foreigners who worked for the Comintern, the ECCI, or exiled fraternal parties used a common political rhetoric in an alien culture to fight battles over international, national, and intraparty issues. They worked in international bureaucracies, whose personnel spoke different languages and had varying backgrounds. In this context, they sought to administer the worldwide Communist movement in a way that balanced the "correct" line of the USSR and VKP against the unique realities of each country.

However powerful the identities and divisions within the Comintern, the VKP provided a common supra-identity for all those affiliated with the Comintern. Nowhere was this more evident than within the ECCI party organization. In early 1935, Dimitrov described that body as possessing a "special character" because "out of 468 members of the party organization, 280 are foreign comrades of different parties."[47] For members, the demands of party discipline were paramount. Party discipline and the homogeneity of party rhetoric during the Stalin era served to mask individual perspectives and opinions, making it difficult for historians to ascertain the dimensions of wholesale belief, selective belief, careerism, opportunism, and fear among Communists.[48] The documents in this volume regrettably shed limited light on private opinions and attitudes. But that need not blunt our ability to appreciate why they behaved as they did. To comprehend the behaviors of the groups and their members, theories of social psychology, particularly those relating to obedience to authority, group identity, and group behavior, are particularly fruitful. A brief discussion of the theories that inform this work is therefore appropriate.

Party discipline was a defining feature of Communist Party, especially VKP, membership. The member parties of the VKP and the Comintern demanded that party members adhere to and carry out the policies and directives of party authorities. Whereas strict party discipline distinguished Communists from members of most other political parties, it served to routinize a universal behavioral tendency—obedience to authority. As Stanley Milgram's classic experiment on obedience to authority demonstrated, human beings, regardless of class, race, age, and education, possess a powerful tendency to obey authority, even when the consequences of doing so inflict harm on others. As long as people acknowledge an authority to be legitimate and accept the authority's orders as being consistent with the setting from which authority is derived, people will obey orders even if doing so induces in them considerable strain and tension. The tendency for human beings to obey is a powerful one.[49]

Members of Communist Parties willingly joined those parties and hence explicitly acknowledged the authority of the party and their superiors within it. Obedience flowed naturally from the situation. Within Communist Parties obedience to authority was a collective behavior, as well as an individual behavior. As such, it provided a powerful inducement to conformity.[50] That disobedience could result in expulsion from the party reinforced members' obedience.

Obedience to authority plays an important behavioral and interpretive role in any history of the Comintern. Members of the Comintern acknowledged the VKP as the supreme authority on political matters and Stalin as the personification of the VKP. The Comintern's leaders derived their authority from the VKP's leaders. Each invoked Stalin, the Central Committee of the VKP, or some other authority in the political hierarchy to justify and rationalize their behavior. The staff of the ECCI and the members of the party organization did the same. In so doing, they behaved the same way as ordinary people everywhere do in the face of authority. Party discipline was a distinctive feature of Bolshevism, but its consequences—obedience and conformity—were universal.

No less important than party discipline was group identity and behavior. Although the VKP was the governing party after 1917, it retained many characteristics common to social movements that do not possess state power. As with religious movements, cults, and sectarian political movements, VKP members constituted a small minority of the national population and shared a distinctive and internally coherent worldview—Marxism-Leninism—from which they derived a shared set of values and assumptions and common frames of reference. The VKP promised a better life for its members and society, provided an avenue for social and economic mobility and status for those formerly denied both, and offered a specific set of values and social norms that helped members give their experiences meaning. Like many social movements, the VKP fashioned its identity both from its values and worldview and from its response to perceived enemies. The members of the fraternal parties shared the VKP's values and worldview. Because they did not wield state power in their countries, their parties were more obviously social movements. But for members of those parties living in the USSR, VKP membership provided a measure of prestige and influence that served to heighten their identification with the VKP. The Comintern was the Soviet institution in which the values and social norms of a ruling party melded with those of a social movement.

The members of social movements who share an internally coherent worldview derive values and assumptions from it that often provide rigid standards of judgment, which can breed intolerance of perspectives that question or threaten beliefs. Party members internalized the VKP's standards, attitudes, frames of reference, and social norms.[51] Living in the USSR, where the VKP monopolized the media, enhanced their internalization of these norms and values.

The demands and strictures of party discipline ensured compliance with social norms. Reinforcing this acceptance was the selective and elective nature of party membership; that is, people had a predisposition or reason for wanting to join the party, but the party decided who would be allowed to do so. The party could, and did, expel from its ranks those who criticized party values or failed to comply with its social norms. Party discipline was a very powerful means of reinforcing the VKP's values, frames of reference, and social norms.

For party members at all levels of the party hierarchy, party discipline and personal beliefs were inextricably intertwined. This did not mean that party members were automatons. On the contrary, members chose to join the party and accepted its values, assumptions, and social norms. But as individuals with differing personalities, abilities, backgrounds, educational levels, and experiences, they embraced some attitudes and values more closely because they were of "personal significance." Although this process of selective identification helps to explain differences in individual party members' perspectives and behaviors, more important for our purposes is a "psychological consequence of this identification of the self with the social world": "that a person depends upon external social circumstances for his personal stability." As members of the ruling party, VKP members had a material, social, political, and personal status that was a function of party membership. Because status and self-identity result from both social recognition and individual achievement, the psychological ties that bound VKP members to the party and its worldview were very strong.[52]

The values, assumptions, frames of reference, and social norms of the VKP defined the mental context of individual party members. That mental context, in turn, enabled party members to interpret and ascribe meaning to their experiences, a need central to all humans.[53] Indeed, belonging to the party served several human needs: it validated the individual's search for meaning, provided a means of reducing uncertainty, and provided consensual validation to all members.[54]

In this volume I focus on the years 1934 to 1939, a period in Soviet history defined by an increasingly uncertain domestic and foreign environment. Uncertainty and unpredictability create anxieties and a heightened need to find stability and meaning; they create a critical situation that many people have an inadequate mental context to interpret. The more directly someone's status or ego is involved, the more critical is that person's situation. Such situations make people susceptible to suggestion. People are particularly susceptible to suggestion when it is offered by an authority and when they have "no adequate mental context for the interpretation of a given stimulus or event [or] when [their] mental context is so fixed that a stimulus is judged by means of this context and without examination of the stimulus itself."[55] To interpret a bewildering situation or event, people commonly accept explanations so long as they do not conflict with their standards of judgment and frame of reference. In such situations, slogans and symbols can be very effective. The more specific the slogans and symbols are, the more likely they are to be effective, because it is easier for people to conceptualize specific ideas than to understand more abstract or complex causes. But slogans or symbols are effective only if they fit mental context and frame of reference and add meaning.[56]

In a critical situation people are also susceptible to explanations that interpret it as resulting from a conspiracy. Believing in a conspiracy enables individuals and groups to explain the seemingly inexplicable. So long as the conspiracy theory does not contradict the members' frame of reference and mental context, it will be seen as plausible.[57] When recognized authorities propagate a conspiratorial explanation for an uncertain situation, the power of that explanation increases, particularly if elements of it resonate with the beliefs of the group.

The need to discover meaning in a situation generally increases with the need to preserve the status of the individual and the group. Hence the actions of individuals and the group reinforce and validate each other. When a person's social identity is threatened directly or indirectly, that person commonly develops a stronger identity with a group.[58] The result is that the behavior of members of a group becomes increasingly defined by the needs of the group; individual behavior becomes increasingly circumscribed. Such a self-validating dynamic creates a sense of universality and increases the pressure on individuals to support the group and to conform. To not do so threatens an individual's identity and status.

Given that the VKP controlled the means of communication and the armed might of the state and that party discipline meant that rank-and-file members had to carry out the party line on any given issue, it may seem unnecessary to apply theories of social psychology to gain insight into how local party organizations and party members behaved and why they behaved as they did. But the claim that coercion alone is sufficient to explain behavior rests more on assumption than on evidence and implicitly denies the role and nature of consent, which contributed to these behaviors. Social psychology offers a useful theoretical perspective because it allows us to view party discipline as a social norm, to appreciate the impact of party propaganda on people's behaviors, and to focus on what was said and done as expressions of group values and concerns. In short, it allows us to view the behaviors not simply as Soviet or Stalinist behaviors but as universal human behaviors. Because words convey values and assumptions, because they have and give meaning, these theories provide a tool with which to penetrate the VKP's rhetorical homogeneity. Because the leaders or members of local party organizations often influenced the ways political campaigns ordered by party leaders were implemented, appreciating group behavior is important. Pronouncements from Stalin and the Politburo were often rather general. It was left to those lower down in the political hierarchy to interpret those pronouncements as they deemed appropriate. How they did so provides some insight into why they did so.

Using Enemies to Forge a Communist Identity

Prior to the adoption of the Popular Front, the Comintern devised for its member parties offensive policies that sought to hasten revolution. The Popular Front was qualitatively different. It was a defensive policy designed to stem the spread of fascism. The shift from offensive, revolutionary policies to a defensive policy speaks volumes about the mounting anxieties and fear of war that gripped the USSR after 1933. But these were not the only policies that defined the political life of the Comintern. From 1919 the Comintern organized and directed a series of political campaigns that sought to discredit socialists and Communists to its right and left who opposed it, its policies, or those of the VKP leadership. The political struggles within the Bolshevik Party (and to a certain extent within the German CP) defined who was the "enemy" at any given historical moment.

By harshly condemning the "improper" viewpoints and political behaviors of those who disagreed with the VKP and the Comintern, these destructive political campaigns defined what Moscow believed to be the proper and improper political behaviors and identities of true Communists. The campaigns identified which parties, groups, and individuals were "enemies" who warranted the scorn or approbation of Communists and explained, in arcane detail, why they were "enemies." Identifying "enemies" and explaining why they were enemies was an important means by which the VKP and Comintern created a true Communist identity. By adhering to and internalizing political policies and behaviors enunciated by the VKP and the Comintern and by eschewing and condemning the policies and behaviors of the perceived "enemy," members internalized this identity and the assumptions and values that underlay it.

Defining enemies was important to the VKP, which regularly recruited new, politically unseasoned people to its ranks. But doing so was also essential to the Comintern, many of whose members lived outside the USSR in pluralist political cultures where the centrifugal pulls of political legitimacy, public debates, and political pragmatism were often strong. For such people, commitment to the cause was a precondition for party membership, but defining the errors of those to the party's right and left provided the means by which party identity and loyalty were formed.

The Bolsheviks and the Comintern saw multitudes of political enemies to their political right and left. The virulent campaign against Social Democrats was one of the means by which the Comintern sought to protect its newly formed member parties from becoming reformist and to solidify their revolutionary identity. Lenin had long railed against Social Democracy as a tendency that eroded the élan and vigilance of revolutionary socialists. Reflecting this view, the seventh of the Twenty-One Points insisted on the need for Communist Parties "to recognize the necessity for a complete and absolute break with reformism" and stated unequivocally that "without that no consistent Communist policy is possible."

Although ideological imperatives help to explain the Comintern's struggle against Social Democracy and reformism, they were not the only reasons.

Prior to 1918, there was no counterpart anywhere in the world to the Bolshevik Party. Most of those who joined the newly formed Communist Parties came out of more moderate Social Democratic traditions. Within the newly formed fraternal parties, the ECCI, and the VKP were former Social Democrats, Mensheviks, Bundists, Socialist Revolutionaries, and members of other radical and reformist parties. Forging a shared Communist identity among comrades who had had personal and political ties to other parties was essential.

The VKP and the Comintern also conducted political campaigns against enemies to the left of the Bolsheviks. Lenin's blistering 1920 pamphlet *"Left-Wing" Communism: An Infantile Disorder,* made clear what he perceived to be the dangers of excessive radicalism to the Communist movement.[59] From the mid-1920s the political struggles within the VKP defined the threats from the emerging left oppositions—first Trotskyism (1923–1927), then Zinovievism (1925–1926), and then the united Left Opposition (1926–1927), all referred to collectively as Trotskyism. The leaders of the VKP and the Comintern went to great lengths to enumerate the Trotskyists' errors for two important reasons. The first is that, within the VKP and many fraternal parties (e.g., the German, Polish, and French CPs), Trotskyism enjoyed considerable popularity. Although the opinions of fraternal parties were of secondary importance to the struggles within the VKP in the 1920s, they were not without influence, and oppositionists used their foreign comrades to buttress and legitimize their struggle. In the late 1920s, Stalin and his supporters viewed the Trotskyists in the USSR and abroad with considerable anxiety.[60] The second reason was that the Trotskyists used Leninist logic and Bolshevik rhetoric to critique the VKP and the Comintern from a Marxist-Leninist perspective. That the Trotskyists used a shared language and shared assumptions to criticize the policies and behaviors of the party majority made their arguments all the more powerful and dangerous. That they were willing to appeal directly to workers, in violation of party discipline, made their political behavior unacceptable. In the eyes of VKP and Comintern leaders, the threat that the Trotskyists posed was a grave one. Identifying the Trotskyists' errors and explaining why they were errors became a Bolshevik and Comintern cottage industry.

With the emergence of the so-called Right Deviation in 1928, led by Bukharin and Aleksei Rykov, VKP and Comintern leaders conducted new campaigns against what they perceived as the reformist danger. As during the anti-Trotskyist campaign, the ECCI urged fraternal parties to identify Rightists and expel them from the party. Yet the campaign against the Rightists never achieved the virulence of that against the Trotskyists, primarily because the former abided by the rules of party discipline whereas the latter refused to do so.[61]

The seemingly arcane quality of the VKP's and ECCI's destructive political campaigns must be understood within the context of the forging of a proper Communist identity. Social Democrats (and other reformists) and Trotskyists (and other "infantile" revolutionaries) were the political Scylla and Charybdis between which those who sought to become true Communists had to steer. The leaders of the VKP believed that they knew how to steer properly between these dangers, to maintain the proper revolutionary course. The Comintern shared and popularized this belief. Hence party discipline, adherence to the policies enunciated by VKP and Comintern leaders, was essential to remaining a "real Bolshevik." The definitional and didactic purposes were what made political campaigns so important and so virulent. Yet in forging the proper political identity, the VKP and the Comintern created a polarized political worldview in which all political enemies became equally menacing, equally dangerous, and deserving of equal disdain. The extent to which the Popular Front softened that worldview varied from country to country, but it never eliminated it. Within the USSR after 1934, that Manichean perspective deepened.

CHAPTER TWO

The Kirov Murder and the Call for Vigilance

If you believe certain words, you believe their hidden arguments. When you believe something is right or wrong, true or false, you believe the assumptions in the words which express the arguments. Such assumptions are often full of holes, but remain most precious to the convinced.

— FRANK HERBERT

It was a paradoxical atmosphere—a blend of fraternal comradeship and mutual distrust.

— ARTHUR KOESTLER

ON 1 DECEMBER 1934, Leonid Nikolaev entered the headquarters of the Leningrad party organization and strode to the hallway outside the office of Sergei Kirov, the party secretary, a Politburo and Central Committee member and one of the USSR's most powerful men. When Kirov entered the hallway, Nikolaev drew his revolver and shot Kirov. The murder electrified the country.

The Kirov murder is to Soviet history what the Kennedy assassination is to American history. Although certain facts are known, many questions remain. Those questions have given rise to considerable scholarly debate.[1] I hope here to examine how Kirov's murder and the Politburo's reactions to it affected the Comintern and the ECCI apparatus.

After the murder the Comintern leadership diligently pursued two lines of action. The first was to act as the agent of the VKP. The leaders issued a steady stream of encoded telegrams to fraternal parties regarding the murder, telegrams that faithfully reflected the party leaders' accusations about the murder and that urged fraternal parties to heighten political vigilance. After Kirov's murder, the ECCI became the central agent in the international campaign against Trotskyism. For the Comintern, directing that international struggle was not a new role, but the virulence of that campaign had intensified. The campaign, which continued through the decade, contributed not only to struggles within the fraternal parties but, ironically, also to the mass repression in 1937–1938.

From December 1934 the ECCI devoted considerable effort and energy to ordering its fraternal parties to expose the dangers posed to the USSR by domestic and foreign "enemies." Shortly after the murder, the Politburo charged that the assassin was part of a White Guard conspiracy. More than a hundred alleged White Guardists were arrested and executed.[2] Telegrams from the ECCI to its fraternal parties conveyed its version of events. Then, in mid-December, the Kremlin charged that Grigorii Zinoviev, Lev Kamenev, and other former Zinovievite oppositionists had been arrested for their alleged role in a conspiracy to murder Kirov, a conspiracy that the Politburo asserted was linked to the exiled Trotsky and had operational centers in Leningrad and Moscow.

In the West some newspapers expressed outrage at the lack of public trials for the White Guardists and at their execution and published allegations that one hundred workers had been executed along with the White Guardists.[3] They also raised a series of questions about the Kremlin's shifting blame for the murder from White Guardists to former oppositionists and condemned the arrest or exile of former oppositionists.[4] This outrage and the questions posed created confusion and problems within fraternal parties, which were unable to answer the questions or to explain the inconsistencies of the Kremlin's different versions of the crime. They beseeched the ECCI for answers. But the ECCI was also unable to answer the questions, or was at least unwilling to break from the official line, and simply told the comrades to present the case more forcefully.[5]

Other ECCI telegrams, however, took a strident, offensive tone in ordering fraternal parties to heighten their political vigilance so as to expose and expel former oppositionists whose behavior or attitudes raised questions about their political loyalty. The ECCI also ordered the parties to organize mass campaigns against Trotskyists. Examining a few selected telegrams will suffice to convey the ECCI's role in directing the anti-Trotskyist campaign abroad and to appreciate how the ECCI's role as the agent of repression began to unfold.

Document 1 is a telegram from the Communist International of Youth (KIM), the Comintern youth organization, to Gilbert Green of the Communist Party of the United States of America (CPUSA), general secretary of the

CPUSA's National Executive Committee of the Communist Union of Youth from 1934 to 1940.[6] Similar telegrams were sent to other party and Communist youth organizations abroad. The accusations in the telegram against "the counter-revolutionary work of the remnants of the former Zinoviev-Trotskyist opposition" are familiar. But its charge that former oppositionists "prepared to murder Stalin and his co-workers" presaged charges that would be brought against Zinoviev, Kamenev, and the other defendants at their August 1936 trial. The call to "achieve the complete expulsion of the trotskyists from the workers' movement" was a common one in the Comintern's telegrams to its fraternal parties from late 1934, as was its unbridled praise of Stalin.

Document 1

Telegram from the Comintern's youth organization to Gilbert Green, CPUSA, regarding the struggle against oppositionists, 1 January 1935. RGASPI, f. 495, op. 184, d. 26, outgoing 1935g. to New York, ch. 1, l. 1. Original in English. Typewritten. Stylistic errors in the original.

1 January 1935
To New York Youth CC Green

The investigation of the murder of Kirov brought out the deathly picture of the counter-revolutionary work of the remnants of the former Zinoviev-Trotskyist opposition which lost all hopes of the support of the masses and prepared to murder Stalin and his co-workers and gain the downfall of the Soviet power by intervention of the imperialists.

Trotsky—one of the chief organizers and spirit of this criminal fascist group—carries full responsibility for the killing of Kirov. Broadly explain to the toiling youth, especially the socialist, the counter-revolutionary fascist character of the role of Trotsky and the trotskyists. Achieve the complete expulsion of the trotskyists from the workers' movement.

With everyday work, continually explain the great role of Stalin[,] continuer of the work of Marx-Lenin, the genial organizer of the victory of socialism in the USSR, the loved leader of the international proletariat.

Point out that Stalin as a great leader and friend and person is surrounded by the love of hundreds of millions. Call to the youth to study the genial works of the life and struggle of Lenin-Stalin, educate themselves in a Leninist-Stalinist quality, work in the spirit of the unlimited trust and love for Stalin and his co-workers—members of the Political Bureau of the CP SU.

YCI[7]

Almost daily in January 1935 the ECCI sent telegrams to its fraternal parties pressing them to "strengthen the struggle against the representatives and defenders of the Trotskyist-Zinovievite bloc" and "show the responsibilities of local enemies of the Soviet state and the party for creating illegal groups and carrying out counterrevolutionary terrorist acts in union with the imperialist interventionists so as to overthrow Soviet power."[8] Some telegrams directed the parties to conduct campaigns against specific individuals or publications that disputed the Kremlin's version of Kirov's murder. Others indicate that the ECCI was monitoring the coverage of the Kirov murder and its political aftermath in the Communist press to ensure that the articles conveyed the Kremlin's version of the events and did not run "slanderous anti-Soviet" articles from bourgeois presses.[9]

The Political Commission of the ECCI's Political Secretariat sent **Document 2** to ten Communist Parties in Europe and to the CPUSA. It represents the anxieties and concerns expressed in some ECCI telegrams sent in late 1934 and early 1935. Moscow's primary concern was to counter the "insolent lie" published abroad claiming that "hundreds of workers" and other innocent citizens had been executed. The ECCI's leaders asserted that such slanders were part of an "anti-Soviet campaign" organized by an "anti-Soviet bourgeois front." To counter this campaign, they urged member parties to take to the pulpit and explain to the masses that "in fact" those executed were "terrorists who had infiltrated the Soviet Union from abroad." This telegram conveys succinctly the Soviet belief that "enemies" encircled and had penetrated the USSR and that they availed themselves of any opportunity to destabilize the government and murder its leaders. The ECCI's solution was to order its adherents to "explain better to the masses" the "facts" about "the shooting of terrorists" and the "white terror."[10] But the most intriguing aspect of the telegram is what it does not contain: although it condemns "White Guards," nowhere is the alleged Zinovievite-Trotskyist conspiracy mentioned. The difference between the villains in Documents 1 and 2 suggests that there was some confusion within the ECCI (or possibly between the leaders of the ECCI and the KIM) over who the villains were—but no confusion over the role of the ECCI as the Politburo's agent.

Document 2

Telegram from the Political Commission of the ECCI Political Secretariat to the Communist Parties of France, Belgium, England, Czechoslovakia, Holland, Sweden, Norway, Denmark, Switzerland, the United States, and Greece on counteracting the anti-Soviet campaign abroad in connection with the executions related to the case of S. M. Kirov, 9 January 1935. RGASPI, f. 495, op. 184, d. 55, outgoing telegrams for 1935, general directives. Original in German.[11] Typewritten with signatures.

---

9 January 1935.

It is essential to make more active and aggressive the unmasking of the anti-Soviet campaign in connection with the shooting of the counterrevolutionary terrorists. Explain better to the masses that the reformists' and other [groups'] resolutions of protest against the shooting of terrorists are, in fact, an open demonstration within the framework of the anti-Soviet bourgeois front, a defense of and solidarity with the White Guards, the worst enemies of the working class [and] the proletarian state. Explain that the violence against white terrorists was undertaken in the interests of protecting millions of workers from a cruel class enemy and is an act of genuine humanism. While doing so, it is necessary to make good use of the telegrams published on 5 January in the newspapers. In order to confuse the masses, French reformists are talking about the execution of hundreds of workers. It is necessary to decisively refute this insolent lie. Those executed were accessories to Kirov's murder and were linked to other White Guard terrorists who had infiltrated the Soviet Union from abroad with bombs and explosive charges with the goal of organizing attempts on the lives of the representatives of Soviet power. We cannot limit ourselves to a press campaign only. It is important to raise a wave of protest among the organizations of socialist parties [and] reformist and other trade unions against the position of the leaders of these organizations. For this purpose, it is necessary to use these local organizations of the Union of Friends of the Soviet Union. Encourage the sending of telegrams of support, resolutions from delegations of reformist and revolutionary organizations, from committee meetings, from production collectives, etc., to Soviet representatives. It is essential to provide better information about the facts of the white terror, which in some countries has grown to an unheard-of scale, while giving a free hand to the friends of those who protest against the shooting of the White Guardsmen.

Polit[ical] ***Commission***
Gottwald, Knorin, Gerish
< . . . >

ECCI officials carefully monitored how fraternal parties covered the events in the USSR following the murder. When they saw undesirable tendencies, they were quick to criticize the erring party, as **Document 3** indicates. This telegram contains criticism of the Politburo of the Italian Communist Party for an editorial that appeared in its theoretical journal, *Lo Stato Operaio*, published from its headquarters in exile in Paris.

Document 3

Telegram from the Roman Lendersecretariat to the Politburo of the Italian CP in Paris, 9 February 1935. RGASPI, f. 495, op. 184, d. 37, outgoing telegrams for 1935 to Paris, l. 20. Original in French. Typewritten with signature.

9 February 1935
Paris
P.B. of the Italian CP
We call your attention to the editorial article in "Stato Operaio"[12] mistakenly connecting the Kirov murder to alleged domestic difficulties in the USSR, instead of stressing the grandiose victories of socialist construction, the growing danger of imperialist aggression against the USSR, the unanimous mobilization of the masses around the VKP(b). The article does not concentrate fire against the activities and counterrevolutionary campaign of the Trotskyists and Social Democrats. We demand an intensification of the campaign against Trotskyists and Social Democracy in all party publications in connection with the Kirov murder.
Rom[an] Secr[etariat]

Abramov

Telegrams such as these were common fare in late December 1934 and early 1935. Although their purpose was to direct the political activities of the fraternal parties abroad, they also reflected the political line enunciated by the leaders of the VKP and the ECCI. Regardless of which version of the murder was conveyed, they both illustrate party leaders' anxieties about the foreign threat to the USSR, as well as the roles of the ECCI as faithful mouthpiece of the Politburo and director of the international Communist campaign against Trotskyism and Social Democracy. The vigilance campaign within the Comintern following Kirov's murder shows the logic and dynamics of this role.

Among Communists, Kirov's murder was shocking and bewildering, and evoked considerable confusion and anxieties. In accordance with Politburo directives after the arrests of Zinoviev and other former oppositionists, many party committees launched investigations of former oppositionists within their own ranks.[13] This was especially the case within the party organization of the ECCI. These investigations constituted the Comintern's second line of action in the aftermath of Kirov's assassination, its work as the instrument of repression. Within the ECCI apparatus, a series of party meetings took place in late December 1934 and early 1935 at which discussions of Kirov's murder and accusations against some former oppositionists occupied center stage. These meetings had a special sense of urgency because not only had Zinoviev, the former chairman of the Comintern, been arrested, but so had Georgi Safarov.[14] Safarov had been expelled from the VKP in 1927 for his participation in the Left Opposition. He was readmitted in 1928 and had worked in the ECCI apparatus since 1929. The arrests placed their former coworkers and former oppositionists who worked in the ECCI apparatus in an uncertain and politically vulnerable situation. The arrests also raised explicit and implicit questions about the leaders and cadres of the ECCI. Understandably, the ECCI and its party organization responded decisively to the Politburo's calls to heighten political vigilance. Appreciating the dynamics of these meetings provides insight into the power of party discipline, the mistrust evidenced in uncertain situations, normative party behaviors, and the expressed beliefs and social norms that constituted the political culture within the ECCI party organization prior to Kirov's murder and that intensified after it.

Before turning to the reactions and behaviors of the members of the ECCI party organization after Kirov's murder, two points deserve mention. The first is that we know today what Soviet citizens at the time did not—that there is still no evidence that any kind of conspiracy to murder Kirov existed. Just as we have no evidence of a conspiracy, they had no evidence that there was not one. On the contrary, the evidence available to them indicated that a conspiracy existed. The accusation that former Zinovievites and Trotskyists were complicit in Kirov's murder placed them outside the bounds of the party. It transformed them from former oppositionists, former errant comrades, into "enemies," the first significant step in their dehumanization.

The second is that historians must interpret the past on the basis of the available evidence. The following documents convey clearly that rhetorical homogeneity was a feature of party discourse under Stalin. Different historians might interpret this rhetoric in different ways. Some might view it as evidence that whatever doubts party members harbored, they were too afraid to express them and hence adhered to party discipline and used the rhetoric as a means of self-defense. Others might view the homogeneous rhetoric as evidence that party members believed entirely what they said, that the rhetoric faithfully reflects their understanding of reality. Without evidence of a person's private thoughts, either interpretation tells us more about the historians than it does about historical reality. Historians are better served by interpreting the rhetoric in the historical context in which it was spoken, by examining which aspects changed and which remained the same over time, by assessing nuance and tone, and by appreciating that words convey and give meaning, that they express shared beliefs, anxieties, and fears, and that they can mask emotions and opinions. "Speaking Bolshevik" was not only essential to personal advancement and group identity but also crucial in shaping and expressing identity.[15]

The rhetorical homogeneity also serves as a vivid reminder of the centrality of party discipline and the consequences of violating it. Party discipline had been a defining feature of Bolshevism since the founding of the party and was required for Comintern membership. It also served as a powerful agent of socialization. While shared beliefs, experiences, and hopes made compliance of party members voluntary, the consequences of violating party discipline served to enforce what the VKP's leaders deemed acceptable. As Cominternists well knew, violations of party discipline could result in expulsion. Trotsky, Zinoviev, and many of their supporters, including some who worked in the ECCI apparatus in 1934, had been expelled from the VKP or fraternal parties for violations of party discipline. By 1934 the importance that Stalin and the leadership attached to party discipline was obvious. Even minor infractions of party discipline could result in expulsion.[16]

Party discipline also served a normative, didactic role. Prior to party meetings, the leaders of a party organization decided who would address the meeting, who would present which reports, and what the contents of the reports would be. To be selected was both an honor and an obligation. The most trustworthy and disciplined members were chosen. Their selection ensured that the party line was expressed. The enunciation of the party line in meeting after meeting, in the press, and on the radio had the cumulative effect of legitimizing that line, or at least aspects of it. That coworkers, comrades, and friends gave the reports reinforced the sense of universality.

Among those in the ECCI party organization who had worked under Zinoviev were people who no doubt found the charge that he had conspired to kill Kirov to be incredible. They did not voice their doubts. But the same people may well have believed that foreign conspiracies threatened the USSR and that Stalin would not fabricate such accusations. For loyal Bolsheviks, sharing certain beliefs and doubting others must have been very disorienting.

The allegation that former oppositionists conspired against the party resonated among its members. For more than a decade, VKP and fraternal party members had condemned various oppositionists' lack of party discipline and their anti-party behaviors. Violation of this central tenet of party culture predisposed party members to accept leading officials' statements that some former oppositionists still harbored anti-party sentiments. The Riutin Platform of 1932—which condemned Stalin and his policies—Trotsky's efforts in that year to revive the Left Opposition, and the existence of smaller opposition groups and platforms reinforced the perception that opposition to the party line remained a real threat.[17] The press presented the existence of a conspiracy to murder Kirov as an established fact and noted that the evidence in support of it was sufficient to convince the police to arrest the accused. "Real Bolsheviks," predisposed as they were to view opposition as a threat to the party, had little reason to doubt their leaders' assertions. To appreciate that some party members accepted the notion of a conspiracy of former oppositionists does not mean that all did. For those who entertained doubts, the accusations were surely bewildering.

The claim that anti-Soviet conspiracies threatened the USSR was not new in 1934. The foreign interventions of 1918–1920 and the invasion by Poland in 1920 were vivid memories for Bolsheviks, foreign Communists, and Soviet citizens. Those invasions confirmed the party leaders' assertion that capitalist states hated the USSR and intended to use any means to eradicate the world's only socialist state. Early in the Soviet experience, the threats posed by capitalist encirclement became a political assumption and a staple of official propaganda. The war scare in 1927 reinforced that fear, as did the military clashes over the Chinese Eastern Railway in 1929 and the ensuing Manchurian crisis.[18]

In the late 1920s and early 1930s in a series of show trials the defendants were convicted of belonging to anti-Soviet groups directed from abroad.[19] Stalin used the trials to assert that the enemies of the Soviet state had altered their tactics but not their goal, as his comments in 1928 made clear: "Earlier . . . international capital thought to overthrow Soviet power by a direct military intervention. The effort was unsuccessful. Now it is trying, and will try in the future, to weaken our economic might through invisible, not always noticeable, but quite powerful economic intervention—organizing wrecking, preparing various kinds of 'crises' in different branches of industry, and by these means facilitating the possibility of future military intervention."[20] Indeed, in the late 1920s and early 1930s, Stalin and other leaders often attributed the problems hindering the realization of party policy to alleged enemies of Soviet power—"wreckers," "saboteurs," and other "hostile elements" who served foreign interests. Stalin and other party leaders believed that neighbors threatened the USSR. In a September 1930 letter to Molotov, a Politburo member, the chairman of the Council of People's Commissars and his close ally, Stalin candidly expressed his belief that Poland and other border states were preparing for war against the USSR.[21] After Hitler came to power in 1933, the fear of the foreign threat intensified, and for good reason—Hitler made no secret of his anti-Bolshevism and his desire to create lebensraum in the east for his thousand-year Reich.[22] By late 1934 the Nazi party was securely in power. Poland's efforts to play Nazi Germany and the USSR off against each other only convinced many in the Kremlin that Poland harbored hostile intentions. Such a threatening environment provided fertile ground for mistrust, spymania, xenophobia, and conspiracy theories.

Party members, including members of fraternal parties who lived in the USSR, either accepted or did not publicly dispute these explanations, thereby legitimizing the belief in conspiracies, foreign or domestic, that was to have such tragic consequences. Why they did so is understandable. Their leaders and the press repeatedly warned about the foreign threat and the conspiracies behind it, and they had no access to independent sources of information and analysis. Propaganda is effective, and in one-party states, values and perspectives can be readily induced. The party's control of the media, educational system, police, judiciary, and economy gave it enormous powers to inculcate values, perceptions, and social norms and to shape behaviors. Even if some were aware of the contradictions and inconsistencies of the conspiratorial explanations, there is no reason to assume that they would have rejected Stalin's and their leaders' explanations. The intellectual beauty of conspiracy theories is that the contradictions can be made to fit the theory.

The overt and subtle pressures to use official rhetoric are obvious. Less obvious is the extent to which people internalized these values and perspectives. We can never be sure whether a particular person believed everything that he or she said. But the evidence does allow us to determine how they behaved. Within the ECCI apparatus, rhetoric and behavior were inextricably linked. Words and deeds have consequences. The consequences may not have been intended, but they were real. Tragically, in this period the consequences of "safe" rhetoric and behavior helped create a situation that placed many people at mortal risk.

Although the predisposition to believe in hostile conspiracies ran deep among Communists in the USSR, that belief is insufficient to explain the reactions and behaviors of many party leaders and members to Kirov's murder. His murder represented a new threat of qualitatively different dimensions. Heretofore Zinovievites, Trotskyists, and other oppositionists had engaged in political opposition, not conspiracy to commit murder. They had opposed party policies; they had violated party discipline. Even when their loyalty to the state was questioned, they had never been accused of engaging in criminal acts against the USSR.[23] Although those arrested after Kirov's murder had formerly been oppositionists, at the time of their arrest they were party members in good standing and held responsible party or state positions. The allegation that enemies of the USSR existed within the party shocked, bewildered, angered, and upset party members. Those reactions and the demands of party discipline help to account for the fearful and belligerent tones that characterized party meetings in late December 1934 and early 1935. In hindsight, the allegation that former and once-forgiven oppositionists had moved beyond intraparty struggles and had joined forces with external enemies of the USSR made the political aftermath of the Kirov murder an especially dangerous precedent. But at the time, its immediate effect was to warn of a qualitatively new danger posed by old antagonists against which the VKP had to once again be vigilant.[24]

The allegation that an international conspiracy was involved in Kirov's murder lent credibility to those within the Central Commmittee and the ECCI who maintained that foreign agents had penetrated the ranks of political émigrés. The leaders of the ECCI and many staff members were quite aware of this viewpoint. In March 1932 the Organizational-Instructional Department of the Central Committee of the VKP sent a circular to the ECCI that stated: "In connection with the contemporary international situation of the USSR, in short order organize an accounting and verification [*uchet i proverka*] of political émigrés on the territory of the USSR. Guide this work in two directions: 1) the identification of cadres who can be of use to fraternal parties [abroad], 2) the struggle against provocation and espionage."[25] The 1932 verification of émigrés was carried out by regional VKP organizations with the participation of the fraternal parties' representatives in the ECCI. Information on suspicious political émigrés thus generated was sent to the Cadres Department of the ECCI, where the staff recorded it in their files on people and, in some cases, forwarded it to the security organs. From 1933, the Politburo and security organs became increasingly suspicious of certain émigrés living in the USSR. In that year, there were arrests of Polish émigrés and Polish CP members on charges of espionage. The security organs also kept a watchful eye on German émigrés, some of whom were arrested.[26]

The 1932 verification was not the only source of disquieting information about the political reliability of some émigrés. Denunciations and reports from local VKP and fraternal party organizations charged that "provocateurs," "irresponsible hooligan elements, and even police agents" disguised themselves as political émigrés.[27] More ominous was the report presented to a meeting of the ECCI Secretariat on 25 October 1934 by Anton Krajewski, a leading Cadres Department official. Krajewski reported: "Under the guise of émigrés, they [foreign intelligence services] send here secret agents who work very well and very easily under the guise of victims of political terror [in their native countries]. Then they turn out to be provocateurs ... this channel of espionage against the USSR is in general the organization of espionage and provocation of an international general staff [*masshtab*]." He also stated that the police provoked factional struggles within Communist Parties abroad and concluded that some participants in former factional struggles might be police agents.[28]

Such an assertion by a Polish émigré and high-ranking Cadres Department official served to validate the fears of those in the Central Committee and the ECCI who suspected that spies and enemies existed among the émigrés and within the VKP and fraternal parties. The allegations raised in Krajewski's report imbued a special sense of urgency into the calls for vigilance that followed Kirov's murder. More to the point, Kirov's murder and the charges against Zinoviev, Safarov, and the rest suggested that the enemy was within the gates. Vigilance was imperative.

On 26 December, several days after Safarov's arrest, the party committee of the Comintern's Publishing House for Foreign Workers held an open party meeting.[29] The meeting, like all VKP committee meetings, had a ritualistic structure. A carefully selected comrade presented the main report, which set the agenda and the political parameters of the discussion. That report took its logic and rhetoric from the pronouncements of VKP leaders on the issue at hand. Other comrades then addressed the meeting and elaborated on aspects of the main report. At this meeting, as at many others, the reports and comments conveyed constructive and destructive messages by identifying positive goals and what had to be overcome and improved to attain them. Those messages reaffirmed the correctness of party policy.

Three other notable features characterized this and subsequent party meetings. The first was the importance attached to one's political past, especially past support for a former opposition. The political pasts of party members had always been important to Communists, but as the vigilance campaign intensified, their importance increased. The second, related feature was that former oppositionists were expected to engage in self-criticism and to denounce other former oppositionists who they alleged had not truly overcome their oppositional tendencies. For former oppositionists to attack other former oppositionists was a significant change in the political ritual; in the pre-Stalin era a simple recantation of one's errors had been acceptable penance. Not every former oppositionist fully embraced the new ritual, however. The third feature was the Politburo's insistence on raising political vigilance, which animated the participants and sharpened their rhetoric, thereby upping the political ante for all.[30]

Of the 206 people who attended the meeting of the party committee of the Publishing House for Foreign Workers, 67 belonged to the VKP, 7 to the Komsomol, and 50 to fraternal parties; 82 were non-Communists. Boris Ya. Menis, deputy director of the publishing house, opened the meeting with a report on the Zinovievite-Trotskyist opposition. Eighteen people participated in the ensuing discussion, four of whom were former oppositionists. After Menis's report, Claude-Joseph Calzan, a candidate member of the Politburo of the French CP and an editor in the Press and Propaganda Department of the ECCI, addressed his comrades. Calzan's comments sought to balance self-criticism of his past political mistakes with a measured call for greater party vigilance. He admitted having formerly supported the Zinoviev opposition, but upon recently learning of their alleged ties to "fascists," he had demanded that oppositionists "should be harshly rebuffed" (*dolzhen byt dan samyi zhestokii otpor*). In light of Zinoviev's arrest, he perceptively concluded that "former oppositionists should be afraid." Nonetheless, he expressed doubt about the Kremlin's version of the murder by suggesting that it might have been a "personal act." Another former oppositionist, Regina Budzynska, who also admitted her past oppositional activities, condemned the Zinovievites for not recognizing the victory of the party line and for seeking to "destroy our ranks." She too called for greater vigilance. The party committee's decision to have former oppositionists address the meeting and condemn the arrested underscored the perceived danger. But it also exposed the former oppositionists to attack.

Several speakers enthusiastically responded to their calls for vigilance by criticizing Budzynska's and Calzan's comments and accusing others of having ties to "suspicious" elements. Among them was Comrade Rakow, himself a former Trotskyist.[31] After stating that he had corrected his errors, he charged that Calzan's comments were too mild and that Calzan was mistaken if he believed that Kirov's murder was "a personal act." In the aftermath of Kirov's murder, Rakow announced, it was better to shoot a hundred people than not to shoot one fascist enemy. But Rakow's hard line did not eliminate him from suspicion. Comrade Vainer reminded the meeting that "at one time, [Rakow] zealously defended the opposition." Kreps, the director of the publishing house, said that for Budzynska to call oppositionists "fascists" and "murderers" was not enough; she "should speak in detail about her own participation in the opposition." Raiskaya called for the expulsion of Pyatgorsky from the Komsomol because he allegedly "belonged to various oppositions abroad."

Although former oppositionists came under attack, members of the fraternal parties received special attention from some of their Soviet comrades. Comrade Dobrovolski suggested "strengthening vigilance not only within the VKP but also within the fraternal parties." Arthur Valter joined Calzan's critics, accusing him of not being sufficiently Bolshevik and of not fully "appreciating the political significance of Kirov's murder." He then named several fraternal party members who worked in the Roman Section of the ECCI (which oversaw the west European fraternal parties) who had "very suspicious ties [to oppositionists]. . . . It is necessary to uncover these ties." Vainer denounced the Belgian member Macsschalek because he considered the latter's proposal from the floor calling for "the execution of [Kirov's] murderer incorrect." Germer described Macsschalek's view as that of "an opportunist, a Social Democrat, but not a Communist."

Not everyone at the meeting endorsed the attacks on fraternal party members. One who did not endorse the attacks was himself foreign-born. Franz Morriens, a founder of the Belgian CP and the head of the Roman Section, which Valter had criticized, cautioned against excessive criticism of foreign comrades: "It is necessary to take foreign comrades as they are." No one else who spoke endorsed his opinion.

Menis, in his closing remarks, put all former oppositionists on notice: "We should hear the voices of all those former oppositionists who did not speak today." Those in attendance then passed a resolution condemning the Zinovievite-Trotskyite opposition, any opposition to the party line, "double-dealers" (who publicly supported the party line but in reality struggled against it), the "fascist terror" against party leaders, and, in particular, the murder of Kirov, "one of the best sons of the party of Lenin." The resolution demanded "of all members of the collective heightened political vigilance" and called for "death and disgrace to the enemies of the working class, to the agents of the Zinovievite-Trotskyist opposition."

Next, those in attendance turned their attention to Comrade Germer's report on the case of Noah Borowskii, the German editor and translator of N. Popov's *Outline History of the All-Union Communist Party (Bolshevik)*. Borowskii had once sympathized with the pro-Bukharinist Brandler opposition within the German CP and with the ideas of the Austrian socialist Otto

Bauer, whose anti-Bolshevik views he allegedly had smoothed over in his translation. Borowskii admitted that "he had made many mistakes, gross political mistakes, but he was never a double-dealer"—a very important distinction. He claimed that he had struggled against Brandler, though not forcefully enough, and that he had learned "vivid lessons" from the review of his case by the party organization. At the end of the meeting Borowskii contritely stated "that he was not a real Bolshevik." His comrades agreed; consequently, he was expelled from the German CP.[32]

At a meeting of the same party committee five days later, Macsschalek, Budzynska, Calzan, and Borowskii all gave penitent speeches. No one who spoke after them had anything complimentary to say. Comrade Boldano exclaimed: "We don't have the right to believe anyone without requiring verification." Fainberg said: "Calzan gave a declaration that has no value and [expressed] completely petit bourgeois thought. This may be the first link in the chain. Petit bourgeois—this is Menshevism, but Menshevism—this is counterrevolutionariness [*kontrrevoliutsionnost'*] and murder." The meeting ended by condemning Macsschalek's speech and sending Budzynska's case back to the party committee for further action. She was expelled from the party and arrested in March 1935.[33]

These two meetings provide intriguing examples of how the party groups within the ECCI responded to the VKP leaders' demands for heightened vigilance in the aftermath of Kirov's murder. In accordance with party discipline, comrades expressed themselves in the current party rhetoric. Former oppositionists were prominent among the speakers. Their self-criticisms and attacks on their comrades played an important role in the ritual and in affirming the need for vigilance. Amid the rhetoric some comrades expressed doubt about the official version of the murder, but most asserted that conspiracies of oppositionists and fascists existed and directly threatened the USSR. Although some Soviet-born, former oppositionists were criticized, the members of the fraternal parties received the brunt of the speakers' criticisms. Clearly, some were unwilling to take their comrades "as they are." The party committee leaders consciously chose these comrades as scapegoats. Scapegoating them both reflected and contributed to an emerging suspicion of foreigners, which in turn reinforced, consciously or subconsciously, the allegation that foreign conspirators threatened the VKP and the USSR.

The 26 December meeting was but a prelude to a joint meeting of the ECCI party and Komsomol organizations held two days later. Its purpose was to consider the case of Ludwig Magyar, a Hungarian Communist who had participated in the short-lived Hungarian Soviet Republic of 1919 and who, after being released from a Hungarian prison as part of a prisoner exchange, emigrated to the USSR in 1922 and joined the VKP. In the mid-1920s, Magyar was a Comintern official in China; upon his return to Moscow, he worked in the Eastern Lendersecretariat, which directed Communist activities in China and other Asian countries. From 1925 until 1927, Magyar supported first Zinoviev's New Opposition and then the United Opposition created by the alliance of Trotsky's and Zinoviev's supporters. Although he criticized the opposition in 1927, thereby escaping expulsion from the party, Magyar continued to maintain close personal relationships with Zinoviev, Safarov, and other former oppositionists, relationships about which Pyatnitsky, one of the most powerful members of the ECCI, had previously warned him.

What triggered the investigation of Magyar was the arrest of his friend and coworker Safarov. Both Safarov and Magyar had supported the Zinovievite and Left Oppositions in the 1920s, had served together as Comintern representatives in China, and had worked together in the Eastern Lendersecretariat. Several speakers at the 28 December meeting referred to the existence of a Safarov-Magyar oppositional group, although Magyar himself referred to this as the "so-called Safarov-Magyar group."

As the transcript of the 28 December meeting indicates (see Document 4), Magyar's maintenance of close friendships with Zinoviev and Safarov "proved" that he was not a "real Bolshevik." He freely admitted that he had frequently had "political discussions" with Zinoviev, who at the time of his arrest served on the editorial board of the VKP's theoretical journal, *Bolshevik*. Prior to Zinoviev's arrest, his and Magyar's friendship had not been an "anti-party activity." Nor had Magyar's friendship with Safarov. But after Safarov's arrest, Magyar gave money to Safarov's domestic so that she could take Safarov a package in prison. While this act of friendship may have been politically naive, Magyar had immediately informed the second secretary of the ECCI party committee, Fyodor Kotelnikov, that he had done so. Neither of Magyar's actions would seem to have necessitated his "political execution," but they did. Why? What had changed?

What had changed dramatically after Kirov's murder was the political climate. Demands by Stalin and the VKP leaders for heightened party vigilance, the allegation that an anti-party conspiracy by VKP members contributed to the murder, and the arrests of former and current members of the ECCI apparatus all helped create a new and politically vulnerable climate. Magyar was a logical scapegoat.

Before turning to the transcript of the meeting, several comments are appropriate. **Document 4** reproduces portions of the stenographic report of the 28 December 1934 joint meeting of the party and Komsomol organizations of the ECCI. It captures the atmosphere of an important historical moment and conveys in detail the reactions of the speakers to Kirov's murder, Zinoviev's and Safarov's arrests, the fears and suspicions that gripped many Cominternists, and their views on what actions needed to be taken and why.

The meeting was obviously a political ritual. The leaders of the ECCI party organization had decided to expel Magyar before the meeting took place. The meeting was not for Magyar's sake but for the sake of the members of the party organization. It served many purposes: it reaffirmed VKP values and norms, it protected the leaders of the organization from any allegation that they were "soft" on potential enemies, it made clear to all in attendance what defined the proper Communist identity, and it condemned those who placed personal ties above party needs. The meeting opened with Kotelnikov presenting the report on Magyar. Kotelnikov, the man in charge of party cadres in the Eastern Lendersecretariat, where Safarov and Magyar had worked, and the second secretary of the ECCI party committee, had understandable personal reasons for demonstrating his vigilance. His report set forth Magyar's alleged crime, the political parameters of the ritual, and the primary message—the need for heightened political vigilance. Following Kotelnikov's report, Magyar engaged in what had become ritualistic self-criticism. Then a series of speakers paraded to the rostrum.

One after another they denounced Magyar for his previous oppositional activities and alleged oppositional tendencies, for not being honest about his relationships with Zinoviev and Safarov, for his failure to appreciate those men's "real" intentions, for his lack of party discipline, for the explicit doubt that giving money to Safarov's domestic cast upon the VKP and the NKVD, for his defense of Safarov during the 1933 purge of the party organization—in short, for not being a "real Bolshevik." Through rhetoric and votes, his comrades conveyed to all present that *he* had betrayed *them*. Many who addressed the meeting were prominent ECCI or VKP members of long standing, Soviets and foreigners alike, who had internalized party values. Their speeches served to legitimize Magyar's scapegoating and to protect their status. Others who spoke had formerly supported an opposition. Their condemnations of Magyar served to assure their comrades that they were loyal party members and, by so doing, to defend their status. The logic and rhetoric used by both groups to condemn Magyar conveyed their anxieties and their public acceptance of the leadership's assertions that some former oppositionists posed a threat to the party. Together, they behaved like a lynch mob.[34] Manuilsky put it bluntly: "Here, comrades, a political execution is taking place."

Magyar himself played a crucial role in the ritual. He did not so much defend himself as try to explain his behavior—as he put it, to "argue against some formulations . . . not over the political essence of the question." In fact, Magyar's comments to his comrades indicated that he too had embraced, albeit incompletely, the values and norms of the party and that he understood that his behaviors, however innocuous, challenged them. He told his comrades that the facts presented in Kotelnikov's report are "quite sufficient to expel me from the party." Magyar attributed his errors and allegedly anti-party behaviors to the fact "that I am still very much the petit bourgeois, that I have a lot of blue-blooded individualism, that I set my opinions, my judgments, against the opinion of the party and the judgments of our authorities. . . . I have maintained a liberal–blue-blood friendship with members of the former anti-Soviet groups. . . . My whole behavior again revealed my petit bourgeois individualism, . . . which I brought with me from that social milieu from which I came." In short, Magyar confessed that he had not fully internalized the party's values, that he was not a "real Bolshevik," that he deserved to be expelled from the party. By so doing, he absolved his comrades and validated the correctness of their actions and beliefs. He also fueled suspicions within the party organization by naming others who shared his political views and activities and by echoing Stalin's view that former oppositionists had adopted "new forms and new methods that . . . led to terror." Such statements reinforced the logic of the political crackdown after Kirov's murder and validated his comrades' decision.

Although Magyar's admission of errors conformed in many respects to what the party expected of its members, he did not play his role well. His tactic of arguing against "some formulations" indicated to those present that he was not a "real Bolshevik." A "real Bolshevik" would not have contested any aspect of the party's judgment, would have fully confessed his errors, and would have sought his comrades' forgiveness. Contesting "some formulations" exposed Magyar to accusations of being a "lawyer," of manipulating the "facts" to serve personal ends, of confusing political and juridical guilt.[35] Magyar's deviation from the ritual script, like Calzan's and Macsschalek's two days earlier, exposed him to vicious attacks from his comrades and suggests that foreign-born comrades' internalization of VKP values and rituals was incomplete.

What made Magyar a scapegoat was not that he was foreign-born. More than half the members of the ECCI party organization were foreign-born, and foreigners were the Comintern's constituency; two-thirds of those who addressed the meeting and condemned Magyar were foreign-born. Scapegoating foreign-born comrades to prove vigilance would not have reduced, but rather increased, the political vulnerability of the ECCI party organization. In late 1934 being foreign-born did not make one "suspicious," an "Other." Nonetheless, there were undertones. Certain comrades asserted that oppositionists "lived as if they were in emigration," and warned that the "facts have shown what . . . these emigration moods could change into."

Magyar was clearly a scapegoat, but let us consider why he was made a scapegoat and what making him one reveals about the those who did so. For many party members, whose status and identity were dependent upon VKP membership and on retention of power by the party, Kirov's murder was an attack not only on the party but also on themselves.[36] That so powerful and popular a leader had been gunned down left party members searching for an explanation. The Politburo and the NKVD provided just that. In fact, they provided two explanations—a White Guard conspiracy and a conspiracy of former oppositionists. Both groups had engaged in anti-party activities in the past, and both had ties to "hostile elements" abroad, as the explanations underscored. Every party member knew that the White Guards had fought to overthrow Soviet power, that Zinoviev and Trotsky had repeatedly opposed the party, and that Trotsky continued to do so even in exile. Because both explanations of the murder resonated with what many party members already knew, the accusations enabled them to give meaning to a seemingly inexplicable event.

Many who spoke at the meeting expressed that they had not previously known the "real Magyar," they had not understood his "real" anti-party, counterrevolutionary activities. But now that they knew what threats existed, they swelled the chorus of calls for greater vigilance. Magyar himself validated the importance of knowing the "real" person and appreciating "real" intentions: "Speaking about my personal connections with these people, I would like to say, comrades, that . . . we discussed political issues only, and I failed to discern in these conversations, during these meetings, the real attitude of these people." The goal of the vigilance campaign was to discover the "real" attitudes of opponents of the party line—past, present, and potential. Magyar's comments served to legitimize the need for vigilance among those attending the meeting.

Although the vigilance campaign put former oppositionists on the defensive, those who addressed the meeting expressed hard-line and moderate attitudes toward former oppositionists. Such a spectrum of opinion was still possible to find in late 1934. Some supported the hard-line position expressed by Otto Kuusinen, an ECCI member and leader of the Finnish CP, who demanded from his comrades higher "vigilance in our work . . . organizational and political vigilance." He warned them: "Trust in the word of no one, especially former oppositionists." Fritz Heckert, a German CP and an ECCI member, was equally harsh. He asserted that "our class vigilance is not as up to the mark as the situation requires," and urged his comrades to recognize "that Magyar also bears responsibility for what Zinoviev's group has done. . . . People who were members of this group, who advocated such a criminal policy, are therefore accessories to the crimes committed. They cannot be tolerated in the ranks of our party." To hard-liners, former oppositionists were a fifth column within the VKP.

Others took a more moderate position. Magyar had asserted that "it was impossible to trust our words, the words of the former Zinovievite opposition." Alikhanov, a Cadres Department official, rejected his assertion and asserted instead that "we know people who have honestly dissociated themselves from Zinoviev. We also know people who have proved their honesty by [their] deeds, by the struggle against the Zinovievites." During and after the meeting others, including Stalin in 1937, made the same point—that among former oppositionists there were many good Bolsheviks. Nonetheless, the hard-liners dominated the meeting.

Although Alikhanov took a moderate stance on former oppositionists, he shared the widely held view that a party member who placed his personal interests or views above those of the party revealed "his anti-party nature." Magyar had defended giving money to Safarov's domestic as evidence of his "petit bourgeois individualism." Alikhanov and others rejected that defense. Alikhanov asserted that after Kirov's murder, Magyar "thought about himself, about . . . how to conduct himself to divert the attention of the party organization away from himself." By juxtaposing individual self-interest against the interests of the party, Alikhanov underscored the importance of party discipline and the primacy of the group. For party members, any distinction between the political and the personal was a false one.

That juxtaposition implicitly raised another, which Magyar expressed in this way: "My whole behavior again revealed my petit bourgeois individualism, my blue-blooded individualism, which I brought with me from that social milieu from which I came." Magyar may have been a VKP member, but he had

lived most of his life in a very different social and cultural milieu. He was a Bolshevik, but he was also an émigré, a man who had come of age in a culture
where friendships and political beliefs were not mutually exclusive. Like all
émigrés, he brought to the USSR social mores different from the Russian ones,
and a different cultural frame of reference. Both Magyar and the ECCI party
organization were aware of these differences: "During the first purge that I
went through after being exchanged [for Hungarian prisoners], comrades,
members of the purge commission warned me about it ["my petit bourgeois
individualism"]. . . . You remember my last purge [1933], when c. Solts again
pointed this out." Raising party discipline implicitly meant rejecting Morriens's plea "to take foreign comrades as they are." As Kuusinen put it, "Real
Bolsheviks" subordinated "personal interests" to "party interests" and "we,
foreign Communists, need [to learn] this lesson."

Several speakers expressed concerns about the political reliability of fraternal party members, especially those members who had once sided with an opposition or who had served time in a foreign prison. Béla Kun, leader of the
Hungarian CP, ECCI member, and émigré, offered a portent of things to come
when he expressed his suspicion that his countryman, Magyar, may have been
released from prison in order to become an enemy of the USSR. The suspicion
that refugees who had served prison terms abroad may have become enemy
agents to secure their freedom appeared frequently in the late 1930s, especially
within the police. That an ECCI member expressed such a view suggests that
other ECCI members shared his suspicion. Another speaker, Sinani, went so
far as to state that the 1933–1934 party purge had not sufficiently revealed the
"anti-party" behaviors of those who had once belonged to other parties or of
those members of fraternal parties who had once supported an oppositional
group. He believed that a more thorough review of party members was in order.[37]

Bronkowski, a Pole and a prominent Comintern official, also offered some
rather critical comments about political émigrés. He said that "in the individual parties there are a number of people who have committed mistakes,
demonstrated their political inconsistency in other parties, and can serve as the
basis for anti-party activities of the different anti-party elements here in the
USSR and in the VKP(b)." He singled out Poles and Hungarians who had either been "in the opposition" or had been "deviationists." Such people, who
"do not demonstrate their loyalty to the party" or who "retain false views,"
provided "fertile [ground] for the seeds of anti-party opposition." The only
way to defend against these forces was "to improve our vigilance."

Bronkowski's sowing of doubts about the reliability of political émigrés, in particular Poles and Hungarians, reflected an existing concern and portended what was to come. For at least five years the VKP delegation to the ECCI had suspected that police agents had infiltrated the Polish party and had authorized the security organs to take appropriate measures to counteract them.[38] In the early 1930s quite a few Polish Communists living in the USSR had been arrested and charged with being enemy agents. Several of them had been executed in 1933 and 1934.[39] Only two weeks after Bronkowski's comments, the ECCI finished its investigation into "significant organizational weaknesses" that afflicted the Hungarian CP. (Bronkowski knew of the investigation.) Its resolution condemned Comrade Gold, a member of the Central Committee of the Hungarian CP and its representative in the ECCI, whose "opportunistic line" on doubling party membership "could only serve the object of provocation, to open wide the doors to the infection of the party by police spies." The resolution noted that the police had "already succeeded in disturbing party work."[40] In short, Bronkowski's and others' comments reflected the concern of the VKP and the ECCI about the reliability of members of these two fraternal parties in particular and implicitly of all fraternal parties, a concern that would deepen from 1935.

We need not take the strident rhetoric at face value to appreciate that many in attendance believed that Magyar, Safarov, and others posed a threat. To their former coworkers and to former oppositionists, they posed a personal threat. To those who were sincerely shocked at the two men's alleged antiparty behavior and double-dealing, they posed a threat to the party. The ECCI leaders no doubt feared that Safarov's and Magyar's cases would raise questions about their stewardship. Kun expressed this anxiety directly: "The quality of our leaders . . . is higher than ever. We now have to rally around this Comintern leadership . . . weed out the roots, eliminate all of the remnants of Zinovievite methods." In such an uncertain situation, vigilance and defense of the party served a host of personal and political needs.

Document 4 conveys much about the beliefs, emotions, and behaviors that made up key aspects of the party mindset, which in turn provided an important cultural precondition for the mass repression. Those who spoke at the 28 December meeting accepted, truly or rhetorically, the political logic underlying the charge that a conspiracy of former oppositionists linked to "enemies" abroad engineered Kirov's murder. That allegation justified the repeated calls for heightened vigilance, calls that resounded like a Greek chorus. Precisely who believed or did not believe the allegation is today impossible to determine. But by their words and behaviors, they validated it and the calls for vigilance and legitimized the directives of the VKP leaders. They thereby created a sense of universality that supported the primacy of the party and the need for greater vigilance.

Document 4

Protocol of the closed joint meeting of the ECCI party organization of 28 December 1934 regarding the case of Magyar, and a resolution about the expulsion of Magyar from the VKP, 29 December 1934. RGASPI, f. 546, op. 1, d. 257, ll. 32–135. Original in Russian (Fritz Heckert's speech in German). Typewritten.[41]

29 December 1934
PROTOCOL No. _____
OF THE CLOSED JOINT MEETING OF THE ECCI PARTY ORGANIZATION AND THE ECCI KOMSOMOL ORGANIZATION of 28 December 1934.

PRESENT: . . . members
PRESIDIUM: Party Committee and Political Commission
PRESIDING: c. Chernomordik
AGENDA: The Magyar case (Report by c. Kotelnikov).

SUBJECT OF HEARING:
1. The Magyar case. (Report by c. Kotelnikov)

KOTELNIKOV: Comrades, each of you read yesterday the indictment of the actions of the counterrevolutionary group of the Zinovievite-Trotskyist bloc. When reading this document, each of us saw the display of the foulest actions of these renegades, traitors, counterrevolutionaries. The goal set by this counterrevolutionary group was to eliminate the leaders of the party, the leaders of our proletarian state by terrorist means. They aimed at the leaders of the party. And only vigilance was able to guarantee against the villainous hand murdering the headman, the leader, our great beloved com. Stalin.

You know that this counterrevolutionary group snatched from our ranks a favorite, a tribune, a party leader, com. Kirov. To accomplish this villainous act, they recruited forces of the < . . . > defeated, yet active Zinovievite factional, anti-party, anti-Soviet counterrevolutionary group. In order to conduct their active struggle against our proletarian state, this counterrevolutionary group linked itself with representatives of bourgeois countries to struggle against Soviet power.

This document clearly shows what those who chose the road of struggle against the party are capable of. It shows where the logic of factional struggle leads.

Comrades, it was only days ago that we discussed the case of a former member of our organization, the counterrevolutionary Safarov.

We unanimously decided to expel him [from the party]. We unanimously decided to approve the measures that the organs of the proletarian dictatorship are taking against Safarov and other counterrevolutionaries.

Com. Manuilsky in his report about counterrevolutionary group activities[42] called for [strengthening] our militant Bolshevik Party vigilance. It was especially necessary since Safarov, a liar and a counterrevolutionary, spent year after year in the ranks of our organization, and we proved incapable of unmasking this counterrevolutionary until he was arrested. Naturally, this appeal by com. Manuilsky found a due response, could not but find a due response in the heart of every party and Komsomol member. Thus, the party group of the Eastern Secretariat,[43] following com. Manuilsky's appeal, raised once again at its meeting the question of how it was possible that Safarov, after working with the same people for several years, could not have been exposed by those people. And this party group failed to find the right answer, which is that the party group displayed insufficient party vigilance.

In addition to that, the party group examined the Magyar question. And now, as com. Chernomordik has announced, the Magyar question is on today's agenda. I will examine in detail why it is that today the party committee raises the Magyar question.

You know Magyar. But we have not known him well enough; we knew him badly. And that superficial knowledge prevented us from fully and completely understanding Magyar as a party member, as a Bolshevik. Today we can state, firmly and resolutely, that Magyar was not a Bolshevik, not a real Communist, not a Communist [at all].

What are the facts? First, Magyar's connection with Zinoviev, **Safarov**, Gorshenin. The names of these people are familiar to you: they are on the list, they are mentioned in the resolution adopted by the organs of the proletarian dictatorship [NKVD]. These people have been exiled as counterrevolutionary elements. Until recently, Magyar maintained ties with Zinoviev. I repeat, Magyar maintained ties with Zinoviev until the last moment. Their meetings took place when Zinoviev worked on the board of "Bolshevik."[44] They continued to meet after Zinoviev was kicked off that board. They were meeting even after com. Kirov was killed.

Where did those meetings take place? They took place in the editorial office or in the street. As it happens, these former comrades in arms in the struggle against the party, against the leadership, against com. Stalin, found a time and place to meet. They met despite com. Pyatnitsky's repeated categorical warnings to Magyar against maintaining connections or meeting with Zinoviev. These warnings notwithstanding, Magyar continued to meet with Zinoviev, this miscreant, factionalist wrecker. His counterrevolutionary activities are well known to the party and the working class of not only our country. In his capacity as a Comintern official, Magyar had no practical need to see Zinoviev. Their meetings could not but bring about certain harm.

What brought them together? What brought Magyar together with Zinoviev? At the meeting of the party group of the Eastern L[ender] S[ecretariat] and at the party committee [meeting], Magyar claimed that during his meetings with Zinoviev, he discussed politics only, that he could not discuss other issues. In Zinoviev, Magyar discovered a consultant on the questions of international politics, on the questions of theory. "Consultant" Zinoviev discovered a patient who struggled with him against the party for many years. And if Magyar was capable of really breaking [with Zinoviev] ideologically and organizationally, if he could overcome and understand the essence of this Zinoviev, he would have never joined him.

From this flows the conclusion that Magyar shared common ideological conceptions with Zinoviev. Magyar returned to the VKP(b) having not completely abandoned his factionalist ideas. Magyar still remained a Zinovievite; the residue of factionalist ideas remained deeply implanted in his consciousness. There is no other way to explain it. I repeat, the fact that Magyar and Zinoviev were former active factionalists served as a prerequisite for their meetings, drew Magyar into receiving consultations from Zinoviev. Magyar's repeated meetings with Zinoviev did nothing to help the party to expose the [real] person [and] the double-dealing and treachery of Zinoviev. He signaled nothing to the party. Magyar and Safarov are two inseparable, closely knit links of the common struggle against the party. Magyar and Zinoviev. The Safarov group—Magyar, Safarov, < . . . >, Vardin. It survived as a group and continued to struggle against the party even after the Fifteenth Congress.[45] However, when Magyar was asked at the party meeting of our group, why this Safarov-Magyar-Vardin group made its statement later than Zinoviev's group, Magyar asserted that, in contrast with Zinoviev's group, this group had no plans to conduct an anti-party struggle, but rather to return to the party honestly and with no [intention of] double-dealing. Having been out of the party's ranks after the Fifteenth Congress, they considered it honest to continue the struggle against the party. This group defies the [party] leadership [*bezvozhdentsy*].[46]

(KNORIN: [A group] of which Rumiantsev was a part.)

Comrades, what does Magyar think about this active factional struggle against the party? They "honestly" remained out of the party ranks and against the party, and only in the late summer of 1928 did they again fraudulently sneak into our party. Year after year they "honestly" remained in the ranks of our party and continued their double-dealing. And now we see the names of these "honest" people in the indictment, referred to as counterrevolutionaries.

We see how they are sent by the organs of the proletarian dictatorship into administrative exile and how this "honest" Safarov, this "honest" Vardin,

and this "honest" Magyar continue their ties with Zinoviev. Damn this honesty. There is no place in our Bolshevik Communist Party for such "honesty."
It is a pity, comrades, that they have been able to deceive our party for a long
time. Such "honesty" dulled Magyar, destroyed his Bolshevik flair, and upon
receiving from Zinoviev the charge [to engage in] factionalist struggle, his old
background took over.

They arrested Safarov. Magyar is the first to learn about this arrest. And
again it so happens that Safarov's maid rushes to Magyar to inform him first.
Why Magyar? Again, their connection can provide the answer to this question, their connection in the enduring struggle against the party. Safarov, the
counterrevolutionary, is taken to Leningrad. Magyar provides material support to Safarov through that very housemaid. Why Magyar? Why would Magyar display philanthropic sentiment toward a person arrested for his counterrevolutionary activities by the organs of proletarian dictatorship? This fact
cannot be considered as anything other than an anti-party, anti-Soviet action
by Magyar.

The Comintern party organization meeting is held. Well, not only in the
Comintern; throughout our country party meetings are taking place and are
actively reacting to the counterrevolutionary activities of this counterrevolutionary group. Magyar remains silent. You remember the big [December]
meeting in MAI[47] when the assembly room could not seat all the comrades
eager to take an active part, eager to express their indignation about the counterrevolutionary activities of Safarov and other members of the counterrevolutionary group.

Magyar stayed out of this activity. Magyar cut himself off. Magyar claims he
did not know about it. But it is hard to believe, comrades. It does not turn out
that way. From the moment this meeting was announced, I and many other
party committee members were literally besieged by our comrades who had
not been transferred to the VKP(b). They demanded to be allowed to be present at this meeting. News about this meeting spread at lightning speed. Comrades from MAI and other places wanted to be present at this meeting. Magyar, a worker in our apparatus, did not know about it for some reason.

Next, feeling the weight of a number of anti-party, anti-Soviet actions (he
could not but feel it), Magyar remained silent, he did not attend the party
meeting, he did not raise a question to discuss. Only when the [party] group
of the Eastern Secretariat raised the question, pulled Magyar out, made Magyar speak and respond, only then did he start to talk about his conduct. I must
say that neither at the party group [meeting] nor at the session of the party
committee did Magyar give a political evaluation of his actions. And now
Magyar is surprised at the party group and the party committee meeting [and
wonders] why the party group and the party committee consider his political
explanation of his ties to Zinoviev and others totally unsatisfactory. It is very
simple. He failed to tell the party committee and the party group about everything that tied him, united him with and attracted him to Zinoviev and other

counterrevolutionary elements. Magyar tried and still tries to hide behind a formal explanation that they supposedly deceived him, that Magyar was some sort of dummy incapable of understanding the actions and politics of this counterrevolutionary group. Since when has Magyar become such a dummy? The party organization knows Magyar as a politically educated, trained, mature person. And yet today he is trying to present himself to the party organization in a different light.

This will not work. We do not need such an evaluation, such a political revelation. We need a real political evaluation of those facts and actions that Magyar has committed of late. Magyar has not given us an answer as to why he was connected with Zinoviev, why he turned to Zinoviev for consultations, why Magyar was so attentive to providing material support to Safarov, why Magyar was silent until lately, why Magyar failed to help the party to expose the people with whom he, Magyar, was closely connected. For all that, he could feel and understand those people's attitudes better. Magyar does not give any answer to these questions.

It seems that Magyar wants to hide behind this formal answer, to elude, to pretend that he has been an honest member of our Bolshevik Party. This time it will not work. The party organization, the party group, and the party committee have decided to expel Magyar from the party for all his actions.

Magyar is trying to cast suspicion over, to slander, the organs of the proletarian dictatorship. He declared at the meeting that the organs of the [proletarian] dictatorship arrest in bunches and investigate later. No, comrades. The organs of the proletarian dictatorship arrest when they possess enough material and have evaluated those people who deserve to be removed by the iron hand of the proletarian dictatorship from the ranks of the working class and our party, those people who hinder our successful socialist construction, who obstruct overcoming difficulties, who attempt to strike a counterrevolutionary blow in the back of the proletarian state, who plot against the leaders of the party and the working class of our country. That is why Magyar slanders the organs of the proletarian dictatorship.

Magyar declared at the meeting of the party group and at the party committee meeting: "Whatever is being told to you, you will not believe anyway; you will pervert everything." No, comrades, the party organization has no interest in perverting the facts, does not want to and cannot do so. The party organization wants to look into these facts and evaluate them properly.

This is a distrust of the party organization, this desire to cast suspicion over the decisions and materials and then to twist these materials to extricate oneself. However, the party organization possesses a number of specific facts that I have cited. One cannot avoid them, and Magyar, as a former member of our party organization, must respond about them before the party organization.

Comrades, I want to finish my report on Magyar with the following. For the second time our party organization is discussing the actions of our members. We are placing before our audience a second member. The first was [exposed] with the help of the organs of proletarian dictatorship, and the second is being discussed today by the party organization itself. This fact points to the necessity to improve our party vigilance even more, to once again examine and penetrate deeper into our party ranks. We should implement in practice, in deeds, the appeal of com. Manuilsky to the party organization. We should raise our party vigilance, our party work in the common struggle against the smallest manifestation of political indifference and other elements of liberalism toward enemies of the working class.

Comrades, we have to organize more tightly, more strongly, the ranks of our party organization, to rally around the Central Committee of our party, around our beloved leader, great com. Stalin. (Applause.)

CHERNOMORDIK: The floor belongs to com. Magyar.

MAGYAR: Comrades, if I were not standing here but sitting there among you and if I had to vote on such an issue, on the issue of the party membership of a comrade, of a former comrade (I do not know which to consider myself), who is being accused of such crimes against the party, against the working class, against the revolution, against our Soviet country, I, comrades, maybe with a heavy heart but with no hesitation and firmly, would vote for the expulsion of such a comrade, or a former comrade, from the party. But, comrades, when I am speaking before you, I do not plan to defend myself or to deliver a speech in my defense. So, if I argue against some formulations of com. Kotelnikov, it is not over the political essence of the question but over secondary issues, over some practical issues, and later over the most important question, which I will address later.

What do I admit before the party organization? The facts that I am going to admit before you, each of those facts, maybe one-tenth or one-hundredth part of those facts, is quite sufficient to expel me from the party. What are these facts?

The first fact: in 1925–26, when in the USSR, I was an active member of the Zinovievite opposition. When the party sent me to China, I was unable to actively participate in the opposition's activities anymore, but I did not disarm myself before the party, did not recognize my mistakes, and continued to maintain connections with the Zinovievite group. I shared with the Zinovievite group views on a number of vital questions of our policy. It was not today, comrades, that I understood that the Zinovievite opposition was an anti-Soviet, anti-party, Menshevik,[48] counterrevolutionary opposition within our party; I understood it earlier and declared it to the party. As to a factual remark that does not justify me, but rather aggravates my situation: com. Kotelnikov is not quite correct when he says that I returned to the party. I was not expelled from the party; the party was extremely lenient toward me. I received an extremely mild party reprimand for my active participation in the Zinovievite, anti-Soviet, anti-party counterrevolutionary group.

Well, comrades, you know what the Zinovievite opposition turned into. People who participate in politics and whom the party entrusts with such work as the party entrusted to me have no right to seek out, to beg for, to demand leniency for, committing such major political mistakes. If I failed to understand the nature of the Zinovievite opposition then, it is quite clear now what this Zinovievite opposition actually was. This fact alone is sufficient to expel me from the party.

Second fact: after the Fifteenth Congress, I returned to the USSR. I broke with the Zinovievite opposition. [But] I did not come over to the party's position. I was a member of the so-called Safarov-Vardin-Magyar group, if you like.

(KNORIN: The one Rumiantsev was a member of?)

No, worse. As a matter of factual reference: the one Kotolynov was in.

Again, comrades, as a matter of reference, I did not defend the Safarov group before either the party group or the party committee [meeting]. I do not know why comrades insist that I wanted to portray our group as an honest one. I repeat, the Safarov group was as anti-party, anti-Soviet, [and] counterrevolutionary as the Zinovievites, as the Trotskyists.

We broke with Zinoviev not because we wanted to lay down arms before the party. We broke with Zinoviev because he capitulated to the party. We knew that this capitulation was a false one, that he deceived the party. Maybe it would be absurd to say that we were more honest than Zinoviev, that we did not deceive the party while remaining as a group. It could be absurd, but, comrades, let us not pick on specific words.

The Safarov group was an anti-Soviet group, which defied the leadership, an anti-Soviet, anti-party counterrevolutionary group, if you like. Besides that, this group had another quality: it was ridiculous, worthless, it was a wretched group. So, what kind of a "group" was ours? This is the second point.

Third point. In politics, one has to judge people, especially people participating in the workers' movement, not by their intentions but by the results. People must be judged by their deeds, not by their words. I think I must tell you directly that when I participated in the Zinovievite opposition, when I participated in this antileadership group, I did not realize what this could lead to. I did not realize it then. But the point is not this; the point is that in politics one has to judge not by intentions but by results. I referred to the results when I said to the party group and to the party committee that I profoundly felt my political responsibility for having planted at some time seeds that gave fascist shoots, responsibility for the fact that from these kinds of groups emerged bandits who killed a member of the Politburo of our party, com. Kirov. This is what we are responsible for—to a degree to be determined by the party and the organs of Soviet power.

(KNORIN: Not just for this.)

I will say now—a full political responsibility. For this, it is quite clear, I also deserve to be expelled from the party.

Fourth point. In June 1928, I appealed to the party claiming to have recognized my mistakes and to have embraced the correct Leninist policy of the Central Committee. However, I retained personal connections with Zinoviev, Safarov, Vardin, plus some others, had meetings with them, held talks and conversations with them.

(VOICE: Who else?)

I have named them, and, if necessary, I will name them [again]. After that I appealed [to the party], claiming to have recognized my mistakes throughout the whole period—precisely at the time when I met with them most frequently, in the period when I maintained a personal friendship with Safarov. Moreover, when it turned out that we worked together in the same collective in the Comintern, I expended considerable effort to retain Safarov, to the extent possible, in this collective.

Speaking about my personal connections with these people, I would like to say, comrades, that com. Kotelnikov was right when he said that once there were meetings, once conversations took place, they were of an exclusively political character. We discussed political issues only, and I failed to discern in these conversations, during these meetings, the real attitude of these people. I did not recognize it.

I know, comrades, that you do not believe this statement.

(Noise.)

I know it. Yet, I would ask the comrades not to interrupt me, if possible.

(VOICE: You are asking for too much.)

I characterized this fact to the party group and to the party committee, that I consider myself a worthless party member, a person who, from the party's point of view, can be characterized as "some fool [who is] more dangerous than the enemy."

(Knorin: Cheap!)

(Laughter.)

(Knorin: Very smart!)

For this, comrades, I deserve to be expelled from the party.

Fifth point: after Safarov's arrest, I received the maid whom Safarov had sent to me with the news about his arrest. Here I have to give a factual reference that com. Kotelnikov did not provide. This took place on the evening of 18 December, and on the morning of 19 December my first trip was to the party organization, where I informed com. Kotelnikov and com. Mif about this, asking them to further inform the leaders of our collective. Therefore, I did not conceal this fact.

Next. I gave this maid money so that she could go to Leningrad for a meeting and to give [a package to Safarov], since she informed me that Safarov had been transferred to Leningrad. After I did it, I immediately informed the party organization about this act. Similarly, I have never concealed that Safarov's wife, upon her arrival, visited me and talked with me. I am not going to confuse [this] general meeting with detailed descriptions of those relatively unimportant conversations. I say "relatively" because I immediately told everything to com. Kotelnikov and com. Mif and told it to you in detail before the party group and the party committee.

How did I assess this fact and how do I assess it now? This fact revealed that I am still very much the petit bourgeois, that I have a lot of blue-blooded individualism, that I set my opinions, my judgments, against the opinion of the party and the judgments of our authorities, that my conduct was anti-Soviet, anti-party. Well, I committed this anti-party, anti-Soviet action under the conditions that I have explained. For this action I also deserve to be expelled from the party.

I stress that I understand very clearly that each of these actions of mine, separate parts of these actions, is quite sufficient to expel me from the party.

What, comrades, do I not admit? There are, comrades, some specific minor issues, and there is also one question, a most crucial one. Regarding the meeting: I did not attend it. I do not know, comrades, whether I should dwell on this fact in great detail. I did not receive any information about the meeting. I did not know [about it]. I did not know that the meeting would take place and, therefore, I did not attend it.

The second fact, that I cast aspersions on the organs of the proletarian dictatorship: I do not admit it. I do not admit casting aspersions on the organs of the dictatorship of the proletariat. I do not know how comrades there understood me and how my words were written down. The meaning [of my words], my idea, was the following. After it was revealed that members of the former Zinovievite opposition, these fascist scoundrels, killed com. Kirov, I personally considered that it would have been logical to arrest us all and later to examine who is culpable and to what degree. I still think so.

I am very much afraid that you might take this [simply] as big words, empty phrases, but quite sincerely I would consider it fair if my case was also investigated there. They can investigate well, they investigate effectively. This case has to be investigated well and effectively.

Next, comrades, as I have already mentioned, I did not admit to the party group that I tried to portray the Safarov group, the group that defies the leadership, as something better than the Zinovievite, Trotskyist, and other anti-party groups.

(VOICE: Did you want to portray it as an honest group?)

Permit me to explain. Comrades, including com. Kotelnikov in his speech here today, accused me of not displaying any form of initiative, of not expressing my attitude toward this question. Well, comrades, I was in such a position that it was impossible to do the right thing in general. I thought and I think now that if I showed initiative, it would look like an attempt to extricate myself; everyone would have thought that "he's given the game away," but the situation turned out to be . . .

(Fainberg:[49] Is there anything to discuss here?)

The situation was such . . . Comrades, I will not answer heckling comments. The situation was such that it was impossible to trust our words, the words of the former Zinovievite opposition. Prattling before you, before the party—no one can believe us now. Declarations? Delivering speeches? You know, Zinoviev, Kamenev, Safarov, and others wrote articles, spoke from the rostrum at the Congress, were published, gave talks—and here is the result.

(Knorin: There are some who are trusted.)

Now, comrades, I do not admit to the most essential and important point. This is the most essential and important point—whether or not I was a member of the group after 1928, when I came back to the party line. No, I was not a member [of the group]. I do not admit it. Did I deceive the party by coming and saying that I am with the party, that I consider the party line correct, and later affiliated, organizationally or ideologically in any other form, with another anti-party group? Comrades, I do not admit it. I did not belong to any group or grouping, I did not retain a wall between me and the party. This I cannot admit. I do not admit, comrades, that I knew that those people with whom I belonged to the same faction were preparing weapons, were at any time planning a crime against the party. Comrades, I do not speak about the terrorist group. I speak about the political group which the terrorist group grew out of. I do not admit it.

What political lessons did I draw for myself? Comrades, since I reembraced the party line, I have been trying to conduct the party line to the best of my ability. I have struggled against Trotskyism, I have struggled against the ideology of the Zinovievite-Trotskyist opposition. But at the same time, I have maintained a liberal–blue-blood friendship with members of the former anti-Soviet groups and, as it is clear today, anti-Soviet, anti-party groups that continued to exist. I combined work according to the party line with personal relationships with people who were enemies of Soviet power.

Another lesson. Comrades, I knew Zinoviev and what Zinoviev was worth better than anybody else, and, nevertheless, I continued maintaining personal relations with him.

Comrades, I realized earlier that groups, factions, blocs, and plots against the party led to the opposite side of the barricades. I realized this after I reembraced the party line. But what I failed to understand, comrades, was that in the present situation, the struggle against the party, against the policy of the party's Central Committee, the class struggle in general in our country was taking on new forms, adopting new methods, new forms and new methods that, in the final analysis, led to terror. These new forms, these new methods of struggle against the country, against the government, against the party—this is what I did not understand. And it led those people who dragged me, along with themselves, into the dirt, into shame and disgrace before the party and the working class.

Another lesson for me: I understood the correctness of party policy, the policy of the Central Committee, but I tolerated liberal gossip. I myself driveled. I tolerated expressions of agreement with the party line conveyed in a tone that should have indicated to me that there was no [actual] agreement, that [in fact] there was a struggle against the party policy. This, comrades, is important not only for me personally. I realized once again . . .

(At this moment com. Martynov approaches the Presidium, talks to the Presidium, and smiles.)

Comrades, no laughing at civil funerals.

(Knorin: Such a mean speech deserves to be laughed at.)

I will not respond to com. Knorin.

(VOICE: He conducts propaganda in the form of political speech and yet wants us to listen to him!)

I am finishing. I declare once again to this party organization: although these facts are insignificant because they are connected to me . . . My whole behavior again revealed my petit bourgeois individualism, my blue-blooded individualism, which I brought with me from that social milieu from which I came. During the first purge that I went through after being exchanged, comrades, members of the purge commission warned me about it. That proved to be insufficient for me, and I did not learn the lesson. You remember my last purge, when c. Solts again pointed this out. Again, I did not learn the lesson and did not realize, did not overcome, these mistakes of mine.

Another lesson: for a long time I have been on sort of bureaucratic work. I did conduct mass work all the time, but for the most part my work was sort of bureaucratic. I did not work on the ground. I think, comrades, that this is not related to me directly; this is already out of the question in my regard. This question is to be discussed with regards to people of the same social origin as mine, to people coming from the same social environment as I do. They should not stay in bureaucratic work for a long time, comrades. I am finishing.

Comrades, I am finishing and making the following conclusion regarding those actions that I have admitted.

(VOICE FROM THE HALL: And where are those people? Who are you referring to? Which people are of the same origins as you? Who are you addressing?)

I am of petit bourgeois origin . . .

(KOTELNIKOV: The comrades are asking, If [they] are not to be in bureaucratic work, then where ought they to be?)

I am not talking about myself. What I mean is that if they have been in bureaucratic work for a while, they should be sent to lower-level work again, so that they do not stay too long in bureaucratic work. That is no good, either.

Permit me to make a conclusion. I think that for those actions that I have admitted to, I deserve being expelled from the party.

(VOICE: For the work in the past?)

No.

(MARTYNOV: The past is waiting after 1928?)

No. I never said anything like that, and please do not attribute it to me. I have declared that I did maintain, even after 1928, personal connections with

Zinoviev. Haven't I told you that until the last days it was friendship that I maintained with Safarov, until the last days? Actions that I committed after Safarov's arrest, were they in 1928? I have clearly indicated to you the five points that constitute my guilt before the party organization.

(MIF: But did you plant anti-party seeds only before 1928, or before 1928 and since then, too?)

I have declared . . .

(MIF: And what you have been declaring here, aren't these the anti-party *declarations?*)

(VOICE: We want you to tell [us].)

This party organization will judge. However, I declare that I have been working in this organization for six years. You have to prove where in my works I did it. I worked on issues concerning twenty-two parties in the Comintern. Where did I plant seeds? Comrades, you have to prove [that I did] it since I reembraced the party line. Who is capable of proving it?

Let me finish. I deserve to be expelled from the party. However, I declare [this]: since I declared my agreement with the party's policy, I have not consciously deceived the party.

BÉLA KUN: Magyar, our former comrade, as he, I believe, called himself, declared here with rhetorical bombast: "No laughing at civil funerals." It is true, of course, as well as that at civil funerals they deliver graveside orations, not a lawyer's speech.

I do not really know what Magyar was talking about today. To be precise, what did he admit in his speech? He recognized that he deserves to be expelled from the party. I was sitting in the back and did not hear well enough, but I understood that after he started his graveside oration and mentioned civil funerals, he continued on as a lawyer would.

I must say that if, in the near future, I confront a class enemy, stand before the court of a class enemy, I will construct my speech the same way Magyar did here before this clearly hostile audience, before this organization [which is] obviously hostile to him.

I, comrades, am not going to look into particular details. I think that the party organization learned the factual side of this case at the party committee and party group meetings well enough. I would like to dwell a while on characterizing the roots of this group's counterrevolutionary activity, or, it would be better to say, not of the group itself but of Magyar in particular.

I think that Magyar did not really mean that he turned out to be just a fool. Magyar is no fool. Magyar is a clever person. Magyar is an educated person. Magyar is a well-read person. Magyar knows his way around international politics, his way around inner-party life, and so on and so forth.

If he did not assume that he is totally untrustworthy, if he did not assume that one cannot believe their promises, even if they are telling the truth, he would then, obviously, describe differently the sources of that shameful activity that was reflected in his latest actions, reflected in the fact that, after the murder of com. Kirov, after the murder of one of the best leaders of the best sections of the Comintern, he supported the obvious counterrevolutionary Safarov.

He did not want to, but he had to prove sociologically, referring to his social origin, that his evolution was, so to say, historically justified. Naturally, his evolution was rather complex, and clearly, under those conditions in which he worked and grew in the party, it was inevitable and natural that he came to the road of political degeneration, to that political swamp that soaked up the scoundrels of the Zinovievite counterrevolutionary group. By that swamp there stood a guard, a protector of the interests of international capitalism, an ingenious protector of the interests of international capitalism, a representative of a capitalist, probably fascist state. I think it is no accident that Magyar, being liberated by the Soviet state, by the Soviet Union, from the prison of Horthy,[50] the hangman of Hungarian proletariat, found himself in the camp of enemies of the Soviet Union.

I do not want to say that I foresaw it. On the contrary, I must say that I did not foresee it, and during the purge, when I defended com. Magyar, then . . .

(MANIS: Yes, yes, we remember.)

. . . I then tried to explain it in such a way that he, as an intellectual, was acting according to the motto To be on the side of the weak in the presence of the strong. But, comrades, such a psychological approach was wrong. It is possible that I could not see through Magyar. I repeat, Magyar was considered a learned man, a specialist on issues of international politics, international economics, a person who read a lot. He was considered a Marxist. And it turns out that the more he read, the more harmful to the party he became. What kind of Marxism is it if it is harmful to the party? Probably someone would say that Magyar wrote many articles. He himself said, Let them prove where in my writings, in my work, I planted anti-party seeds. What kind of lesson should we learn from this? That we can write whatever we like and do whatever we like. However, one can write one thing and do the other.

This is the first lesson we should learn. Our vigilance should not be aimed at what is being written, as usually happens. Our vigilance should be aimed, first of all, at what is being done. This is exactly what com. Stalin has said and written, that one has to test the Social Democratic leaders of the Second International not by their words, not by their writings, but by their deeds. It refers to this case as well. Then, of course, we will never fail to foresee the further evolution of such people who write one thing and do the other.

In his speech Magyar said that he worked and wrote and that one can examine his work and what he wrote. This reminds me of the methods of Zinoviev's leadership in the Comintern. If you permit me, I would like to dwell on this in a little more detail. Zinoviev, as an anti-Soviet element, as a counterrevolutionary, has now been completely exposed. However, there are some very compelling political reasons to look into the question of Zinovievite methods of leadership in the Comintern.

What characterized the Zinovievite methods of leadership? Only a few know about it. Those who occupied positions of leadership in the Comintern at the time of Zinoviev, those who have to carry out the work of exposing completely the Zinovievite methods, have taken a sort of monopoly position on this issue. Zinoviev always had two pockets and two perspectives.[51] This is the main method of the Zinovievite leadership: to have two pockets and in each pocket to have one perspective. And, depending on what is to be emphasized, pulling out this or that perspective. This is what is called the Zinovievite leadership.

However, comrades, this was connected with another major method of leadership by Zinoviev. He repeatedly made statements about implementing the Leninist line in the Comintern himself or being Lenin's deputy in the Comintern.

Zinoviev always had two pockets and two perspectives; however, he always had one policy toward the Comintern's cadres. Of course, he did not manage to deceive the Comintern's cadres, the cadres of Communist Parties. Many of us remember how, at the time when the implementation of the United Front tactics began, Zinoviev supported these tactics before Lenin and [at the same time] tried to persuade us to speak up against the United Front tactics at the preliminary meeting.

This kind of unscrupulousness, comrades, was the basic tone of today's speech by Magyar. I wrote everything correctly, I behaved properly, and yet I deserve to be expelled. How can one understand it? Isn't it the final stage of political degeneration? Isn't it an attempt, a new attempt, to hide behind the expulsion and leave the back door [open] in order to come back to the party at a time when vigilance is lower than it is now? This is the real ideological connection with Zinoviev and those methods that Zinoviev employed in the Communist International. Comrades, vigilance alone, decisions alone, are insufficient to [struggle] against these methods. We have to expose completely the Zinovievite methods of leadership and to oppose them with the new, truly Bolshevik methods of leadership that are being employed in the Comintern with more and more success since Zinoviev's removal. Probably we still have shortcomings. But I have to say that the quality of the Comintern's leadership is now higher, much higher, than it was under Zinoviev. If we look back, [we see nothing] but the policy of two pockets and two perspectives that surfaced, for example, when Zinoviev, at the time of the Anglo-Soviet Committee, declared that the route of the revolution had been changed, [that] we are going toward the revolution on the road of the British trade unions. But then, six months later, [he] accused the party of opportunism because it created the Anglo-Soviet Committee. Besides that, an important method of Zinovievite leadership was dilettantism, despite the fact that many [people] wanted to create a picture of Zinoviev as a superhuman, a great leader who guided the Comintern at a very high level. I think that we do not have to be ashamed of our leadership. On the contrary, the quality of our leaders, of our leadership, is higher than ever. We now have to rally around this Comintern leadership and, under the direction of these leaders, weed out the roots, eliminate all of the remnants of Zinovievite methods. Then, I think, we will be able to foresee such developments as Magyar has gone through, toward that swamp where there are undoubtedly still scoundrels of the Zinovievite anti-Soviet group. To drain this swamp, [the support of] the power of the Soviet and international proletariat under the leadership of our great leader, com. Stalin [will] surely [be needed]. I, comrades, vote for expelling Magyar.

(Applause.)

CHERNOMORDIK: A suggestion has been received to fix the time limit to ten minutes. (Accepted.) . . .

HECKERT: The last weeks have shown that our class vigilance is not as up to the mark as the situation requires. Therefore, we must be more alert than ever to each word said by our comrades. Magyar said here that the group to which he belonged intended to be honest with the party. In this regard he said straightforwardly: "We know that Zinoviev's declaration was hypocritical toward the party." The party believed Zinoviev's statement to be honest. Magyar considered it hypocritical. Despite this, Magyar maintained connections with this hypocrite until the very last days. It is a rather strange kind of attitude of a Bolshevik toward the party.

Today Magyar said also that the Zinoviev group fooled him. Meaning that he was an unfortunate fool, that he was fooled by a scoundrel. But he knew that Zinoviev intended to fool the party with his behavior. Thus, he did not need to mention that petty trick with which he himself was fooled. He contradicts his own statement.

But this trickery of the last weeks has shown us that we need to display the strictest vigilance toward all the groups. The case is not just that someone said that he was merely a passive fellow traveler. We know, not just from this case, how factionalist groups behave. Magyar himself said that any such group eventually finds itself on the opposite side of the barricade. Nevertheless, he joined this group. And now he is surprised to find himself on the opposite side of the barricade.

Now he wants to explain everything by his petit bourgeois origin, by his aristocratic ideas, by his hypocritical views. This is too superficial. Take a look at this group of Zinoviev's. It has never been connected to the proletariat; otherwise, it would have never been able, especially in the current situation, to come to such a wild idea as to develop a new opposition on the old platform. But Zinoviev is very well known. For many years he duped the Comintern with his theory of two perspectives. He was expelled from the party three times, and three times he appealed [for readmission]. Three times he betrayed the friends to whom he was tied. And such an educated man as Magyar considered Zinoviev a distinguished personality, from whom he received advice. I am completely unable to understand it. It can be explained by the arrogance of an intellectual who despises the proletariat, who thinks that politics can be made at the expense of the proletariat, not for its sake. We have clearly seen it with the example of Safarov. This man's arrogance was so excessive that he even despised the organs of the Comintern. He would give directives to the parties behind the back of the responsible organs. Parties' representatives did not exist for him. And if he was reproached for this, he felt offended. Only a person who has completely separated himself from the proletarian class can demonstrate such an attitude. Therefore, we have to admit today that Magyar also bears responsibility for what Zinoviev's group has done. It cannot deny its responsibility for Nikolaev and his shots in the back. And people who were members of this group, who advocated such a criminal policy, are therefore accessories to the crimes committed. They cannot be tolerated in the ranks of our party. [. . .]

GURALSKY: Comrades, I was an active member of the anti-Soviet Zinovievite-Trotskyist opposition. I was expelled from the party by the Fifteenth Party Congress. Probably this expulsion from the party was the very best and the most serious lesson that I have received from the party, which made me not only break with the opposition and personally with its members but also thoroughly review all [my] incorrect conceptions on all major questions.

When I was listening to Magyar today, I was thinking: This person has not yet thought seriously about what the expulsion from the party means. Magyar brought forward three points that he wants to use to morally threaten [us]. If I had ever followed even one of these three points, I would never have become an honest party member.

The first point: The situation is such that I cannot act in a right way. Is this the point of view of a revolutionary? It is the point of view of scum, of degenerates. There is no such situation in which a person cannot say to himself: I must serve my proletarian class. There is no such situation. If a person claims that there is a situation in which he cannot properly serve his class, it means that he has lost himself, that he cannot find his way.

Magyar's second statement is of a similar nature: They will not believe me anyway. I am sure that Zinoviev managed to keep whole groups in the opposition precisely by maintaining this point of view—they will not believe you—with the point of view that a correct position is not possible. And finally, it is not true what Magyar says, that he does not consciously deceive the party. Isn't he deceiving the party and himself today? He does, fully and completely. Today in his speech Magyar, on the one hand, covered up the role of the Zinovievite faction and, on the other, did not explain what connected him with the Zinovievite faction.

Comrades, was it just because of personal relations that Magyar wanted to consult Zinoviev on every major problem of the Comintern and international politics? I declare: No, that was the old conception of the Trotskyist-Zinovievite opposition, a conception that does not recognize the whole Stalin-

ist epoch in the VKP(b) and in the history of the Comintern. This was the opposition's basic position, that from the time of Zinoviev's departure [from the
Comintern] the history of mankind has collapsed. There is not a million-
member party. This is a Trotskyist point of view. This is what Zinoviev em-
bodied in the fascist shot. There is no party left, only its elite. There is no
more history of the immense victories of socialism. There is no more history
of the transformation of the Comintern from a small German-French party
into a world party. What is the Comintern? When I came to work in the Comintern, I heard rumors that Zinoviev had told different people with whom to
work and what to do. There is no Stalinist epoch, there is no new era of the international workers' movement, there is no new epoch of the creation of a
world party, there is no VKP(b), no industrialization, no collectivization.
Only on this basis could anyone step away from the Comintern to a perpetual
reading [of Zinoviev's thoughts]. But what does Zinoviev say, what does Zinoviev know, about Lenin's opinion on the global questions? The revolutionary policy became a secret of Zinovievite renegades and not the political line
of the Comintern and the VKP(b).

I do not want to deal with the question of whether or not Magyar thought
this over. He felt that way. I remember times [when I was in] the opposition
when we felt this not in a revolutionary but in a counterrevolutionary way.
And he was ten years further along. That is why I think that Magyar has to understand that he has adopted the major Zinovievite position, that there is no
Stalinist epoch.

Second, what did the work of the Zinovievite-Trotskyist opposition consist
of? It lived a near-party life; it lived as if it were in emigration. The facts have
shown what this near-party life, these emigration moods, could change into.
Magyar supported these moods, he displayed support for them twice. He supported them when he shared his impression with Zinoviev that there are people in the Comintern who are with him [Zinoviev], who are waiting for him,
who seek his advice. He supported them when he committed an anti-Soviet
act by lending money to Safarov.

I am interested not only in the anti-Soviet side of his action; I am also interested in the political side of it. Zinoviev and Trotsky say: The people would
support us, but the party elite does not let them. Magyar supported this thesis, he supported this idea, and this is extremely important. Magyar still has
not thought deeply enough about this question, he is still hostile, he has not
yet overcome [his mistakes], he does not yet feel the atmosphere that we have
here, he thinks, "Maybe I am giving my game away, too." He still thinks that
he is in the enemy camp, he has not yet overcome this, he is still standing
firmly by the position of the Zinovievite opposition.

Comrades, it seems to me that this is the most important and the most
harmful [thing] from which the embellishment proceeds. He portrays the
case in this way: a small group, a group of fascists, a hated group, wanted to
kill Kirov. And this group wanted to kill the party's leader, the best person

created by the proletariat. And, on the other hand, in light of these hostile ideas < . . . >

Comrades, I am ashamed to admit that I was in the ranks of the opposition, but I do not feel any guilt at all in this case. One cannot interpret this question so hopelessly: I planted wrong ideas, and ten years later terrorists grew up. No, the case is different. I think that if Magyar had disarmed today, if he had been able to understand it, he would have come and told the meeting. He would then have fulfilled his role if he had revealed everything he knew [and] why those ideas were mistaken. Then all of us, knowing the milieu, would [be able to] expose not just the ideologists but also the direct perpetuators and instigators of the murder.

Have they not provoked hatred for ten years? Have they not been saying, for ten, eleven, and twelve years that all danger is in the hated party elite? Have they not been inciting the mood that everything that has happened in the Soviet Union, in the Comintern, is a failure? Have not Zinoviev and others been trying to prove that probably the October revolution was Lenin's mistake, that Trotsky was right, that there is no way out? All these are facts. Zinoviev and Kamenev are finished, morally and politically, in the eyes of the proletariat and the peasantry of the [Soviet] Union and in the eyes of the revolutionary workers. And this is what Magyar failed to understand. He should have understood this and proceeded from this point of view to reevaluate his own connections, to explain to himself that politically they meant not what he wanted, not what he thought, not what he felt, but what they had become politically. Politically, they have become a force hostile to our party. That is why I think (I was not cited quite correctly here; I do not know the facts) that, as they said, Magyar represents a mixture of political mistakes, of well-known philistinism and apoliticism. I heard Magyar, I already know the major facts, and it is clear to me that this is [an expression of] Zinovievite degeneration. And let Magyar understand that for the party that clearly wants to remain a revolutionary party, a party of the second round of wars and revolutions, there is only one way: to close its ranks, to forge vigilance, to more actively pursue ideological integrity, to watch very carefully, to judge people by their deeds, to never tell people that there is no way out but to see the situation as it is. Only such a party will be able to fulfill its obligations.

(VOICE: And what shall we do with Magyar?)

Expel him from the party. It is clear.

KON SIN: In his speech Magyar called himself a fool. But he has been masking himself as a fool for a number of years now. Coming to this meeting today, he continues to act in the same way and today, too, he was masking himself as a fool. Magyar said today in his speech that he has been working for a long time in the Comintern, for six years, but in fact he has been working for the benefit of our class enemy. Magyar struggled and continues to struggle against the party, against the CC of our party, against Soviet power, and we can say that Magyar also struggles against the Chinese party and supports counter-revolutionary Trotskyists.

At present, the Chinese Communist Party is at the head of Soviet power in China and the Chinese Red Army, under its leadership, organized Soviet power and the Red Army. Magyar claimed that there are supposedly groups in the Central Committee of the Chinese Communist Party. Our class enemy also charges that the CC of the Chinese Communist Party, that our CC, is Stalin's faction. Magyar also considers the CC of the Chinese Communist Party [to be] a faction, a group.

In the Chinese Soviet regions, the counterrevolutionary Kliuev has been exposed. He was arrested. However, when Magyar and Safarov learned [about it], they claimed this arrest was wrong, they thought that Soviet power in China oppresses good comrades. Thus, they, too, supported the Chinese counterrevolutionary Trotskyists. Safarov and Magyar suggested sending a telegram [demanding] the liberation of this counterrevolutionary Trotskyist. Therefore, we can see that Safarov and Magyar not only struggled against the VKP(b) and against the CC VKP(b) but at the same time, via the Comintern, struggled against the fraternal parties and against the Communist Party of China.

Therefore, not only do we have to direct our wrath against Safarov, against Magyar, against our class enemy here, but our foreign comrades at the same time have to take note that, in the capitalist countries, those connected with Magyar and Safarov should be exposed. We must also raise class vigilance toward these elements. You have seen that even now Magyar acts like a fool in order to deceive our party, to deceive us. Today at this rostrum Magyar behaved very modestly, very pathetically, as if he wanted to present himself to our party committee as a Communist in order to deceive you once again and to continue struggling against our party.

I think that there is no difference between the crimes of Magyar and Safarov and that of the murderer of com. Kirov, Nikolaev. Therefore, I think that it is not enough to expel him from the party. I think it will be very regrettable if he is not arrested now.

KNORIN: Comrades, when on the evening of 1 December the news about the murder of com. Kirov spread, the heart of each Communist was filled with deep sorrow and anger because it was clear that the enemy inside the country is still alive. The enemy inside the country is still alive.

But the sorrow that filled the heart of each Communist became even more bitter when we read, on 16 December, the resolution of the Moscow and Leningrad [party] committees indicating that the murderers of com. Kirov were party members, that the enemy dwelled in our own house, that the enemy turned out to be inside the party.

More than thirty years have passed since the creation of the Bolshevik Party. The eminence of Lenin was demonstrated when he immediately managed to discern in the first minor contradictions of statutory and programmatic questions another party, the Menshevik party, a party that works against the revolution, a party that has become the worst enemy of the proletarian revolution, the Menshevik party.

Stalin's great intellect and intuition were demonstrated twenty years later when, in 1923, at the time of the opposition's first actions, he discerned in them a new Menshevism, neo-Menshevism, the beginning of the new anti-party group, an anti-Soviet party, a counterrevolutionary party.

More than thirty years of development have brought Mensheviks to form a bloc with all sorts of trash, with the counterrevolution. They were with Kolchak, with Denikin, Bulak-Balakhovich, with all sorts of rabble that attacked the Soviet Union.

More than ten years of development by the Zinovievite opposition have demonstrated that this group, this anti-party group, managed to form a bloc with the most ignoble elements inside the country, with the last fragments of the counterrevolution inside the country, and with the foreign bourgeoisie.

At present, in the conditions of the dictatorship of the proletariat, in the conditions of sharpened class struggle, counterrevolutionary groups develop, form faster, much faster than in the previous historical period.

Here Magyar delivered a speech that cannot be called anything other than ignoble, infinitely ignoble and impudent, in particular those arguments that he brought up and from which his expulsion followed. If the case was such [as Magyar portrays it], neither of these arguments would justify his expulsion.

It was a cleverly organized, defensive speech. Our comrades have absolutely correctly indicated that today we expel Magyar, exile Safarov [and] banish Zinoviev not for those seeds of distrust toward the party, of opposition to the party, which they planted in 1923–1925. Magyar applied to that period all those definitions that we attach to his group today. Then we referred to those groups as no more than a Social Democratic deviation in our party. Then it corresponded to the actual situation. In 1923–24, it was still a group within the party. By 1927 it had already grown into a different party. It was then that we had to raise a question of expelling them from the party. Organizationally they had formed themselves as another party. Then we had to remove them from the party's ranks.

Around which questions did they organize themselves? Around all major questions, being the enemies of Socialist construction in our country, being enemies of Socialism, as a party, a group that wants to lead our country back to capitalism. They were expelled in late 1927. In 1928 a significant portion of them was readmitted. Magyar avoided expulsion. However, all the double-dealing of this group can now be seen. We have in our possession a letter from Zinoviev to Rumiantsev,[52] a leader of the Leningrad center of the Zinovievite oppositional scum. In this letter, Zinoviev advises Rumiantsev to rejoin the party, that he file an application in such a way that the CCC [Central Control Commission] would admit him, that he write whatever is necessary, whatever the party would require [from him to be able] to return to the party. Because, he says, the party is facing new difficulties, and the party will need us to struggle for Leninism, i.e., for the Zinovievite oppositional line. This is what Zinoviev wrote to Rumiantsev. This is how he instructed his buddies to return to the party: to capitulate formally in order to struggle against the party.

Of course, one of the conditions was to retain all connections, not in the form of a broad structured organization but in such a way as to be able to survive, to bide one's time to struggle against the party. At the same time, Zinoviev was writing his famous variants regarding which ways he could take: One with Trotsky outside the party, to struggle against the party from the outside. Another way, according to Trotsky, to struggle against the party from inside the party, as Trotsky did. The third way, he says, is to capitulate to the party. It means capitulation. This is the central line that Zinoviev planned at that time.

We exposed it one more time. As soon as Zinoviev sensed some oppositional groups, there he was, he came knocking again [at the door]. We also smashed that group completely. It got no response in the country. A dozen counterrevolutionaries were exiled. Those who maintained connections with them, like Zinoviev, Kamenev, and others, were punished.

It seemed that we had finally defeated the opposition, destroyed this group. But some minor fragments remained, and that is why, by no accident, they were repentant at the Seventeenth Congress.

Yes, they were defeated. Nothing was left but some isolated people, miserable scoundrels who wormed their way into cracks of the party, who were hostile to the party. However, these people maintained connections with each other. It took only a short time [after they were] back in the party to reestablish old friendships; they reached out to those who remained in the old positions. The case is not as simple as Magyar described it here.

The Leningrad center, part of which directly organized the attempt on com. Kirov, this Leningrad center maintained connections with Moscow, with the Moscow center that was headed by Zinoviev, the ideologist, the leader, the unifier of forces within the party to struggle against the party, to struggle against the dictatorship of the proletariat, for the return to capitalism. Their program was a program of returning to capitalism.

Magyar did not belong to this leading center. It is obvious, and one should not call him a leader. He is not fit to be a leader. He is far too insignificant. He is much more obscene than a leader. But what in general was the essence of the organization, the essence of the opposition's existence?

The people, the leaders, the bosses, maintained connections; they reached out to those who supported old concepts, old positions, who could be reliable, who could be selected to make a move as soon as the situation was favorable, as soon as new difficulties were created.

One of the accused admits: "We watched for some sort of contradictions in the party leadership. We relied on any opening to help us come to the leadership, to come to power. That is why we preserved our cadres, why we established connections with everyone who was against the party leadership, who had an oppositional sentiment. Until the very last moment, we cherished hopes that in this way, through some disagreements, through some difficulties, we would be able to rise to [positions of] leadership and turn the country onto another road, onto our road."

And so I am asking, Did Magyar belong to this organization that was not based on solidly shaped cells but was an organization built on connections, on gathering forces? Yes, he belonged to this organization.

Probably, obviously, he was not in its leadership, but he did belong to this organization. Hence, Zinoviev's connection with him. Zinoviev is not an apolitical person, he is not a person whose relationships were based on personal friendship and acquaintance. This connection is political, this connection is organizational, this connection meant gathering their people, their forces. That is why the Rumiantsevs and Kotolynovs were coming to Moscow, to establish ties with the Moscow elements. That is why Muscovites traveled to Leningrad to establish ties with Leningrad groups.

Let us take another question. It is quite clear that Safarov has not always been connected with the centers of this counterrevolutionary group in the same way. They say that his connections to this group in late 1933, in 1934, became more frequent, became stronger, [and] that since that time he has become more outspoken, more open with his counterrevolutionary views on questions regarding the Soviet Union, as well as on questions regarding the Communist International. Here is the question: The people who were constantly exchanging their political opinions, how could they have not known it? People who engaged in anti-party, anti-Soviet conversations in their environment, how could they not know about it, not see it? Nobody would believe it.

(MAGYAR: It did not happen in 1934.)

In 1934 you were engaged in anti-party conversations outside the Soviet Union. In 1934 you were waging a campaign and a struggle against the German Communist Party. You transferred the Zinovievite concepts here when speaking about the concentration of leadership, about transferring the leadership to the conciliators,[53] etc. You did it there. These are proven facts that you cannot escape.

Your role here was one of providing connections and information on the international questions, as well as the role of a transmitter. This is the state of affairs. You want to deny it. It won't work. I will dwell on this question later. This case is rather serious. One can, and should, speak only about that which today is quite clear, is obvious: that this political connection was [also] an organizational connection, which means that Safarov and Magyar belonged to a particular political anti-Soviet organization. It is the only way to see it. We are not little children who believe that friendly conversations between two seasoned politicians who, over the course of many years were tied together by shared political concepts, would not lead to some further goal. This is not the case. And if in 1934 there were still people in the Zinovievite opposition who dreamed of returning to the party some day, this was the common course for the whole Zinovievite group. And, as it was in 1923 and as it was in 1934, this organization, these ties, nurtured the Leningrad group of Rumiantsev-Kotoly-nov-Nikolaev. They supported this group in those forms of struggle that it took on. This is the essence of the question.

If Zinoviev and Kamenev had sincerely returned to the party, if Zinoviev and Kamenev had said that they capitulated to the party, there would have been no Rumiantsevs, Kotolynovs, or Nikolaevs. They would have not been able to organize themselves and to organize their attempt [on Kirov]. If at the Seventeenth Party Congress this had been seriously exposed, if it had been terminated once and for all, if these elements, with their anti-Soviet counter-revolutionary activity, had not grouped around Zinoviev, the Leningrad group of Rumiantsevs and Nikolaevs would not have been able to count on Zinoviev. This is the essence of the question.

This group was small, it was insignificant, but it inflicted a heavy blow on us. We can say now that we have definitively finished with the opposition within the party once and for all. We are united, and no group can shake the powerful unity of the party. No group can incapacitate the forces of our party.

Let us take what Stalin said two years ago about the kulak. Now it is no longer the big-bellied kulak who comes out in open struggle against the So-viet power. And the inner-party enemy now is not as it used to be several years ago when the opposition was openly led by Zinoviev, Trotsky, etc. The inner-party enemy is now hiding. Like a kulak in a kolkhoz, he is trying to be a steward, to be a keeper of some property, to work on some editorial board in order to smuggle its contraband, in order to say we are still alive, do not forget us, we still exist, count on us.

Such is our inner-party enemy today. Against this enemy other, harsher methods of struggle are needed, and higher vigilance is required of each of us. We are a strong party, a powerful party, and no one can reverse our country's course. Let the Kotolynovs and all others preach the return to capitalism, let them preach about intervention. Under Stalin's leadership, we will move for-ward at a faster pace. (Applause.) [. . .]

ALIKHANOV: During Magyar's speech we here in the Presidium were laugh-ing—not about Magyar's speech but rather about Martynov's insisting that we give him the floor. And we were saying that Martynov should not be given the floor because he was ill. The laughter was about Martynov's persistence, not Magyar's speech.

(MAGYAR: In this case I am very sorry.)

Of course, there is not much that is funny, to say nothing about joyful, re-garding your speech. I think that com. Burzynski is not rejoicing any more than all of us attending this discussion of Magyar's speech are. It's true that there is nothing funny, but does Magyar think that we came here to cry? Does he think that we came here to shed tears? No, comrades, we came here not to cry but to expose the anti-party nature of Magyar, to expose Magyar's dishonest behavior, his dishonest behavior the day before yesterday, and yesterday, and at today's meeting. This is how I understand our task in light of those facts of which I became aware in relation to Magyar. I am not going to distort these facts, since they have been discussed enough today.

Magyar also assesses these facts, but he derives from them a different conclusion than a Bolshevik should. Was Magyar speaking here honestly? Did he speak sincerely at our meeting today? What was he saying? He was saying that one cannot believe the declarations of anyone who once was in the Zinovievite opposition.

This is not correct. We know people who have honestly dissociated themselves from Zinoviev. We also know people who have proved their honesty by [their] deeds, by the struggle against the Zinovievites. Therefore, it is not correct that one should not believe their declarations, as Magyar says. Is he saying it sincerely? No, he is not speaking sincerely, because if he sincerely thinks that one cannot believe their words, then why did he try for a whole hour to whitewash himself through skillful arguments and intricate maneuvers to prove that he was not guilty of what he is accused? It was an insincere speech.

Is it honest on Magyar's part for him to call himself a fool at the party meetings the day before yesterday, and yesterday, and today? It is dishonest and insincere. It needs no proof. Don't we know Magyar?

Is it honest of Magyar to put forward the thesis that the guilt of the opposition's leaders, of Zinoviev and others, the guilt of the active participants of the Zinovievite group and Magyar's ties to these vile murderers, lies not in the present but in the past activities of the opposition? Is his declaration sincere about them planting seeds then, and that now there are fascist sprouts?

I think, comrades, that it is clear that the question here is not only about the opposition's past. We have enough facts proving not only that they planted [seeds] some time ago but that they have been tending those sprouts in the present. These facts are known to the whole country, these facts are known to Magyar. Is it honest on his behalf to declare in his speech that it is only relevant to what he did some time ago? Is it honest to shield himself, and Safarov, and Yevdokimov—i.e., those who are now under investigation and those exiled?

This speech is dishonest and insincere. It is fairly clear to all of us.

Magyar said that he helped Safarov after his arrest and clearly characterized this act. He said he committed a counterrevolutionary act. That's what he said. But is he saying it honestly? No, comrades, not honestly. Because this man explains this counterrevolutionary act by his petit bourgeois individualism, that it was precisely this petit bourgeois individualism that pushed him, Magyar, to support Safarov when Safarov was arrested.

Who is going to believe it? How is individualism related to this? In my mind, by this act he revealed not individualism but collectivism. Collectivism toward whom? Toward the counterrevolutionary Safarov. Why would Magyar need to express this feeling of his in such a way? Why would Magyar be concerned about Safarov's arrest, about his exile, be concerned that his feet not get cold, take the trouble to buy him something and give him money?

Why is this petit bourgeois individualism and not an expression of solidarity with Safarov? He knew Safarov well, perfectly well, and if he, as he says, had any doubts about Safarov or Safarov had cheated him, then, after Safarov was arrested and Magyar not, would it not have become clear to Magyar that to express solidarity with Safarov meant expressing solidarity with Safarov's line? And he speaks at the party meeting and tries to explain the counterrevolutionary act as a result of petit bourgeois individualism. It is dishonest, comrades. Does Magyar not understand that it has become clear to the party organization, and not just to the party organization but to the entire working class, to the whole country, that the Zinovievite counterrevolutionary group organized the murder of com. Kirov? Didn't Magyar try here to deny this fact, to interpret it in a different way, as if it was not the case that the Zinovievites organized [the attempt], that somebody else utilized the Zinovievite ideas? As if it was not the case that the Zinovievites had their terrorist group not just in Leningrad but [also] had their own Zinovievite center in Moscow, and that these were connected. It is all clear. Magyar is trying to confuse these explanations, to disavow the facts that have become so obvious to our whole country.

The last point. I want to talk about another side that was not stressed and that, in my mind, is characteristic of Magyar. I am referring to Magyar's method of self-defense. What did Magyar think about com. Kirov's murder? Did he think the same way as all party members? Was he overwhelmed by the same grief and indignation as the whole party and the entire working class? No, comrades. No, because as Magyar claimed here, he was thinking then not about Kirov but about himself. He said: If I spoke, if I came to the party organization and said that I, as a former member, as an active member of the Zinovievite opposition, bear responsibility for this vile act, then they would say: "He has given his game away." This is what he thought. He thought about himself, about how to conduct himself so that no one would think that he was giving away his game, how to conduct himself to divert the attention of the party organization away from himself, not how to take any initiative to honestly declare that he bore responsibility. Instead, he decided to sit quietly on the fence, to ride out the storm, to hold out until the party organization called on Magyar and told him: Report, what did you do? Prior to this event, how did you behave toward those people who had ties to terrorists?

From here on begins the exposure of Magyar. The unmasking of Magyar revealed his anti-party nature. I think it is more than clear to us, and that we have to say unanimously: There is no place for Magyar in the ranks of our party. (Applause.)

KUUSINEN: Comrades, I took the floor in order to emphasize some of the principal lessons of this case, lessons that are important to all of us.

The first lesson relates to our attitude toward the class enemy. The second lesson is our attitude toward the party.

In our apparatus, yes, in the Eastern Secretariat itself, there was a worker connected to the terrorist, counterrevolutionary opposition. Our great leader, one of the greatest leaders of our Soviet power, com. Kirov, fell victim to this organization. And Safarov, who, as it now has turned out, was nothing but a political agent of this vile counterrevolution, had worked by our side for many years.

What conclusions can be drawn from this? Only one conclusion: to heighten political vigilance in our work, to improve organizational and political vigilance.

We talked with Safarov only about questions of current work. However, I remember one personal conversation with him three or four years ago. It was at the time of the first successes on the kolkhoz front. Then Safarov, after the discussion of some resolution, wanted to add something and said it, or so it seemed to me, in a very sincere manner. But we now know that it was a false sincerity. He said that after all those victories on the peasant issue, only then did he finally understand what a harmful and criminal position he had maintained in the past. It was all lies. He was consciously deceiving us. All that sincerity was false. And the conclusion is: Never take anybody's word, especially that of the former oppositionists, at face value.

Mif mentioned Safarov's book here. This question was raised here at the [party] cell [meeting]. I think that Mif should not have raised this question now. We exposed Safarov's book and qualified it as a Right-Opportunist deviation. The cell made this decision. Possibly the resolution was not completely worked out, but I want to say that if we acted on all questions as we did on this question, that would be sufficient. If we exposed [everyone] to the same extent as we tried to expose Safarov, it would be good.

Now more than ever we need political vigilance. But this is not the most important [aspect of] our attitude toward Safarov. He displayed a kulak deviation more than a Trotskyist deviation. Today I am absolutely sure of that. He did struggle against Trotskyist views, but he demonstrated a rugged Right-Opportunist deviation.

But we failed to see his fraud in his current work for many years. Did his Menshevik Zinovievite conception negatively affect current work in the Comintern? This question has to be raised. I think that in general the answer is no. As to the resolutions, Safarov wrote very many draft resolutions; but our attitude toward his projects was one of mistrust. I think there was a mistrust on our side; we corrected [those drafts], and I think that if one were to check them, there would be little of Safarov's personal opinions in them. We distrusted him and, of course, would not permit him to develop a political line of his own. But what I am particularly worried about is that he had the opportunity to speak in the KUTV school [Communist University for Toilers of the East].

(VOICE: This is right.)

Or with some colonial comrades, with whom he had an opportunity to speak without witnesses, without anyone from the Eastern Department being present. There is a possibility that he could have palmed off his Zinovievite views. Therefore, we will need to check this out in the Eastern Department.

However, there is no more need to discuss here the agent of the counterrevolution Safarov, simply because the question raised here is not directly [related to Safarov] but to Magyar. Until recent years, we have considered Magyar a capable and useful worker. What we have learned was a complete surprise to us. And the fact that we have only now learned about his ties to Safarov and Zinoviev and other members of this counterrevolutionary center demonstrates the lack of political vigilance. Magyar stressed in his speech here that there was a lack of political vigilance. Magyar stressed in his speech here that he did not belong to this Zinovievite group. However, one can see from the testimony of one of the arrested counterrevolutionaries that they possessed information that Magyar belonged to their group or had connections with their group. Where is the truth here? Magyar himself says that one cannot take words for face value. Do I want to say that I believe that arrested counterrevolutionary more than [I believe] Magyar? No, I do not want to say that. It is possible that Magyar is right. But it can also be that Magyar and that counterrevolutionary are both right, that Magyar belonged and [at the same time] did not belong to the group; it is very possible. As com. Magyar himself stated here, his attitude toward the leading members of this group was one of conciliation to the extent that they might have considered him, if not a member of the center, nonetheless a member of their periphery.

One can consider Magyar a member [of the group] who attached himself to them; however, Magyar takes a juridical view of the case, whereas we are talking of its political aspect. Magyar had a friendship with Safarov. Besides that, he sustained his friendly relations with Zinoviev and some other members of this counterrevolutionary opposition. The result was that he did not tell everything about the conversations that they had to the leaders of the party and to the leaders of the Comintern. He now says that at least the tone [of those conversations] was anti-party and anti-Soviet. However, when Magyar spoke to us or to any other comrade, he gave an impression of a very open comrade who tells everything. It turned out that he talked about everything except the anti-party moods and anti-party tone of Zinoviev, Safarov, and others.

He says that he and Zinoviev had only political conversations. But this is the most important [kind of conversation]. And you had a personal friendship with Safarov. Is it conceivable then that you did not know Safarov's mood, his anti-party, anti-Soviet mood? This friendship of yours with Safarov, who was directly connected with the counterrevolutionary group, was, as it has turned out now, an indirect link to the group that committed a vile terrorist murder. Magyar, such a friendship results in hands being spit on with blood.

The basic obligation of each party member is to not maintain such friendships and such personal relations, which even for a moment [might betray] the slightest overtones, might be embarrassing to reveal to the party. How else will the party be able to conduct its struggle if we do not educate our comrades in such a party spirit? We have to rally closer than ever around the Bolshevik Stalinist party, around Stalin, whom these vile counterrevolutionaries also wanted to kill. It is also a necessary lesson for us.

Also revealing is Magyar's attitude toward the party, and even toward Soviet power, at the time when Safarov was arrested. It often happens that when our comrades are arrested in the capitalist countries, we become worried, we want to take some immediate measures to alleviate their situation, etc. But here a person was arrested under Soviet power, under the dictatorship of the proletariat as a result of a real crime committed, and Magyar becomes worried, he wants to, he tries to help him. He does not sufficiently trust the organs of Soviet power, their fairness, the results of their investigation.

He tries to intervene to counterbalance these actions. How can this be compatible with party membership? How can this be in the least compatible with a Soviet mentality? Com. Magyar said here several times that he deserved to be expelled from the party. I share the opinion that the decision about the expulsion has to be taken. However, this conclusion of Magyar's is not complete. If a comrade still retains remnants of party consciousness, he should not only draw a conclusion like "I deserve to be expelled from the party." Even if he might have committed a grave crime, he can still ask the party organization, "Even though my fault is such that I deserve to be expelled from the party, I am asking you, since I consider that I still have party consciousness, that I can still be useful to the party, I am asking you to readmit me to the party." I have not heard such an appeal from Magyar. I was waiting for him to make such an appeal; I would have been delighted to hear it. Maybe he considered that it would be humiliating. Anyway, I think that his conclusion, "just expel me from the party," is a non-party one. It cannot be explained other than as a lack of party consciousness, a lack of a truly Bolshevik attitude.

Personal relations, personal interests, no matter how cherished they might be, must be unconditionally subordinated to party interests. There is no other attitude for a Communist. It is natural to old Bolsheviks—they do not even have to think about it—but all of us, we foreign Communists, need [to learn] this lesson. We must develop in ourselves a party discipline, an iron discipline. Not a mechanical but a living discipline. We have to educate ourselves in the spirit of always subordinating personal interests and personal friendships to the interests of the party. And what are the party's interests? They are simply the interests of the revolutionary class, the interests of the revolution, the interests of the workers' cause.

At another meeting a couple of days ago, com. Manuilsky reminded us about the example of the civil struggle that the movie "Chapaev"[54] demonstrated. Comrades from KIM reacted enthusiastically to the mention of this example. What sort of lesson can be derived from this example? It is a lesson from the times of the Civil War, when people thought that the most cherished, the most important [goal of all] was the cause for which they struggled, when they did not think for a moment that one could put some personal interests before their dedication to the cause. They do not think about their private life; they sacrifice it. But we still have another anti-Soviet war waiting for us. How are we going to face it if we do not educate ourselves and all the rest in this spirit? This lesson is even more important than before. We have to learn this lesson and never forget it for a moment. We have to educate all young comrades in the spirit of these lessons. (Applause.)

BRONKOWSKI: Comrades, as soon as the first word spread about the foul murder of one of the Bolshevik Party leaders, com. Kirov, it was immediately followed by the rumor among the party activists, to whom Magyar belonged at that time, that it was committed by a party member. This news, I must say, spread among the party activists very rapidly. Our first move, our first thought, was to look around, to look at our ways and at the activities of different degenerates, different groups that nurtured the kind of renegades who went so far as to embrace a foul act like the murder of com. Kirov.

And what was Magyar doing at that time? Magyar visited Zinoviev to conduct political discussions. What was Magyar doing after the whole group was exposed, when it was determined who was responsible, politically responsible, for this foul act, and when after that, one of the responsible organizers connected with this group, Safarov, was arrested? He was organizing help for Safarov.

What was Magyar doing when at the party cell [meeting] a question was raised not only about Safarov but already about Magyar? He was actually defending, covering up for, Safarov, covering up for himself.

I ask you, comrades, in the current situation, when there is no other way left for the scum of the anti-party groups to struggle against the party but through underground counterrevolutionary struggle that embraces terror, at this moment can there be a better lesson than this open display of solidarity with and support for those who are responsible for this foul murder, who in one or another way are connected with the organizations, with the executors of this crime?

It seems to me that this alone is quite sufficient to assess the role of Magyar. And Magyar did belong to the group to which also belonged the direct organizer of the murder, Kotolynov, who directly passed on the revolver that fired the deadly bullet at Kirov.

If this person had even an iota of party consciousness and party responsibility left, would he not be compelled to think about all of the connections that he might have had in the past and in the present, and then to come to the party organization, to go to the Soviet organs, and to ask [them] to investigate to the end everything that might help illuminate the real role of the inspirers of the murder and of the murderers themselves? Did Magyar do it? We know that he did not do it. We know that what he did was, in fact, as they said here, to express solidarity with the organizers of the killing and its political inspirers. This is the way to describe the essence of this case in its present form. I think that this is sufficient for a verdict on a former party member.

I am not going to speak about Magyar's false and deceitful stories about his ties to Zinoviev. Com. Heckert has explained to us very clearly the point that, given Magyar's assessment of Zinoviev, an assessment of him as a double-dealer when all the time he was giving false testimony to the party, given such an assessment of Zinoviev, Magyar's visits to one of the very important political workers of the Comintern could not have had the character of consultations, or political discussions about general topics of party life; they could only have had a group character.

Com. Magyar is actually trying to reduce everything to his liberalism, to his petit bourgeois origin. I think it is not the liberalism of Magyar. In fact, Magyar is counting on the liberalism, the remnant of that liberalism that still survives in many of us. This liberalism reveals itself when, out of tolerance, in particular with respect to the comrades with an anti-party past, we do not attempt to look for the political roots of [their] political essence and thus become incapable of revealing their true faces. I think that the conclusions for us, the Comintern workers, have to be particularly acute, since our vigilance has to be higher [and] sharper than in other places, than in any other party organization. Why? Not only because we have Safarov and Magyar, not only because we have had someone else before. It was said here that Zinoviev has not played [his] final role in the Comintern. But if we are to assess this role in the past, we will have to approach it from the viewpoint of which heritage, which remnants of it we still retain. And it looks as though there is still something left. [This role has to be assessed] in the Comintern in particular. < . . . >[55] It is possible that such people with anti-party pasts are attracted to the Comintern because it is hard for them to get on in the VKP(b), where it is easier to reveal their [true] face by directly judging their work for socialist construction. Finally, because in the Comintern we are dealing with a great number of parties. With rare exceptions, in the individual parties there are a number of people who have committed mistakes, demonstrated their political inconsistency in other parties, and can serve as the basis for anti-party activities of the different anti-party elements here in the USSR and in the VKP(b). There are two kinds of such elements, and it is worth mentioning them here.

There are Poles, there are Hungarians, there are other nationals who have worked closely with the VKP(b), who have revealed their political face here. They had been in the opposition before, had been expelled from the party, and came back later. Many of them, I can name them, do not want to reveal their faces, do not demonstrate their loyalty to the party through everyday work, i.e., in the socialist construction, where they had been exposed and expelled, i.e., as in the VKP(b). They are either working in other parties or conduct work in the Comintern. Such tendencies are noticeable because the easiest way to reveal such people's faces is through practical work of socialist construction. It is in such work that it is easiest to expose them. This is the first point.

Another type of comrade are those who, on the contrary, revealed their inconsistency, were deviationists and transferred to the VKP(b) in order to reeducate themselves in the environment of the Bolshevik Party and to reveal their faces. This kind of comrade considers it possible to retain false views regarding foreign parties while remaining VKP(b) members. Is it compatible? Hardly, and it represents that particular ground that is so fertile for the seeds of anti-party opposition of a different kind since the VKP(b), the leading section of the Comintern, for the most part determines the line and attitude toward these or other parties. Discontent with any particular party and the Comintern cannot [help] but influence strongly the attitude toward the VKP(b) and its leadership.

We will have to improve our vigilance along this line; we will have to do away with liberalism. Only on this basis will we be able to move forward, having purged our apparatus of the Magyars. We have to purge ourselves of the Magyars as soon as possible. Only then will we be able to actually strengthen our cohesion and to further advance our work, [which is] aimed at bringing the proletariat closer to world revolution, basing ourselves on the example of the VKP(b) and under Stalin's leadership. [. . .]

MANUILSKY: Everything substantial has been said. Magyar, for the last time—he is now citizen Magyar, and you still have to earn [the right] to be called a citizen of the Soviet Union—citizen Magyar asked here at the party meeting for a pass to the [ranks of] non-party members. You will be granted this pass.

I am not going to dwell on this question any longer. I want to draw some political conclusions from what has happened here.

When citizen Magyar spoke here, he said that it was a civil funeral taking place here. No, citizen Magyar, we do not serve civil funerals for Magyars. We have lived through a big funeral, a funeral that stirred the entire party, that stirred all of the workers and kolkhoz peasants of our country. Here, comrades, a political execution is taking place, the execution of a man who deceived the working class, who cheated the benevolence of the party that had forgiven him and accepted him unconditionally to its ranks. In this sense it is a political execution that is taking place here, and we must say plainly and clearly what we are accusing Magyar of. Do you want to know, citizen Magyar, what we are accusing you of? Try to deny it! We are accusing you, and this is a major political accusation, of having the blood of com. Kirov on your hands and on the hands of that group to which you belonged, on the hands of the group of former Zinovievite opposition. Try to wash that blood out! (Applause.)

You did not need to deliver those sorrowful, penitent speeches. Even if you cried from this rostrum, you would not have been able to wash this blood off the hands of the Zinovievite opposition, wash off this political, moral-political responsibility.

It is not important whether it was Magyar or Zinoviev or anybody else from the former Zinovievite opposition, whether it was Kotolynov or Shatsky (who then shadowed [Kirov]) who put the revolver into Nikolaev's hands. Who is Kotolynov? Kotolynov developed out of that ideological school whose leaders were Zinoviev and others. Where was citizen Magyar's ideological vigilance? That group of criminals that dared to attempt the life of com. Kirov grew and developed in this rotten swamp, in underground circles, in the circles directed not against the class enemy, which the German party is struggling against now, but in the underground circles directed against the dictatorship of the proletariat, in the circles where everything is poisoned by the miasma of distrust, gossip, slander against the party, against the working class, against socialism. They say that Zinoviev was an ideologist of this group. But is Zinoviev the only one responsible? No. This whole movement that had been conducting the struggle against the party for a number of years is responsible. It is from here that this miasma grew. And this is the first accusation, citizen Magyar, that the party brings against you, and you cannot wriggle out of it.

Second. Magyar said here that after Kirov was shot, it became crystal clear to him that the opposition had degenerated into an anti-Soviet, White Guard, fascist group. It became clear to you only now? Then tell all the comrades who are present here what happened on 7 November 1927? Here on the streets of Moscow anti-Soviet demonstrations took place that we, the party members, had to disperse.[56] It was the day when Trotsky, Zinoviev, and Kamenev were touring the workers' districts. For the first time then this group acted as an anti-Soviet group. And that was not a decisive event for you? You had to wait for the shot at com. Kirov to understand the counterrevolutionary nature of the opposition? This is our second accusation to citizen Magyar.

Citizen Magyar said here that he maintained only personal and private relations with Zinoviev and Kamenev, you see. The one who maintained such relations after 7 November 1927 has no right to come and speak today about personal relations only. It is quite clear that what we have here is maintaining [relations] with an organized group, a counterrevolutionary group that had organized anti-Soviet demonstrations.

We are accusing citizen Magyar of a third point. Magyar said here that he conducted political conversations with Zinoviev but never noticed anything anti-party in those political conversations, you see. Stop it, citizen Magyar, stop it. It is not true.

It is not true, and if from this rostrum here today you talked about what you were actually discussing with Zinoviev, I assure you that there would have been a sudden change in the mood of this party organization that is judging you today. If Magyar had spoken sincerely about what he discussed with Zinoviev, it would have happened. Don't we understand that Zinoviev, who had been conducting the anti-party struggle for a number of years, that Zinoviev and Kamenev, who occupied unimportant positions and were dissatisfied with it, did we really think that they never raised political questions about the change of leadership? Excuse me, no one will believe you if you say so, and in this lies your lack of sincerity toward the party.

Comrades, besides those major accusations, here are the three political accusations that today are being brought against Magyar. And this party trial is to decide today whether Magyar is guilty or not. I am convinced that the party meeting will unanimously say that Magyar is guilty and does not deserve mercy. (Applause.)

There is one more political lesson of tremendous importance, and I want our foreign comrades in particular to understand this political lesson. It is the complete fascist degeneration of Trotsky. It is a new stage in the development of this opposition toward fascism. But is it actually a new stage? No, comrades. Those who witnessed the origins of the opposition in its very first discussions, who followed its development up until the anti-Soviet demonstrations of 7 November 1927, cannot doubt this concept. It is one of the most important political lessons.

I remember, and I want to finish on this, I remember how we all, the delegates to the Seventeenth Party Congress, were listening with particular attention to the speech of Sergei Mironovich Kirov. He was standing at the rostrum, so close, so dear to us, and said: "We have won now, we have gained a number of victories, and our mighty, solid, strong army is advancing, its marching sounding like a militant song. But there are still some fellow travelers lagging in the rear. They are trying to keep pace with this mighty class army. They also want to sing, but they sing out of tune."

Com. Kirov was mistaken in one thing: The fellow travelers turned into white bandits with sawed-off guns shooting [people] in the back. And com. Kirov fell [their] first victim.

Comrades, our great army, called the All-Union Communist Party, is going forward toward new victories, and it is led by the great field marshal, our glorious commander in chief, our beloved Stalin. (Applause.) This army is not afraid of difficulties, it is not afraid of the class enemy, it is not scared by the capitalist world and the Magyars. It will sweep away all those standing in its way. It will, as a powerful wheel of history, smash Magyar and the rest. Our party is going toward new victories under the leadership of our great Stalin. Away with Magyar from the party. Long live the VKP(b) and Stalin. (Applause.)

CHERNOMORDIK: Com. Kotelnikov is forgoing his concluding speech. Are there any declarations?

(None.)

Let me give the floor to com. Alikhanov to announce the resolution of the party committee.

(Com. Alikhanov reads the resolution of the party committee.) (Applause.) CHERNOMORDIK: Are there any declarations or motions regarding this resolution? It is possible to adopt it in principle now. I put it to vote. Who is for adopting the decision of the party committee in principle? All those present here vote, and then, separately, the VKP(b) members. Who is for adopting the resolution in principle? Who is against? Who abstains? (Adopted unanimously in principle.)

(VOICE: I suggest combining both resolutions and then updating them in accordance with today's speech by Magyar.)

A suggestion has been made to combine both resolutions stylistically [and] editorially. Any objections? (None.) Accepted. Second, a suggestion has been made to highlight what is new that was said at the meeting (although I think that Magyar has not added anything new) and to evaluate his behavior at the meeting, based on his speech. (Accepted.)

(GERISH: I suggest changing the paragraph that says that Magyar failed to demonstrate vigilance toward Safarov because he was connected with him.) There is a suggestion to change this paragraph so that it conforms to the whole resolution. (Accepted.)

(ISKROV: I suggest adding the following statement: The fact that Magyar helped Safarov after his arrest is an open manifestation of his hostile attitude toward the organs of Soviet power and proletarian dictatorship.)

It has been [already stated] here. Com. Iskrov suggests giving a sharper formulation by stressing that it is not only the lack of vigilance but an open demonstration against Soviet organs. (Accepted.)

(VOICE: To mention that there was a connection with Kotolynov.)

There is a suggestion to mention the connection with Kotolynov. (Accepted.)

Let us vote [for the resolution] in general. Those voting for the resolution, please raise your hands. Those against . . . Those abstaining . . . (Adopted unanimously.)

Second, I can now announce that the Political Commission made a decision yesterday to remove Magyar from the Comintern apparatus. [. . .]

RESOLUTION OF THE GENERAL MEETING OF THE PARTY ORGANIZATION OF THE ECCI APPARATUS ABOUT THE EXPULSION OF MAGYAR FROM THE PARTY.

Having heard and discussed the information of the representatives of the party committee and the party group of the Eastern Lendersecretariat regarding the behavior and actions of Magyar, and Magyar's explanations, the general meeting resolves:

Magyar, along with all active participants of the Zinovievite-Trotskyist bloc, as a participant and supporter of this bloc, bears full responsibility for the vile murder of com. Kirov, which was carried out by the black hundreds [*chernosotennoe*] of the Zinovievite counterrevolutionary group. Along with Zinoviev, Yevdokimov, Bakaev, Safarov, and others, Magyar's hands are stained with the blood of Kirov, a friend and comrade-in-arms of the great Stalin.

Magyar, who has not been exposed by the organs of the proletarian dictatorship [NKVD], who is still carrying his party card, who is aware of his full responsibility for the fascist, black hundred action by the scum of the Zinovievite group, has not taken a single step to admit this responsibility before the party organization in order to assist the party and organs of proletarian dictatorship in thoroughly exposing all the participants, all direct and indirect perpetrators [of the crime], all the organizers and inspirers of the assassins of the popular tribune, of the assassins of one of the leaders of our party.

And even after the whole country had already recognized in Nikolaev, Kotolynov, Rumiantsev, and others the familiar vile image of the Zinovievites, Magyar was preoccupied with only one concern: how to hide himself, how to remain silent and keep a low profile, how not to stick out in order to save his own skin, in order not to attract any attention to himself.

Only after the ECCI apparatus party organization, on its own initiative, demanded that Magyar speak and explain his ties with the counterrevolutionaries of the Zinovievite-Trotskyist bloc was Magyar obliged to speak and to abandon [his] tactics of dishonest silence. But he replaced [that silence] with the no less dishonest tactics of insincere, hypocritical behavior before the party organization, tactics of unscrupulously defending himself and Zinoviev, Safarov, and Co.

The whole anti-party behavior of Magyar derived primarily from the fact that he, until the very last day, maintained permanent connections with Zinoviev, Safarov, Vardin, Gorshenin, and other members of the counterrevolutionary group. Magyar maintained ties to these elements despite the timely and categorical warning of c. Pyatnitsky and despite the fact that this connection could not be justified by any practical necessity arising in the Comintern apparatus. On the contrary, [this connection] hampered the work of our apparatus.

By maintaining permanent connections with Zinoviev, by consulting with him about vital political questions (the construction of socialism in one country, the role of Stalin, the murder of c. Kirov, Lenin's opinion about the military alliance, etc.), Magyar tried to prove to the ECCI party organization that Zinoviev held correct party positions on all questions.

By maintaining close, friendly relations with Safarov, discussing vital political problems with him, Magyar is trying to prove that Safarov had no anti-party or anti-Soviet views or moods.

Although Magyar maintained close, personal, intimate, and permanent relations with these traitorous elements and was no doubt aware of the real moods of these counterrevolutionary elements, not only did he fail to promptly signal the party about them, but at the party meetings he did not expose them politically or assess the true worth of the anti-Soviet Zinovievite group's actions [nor] his own connections with the group's leaders and members. The general meeting deems Magyar's attempt to portray himself as a "disoriented fool" and to thereby justify his anti-party behavior an obviously calculated maneuver by which Magyar attempted to obscure the case and to avoid party responsibility.

The meeting notes Magyar's insolent attempt to portray, in retrospect, the group of Magyar, Vardin, and Safarov, to which belonged Kotolynov, a direct organizer of the murder, as the most honest and sincere part of the Zinovievite opposition.

The general meeting notes with disgust the counterrevolutionary behavior of Magyar as reflected in his maintenance of relations with Safarov after his arrest. He gave advice to people close to him and gave money to Safarov, who had been arrested in connection with com. Kirov's murder. This miscreant, anti-Soviet act of Magyar is nothing but an [open] demonstration by Magyar against the organs of proletarian dictatorship and their struggle against the scum of Zinoviev's counterrevolutionary group.

Considering that Magyar is an alien and hostile element in our party, who has retained ideological-political and organizational ties to the Zinovievite counterrevolutionary group, [the party meeting resolves to] expel Magyar from the VKP(b).

The transcript of the meeting conveys vividly two key aspects of the party mindset at the time. One was that criticism of the party and its political line had become a "counterrevolutionary act" that led to the "opposite side of the barricades." Even doubts ("liberalism") constituted an anti-party act because they led to "counterrevolutionary" views. In short, any opposition to the party constituted an "enemy" activity. But as several speakers stated or implied, this ideal vision of the party had not yet been achieved. Only by rallying "even closer around the CC, around Stalin," by raising vigilance, and by strengthening party discipline could the goal be realized. For those who had internalized the assumptions and values of the party, who believed the case against Magyar to be a compelling one, the end justified the means. But the price of party purity was steep. Heightening vigilance meant sowing more mistrust and suspicion among comrades.

The second aspect was the expressed belief that hostile conspiracies existed within the VKP and the USSR. Several speakers' descriptions of how defeated oppositionists formed an anti-party conspiratorial group clearly express the causal logic that underscored that belief. That the Bolsheviks prior to 1917, and some fraternal parties at that moment, employed conspiratorial methods to survive police repression made that logic easy for those present to understand. But conspiratorial work is not the same as the conspiratorial mindset.

Although the explicit purpose of the meeting was to expel Magyar, it served a more important purpose: to convey to all present what Stalin, the Politburo, and the ECCI leaders believed constituted proper and improper party behavior. The didactic and symbolic power of the ritual and the rhetoric was significant. The meeting reaffirmed the centrality of the party, its assumptions, values, mores, and social norms. It conveyed that only through the party could the dreams of individual Communists be realized and only by proper party behavior could the "counterrevolutionary" threats to those dreams be repulsed. The party elite defined the political tasks and tone of the post-Kirov years, but the ECCI leaders and cadres responded willingly and decisively.

Over the course of the next several months, the ECCI party organization investigated other comrades. All were expelled from the party and soon after were arrested.[57] During that period others who had aroused suspicion would have to account for their behavior.[58] The logic and consequences of vigilance had begun to unfold.

Following the 28 December meeting, party groups within the ECCI held meetings at which calls for vigilance were common fare. The resolution passed at the 4 January 1935 meeting of the party group in the Polish-PriBaltic Lendersecretariat is representative. The resolution proclaimed that "the high point of vigilance demands from us familiarity with the daily lives of each member of the party group and with his political physiognomy, a systematic review of all comrades."[59] Ascertaining the "political physiognomy" of each comrade was the purpose behind the periodic purges of VKP members.[60] That Safarov and Magyar (and others "unmasked" in 1934–1935) had passed through the 1933–1934 purge only to be later "unmasked" as Zinovievites underscored for many the importance of learning "the daily lives of each member . . . and his political physiognomy." This held true for ECCI members as well as the rank and file. In 1934, Béla Kun had praised Magyar as "one of the best workers in the ECCI apparat."[61] At the 28 December meeting, Kun denounced Magyar as a counterrevolutionary. Safarov and Magyar had become symbols of the need for greater vigilance in the aftermath of Kirov's murder.

In mid-January 1935 the CC circulated a secret letter on the "lessons learned from the events connected with the foul murder of Comrade Kirov."[62] The letter increased the pressure on party organizations to raise political vigilance. On 16 and 20 February the ECCI party organization held closed meetings devoted to the lessons learned by that body from the murder and its aftermath. The latter meeting was convened after the investigations into certain party members had been completed. Although full transcripts of the meetings exist, the focus here is on the speeches of Georgi Dimitrov, rising star of the Comintern, who would be elected its general secretary in August, and Osip Pyatnitsky, a member of the ECCI's Political Secretariat.[63] Both men spoke at the 20 February meeting. Because Dimitrov would soon be general secretary, only his comments are reproduced in full in **Document 5**.

Document 5

Dimitrov's speech to the 20 February 1935 general closed meeting of the ECCI party organization, dedicated to the lessons flowing from Kirov's murder, 9 March 1935. RGASPI, f. 546, op. 1, d. 274, ll. 93–96. Original in Russian. Typewritten.

[. . .]

9 March 1935

Secret.

DIMITROV. (Applause.) Comrades, as we saw from the report at the last meeting,[64] through a common effort our party organization has conducted a serious Bolshevik self-cleansing in connection with the lessons that we all, all the Comintern, learned from the foul murder of com. Kirov. And let not the penitent transgressors like c.c. Guralsky, Kurella,[65] and others attempt here to reduce this work, which is extremely important for the party organization, to a trifle, reduce it to "legends" and personal squabbles. This question is too vital for anybody from our party organization to be able to diminish the importance of the work done.

That which has already been done, as well as all those suggestions that the party committee has made to the party organization and those to be adopted at today's meeting—all this is good. Yet, I ask, Will it be sufficient? And I permit myself to answer straightforwardly: It is not yet sufficient. It is insufficient, not only because there was no chance to clean out at one stroke everything rotten that probably still exists in our ranks. We will have to work on it in the future, to expose it and flush it out. Whatever has already been done is also not sufficient because our party organization is not an ordinary VKP(b) organization. Our party organization has a special character.

First, the composition of our party organization is international. Out of 468 members of the party organization, 280 are foreign comrades, members of different parties from all parts of the world. Second, this is a party organization of the workers of the Comintern apparatus, who work for the leadership of the world Communist movement. Thousands of ties, thousands of roads lead from Mokhovaia[66] to all the countries of the world—to China, to Germany, to Spain, and to the Balkans.

The work of the members of our organization is directly linked to the life, to the situation, to the struggle of the Communist movement in all countries. Naturally, the class enemy attempts by all means to sneak into our ranks, has attempted, is attempting, and will attempt to find conscious or unconscious tools within our own ranks, is paying and will pay attention to Mokhovaia, to our organization, to the members of this organization.

Comrades, if this is correct, and it is no doubt correct, then the question is, Do some special tasks for our party organization derive from this? Should our work regarding the raising of Bolshevik vigilance, the struggle against the enemy's new methods of work, be of the same character as, for example, in the party organization of some factory or some Soviet office? No. We need special measures, special methods to protect the Comintern apparatus from infiltration by the enemy's agents and from the danger of double-dealing. As far as I know, insufficient attention has been paid and is being paid to the special tasks and the special demands that our party organization faces. Whereas in other party organizations Bolshevik vigilance and the strengthening of vigilance is necessary, in our organization this vigilance must be even higher. Whereas in other places it is vital to verify people, the constant verification of people here is even more important. We see that in the Comintern apparatus, there are working many foreign comrades who are members of our organization and who in their countries, in their parties, used to occupy or still occupy leading positions and are more or less important leaders there. They usually think that they possess significant political experience and do not pay sufficient attention to connecting themselves more closely and directly with the VKP(b), with party life in the Soviet Union.

It is not a secret that a number of foreign comrades who have been living and working here for years do not study Russian. Sometimes they do not know a word of Russian. Yet they feel that it is necessary to familiarize themselves with the life and work of the Russian Bolshevik Party and the socialist construction in the USSR, to use the tremendous experience of the Russian comrades. It is good and correct that the suggested resolution points to the necessity to intensify the study of the history of the VKP(b). Given the special character of our party organization, it is also necessary to pay serious attention to the study of the struggle against deviationists, against factionalists, and against enemies in other fraternal parties, using the experience of the Communist movement in other countries for the struggle against the class enemy.

In our ranks, comrades, there are still many revealing petit bourgeois prejudices. Two such cases were discussed here. Any member of our organization who values his personal ties and places his personal situation above that of the party, who, owing to false comradeship, does not conduct a struggle against intrigues, squabbles, and plans aimed against the party and the Comintern, is not a revolutionary and not a Bolshevik. He who does not notify, who does not promptly signal, the party organization about any such danger is an accessory to the enemy. We urgently need Bolshevik reeducation. Members of the party organization, notwithstanding their skill, notwithstanding those positions that they used to occupy or now occupy in this or that party, have to reeducate themselves in order to subordinate their personal life, all personal ties and actions, to the interests of the party. The party is everything for us—this is our slogan, this is our Bolshevik law that we must follow in all our actions.

Comrades, in connection with the resolution suggested here, I would like to make a special proposition: To charge the party committee, in light of the special character and tasks of our party organization, to discuss measures to strengthen political-educational and instructional work, as well as other organizational measures that are necessary, in order to ensure Bolshevik vigilance and a Bolshevik reeducation of the members of our party organization, to oblige the party committee, after discussing these measures and working out a concrete plan of work in this direction, to give suitable proposals to the party organizations in order to thereby mobilize the party organization to struggle to raise our work to an even higher level. Upon completion of the first phase of our Bolshevik self-cleansing, we have to provide a more formidable basis for the future struggle against the agents of the class enemy, against double-dealing, against spinelessness, against slackness, against squabbles, against anti-party gatherings, against everything that can be useful to the enemy and harmful to our party and the Comintern. (Applause.) [. . .]

Later, Pyatnitsky addressed the meeting.[67] His comments echoed many of Dimitrov's points, although he embellished his comments with many more details. Like Dimitrov, Pyatnitsky viewed heightened vigilance within the ECCI apparatus and the party organization as essential in light of the Comintern's unique international composition: "Vigilance in the CI apparat should be many times higher than it is . . . double-dealers say one thing and do another. It is impossible to believe them." Whereas Dimitrov spoke in general terms about why vigilance was necessary, Pyatnitsky peppered his comments on the need for greater vigilance with examples of specific individuals whose former deviations and present behaviors posed serious dangers to the ECCI. Although he criticized both the Polish and the German parties, he devoted special attention to German Communists who, not appreciating the dangers posed by oppositionists, had become "conciliationists," that is, people who ostensibly sought to reconcile the critiques of former oppositionists with the party line.

He noted that the German Communist Party, in particular, often sent to the ECCI comrades who had been oppositionists and who remained conciliationists. Such people posed a special threat to the ECCI, because, he said, they often violated the code of secrecy by passing on information to oppositionists. Pyatnitsky also expressed satisfaction that the party committee had recently expelled double-dealers from the party, but he issued an especially ominous warning to former oppositionists and conciliationists: "Lenin said that if a comrade admitted his mistakes and worked well, it was not necessary to remember the mistakes." But with all deference to Lenin, he noted: "I am of the opinion that whoever lied once to the party, even on an insignificant occasion, is capable of lying a second time on a more serious occasion."[68]

Pyatnitsky also made some harsh comments about political émigrés. He reiterated Dimitrov's expressions of incredulity and frustration that many foreign comrades who lived in the USSR did not learn the Russian language and did not engage more actively in Soviet life. He shared Dimitrov's view that enemies tried to use the émigré communities as a cover to penetrate the ECCI apparatus. Both men's concerns about the foreign comrades were part of a larger concern about the quality of cadres in general. Pyatnitsky frankly expressed his fear that an insufficient number of cadres were both capable and politically reliable: "We do not have a sufficient number of qualified cadres who were never in any sort of opposition in the fraternal parties." Vigilance was necessary to deter the penetration by "hostile elements," but it alone was not sufficient. As Dimitrov put it: "There was no chance to clean out at one stroke everything rotten that . . . exists." More sustained efforts were required.[69]

Both men believed that a two-track approach was necessary. On the one hand, it was necessary to verify the members of the party organization to expose double-dealers; that is, vigilance had to be raised. Dimitrov, more so than Pyatnitsky, stressed the necessity for a verification of the ranks of the ECCI party organization and the fraternal parties. That call reflected not only the CC's position but also Dimitrov's long-standing intolerance of the former Left Opposition.[70] On the other hand, only sustained political education and enlightenment would ensure that the quality of cadres improved. According to Dimitrov, "Any member of our organization who values his personal ties and places his personal situation above that of the party . . . [is] not a Bolshevik." Political education was essential if such "petit bourgeois prejudices" were to be eradicated. Such "petit bourgeois" attitudes also gave rise to "squabbles," which Dimitrov twice condemned as being "useful to the enemy and harmful to our party." Pyatnitsky stressed even more forcefully the need for better political education for foreign comrades. Echoing the recommendation of the CC's secret letter on the Kirov murder, both men called on their comrades "to pay serious attention to the study of the struggle against deviationists, against factionalists, and against enemies." The recommendation that a two-track approach to the problem—vigilance and education—was necessary echoed the views of Stalin and the party leadership on how best to improve the quality of cadres.[71]

The 20 February meeting ended with the passage of a rather lengthy resolution,[72] several aspects of which warrant attention. The first is that it proclaimed that the "ECCI party organization is politically healthy and has been correctly conducting the general line and specific directives of the VKP(b)." While it also noted that "in light of revelations about the Zinovievite counter-revolutionary terrorist group," it was essential to increase vigilance and party activism, the call for increased vigilance was implicitly offset by an expressed sense of closure and a belief that the party organization had weathered the recent crisis and had reduced its political vulnerability. The party committee had responded to the "appeal by the VKP(b)" by finding some alleged oppositionists in its midst and expelling or reprimanding them. It had proven its vigilance and, by so doing, underscored the importance of party discipline and legitimized the need for vigilance. Its self-proclaimed success did not, however, negate the need for continued vigilance. To achieve that goal, it was essential to improve the quality of political education. Such knowledge was essential to forge the correct Communist identity.

The punishments meted out to the members of the ECCI party organization, whose shortcomings and supposedly nefarious activities the committee had recently exposed, deserve note. In the six months after Magyar's expulsion, twenty-three members were punished. Nine were expelled from the VKP or a fraternal party. Five of them had been arrested by mid-1935. The remaining fourteen received party reprimands or punishments. As a result, the ranks of the party organization shrank by 2 percent (from 468 to 459 members).[73]

The political impact and legacies of the 1934–1935 vigilance campaign cannot be adequately quantified and were more profound than the percentage suggests. Stalin's and the Politburo's willingness to arrest large numbers of party members had a startling effect.[74] Vigilance against oppositionists, factionalists, deviationists, and double-dealers had been an identifying feature of Bolshevism since at least 1918. But Kirov's murder dramatically changed the political climate; the arrests reflected that change. The allegation that former oppositionists engaged in an anti-party conspiracy with ties abroad resulted in their being subjected to increasing scrutiny. The explicit lesson was that stricter party discipline was mandatory for all.

That the purported conspiracy to murder had ties to "enemies" abroad injected a xenophobic quality into the vigilance campaign and exposed latent tensions between Soviet-born and foreign-born comrades. That more than half of those who were reprimanded or expelled from their parties in February 1935 were foreign-born suggests that, even within the headquarters of the Communist International, national identity was a crucial and potentially divisive identity. It was not so stated. Rather, euphemisms were used: people for whom "the party is everything"; people who retained vestiges of "petit bourgeois prejudices" or "blue-blooded individualism." Magyar retained his blue-bloodedness and hence was not a "real Bolshevik." But as Magyar noted, cultural frames of reference and mores are not easily overcome. Just as political émigrés could not completely purge themselves of their mores, neither could their Soviet-born comrades completely overcome their perceptions of those raised in capitalist countries, of those who lived in émigré enclaves and had not learned Russian, of those who hesitated to subject personal relations to party discipline.

To be a "real Bolshevik," foreign-born comrades would have to completely internalize the VKP's values and mores. To be a "real Bolshevik," all comrades would have to be more vigilant against those who, "in the past, had struggled against the party," who maintained "close, friendly relationships" with former oppositionists or conciliationists. Within the ECCI party organization, the lessons of the Safarov-Magyar affair were clear, and helped define the characteristics of the emerging out-groups. We see them in the main players: the perennial oppositionist, Safarov, whom the party had forgiven, and Magyar, who carried "my petit bourgeois individualism . . . from that social milieu from which I came."

CHAPTER THREE

The Search for "Hostile Elements" and "Suspicious" Foreigners

> Under the guise of émigrés, they [foreign intelligence services] send here secret agents who work very well and very easily under the guise of victims of political terror [in their native countries]. Then they turn out to be provocateurs . . . this channel of espionage against the USSR is in general the organization of espionage and provocation by an international general staff.
>
> — ANTON KRAJEWSKI

THE COMINTERN held its Seventh Congress in Moscow from 25 July to 20 August 1935. Its most significant decision was to abandon the stridently sectarian policies of the Third Period (class versus class, and "social fascism") and to organize an anti-fascist Popular Front that would include all people and parties committed to opposing fascism.[1] Preparatory meetings for the Congress occupied the ECCI for much of the spring and summer of 1935. The Congress also elected Dimitrov to be the general secretary and approved a series of organizational measures that he had proposed. Over the next few years the Comintern's fortunes reached their zenith. Popular Front governments were elected in France and Spain, and participation in Popular Front activities in Europe and the Americas increased sharply.[2]

After the Congress, political anxieties that had concerned the Central Committee and the ECCI in early 1935 reasserted themselves. Chief among these was concern about the political reliability of émigrés. Soviet security and intelligence agencies had been aware for some time of efforts by Germany and neighboring countries to use disinformation and espionage to destabilize Soviet politics.[3] More seriously, from 1933, suspicions that émigrés, especially those from Poland and Germany, engaged in espionage and various anti-Soviet activities deepened within the VKP leadership and security organs. The number of arrests of émigrés for such reasons began to grow.[4] In a September 1935 speech to party secretaries, Nikolai Yezhov, a secretary of the Central Committee, head of its Department of Leading Party Organs (ORPO), and an ECCI member, pointedly expressed his conviction that some émigrés living in the USSR were foreign agents. Echoing Krajewski's earlier allegations, Yezhov told his audience that "foreign intelligence officers, saboteurs, knew that there is no better cover for their espionage and subversive operations than a party card, and they relied on that fact. For this reason, it is necessary to hide behind a party card at whatever cost. And they utilized every means of deception in order to obtain a party card for a spy or a saboteur. We can assert firmly that Poles, Finns, Czechs, and Germans have been openly gambling on this."[5]

Yezhov's ominous assertion came during his comments regarding Trotskyists, who "it seems to me . . . undoubtedly have a center somewhere in the USSR."[6] In Yezhov's mind, the two groups—spies and Trotskyists—shared similar goals and methods of operation. To him, there was little difference between them. His speech was therefore a call to identify and expel all ideological enemies from the VKP.

Krajewski's 1934 report on émigrés acting as spies, Yezhov's comments, and revelations during the VKP's 1935 verification of party documents (proverka) that large numbers of party cards had been forged or were missing and that non-party members, Soviets and foreigners alike, illegally possessed cards[7]— all these brought to the forefront the issue of the political reliability of émigrés, in particular those who belonged to the VKP. The concern of the VKP leaders over this issue is evident in their efforts to restrict immigration to the USSR. A Politburo resolution of 1 December 1935 sought to stem the entry of émigrés from Poland, west Ukraine, and Lithuania. It cancelled all approvals for entry that the ECCI and MOPR had issued and ordered VKP *oblast* committees not to accept anyone from the Polish section of the Comintern without the explicit approval of the Central Committee in the person of Yezhov.[8] By late 1935 many VKP leaders had become convinced that political émigrés posed a serious threat to the party and to national security. Perceptions that aliens were subversive deepened. As they did, pressures on the ECCI mounted.

In late 1935 the ECCI Secretariat ordered that a report on political emigration to the USSR be prepared for presentation to the Plenum of the VKP Central Committee in December. Manuilsky, the Central Committee representative in the ECCI and the ECCI secretary responsible for cadres, drafted the report, which Dimitrov read and edited.[9] The Politburo or the Central Committee had undoubtedly requested the report. In the report to the Plenum, Manuilsky repeated many of the assertions and concerns expressed by Krajewski, Yezhov, and the Politburo. He began by stating that "the main reason for the obstruction of political and educational work among the ranks of political émigrés is the degeneration [razlozheniia] within and the entry of enemies into the ranks of the Polish, Hungarian, Finnish, and other political émigrés." He criticized MOPR, which had formal responsibility for political émigrés, because it provided "no guarantee against penetration by hostile elements; on the contrary, it facilitates avowed enemies' legal entry into the USSR. The enemies of the USSR and the Comintern use political emigration as a channel [kanal] for penetrating their agents into the USSR and even the VKP(b)." "Facts" uncovered during the 1935 proverka revealed that "the admission of members of fraternal Communist Parties into the VKP(b) gave hostile elements the opportunity to receive party cards." Manuilsky claimed that some fraternal parties had made it a practice to send to the USSR people who had committed "political mistakes and crimes" in their native countries. By so doing, those parties had allowed "suspicious" elements to enter the USSR. In light of the potential dangers, he noted with shock that "not a single organization has an even somewhat accurate accounting of political émigrés or even those admitted to the VKP(b)."[10]

Manuilsky then recommended a series of measures to ensure the political reliability of those admitted to the USSR. He detailed the criteria that a potential political émigré should have to meet before being admitted to the country, suggested a review of all political émigrés and members of fraternal parties living in the USSR, urged improving political and cultural work among émigrés, and recommended guidelines that members of fraternal parties should have to meet before being admitted to the VKP.

His report and the announcement at the Plenum that the party membership screenings of 1933–1935 (the purge of 1933–1934 and the proverka of 1935) had revealed that missing and doctored party cards were in the hands of "enemies of the USSR" convinced the Central Committee of the need to act.[11] It passed a resolution that—after noting the penetration into the VKP of enemies in the guise of political émigrés and members of foreign parties—ordered an exchange of party documents (obmen partdokumentov) to ferret out all hostile elements.[12] The possibility that the party might be threatened from within and that spies, saboteurs, and enemy agents threatened national security demanded vigilant action.

The Plenum of the Central Committee jolted the ECCI into action. As the organization with overall responsibility for the fraternal parties and émigrés, it assumed a central role in identifying and exposing "hostile elements." In late December 1935 the ECCI Secretariat issued a resolution on the admission of members of fraternal parties to the VKP. Any such admission, it stated, would be accepted only after a thorough review of the applicant and a special recommendation from the applicant's Central Committee.[13] In early 1936, the ECCI ordered a series of political and administrative operations aimed at exposing any "hostile" or "suspicious elements" among émigrés, refugees, and foreign students.

On 3 January 1936, on behalf of the ECCI Secretariat, Manuilsky wrote to Yezhov expressing the ECCI Secretariat's deep concerns about "the penetration of the territory of the USSR by spies and saboteurs, disguised as political émigrés and members of the fraternal parties." His letter speaks for itself.

Document 6

Letter from Manuilsky to Yezhov regarding measures against "spies and saboteurs disguised as political émigrés," 3 January 1936.[14] RGASPI, f. 495, op. 18, d. 1147a, ll. 1–3. Original in Russian. Typewritten with handwritten additions.

Top secret
Sent to c. Yezhov.

3 January 1936

Dear Nikolai Ivanovich!

I ask you to receive me in the coming days on the question of measures to take against the penetration of the territory of the USSR by spies and saboteurs, disguised as political émigrés and members of the fraternal parties. ***Before the meeting***, I would like to identify the range of questions ***to be*** discussed ***with you***:

I. ***On the closing of the "green" frontiers.***

To close the so-called green passages[15] across the border not only to the Poles but also to the Finns, Latvians, Lithuanians, Estonians, for [they have] parties prone to provocation (the Romanian party has no "green passage"). The "green passage" should be used only ***in exceptional cases***, each time with the special permission of the CC VKP(b).

II. ***Limiting the influx of political immigration to the USSR.***

To limit the influx of political émigrés to the USSR, give to the fraternal parties a political explanation of [the need for] it as a measure necessary to fight mass desertion from the battlefield of class struggle and [to reduce] the danger of the exposure of party cadres. To that end, it is necessary:

a) to admit to the USSR only those individuals who would be personally known by the CC of the corresponding party and the Comintern and who would have special permission and a recommendation from the CC of their party to leave for the USSR, and only in cases where there is a threat of harsh repression in their country and of persecution in other capitalist countries. *It is also necessary to envisage the possibility of admitting* [to the USSR] sick comrades in need of special treatment, who are sent to the USSR by petition of the CC of the corresponding Communist Party and with the consent of the VKP(b) CC, and after the treatment is over, that comrade would immediately return to [his] country;

b) in connection with limiting the influx of émigrés to the USSR, to envisage the possibility of granting MOPR an extra hard-currency subsidy to render support to the émigré community abroad;

c) to forbid the international organizations to keep foreign tourists or assist them in staying on the territory of the USSR after their stay in the USSR is over;

d) to oblige the Comintern and other international organizations not to keep in the USSR students eliminated from competition or graduating from the international schools;

e) to oblige the Comintern and other international organizations to stop the practice of keeping *individuals* suspected of provocation or spying on the territory of the USSR (except in those cases where there is an appropriate instruction from NKVD organs);

f) to abolish the MOPR Legitimization Commission and transfer its functions of granting admissions to and legalizing stays in the USSR to the special USSR CEC [Central Executive Committee] commission;

g) to deprive the MOPR representatives abroad of the right to give [people] recommendations to enter the USSR, reserving this right to the CC of the respective parties only;

h) to let stay on the territory of the USSR only those defectors, crossing the border on their own, who would pass the most careful verification by NKVD organs and receive permission and a recommendation from the CC of the respective party.

III. Registration and verification of political emigration.

Undertake measures to register and verify all political émigrés settled on the territory of the USSR. To that end:

a) for political émigrés who are VKP(b) members, establish a special verification [*proverka*] of them during the exchange of party documents;

b) create special commissions for the verification of political émigrés in every city and town where there are political émigrés;

c) establish a system of special registration for political émigrés, concentrating on the registration of the political émigrés who are VKP(b) members in [their] party organizations, and the rest of the political émigrés in the MOPR organs;

d) oblige the Comintern to take measures to send from the USSR those political émigrés **not threatened by harsh repression** to [their] respective countries;

e) take measures to deport from the USSR those political émigrés who, while not being sick, systematically avoid working and live parasitically at MOPR's expense.

IV. Organization of political and cultural work among political émigrés:

a) entrust political work among political émigrés to local party organizations, taking this task away from trade union and MOPR organizations;

b) oblige the Comintern to plan a series of political activities aimed at the preservation and Bolshevik education of the émigré cadres from the illegal fraternal communist parties in the USSR;

c) turn KUNZ[16] (Communist University of the Peoples of the West) into an international school for the preparation and education of the fraternal communist parties' reserve cadres.

V. Replacement of the current MOPR leadership.

Replace the current MOPR leadership for not coping with its tasks and, following the Comintern's example, create a secretariat composed of a number of foreign comrades, with a sufficiently strong and authoritative VKP(b) representation, to be entrusted, together with the NKVD organs and the ECCI Personnel Department, with the task of the careful verification of all political emigration [*sic*] already in the USSR, as well as [those] arriving in the USSR.

In addition, I would like to discuss with you the question of measures of verifying the Polish Communist Party, which, as you know, in recent years has become the major supplier of spy and provocateur elements to the USSR.

I await your answer.[17]

The letter clearly indicates that Manuilsky and the ECCI leaders had serious concerns about fraternal party members and other foreigners who resided in the USSR, especially those who had become VKP members.[18] Although the party might be able to examine the pasts of its members, the threat posed by enemy agents "disguised as political émigrés," students, or employees in factories and offices, required nothing less than reviewing all political émigrés, refugees, and students. That task necessitated creating special commissions "in every city and town" to examine each foreigner. In this way, anxieties about foreigners became generalized within the party and society.

But reviewing all foreigners ran the risk of putting the ECCI in a politically vulnerable position. The discovery of "suspicious" or "hostile elements" among its charges might raise questions about the political oversight work of the

ECCI and thereby place it under scrutiny. Having provided materials that helped to define the resolution of the Central Committee Plenum, the ECCI had no choice but to investigate its charges. Doing so carried risks. Manuilsky's recommendations sought to minimize those risks by transferring responsibility for accepting future émigrés to a special CEC commission and by having the NKVD approve the admission of all future émigrés. He also provided a potential future scapegoat, MOPR, should the verifications of émigrés living in the USSR produce any embarrassing revelations. His recommendations to strip MOPR of responsibility for admitting foreigners and for conducting political work among them served as a preemptive defense of the ECCI.

At the time that Manuilsky wrote to Yezhov, the Central Committee was pursuing two parallel policies to improve the quality of cadres: reviewing party cadres and investigating any evidence of suspicious behavior, and upgrading the political education of cadres. As Dimitrov's and Pyatnitsky's comments to the February 1935 party committee meeting made clear, the two policies were interdependent.[19] Although Manuilsky's letter to Yezhov reflects these two tactical lines, his recommendation to close the green frontiers, to limit political immigration, and to register and verify all political émigrés in the USSR no doubt strengthened the hands of those who advocated vigilance.

Manuilsky was among them. In a 2 January 1936 letter to A. A. Andreev, a Politburo member and a secretary of the Central Committee, he announced that the ECCI Secretariat would soon propose to the Central Committee a "reorganization" of the Communist University for National Minorities of the West (KUNMZ, wrongly cited in the letter), which provided cadres who qualified with political education. Although the influx of émigrés strained the capacity of the school, Manuilsky was more concerned about the political reliability of the students and staff. He informed Andreev that the Secretariat advocated a verification of all students and staff in the KUNMZ and other party schools under ECCI control before the reorganization was carried out. That verification occurred in 1936, parallel with a verification of the fraternal party members living in the USSR.[20]

From January 1936 the ECCI leaders and the Cadres Department acted to fulfill the charge of the Central Committee to identify "suspicious elements" among the émigrés. Doing so required raising vigilance and improving verification. At a 19 January 1936 Cadres Department meeting to discuss issues relating to political émigrés and cadre policy, Manuilsky urged those in attendance "to plan together with us a series of measures that in the future will prevent suspicious and undesirable elements, agents of the class enemy, to penetrate into Soviet territory and the ranks of the VKP(b)."[21] Shortly after, he wrote to Yezhov informing him that the ECCI Secretariat had ordered the verification of political émigrés. He claimed that the operation would be completed by 8 March (a wildly optimistic forecast) and that some nine to ten thousand people had already been reviewed. But, he noted, there were an unspecified number of people about whom neither the Cadres Department nor MOPR had any information. To aid the ECCI apparatus and "the appropriate Soviet organs" (i.e., the security organs), Manuilsky deemed it essential "to establish the precise whereabouts of political émigrés and to collect in one place all existing materials on each of them, [and] to create a series of commissions of VKP(b) members that should verify each political émigré personally on the basis of existing references received from [fraternal] parties and local VKP(b) organizations where a given émigré had worked or is working."[22] These commissions carried out their work throughout 1936 and early 1937. They did so under increasing scrutiny from the Central Committee. Based on Manuilsky's and Yezhov's reports that some émigrés posed a serious threat to national security, the Central Committee passed a resolution in February that ordered the creation of a special commission to oversee the verification of foreigners living in the USSR. Its members were Manuilsky, Yezhov, and M. I. Gai of the Special Department of the Main Administration for State Security. In March the commission accepted Manuilsky's suggestion and voted to review the foreign sections of the Comintern, starting with the Polish section.[23]

In preparation for the verification of émigrés, the ECCI Secretariat instructed the representatives of the fraternal parties to draw up proposals detailing how they would verify their compatriots residing in the USSR and how they would control future emigration to the USSR. On 23 January, Zigmas Angaretis, an Old Bolshevik and the representative of the Lithuanian Communist Party (CPLith) in the ECCI, sent to Moskvin, a candidate member of the ECCI Secretariat, a memorandum outlining his ideas on how best to realize the Secretariat's goals.[24] Manuilsky's dubbing of the Lithuanian CP as a party "prone to provocation" created considerable pressure on Angaretis to satisfy his bosses. His attempts to do so and Moskvin's handwritten reactions in the margins are shown in **Document 7**. Angaretis's proposals make clear that he interpreted his charge broadly. His proposals addressed the verification of émigrés living in the USSR, the selection of future émigrés, the raising of vigilance within the Lithuanian CP, political education, and other issues. The range of his proposals illustrates how VKP members understood the connections between the campaigns to improve party cadres, to ferret out "suspicious" or "hostile elements," and to enhance Soviet security. They also indicate that some foreigners would still be admitted into the USSR, although the selection process had to be improved.

Document 7

On the policy regarding cadres and measures to raise the vigilance of the Lithuanian CP, 23 January 1936. RGASPI, f. 495, op. 74, d. 369, ll. 1–8. Original in Russian. Typewritten with handwritten comments.

To c. Moskvin[25]
23 January 1936
Top secret

ON THE POLICY OF CADRES AND MEASURES TO RAISE
THE VIGILANCE OF THE CP LITHUANIA.

1. On the system of selection and admittance of the political émigrés from Lithuania to the USSR.

As a rule, beginning in 1928 political émigrés from Lithuania were being sent to Germany and partly to Latvia and other bourgeois countries and, only as an exception, to the USSR. But there have been too many of these exceptions. These measures have reduced emigration from Lithuania. After the fascist coup in Germany, political emigration to the capitalist countries almost stopped, but political emigration to the USSR has hardly increased. However, the number of escapees from prisons has increased (1935), which creates doubts among us regarding the escapees.

Suggestions:

1) In the future, send political émigrés to the USSR only as an exception in order that those coming to the USSR go back after some time. [In margin: ***Who is responsible for sending political émigrés to the USSR? It is not pointed out that only absolutely tested comrades can be sent to the USSR, and only in exceptional cases.***]

2) Send to the USSR only the more active party members, who need to be "hidden" from the eyes of the police.

3) As a rule, after release from prison, keep [them] in the country [Lithuania], as has been the case until now. After six–twelve months, send a portion [of them] to study in the reorganized KUNMZ.

4) As a rule, the so-called failures should not be sent to the USSR, because precisely this category has provided the largest percentage of the suspicious element, and frequently the so-called failures turn out to be fictitious.

5) Those escaping from Lithuania to the USSR are to be sent back after they

have been verified. [In margin: ***In this case, is it necessary to expel from the party?***]

6) For the verification of the political émigrés coming to the USSR from Lithuania, create a commission composed of [ECCI] Cadres Department representatives, a representative of the CC CPL[ith] and [one from] the MOPR CC. [In margin: ***The deadline is not indicated.***]

7) Political émigrés can be sent to the USSR only with the consent of the Secretariat of the CC CPL[ith]. Local [party] organizations may not give permission to leave the country.

8) If there exists any kind of suspicion about anybody, that person may not be sent into political emigration.

2. About the verification of political émigrés from Lithuania who are already in the USSR.

1) With the cooperation of the ECCI and CC MOPR, the Lithuanian section should collect all data on the political émigrés in the USSR, their work, party affiliation, etc. Take [the years] 1926–1935 as a starting point.

2) Check the political identity of all suspicious political émigrés. The Lith[uanian] section should send all of its concerns regarding suspicious political émigrés to the Cadres Department.

3) Political émigrés who have already transferred to the VKP(b) or been admitted to the VKP(b) on the regular basis [i.e., under the old rules] should be checked especially carefully. It is important to present to the ICC issues concerning those party members about whom there may be doubts, those whose recommendations may have been mistaken, and those doubtful political émigrés who were admitted to the VKP(b) on the regular basis.

3. On utilizing the political émigrés in training the CPL[ith] reserve [cadres].

1) Send the best political émigrés to study in a two–three year special program in the reorganized KUNMZ so that after the course is over, at least part of them, if not all of them, can be sent to work in Lithuania. [In margin: ***What kind of reorganization?***]

2) For some political émigrés already living in the USSR, Moscow, organize night courses for them to study special subjects, i.e., a history of the CP Lithuania, mass work, and party construction, at the reorganized KUNMZ.

3) Involve certain political émigrés in the work of the sections.

4. On measures in the struggle against the infiltration of alien elements and agents of the class enemy from the CPL[ith] and Lithuanian emigration into the USSR and the VKP(b).

Referred to, in part, in sections 1 and 2. In addition:

1) Work out stricter rules on political emigration. Make it a rule that nobody can come to the USSR as a political émigré without the consent of the ECCI Cadres Department and the CC CPL[ith] representative.

2) Only tested [candidates] who have spent at least two years in the CPL[ith] (if a worker) or four years (if not a worker) can be recommended to

the VKP(b). Others should either be expelled from the CPL[ith] or be considered as having automatically ceased their membership in the party. [In margin: ***Those living temporarily in the USSR are exceptions.***]

If a political émigré received a recommendation for the VKP(b) from the CC [of the CPLith], but the CC representative in the ECCI refuses to give a recommendation, the interested party member has the right to appeal the conduct of the CC representative of the CPL[ith]. [In margin: ***This is wrong. In such a case, the representative himself should contact the CC.***]

5. On political measures in the struggle for the legalization of CPL[ith] activity and the legalization of our cadres.

Until now, we have partially legalized our trade union activity by working in mass organizations organized by the fascists, utilizing some of the fascists' activities (e.g., the question of the workers' *starostas*,[26] the workers' chamber [*palata*]), etc. Also, by organizing meetings at the enterprises on the spur of the moment, sending out workers' delegations on different occasions, etc. Most of our cadres are living illegally. Those released from prison live legally and, if arrested again and there is no material evidence, usually get one–three months (if something is found, they get ten–fifteen years). As a rule, we send those who live legally to the school (MLSh).[27] Therefore, the course is short (7–8 months), so that after they return it will be easier to live legally and easier to explain their temporary absence (e.g., by saying that he went to work in the countryside or other place after losing a job).

In addition it is essential to:

1) Try to organize various legal and semilegal organizations.

2) To see to it that all secretaries of the regional committees are living legally.

3) To make broader use of various fascist activities among the workers, etc. [In margin: ***This is not clear. <. . . > of Angaretis.***]

6. On the order of admission to the party.

As in many other countries, we have had a sectarian approach to admitting new members to the party and simultaneously have done a bad job of investigating those admitted to the party. We in Lithuania have repeatedly given directives: admit more, investigate better. It is essential to conduct work among the masses better and to better ***promote*** the non-party activists. With this aim, meetings of the non-party activists in the town and in the country should be called more frequently.

1) All party cells should be surrounded by non-party activists already involved in struggle ***and work***. New party members are to be recruited from among these activists.

2) Each party cell that admits a new party member must know him well. It is important to verify with particular thoroughness those who have recently come to that particular region. If nobody knows the candidate's past, he should not be admitted to the party. [In margin: ***The role of higher party bodies in admission to the party?***]

3) If someone recommends a dubious person to the party, knowing that there are certain doubts about him, [the recommender] should be expelled from the party. [In margin: **Who recommends?**]

4) Former members of other parties, nonproletarian elements, and those workers who have not yet been tested in the struggle and in practical work are to be admitted <u>as candidates</u> for at least six months. [In margin: **The institute of candidates—it is a Lithuanian invention.**]

Candidates cannot become cell members. The cells can be formed only of party members, while candidates work under the direction of the cells or committees. Candidates to the party and others sympathetic to us can form special groups of sympathizers or party assistance groups, in which, if possible, a party member should work. Candidates and sympathizers should be introduced into various mass organizations.

5) It is obligatory for candidates and members of groups of sympathizers to participate in some sort of work and to raise [the group's] political level. [In margin: **Thus, first** [come] **those activists who are not party members, then sympathizers, and finally party members. This is wrong.**]

<u>7. Training young party members.</u>

1) All those recently admitted to the party should be introduced to the rules of conspiracy so that they know how to behave after being arrested and in court.

2) It is necessary to <u>better</u> organize political education work among young party members.

COMMENT: Something is already being done in this respect, but it is still too little. [In margin: **This kind of work** [ought to be conducted] **with all party members.**]

<u>8. On the system of investigating our cadres and the members of our party.</u>

1) Oblige the CC and regional committees' secretaries to continually investigate the composition of the party committees, to check on activists and their pasts, to provide information on the activists, to investigate how the committee members and other activists joined the party, how they were promoted at work, etc. Carefully check whether or not activists had been members of any political groups, had any connections to Trotskyists, for example (especially in Kovno, where there is a Trotskyist organization), how they behaved after being arrested, during the trial, etc. It is important to study <u>indictments</u> and newspaper information on the arrested [and] to collect information about the trials. If agent provocateurs or other enemies of the party (Trotskyists) who sneaked into the party are discovered, it is vital to investigate carefully who they brought into the party, who they promoted to the leadership, in order to facilitate the purging of the undesirable elements.

At this time, it is important to know how the party members and activists understand the tactics of the United [Popular] Front, how they conduct the work among the masses, how they conduct the struggle against sectarianism, etc. In general, it is essential to carefully verify all activists. The first steps in this direction are already being taken.

9. On the system of promotion.

Until now, we have not promoted new cadres very systematically. Frequently our comrades would not look at the way the person works but at the way he speaks. If the leadership of local organizations was taken over by sectarian elements, as a rule **they** promoted not only sectarians but, frequently, doubtful elements, as, for example, [happened] in 1934 and partly in [19]35 in Kovno and other places. [Our comrades] did not verify carefully enough the past of the one being promoted, or would simply say, "There is no one to be promoted in place of the arrested," and would sometimes promote those already removed from the leadership.

Every committee, every committee member, has to select in advance those activists who, if necessary, could be promoted to the committee. Special attention should be paid to these potential committee members: they have to be involved in active work and the work of the committee, they should be politically fortified, and so forth. They should be thoroughly and carefully verified well in advance. Here in Lithuania it has been repeatedly pointed out that every committee member has to have his own deputies and assistants, to bring them up as future leaders of the local organizations. It is also essential to organize special political education classes for them. Little has been done in this direction yet.

10. On the system of unmasking undesirable, suspicious elements and their isolation from the workers' movement. [In margin: **The whole section is written badly.**]

To make the unmasking of suspicious elements easier, trials and indictments are to be studied, [and] certain party members are to be checked in the card index*?*. Hundreds of okhranka agents, policemen, agents provocateurs, traitors, have been announced in the press and some pamphlets. Besides, several hundred agents of the tsarist okhranka, some of whom also worked in the Lithuanian okhranka, have been announced in the press (and in pamphlets).[28] For the purposes of isolation, certain party members are being removed from underground work, or being gradually removed, first from responsible work, later from underground work, and eventually being expelled from the party. The okhranka is trying to confuse us by arresting party members whom they later expose as agents provocateurs in order to better conceal their most valuable agents, e.g., by keeping an arrested provocateur in prison while releasing the rest so that suspicion falls upon those released. Therefore, we sometimes had to remove from underground work for several years those party members about whom nobody had any suspicions [that they were engaged in] provocation. Sometimes whole organizations, not just individual cells, are dissolved. [In margin: **when? which?**] Regarding agents provocateurs, there are directives to boycott them in prison as well as on the outside. [In margin: **It is not sufficient just to boycott agents provocateurs.**] Traitors are expelled not only from the party but also from political prisoners' organizations (in this respect, mistakes are also made, and some individuals have developed a liberal attitude toward provocation).

11. On the system of testing and verifying individuals whose loyalty and party honesty raise suspicions.

To test those individuals about whom suspicions arise, after removing them from leadership work we send them to low-level work in their cells so that they cannot contact others at their workplace who engage in underground work. Some of them later return to their work; others are eventually expelled. Sometimes those under investigation [who have been] removed from underground work continue legal work among the masses. Or they are advised to move to another region where there is either not yet a party organization or it has been destroyed, so that they can prove [their] loyalty to the party by their active work and rebuild the organization there. This kind of probation is also applied to those comrades about whom there have been no suspicions but who have systematically worked badly. At the same time, their past is verified and material is collected. In the past, a whole series of such party members were sent to the USSR, where they made it into the VKP(b). This is to be recognized as a grave error. Some of our comrades think as follows: it is hard to investigate in our country; it is easier to investigate in the USSR. As a rule, such "investigations" should be prohibited.

CONCLUSION.

Finally, some words about what we have been doing to better verify our cadres, political émigrés, and all those about whom there was some doubt or suspicion.

All materials are being reviewed and new ones are being collected; directives are being given to verify the information about certain individuals.

The CC Secretariat should thoroughly verify all the CC apparatus (instructors, technicians, etc.), as well as the secretaries and members of the regional committees. [In margin: ***And who is going to verify members of the CC Secretariat?***] The secretaries and individual members of the regional committees should verify their own apparatus as well as the members of subcommittees and the cell secretaries. Likewise, every person about whom there is the slightest doubt is subject to special investigation. Who should be removed from responsible positions and underground work or expelled from the party is being indicated.

Obviously, because it is illegal to conduct party work, we will not be able to investigate all the party members. However, our measures will raise the vigilance of the cells.

A series of measures is to be taken in regard to the Komsomol and the Red Aid, through which the Trotskyists and other agents of the class enemy attempted to infiltrate our ranks.

25/I-36

Angaretis
Angaretis

Both the spirit and specific recommendations of Angaretis's memorandum reflected the demands of the Central Committee and the ECCI Secretariat to improve party cadres, to verify party members, especially émigrés who had become VKP members, and to verify all émigrés in the USSR. It would seem that Angaretis had done a good job. But judging from the handwritten comments in the margins, Moskvin was less than satisfied with aspects of it. Many of them were legitimate queries, but his question "And who is going to verify members of the CC Secretariat?" indicates that, to Moskvin, no foreign comrade was above suspicion. That the Lithuanian party had had no systematic procedures for verifying and approving émigrés to the USSR underscored the need for the proverka of émigrés. It also undoubtedly raised implicit questions about the reliability of those already in the USSR, especially those who had "systematically worked badly" yet still "made it into the VKP(b)." The knowledge that precisely such people carried party cards worried the VKP leadership. Indeed, the tone and substance of Angaretis's comments regarding the political problems faced by the Lithuanian CP (and implicitly by all illegal parties), the presence of agents provocateurs within the VKP, doubts about those who had been arrested, and the need to check "especially carefully" the Lithuanian émigrés who belonged to the VKP reinforced mounting anxieties about the political reliability of émigrés. The case of the Lithuanian CP posed special dangers because some of its members had used the green passages to cross the border that divided capitalist Lithuania from the USSR. Finally, Angaretis's concern about the political reliability of escapees from prisons echoed that already expressed by some ECCI members as to whether some Communists who had been imprisoned abroad had made deals with their captors in exchange for their freedom.[29] Political arrest in capitalist countries, once a respected battle scar, now aroused suspicions.

Moskvin's critical comments and queries aside, the way Angaretis's proposal mirrored the concerns of the Central Committee and the ECCI Secretariat is striking. Many of his recommendations were identical to those contained in those organizations' directives. Party discipline demanded nothing else. But the tone of Angaretis's report, his expressed suspiciousness and fear of agents provocateurs and enemy agents, and his insistence on the need for continual investigations and verifications of party members strongly suggests that he was motivated not simply by party discipline but also by a belief that enemies threatened the USSR, VKP, and Lithuanian party. As a Bolshevik in good standing for thirty years, Angaretis had internalized party assumptions, values, and perspectives. Party discipline was a social norm for him. After three decades of operating in the underground as an Old Bolshevik and Lithuanian CP leader, distrust and suspiciousness had become normal. It was people like Angaretis whom the ECCI Secretariat charged with overseeing the verification of their comrades residing in the USSR.

In light of the concerns repeatedly expressed by the ECCI Secretariat in late 1935 and early 1936, its 26 January 1936 resolution calling for "the utmost improvement of vigilance in all sections of the Communist International and of the measures against the infiltration of their ranks by agents provocateurs and agents of the class enemy" is hardly surprising.[30] That issue would increasingly occupy the ECCI's energies as 1936 progressed.

Ferreting out the "agents provocateurs and agents of the class enemy" who had infiltrated their ranks was the charge given to the commissions created to verify those members of fraternal parties living in the USSR. But the ECCI Presidium was also concerned about identifying how such people entered the USSR and VKP. To address this problem, on 19 February 1936 it drafted a resolution ordering the ICC to conduct an investigation into the "criminally careless attitude on the part of the representatives of the fraternal parties in the ECCI toward giving recommendations for the transfer" of fraternal party members to the VKP. The resolution instructed the ICC that the goal was to bring to "party responsibility all those representatives of the various parties and other persons who had recommended or helped in transferring to the VKP" allegedly "suspicious" or "hostile elements."[31] Henceforth the representatives of the fraternal parties in the ECCI were on notice. Although that might have ensured greater vigilance and closer verifications in the future, the resolution could not undo what had already been done.

As Manuilsky's letter to Yezhov made clear, the ECCI Secretariat believed the Polish Communist Party to be "the major supplier of spy and provocateur elements to the USSR." Although that perception ultimately determined the fate of the CPP and many of its members, historically relations between the CPP and the Comintern, and between the CPP and the VKP, had been more positive, albeit complex.[32] In Lenin's time, the CPP had played an active and leading role in the formation of the Comintern and the working out of its major policies. Many Poles who had lived in Russian Poland before the revolution were longtime VKP members and held leading posts in that party and the Soviet government. Prominent members of the CPP, which from the early 1920s was the largest Communist Party in Eastern Europe, held leadership positions in the Comintern. Such credentials were a source of pride for Polish Communists.

But not all was rosy for the CPP. Stalin and some of his lieutenants viewed it with suspicion, if not antipathy. The precise reasons for Stalin's attitude are unclear, but several factors deserve note. During the Russo-Polish war of 1920, Trotsky and others harshly criticized Stalin's performance. For his part, Stalin countered that the inability of the CPP to support the advance of the Red Army on Warsaw played a major role in the rebuff of that advance by the Polish army. During the intraparty struggles following Lenin's death, the leaders of the Polish CP expressed disagreement with the methods employed by Stalin and the Central Committee majority, and supported Trotsky's positions as they related to the Comintern. Stalin was hardly impartial to a party that had openly sided with his major rival. At the time, he dubbed the Central Committee of the Polish CP the "Polish branch of the opportunistic opposition in the RKP(b)" and during the Fifth Comintern Congress in 1924, he succeeded in forcing changes in its leadership.[33]

The historical origins of the Polish CP also contributed to Stalin's and others' doubts about it. More so than in other fraternal parties, its growth resulted from large segments of several established political parties (e.g., Polish Socialist Party–Lewica, Social Democratic Party of the Kingdom of Poland and Lithuania, Bund, etc.) joining the newly formed party.[34] Although members pledged their loyalty to the Communist Party, they carried with them political mores and behaviors from other parties that had markedly different political cultures. This fact divided the Polish CP in the 1920s; some members were loyal to the reigning Moscow leadership, others to Trotsky and the German Left Communist group (the Fischer-Maslow group), still others to the ideas of Rosa Luxemburg. Political divisions within the Polish CP ran deep.[35] Such political pluralism within a Communist Party raised Moscow's suspicions. In addition, within the Comintern, the Communist Party of the Western Ukraine (CPWU)[36] and the Communist Party of Western Belorussia (CPWB)[37] were formally under the Polish CP. The terms of the 1920 treaty ending the Russo-Polish war drew the borders between Poland and Soviet Russia such that many Ukrainians and Belorussians, who had previously lived under Russian rule, became Polish citizens. Peasant resistance and nationalist and Communist movements were regular features of the political landscape of eastern Poland. The Polish police kept a watchful eye on such movements and, when possible, infiltrated them. In the years following the treaty, especially in the 1920s, the legal and illegal movement of people across this border was common. As Manuilsky's letter indicates, the Soviet government maintained approved green passages through which Communists passed into and out of Poland.

Exacerbating the suspicion that there were Polish agents among the Polish émigrés and refugees was the complex and often tense diplomatic relationship between Poland and the USSR. As early as 1930, Stalin believed that Poland was preparing for war against the USSR, a fear that deepened after Hitler's ascension to power in 1933.[38] In the interwar years Warsaw sought to defend national independence by pursuing a foreign policy that counterposed the USSR and the Western European powers—Great Britain in the pre-1933 period, and Great Britain and Nazi Germany after 1933. Moscow viewed Poland's diplomatic maneuverings vis-à-vis Nazi Germany with increasing concern.[39]

Stalin and other VKP and ECCI leaders often viewed the Polish party with a suspicious eye.[40] From at least the late 1920s, the VKP delegation in the ECCI suspected that police agents had infiltrated the Polish CP. An early May 1929 report from Mitskevich-Kapsukas provided material to support that suspicion. Entitled "The Work of Polish Wreckers," the report expressed concern over the growth of factionalism and the increasing influence of former Mensheviks within the Polish CP. It asserted that a wide network of provocateurs had weakened the party's ability to function and that Polish police had hamstrung many organs of the CPWU and CPWB. When the VKP delegation in the ECCI met in Stalin's office on 14 May 1929, it resolved: "To take all essential measures for protecting the CC CPP from provocations corroding the [Polish] party. To ask the Collegium of the GPU [state security organ] to take measures for exposing provocateurs in the CPP."[41] From that point on, Soviet security organs kept a watchful eye on the Polish CP. Those organs believed that Polish disinformation and espionage networks were active in the USSR.[42] Annually in the early 1930s, the GPU-NKVD and the ECCI accused individual Polish CP members of being police agents. Arrest and expulsion from the party followed shortly thereafter. Consider the case of Jerzy Sochacki.

A member of the Politburo of the Polish CP and its representative in the ECCI Presidium and Political Secretariat, Sochacki was arrested on 14 August 1933. On 4 September he committed suicide in prison and left a note proclaiming his innocence. On 10 October, Pyatnitsky sent to Lazar Kaganovich, a VKP Politburo member and one of Stalin's staunchest allies, a draft declaration by the Central Committee of the Polish CP asserting that Sochacki was a provocateur. Jan Bielewski (aka Jan Paszyn), a member of the Politburo of the Polish CP, composed the declaration; Genrikh Yagoda, deputy chairman of the OGPU, and Ya. Agranov, Yagoda's deputy, approved it. Stalin ordered the draft to be revised. On 22 October, Pyatnitsky sent the revised text to Molotov for Stalin's approval: "The draft declaration of the CC CP Poland concerning Sochacki-Bratowski was sent to Stalin. We compiled the declaration and ask you to review it and indicate if it is fit to publish. I request that you review the draft as soon as possible because we fear that the bourgeois press is beginning a campaign around Sochacki's arrest."[43] The declaration was published soon thereafter.

Throughout the 1930s, Soviet security organs maintained that provocateurs and Polish counterintelligence agents, in particular agents of the Polish Military Organization (POW),[44] had infiltrated the Polish CP and its Central Committee. They used their agents and network of informers to monitor Polish CP activities, a practice that yielded valuable intelligence but also no doubt encouraged agents to see nefarious activities in the benign and their informants to settle personal scores. When the security organs deemed it appropriate, they informed the ECCI about its investigations, which from 1933–1934 on resulted in the arrests of hundreds of Poles.[45]

The ECCI was well aware of the suspicions and arrests of Poles. In February 1936, for example, Dimitrov's Secretariat received a letter from Bronislaw Berg (aka Witold Zaltsburg), who had been arrested in December 1934 and sentenced to five years in the gulag. Berg wrote, "During the past two years, several hundred Communist and non-Communist Poles, many of whom were political émigrés from Poland, were arrested in Ukraine. The arrested, including me, were charged with belonging to the Polish counterrevolutionary organization POW."[46] He wrote of harsh treatment, including cold water baths, uninterrupted interrogation, and physical abuse, that resulted in his signing a confession that compromised Polish CP leaders, including its general secretary, Julian Lenski. Berg asked that his letter be shown to members of the VKP's Politburo, whom he believed had no knowledge of the affair. Instead, Dimitrov showed the letter to Manuilsky, who sent a copy to the NKVD.[47] Given Berg's graphic description of the arrests and torture of hundreds of Poles, the ECCI leaders were well aware of the situation, yet they appear to have done little or nothing to investigate whether the arrests were warranted. On the contrary, their behavior toward the Polish CP suggests that suspicions of the Polish ran deep among the ECCI leaders.

By early 1936 the long-standing allegation that "enemy agents" had penetrated the Polish CP had become an assumption among many within the VKP, NKVD, and ECCI. In January 1936 an unsigned "Resolution on CPP Organizational Issues," which circulated among the ECCI members, reinforced that assumption. The resolution claimed that "alien elements obstructed the leading organs" of the Polish CP and accounted for the party's "incorrect policy of cadre selection." "The chief mistake of this policy during the first years of the party's existence included its incorrect relations to those elements who left other parties, especially those released from Pilsudskyist [i.e., Polish] prisons." These people, it asserted, soon took "leading posts" in the party and later in "the leading organs of the party. . . . By such means, agents of the *Pilsud-shchina*,[48] UVO [Ukrainian Military Organization] [and] okhranka penetrated the party. . . . In the last five years we have removed more than forty provocateurs and suspicious types from the central apparatus."[49] Vigilance was the watchword of the Cadres Department and increasingly the Polish CP was the object of its attention.

The evolution of the conviction that Polish intelligence agents had penetrated the Polish CP provides an intriguing example of the ways in which anxieties and suspicions were transformed into beliefs. In 1929, Stalin and the VKP delegation to the ECCI had suspected "provocations" within the Polish CP and had ordered the GPU "to take measures for exposing provocateurs." That ever-vigilant organization compiled and, by various means, "discovered" such people, whom it tortured into signing confessions that were presented to the Central Committee and the ECCI as "proof" that enemy agents had in fact penetrated the Polish CP. That "proof" transformed the suspicions into the assumptions upon which the VKP's Politburo, the NKVD, the ECCI, and the Cadres Department acted. Although Stalin's role in initiating the process was crucial, the VKP, NKVD, and ECCI each played essential roles, too. Even those who may have harbored doubts acted as though the allegation was valid, thereby legitimizing it. What is not clear is how many Polish CP leaders shared the assumption. This brief background provides a context in which to appreciate Document 8.

Document 8 is the January 1936 resolution of the ECCI Secretariat on the Polish question. According to Comintern practice, a delegation from or a representative of a fraternal party periodically presented a report on party affairs to the appropriate ECCI secretary or, in some cases, to the entire Secretariat. In late January, Julian Lenski, general secretary of the Polish CP and member of the ECCI Presidium, delivered that report. The Secretariat then held private discussions about it and issued its resolution, which addressed an array of issues. For our purposes, the most noteworthy of the Secretariat's concerns are the familiar ones.

The Secretariat viewed the situation in the Communist Party of Poland as "extremely serious, requiring urgent radical measures to improve the party and strengthen the leadership." What most concerned the Secretariat were the dangers posed by the "agents of the class enemy," the "disorganizing work of the Pilsudshchina," and the "remnants of sectarianism." Given the Comintern's sectarian tradition, the last concern may seem disingenuous. But in Comintern parlance, sectarianism referred to those people within a Communist Party who held so-called leftist positions that deviated from those of the Comintern. The resolution conveys succinctly how the ECCI Secretariat viewed the problems that it thought afflicted the Polish CP and sets forth its belief that the Polish government had infiltrated its agents into the party. Given its assumptions, the notion that agents of the class enemy had disguised themselves as émigrés and entered the USSR followed logically.

Two of the Secretariat's recommendations deserve special note. Its call for a "systematic verification" of all members of the Polish, Western Ukrainian, and Western Belorussian Communist Parties reflected the early 1936 directives of the Central Committee and the ECCI Secretariat. But its call to "dissolv[e] the Polish section of the Comintern, which, owing to the lowering of its Bolshevik vigilance, has failed to prevent infiltration by spies and saboteurs into the VKP(b)," was a radical and ominous solution to what the Secretariat viewed as a persistent problem.[50]

Document 8

The 28 January 1936 resolution of the ECCI Secretariat on the Polish CP, 28 January 1936. RGASPI, f. 495, op. 18, d. 1071, ll. 5–8. Original in Russian. Typewritten with handwritten additions.

SECRET
FINAL TEXT
Resolution of the ECCI Secretariat of 28.1.1936 on the Polish Question[51]
Having heard the report by com. <u>Lenski</u> on the work of the CP of Poland after the Seventh Comintern Congress,[52] the ECCI Secretariat considers the situation in the Polish Com[munist] Party extremely serious, requiring urgent radical measures to improve the party and strengthen the leadership in the center and at the local level.

Pointing out the positive achievements of the CPP in implementing the United [Popular] Front tactics in accordance with the decisions of the Seventh Congress, the party's successes in leading the strike movement of the Polish proletariat, [and] the strengthening of the party's position in the trade unions, the ECCI Secretariat charges the CPP leadership to subject the weaknesses and political mistakes that facilitated the saturation of the party with agents of the class enemy to broad critique and to decisively oppose any [attempt] to disguise them, which can only impede the improvement of the party.

The ECCI Secretariat believes that the CPP's political activity at this time should derive from the unresolved tasks of the bourgeois democratic revolution in Poland, the struggle for which will tie the Communist Party to the millions of laboring masses and will help it to become a decisive factor in the life of its own country. The ECCI Secretariat suggests that the CC define the party line at the next plenum **on the basis of the Seventh Congress decision and**[53] in accordance with the CI [Communist International] program, which defines the broad array of tasks of the bourgeois democratic revolution in Poland and the resulting political, tactical, and organizational guidelines.

The ECCI Secretariat considers the intensification of the struggle against sectarianism to be essential. The remnants of sectarianism, which by its leftist phrases often encourage passivity in relation to the concrete enemy, have prevented the party from opportunely developing the struggle against the fascist constitution now in preparation.

Despite the daily heroism of the rank-and-file Communists, the long-standing disorganizing work of the Pilsudshchina in the ranks of the CPP has weakened the party's capacity for struggle and has systematically undermined the growth of its influence among the broad masses of toilers. This demoralizing work of the Pilsudshchina and other agents of the class enemy led to a periodic destruction of the party's proletarian core, delayed the overcoming of the nationalist illusions by the masses, narrowed the party's influence in the countryside and among the oppressed peoples, and hampered the development of a mass struggle against the fascist dictatorship.

For many years, party leaders did not give the proper Bolshevik rebuff to the demoralizing work of the Pilsudshchina and did not order a systematic struggle against Pilsudshchina ideology and other kinds of nationalist ideology hostile to laborers' interests.

The current party leadership failed to overcome the saturation of the party [with class enemies] that had been allowed by the former leadership of Warski and Kostrzewa, [and] overlooked the dirty game of the Pilsudskyite agents (Żarski, Sochacki, etc.), who consciously stirred up the factional struggle in order to undermine the CPP's authority by discrediting its leaders in the eyes of the masses. On the other hand, the current party leadership, having broken with the rightist opportunistic idealization of the Pilsudshchina, failed at the same time to tie its internationalist aims to the nationalist feelings of the masses. Using the leadership's inadequate vigilance and national nihilism as a cover, and in accordance with the Pilsudshchina's tasks, the agents of the class enemy who had infiltrated the party have helped to portray the CPP as a party alien to the Polish people and indifferent to the national fate of Polish workers and peasants.

In conducting the essential struggle against the right-opportunist directives of Kosheva and against counterrevolutionary Trotskyism, the party leadership, which has not overcome the remnants of the factional struggle, did not provide sufficiently effective measures to purge the party of the rotten elements of a semi-Trotskyist character, who are directly linked to the class enemy's network of agents of the class enemy.

As a result, healthy proletarian elements in party organizations were frequently pushed aside, their places taken by politically immature petit bourgeois intellectuals untested in the struggle, who by their permissiveness toward the internal party struggle created a fertile ground within the party for the pilsudchiks to recruit agents.

These petit bourgeois fellow travelers, who are politically emasculated, riddled with skepticism, and lacking faith in the power of the working class, used their influence in the party to plant distrust **toward the VKP(b)**, toward the Comintern. They hampered the education of the party's youth in the spirit of honesty and sincerity toward the Executive Committee of the Comintern.

In the light of this, the ECCI Secretariat resolves to suggest to the CPP leadership:

a) removing from the CC those individuals whose past and present activities warrant a lack of complete trust;

b) organizing a systematic verification of all CPP activists both in emigration and in the country; extending this verification to all CPWU and CPWB activists;

c) dissolving those levels of party organization most infected by provocation;

d) dissolving the Polish section of the Comintern, which, owing to the lowering of its Bolshevik vigilance, has failed to prevent infiltration by spies and saboteurs into the VKP(b);

e) reviewing the CPP's organizational structure with the aim of reducing the upper levels of the organization, reducing the size of the bureaucracy [which is] not necessary in the illegal conditions, removing all suspicious and untrustworthy individuals from all levels of the party organization, [and] firmly steering a course to strengthen the internal leadership in the country;

f) strengthening the regional leadership, in particular in the major industrial districts; to consider as obligatory a careful selection and registration of regional committee secretaries and the provision of real support to the regional committees; pursuing a decisive policy of proletarianization of the party [and] of educating worker cadres to become leaders of the party organizations;

g) the Political Bureau of the CC CPP should convoke a plenum of the party's CC[54] to work out concrete measures to protect the party line from sectarian deviations, to carry out a correct cadres policy and a relentless struggle against provocation and demoralizing elements. The plenum should be held in an atmosphere of bold Bolshevik exposure of all of the party's ills, in accordance with this resolution.

The CC plenum's resolution on the improvement of the CPP should be submitted to the ECCI Presidium for approval. Expressing confidence in the CC CPP Political Bureau, the ECCI Secretariat is deeply convinced that the implementation of this resolution will assure a radical change in all the organizational policy and cadre policy of the party.

The ECCI Secretariat has decided to bring this resolution to the notice of the CC CPP plenum only.

31 January 1936.
? 28/I-36 ?

> *Final text*
> *G. Dimitrov*
> *D. Manuilsky*
> *Ercoli*
> *Moskvin*

Kuusinen

The ECCI Secretariat obviously viewed the condition of the Polish CP to be "extremely serious." The short interval between Lenski's presentation of the report (28 January) and the issuance of the resolution (31 January) suggests that the ECCI secretaries already had well-formed opinions about the party. Taken together, the condemnations and recommendations in the resolution placed the Polish CP in a very tenuous position. On the one hand, to forge the proper Communist identity, the ECCI ordered the party to intensify the struggle against "sectarianism," right opportunism, "counterrevolutionary Trotskyism," and "rotten elements of a semi-Trotskyist character." In short, the CPP was to purge anyone who had expressed doubts about or critiqued the political line of the Comintern and the VKP. On the other hand, the demands of the Popular Front and the tasks of the "bourgeois democratic revolution" in Poland required that the Polish party forge political coalitions with parties and organizations with whom it shared a common enemy. To be successful, such coalitions required that party members engage in political actions that threatened to dilute the political purity demanded by the Comintern. Finding the proper way to balance these centrifugal and centripetal forces created a dilemma. Failure to do so would provide more "evidence" of just how "serious" the condition of the party was. That challenge must have been all the more daunting to the party leaders because they had been appointed by the ECCI Secretariat.

The Polish CP was not the only fraternal party that caused concerns for the ECCI. For much of 1936 so, too, did the Hungarian party (CPH), although the problems afflicting it differed substantially from those of its Polish neighbor. The problems of the Hungarian CP came to the fore in December 1935, when some members of its Central Committee and their supporters met with ECCI officials and denounced Béla Kun, the party leader and, until 1935, an ECCI member, for refusing to implement the Comintern's Popular Front policy. In a letter to the Central Committee of the Hungarian CP, Kun accepted partial responsibility. Two days later he appeared before an enlarged meeting of the ECCI Secretariat where ECCI leaders and Kun's rivals in the Hungarian CP subjected him to harsh criticisms and accused him of several serious political mistakes. In January 1936 leaders of the anti-Kun group announced that they had formed a "temporary leadership of the CP of Hungary." Over the course of the next eight months the ECCI investigated allegations that Kun and his allies had refused to implement Comintern policies and had engaged in incessant personal squabbles that fostered factional struggles within the Hungarian CP, thereby enabling Hungarian police agents to infiltrate its ranks and disrupt its work. (See "The Case of Béla Kun" in Chapter 7.) Accusations that police agents had infiltrated the Hungarian and Polish parties, as well as other problems that bedeviled these and other parties, served to reinforce the anxieties of ECCI leaders about the political reliability of their foreign-born comrades.

Although the ECCI devoted much attention in early 1936 to monitoring the activities of fraternal parties and to organizing the verification of the fraternal party members living in the USSR, it had not slackened its international campaign against Trotsky and Trotskyism. On the contrary, vigilance against "counterrevolutionary Trotskyism" and verification were complementary policies. **Document 9** conveys concisely the ongoing obsession of the Comintern and the VKP with the perceived dangers that Trotsky and his followers posed to the USSR. What prompted Document 9 was the publication of articles by Trotsky in a Hearst newspaper in the United States.

Document 9

Telegram from the ECCI Secretariat to the Communist Parties of the United States, England, France, Belgium, Spain, Greece, Holland, and Norway and to the South American Bureau on Trotsky's bloc with Hearst, 23 January 1936. RGASPI, f. 495, op. 184, d. 77, general outgoing telegrams for 1936, l. 290. Original in German. Typewritten with signatures.

<u>Top Secret</u>

To the Communist Parties of the United States, England, France, Belgium, Spain, Greece, Holland, Norway. South American Bureau

Trotsky is carrying on a libelous campaign against the Soviet Union and Stalin in the Hearst press. On 19 January, Trotsky began to publish in the "New York American" a series of articles in which he accuses the Soviet government of imprisoning and torturing "innocent" Trotskyists and asserts that Stalin and the Comintern aided Hitler's rise to power. You should use this fact of a bloc between Trotsky and Hearst, the vilest anti-Soviet instigator, the supporter of Hitler, and the local coordinator of American fascism, to further expose the counterrevolutionary role of Trotsky, who is the accomplice of fascism in the struggle against the proletarian revolution and the Soviet Union. At the same time, you should hasten the separation of all honest elements from Trotskyist groups. During this [campaign] condemning Trotsky's bloc with Hearst, determine who still exhibits sympathies with Trotsky.

Secretariat

5 February 1936

G. Dimitrov
D. Manuilsky
M. Moskvin
<. . .>

The ECCI leaders used the publication of Trotsky's "libelous" articles and his charges that "Stalin and the Comintern aided Hitler's rise to power" as further evidence that Trotsky was an agent of fascism. The fact that William Randolph Hearst's newspapers espoused a very conservative editorial line, with continual attacks on the USSR and approbation of the economic successes of Nazi Germany, made Hearst a powerful propagandist for fascism in Moscow's eyes. Yet the ECCI Secretariat also sought to turn Trotsky's articles to its advantage by using the reactions of fraternal party members as a litmus test to separate "honest elements from Trotskyist groups" and thereby enable fraternal parties to cleanse their ranks of "unreliable" members.[55]

That political litmus test and the directives to the Polish CP shared a common goal—to temper party discipline in order to eliminate the political temptations that accompanied the Popular Front. The success of the Popular Front depended on its being inclusive, on its forging political alliances with an array of social classes and political parties and groups. Yet being inclusive exposed party members to political forces and temptations that might potentially weaken their discipline and resolve. The anti-Trotskyist campaign became a means by which the ECCI hoped to steel its followers abroad, to harden their commitment. The centripetal force of party discipline was supposed to counteract the centrifugal forces that fraternal parties faced in their native countries. One of the major goals of the anti-Trotskyist campaign was to distinguish "real" Communists from those who used Bolshevik rhetoric to criticize Bolshevik policies. As the campaign unfolded, the meaning of the term Trotskyist became diluted. That Moscow believed Trotsky had become a fascist ally meant that rhetorically and politically, the term Trotskyist became a generic term of condemnation. It nonetheless served valuable functions—to separate Communist Party members from "leftists" who used Marxist-Leninist rhetoric, to separate supporters of the USSR from its radical critics, and to solidify a Communist identity.

The Secretariat realized that the proverka of the fraternal party members and émigrés living in the USSR would require considerable administrative resources and their efficient use. In early 1936 it discussed and resolved a series of administrative issues to enable the ECCI apparatus to carry out that proverka.

The most pressing task was to define clearly the roles and responsibilities of the relevant ECCI organs. On 11 February the Secretariat issued "Regulations on the Cadres Department," which reorganized that department and redefined its functions. Although Manuilsky had political and administrative responsibility for the Cadres Department, Krajewski and Chernomordik oversaw the cadres and operations of the fraternal parties. The regulations gave the Cadres Department responsibility for all aspects of cadre affairs and cadre policy implementation, including "registration and study of the cadres of the Comintern," "verification of the fulfillment . . . of cadre policy," organizing international schools and training cadres, aiding fraternal parties in "educating, preserving, and promoting new cadres," "study of the enemy's methods of work," assisting "in the struggle against provocation and espionage," enhancing "work among political refugees with the aim of exposing hostile class elements who have penetrated their ranks," and organizing the "verification and formal completion of transfers from one foreign Communist Party to another and the preparation of material for transfers to the VKP."

The regulations gave the Cadres Department responsibility for implementing all aspects of cadre policy, which the ECCI Secretariat formulated: The "cadre policy of individual parties is drawn up under the direct guidance of the ECCI secretary, who is responsible for a given country." Although the ECCI Secretariat formally determined cadre policy, Dimitrov and Manuilsky were responsible for "final decisions on questions of cadres."[56]

In other resolutions, the Secretariat delineated more precisely the role of secretaries responsible for the fraternal parties in the Cadres Department, a task it deemed essential in order to "strengthen it [the department] during its reorganization" and "to heighten vigilance in relation to the enemy." It ordered the secretaries to play a more active role in the fulfillment of cadre policy and the secretariat to participate more actively in the work of the Cadres Department, especially the verification of cadres.[57] An 11 February 1936 directive clarified the responsibilities of the representatives of the fraternal parties.[58]

The redefinition and delineation of responsibilities reflected Dimitrov's efforts to centralize and rationalize Comintern cadre policy in general and the verification campaign in particular. They paralleled Stalin's simultaneous efforts to achieve the same goals within the VKP. Both efforts resulted in the creation of centralized administrative mechanisms that later facilitated repression. The available evidence provides no reason to believe that these reorganizations served any purpose other than their stated intentions: to make the implementation of cadre policy more consistent and to improve the quality of cadres both by better education and by vigilantly exposing "suspicious" or "hostile elements" within their ranks. Although the Cadres Department later became an instrument of repression, there appears to have been no a priori plan to use it as such.

Document 10 illustrates clearly how such administrative reforms sought to ensure vigilance. The document conveys yet again the ECCI Secretariat's worries about the political reliability of émigrés and reiterates the policies that the ECCI Secretariat had crafted to expose "hostile elements." In particular, it requires the Cadres Department to order the deportation from the USSR of any "individuals suspected of provocation and espionage." That the resolution called for deportation as opposed to arrest indicates that in early 1936 the ECCI Secretariat considered administrative solutions to the problem to be sufficient in most cases. What underscores the importance of these issues, and makes the document unique, is its addendum. To ensure that the Cadres Department staff read the directive and appreciated its importance, the Secretariat required each staff member to sign a supplementary page attached to the resolution acknowledging that he or she had read it. Requiring staff members to do so bound them to implement the policy; efforts to honor that oath would later fuel the mass repression. But in early 1936 the addendum ensured that the department staff understood their redefined responsibilities. The addendum also served a political purpose: signing it made the signatories the responsible parties, thereby protecting the ECCI Secretariat from culpability should the Cadres Department fail to fulfill its role.

Document 10

Resolution of the ECCI Secretariat on the obligations of the Cadres Department with regard to émigrés, 3 March 1936. RGASPI, f. 495, op. 18, d. 1073, ll. 121–123. Original in Russian. Typewritten with handwritten additions. Attached is a sheet of paper signed by Cadres Department staff members who, by their signatures (some illegible), acknowledged reading the resolution.

Top secret
Final text
G. Dim[itrov]
RESOLUTION OF THE SECRETARIAT

1. Oblige the Cadres Department to discontinue the existing practice of keeping on the USSR territory individuals suspected of provocation and espionage, making an exception only in those cases where the appropriate organs demand it.

2. Suggest that the Cadres Department work out and implement a series of measures to send back to capitalist countries all individuals who have not demonstrated in the past the necessary Bolshevik firmness and loyalty to the party—first of all, those suspected of espionage and provocation.

3. The Cadres Department should take measures to thoroughly improve the selection of students for the international schools in order to decrease, to the maximum extent possible, the number of those who are unable to return to work to their country.

4. Discontinue the practice of keeping in the USSR those who, for different reasons, at the time of either admission or graduation, had dropped out of the international schools. Take measures to return to their countries all those individuals who had studied in the international schools and had stayed on USSR territory.

5. The Cadres Department, together with representatives of the parties, should work out a series of measures to prepare reserves [party members] and to send back to their countries all comrades from among the political émigrés who can be used for work in their countries. Plan similar measures to use in their own countries the political émigrés who find themselves [currently] staying in capitalist countries.

6. The Cadres Department is to assure that the parties firmly follow the line of keeping in their countries those comrades who had already served their term [in prison] and are not threatened with extremely harsh repression.

Conduct a decisive struggle against keeping in the USSR those party and

Komsomol members who left their countries without the special permission of the party CC, [making them] deserters from the battlefield of the class struggle. These individuals should not be considered to be party members, and no trust or help should be rendered to them.

7. The Cadres Department, together with the Propaganda Department, should work out a series of measures on the systematic education of the political émigrés and to shield them from the influence of alien elements and demoralization.

Resolution of the Secretariat
Read by:
< . . . > 10/III-36
Andreev 10/III-36
< . . . > 10/III-36
Cichowski 10/III-36
Palkina 11/III-36
Blagoeva [10/III-36]
Lebedeva 10/III-36
Golubeva [10/III-36]
Zonbert 20/III-36
< . . . > 20/III-36
< . . . > 1/IV
***Gopner**[59]

By spring 1936 the verification of fraternal party members, émigrés, and foreign students residing in the USSR had been going on for several months. It is fair to ask whether the early results provided the Comintern leaders with any evidence to justify their and the Central Committee's suspicions. Available evidence suggests that ECCI officials believed that there was. A Cadres Department report entitled "Preparation and Retraining of Cadres" offers insight into the kinds of evidence that ECCI members believed made the case for greater vigilance. Although the report is nominally devoted to the training of cadres ("one of the most important problems of party development"), most of its contents consist of evidence of "how the class enemy penetrates our schools." Its Janus-like quality underscores the belief of the Politburo and the ECCI that educating cadres better and unmasking enemies more vigilantly were the twin pillars of a sound cadre policy.

As a result of the verification of the staff of the Marx-Lenin School, the Cadres Department ordered the removal of twenty-eight people. The report provided information on eleven of them to illustrate the types of people who warranted dismissal. Among those eleven was a Dekapolitov, a former captain in the tsarist army who had been arrested in 1919 for counterrevolutionary activities but had escaped to Poland, where he enlisted in the Polish counterintelligence service. He later entered the USSR and, posing as a worker, enrolled in the Marx-Lenin School. It is not clear how long he had resided in the USSR. Others included the school librarian, whose husband and brothers were Polish army officers; a Red Army deserter who had fled to Latvia; a former aristocrat who had sided with the White Army and maintained close ties to people in Germany; and the leader of an anti-Soviet peasant uprising. What made those removed dangerous in the eyes of the Cadres Department were their pasts: they had hidden their class-alien pasts or, at one time, had engaged in anti-Soviet activities. It is not clear whether they had continued such political activities, nor whether they were active enemy agents. But those implementing the verification obviously shared Pyatnitsky's belief that "whoever lied once to the party . . . is capable of lying a second time on a more serious occasion."

The Cadres Department concluded that the verification of the students at the Marx-Lenin School "revealed facts not previously known by the directing organs of the specific [fraternal] parties. For example, service in the police abroad, service as volunteers in expeditionary armies [during 1918–1921], holding posts in fascist organizations, ties to provocateurs, etc." The report also noted with alarm that a significant percentage of the students (20–60 percent, depending on the year of study) remained in the USSR after the completion of their studies, although they were supposed to return to their native countries. Among them were people like Yasinskii, a Polish CP member who had hidden the fact that he was an officer in the Polish army during the Russo-Polish War, and Karl Hahn, a German CP member whose two sisters and two brothers were members of the Nazi Party.[60] According to the new cadres policy, such people should have been deported, but undoubtedly some were referred to the NKVD.

The mid-1936 verification of the staff and students at the Communist University for National Minorities of the West revealed other cases that the Cadres Department found disturbing. Among them was that of Alexander Kravchuk, a member of the CPWB from 1930, whose unauthorized entry into the USSR and alleged ties to Polish police caused sufficient concern for the verification commission to make this recommendation: "Arrest and carry out an investigation." The case of Erik Eisen (aka Weinberg), a German CP member from 1930, also deserves note. Eisen had directed a party group in Hamburg until his arrest in December 1933. He admitted telling his interrogators that he had secret ties to the Comintern and that "the Gestapo proposed to him a [arrangement for] secret cooperation. . . . He was then released. After his release from prison, he fled from Germany to the USSR."[61] Eisen denied making a deal with the Gestapo, but his release from prison raised suspicions in the Cadres Department. That both men had been admitted to a party school only a few years earlier underscores how dramatically vigilance and the attitude toward foreigners had changed by 1936. To the advocates of vigilance, such cases proved how lax admission policies had been and how important thorough verification was.

What made this and other anecdotal evidence alarming to ECCI officials was that the Cadres Department had no clear idea about how many political émigrés lived in the USSR. The ICC and the Cadres Department made inquiries of representatives of the fraternal parties in early 1936 and discovered that since 1920 a minimum of 35,372 to 37,372 political émigrés had taken up residence in the USSR. Some 20,000 of them (between 19,600 and 21,600) came from states bordering the USSR and from Germany. Roughly a quarter of them (between 9,307 and 10,707) had joined the VKP; Germans (2,600), Poles (2,000), and Americans (2,000–3,000, many of Finnish origin) constituted a majority of the transfers to the VKP. These figures are underestimates of the numbers of émigrés and transfers to the VKP. Thirteen fraternal parties (including those of Bulgaria, China, and Romania, from which sizable numbers of émigrés had entered the USSR) provided no information; parties that had provided information acknowledged it to be incomplete. The Cadres Department had no information whatsoever on the number of political émigrés and transfers to the VKP from eight countries (including Hungary and China). In the case of Bulgarians, it had no information on the number of political émigrés but reported that between five hundred and eight hundred Bulgarians had joined the VKP. Surely as disturbing to the Cadres Department officials was the complete lack of information from twenty-one of the twenty-four reporting parties on how many people transferred to the VKP had been recommended for removal. The incompleteness of the data no doubt raised questions within the Cadres Department and among the advocates of vigilance about the ability of representatives to account for their charges and about the possibility that "secret agents" "under the guise of émigrés" had become VKP members.[62]

Such uncertainty about how many émigrés lived in the USSR and belonged to the VKP strengthened the resolve of Yezhov and other Central Committee members to constrict immigration to the USSR. During the first half of 1936, MOPR received 314 requests for entry into the USSR; more than half of them came from Poland (90), Germany (44), and Austria (35). (The ECCI received similar requests.) MOPR, in turn, petitioned Yezhov for permission to admit 117 of that group. The procedure was that MOPR (or the ECCI) sent requests to Yezhov's office for approval. How many of the 117 were approved is unclear, but when approval was granted, that office requested the NKVD to telegram permission for a visa to the Soviet embassy in the respective country.[63] That Yezhov's office approved only a portion of MOPR's requests suggests that it was carefully screening foreign applicants. But the fact remains that during the first half of 1936, as doubts about the political reliability of émigrés deepened, foreigners were still being admitted to the USSR. Vigilance, not xenophobia, was the order of the day.

For its part, the Cadres Department practiced vigilance by maintaining and updating lists of "doubtful individuals" in Soviet emigration. One such list, dated 28 May 1936, contains the names of 201 German émigrés accumulated over the course of four years. The department compiled the list from denunciations it had received, answers sent in response to inquiries, and other unspecified sources. Next to each name were recorded the "brief contents" of the alleged infraction, such as former oppositional activity or hostile attitudes toward the USSR. Among those on the list was Valentin Olberg, who would later be a defendant at the August 1936 show trial. On 28 February 1936 the Cadres Department answered a NKVD inquiry by stating: "In 1932 he was expelled from the party [German CP], after which he joined the Socialist Workers' Party [a Trotskyist party]. He has ties to Trotskyists and Russian émigrés."[64]

This was the second report on Olberg that the Cadres Department sent to the security organs. The first had been sent on 11 June 1932 and explained the reasons for his expulsion from the German CP. According to that report, in 1932, Olberg's Berlin apartment had been searched by some comrades, who discovered a large quantity of letters and postcards from Trotsky and his son, Sedov. Information in the correspondence indicated that Olberg, a leader of the local party organization, participated in the publication and distribution of Trotsky's newspaper, *Bulletin of the Opposition,* and maintained contact with Trotsky's supporters in the USSR and other countries. Based on this, the Central Committee of the German CP had expelled him from the party and sent the relevant materials, including the names of the eleven addresses in the USSR to which Olberg had sent Trotskyist materials, to the ECCI, which, in turn, forwarded them to a security organ (OGPU). Yet in 1935, Olberg had entered the USSR without the aid or knowledge of the ECCI or MOPR and had secured a job at the Gorky Pedagogical Institute. How he accomplished this is unknown. On 5 January 1936, Olberg was arrested. His arrest triggered the arrests of 508 alleged Trotskyists by April 1936.[65] At the August 1936 show trial, Olberg confessed to working for Trotsky and preparing an attempt on Stalin's life.[66]

Evidence such as Olberg's arrest and the verification of the Comintern schools created serious concerns for the ECCI and strengthened the argument that "enemy agents" and "hostile elements" had penetrated the VKP and USSR. It provided an impetus to ensure that the verification of the members of fraternal parties and émigrés living in the USSR was thoroughly carried out. Nor was the ECCI apparatus above suspicion. In January 1936 the Secretariat created the Commission for the Verification of the Qualifications of the ECCI Apparatus, chaired by Moskvin. Over the course of that year it reviewed the files of 387 people who worked in that bureaucracy.[67]

Believing that "enemies" posed a domestic threat and issuing directives defining the responsibilities of those organs charged with ferreting out the enemies did not mean that the vigilance campaign proceeded efficiently. In fact, a June 1936 letter from Skulski, a member of the Politburo of the Polish CP and the head of the commission to verify Polish members in the USSR, to Dimitrov, Manuilsky, and Moskvin suggests that, despite their repeated calls for vigilance, the three most powerful ECCI members were at times obstacles to the fulfillment of their own orders. Skulski began his "top secret" letter by stating that the commission to verify the Polish CP had been "working on the verification of party émigrés almost nonstop (15–18 hours a day)" and that they had identified 102 people who should be returned to Poland. But, he complained, the commission "had been waiting for dispatch orders for more than half a year." Skulski deemed these 102 people "very necessary" to party work in Poland and noted that maintaining them in the USSR was costing "about 50,000 rubles a month." He pointed out that, although the members of the verification commission had discussed this issue with Manuilsky, Moskvin, and Krajewski several times, "these 102 people still remain in place." And so, he concluded, "yet again I urgently ask you to resolve the issue of dispatches for these 102 people . . . [and] to give me clear directives about what to do with these people."[68]

Given the ECCI's long-standing concerns about the quality of political émigrés from Poland, one wonders why the Cadres Department had not issued dispatch papers for these 102 people. The Secretariat's directives stated that "suspicious" émigrés should have been returned to their native countries as quickly as was safely possible. The Cadres Department staff had signed a paper indicating that they had read and understood these directives. Yet here were 102 Poles slated by the verification commission for return to Poland who remained in the USSR. Perhaps the NKVD was the obstacle. The available evidence sheds no light on this issue.

As Skulski had indicated, the verification of the members of parties in the Polish section continued. On 16 July 1936 he sent to Dimitrov, Manuilsky, and Moskvin a progress report on the results of the first stage of the verification (from 1 April to 15 July). Three commissions were conducting the verification: one each for the Polish, Western Belorussian, and Western Ukrainian parties. The first had reviewed 650 of the "more than 3,000" Polish CP members who resided in the USSR; the second had reviewed 520 of the "more than 1,800" of the CPWB members living in the country; for the third, Skulski reported, he had "no information." At that point, the Polish commission had reached decisions on 475 people and sent recommendations on 400 of them to the Cadres Department for ratification; the Western Belorussian commission had reached decisions on 520 people and sent recommendations on 250 to the Cadres Department. The Polish commission decided that 140 people (35 percent) should be returned to Poland, but that 77 of them should not be permitted to have any ties to the party there. It also recommended that 166 people (42 percent) be allowed to remain in the USSR and that materials on 77 people (19 percent) be sent to the NKVD. That more than one-fifth (22 percent) of the Poles reviewed were suspicious enough to be investigated by the NKVD or denied the right to even contact the party back home surely raised eyebrows in the ECCI and Cadres Department and reinforced long-standing suspicions about the Polish CP.

In his cover letter, Skulski posed a series of questions that revealed his concerns about returning 140 émigrés to Poland. How, he asked, will the Polish press exploit the sending of Communists back from the USSR? Because most of them "honestly and conscientiously participated in socialist construction," how will the Polish press exploit the "soul-less" behavior of the USSR toward Communists? How will those deported from the USSR live and work in Poland? What will happen to their families ("a majority of the children were born here")? Skulski also expressed concern about the dangers that the expulsion of those people might pose to the USSR. Once again he asked the Secretariat to provide advice on these and other issues and assured it that the verification would continue apace.[69]

Less than two weeks after Skulski's report, the Secretariat of the Central

Committee of the VKP sent a letter to all party organizations above the district (*raion*) committee level that dramatically changed the verification and vigilance campaigns. Dated 29 July 1936 the "top secret" letter stated that "new materials obtained in 1936" proved that Zinoviev and Kamenev, "in a direct bloc with Trotsky" dating back to 1932, had planned not only the murder of Kirov but also "attempts on the lives of other leaders of our party, primarily Comrade Stalin." The letter devoted special attention to the conspiratorial, counterrevolutionary activities of Trotsky and Trotskyists and suggested that enemies had penetrated the party apparatus. It informed party committees that the conspirators' trial would take place in August and urged them "to rivet attention on the tasks of all-around heightening of Bolshevik revolutionary vigilance." It ended by announcing that "under present conditions, the inalienable quality of every Bolshevik must be the ability to detect the enemy of the party, however well he may be masked."[70]

As **Document 11** below indicates, Kotelnikov, secretary of the ECCI party committee, took the allegations in the letter and its call for vigilance very seriously. He had good reason to do so. Two of the defendants at the August show trial—Fritz David and Moise Lurye (Emel)—had worked in the ECCI apparatus, and one—K. Berman-Yurin—belonged to the German CP. The ICC had expelled David from the German CP in 1935. Even though Kotelnikov maintained that in David's case, the party committee had acted correctly, neither it nor the ICC had unmasked the "true" nature of David's alleged activities, which put both organizations on the defensive. As Kotelnikov noted, this was not the first time that the NKVD had "unmasked . . . enemies" before the party committee had done so. Kotelnikov's purpose in writing the letter appears to have been to defend his and the party committee's failure to do so.

Document 11

Memorandum from F. Kotelnikov to Dimitrov, Manuilsky, and Moskvin about the work of exposing "the wreckers in the ECCI," 11 August 1936. RGASPI, f. 546, op. 1, d. 369, ll. 6–11. Original in Russian. Typewritten with handwritten additions and signature.

[. . .]

11 August 1936.

Top secret.

TO THE GENERAL SECRETARY OF THE EXECUTIVE COMMITTEE OF THE COMINTERN Com. DIMITROV, AND c.c. MANUILSKY AND MOSKVIN.

In the course of the verification and exchange of the party documents,[71] our party organization of the Comintern Executive Committee apparatus, as an integral part of the united, monolithic Leninist-Stalinist party, examined its ranks and purged those of them [deemed] unreliable, those unworthy of the great honor of being a Communist Party member. [The party organization] exposed and expelled from its ranks a group of degenerates who became traitors to and enemies of the party and the working class.

To our shame and disgrace, in our organization, in the Comintern Executive apparatus, [we discovered that] for a long time we had not unmasked the vilest enemies of the workers' party, who, by means of terror, set for themselves the goal of depriving the party and the proletariat of the best, most precious, dearest, beloved—leader, friend, and teacher, com. Stalin.

As is clear, the resolute call by the party, by com. Stalin, to improve Bolshevik revolutionary vigilance, Bolshevik watchfulness, agility, and intransigence has not penetrated into the depths of the hearts of the Bolshevik rank and file [nor] the highest-ranking members of our organization. The proof of this are the recent [and] blatant facts regarding F*ritz* D*avid*, the miscreant agent of the counterrevolutionaries Trotsky-Zinoviev-Kamenev, who stretched their bloody hands toward the heart and brain of the working-class party, toward the VKP(b) Central Committee, and toward [its] leader, com. Stalin.

The recent letter from the Central Committee and the editorials in "Pravda"[72] oblige us, above all else, to improve Bolshevik vigilance, to learn to recognize the enemy, to safeguard the purity of party ranks. The verification and exchange of party documents demonstrate that both our party organization and our party committee have not been adequately fighting, and are still not adequately fighting, to implement this directive and appeal of the party.

Those unmasked and expelled from the party.

Before the verification of party documents, the counterrevolutionary elements Safarov, Magyar, and Sinani were expelled from the party. The party organization failed to expose Safarov before his arrest. Magyar and Sinani were exposed and kicked out of the party before their arrest. It was a long time before this double-dyed, counterrevolutionary triad was exposed.

During the verification of party documents, 27 members were purged from our party organization and from the party organization of the Publishing House. Among them were Meshkovskaia and Gomez, who used to work in Wang Ming's Secretariat and, earlier, with Sinani. They were later arrested as overt enemies of the party and the people. Two enemies, Stasiak and Gulko, were not exposed by us but removed by the NKVD organs.

During the exchange of party documents, four members and three candidate members of our organization were expelled from the party. The reason for the expulsion of Gurevich, Gurianov, and Neibut was their affiliation with Trotskyism in 1923 and 1927, and [their] concealment of this during the verification of party documents. Nikolaeva [was expelled] for continuing to defend the innocence of her husband,[73] who had been arrested and sentenced to ten years for wrecking. Candidate members: Romanov [was expelled] for being a moral degenerate (he was married five times) and for violating [the rules of] conspiracy; Arakcheev, for concealing from the party the fact of the arrest and exile of his father, an active SR; Portnoy, [who was] mistakenly admitted as a VKP(b) candidate [member], for having close ties with Atanasov (Atanasov recommended his candidacy) and for his suspicious behavior abroad, [in particular] his attitude toward a provocateur.

The question of the party membership of members of our organization, Furschik, Nauzer, Abramian, still remains unresolved. It is possible that the question of Blumfeld will arise with theirs because their Trotskyist friends have been arrested.

The conclusion suggests itself that we still do not know each member and candidate of the party well enough. Through more careful and serious examination, we will uncover those who have no place in our party.

The task remains to examine the members of the [party] organization over and over again. This task is within [our] powers and is quite feasible if only we secure a real improvement of Bolshevik vigilance in the party organization and of party awareness of each member and candidate member of the party.

The case of F*ritz* D*avid* and H*einrich (Süsskind).*

In this report, I consider it absolutely necessary to raise the question and shed light on the case of F*ritz* D*avid* and H*einrich (Süsskind)*. This is dictated above all by the fact that these two enemies of the party *and* the working class were members of our apparatus and [that] F*ritz* D*avid* was getting ready and waiting for the moment to accomplish his foul plan. The party organization had opportunely raised the question of the inadmissibility of retaining them in the ECCI apparatus. On the basis of party self-criticism, without respect of persons, let us, as our leader and teacher com. Stalin teaches us, characterize the case as it was.

Let us start with the case of F*ritz* D*avid*. On 9 July 1935, on the eve of the Congress,[74] I interrogated F*ritz* D*avid* for several hours, and everything was recorded. It was discovered that he, as an active Menshevik until 1919, had been arrested by the organs of the ChK [Cheka] for counterrevolutionary activities. In 1926 he left for Germany in order to infiltrate the Communist Party. He succeeded, and from there he began his political career. I will not set forth everything that was written down in the stenographic report because it is impossible to read it all. I sent the stenographic report, along with the memorandum, to [comrade] Pyatnitsky in the Political Secretariat with a request to discuss and resolve the question of F*ritz* D*avid*. Some time later, this report was returned to me with Pyatnitsky's note "return to the party committee."

I also sent the stenographic report to the NKVD organs in July 1935.

The commission to select the apparatus to work at the Seventh Congress, of which I was the chairman, resolved not to let F*ritz* D*avid* attend the Congress. This decision by us was repealed, and he, this vilest enemy of the party and the working class, attended the Congress. When one reads the [29 July] letter of the Central Committee, one feels truly terrified by the opportunity we granted to the enemy by letting him attend the Congress and retaining him in the ECCI apparatus. This lesson should teach us a lot—above all, to be vigilant and intransigent toward our enemies.

There is a second case, H*einrich (Süsskind).* In the resolution of the party committee of 11 January 1935, we resolved that he be expelled by the International Control Commission from the Communist Party of Germany as a double-dealer and that he be removed from the Comintern apparatus. I refer to this second case in order to demonstrate once again how insufficiently vigilant we proved to be. I have attached the resolution of the party committee of 11 January 1935 to this [report].

I have also attached the ICC resolution on him of 25 January 1935.

Isn't it sufficient not to let him within gunshot of the Comintern? No, because at someone's initiative he became a worker in the Comintern apparatus. Several days later, he was arrested as an enemy.

What conclusion [can we draw] from this? The party committee had opportunely raised the question about these two counterrevolutionaries, and it was right.

We ought to determine who was personally responsible, at whose initiative they started working in the apparatus, and draw the appropriate conclusion, which will serve as a lesson, and to educate the whole collective of party and non-party [members] of the ECCI apparatus.

Selection of the workers to the apparatus.

The examination of the composition of the party organization during the verification and exchange of party documents provided the opportunity to learn that there are currently sixteen members of the organization who, in 1923, had Trotskyist vacillations. Three of them had rightist vacillations in 1929.

Aleksandrova, who was recently hired by the ECCI apparatus, earlier, between 1916 and July 1917, was a member of the interdistrict organization of S.D. [Social Democrat] (Internationalists).[75] In 1923, in Marxism classes, she had Trotskyist vacillations. I think that the leadership did not know about her Trotskyist mistakes when deliberating the question of her admission to work in our party apparatus. The Cadres Department also failed to mention her Trotskyist waverings in its memorandum to the Secretariat.

In conclusion, I want to emphasize that the conclusions that are made based on the results of the exchange of party documents in our organization, as well as general tasks that our party organization is facing, can and must be carried out actively. For their most successful and timely implementation, it is necessary to have a strong and authoritative party committee and the direct support of its work by the leadership. Three members of the party committee have recently left the party committee. It is necessary to fill [these positions] in the party committee, to elect active and authoritative comrades.

Secretary of the Party Committee of the ECCI party organization:
F. Kotelnikov
F. Kotelnikov

Several aspects of Kotelnikov's letter deserve note. First, he argues that in the cases of David and Heinrich (Süsskind), the party committee had been vigilant and acted properly. Yet, to his shock, both men continued to be active in the Comintern. He strongly implies that Pyatnitsky, who had opposed the adoption of the Popular Front and had been transferred to work in the Central Committee in 1935, had intervened at least once to set aside the party committee's doubts about Fritz David. Although Kotelnikov's rendition of the facts in David's case may be accurate, he defended his and the party committee's behavior by accusing others, an all-too-common political behavior that would later have dire consequences for many accusers and accused. It is also noteworthy that Kotelnikov had sent copies of the materials on David and others, such as Olberg, to the NKVD. In this way, the police accumulated materials that it would use during the mass repression.[76]

Kotelnikov's data on the number of members of the party organization expelled during the 1935 verification and the 1936 exchange of party documents suggest that these administrative procedures were not yet full-blown witch hunts, but rather the scapegoating of former oppositionists in an effort to prove the vigilance of the ECCI party committee.[77] In spring 1935 the ECCI party organization had approximately 460 members. According to Kotelnikov, during the 1935 verification, the party organization expelled 27 people (6 percent). All 27 had worked in one department (the Publishing House of Foreign Workers), and most were foreigners; the NKVD had arrested two of them before they were expelled. Fewer than 2 percent of the members of the party organization (all of whom were native-born) were expelled during the 1936 exchange of party documents; it seems that all were expelled in August—that is, following the Central Committee letter of 29 July. All told, less than 8 percent of the members were expelled in 1935–1936.

While that proportion may not constitute a witch hunt, the effects of those expulsions, the August show trial of Zinoviev, David, Lurye, Berman-Yurin, Olberg, and the rest, and the ongoing verification of fraternal party members living in the USSR were profound. The effects are discernible in the tone of Kotelnikov's report. Whereas the 20 February 1935 resolution of the party organization, passed after the Magyar affair, had proclaimed the party organization "politically healthy," Kotelnikov's August 1936 assessment provided no sense that such was the case and no sense of closure: "We still do not know each member. . . . The task remains to examine the members of the [party] organization over and over again." In light of the August trial and the preliminary results of the verification of émigrés, greater vigilance and party discipline were essential. The need to "know each member" took on a heightened sense of urgency.

Kotelnikov ended his letter by implying that the ECCI Secretariat had heretofore not done enough to ensure the "successful and timely implementation" of VKP directives. He was not the only person to challenge its political leadership, albeit for very different reasons.

Document 12 below is a 17 August 1936 "top secret" letter to Dimitrov, Manuilsky, and Moskvin from Skulski, the representative of the Polish CP. This time Skulski wrote to protest what he believed to be unwarranted attacks on his party's alleged lack of vigilance regarding comrade Buzynski.[78] The allegations were made at a party organization meeting during the August trial. Skulski argued strongly that the charges against the Polish CP group in the USSR were unfounded, because its verification commission had spoken personally to Chernomordik (one of the Cadres Department heads), Manuilsky, and Moskvin about the commission's recommendation to expel Buzynski. Either these three did not take the case seriously enough to act on it, or they simply failed to respond to it in a timely manner. Nor did they respond to other evidence presented by that commission; in fact, in several cases, Moskvin appears to have ignored evidence. Skulski's criticisms of Moskvin are particularly sharp. He was angry that none of the three had defended the Poles by presenting what he saw as the facts of the case. His argument that, "having learned from bitter experience," the Poles had been more vigilant in rooting out suspicious elements than the ECCI leadership or the Cadres Department is convincing. If so, given what awaited the Poles, a tragic irony underscores an essential feature of the period: that Communists, regardless of their nationality, believed in the foreign threats to the USSR and VKP, or at least acted in accordance with that assertion.

Document 12

Letter from Skulski to Dimitrov, Manuilsky, and Moskvin, 17 August 1936. RGASPI, f. 495, op. 74, d. 399, ll. 11–12. Original in Russian. Typewritten.

KDKPP [. . .]

To: Com. Dimitrov
Com. Manuilsky
Com. <u>Moskvin</u>

At the 15 August 1936 ECCI party organization meeting, upon hearing the Buzynski case, some comrades harshly attacked the Polish section for not signaling its concerns about Buzynski. Even some party committee members (c.c. Chernomordik and Kotelnikov) reproached the Polish section for failing to inform the party committee about the Buzynski case in a timely manner.

Since these comrades, especially c. Chernomordik, had been informed about our conclusion on Buzynski (regarding [his] dismissal from the ECCI apparatus and expulsion from the VKP(b)) one month before the meeting, on 14 July 1936 to be precise, and must have not paid sufficient attention to our conclusion, I consider their behavior at the meeting improper. It was especially improper since I had talked with c.c. Manuilsky and Moskvin about the Buzynski case a month ago (15 July 1936), and we had agreed that Buzynski should be removed from work.

It is strange that instead, Buzynski received a pass to a health resort, and the Polish section was later criticized for insufficient vigilance.

It is completely understandable that I was not able to protest at the general meeting, because I considered it inappropriate. But I thought that some of the ECCI leaders present at the meeting would have found the opportunity to note that this time, the Polish section had not stood around gaping and, after a lengthy verification of Buzynski, had raised the issue of his removal from the ECCI apparatus and his membership in the party in a proper party order (ECCI leadership, Cadres Department).

But unfortunately, nobody mentioned that even though it could have been done in a proper way, the more so because we (having noticed the dragging out of the Buzynski case in the Cadres Department) had sent, on 27 July 1936, a copy of our resolution on Buzynski to the CC VKP(b); but it was kept by com. Moskvin until the investigation of the correctness of our accusations against Buzynski [could be completed]. It seems to me that our letter with a copy of the resolution on Buzynski is still being kept in the ECCI apparatus (in Moskvin's Secretariat).

In this connection, I want to remind you that the final resolution of the question of party membership of some members of the Leontiev group (the formation of an anti-party clique and suspicion of provocation) has been delayed for eight months already because, in accordance with com. Moskvin's order, the correctness of our suggestions regarding those of the group living in Moscow is still being verified. Meanwhile, those [members of the Leontiev group] living in the BSSR [Belorussia] have not only been expelled already from the VKP(b) but been arrested and condemned by the appropriate organs to varying terms of imprisonment.

I would also like to remind you that the investigation of the Khavkin-Valter case, which had been initiated by us in connection with his Menshevik past and Trotskyist affiliation, has been delayed for half a year already. In February our P[olitical] B[ureau] charged me with raising this question with com. Moskvin, which I did promptly. Com. Moskvin charged com. Krajewski with verifying the correctness of our accusations, yet Valter continues to work in the OMS. Besides—at a time when the ECCI leadership was aware of the new materials on the Trotskyist-Zinovievite bloc—he has been sent on a trip abroad, before I knew anything about your decision on his party affairs.

Since we, having learned from bitter experience in the past, have considerably heightened our vigilance, we request most strongly that you guarantee that the results of our vigilance will be acted on, and not give cause, to the extent possible, to the generally unjustified attacks on us for any supposed lack of vigilance.

In conclusion, I ask you to inform me about any directives or observations regarding our insufficient vigilance, if you have any, and to contribute to cessation of the groundless attacks against the Polish section at the general meetings of the party organization, attacks that unjustly put us in a difficult situation.

Representative of the CP Poland in ECCI
Skulski
SKULSKI
17 August 1936

Skulski's letter hints at two notable issues. The first is that the members of the ECCI Secretariat, who were quick to issue orders to raise vigilance, were themselves slow to resolve certain issues that resulted from the vigilance campaign. Why they were slow is unclear. Whatever the reasons, Skulski's attack on them was surely unwelcome. The second is that his account of the meeting suggests that Polish Communists, who had long been the object of suspicion, made an easy scapegoat for comrades eager to prove their vigilance. Precisely to overcome those suspicions, Skulski asserted that the Poles had "considerably heightened" their vigilance. But doing so provided no "guarantee" that the results of their vigilance would be acted on. His letter conveys succinctly that the Polish CP had become an out-group within the ECCI and apparatus. Skulski's frustration with the Catch-22 position in which the CPP and Poles in the USSR found themselves is evident. Yet there was obviously little he could do to change it, except to be more vigilant.

In the first half of 1936 four important developments helped to set the stage for the mass repression of 1937–1938. The first was that the Cadres Department and the ECCI Secretariat, in their reports to the Central Committee, raised serious doubts about the political reliability of émigrés, especially those who had joined the VKP. During 1936 the suspicion that foreigners, aliens, posed a threat to the VKP and Soviet national security mounted. Given that many in the Central Committee and the Politburo already harbored such suspicions, the cause and effect relationships between the ECCI reports and Central Committee concerns are unclear. Unraveling them is perhaps less important than appreciating that leading members of the VKP and the ECCI shared these concerns and fueled each others' anxieties. The verification of all émigrés in the USSR, especially those who were VKP members, and the growing suspicions of certain groups, especially émigrés from Poland, deepened the spymania and hastened the transformation of suspicions into xenophobia. The second is that the ECCI had implemented a series of reforms and policies designed to centralize cadre policy and accountability. It did so both in response to Central Committee policy and of its own accord. By so doing, it created the administrative apparatus and procedures that later generated materials used to arrest large numbers of people. The third is that the ongoing verification of foreign émigrés not only deepened VKP leaders' anxieties about foreigners but also demonstrated the power of party discipline. The still incomplete verification of the Polish émigrés offers an appropriate example. The verification commission consisted of Poles who were VKP members. Some of them shared VKP leaders' concerns that "enemy agents" had infiltrated the USSR and the party. VKP membership, not nationality, determined their political behavior. Whatever Lenski, Skulski, and other Polish CP leaders were later accused of, their behavior during the 1936 verification makes clear the extent to which they were "real Bolsheviks" for whom the perceived threats against the USSR demanded vigilance. Finally, the August 1936 trial of Zinoviev, David, Lurye, Berman-Yurin, and others fused the escalating suspicions of foreigners to the long-standing anti-Trotskyist campaign. The intertwining of political vigilance and mounting xenophobia would continue over the next eight months and lead to tragic and devastating consequences.

CHAPTER FOUR

Campaigns Converge, Anxieties Deepen

Our apparatus has to be crystal clear and to consist of people [who have been] thoroughly tested. We know that the enemy is trying to infiltrate us. We can guard ourselves from the penetration of alien elements only through firm vigilance toward each and every [person] working with us, coming to us.

— ANNA RAZUMOVA

The Cadres Department is sending to you a memorandum, "On Trotskyists and other hostile elements in the émigré community of the German CP." We here mention only the most typical cases. Actually, the work on exposure is in progress, and a much larger number of these kinds of elements has already been revealed.

— MOISEI B. CHERNOMORDIK

THE AUGUST 1936 SHOW TRIAL intensified the Comintern's struggle against Trotskyism. On trial were Zinoviev, Kamenev, David, and others, labeled the Anti-Soviet United Trotskyist-Zinovievite Center. According to the evidence presented by Andrei Vyshinsky, the state procurator, the defendants had participated in a terrorist organization, directed from abroad by Leon Trotsky, whose members had murdered Kirov and planned the assassinations of Stalin and other party leaders. We now know what those within the Comintern did not—that there is no evidence that such a conspiracy existed.[1] The trial, like those in January 1937 and March 1938, was designed to convey to citizens the dangers, internal and external, that threatened the USSR. The foreign threat was central.

In court the defendants confessed to the charges, and all were sentenced to death. The trial was a national and international media event. Newspapers published lengthy excerpts from the trial transcript. Newspapers, party com-

146

mittees, trade unions, and other organizations demanded the execution of these so-called enemy agents and terrorists. Living in a society in which the party controlled the media, it is hardly surprising that many citizens believed the charges. The state had presented seemingly convincing evidence, and most important, the accused had confessed in a public court. Some people may have harbored doubts about the trial, but if they did so, they kept them to themselves and behaved as though the charges were real.[2] Public pressure to do so was substantial; large numbers of demonstrators massed in Red Square and demanded that the defendants be executed.

To many within the Comintern and the VKP, the "evidence" presented at the trial was undoubtedly shocking and bewildering. The verdict propelled the ECCI and its party committee into action. The trial had a special impact on the Comintern. Not only had two defendants—Fritz David and Moise Lurye—formerly worked in the Comintern apparatus, but the "proof" of an international Trotskyist conspiracy put the Comintern, the agent of the international anti-Trotskyist campaign, on the defensive. The trial underscored the need to heighten the anti-Trotskyist and vigilance campaigns and the verification of fraternal party members. The Comintern's roles as agent and instrument of repression intensified commensurately. The telegrams from the ECCI that defined those campaigns mirrored faithfully the Politburo's interpretation of the trial. **Document 13** represents the tone and contents of the flurry of telegrams that the ECCI sent to the fraternal parties during and shortly after the trial.

Document 13

Telegram from the ECCI Secretariat to the Communist Party of Great Britain on the lessons of Trotskyist "counterrevolutionary activity" as revealed by the August 1936 trial, 20 August 1936. RGASPI, f. 495, op. 184, d. 15, outgoing telegram 1936 general, ll. 61–62. Original in Russian. English translation by ECCI translators with handwritten additions. Typewritten.

[. . .]
England
Trial gang Trotzky-Zinoviev unveils picture [of] huge crime of these mean degenerates stop These abominable traitors of workingclass, recognising all hope lost regards failure [of] socialist construction and having no support within country made terror to chief method of their conterrevolutionary activity stop Now it has been clearly established that criminal murder of Kirov has been prepared and carried through according to direct instructions of

Trotzky and Zinoviev, that according to their immediate instructions have been prepared a serie[s] of other terro[r]istic actions against leaders of CPSU [VKP] and Soviet State, in first place against comrade Stalin stop Now it has been ascertained documentarily that they have established direct connections with the fascist GESTAPO in order to carry through their terroristic activity stop RUNAG[3] will inform fully about course of trial Point out newspapers necessity [to] utilize widely this material in order to tear off definitively mask of mean agent of fascism stop With facts in hands prove, that trotzkism is vanguard [of] conterrevolutionary bourgeoisie, that he maintains open connections with Hearst press in United States of America and se[p]erate connections with fascist GESTAPO, that to-day he endeavours in Spain through criminal game with most extreme slogans to facilitate intervention of german and italian fascism and playing into the hands of fascist rebels, that he is acting as arch enemy [of the] Soviet Union and participates in preparation [of] war aggression against Soviet Union, that he is doing sabotage work in workers movement, that he is pursuing policy of desorganization [of] working class, its scattering, that he penetrates into workers organizations in order to disrupt united and people's front [Popular Front], that he is acting in the interest of the defeat [of the] working class, in order to act hereafter [in] Communist Parties and workers movement stop Unmask fascist aggression of Trotzky's home framed up by Trotzky himself together with fascists[4] in order to hide on eve of judgment over his terroristic gang[,] his connection with fascism and to present himself as a victim of fascism stop Necessary now to secure full liquidation of trotzkism stop With all forces carry on struggle against all those, who during trial support terrorists of Trotzky stop Secure that socialist and antifascist organizations and press take position against this fascist gang stop Raise question terroristic counterrevolutionary activity trotzkism in meetings [of] party and workers, give broad publicity resolutions voted in these meetings stigmatizing trotzkist gang and conveying greetings to working class USSR and Stalin, great leader workers whole world.

    Acknowledge receipt. Secretariat

20/VIII/36

Australia: Zash, Plume, Rozent, Reizinger, Koralov 26/III

[. . .]

 The telegram is self-explanatory, but certain points deserve to be highlighted. From late 1934 the ECCI had charged in its telegrams that Trotsky had colluded with the Gestapo in an anti-Soviet campaign. The trial "proved" that Trotsky and his supporters within the USSR actively participated in this conspiracy. After Kirov's murder Zinoviev and Kamenev had been convicted only of moral complicity, but at the August trial they confessed to direct participation in a terrorist organization. The convictions injected a sense of urgency into the anti-Trotskyist campaign. As in earlier telegrams, the ECCI sought to direct the campaign abroad by ordering the fraternal parties to use the "facts in hand" to "secure full liquidation of" Trotskyism.

Document 13 also conveys the Comintern's allegation that Trotsky and Trotskyists had not confined their "counterrevolutionary" activities to the USSR, that they had also sought to sabotage and disorganize workers' organizations and to facilitate intervention in Spain by German and Italian fascists. Before the mid-1930s the Comintern had devoted little attention to Spain. The Communist Party there had been very small and politically weak. But after the Spanish Revolution of 1931 and especially after the election of a Popular Front government in early 1936, the Comintern paid increasing attention to Spain. The outbreak of the Spanish Civil War in July 1936 catapulted Spain to the top of the Comintern's agenda. From then until the Spanish fascists' victory in early 1939, that war occupied much of the ECCI's attention and energy.[5] It also epitomized the threatening international context in which the various show trials and repression unfolded. The Comintern organized the International Brigades of volunteers who went to Spain to defend the legally elected Popular Front government. Germany and Italy quickly rushed military matériel and troops to Spain to support the rebels, thereby transforming the Civil War into a European struggle. The USSR offered first political and then military support to the Spanish government. In this struggle between the left and the right, Trotsky's criticisms of the Spanish Popular Front government and the Comintern's Popular Front policy provided the evidence that the Comintern used to label him the archenemy of the Soviet Union.

Maintaining a broad and cohesive Popular Front was important to the struggle against Spanish fascism. Yet the insistence in the telegram that fraternal parties abroad ensure "that socialist and antifascist organizations and press take position against this fascist gang"—that is, the defendants in the August trial—served only to weaken the Popular Front. Most "socialist and antifascist organizations" abroad were highly critical of the trial and the verdict. The ECCI's demand that its adherents insist that such organizations condemn Trotsky and his "fascist gang" divided Popular Front supporters. In Moscow, the refusal of these organizations to accept the trial as fair and to condemn the "trial gang" reinforced an increasingly Manichean worldview and deepened the sense of isolation and uncertainty.

Whereas most of the telegrams in August 1936 echoed the themes found in Document 13, others illuminate the extent to which the ECCI Secretariat acted as the Politburo's agent in the campaign. **Document 14** provides an intriguing example. The ECCI Secretariat sent it to Earl Browder, the leader of the CPUSA, but similar telegrams were sent to other fraternal parties.

Document 14

Telegram from the ECCI Secretariat to Earl Browder, CPUSA, 25 August 1936. RGASPI, f. 495, op. 184, d. 34, outgoing telegram 1936 to New York. Original in English. Typewritten.

---

25 August 1936
New York
Browder.
   Articles of Radek,[6] Piatakoff[7] and Rakowski[8] published in *Izvestiia* and *Pravda* August 21 must be published in whole in *Daily Worker*[9] and all Communist press. Secretariat.

Document 14 appears to be a straightforward effort by the ECCI Secretariat to direct the conduct of the international anti-Trotsky campaign, to silence critics abroad, and to convince skeptics of the validity of the trial. It served those purposes. But in this case, there is more than meets the eye. Radek's, Pyatakov's, and Rakovsky's articles denouncing the defendants were published on 21 August, during the trial. The next day (and three days before the telegram was sent), Vyshinsky informed the Central Committee that there was sufficient evidence to investigate the three men's relations with the opposition. Whether or not Manuilsky, a Central Committee member, or the ECCI Secretariat knew of Vyshinsky's recommendation is unclear. The ECCI Secretariat's telegram ordering the fraternal parties abroad to publish the articles served to buttress the official version of the trial. Following the three men's arrests, the published articles provided "evidence" that they were "double-dealers" who denounced others while engaging in anti-Soviet activities. There is no indication as to whether the Secretariat itself made the decision to order the publication of these articles or whether the decision was made for it. What is clear is that, wittingly or unwittingly, the Secretariat acted as Stalin's and the Politburo's agent.

   At the same time that the ECCI instructed fraternal parties abroad on how to conduct the anti-Trotskyist press campaign,[10] it continued its efforts to purge Trotskyists from the ranks of fraternal parties. On 26 August, Moskvin drafted directives for the leaders of the Lithuanian CP that stated that the "trial showed that many Trotskyists come from Lithuania. It is essential to verify that Trotskyists have not yet penetrated the CPLith, for in past years an excess of Trotskyist émigrés [to the USSR] have been discovered."[11]

After the trial, various ECCI organizations met to discuss its implications. At a meeting of the ECCI Presidium, Ercoli (Togliatti), an ECCI secretary and the leader of the Italian CP, presented a report entitled "The Lessons of the Trial of the Trotskyist-Zinovievite Terrorist Center." In it he argued that the trial proved the necessity for heightened vigilance, which he called "an act in defense of democracy, peace, socialism, [and] revolution."[12]

On 26 August the party group of the Secretariats held an open meeting to discuss the implications of the trial.[13] **Document 15** presents portions of the protocol of that meeting. Anna Razumova, who would herself be arrested in 1938, delivered the main report.[14] Her comments focused on the dangers posed by the "terrorist gang" and the necessity of raising vigilance "in deeds, not in words." "We talk about vigilance and pass resolutions at each meeting, only to forget about them later." She implies that before the August 1936 trial, some of her comrades had engaged in rhetorical vigilance only to formally fulfill the demands of party discipline. Razumova was not such a person. For her, vigilance was not simply a duty; it was a necessity. She presented as fact that enemies sought to penetrate the ECCI apparatus and that dubious elements who had hidden their past oppositional activities still existed within the apparatus. Therefore, she urged her comrades "to help our NKVD organs" to unmask not only the Trotskyists but also former Rightists. For Razumova, "the real meaning of vigilance" necessitated knowing more than how people worked; it also necessitated knowing "the people themselves." For her, vigilance was imperative if the VKP was to be protected from its "enemies." Her demand that comrades had to know "the people themselves"—that is, that they had to delve into people's private lives—portended an ominous new phase in the vigilance campaign. Henceforth, people's private and public lives warranted equal scrutiny.

Consistent with her call for vigilance "in deeds" and her pledge to help the NKVD, she denounced the wife of a comrade (Servet) who was friends with the wife of one of the defendants in the August trial. Servet, in turn, presented an explanation of this relationship and engaged in self-criticism. Others who addressed the meeting followed Razumova's and Servet's examples: they called for greater vigilance, engaged in self-criticism and self-defense, and leveled accusations against others. Such behaviors were the norm in this ritual, which took place amid considerable political uncertainty.

Document 15

Protocol of the 26 August 1936 meeting of the party group of the Secretariats. RGASPI, f. 546, op. 1, d. 340, ll. 52–56. Original in Russian. Typewritten with handwritten additions.

To the file
PROTOCOL No. *14*
Of the 26 August 1936 open meeting of the party group of the Secretariats.
Present: Razumova [. . .] Lang, Magnuson, Yanson,
[. . .] Servet, Mirov [. . .]
Agenda: 1. On the trial of the Trotskyist-Zinovievite
gang of terrorists.
2. Information about the last party committee session
a) MIuD,[15] b) implementing the conversion.

HEARD: 1) Report of com. Razumova about the results of the trial of the Trotskyist-Zinovievite terrorist gang. Referring to vigilance, com. Razumova stresses the importance of this problem here in our organization. Our vigilance has been expressed by emphasizing the question of observing the rules of conspiracy.[16] We have achieved this in that comrades are now more alert and responsible regarding the storage of secret documents, but we have paid little attention to the people themselves. We are responsible for failing to expose the scoundrel F. David and his friends, which left an indelible mark on us. We talk about vigilance and pass resolutions at each meeting, only to forget about them later. Our apparatus has to be crystal clear and to consist of people [who have been] thoroughly tested. We know that the enemy is trying to infiltrate us. We can guard ourselves from the penetration of alien elements only through firm vigilance toward each and every [person] working with us, coming to us. A number of party meetings held by us [have] revealed, however, that in our apparatus there are still individuals who have not been sufficiently investigated, who were hiding their past affiliation to the **Trotskyist opposition** and to factional groups in the fraternal communist parties, and who remained friends of and close to David, Emel [Lurye], etc.

Com. Razumova cites a number of concrete examples of lack of vigilance such as, for example, the election of the former Trotskyist Shtorm as chairman of the meeting dedicated to the trial. Later in the meeting, this Shtorm gave the floor to a recently expelled party member, the Trotskyist Gurevich, who was not even working in our apparatus.

[Razumova cites] the example of the loss of a foreign comrade's documents by one of the SS [Sluzhba Sviazi—Communications Department] workers who failed to report this fact, even to his boss, for three days.

There is a very serious problem, says com. Razumova, within our own group, with com. Servet, whose wife used to be a friend of the wife of Emel (M. Lurye) and met with her. When he was talking about his former mistakes, it never occurred [to Servet] to mention his membership in the Barbé-Celor group,[17] which has now slid, together with Doriot, into the fascist camp, [or to mention] that Lurye's wife (arrested several months ago) visited his house and met with his wife.[18] Is it the right thing to do? Does it mean that the comrade finally realized the terrible danger of this "liberalism" toward those arrested and the real meaning of vigilance?

Later com. Razumova speaks about the struggle that our [party] organization waged against the Trotskyists and the Rightists in 1929, about the connections of our Rightists with those abroad, about the necessity to carefully inspect what is being done in this area, about the need to help our NKVD organs to reveal the remaining connections between the Rightists and the Trotskyists.

Saluting the tribunal's decision and the carrying out of the verdict, com. Razumova calls on our comrades to be vigilant in deeds, not in words, and asks us to help our party organization in exposing enemies of the party and those who have attached themselves to our apparatus.

SPEAKERS:

SERVET: The facts of the latest events demonstrate that, first of all, we have to know those people with whom we are working. We know little about the past of certain comrades, and as a result, we are not always able to strengthen [our] vigilance. For example, I did not know that in the past, Shtorm used to be a Trotskyist. Similarly, I did not know the pasts of David and others who worked in the apparatus. Today I realized that I maintained relations with counterrevolutionaries who have now been shot, and it was my mistake not to tell [about them]. However, I met them only at work. M. Lurye's wife [was] from the Radio Communications [Department], and we analysts had to discuss with them a number of questions. Present at these discussions were: M. Lurye's wife, Frumkina, De Boeck, Garnier. Some of these meetings took place in my apartment. Later my wife transferred to work in Radio Communications. She worked under the leadership of the M. Lurye's wife, and they established friendly relations. I saw him [Lurye] once in Germany at the Conference on Agitation and Propaganda, but I was not acquainted with him. Here I met him only occasionally in the Park of Culture and Recreation, and sometimes in the Soiuznaia [Hotel],[19] since we lived close to each other. I did not know his political background; I did not know that he was a Trotskyist before. It was my mistake not to inform the party organization about my connections, but I did not do it because I had no political connections [at all]. C. Kotelnikov was right when he said that I did not demonstrate unfailing vigilance.

MAGNUSON: Some German comrades share an opinion that only com. Pieck is responsible for the F. David case. It is not correct. The German comrades have to help c. Pieck, to signal him about facts that they might be aware of. I want to tell what I know regarding David. Some time ago, Karolsky and I were charged with organizing the publishing of a newspaper. Karolsky wanted to invite David to do this work, but I objected, and as a result, David was not given this job. I informed c. Zholdak, the party secretary of the organization where Karolsky works, about this case. . . .

LANG: [He] focuses on the international significance of the recently concluded trial of the ignoble murderers. When we talk about revolutionary vigilance, we have to admit that it is a shame that in our organization there were people like Fritz David, who strolled about at the Seventh Congress of the CI and was able to work in our apparatus for several years without being exposed by anybody.

We have still not sufficiently exposed the Trotskyists in the Communist press; we have not sufficiently explained their role to the masses.

Regarding c. Servet: he should have explained the role of Barbé-Celor, and in particular, he should have informed the party organization about his connections with the Emel [Lurye] family. In the eyes of some foreign comrades, Trotsky and Doriot and other [Trotskyists] played a certain role in the revolution, and therefore, they still enjoy authority. Our task and the task of the fraternal Communist Parties is to explain to the broad masses what has happened to them lately and what they have come to be. For example, in Austria Trotskyists are trying to join the Leftist organizations and conduct their policy there. We have not yet sufficiently explained to the broad masses the decisions of the Seventh CI Congress, and therefore, Trotskyists are sometimes able to confuse people. We have to expose Trotskyists everywhere. Com. Lang says that it is not clear to him how it was possible that Gurevich, the Trotskyist expelled from the party, could still enter the building. Why did they not cancel his pass?

YANSON: [He] thinks that the question of vigilance is of great importance, especially in the Chinese section. Trotskyists in China, according to information received [from there], conduct a struggle against the United [Popular] Front. They are also connected through their activities with the Japanese police.

Safarov and Magyar managed at some point to train their people and to send them into the country. Trotskyists have always used the method of deception; therefore, the struggle against them has to be systematic. It is especially important to pay attention to the former Trotskyists abroad. We also have many former Trotskyists who were expelled from the universities and who stayed in the USSR. We have to closely watch these people, since there has already been an attempt to murder c. Wang Ming. Hence it is necessary to demand that the Cadres Department verify all the émigrés in the USSR [and] verify all of the students here.

MIROV: [He] tells about how once, during a meeting of the political education class that he led, there arose a question of how to better develop vigilance in a situation where the enemy skillfully masks himself, when he denounces another in order to shield someone else and protect him for future work. In order to recognize the enemy, one has to be a clever Bolshevik, one has to be well equipped ideologically and be stronger than the enemy. We also need to be cautious because we are still living in the conditions of class struggle. For example, there are recent reports from Spain that there are a growing number of spies in the government camp who provide information to the rebels. War is being prepared, it is inevitable, and on the eve of the war spies become more active. The trial of the Trotskyist-Zinovievite gang clearly took place on the eve of the war, and therefore, caution is essential. Are we up to it? While in the apparatus Fritz David and others caused doubts among many [comrades], but everyone concealed these doubts. Today's editorial article in "Pravda" gives us a directive. "One has to listen to the voice of the masses." One has to be cautious toward everyone. If a person is suspicious, it is necessary to signal the party organization. It is essential to build an iron wall around our leaders. Vigilance means not only to warn but also to complete work once started.

Later c. Mirov informs the party group that he had never been a member of any opposition, but until 1926 he worked with Zinoviev [in the ECCI apparatus]. However, during the discussion in the Secretariat, relations [between them] became strained, and he was removed from work. After leaving the Secretariat, he met neither Pikel nor Bogdan nor any of Zinoviev's former cadres. While working for the past few years in the ECCI apparatus he was a party committee member and the secretary of the party group, and he led an active struggle against the united Trotskyist-Zinovievite opposition. . . .

RESOLVED: To charge c.c. Razumova and Koker to work out a resolution on the basis of the concrete proposals of com. Razumova and those resulting from the discussion; to approve it by referendum and to attach it to this protocol.

2) HEARD: Report by com. Razumova about the last meeting of the party committee.

3) RESOLVED: To take the information into consideration. To pay serious attention to the organization of the demonstration on 1 September;[20] all comrades who will not be working have to participate in the demonstration. [. . .]To name the flank men. To ensure the timely exchange of bonds.

Chair: *Razumova*
Razumova
Secretary: Koker
Koker.

[RESOLUTION]

1) To consider it necessary to inform the party committee about the report of c. Magnuson regarding the incident when c. Karolsky tried to admit F. David to work, and only after c. Magnuson strongly objected, was David not admitted to work.

2) To ask the party committee to review again the case of c. Servet, because the party group considers the question of the friendly relations between Emel's [Lurye's] wife and c. Servet's wife has not been sufficiently clarified and that c. Servet has not fully recognized his liberalism toward those arrested and does not understand the importance of vigilance toward the enemies.

3) To hear at the party group [meeting] more detailed, individual reports of comrades. In addition, to oblige the secretary of the party organization to talk to specific comrades from time to time and, in suspicious cases, raise a question at the party group [meeting].

4) On the basis of the suggestions by com. Yanson, to ask the party committee to raise, when appropriate, the question of: a) watching Trotskyists who were expelled from the universities and have stayed in the USSR; b) observing those people who were at some point sent to China by Safarov and Magyar; c) verifying the students who are staying here; d) improving the hiring of workers in the ECCI apparatus by getting to know personally each candidate, and not on the basis of [his] papers.

5) To ask the party committee to find out who was responsible for the fact that Gurevich, who had been expelled from the party and no longer worked in the apparatus, had a pass to the building in his possession for a long time.

Each comrade is to be obliged to keep an eye on his surroundings and to warn the party organization in a timely manner about all suspicious findings.

In many respects, the contents of Document 15 are depressingly familiar, which suggests that the trial did not mark a radical break with previous policies and behaviors. Denunciations of comrades, as before, necessitated investigation. Suspicions expressed about foreigners and contacts with foreigners while abroad were common. The call for a verification of all foreigners—seemingly an odd recommendation, because that operation was already under way—was not new, nor was calling on "each comrade . . . to warn the party organization . . . about all suspicious findings." In fact, all the themes and behaviors that were to play so devastating a role in 1937–1938 were already frequent within the ECCI apparatus and party committee in mid-1936 and had been for some years. What had changed with the trial was the heightened sense of urgency and apprehension regarding the anti-Trotskyist and vigilance campaigns.

Yet certain aspects of the meeting deserve note. Those denounced at the meeting were denounced because of their associations with convicted enemies: in Servet's case, his wife's association with Lurye's wife; in Karolsky's case, his earlier support for Fritz David. Associations with convicted enemies (or their families) made it easy to choose scapegoats. And given the demands for vigilance, some scapegoats were necessary. That both Servet and Karolsky were foreigners may have made it easier (at least subconsciously) for Soviet comrades to denounce them.

Charges of having ties, however innocuous and explicable, with enemies required that the accused engage in self-criticism. As a rule, those who did so claimed that they had been ignorant of the recently revealed enemy's past. For people like Servet, who had adhered to the party-prescribed rules and behaviors, the allegations that they consorted with "enemies" induced considerable confusion. The best defense was to adhere even more strictly to the rules. Servet expressed this confusion and behavior most succinctly: "It was my mistake not to inform the party organization about my connections [with Lurye and his wife], but I did not do it because I had no political connections [at all]. C. Kotelnikov was right when he said that I did not demonstrate unfailing vigilance." In light of the trial and more strident calls for vigilance, party discipline and self-defense required that comrades be more suspicious of one another, that they question the motives behind each other's party rhetoric because the "enemy skillfully masks himself" with seemingly proper phrases, that they view with suspicion all social and work relations because "enemies" used those relations as a tactic for recruiting people. Party leaders used the search for "enemies" to obliterate the distinction between public and personal lives. Vigilance and suspiciousness had become synonymous; they had become the surest means of defending the group and the individual in the uncertain environment that succeeded the August trial. Razumova's call for vigilance in deeds, not in words, became essential for party members who sought stability in an increasingly chaotic political world where "war is being prepared." Suspicion and mistrust had become defining features of comradeship.

Self-criticism was an act of confession, an admission of fallibility, and an appeal to the collective for help in mending one's ways and remaining worthy of the honor of party membership. Servet's admittedly confused and tragic admission exemplifies the importance of self-criticism as confession and exculpation. But self-criticism also served as an accepted means of denouncing an accused or convicted person for having hidden his or her ties to the opposition.

Finally, Lang's observation that Trotsky and other oppositions "still enjoy authority" and hence "our task and the task of the fraternal Communist Parties is to explain to the broad masses what has happened to them lately and what they have come to be" reminds us that the anti-Trotskyist campaign had two goals: to condemn perspectives and behaviors that the VKP leaders deemed a threat and to educate party members by identifying what constituted "proper" Communist characteristics.

The importance of the trial in animating the Comintern's anti-Trotskyist campaign is also clear from a series of documents that the ECCI sent to fraternal party leaders after it. In late August the ECCI Secretariat sent to the leaders of the British and French parties a letter explaining the conclusions to be drawn from the August trial and how to use them "for the political liquidation of Trotsky and Trotskyism." **Document 16** is the letter that the Secretariat sent to Thorez and Pollitt (the general secretaries of the French and British CPs respectively) instructing them on how Communist delegates to the upcoming Brussels Peace Congress should conduct the anti-Trotskyist campaign. That congress was one of a series of Popular Front forums attended by representatives of Communist, socialist, and anti-fascist organizations.

Document 16

A letter from the ECCI Secretariat to the leaders of the British and French CPs regarding the conclusion of the August 1936 trial and the upcoming Brussels Peace Congress, 28 August 1936. RGASPI, f. 495, op. 184, d. 15, outgoing telegrams for 1936, special, ll. 72–76. Original in Russian. Typewritten with handwritten corrections.

Top secret

28 August 1936

1. It is essential to use the trial of the Trotskyist-Zinovievite terrorist gang for the political liquidation of Trotsky and Trotskyism as a fascist agency that, in capitalist countries, masking itself with radical phrases, disorganizes the workers' movement and, in the USSR, organizes terrorist acts against the leaders of the country of socialism. The bureau in Paris is to take leadership of this campaign in its hands, using the arrival of Communists from many countries to the Brussels Peace Congress.[21] It is essential that Thorez and Pollitt instruct each of the groups of Communist delegates from different countries in Brussels on how to conduct this campaign.

2. It is essential to inform public opinion as broadly as possible about the results of the trial, which has indeed shown that:

a) Trotsky and Zinoviev, nourishing unrestrained hatred toward the party, lacking any ideological or political program to counterpose against the party, lacking any support among the masses, promoted terror as the only method of struggle against the party leadership. All of their counterrevolutionary, bandit activities were aimed at reaching personal, mercenary goals—to force their way to power at any cost;

b) Trotsky and his gang, mixed together with the Gestapo spies, subversives, and agents, were preparing attempts on the lives of com. Stalin and other outstanding leaders of the USSR;

c) they killed com. Kirov, treacherously hiding themselves behind the physical executor of this brutal act—Nikolaev;

d) they acted in concert with the Gestapo, i.e., German fascism, the worst enemy not only of the German but the working class of the whole world. They *cultivated* the practices of the fascist guards, who, as is well known, had eliminated all the Gestapo agents after the Reichstag fire;[22]

e) Trotsky's and Zinoviev's terrorist activity was closely linked to their goal of the USSR's defeat in case of aggression by the German and Japanese imperialists against it. They set for themselves the goal of contributing to the imperialists' victory over the workers and peasants of the USSR.

All this was proven and confirmed at the trial by the confessions of the accused in the presence of the representatives of the international press.

3. Along with this, Trotsky and his supporters are playing a role in wrecking *the workers' movement* in capitalist countries:

a) with their foul and dastardly campaign against the USSR, against the Bolshevik Party and its leaders, they are trying to undermine the trust of the international working class in the USSR and turn the masses toward the fierce enemies of the workers—the fascists;

b) they are the enemies of working-class unity, enemies of the rallying of the masses into a solid anti-fascist front. They disperse the workers' movement into small and minuscule groups trying to weaken the working class and facilitate the victory of fascism;

c) in Spain, their adventurist policies are pushing the revolutionary people toward defeat and are facilitating the intervention of German and Italian fascism;

d) wherever Trotskyism entered a mass workers' organization, it either attempted to destroy them or did destroy *them* from within (French Socialist Party,[23] Belgian "Young Guard," trade union organizations, as, for example, leftist teachers' union in France, etc.);

e) everywhere Trotskyists are mixed together with the police agents. This is the case in Greece, in China, where Trotskyists are serving the Japanese elements, in the countries of Latin America, etc. In Poland, the police reprint Trotsky's books in order to confuse the ranks of the workers' movement. In Norway, a few days before the trial, fascists staged a search of Trotsky's house in order to create the impression among the workers that Trotsky is the victim of fascist prosecution and thereby to help to keep him afloat politically.

It is no accident that the fascist press, "Volkischer Beobachter"[24] in particular, comes to Trotsky's defense, thus revealing once again his role as a zealous champion of the fascist plans;

f) having established, in the "underground," connections with the secret agents of different countries, Trotsky openly contributes to the newspaper of the American fascist newspaper trust "Hearst," which is the foulest disseminator of slander against the USSR and the workers' movement in the whole world;

g) Doriot, Trotsky's comrade in arms in France, is a rabid enemy of a united front with the Soviet Union. He fights for an alliance of Republican France with Germany. Since the dissolution of the Croix de Feu,[25] he is organizing a new fascist party and creating militant fascist organizations.

4. The struggle against Trotsky and Trotskyism, the vanguard of the counterrevolutionary bourgeoisie, which carries out the directives of fascism to penetrate the working masses, should be the cause not only of Communists but also Socialist parties, every worker organization, every democratic organization, every honest politician, struggling against fascism. The struggle against fascism [should read: Trotskyism] is an integral part of the anti-fascist struggle of the international proletariat.

"To defend base terrorists means to help fascism," wrote com. Dimitrov. He who directly or indirectly defends Trotsky and his terrorist gang in fact serves German fascism and contributes to the realization of its plans, helps Generals Franco and Mola and other rebel generals in Spain, [and] is an enemy of the Spanish workers and peasants fighting fascism.

5. Based on com. Dimitrov's article "Defending Base Terrorists Means Helping Fascism,"[26] it is essential to repulse the reactionary leaders of the Second International,[27] who, at the moment of the creation of the united front of the international proletariat around the heroic struggle of the Spanish people, are trying to undermine the unification movement with their defense of the terrorists.

Everywhere, Socialist workers who hate fascism and are ready to fight it approve of the verdict of the Soviet Union. The Spanish Socialist and Republican parties, which are carrying out an armed struggle against fascism, enthusiastically welcome the verdict [passed on] the Trotskyist-Zinovievite terrorist gang. The defense [of that gang] offered by the reactionary leaders of the Second International is a hostile demonstration against the USSR and international communism. When fascists in France attacked Blum,[28] Communists of all countries came forward in Blum's defense against the fascist scoundrels. The reactionary leaders of the Second International are siding with the fascist scoundrels who killed com. Kirov and are prepared to assassinate com. Stalin, [who are] against the land of the Soviets, against com. Stalin and Kirov. Let workers judge the behavior of Communists and reactionary Socialist leaders by their deeds.

6. The campaign against Trotsky has to parallel the mobilization of the sympathies of the working masses toward the Soviet Union, the VKP(b), and the leader of the international proletariat, com. Stalin, who, because of his selfless service to the international working class, is so hated by the world bourgeoisie and its fascist agents. The international working class has to form a wall of steel around the USSR, to shield its great leader from the vile intrigues of the class enemy, to surround their Stalin with an impenetrable wall of love and self-sacrifice.

7. All of the activities of the Trotskyist agents revealed at the trial point to the necessity of raising Bolshevik vigilance in every area of struggle.

Trotskyists, following their teacher's example, are seeking to penetrate the ranks of Communist Parties and carry out their provocations from within.

Bolshevik vigilance in the selection of cadres, in particular to the leading organs, has to nip in the bud any possibility for activities by the agents of Trotskyism and those assisting them.

Document 16 conveys not only the bill of particulars against Trotsky and his supporters but also the political logic that animated the anti-Trotskyist campaign, a logic that the August trial had validated. The most striking aspect of the document is the fear that permeates it—fear of fascism, fear of Trotskyism, fear of enemy agents within the USSR, and fear of war. These fears fueled the increasing suspicions, calls for vigilance, and widening repression.

Document 16 also sheds light on the self-destructive nature of the conspiratorial mindset. The goal of the Brussels congress was to generate broad-based support for the embattled Spanish Republic and for the anti-fascist Popular Front. Central to its success was winning the support of liberals, radicals, Social Democrats, and supporters of the Second International. However, the August trial had outraged many such potential supporters, who viewed it not as "an act in defense of democracy, peace, socialism, [and] revolution" but for what it was—political repression. Liberal, radical, and socialist newspapers condemned the trial. Indeed, one purpose of Document 16 was to provide Communists abroad with arguments and evidence to counter criticisms of the trial. In preparing the evidence, antipathy to Social Democrats came to the fore. Although the juxtaposition of Spanish socialists, who were committed to "an armed struggle against fascism," and the "reactionary leaders" of the Second International (as opposed to its rank-and-file members) sought, however lamely, to maintain the anti-fascist alliance, the description of the leaders of the Second International differs little from the earlier "social fascist" formulation. Such political reversion served to erode the Popular Front and, as that process accelerated, to reinforce Moscow's sense of isolation.

Nor was this formulation an aberration. The ECCI Secretariat sent to the leaders of the French, English, U.S., Dutch, Swiss, Norwegian, Swedish, and Belgian parties an encoded telegram stating that the "campaign surrounding the trial of the Trotskyist-Zinovievite terrorist band is developing weakly . . . international reaction has raised a furious anti-Soviet howl. At anti-Soviet demonstrations, leaders of the Second International give speeches" condemning the trial and the USSR.[29] Dimitrov made similar claims in his article entitled "Defending Base Terrorists Means Helping Fascism," published in the journal *Communist International*.[30] The man who during the 1933 Leipzig trial had learned how prosecutors can distort and falsify evidence and who apparently harbored doubts about the trial,[31] now proclaimed the clarity of the "documents, facts, real proof" presented at the August trial. Dimitrov argued that because the defendants had the right to defend themselves, their confessions stood as proof of their guilt. He went on to vilify those Social Democratic leaders of the Socialist Workers International and the International Association of Trade Unions who had sent a telegram to the Soviet government protesting the August trial. Such rhetoric and accusations alienated Social Democrats and other non-Communists and weakened Popular Front coalitions in various countries. By defending the legitimacy of the August trial, Dimitrov and the ECCI undermined the policy deemed essential to the defeat of fascism and the defense of the USSR.

On 23 August, the day before the August trial ended, the Cadres Department sent a report to Dimitrov on the results to date of the verification of fraternal party members and émigrés living in the USSR. According to the report, "The Cadres Department has sent to the NKVD material on three thousand people suspected as spies, provocateurs, wreckers, etc. The fact is that the Cadres Department has conducted much work during the verification of party documents to unmask significant numbers of enemies who penetrated the VKP(b). It is also a fact that a whole series of outstanding cases concerning . . . provocateurs and alien anti-party elements in the Polish, Romanian, Hungarian, and other parties were supplied properly and quickly to the Cadres Department. In the Central Committees of a series of parties, with the help of the Cadres Department, alien elements and agents of the class enemy were exposed."[32] Several aspects of this report are striking. The first is the Cadres Department had sent materials on three thousand people to the NKVD. In this way, the NKVD files mushroomed. Among the three thousand were members of the Central Committees of a "series of parties." Their inclusion among the three thousand put fraternal parties, especially the Polish, Hungarian, and Romanian parties, and their members living in the USSR at increased risk. What kind of help the Cadres Department offered the unnamed fraternal parties is unclear, but no one could accuse it of lacking vigilance. Nor is it clear who supplied the information on the alleged provocateurs and alien anti-party elements. The language of the report suggests that many of the names on the list were VKP members; however, it implies that all were foreign-born. Whether or not this was the case is unclear, but there seems little doubt that foreign-born comrades made up the preponderance of the three thousand. The report provided evidence that transformed émigrés, especially those from neighboring states, into a threatening Other.

At a 29 August Cadres Department meeting, Chernomordik told about the report, then ordered the staff "to prepare old lists of Trotskyists and suspicious people in emigration" in the USSR.[33] Six days later he sent a list to the ECCI Secretariat: **Document 17**, a list of "Trotskyists and other hostile elements in the émigré community of the German CP." He undoubtedly also sent a copy to the NKVD and the ORPO. Across Chernomordik's cover letter, Dimitrov wrote "carry out and report on the results of the verification of the German émigrés." Echoing a theme expressed earlier by others, Chernomordik asserted that "among the German émigrés in the USSR there are people who were known in the CPG as active Trotskyists and factionalists before their arrival in the USSR." The material in the document represented "only the most typical cases" and announced that "a much larger number" of "hostile elements" had "already been revealed." Lists such as these constituted "proof" of the 1934 allegation by Krajewski (Chernomordik's coworker) that secret agents had penetrated the USSR "under the guise of émigrés." Document 17 reproduces portions of this lengthy document, the value of which rests in which types of evidence are presented and how Chernomordik interpreted that evidence.

In the course of two weeks, Cadres Department officials produced "evidence" that the two perceived threats to the USSR, VKP, and Comintern—foreign-born "spies, wreckers, [and] provocateurs," and "Trotskyists and factionalists"—were very real and very numerous.

Document 17

Cadres Department memorandum "On Trotskyists and other hostile elements in the émigré community of the German CP," 4 September 1936. RGASPI, f. 495, op. 74, d. 124, ll. 11–31. Original in Russian. Typewritten with Dimitrov's handwritten comments and underlines.

[. . .]
4 September 1936.

Top secret.

1936
To c. Sergeyev
Carry out and report
on the results of the verification of
the German émigrés.

9. 36. GD [Georgi Dimitrov][34]

> To: <u>Com. Dimitrov.</u>
> <u>Com. Manuilsky.</u>
> <u>Com. Moskvin.</u>

The Cadres Department is sending to you a memorandum, "On Trotskyists and other hostile elements in the émigré community of the German CP."

We here mention only the most typical cases. Actually, the work on exposure is in progress, and a much larger number of these kinds of elements has already been revealed.

> ***Chernomordik***
> Chernomordik.

[. . .]
2 September 1936.

Top secret.

MEMORANDUM

ON TROTSKYISTS AND OTHER HOSTILE ELEMENTS IN THE ÉMIGRÉ
COMMUNITY OF THE GERMAN CP

Among the German émigrés in the USSR there are people who were known in the CPG as active <u>Trotskyists and factionalists</u> before their arrival in the USSR:

1. <u>SOLOMON MUSCHINSKI</u> (STSALMOSH)[35]—a member of the CPG from 1921, an active <u>collaborator of Ruth Fischer-Maslow</u>'s, a member of the Korsch opposition;[36] throughout his party membership, maintained close ties with [those] expelled from the party as ultra-Leftists and Trotskyists. As early as 1931, there was a rumor in the party that his brother was a Polish okhranka agent and that he, together with his brother, was trading cocaine in Khemnits, etc. According to the German section, he was already trying to get some party work assigned to him, but was denied it, under different pretexts, owing to his lack of credibility.

After the arrest of Berman-Yurin, his wife, Sonja Fichmann, told Koska (the CPG member) that at the time of Koska's visit to Berman-Yurin's apartment, the latter was talking in Russian over the telephone with Muschinski (Stsalmosh). This fact is evidence of Muschinski's connection with Berman-Yurin.

Muschinski came to the USSR in 1931 via the trade delegation with which he had worked in Berlin. <u>Expelled from the VKP</u>(b). He asked Koska for a recommendation, but he refused.

<u>On 26 April 1936 the German representative sent to the Party Control Commission a positive recommendation [of Muschinski] as a CPG member</u>, alluding to the positive recommendation of [his] party cell. His place of work is unknown; recently he lived in the Mirovoy Oktiabr apartment cooperative.

2. <u>RUNDOLF GERTSEL</u>[37]—a member of the CPG from 1919; before that a member of the PPS [Polish Socialist Party] and the German SD [party]. Before

1933, [he] was an active Brandlerian,[38] [a fact] that he had concealed in his autobiography. [He] came to the USSR in 1934 from Paris, without party consent. His [home] address and place of work are not known.

3. HERBERT ENGELHARDT (WILHELM REISS)—a member of the CPG from 1924. Known as an active fractionalist and a member of the ultra-Leftist group in Saxony. In 1927–28, [he was] a member of the Wedding opposition.[39] Recommended to the party by Renner, who was expelled for Trotskyism. In 1931, [he] came to the USSR, [after] being supposedly persecuted for stealing arms, but he was not given political émigré status. [He] works in a plant in Kolpino, Leningrad region.

4. NOAH BOROWSKI—a member of the CPG from 1919. Worked in Khemnits-Leipzig. Expelled from the party in 1929 as an active member of the Brandler group; worked on the Brandlerian newspaper "The Workers' Politics." Before his arrival in the USSR (i.e., before 1931), he remained closely connected with the Brandler group. Readmitted into the CPG in 1933. While working in and translating for the Foreign Workers' Publishing House in December 1934, he tried to integrate anti-party ideas into Popov's book "History of the VKP(b)," omitting those parts [of the book] that described Kamenev's behavior during the trial of the Duma faction, his strikebreaking in October, etc. His last place of work is unknown; his wife is still working in Moscow for the "Deutsche Zentralzeitung."[40]

5. LEW SÜSSKIND—a writer, he came to the USSR from Copenhagen in 1934. It is known that after his arrest in the winter of 1933, he passed on to the Gestapo the addresses of Communists, and after his release, he publicly declared that Communists were not tortured. After his release, he visited one of the leaders of the storm troopers and gave him presents. In an article in an American newspaper, [he] described the revolutionary activities of a certain Deivits. [He] had connections with a certain Moishe Livshits, who had a reputation as a provocateur and who played a suspicious role in connection with the USSR. It is known that Süsskind gave Trotskyist speeches in the Berlin Jewish Club [and] received and distributed Trotskyist literature in Dannemark [Denmark]. After Süsskind's departure from Germany, a group of German political émigrés to which he belonged was expelled from the party for Trotskyist activity.

   After his departure from Germany, he went legally [i.e., with his own passport] from Copenhagen to Paris and back via Germany. Currently [he lives] in Minsk.

6. PETTER, ERWIN—a member of the CPG from 1927 to 1928, expelled from the CPG as a Trotskyist. He took part in the attack on Wilhelm Pieck during his speech in Ratenau. Despite his continual Trotskyist activity in the CPG and despite the fact that the CC CPG in its letter of 10 January 1930 refused to give Petter a recommendation to the VKP(b), he joined the party, evidently while he was working at the Mostremass plant[41] in Moscow. [He was also] sent to the University of the Peoples of the West, from which he graduated in 1934.

The question of his attack on c. Pieck was raised during the purge in the university. However, in view of c. Pieck's statement that no importance should be attached to it, the German section did not discuss this question. Recently [Erwin] worked in Prokopievsk in the Kuzbass as an instructor among foreign workers. In October 1934 an evaluation of Petter corresponding [to the above] was given in response to the inquiry from the appropriate organizations. [. . .]

8. ERNST HESS (LEO ROTH)—a member of the YCL [Young Communist League] of Germany, expelled from the YCL in 1926 for Trotskyism. Between 1926 and 1928, [he] was one of the leaders of the Korsch opposition, after the Pappelplatz group split from the German YCL. Admitted to the CPG in 1929; in 1930, he began to work in its underground apparatus and, after that, in the CC CPG.

[He] came to the USSR in November 1935 on the order of the CPG (representative) to work in the apparatus. HESS is married to the daughter of Von Hammerstein, a colonel-general of the German Reichswehr. He receives mail from abroad at the address of Nati Steinberg, with whom he maintains close relations. [. . .]

10. OTTO KNOBEL (OTTO BRANT)—a former worker of the YCL of Germany who worked in the International Publishing House for Youth in Germany and who, in 1933, emigrated to Paris without party consent. [He] was not granted political émigré status, returned to Germany, and then emigrated again. In Paris, [he] was involved with the Trotskyists. [He] moved to Copenhagen to work, where he was not connected to the party and did not establish connections with the émigré community. In Copenhagen, [he] worked in the publishing house of Wilhelm Reich, who had been expelled from the CPG for Trotskyism. According to him, he broke with Reich over personal differences. However, according to some party comrades, he went to Berlin with Reich's consent and, a month later, in late 1935, came to the USSR via Intourist without connections and without party permission. He was so close to Reich that he read [Reich's] letters to Trotsky and even mailed them himself.

In April 1936, the Cadres Department reported Knobel's past to the responsible organs. His last address [was] Hotel Novomoskovskaia.

11. LADISLAUS STERN (PAUL STEIN)—a member of the CP Hungary from 1918–21, CP Austria from 1922–29, CP Germany from November 1929. From 1924, he revealed himself as an active Trotskyist. At the party meeting in 1927, he protested the expulsion of Trotsky. In 1928–29, he worked with the Trotskyist group of Iakov Frank, Iza Strasser, Raisa Adler. At party meetings, he spoke openly as a Trotskyist, defended the theory of permanent revolution, and stood by the platform of the Russian opposition. In that period, he personally sent a package of books to Trotsky. In June 1929, expelled from the CP Austria for Trotskyism. Deported from Vienna in June 1929. In August 1929, after making an oral declaration recognizing his mistakes to the Berlin district committee and appealing to the CC CPG for reinstatement to the party,

he was admitted to the CPG in November 1929 with the agreement of the CC CP Austria. According to the German section, nothing "reprehensible could be attributed to him during the period of 1929–1931 (in Berlin)."

From May to August 1931, while doing underground work in Hungary, [he] was reprimanded for violating the rules of security.

[He] has been living in the USSR since January 1932, because he was prohibited from staying in Germany. [He] arrived with the permission of the CPG and CP Hungary. [He] works in the "Deutsche Zentralzeitung" in Moscow.

12. SOBOLEVIC A. (Abrascha, SENIN)—according to his own words, a member of the YCL of Lithuania from early 1921; however, according to [his written] statement of 18 June 1931, from 1920–21. According to some sources, he conducted disorganizing work in the YCL of Lithuania and had a reputation as "a disorganizer with adventurist propensities." A CPG member from 1924. He claims that his Trotskyist activities started in 1929, but according to our sources, he joined the Trotskyists much earlier and in 1929 was expelled from the CPG as a Trotskyist. In 1927, Sobolevic traveled from Germany to the USSR, probably to establish contacts with the Russian Trotskyists. In 1928, he and the Trotskyist Frank from Vienna (originally also from Lithuania) offered their services to the CP Lithuania, but at that time Sobolevic's friend Glavatsky was expelled from the CP Lithuania.

Frank and Sobolevic protested against this expulsion, and it turned out that in 1928, Sobolevic had already traveled to Lithuania to contact Lithuanian Trotskyists. Sobolevic contributed to Trotskyist newspapers in Germany and France, traveled to Turkey to see Trotsky, and returned to Germany, where he organized Trotskyist groups in several cities, including Leipzig. Once again he went to the USSR, via Inturist, after which he published a series of articles hostile to the USSR in a Trotskyist newspaper. His wife, who worked for Inturist, helped him to leave the USSR for abroad.

In 1932, Sobolevic and his brother (Ruvim Sobolevic, Roman Vell) published an article against Trotsky in the Trotskyist press and after that tried again to join the party. In 1932, Sobolevic came to the USSR, joined the VKP(b) (dating his party membership back to 1931), and worked as an editor of "Das Neue Dorf" in Kharkov.

In April 1934, the Cadres Department sent c. Shkiriatov a report about Sobolevic's Trotskyist activities and comments by c. Angaretis about the incorrect information in Sobolevic's autobiography. At the same time, the Cadres Department sent all of the necessary information on Sobolevic to the responsible organs. After December 1935, these organs [made] new inquiries. The Cadres Department sent to the responsible organs a statement by Ludwig Brucker unmasking Sobolevic as an agent of Trotsky. It mentions, among other things, that according to Sobolevic, "The old man (Trotsky) continues to trust him in the same old way."

The fate of Sobolevic, who was expelled from the party in February 1936 in Kharkov, is unknown to us. [. . .]

14. PAUL WEISS—a member of the CPG from 1924 to 1930. The party was aware of his rightist position in the past, after the Sixth [Comintern] Congress. On 15 May 1930, WEISS arrived with the approval of the CC CPG and was immediately sent to the Philosophy Department in the [Institute of Red] Professors with the approval of D. Riazanov, even though he is a musician and artist by training. In 1930, he was admitted to the VKP(b). Weiss was expelled from the party for Trotskyism in 1935. He and his wife, Vera Emerikovna Weiss, a VKP(b) candidate member from 1931, remained Czech citizens without party permission. His wife worked as a party cell technical secretary. All the time they were both connected to the Czech consul in Moscow. It also turned out that Weiss later worked in the music section of Gosizdat [State Publishing House]. In 1934, the Kun commission[42] discussed the question of Weiss's trip abroad (on behalf of Gosizdat), but that trip was canceled.

What happened to him later, we do not know. His address is 54 Bolshaia Pirogovskaia, apt. 230.

15. ELZHERS, ALBERT (LEO BERMAN)—Berman-Yurin's brother, a member of Poalei Zion from 1917–1928, a member of the CPG from 1927. Came to the USSR in April 1933 with a trade delegation. Connected to Fritz David and Berman-Yurin. In the past, [he] worked as an instructor of mass cultural work in the VTsSPS [All-Union Central Council of Trade Unions]; [he] was fired from there in August 1933. His old address (1933) is 9 Chernigovsky pereulok, apt. 13.

16. NATHAN NEIMAN—a member of the CPG from 1923. [He] came to the USSR in December 1934 and was denied émigré status. In his recommendation he refers to Fritz David, with whom he could not have had any party connection. He entered the USSR via the German section thanks to Fritz David. [He] worked in the OGIZ [Association of State Publishing Houses for Books and Periodicals] scientific research institute, 28 Varlovaia [Street].

17. HOFFMAN, INGA—the wife of N. Lurye, a member of the CPG from 1926. [She] came to the USSR in 1932 with her husband N. Lurye—Hans Wolf. Regarding her work in the CPG, the German section knows only that she held a series of party duties of a technical character. She has a recommendation to the VKP(b) from Leo Berman (Elzhers, Albert).

18. SONJA FICHMANN—Berman-Yurin's wife, a member of the CP Romania from 1919–23, a member of the CPG from 1923. [She] came to the USSR in 1923 on a trade delegation trip. The German section characterizes her as an active party worker.

The Cadres Department knows the following facts: when in Berlin, Fichmann vigorously opposed the expulsion of a Trotskyist named Rosov from the party.

One Arnold Gubb, a former CPG member who was suspected of provocation and later found his way to the storm troopers, also enjoyed Fichmann's protection.

Fichmann, together with Berman-Yurin, tried persistently to talk c. Goldzweig, who now works in the IMEL [Institute of Marx, Engels, and Lenin],[43] out of going to the USSR, by making arguments such as: "Where are you going? It is so bad there." When she worked at the [newspaper] "Za industrializatsiiu,"[44] Fichmann had access to materials from military factories and reportedly visited those factories more than once.

According to Golda Frölich, a VKP(b) member, Fichmann offered a room to Freilich's sister, in which, it turned out, [the sister] lived with [a person] exiled for Trotskyism for three years. Currently, CPG member Vinter and her husband, the recently arrested HARTMANN, live in this room. Address: 29 Usachiovka, korpus 7, apt. 366.

19. HAUSCHILD, ROBERT (HAUS, RUDOLF)[45]—a member of the CPG from 1918. Between 1924 and 1934, he was loosely connected to the party organization and party work. Maintained close connections with Trotskyists and Brandlerians. In 1928, published a military-political magazine "Die Gruhne Front." Despite a CC CPG decision, he tried to maintain the newspaper by financing it with the help of German and foreign Brandlerians. From 1928–29, he was known in the CPG as a conciliator.

According to c. Ercoli's secretary, c. Petterman, in 1930, Hauschild expressed in conversations "doubts about the possibility of building socialism in one country," talked "about the possibility of a Thermidor as a result of degeneration of the proletarian dictatorship," "about the likely necessity to 'overcome' the CPG and the Comintern, which had proved to be incapable of moving the revolution forward." "Seriously doubted the importance and the role of Stalin, unscrupulously discredited Ernst Thälmann, as well as the other comrades from the party leadership." Com. Petterman claims that Hauschild maintained permanent contact with various oppositional elements in and around the party, in particular with Walter Frölich, Kurt Heinrich (Süsskind), Robert (Volk, Karl), Frenzel, Greve, Herbert,[46] Bringdolg (Switzerland). During his trip to France, he tried to talk with Souvarine. Came to the USSR in 1932, with the permission of the CC CPG. [Currently he] works for "Izvestiia."

In August 1934, in response to an inquiry from the responsible organs, the German section reported that "Hauschild has been a CPG member from 1919, a writer, and currently works in the Fourth Department." In October 1935, the same [information], as well as [information] that, from 1929–31, he joined the conciliators, was given in response to a second inquiry. In February 1936, the following reference was given: "Already during the world war, he belonged to the Socialist youth and worked in close contact with comrades from the Spartacist Union. During the world war, [he] was imprisoned several times for his political beliefs and work. After 1919, [he] belonged to the CPG. After the Sixth [Comintern] Congress, between 1928 and 1930, he belonged to the conciliators. For about eight years [he] has specialized in military issues."

20. HAUSCHILD, HILDE (LOEWEN)—a member of the CPG from 1922. In

1931, an instructor in the eastern <u>subdistrict committee in Berlin</u>; she worked for the "Die Gruhne Front" magazine published by her husband. At one time, the CC CPG received a statement by Eigin, c. Schoenhaar's technical secretary, that she "works for the class enemy." In 1930, <u>she tried to spy</u> on some party workers in the interests of her husband's magazine (connections to the police, etc.). Between 1928 and 1932, [she] disagreed with party policy and belonged to the conciliators. In 1933 (already in the USSR), [she] was reprimanded by the ICC <u>for blabbing about secret addresses</u>.

In 1934, the German section responded to an inquiry from the responsible organs that Hilde Hauschild was a CPG member from 1922, had come to the USSR with CC CPG permission, and was working as an <u>editor at the International Radio</u>. In February 1936, it repeated the same information and added that she was an active CPG worker and had belonged to the conciliators from 1928 to 1930.

21. <u>PAUL HEINZ (Rakow's brother)</u>—a member of the CPG, he maintains continual ties with his brother. Came [to the USSR] <u>via the OMS</u>, recently worked as an instructor among foreign workers in the Postyshev (formerly Grishino, mine no. 1). The CPG delegation states that according to c. Stucke (Tselner), who went there to conduct propaganda work, Paul Heinz <u>has two passports—German and British—and boasts of his former</u> underground work and his <u>current ties to the NKVD</u>. "At a study group [he] asked a question through his wife: What mistakes did Thälmann commit in 1932?"

22. <u>HEINZ MÖLLER (ASIATICUS)</u>—[He] came [to the USSR] with a Polish passport under the name of Schiff. [He] came in order to file an appeal. [He] had been [in the USSR] with the same objective in 1927. [He] is a CPG member and was a VKP(b) member, but was expelled in 1927 for his Trotskyist position on the Chinese question. <u>An active Brandlerian</u>. After expulsion from the party, [he] went to China and worked <u>in Shanghai</u> as a journalist. According to the Cadres Department (of the Chinese section), [he] went to China to work in the newspaper of a certain Isaacs, who is a direct agent of Trotsky in China (and went <u>to see Trotsky in Norway in 1935</u>). Isaacs's newspaper, "<u>China Forum</u>," was published in Shanghai for some time as an American-Chinese newspaper, and Asiaticus worked there. But this newspaper was closed because the <u>CC CP China publicly dissociated itself from this newspaper</u>.

<u>Asiaticus escaped to Norway with party money</u>. In his statement asking to be readmitted to the party, [he] lists all the newspapers for which he had worked, but fails to mention the abovementioned facts. The Chinese comrades claim that Asiaticus has a <u>reputation as a police agent</u>. The fact that, in his statement, he refers to the connection to and the support of the Communist organization in China speaks, according to the Chinese comrades, against him, because it is known that in Shanghai there is only a police agency disguised as a Communist organization. [He] <u>works as a full-time correspondent of "Izvestiia" and TASS</u>.

The Cadres Department has taken appropriate measures. [. . .]

26. ILIAS SARCHIN (WALTER BERGER)—Berman-Yurin's closest friend. According to Karl Höflich, [he] belonged to Berman's group in Germany, after which, in 1931, [he] was sent to [work in] Lesoexport [the State Timber Export Company] in Leningrad. In 1932, he traveled to Berlin.

27. WILLI RABE (REAL NAME, PAWERA)—a worker; a member of the CPG from 1926. From 1930, he worked in the CPG apparatus. From 1930 until the end of 1933, an active member of the conciliators' faction, received financial support from them, [and] attended all the faction's meetings. Being a CC courier, [he] surveyed and passed over to the conciliators all of the CC's mail regarding the conciliators. [He] came to the USSR in 1933, studied in the MLSh. [He] concealed from the party his work on behalf of the conciliators and was unmasked in 1934.

[He] had connections with Fritz David from trade union work in Germany and continued to maintain these connections in Moscow. Referred to Fritz David's recommendation and regularly read the fascist press in his home. Since then, he has not provided the German representative with any explanations of his relations with Fritz David. [He] works at the Sacco and Vanzetti factory in Moscow.

28. NEWIJASHEVSKI, FAIBISH (PAUL WEIZENFELD)[47]—originally from Gorodnia, Ukraine. From 1917 to 1920, a member of the Poalei Zion. In 1920–21, was in emigration in Lithuania, [and stayed] in Memel until 1923. A member of the CPG after 1926. According to his statement, he was exiled to the USSR in April 1933 as a Soviet citizen. Com. Angaretis claims that Weizenfeld stayed in Lithuania as a White émigré. Recommended by Fritz David, Leo Berman (a brother of Berman-Yurin), Alexander Emel [Lurye], Brucker (who provided this information), Osher Tikushinski.

29. EMIL POTRATZ (HERBERT KRAMER)—a member of the CPG from 1920. Came to the USSR as an émigré in June 1933. He recommended Alfred Kuhnt, known from the trial of the Trotskyist-Zinovievite gang.

Here in the USSR, Potratz, who used to be an active CPG worker, has an awful reputation (organization of drinking bouts, connections with the worst elements among the foreigners). His wife writes to Germany that there is hunger here and each time repeats that she wants to go back. All this time Potratz has been seeking Soviet citizenship. He works in a foreign bureau of the Novokramatorsky machine-building plant in Donbas.

30. FRITZ PALENSCHAT—a member of the German YCL from 1922, a member of the CPG from 1928. In 1928 and 1930, worked in the underground organizations (in the storm troopers and in the Reichswehr). Came to the USSR in February 1934, recommended by Ernst Mansfeld, who was arrested in the USSR. In conversations, [he] advocates the idea of individual terror. His wife frequently travels to Germany. [He] works at the Stalin plant in Leningrad [and] lives at: Kamenostroevskii, 49 Glavnaia alleia, apt. 16.

31. HARTMANN ("Pravda"'s correspondent in Berlin)—according to Rich-

ard Paschke, a CPG member working for "Pravda" in Berlin, [Hartmann] had much closer connections with David than were necessary for his work. Allegedly, "Pravda" occupied his Berlin apartment, where David used to live. Hartmann also met with Wollenberg, a Trotskyist expelled from the party, who is now in Prague conducting active counterrevolutionary work. Moreover, he had connections with Magyar during Magyar's stay in Berlin. He was visited twice by Berman-Yurin. Hartmann is currently in Moscow, [living] in the Hotel Savoy, and works for TASS.

32. GINZBURG, MEER (KARSKI, PAUL)—a member of the CPG from 1928. Came to the USSR in 1931 with the trade delegation and was sent to work in the Scientific Research Institute of the Monopoly of Foreign Trade. On the recommendation of the CC CPG, [he] was transferred to the VKP(b) in 1931. According to recently received information [and] according to the statement of CPG member Johanna Zorn, [he] was the closest friend of Natan Lurye and visited N. Lurye in Cheliabinsk.

According to the statement of the party committee of the Institute of Foreign Trade, [he] was expelled from the party as an alien element during the verification of party documents in 1936. Based on the information provided by the German section, the Cadres Department responded to an 8 May 1934 inquiry from the responsible organs [by saying] that he was an active party member and conducted a struggle against the Trotskyists and Brandlerians. The German section gave [him] a reference not only on 22 December 1931 but also on 28 January 1936, based on the reference of the party cell of the trade delegation, [but] without taking pains to verify that information.

The characteristics of the political émigrés who are CPG members [and] who have been arrested by the NKVD makes evident the level of [enemy] saturation of German emigration in the [Soviet] Union. We already know about fifty people [who have been] arrested.

Among those arrested are Willi Leow, a former CC CPG member and party member from 1920; a number of CPG members who had been in the party for 17–15 [sic] years . . . ; ten people who have been in the party from 1919–1922; twelve people—from 1923 to 1929, etc.

But most important is that many of them had been recommended for jobs by the German section as political émigrés, as party members, and most of them were in good repute within the section until the very last moment, until their arrest.

Moreover, the Cadres Department continues to receive information about a whole series of individuals among the German political émigrés [who are] suspicious, maintain connections with those arrested [or] put on trial, suspected of serving in the Gestapo, suspected of provocation, etc. Most of these people are currently in the USSR. [. . .]

Given that it is unacceptable to delay reporting on these people until the final investigation of their fates or even ascertaining their current location (unknown, in some cases, even to the German section), we consider it necessary, besides being a matter of urgent police investigation, to draw certain conclusions on the basis of these materials.

As the above facts demonstrate, the absolute majority of the aforementioned CP members were Trotskyists and Brandlerians in the past, who were expelled from the party and retained close contacts with anti-party elements and with the people who conducted anti-party work in the USSR. They came to the Soviet Union in 1931–1934, years of fascist growth, the activization of Trotskyism and its conversion into a direct agency of fascism. Indeed, in 1930, three people came, in 1932—eleven people, in 1933—eleven people, in 1934—thirteen people, in 1935—five people.

Already now, on the basis of the existing materials, it is possible to trace certain connections between these people and known groups in our country.[48]

Indeed, there is a connection between Fritz David and Berman-Yurin and [all the following:] Leo Berman (Berman-Yurin's brother), Inga Hoffman (Nathan Lurye's wife), Solomon Muschinski, who was connected to Berman-Yurin in Moscow, Nathan Neiman, whose arrival in the USSR was made possible with the assistance of Fritz David via the German section, Sonja Fichmann—Berman-Yurin's wife, Sara David, Ilias Sarchin—Berman-Yurin's closest friend, Willi Rabe, who came [to the USSR] in 1933 and maintained permanent relations with Fritz David, Newijashevski (Paul Weizenfeld), who has a recommendation from Fritz David, Leo Berman, and Emel [Lurye].

On the other hand, Emel Potratz, who came in June 1933, recommended Alfred Kuhnt, who used to bring Trotsky's letters to Moscow. Alfred Kuhnt himself, a CPG member from 1923–27, expelled in 1927 for participating in the activities of the Trotskyist center and again admitted to the CPG in 1929, came to the USSR in 1932 as an émigré. He claimed that he had been charged with killing one Nazi, presumably in an armed clash. However, it was not a clash, but a drinking bout.

A group of émigrés from Poland and Lithuania, who came from different places and under different pretexts to join the German party and, through it, came to the USSR as political émigrés, merit attention. Indeed, Leo Berman, the Poalei Zion member between 1917 and 1926, is from Minsk; Hoffman, Inga, is from Kovno; Nathan Neiman is from Warsaw; Noah Borowski is from Peski; Rundolf Gertsel, the PPS [Polish Socialist Party] member between 1912–1925, is from Tsarnov; Sobolevic A. is from Lithuania; Lew Süsskind is from Poland; Solomon Muschinski is from Poland; Newijashevski (Paul Weizenfeld), a member of the Poalei Zion from 1917 to 1920, is a Lithuanian émigré. Baer Sima is from Vilno. Skrobic, Samuel, a member of the Bund from 1912 to 1932, is from Poland. Some of these people are connected to each other, as shown above.

A significant number of these people have settled in Moscow and work in the press and publishing: Hauschild, Robert, for the newspaper "Izvestiia"; Weiss, Paul, in the Gosizdat's Music Section; Sobolevic, editor of "Das Neue

Dorf" newspaper. Lew Süsskind is a writer, Noah Borowski [works] in the Foreign Workers' Publishing House, his wife [works] for the "Deutsche Zentralzeitung"; Paul Stein [works] for the "Deutsche Zentralzeitung"; Sonja Fichmann [works] for the newspaper "Za industrializatsiiu"; Hauschild, Hilde, is an editor on the International Radio; Nathan Neiman is in the OGIZ Scientific Research Institute; Heinz Möller (Asiaticus) works, according to his statement, as a full-time TASS and "Izvestiia" correspondent; Hartmann works for TASS.

Another portion [of them] work <u>in factories</u>: Herbert Engelhardt—in a plant in Kolpino, Leningrad district; Petter Erwin, in Prokopievsk, Kuzbass; Paul Heinz, in the Donbass, in the Grishino mine; Schweiger, in the Kharkov tractor plant; Fritz Palentschat, in the Stalin plant in Leningrad; Georg Blumfeldt, in Metrostroy, etc.

The <u>German delegation</u> has not applied itself to verifying those coming to the USSR, to selecting them carefully, and has failed to organize the investigation into cases of clearly suspicious elements. In a number of cases, it permitted <u>direct agents of Trotsky and the Gestapo</u>, agents provocateurs, and spies <u>to enter the USSR</u>, often even failing to warn the Comintern and other organizations and showing no further interest in them.

It was with the explicit consent of the German section that Hoffman, Inga; Nathan Neiman; Noah Borowski; Steinberger, Nati; Ernst Hess (who even came at the CPG's invitation); Paul Weiss; Ladislaus Stern; Hauschild, Robert; and Hauschild, Hilde, came to the USSR, despite the fact that the CPG was aware of the Trotskyist past of these people, most of whom had been expelled from the party.

The German delegation failed to warn about the arrival direct from Copenhagen of such people as <u>Otto Knobel</u> and <u>Lew Süsskind</u>. The [German] section learned about the open, anti-Soviet activities of a number of arrested and suspicious people, those who had connections with the German embassy, agents provocateurs, and criminal elements only after they had been exposed without the participation of the section.

Taking into consideration the large number of German political émigrés in the USSR, their saturation [with enemies], as well as the substantial ignorance of the German section and its poor organization of the verification of political émigrés, it is essential:

1. To oblige members of the CC CPG (c.c. Pieck, Florin, Weber) to personally conduct, within a month, the verification of all German political émigrés and to provide, under c. Pieck's personal supervision, a report on each of them.

2. To investigate without delay all existing materials on German political émigrés.

To present to the commission on the political émigrés the question of each of the people mentioned here in order to decide on their future fate.

CADRES DEPARTMENT.

Several aspects of the document deserve note. One is that the Cadres Department had apparently known about the previous factional activities and associations of most, if not all, of the people named. Given that German émigrés had already been arrested and given, too, the belief that the "level of [enemy] saturation" among German émigrés was believed to be substantial, why had it waited so long to alert the Secretariat of these "Trotskyists and other hostile elements"? The most plausible answer is that the August show trial spurred the Cadres Department into reexamining its files with a more vigilant and suspicious eye than had heretofore seemed necessary. The trial had increased the political vulnerability of all party organizations, especially the Comintern. Heightened vigilance appeared the best guarantee of personal and institutional self-defense. But vigilance was a double-edged sword: The more "suspicious elements" Cadres Department officials discovered, the more they exposed their own organization to increased scrutiny. Chernomordik sought to deflect attention away from the department by highlighting the "substantial ignorance of the German section and its poor organization of the verification of political émigrés," a criticism for which he provides considerable evidence. Criticizing that section and denouncing German "Trotskyists" and émigrés may have seemed to make political sense at the time, but doing so increased NKVD suspicions of all émigrés and of the institution responsible for them—the Comintern. Dimitrov's order to "carry out and report on the results of the verification of the German émigrés" suggests that he appreciated the political danger.

Document 17 makes clear that double-dealers and those who hid their past behaviors were, as always, cause for serious concern. It also conveys graphically the logic of guilt by association that pervaded the mass repression. Several people warranted inclusion in the list for past associations or friendships with Fritz David, Berman-Yurin, or N. Lurye. Based on people's associations with these three men, Chernomordik constructed an alleged network of ten people whom he claimed posed a danger to the USSR. The memorandum also provided so-called evidence to substantiate suspicions of émigrés from Poland and Lithuania and the German CP's judgment about who to send to the USSR. Finally, the working assumption behind the document was portentous— namely, that not only Trotskyists but anyone who had at one time sided with any opposition or criticized the Comintern, CPG, VKP, or Stalin was worthy of suspicion.[49] Trotskyists were the major threat. Chernomordik's report provided "evidence" that there existed a Trotskyist network among German émigrés living in the USSR and that some of the émigrés had personal links to Trotsky. Such "evidence" lent credence to Yezhov's opinion that the Trotskyists had a center somewhere in the USSR.

It is worth pausing for a moment to consider what constituted "proof" that those listed in the memorandum were "Trotskyists" or "hostile elements." The range of evidence presented was quite wide. For example, some people were known former oppositionists, had entered the USSR illegally, or had been denied émigré status. But much of the "evidence" presented was of the sort common to denunciations. A common formulation was, "it is known that" so-and-so engaged in some nefarious political activity or had associations with suspicious people. The anonymous quality of the formulation suggests that Chernomordik may have culled the evidence from personal denunciations. Associations (familial, personal, or political) with convicted enemies or former oppositionists constituted another type of evidence. Indeed, associations provided the evidence that Chernomordik used to construct the networks that he presented late in the memo. Other "evidence" included rumor, secondhand information, denunciations, early release from prison, contacts with the embassy of one's native country, and correspondence from or to "suspicious" people abroad. The materials available do not permit us to track down the source of this alleged evidence, which the Cadres Department "continues to receive." Including the allegations in an official memorandum gave the evidence and accusations bureaucratic and political legitimacy—the aura of proof.[50]

More problematic for the historian is how to assess the allegations that some named in the memo had belonged to or were associated with Nazi storm troopers, active Trotskyist underground networks, or other groups. The available evidence is insufficient to dismiss the allegations out of hand, but the logic that led to the inclusion of others in the list suggests that skepticism is not unwarranted.

Document 17 was not the only list of suspicious elements among the German émigrés compiled after the August trial. There were, among others, a September 1936 list, "About bad elements among the CPG active in Moscow," and a January 1937 list of Gestapo agents and anti-Soviet and counterrevolutionary elements.[51] The German compilers of these lists, Albert Müller (aka George Bruckman) and Edna Mertens (Margarete Wilde), who worked in the Cadres Department, later perished in the repression. Nor were Germans singled out; other lists of people, grouped by nationality, were also compiled. Herein lay one of the most notable changes produced by the August 1936 trial: it transformed suspicions about certain émigrés into xenophobia. Prior to the trial, the implicit assumption had been that most émigrés were politically reliable, although some "enemies" had penetrated their ranks. The proliferation of lists by nationality compiled after the trial indicates that being a foreigner, especially from Germany or a border state, was sufficient to warrant suspicion. As suspicions mounted, more lists of "suspicious" émigrés were compiled and sent to the NKVD. The existence of the lists validated the earlier suspicions.

Document 18 underscores this point. It presents portions of a list of members of the party committee of the ECCI apparatus, "formerly in other parties, having Trotskyist and Rightist tendencies." Kotelnikov, secretary of the ECCI party committee, compiled the list based on a review of party cards.[52] His list highlights how a person's political past had become a key criterion by which to separate "real Bolsheviks" from an evolving Other. It is the logical culmination of the opinion held by some VKP leaders that party members who had once belonged to another party tended to join "counterrevolutionary groups."[53] Although the list consists only of VKP members who had previously belonged to other parties, almost two-thirds of them were émigrés. Since Communist Parties had not come into existence until after World War I, it is hardly surprising that many foreign-born members had formerly belonged to other parties. Kotelnikov seems to have ignored the restrictions imposed by history. The list reflects his conscious or unconscious anxieties about political émigrés within the party, anxieties that the list fueled.

Kotelnikov's list was not of people who had been "Trotskyists" or "Rightists" in the past but rather of those "having Trotskyist and Rightist tendencies." What constituted a tendency? Some, like Bortnowski, had simply had doubts about a policy, often many years earlier. Others had belonged to the ECCI party organization in 1923 and had voted for a resolution later deemed to be of a Trotskyist character. Still others had received party punishments for personal rather than political infractions. It appears that Kotelnikov's criteria were quite elastic. But inclusion in the list transformed "doubts" in the 1920s into oppositional "tendencies" in September 1936; in 1937–1938, the NKVD would transform those "tendencies" into "crimes." Given that many included on the list had never before exhibited "Trotskyist or Rightist tendencies," we can wonder at Kotelnikov's motives for including them. In essence, his list was a mass denunciation, presented in the guise of party vigilance and discipline. That Kotelnikov included not only workers in the ECCI apparatus but also its leaders demonstrates his vigilance. Among those included were ECCI members Walecki (a Pole), Béla Kun (a Hungarian),[54] and

Kuusinen (a Finn) and the heads of the Cadres Department (Krajewski and Chernomordik). It is impossible today to ascertain whether Kotelnikov included some on the list simply because he disliked them. But personal motives should not be ruled out.

Across the top of the first page of Document 18, Kotelnikov wrote: "(Sent to the NKVD leadership)." Whether he did so on 4 September 1936 is unclear. Kotelnikov probably also sent the list to ORPO, that is, to Yezhov's office in the Central Committee. Kotelnikov later recorded the fates of forty-five of the eighty-seven people named on the list. Next to the appropriate name he wrote in red pencil "arrested" (abbreviated either as "ar" or "arrest"). Next to other names he made various notations, such as "working in another organization," "working in the ICC," "working," "dead," or "abroad." There is no indication as to when he made these notations, although internal evidence suggests that he did so no earlier than mid-1938. Nor is it clear whether his notations reflect the fate of everyone on the list. The tragedy is that, based on Kotelnikov's evidence, few of those who were later arrested appear to have committed offenses more serious than losing a party card, receiving a reprimand, vacillating on an issue, or belonging to another party before a local Communist party existed. Indeed, given the NKVD's propensity in 1937–1938 to arrest people with oppositional pasts and suspected "tendencies," it is not clear why more of those on the list were not arrested.[55]

Document 18

List of VKP members "formerly in other parties, having Trotskyist and Rightist tendencies," sent by F. Kotelnikov to the NKVD, 4 September 1936. RGASPI, f. 546, op. 1, d. 376, ll. 30–36. Original in Russian. Typewritten with handwritten additions by Kotelnikov.

Secret.

3 copies
4 September 1936.

To the file (Sent to the NKVD leadership)[56]

LIST
of VKP(b) members formerly in other parties,
having Trotskyist and Rightist tendencies, as well as [those] having
received party reprimands. (The material comes from the new
[party] registration forms.)[57]

Arrest[ed] 1. ALEKSA-ANGARETIS, Zigmont Ivanovich

1) Belonged to the SDP [Social Democratic Party] of Lithuania from June 1906. After October 1906, belonged to the left wing of the SDP of Lithuania.

2) In 1918, he opposed the Communist Party on the question of the Brest peace and was close to the "Left" Communists. [. . .]

Arrest[ed] 3. BRUN, Stefania Stanislav[ovna] [Stefania Brunowa]

1) Belonged to the S.D. Party of the Kingdom of Poland and Lithuania between 1904 and 1910 in Warsaw. [She] left the party because of poor health.

2) [She] belonged to the former minority [group] in the Communist Party of Poland, which now, under the c. Lenski leadership, is heading the CP of Poland.

Arrest[ed] 4. BORTNOWSKI, Bronislaw Bronislawowich

—In 1918, [he] had doubts regarding the question of signing the Brest peace treaty, but [he] promptly overcame [them] and did not belong to the opposition. [. . .]

Ar[rested] 6. BRANN, Lotta

1) Belonged to the Zionist Union of Youth from 1920 to 1925 in Berlin.

2) Reprimanded for a lack of party vigilance and passivity in party life by the Frunzenskii RK [district party committee] in Moscow on 27 March 1936.

Ar[rested] 7. BALOD, Karl K.

—Voted for a resolution of a Trotskyist nature. In 1923, [he belonged to] the ECCI [party] cell [that passed the resolution]. [. . .]

Ar[rested] 10. WALECKI, M. G.

1) Belonged to the Polish Socialist Party between 1895 and 1905; belonged to the [PPS] Lewica party between 1905 and 1918.

2) In 1923, he was among the leadership of the Polish Communist Party. Took a position of actual support of the German Brandlerians and the Trotskyist opposition in the VKP(b), for which he was criticized, along with others, by a resolution of the Polish Commission of the Fifth Comintern Congress in 1924.

Ar[rested] 11. WHEELDON, W. M.

—Belonged to the Socialist Workers' Party of England between June 1919 and July 1920. Derby, England.

Work[s] *in anoth*[er] *org*[anization] 12. WENDT-STOIANOV, F. V.

—Belonged to the German SD Party between 1904 and 1914. Hamburg, Germany.[. . .]

Ar[rested] 14. GERISH, Grigory Moiseevich.

1) Belonged to the Socialist Party of the USA between 1915 and 1919. Philadelphia, USA.

2) In 1923, voted for a resolution of a Trotskyist nature in the ECCI [party] cell.

Works [in the] *ICC* 15. GENINA, Lucia Khristianovna

—Joined the VKP(b) in June 1919 in the party group of the Fifth Latvian Infantry Regiment. During the purge of 1921, she was demoted to candidate [party member] for political illiteracy by the purge commission of the Khamovnicheskii district. Moscow.[. . .]

Wor[king] 17. BLAGOEVA, S. D.

—Belonged to the Bulgarian Tesniak SD Party between 1915 and 1919.

Ar[rested] 18. GOLKE-Rozenfeld.

—Belonged to the SD Party of Germany between 1914 and 1916. Berlin and Danzig.

—Belonged to the Independent Socialist Party of Germany between 1916 and 1918. Berlin.

Died 19. GOLUBEV, V. N.

—Was admitted to the RKP(b) [Russian Communist Party (Bolshevik)] in 1920 by the part[y] commission of the 53rd Infantry Division. In 1922, his membership was automatically discontinued after his party card was stolen and his personal file lost.

Ar[rested] 20. GROSMAN, A. I.

—Belonged to the Polish Socialist Party (Lewica) between 1910 and 1918. [. . .]

Wor[king] 22. ZHEMAITIS, A. S.

—Between 1912 and 1919, he belonged to the Lithuanian Federation of the Socialist Party of America in Pittsburgh and Cleveland, USA.

Ar[rested] 23. ISKROV, P. Kh.

—Cooperated with the Left-sectarian group in the CC CP of Bulgaria in 1930–1934.

? 24. ITKINA, A. M.

1) [She] belonged to the interdistrict organization of the SD (Internationalist) from August 1916 to July 1917. Petrograd.

2) In 1923, at the Marxist school section, she abstained from voting for the resolution condemning Trotskyism.

Ar[rested] 25. KATZ, Aron

—Belonged to the Socialist Party of America between 1904 and 1919.

Ar[rested] 26. KRAJEWSKI, A. P.

—Between 1929 and 1930, he was in the Rightist group of the Polish Communist Party.

Wor[king] 27. KOZHARIN Ya. Ya.

—In December 1919, he was admitted to the party by the party organization of the Murmansk city Soviet RK and KD.[58] In December 1920, his membership was discontinued after the loss of [his] party documents during their transfer from Murmansk to Sevastopol. [. . .]

Ar[rested] 29. KRYMOV, A. G.

—Following the decision of the Chinese Communist Party, in 1925 he became a member of the Guomindang in Shanghai. [. . .]

Wor[king] 31. KUUSINEN, O. V.

—Between December 1904 and August 1918, he belonged to the SD Party of Finland.

Ar[rested] 32. BÉLA KUN M.

1) Between 1903 and 1916, he belonged to the SD Party of Hungary.

2) A Left Communist between January and May 1918, he did not understand Lenin's Brest tactics, and, being a Hungarian, he wanted the revolution to be brought to Hungary "on bayonets."

Ar[rested] 33. KAROLSKY, A. P.

—From 1912 to 1916, belonged to the Polish Social Democratic Party "Lewica."

? 34. LITVAKOV, I. I.

—Belonged to the party of *Zionists* Socialists between 1903 and 1906 in Russia. Between 1906 and 1911, in the Socialist Workers' Party of the USA in Philadelphia and New York. Belonged to the Industrial Workers of the World in 1911–1917. [. . .]

Ar[rested] 39. MERTENS, E. F.

—Between 1923 and 1925, she was active in the Ruth Fischer-Maslow faction. In June 1925, even before the open letter of the ECCI that exposed Ruth Fischer was published, she took a correct party position. In 1929, she was one of the leaders of the anti-party students' group in the International Leninist School.

Abr[oad] 40. MILLER, K. E.

—Between 1925 and 1929, he belonged to the Lovestone group in America.

Ar[rested] 41. MIRONOV, S. N.

—On the decision of the Frunzenskii district [party] committee in Moscow, he was expelled from the VKP(b) ranks for immoral behavior. The P[arty] C[ontrol] C[ommission] of the CC VKP(B) readmitted him to the VKP(b) on 26 May 1936.

Wor[king] 42. MOCHILIN, I. E.

—He was expelled for six months by the purge commission in September 1933 for forging an advance financial report for 89 rubles. The expulsion was approved by the CCC. He was readmitted [to the party] in November 1934 by the CCC VKP(b).

Wor[king] 43. MOREINS, F. F. [Franz Morriens][59]

—Belonged to the SD Party of Belgium between 1916 and 1919.

Wor[king] 44. MONAKHOV, F. I.

1) Belonged to the SR Party in March–May 1917. Petrograd.

2) In 1923, he voted for a resolution of a Trotskyist nature at the general party meeting in the ECCI [party] cell.

Ar[rested] 45. MILTER, Philipp

—In 1923, he voted for a resolution of a Trotskyist nature at the meeting of the ECCI [party] cell. [. . .]

Ar[rested] 47. MINGULIN, I. G.

—He was a Left SR between 1917 and April 1919 in Rostov-on-Don and Kherson, with intermissions between April 1918 and February 1919. A Left SR (borbist) from May 1919 to July 1920 in Kherson and Nikolaev. [. . .]

52. NOVIKOV, P. N.

—Received a harsh reprimand from the Kievskii district party committee in Moscow on 29 June 1936 for a non-Communist attitude toward his wife. [. . .]

Wor[king] 54. PROGER, L. D.

—She was admitted to the VKP(b) in March 1919 by the Moscow City District Committee. In November 1921, the purge commission in Tashkent demoted her to a candidate party member for her [lack of] Communist education.

Ar[rested] 55. PETERMANN, Erna F.

—As a member of the CP of Germany, she had vacillations: she did not understand the meaning of the Right deviation and the necessity of the struggle on two fronts. Leipzig, 1929.

Ar[rested] 56. PESTKOWSKI, S. S.

—In January–June 1918, he supported the group of "Left" Bolsheviks in Leningrad and Moscow on the question of the Brest peace treaty. His participation [in the group] was never formalized but was reflected in his speeches at some meetings.

He participated in the "Democratic Centralism" group in Moscow between April 1920 and January 1923. His participation was formalized; he took part in several discussion meetings of the center and also spoke at some meetings. [He] did not sign documents. [. . .]

Wor[king] 58. REINSTEIN, B. I.

—Belonged to the youth circles of the Narodovoltsy[60] between 1884 and 1886 in Rostov-on-Don and Yekaterinograd. From 1887 to 1892, belonged to the Zurich "circle of young Narodovoltsy" in Zurich, Bern, Paris. Belonged to the American Socialist Party between 1893 and 1917 in Buffalo, USA. In August–September 1917, belonged to the Menshevik-internationalists faction in Petrograd.

Ar[rested] 59. REDIKO, A. G.

1) Between 1917 and 1921, she belonged to the Bundist youth organization Zukumft. Belonged to the Jewish social-chauvinist organization Bund from 1921 to 1922 in Warsaw.

2) She was a *supporter* of the former minority in the Polish Communist Party headed by c. Lenski.

Wor[king] 60. ROGOZHNIKOV, P. G.

—Belonged to the "Left" Socialist Revolutionaries from June 1916 to May 1918 in Zlatoust, Ufa province.

Ar[rested] 61. SUVOROV, S. G.

1) Belonged to the Astrakhan group of Anarchists-Communists in Astrakhan between 1909 and 1912.

2) In 1923, he voted for a resolution of a Trotskyist nature in the ECCI [party] cell.

In 1929, he supported the Right-opportunist positions about the pace of development of industrialization in the country; spoke at party meetings and in the evening [courses at] Sverdlovsk University. [. . .]

Ar[rested] 73. TSOI SHENU [Sheu], V. A.

—Between Sept. 1923 and Feb. 1925, he was a participant in the factional struggle within the Korean Communist Party and supported the so-called Korean Bureau, which was condemned by the Comintern.

Ar[rested] 74. CHERNOMORDIK, M.

—In 1923, when he belonged to the Bureau of the Irkutsk province [party] committee, he voted for delaying until the receipt of the CC VKP(b) directives a discussion of the address by the Petrograd committee that exposed Trotsky. [. . .]

Ar[rested] 76. CHERNIN, I. I.

1) In 1928–1929, he supported the factional activities of the Rightists in the ECCI party organization.

2) In 1929, he was reprimanded by the purge commission for a lack of firmness in 1928–1929 and for supporting the Rightists' factional activities.

3. CHEREPANOV, P. N.

—In 1933, he was reprimanded by the regional party commission of the Moscow military district for losing his party card.

Ar[rested] 78. SHOK, G. A. [Gustav Schock]

1) He was a VKP(b) member in the Neviansk party organization in the Urals between 1917 and 1918. His membership was automatically discontinued because of his departure for Hungary.

2) Between 1913 and 1915, he belonged to the Hungarian SD Party in Pozsony, Hungary; between 1919 and 1920, a member of the Hungarian SD Party in Bratislava, Hungary.

3) On 21 July 1936, he received a harsh reprimand from the Bureau of the Kievskii district party committee for insincerity during the party verification.

Ar[rested] 79. SHTORM, A. K.

—In 1923, he voted for a Trotskyist resolution at the party meeting of the Communist University of the National Minorities of the West [party] cell in Moscow.

Ar[rested] 80. STANGE, A. A.

—In 1930, the purge commission gave him a harsh reprimand for economic activities in the countryside; he did not demonstrate adequate initiative in kolkhoz construction. [. . .]

85. EISENBERGER, I. I.

86)[61] Belonged to the SD Party of Germany from 1912 to June 1919 and to the Independent SD Party of Germany from August 1919 to May 1920.

87) In 1923, he was one of the five German Rightists in Moscow; was a personal friend of Brandler and opposed his expulsion from the CC CPG. He did not understand the connection between the political and organizational lines of the party in 1926 and vacillated on the question of alienation of privately

owned houses, believing that parliamentary success, "popular voting," would grow into the decisive struggle for power.

Wor[king] 86. YASHENKO, F. E.

—She was expelled by the M[oscow] C[ontrol] C[ommission] of the VKP(b) in 1926. On 11 June 1927, the CCC considered her automatically expelled. [She was] readmitted [to the party] by the party troika of the CCC VKP(b), protocol no. 390 of 26 June 1931, her membership to be considered not to have been interrupted.

Ar[rested] 87. YANSON, A. K.

—Belonged to the Socialist Party of the USA (Left wing), from which the Communist Party was organized, between December 1906 and August 1919.

Coming as they did within two days of each other, Documents 17 and 18 indicate how profoundly the August trial had deepened the anti-Trotskyist and vigilance campaigns and fanned suspicions of former oppositionists and foreigners.

Given the ECCI's orchestration of the international anti-Trotskyist campaign and the flurry of ECCI and party committee documents after the August trial expressing heightened anxieties about Trotskyists, it is worth reiterating what explained this obsession with Trotsky and his followers and how the campaign had changed since late 1934. No doubt Stalin's hatred of Trotsky played a major role in defining him and his followers as enemies. But Trotsky was in exile and the movement that bore his name had only some five thousand adherents worldwide.[62] The direct threats posed by Trotskyists to the USSR and Stalin were minimal. To explain Stalin's obsession with Trotsky requires understanding his personal disorders, for which the reliable evidence is still insufficient. There is no doubt that Stalin was in varying measures distrustful, jealous, vengeful, and paranoid. But his demons aside, the campaign against Trotsky and Trotskyists clearly resonated within the VKP and the Comintern, especially their leaderships. Why?

The answer lies less in what distinguished Trotskyism from Stalinism than in what they had in common. Adherents of both claimed to be the true heirs to the Leninist party line. Adherents of both spoke the language of Bolshevism and employed Bolshevik tactics. Adherents of both viewed reform socialists with a contempt comparable to that which Communists reserved for imperialists, the bourgeoisie, reactionaries, and fascists. It was, in fact, these shared attributes that made Trotsky and Trotskyism so menacing and feared within the USSR.[63] Trotsky could legitimately claim to offer a Leninist alternative to the

USSR and the Comintern. Trotsky alone had the international revolutionary credentials to use Bolshevik rhetoric and Leninist logic to attack the USSR and its policies. Precisely because he did so, Trotsky and his followers posed a threat far greater than their numbers suggest. As all Bolsheviks knew from the experience of 1917, numbers did not dictate who would win the hearts and minds of the revolutionary proletariat.

Whereas earlier the anti-Trotskyist campaign had served to define the characteristics of "real Bolsheviks," from 1934 the interweaving of the anti-Trotskyist campaign and the perceived foreign threat made the two all the more threatening. Trotskyism, the hidden "enemy" against which "real Bolsheviks" were to be ever vigilant, became an increasingly amorphous term. Before the August 1936 trial, the VKP and the Comintern more or less used it to designate former and active supporters of Trotsky or his policies. After the trial, it became a "universal designation for the worst kind of enemy," for people who had at one time opposed or harbored doubts about the party line.[64] That Kotelnikov lumped together "VKP(b) members formerly in other parties, having Trotskyist and Rightist tendencies," indicates the extent to which "real Bolsheviks" had come to categorize differences, past or present, as threats. By August 1936 the campaign against Trotskyists began to meld with a growing xenophobia, as a September 1936 Politburo resolution indicates: "The Trotskyist-Zinovievist scoundrels . . . must therefore now be considered foreign agents, spies, subversives, and wreckers representing the fascist bourgeoisie of Europe."[65] Vigilance demanded the "unmasking" and expulsion of alleged Trotskyists and "suspicious" foreigners.

Whereas in the USSR, there was no public debate about the nature and dangers of Trotskyism, Communist Parties abroad had to contend daily with debates over and criticisms of the August trial, the widening repression, and the international anti-Trotskyist campaign in the mass media as well as from Trotsky himself. In October, Trotsky attempted to sue the editors of *Arbeideren* (the newspaper of the Norwegian CP) and *Frid Volk* (a Norwegian fascist newspaper) for defamation. These newspapers claimed that Trotsky was the leader of a terrorist organization. In mid-October, Florin, a member of the ECCI Presidium, sent a telegram to Dimitrov to inform him of the suit and to ask his advice. Dimitrov could offer no advice other than to organize "a large campaign to unmask Trotsky's maneuvers."[66] Such a formulaic response offered little realistic support to foreign comrades, some of whom abandoned the Communist movement as the repression grew in scope.

The charges against the defendants at the August 1936 trial demonstrated the conspiratorial mindset that guided many of Stalin's and the Politburo's policies. Chernomordik's list of "Trotskyists and other hostile elements" among German émigrés and Kotelnikov's list of suspicious members (including Chernomordik) of the ECCI party committee exemplified that mindset and provided the so-called evidence to validate it. Increasingly, the conspiratorial mindset defined party behavior and gave rise to a Manichean worldview.

Few leading Bolsheviks exemplified the conspiratorial mindset better than did Nikolai Yezhov, the ECCI member. In September 1936, Stalin recommended that Yezhov replace Yagoda as the head of the NKVD. His appointment signaled that the search for "enemies" would be intensified. Yezhov's insistence on vigilance and political purity were well known among VKP leaders. From 1926 he worked in the Organizational-Assignment Department (Orgraspred) of the Central Committee and, in 1933, became the head of that department. In March 1935 he headed the Department of Leading Party Organs (ORPO), which replaced Orgraspred. At the Seventeenth Party Congress in 1934, he was elected to the Central Committee, the Central Control Commission, and the Organizational Bureau (Orgburo) of the VKP. Following Kirov's murder, Yezhov accompanied Stalin and other Politburo members to Leningrad to investigate the murder. He soon "took control of the investigation" and "participated directly in fabricating and releasing the story about the special moral responsibility of former members of the opposition."[67] In 1935 he became a secretary of the Central Committee, the chairman of the Party Control Commission, and an ECCI member.

Yezhov's work at Orgraspred, ORPO, and the Central Control and Party Control Commissions had exposed him to various personnel and political problems that afflicted the party. Across his desk had passed reports on the failure of party committees to properly carry out the purges and verifications, reports of the verification of fraternal parties, denunciations by party organizations and comrades of "suspicious" activities or individuals, lists from party organizations of "Trotskyists" and other "hostile elements," NKVD reports on party members who had been arrested and "confessed" to participation in nefarious political activities and groups. Exposure to such materials no doubt deepened Yezhov's belief that Trotskyists, "enemies," and "hostile elements" —native-born and foreign-born alike—had penetrated the VKP and that to expose them required a careful study of people's pasts and their networks of associates.[68]

In 1935, Yezhov expressed that belief in his only "theoretical work." In an essay, entitled "From Factionalism to Open Counter-Revolution," he laid bare his view that sinister conspiracies riddled the party. He asserted that the "Trotskyists and Zinovievites regularly inform each other about their activities . . . [and] have also taken the path to terrorism." Their goal, he claimed, was "to behead the revolution, to wipe out comrade Stalin." Stalin read and marked the essay.[69] In mid-1935, while he headed ORPO, Yezhov instructed Agranov, the deputy people's commissar of the NKVD and the head of the Directorate of State Security, to pursue Trotskyists. According to Agranov: "Comrade Yezhov announced that, according to his own information and in the opinion of the Central Committee of the party, an undiscovered Trotskyist center existed which had to be found and liquidated. Comrade Yezhov gave me sanction to produce a massive operation against the Trotskyists in Moscow."[70] Yezhov's belief in an undiscovered Trotskyist center necessitated that it be found. In April 1936, 508 former oppositionists were arrested; during the spring and summer, the NKVD stepped up its "battle against the Trotskyists." Such arrests validated Yezhov's assumptions and set the stage for the July Central Committee letter that announced the August show trial and called for an intensification of the vigilance campaign. Yezhov wrote that letter.[71]

When Yezhov became head of the NKVD, he brought with him not only his conspiratorial worldview and hatred of those who opposed the party but also his beliefs about which people and groups warranted police investigation, beliefs based on his interpretation of materials received during the previous three years. Before and during his tenure at the NKVD, Yezhov's positions gave him ready access to Stalin, who already shared many of Yezhov's assumptions about enemy conspiracies. The precise relationship between these two men remains unclear, but unquestionably Yezhov was Stalin's man and he acted with Stalin's blessings.

The August trial and reports such as Chernomordik's increased the pressure on fraternal party commissions to complete the verification of their members living in the USSR. Few were as responsive to those pressures as the parties of the former Polish section—the Polish, Western Ukrainian, and Western Belorussian parties—which carried out the verification with determination. Their verification commissions were especially active after the 29 July Central Committee letter. The work of the CPP's verification commission is illustrative.[72] The verification commission compiled biographical information for each known member in the USSR, either from its own records or from materials requested from other agencies. The commission met seven times between 24 July and 29 September 1936 to determine whom to return to Poland, whom to exclude from the party, whom to refer to the NKVD, whom to permit to continue residing in the USSR, and whom to investigate further. At each session the commission passed judgment on groups organized into lists of twenty-five comrades each.[73] It kept careful records of its decisions, which it forwarded to the Cadres Department and to Dimitrov, Manuilsky, and Moskvin.[74] This verification was clearly an administrative procedure. The vast majority of decisions were made on the basis of materials in the files; very few people appeared in person before the commission. Although this sped the process, it magnified the possibilities for arbitrariness. Poor record-keeping, baseless denunciations, political differences, and petty squabbles undoubtedly became the basis upon which some comrades' fates were decided. Considering the political pressure on the commission, its members probably operated on the principle that proving its vigilance was more important than contemplating the quality of the evidence.

In verifying the loyalty of comrades, the Polish commission paid close attention to certain groups of people. Among them were those who had served in the Polish army,[75] people whose stated reasons for emigrating to the USSR were questionable,[76] former students at one of the USSR international schools,[77] people whose past political activities raised suspicions,[78] and those who had previously belonged to another party[79]—categories that the Central Committee or the ECCI had deemed worthy of suspicion. The verification commission often sent letters and supporting materials about cases to the ECCI Secretariat and the Cadres Department. The Cadres Department, in turn, conducted its own investigation into certain Polish comrades, in particular those who had joined the VKP. That department and the Central Committee commission on transfers to the VKP frequently exchanged materials and requests for information on individuals. The Cadres Department also sent some of these materials to the Polish commission, a practice that increased the pressure on the commission to prove its vigilance.[80]

The Western Ukrainian verification commission was also hard at work in August and September. On 13 September, Sevan, the chair, submitted a progress report on its work to date. After reviewing 528 of its 1,139 members living in the USSR, the commission recommended returning 233 (44 percent) to Poland, three-quarters (175) of whom were to be denied any contact with the party. It recommended that only 78 people (15 percent) be allowed to remain in the USSR and that 27 (5 percent) already living in exile "in the Soviet hinterland" remain there. Sevan recommended that 49 people (9 percent) for whom "there are concrete compromising materials" be sent to the NKVD, and noted that 10 of them had already been arrested. An unspecified number of those on whom there were "compromising materials" were allegedly Polish or Ukrainian nationalists, or agents of the Polish Military Organization or Ukrainian Military Organization (UVO). The commission reported that it needed to review again the cases of 131 people (25 percent) "who are unknown to us." Sevan noted that this confusion arose from significant confusion in the records of the Polish and Western Ukrainian parties; some records were known to one party and not the other, or vice versa. Taken together, those who were barred from any future contact with the party, those whose cases were to be forwarded to the NKVD, and those already in exile accounted for 47 percent of the people reviewed.

Sevan used his report to highlight some serious concerns about the CPWU. He believed that the central leadership and all levels of the party organization "need to be serious strengthened," and lamented that "the process of educating new cadres for the middle level [of the party] proceeds much too slowly." Given the large proportion of members whose credentials raised serious concerns, Sevan recommended that henceforth there be a person in each of the party's leading and district organizations who specialized in "the verification and study of cadres."[81]

These findings provided the advocates of vigilance (be they in the Cadres Department, the ECCI, the Central Committee, or the NKVD) with evidence to press for a stricter accounting of émigrés, especially those from the western borderlands, and for raised vigilance.

The preliminary results of the work of the Polish and West Ukrainian commissions were surely on the minds of the ECCI Secretariat members when, on 17 December, Lenski presented to them his report on the CPP's activities in 1936. His report made clear that the party had taken to heart the criticisms and advice contained in the January 1936 report of the Secretariat (see Document 8). Lenski began by highlighting the organizational problems that the party had overcome. He reported that "we have practically restructured the party organization" by reducing the number of members (from sixteen thousand to fourteen thousand in one year) and reorganizing the work of the apparatus. During 1936 the CPP had reviewed the credentials of all its members living in Poland. This had been the first ever review of party members, and Lenski claimed that it had strengthened the party. Although Lenski asserted that the review aided the party in its struggle against provocateurs, he noted that provocation, especially by those with ties to the Polish police and "Ukrainian fascists" still posed a threat. Other problems remained, especially in the Warsaw party organization, where many "old sectarians" who had supported the

Left Opposition in the 1920s remained active. The remainder of his report dealt with issues relating to the struggle for influence in the union movement, moves to advance the Popular Front, aid to Spain, demands for changes in Polish foreign policy, and other policy concerns.[82]

The Secretariat's response to Lenski's report was relatively favorable compared to its response a year earlier. After stressing that the CPP needed to improve its work to aid the Spanish people and to mobilize "all the democratic forces in the country in order to tear Poland away from a bloc with Hitlerite Germany," the Secretariat expressed provisional satisfaction with its efforts to improve the quality of cadres. Nonetheless, much work remained. "Noting the favorable work of the leadership in verifying and cleansing the ranks of the Party and also the successful mobilization of the Party against alien and hostile elements and Trotskyite agents, the Secretariat of the ECCI considers it necessary to systematically continue this work, which has not yet embraced the district organizations. The complete cleansing of the Party from hidden Trotskyite elements is necessary, and there must be further decisive struggle for the isolation of counter-revolutionary Trotskyism in the ranks of the working class. The complete defeat of Trotskyism in the country must be brought about, and the Trotskyite gangs must be surrounded with a wall of hatred of the masses of people, and they must be driven out of the mass organizations, exposing them as agents of fascism."[83]

The Secretariat obviously remained concerned about problems that it believed beset the Polish party. At its meeting on 20 December to discuss the Polish question, it affirmed the importance of "strengthening the party as a <u>Polish</u> party" and formed a commission to ensure that this goal was achieved.[84]

The insistence by the ECCI Secretariat that the anti-Trotskyist campaign be intensified was not confined to the CPP, as **Document 19** indicates. In the aftermath of the August trial, the ongoing investigations by the NKVD and the arrests of former oppositionists gave rise to the mounting condemnation of these activities in Europe and the United States, and the ECCI Secretariat struggled to contain the political damage. The importance of the document rests not in the political guidance provided by the ECCI Secretariat to the fraternal parties abroad on how best to implement the anti-Trotskyist campaign—that had become routine business—but in its insistence that only "the most reliable and politically qualified authors should be entrusted with writing articles against Trotskyism." That directive illustrates succinctly the Secretariat's increasing anxieties about the effective carrying out of its charges.

Document 19

Telegram from the ECCI Secretariat to the Central Committees of the CPs of Czechoslovakia, Switzerland, Holland, France, Belgium, England, the United States, Canada, Sweden, Norway, and Denmark and to Julius (alias of Gyula Alpari) regarding the struggle against Trotskyism, 30 December 1936. RGASPI, f. 495, op. 184, d. 73, outgoing telegrams for 1936, general, l. 4. Original in German. Typewritten.

30 December 1936

The ECCI Secretariat points out the necessity of a systematic struggle against Trotskyists as counterrevolutionary terrorists, Gestapo agents, etc. Along with that, one must refute their slander directed against Stalin, oppose this slander with a broad popularization of his gigantic revolutionary activity [and with] an explanation of his role as a leader of the international proletariat and the workers of the whole world. We also point to the danger that has revealed itself in [the practice of] the Communist press of quoting attacks by the class enemies, especially of Trotskyist tendencies, without providing [those] Communist newspapers a convincing [and] principled answer. One has to avoid giving a detailed, quotation-laden account of the counterrevolutionary slander [and] Trotskyist propaganda, as well as [that published in] other reactionary fascist presses. One should not fall for the class enemy's provocation. It is necessary to give a principled answer and not to turn such fundamental questions of the Communist movement as the struggle against Trotskyism, defense of the USSR, [and the] attitude toward Stalin into sensationalist newspaper fraud and irresponsible journalism. We point out the necessity of thorough control over the editorial staff in order to purge the newspapers of suspicious elements and double-dealers. Only the most reliable and politically qualified authors should be entrusted with writing articles against Trotskyism. The newspaper editor has to carefully read each article himself and be personally responsible for it.

Secretariat

GD

The announcement in January 1937 of the upcoming trial of the Anti-Soviet Trotskyist Center—Pyatakov, Radek, Sokolnikov, Muralov, and others—on charges of committing sabotage under Trotsky's direction propelled the ECCI Secretariat to demand that fraternal parties abroad intensify the anti-Trotskyist campaign. Dimitrov and Manuilsky appreciated fully the political importance of the trial and were privy to some of the political discussions leading up to it. On 4 December 1936 they attended the Central Committee Plenum, where they heard Yezhov's report "on the counter-revolutionary activities of

Trotskyists and rightist organizations—Pyatakov, Sokolnikov, Serebryakov, etc." and heard Stalin state, "<u>The word of a former oppositionist can not be trusted.</u>"[85] On 16 December, Dimitrov met with the Five (Stalin, Molotov, Kaganovich, Voroshilov, Ordzhonikidze) in the Kremlin and heard Stalin's discussion of Sokolnikov's confession.[86] Dimitrov's diary entry in early January that he had read the testimony of Radek and Ustinov establishes his access to materials relating to the trial.[87] Dimitrov and the Comintern leaders understood the political significance of the upcoming trial and urged the fraternal parties abroad to do likewise.

Throughout January the ECCI Secretariat sent encoded telegrams ordering the fraternal parties to assess their members' reactions to the trial in order "to more easily identify enemies who have penetrated the party," to use reactions to the trial for "unmasking Trotskyists and wavering elements for a future purge of the party," and "to verify in this case the ranks of the party [so as to] cleanse it of Trotskyist elements."[88]

As the January trial neared, the Secretariat redoubled its efforts to orchestrate press coverage of the event by the Communist Parties and to repel the expressed and expected criticisms of the trial by bourgeois and Social Democratic presses. **Document 20** exemplifies the tone and content of the Secretariat's telegrams.

Document 20

Letter from the ECCI Secretariat to the leaders of selected Communist Parties regarding propaganda work during the trial of Radek, Pyatakov, and others, 17 January 1937. RGASPI, f. 495, op. 184, d. 19, ll. 4–5, outgoing telegrams for 1937, general directives. Original in German. Handwritten.

Urgent[89]

17 January 1937

The trial of Radek, Pyatakov, and others opens in a few days. It is necessary [to give] **in the Communist press the widest possible convincing explanation of the defendants' confessions. It is necessary to organize a refutation of the arguments of the bourgeois Social Democratic press, which will try to discredit the trial. Immediately initiate a campaign in the press and among the masses against Trotsky and Trotskyism as a terrorist agency, a gang of wreckers, subversives, spies, and accomplices of the German Gestapo. Even before and during the trial, develop a campaign in the press not only by reporting on the trial but also by publishing articles written by** *the party leaders. Accounts of the trial are to be published in the form of your newspaper correspondent's special report.*

Secretariat
GD
Ercoli 17.1.37

Sent to: Thorez—Paris
　　　　Pollitt—London
　　　　Browder—New York
　　　　Gottwald—Prague
　　　　Díaz—Valencia
　　　　Linderot—Stockholm
　　　　P.B. [Political Bureau]*—Brussels*
　　　　P.B.—Amsterdam
　　　　P.B.—Copenhagen
　　　　Julius—Paris

Anxious that fraternal parties abroad be able to counter criticisms of the trial and the mounting anti-Soviet sentiment that accompanied them, the ECCI Secretariat also sent **Document 21** to Julius (Gyula Alpari), the editor of the Comintern journals *Imprecor* and *Rundschau* and the Comintern's press agent in Europe.[90]

Document 21

Telegram from the ECCI Secretariat to Julius in Paris, 17 January 1937. RGASPI, f. 495, op. 184, d. 23, outgoing telegrams for 1937. Original in German. Handwritten.

Urgent[91]
17 January 1937

To Julius—Paris
　During the upcoming trial of Radek-Pyatakov, "L'Humanité"[92] *and "Daily Worker" (New York) are to be considered the main mouthpieces of our campaign. Give all-round support to these newspapers. In addition, you are given the special charge to distribute to the left bourgeois and Socialist presses extracts from and the major points of our reports.*

Secretariat
GD
Ercoli 17.1.37

To deflect any criticisms of the upcoming trial, the Secretariat selected prominent foreign Communists to attend it as observers and correspondents. On 17 January, the Secretariat dispatched an encoded telegram to Maurice Thorez, secretary of the French CP: "In connection with the upcoming Radek-Pyatakov trial, send Paul Valliant-Couturier immediately. He has to leave within twenty-four hours."[93] Valliant-Couturier was the editor of *L'Humanité*, the most important Communist newspaper in Europe, one of the two "main mouthpieces" for the anti-Trotskyist campaign. Two days later, Alikhanov of the ECCI Cadres Department sent a memo to N. I. Kornilev, an official within the Main Administration for State Security of the NKVD, requesting approval to issue press passes for twenty-one people "to work at the trial as correspondents of Communist presses of capitalist countries and as translators." Alikhanov provided a brief biographical sketch of each.[94] Whenever the Comintern wished to invite foreigners to Moscow, it needed NKVD approval to receive visas for them. But this request was a bit different and involved a greater degree of political risk. Although the Comintern could recommend reliable comrades, Alikhanov's memo indicates that the NKVD would decide who would and would not attend the trial. Such actions leave no doubt as to the Secretariat's efforts to direct Communist press coverage of the trial and to ensure that the Kremlin's version of it was faithfully conveyed to the world.

The thoroughness with which the Comintern orchestrated Communist press coverage of the trial was impressive. The Secretariat's plan to have prominent Communist and radical journalists attend the trial indicates the importance that it attached to countering criticism abroad. Toward that end, the ECCI also sought to co-opt left-wing intellectuals abroad, such as Dennis Pritt and Leon Feuchtwanger, to write articles defending the trial. Comintern analysts (*referenty*) daily monitored Communist and other foreign newspapers, and when they encountered articles that warranted a reaction, they alerted their bosses. Before, during, and after each of the three Moscow show trials, the analysts frequently traveled between their desks and the Secretariat's office. When an article warranted a reply in the Communist press, the Secretariat often alerted the party leaders in that country.[95] Such was the case on 21 January 1937, when the Secretariat ordered the British CP to respond to articles written by Lev Sedov, Trotsky's eldest son and adviser, and the editor of the Trotskyist newspaper *Bulletin of the Opposition*. As **Document 22** makes clear, the Secretariat determined who would write the article. In this case, it was Dennis Pritt, a Labour member of Parliament.[96]

Document 22

Telegram from the ECCI Secretariat to the CP of Great Britain, 21 January 1937. RGASPI, f. 495, op. 184, d. 14, outgoing telegram for 1937 to London. Original in English. Handwritten.

21.1.37 17.00

London
Organize answer by Pritt [to] *article* [by] *Siedoff in Manchester Guardian;*[97] *send protest letters against Manchester Guardian, which becomes the tribune of Trotskyist bandits.*
                                   Secretariat

But orchestrating a press campaign does not guarantee successful results. At the trial Pyatakov confessed that he had flown to Oslo to meet with Trotsky at the Bristol Hotel. The European press quickly demonstrated that this was impossible because there had been no such flight on that day and that the Bristol Hotel had been demolished years before the alleged meeting. These and other refutations of the evidence presented at the trial created considerable embarrassment and problems for the fraternal parties abroad. Following the publication of evidence that the meeting at the Bristol Hotel could not have occurred, the Norwegian CP telegraphed Moscow for instructions: "For us this is extraordinarily important. Communicate details of Pyatakov's visit to Oslo." Elena Valter, Dimitrov's secretary, wrote on the telegram: "Message from Ercoli. To this telegram there will be no answer; that is, they have already received directive documents related to the trial. The opinion of the [European] press is divided. Part of the press confirms the fact of the airplane."[98] The lack of an answer frustrated the Norwegians, who again implored Moscow for advice: "Exact details about . . . the flight of the airplane to Oslo are very important. It is impossible to wait for six months."[99] Again, the ECCI sent no reply. Caught as it was between party discipline, the beliefs of its members, mounting political anxieties and fears, and confused fraternal parties, silence was the safest answer.

The ECCI Secretariat's direction of the international press campaign makes clear its role as the agent of repression. But the dimensions and consequences of its role deepened on 21 January, when it sent the following telegram.

Document 23

Telegram from the ECCI Secretariat to Díaz in Spain, 21 January 1937. RGASPI, f. 495, op. 184, d. 12, outgoing telegram for 1937 to Spain. Original in French. Handwritten. Initialed by Dimitrov and Moskvin.

---

21 January [1937] *17:00* [hours]
Spain
Díaz Luis Pedro [José]

Use the trial of Pyatakov and consorts to politically liquidate the POUM and try to obtain from working elements of this organization a declaration condemning Trotsky's terrorist band.

Secretariat
G.D.

n. 35
MM

By ordering the political liquidation of the POUM, the Partido Obrero de Unificación Marxista, the Comintern's long-standing campaign against Trotskyism took on an even more concrete character outside the USSR. Its complicity as the agent and instrument of repression deepened. With this order, the Secretariat hoped to remove a popular critic and rival of Spain's Popular Front government. The POUM was an anarcho-syndicalist party with strong working class support in Barcelona and Catalonia. After the Spanish Civil War began, the POUM exercised considerable power in Catalonia and used its influence to advance social revolution there. POUM leaders frequently criticized the moderate policies of the Popular Front government and its ostensible refusal to fulfill the promises of the Spanish revolution. Although the criticisms and proposals of the POUM were similar to those enunciated by Trotsky, the party was not Trotskyist, although some of its members and leaders had supported Trotsky in the past. Trotsky himself frequently criticized the POUM's actions and its anarcho-syndicalist nature.[100] But in Moscow the similarity of the POUM's and Trotsky's criticisms and proposals seemed more than coincidental. To the Kremlin and the ECCI, the POUM was de facto a Trotskyist party and ipso facto an agent of fascism, hence the linking of the trial of "Pyatakov and consorts," that is, "fascist agents," to the political liquidation of the POUM. The call to "politically liquidate" the allegedly Trotskyist POUM, which was a thorn in the side of the Spanish and Soviet governments, followed logically from the anticipated convictions of the defendants awaiting trial.

Crushing the POUM might also have strengthened the military position of the Popular Front government in Barcelona and Catalonia. Removing a powerful political rival would allow the government to extend its efforts to centralize military operations and political organization, two goals demanded by Moscow and its military advisers in Spain. In short, liquidating the POUM served the political and military interests of the USSR, the major ally and supporter of the Spanish Republic, as well as those of the Comintern, which organized and coordinated the International Brigades fighting in the Spanish Civil War.

The Secretariat's call for the political liquidation of the POUM was, however, not a call for the physical liquidation of its members. The Comintern's goal in January was to destroy its political influence in Spain and among members of the International Brigades. Not until after the POUM uprising in Barcelona in May 1937 did the physical repression of its members begin. Then NKVD agents, not the Comintern, carried out that repression. But the Comintern's call to politically liquidate the POUM set into motion the complex dynamics that contributed both to the POUM uprising and to the NKVD's brutal repression of its leaders and supporters.[101]

If the January show trial precipitated the liquidation of the POUM, Trotsky deserved no less. During the trial, Dimitrov sent to Earl Browder, secretary of the CPUSA, the following telegram.

Document 24

Telegram from Dimitrov and Moskvin to Browder, CPUSA, 26 January 1937. RGASPI F. 495, op. 184, d. 17, outgoing 1937 to New York. Original handwritten in Russian with accompanying handwritten translation into English. Initialed by Dimitrov and Moskvin.

New York
26/I [1937] *12:20* [hours]

Browder
Help Mexican CP rouse whole public opinion against presence of Trotsky in Mexico which is real provocation to all Soviet people and Mexico. The

alliance of Trotsky with Japanese directly targeted against USA and threaten[s] *Mexico too. The same offensive campaign carry on in USA aiming to clear out Trotskyites from all mass organizations.*
        Secretariat
        G.D.
        M.M.

During the August 1936 trial the Soviet government demanded that the Norwegian government extradite Trotsky to Moscow. Rather than cede to Soviet pressure, the Norwegian government placed him under surveillance, virtual house arrest, while it determined what to do. The actions of the Soviet and Norwegian governments prompted Trotsky's supporters and civil libertarians in Europe and the United States to form committees for his defense and to find him a safe political asylum. Efforts to pressure the U.S. government to admit him failed, but the president of Mexico, Lazaro Cardenas, agreed to requests from Andrés Nin, leader of the POUM, and from Mexican and U.S. Trotskyists to grant Trotsky asylum. Trotsky arrived in Mexico on 3 January 1937 and lived there with his wife until a NKVD agent, Ramon Mercador, murdered him in August 1940.[102]

Given that Trotsky resided in Mexico, why did Dimitrov send **Document 24** to Browder in New York? There were two interconnected reasons. The first is that the CPUSA formally oversaw and directed the Mexican CP. Instructions and directives from the Comintern to the Mexican party almost always went through New York. The second is that the campaign to force Trotsky's removal from Mexico was to be an inter-American campaign. The fact that the United States was home to the world's largest Trotskyist party made the active participation of the CPUSA essential.

Document 25 further underscores the importance of the January trial to the Comintern's anti-Trotskyist campaign. Its contents are familiar, but its addressees are not. Šmeral was one of the founders of the Czechoslovak CP, an ICC member and the leader of a prominent Popular Front peace organization in Paris. Willi Münzenberg (Herfurt) was the very successful organizer of a series of broad-based, anti-fascist and anti-war Communist front organizations that played important roles in heightening the Popular Front's popularity in Europe. By directing Šmeral and Münzenberg to have their respective organizations defend the January trial and participate in Moscow's anti-Trotskyist campaign, the ECCI contributed to a reversal of their fortunes. Many who participated in

Münzenberg's and Šmeral's organizations did so because they opposed dictatorial restrictions on basic human freedoms and any state's use of the police and courts to restrict political activities and punish political critics. Many of these people viewed with alarm the Moscow trials, trials that warranted their condemnation and hastened their break with Moscow and its front organizations.

Document 25

Telegram from the ECCI Secretariat to Šmeral and Münzenberg (Herfurt) in Paris demanding the intensification of the propaganda campaign in connection with the Trotskyist center trial, 29 January 1937. RGASPI, f. 495, op. 184, d. 23, outgoing telegrams for 1937 to Paris, l. 108. Telegram in French, typewritten. Handwritten original (l. 108 ob.) written in Russian by G. Dimitrov.

Rec[eived] **29/I 10⁰⁰**

To Šmeral, Herfurt [Willi Münzenberg]—*Paris*

It is necessary to intensify, in every way possible, the explanatory campaign in connection with the trial. Influence systematically the Popular Front press. React skillfully and opportunely to the campaigns of the enemy press. Pay special attention to the Committee of Aid to Political Prisoners and its Trotskyist-anarchist environment. Inform [us] *regularly on the most important stages of the campaign.*

Secretariat.

Despite the flurry of telegrams and activities that preceded the trial, it was only on 23 January, the day the trial began, that the ECCI Secretariat appointed a troika comprised of Ercoli, Shubin, and Ponomarev to coordinate the Comintern's "anti-Trotskyist campaign."[103] Immediately following the trial, an expanded meeting of the Secretariat discussed how the Comintern might best use the trial to strengthen its campaign and established a "commission to work up the resolution."[104] The discussions at these meetings involved little debate about the veracity of the trial—Dimitrov and other ECCI leaders believed that the trial "proved" the existence and intentions of the conspiracy.[105] But Dimitrov's public pronouncements that the defendants were guilty and that Trotsky had directed their sinister conspiracy did not allay his private apprehensions over how the trial had changed the political atmosphere: "Why such a great fuss over the trial? Incomprehensible. An atmosphere has been created of extreme unrest among the population, mutual suspicions, denunciations, and so on. Trotskyism has been killed, why such a campaign?"[106]

Nonetheless, on 5 February the ECCI Presidium approved two resolutions: "The Results of the Trial of the Trotskyists" and "On Carrying Out the Campaign Against Trotskyism" (Document 26). The same day, Dimitrov wrote to Stalin: "In connection with the trial of the anti-Soviet Trotskyist Center, a meeting of the ECCI Presidium, in which comrades Cachin, Valliant-Couturier (France), Linderot (Sweden), Humbert-Droz (Switzerland), Shakhler (Holland), Ulbricht (Germany), and others participated, decided the question of using the trial in the struggle against Trotskyism in important capitalist countries." Dimitrov then noted the passage of the two resolutions and asked Stalin for his "remarks and orders."

The language and logic of the ECCI Presidium's resolution on the results of the trial of the Trotkyists illuminate both the Kremlin's version of the significance of the trial and many Communists' shared fears. The resolution began by noting that the January trial "disclosed to the whole world that Trotskyism . . . has become the international agency of fascism. . . . They fight with the aid of terror, espionage, and subversive acts for the restoration of capitalism in the USSR. They act as the agents of the most reactionary, the most chauvinist, the most imperialistic section of finance capitalism—fascism." The crimes to which the defendants admitted "are such that no honest worker . . . can have any attitude toward such despicable enemies of the people other than indignation, repugnance, and execration."

The resolution then summarized the defendants' crimes, including their "plans for the murder of Comrade Stalin" and "other leaders of the Soviet Government," working to "accelerate the war of German fascism and the Japanese fascist military clique against the USSR," espionage, and sabotaging key industrial sectors. The defendants' "confessions" "proved" that Trotskyists posed a serious threat to Soviet national security and world peace. The resolution asserted that there could be no doubt of the defendants' guilt because the "trial took place publicly in the presence of representatives of public opinion of the whole world, with every possible guarantee of objectivity." It then claimed that "Trotsky and his accomplices are not only the desperate enemies of the Soviet Union . . . they are the disorganizers and wreckers of the working-class movement in every country." It noted that Trotsky opposed the Popular Front in France, that in Spain "the Trotskyites are a component part of the 'Fifth Column' of General Franco [military leader of the Spanish rebels] . . . they try to stab in the back the International Brigades, which are the living embodiment of proletarian solidarity and the international united front" against fascism, that in China they "openly serve the secret police," and that in the United States they "are the sources of supply of anti-Soviet counterrevolutionary slanders for the reactionary Hearst press, Hitler's ally in America." "In many countries the police recruit their agents from among the Trotskyite degenerates; the fascist jailers in Italian, Polish, and German prisons distribute Trotsky's book 'My Life' to demoralize the political prisoners." After decrying Trotsky's and his followers' opposition to Soviet diplomatic efforts "to preserve general peace," the resolution concluded by noting: "The struggle against Trotskyism is a component part of the struggle against fascism. The defeat of Trotskyism is one of the most important conditions for the victory over bloody fascism."[107]

That resolution and the resolution "On Carrying Out the Campaign Against Trotskyism" were supposed to provide the fraternal parties abroad with the evidence that they needed to strengthen their campaign against Trotskyism, to respond to criticisms of the trials in bourgeois newspapers, and to educate party members. **Document 26,** which was approved at the 31 January expanded meeting of the Secretariat and the 5 February meeting of the ECCI Presidium, provided the most recent marching orders for that ongoing campaign. The goals and recommended tactics are familiar, but two points deserve mention. The first is the call to conduct a "verification of the ranks" not only of party organizations but also of non-party organizations in which Communists were active. The goal of the verification was "to expose double-dealing Trotskyist elements." As the perceived threat deepened, the Comintern intensified its struggle against Trotskyists and demanded that only the most dedicated and disciplined Communists remain in the party. But Communist verifications of non-party organizations weakened the Popular Front. So the resolution also stressed the importance of "rais[ing] the ideological-political level of party education." This is the second point. In early February 1937 vigilance and education remained the means by which enemies would be unmasked and political purity would be ensured.

Document 26

Resolution of the ECCI Secretariat sent to member parties of the Comintern on carrying out the campaign against Trotskyism, 5 February 1937. RGASPI, f. 495, op. 2, d. 246, ll. 144–145. Original in Russian. Typewritten with handwritten additions.

__Final text__
5.2.37 GDim

ON CARRYING OUT THE CAMPAIGN AGAINST TROTSKYISM

In connection with the outcome of the trial, conduct a mobilization of the Communist Parties in order to develop a broad, mass campaign against Trotskyism so as to destroy it completely. This must be the task of the whole party and the entire working class. To this end, it is essential that the Politburo of every party plan a series of measures aimed at making the campaign, by its character and scale, not only intraparty in character but one designed for the broadest popular masses. It is necessary to show these masses [that] Trotskyism is an agency of fascism and [to show] Trotsky and Trotskyists as the most dastardly enemies of the USSR, as enemies of the people's liberty and independence, as advocates of the restoration of capitalism in the USSR, and as warmongers. Using the trial materials, this campaign must give a complete and concrete picture of the Trotskyists' counterrevolutionary activities in Spain and France, as well as their wrecking work in the workers' movement throughout the world and in each given country, [and] their attempts to subvert the movement toward the United [Popular] Front and working-class unity. In addition to the trial materials, it is essential to base this mass campaign on the facts of the Trotskyists' counterrevolutionary activity in each specific country, taking into account local conditions and the level of the workers' movement. It is essential to explain, on the basis of the facts revealed at the trial, the harm that is caused in each country by the Trotskyists' subversive activity and by Trotsky's arrangement with German fascism and Japanese militarism. During the campaign, it is necessary to strive to get those people and organizations affiliated with Trotskyism to dissociate themselves from Trotsky as an agent of fascism. At the same time, during the campaign, the broad masses of people must put forward the demand to expel Trotsky from Mexico [and] the demand that Trotsky face the proletarian court of the USSR rather than hide behind the back of agents whom he has recruited.

In addition to party meetings that explain the results of the trial, this campaign should take the form of broad mass meetings in which the most prominent party representatives have to participate, as well as members of other parties and organizations who have expressed a readiness to fight against Trotskyism as a fascist agency. When carrying out this campaign, there should be a differentiated approach to different strata of the population (working class, peasantry, intelligentsia, etc.). The Secretariat considers it very expedient for comrades who were present at the trial—Cachin, Vaillant-Couturier, Linderot, Humbert-Droz, and others—to give speeches in the largest European capitals.

The Secretariat also considers it essential that the parties and their local organizations, as well as Communists working in the non-party organizations, conduct a thorough verification of the ranks of these organizations to expose double-dealing Trotskyist elements and to throw them out of these organizations. At the same time, it is necessary to intensify the explanatory work in all the party and non-party organizations so that the members of these organizations are not left with unanswered questions, and they will be prepared for the struggle against Trotskyism.

The Secretariat recommends that the CCs of the Communist Parties and their agitprop [departments] plan concrete measures to raise the ideological-political level of party education, especially of the illegal parties, both in regard to schools, classes, and the periodical press and in regard to all the publishing activity of the party. In this propaganda work, it is necessary to show the real history of the VKP(b) and the October Revolution, the prolonged struggle of the party of Lenin-Stalin against Trotsky, and to show the evolution of Trotskyism, which has slid down the path of open counterrevolution and is an agency of fascism.

The Secretariat charges the Press and Propaganda Department of the ECCI Secretariat, together with the Editorial-Publishing [Department] of the ECCI Secretariat, to plan a series of publications on the struggle against Trotskyism on the basis of the proposals of the commission appointed by the Secretariat.

Because the political tasks were urgent and documents took time to transmit, two days later the Secretariat conveyed the essential points of Document 26 to the fraternal parties by encoded telegram. **Document 27** is the version sent to the American and British parties.

Document 27

Telegram from the ECCI Secretariat to the CPUSA and British CP on the political tasks in light of the January 1937 trial, 7 February 1937. RGASPI, f. 495, op. 184, d. 19. Special 1937. General Directives. Original in English. Typewritten with handwritten notations.

7.II.1937 13:30 [hours]
New York Trans. Nos. 68, 69, 70, 71
London [Trans. Nos.] ***19, 20, 21, 22***

New York—Browder, London—Pollitt

I. Basing on results of trial mobilize party, working class, democratic forces for entire smashing of trotzkyism, agency of German fascism Japan[ese] militarism, most vile enemy of the Soviet Union, fighter for restoration of capitalism, provocator of war, enemy of liberty and independence of nations.

II. Give concrete picture of counterrevolutionary activities of trotzkyism in capitalist countries, of his fight against united front, peoples front for the purpose of splitting workers movement in interest of fascism especially in France, Spain and your country.

III. During the campaign demand in name of workers organizations, popular masses the expulsion of Trotzky from Mexico and to place himself to [before] proletarian soviet tribunal.

[Use] pressure of masses effect[ively], that organizations and persons influenced by Trotzkyism denounce solidarity with Trotzky and his criminal activities.

Organize meetings with reports on trial by comrades who *were present* on trial. Popularize in widest way resolution of presidium on results of trial, reports of trial and pamphlets on trial. More exact instruction follows.

Secretariat

To n. 6 New York, n. 32 London. zam. Dekebakh 7/II

It was only after the ECCI had passed its resolutions and had transmitted the essential points to the fraternal parties that Stalin and Dimitrov met to discuss the resolution on the anti-Trotskyite campaign. Stalin was critical of the ECCI's efforts. After reminding Dimitrov that "1) You're forgetting that the European workers think that everything's happened because of some quarrel between me and Trotsky, because of Stalin's bad character. 2) It must be pointed out that these people fought against Lenin, against the Party, during Lenin's lifetime," Stalin offered concrete suggestions: "Quote Lenin on the opposition. . . . Quote the defendants' testimony." Then Stalin said: "The resolution is nonsense. All of you there in the Comintern are playing right into the enemy's hands. There is no point in making a resolution; resolutions are binding. A letter to the parties would be better."[108]

The letter that Dimitrov wrote at Stalin's suggestion relied heavily on the ECCI resolution, but there were some expected differences. Dimitrov took to heart Stalin's advice that it highlight Trotsky's oppositions to Lenin and the VKP. He described Trotsky as "the bitterest enemy of Lenin and Lenin's line" and buttressed this assertion with quotes from Lenin. He characterized the defendants in the trial in similar terms and peppered the letter with lengthy quotes from the transcript to illustrate not only the "crimes" of the accused but also their confessions.[109]

Stalin's comments, coming as they did after the ECCI had telegraphed its charges, emphasize an important point. Although at times the ECCI leaders directly sought his "remarks and orders," in this case they decided on their own how to best use the trials to strengthen the anti-Trotskyist campaign. Although the style of Document 26 did not meet Stalin's approval, he did not dispute its political logic or line. As their behavior after the trial suggests, the ECCI leaders believed in the veracity of the trials, in the guilt of the defendants, in the existence of an international anti-Soviet conspiracy directed by Trotsky, and in the threat that a Trotsky-fascist alliance posed to the USSR and international communism. Party discipline and the atmosphere of "extreme unrest . . . mutual suspicions, denunciations, and so on," of which Dimitrov wrote, no doubt also influenced their behavior. To not press the anti-Trotskyist campaign in such an atmosphere, even if, as Dimitrov confided to his diary, "Trotskyism has been killed," would have left the ECCI members open to denunciations. Party discipline, uncertainty, belief, anxiety, the need to find meaning—these and other factors made the political dynamics of the time very complex.

Issuing and executing orders on how to conduct the anti-Trotskyist campaign did not ensure that Moscow's views would prevail. Non-Communist publications throughout the world questioned the authenticity of the January trial and published evidence that exposed the falsehood of some of the evidence presented there. Nor did the campaign always proceed as ordered within the fraternal parties. Some members of fraternal parties raised questions and expressed doubts not only about the trials but also about the very premise of the campaign—that Trotsky had allied himself with fascists. **Document 28** conveys succinctly some of the problems that the campaign encountered in Lithuania. Such skepticism would require heightening vigilance, especially vis-à-vis a party that the ECCI leaders had deemed "prone to provocation."

Document 28

Telegram from Lithuania about work being done to liquidate Trotskyism, 9 February 1937. RGASPI, f. 495, op. 184, d. 8. Incoming telegrams for 1937 from Lithuania. Original in Russian. Typewritten on telegram letterhead. Transmitted in three parts. Initialed by Manuilsky, Angaretis, and Moskvin.

---

9 February 1937
To: Angaretis,
Dimitrov,
Manuilsky
The struggle against Trotskyists, especially after the trials started, has been especially accentuated in the press and in general during the whole six-

month period. Yet the issue of the Trotskyists has not been discussed in all the organizations. The explanatory work has also been weak among the non-party members. Our comrades in the factories frequently lacked courage to repulse the Trotskyists' slander. [The effort to draw] concrete lessons is even worse.

In Kovno, only Geraite has been expelled, and that was done on the sly. Although there is an understanding among party members that the Trotskyists and rotten liberals cannot be party members, one notes doubts [among comrades] about how the Trotskyists managed to sink to fascism and why they confessed at the trial the way they did.

It looks as though not everyone has understood clearly enough that the Trotskyists qualify as agents provocateurs and as the agents of the fascist okhranka. We are also emphasizing [the need] to review dubious elements and to unmask the Trotskyist elements that no doubt exist among them.

In Shantsy (Kovno workers' suburb), two party members had earlier defected to the Trotskyists. Wherever we maintain our connections, there is *no* sympathy toward Trotskyists, although in some places one can sense a lack of firmness toward them. We think that the Kovno [party] organization is not exposing all those places where the Trotskyists are active.

Those expelled from the party are being driven out of the non-party organizations.

In the circles of the Jewish and Lithuanian intelligentsia, there is serious disbelief that the Trotskyists were able to do [what they were accused of] in the Soviet Union and that they have confessed.

We are pressuring the local [party] organizations to consider the struggle against the Trotskyists not as a short campaign but as systematic work.

M[*anuilsky*]
Angaretis
M. M[*oskvin*]

Such doubts were not confined to Lithuania. Worldwide, many non-Communists and even some Communists also expressed "serious disbelief" about the trials and the charges leveled against Trotsky. As criticisms of the trial and the unfolding repression intensified in Western non-Communist newspapers, and as people once sympathetic to the USSR denounced the trials, Moscow's sense of isolation and its belief that Trotskyist influence was growing deepened. As this occurred, the arguments put forth by the advocates of vigilance became more difficult to counter. Those who harbored doubts could ill afford not to be vigilant. Hence, the political dynamics that propelled the vigilance campaign accelerated.

As the anti-Trotskyist campaign was reaching its apex, the verification of the political credentials of the ECCI staff was concluding. In January 1936, at the same time that it had ordered the verification of political émigrés and the fraternal parties, the Secretariat had created a Commission of the ECCI Secretariat for the Verification of the Apparatus and had charged it with conducting a thorough review of the political and work credentials of the apparatus staff. The members of the Moskvin Commission, as it was known within the ECCI, quietly went about their work.[110] On 5 February the Moskvin Commission issued its final report. **Document 29** is the summary memorandum.

Document 29

Memorandum on the results of the work of the commission of the ECCI Secretariat to verify the qualifications of the ECCI apparatus, 5 February 1937. RGASPI, f. 495, op. 21, d. 52, ll. 23–25. Original in Russian. Typewritten with handwritten corrections.

---

5 February 1937

Top secret.

MEMORANDUM
ON THE RESULTS OF THE WORK OF THE ECCI SECRETARIAT'S COMMIS-
SION TO VERIFY THE QUALIFICATIONS OF THE ECCI APPARATUS.[111]

During the time of its work, the commission reviewed 387 cases of workers of the ECCI apparatus and of the international organizations.

The cases reviewed can be broken down according to individual sections and sectors:

1. Workers of the Secretariats	69
2. ICC	2
3. Cadres Department	37
4. Bureau of the Secretariat	25
5. Translations Department	60
6. Propaganda Department	39
7. Public[ations] Sector	15
8. Editorial Board of the *Kommunisticheskii Internatsional*	20
9. Representatives of the parties	26
10. Sections	32
11. Party Committee and Local [Trade Union] Committee	2
12. KIM	1
13. Foreign Workers' Publishing House	11
14. Various international organizations	48

<u>By party composition:</u>

1. Members of the VKP(b)	107
2. Members of the VLKSM [Komsomol]	25
3. Non-party members	66
4. Members of the fraternal parties	189

<u>including:</u>

1.	CP of Germany		92
2.	"	" France	7
3.	"	" England	10
4.	"	" USA	9
5.	"	" Austria	9
6.	"	" Romania	3
7.	"	" Yugoslavia	3
8.	"	" Hungary	3
9.	"	" Latvia	4
10.	"	" Lithuania	3
11.	"	" Italy	4
12.	"	" Turkey	2
13.	"	" Iran	1
14.	"	" Poland	3
15.	"	" Czechoslovakia	8
16.	"	" Norway	2
17.	"	" Brazil	2
18.	"	" Finland	5
19.	"	" Holland	1
20.	"	" Belgium	2
21.	"	" Australia	1
22.	"	" Switzerland	3
23.	"	" Greece	2
24.	"	" Bulgaria	6
25.	"	" Denmark	1
26.	"	" Syria	1
27.	"	" China	1
28.	"	" Cuba	1

Of all the cases that were reviewed, according to the preliminary decision of the Commission, <u>71 people were slated to be removed from the ECCI apparatus and the international organizations.</u>

After additional verification in the course of the Commission's work and after revising its previous decisions, <u>the Commission considers it necessary to relieve from work in the ECCI apparatus and in the international organizations only 58 people</u> (rather than 71 people).

In the Commission's opinion, 14 [13] people, about whom a decision had been previously made to remove [them from work], can be temporarily kept in the apparatus until adequate replacements are found.

<u>Distribution of those to be removed [from work]:</u>

1. The secretaries' apparatus	**7** people
2. The Bureau of the Secretariat	2 "
3. Translations Department	13 "
4. Propaganda "	6 "
5. Cadres "	2 "
6. Editorial and Publishing [Department]	5 "
7. Editorial Board of the *Kommunisticheskii Internatsional*	3 "
8. ICC	1 "
9. KIM	1 "
10. Foreign Workers' Publishing House	7 "
11. Various international organizations	9 "
TOTAL	5**8** people.

<u>The breakdown of those to be removed, by party affiliation:</u>

1. VKP(b) members	10
2. KSM members	1
3. Non-party members	11
4. Members of the fraternal parties	35

including:

1. CP of Germany	19
2. " " Hungary	1
3. " " Austria	2
4. " " Czechoslovakia	1
5. " " Yugoslavia	1
6. " " France	5
7. " " USA	1
8. " " Poland	3
9. " " Belgium	1
10. " " Italy	1
11. " " Sweden	1
12. " " Norway	1

<u>The breakdown of those slated to be removed, by political motives:</u>

1. Ties to the counterrevolutionary group of E[mel] Lurye	6
2. " " " " " " David and Berman	5
3. " " " " " " E. Wendt	3
4. " " " " " " Süsskind	2

5. Trotskyist connections	16
6. Politically unreliable	4
7. Suspicious and not [previously] exposed	11
8. Unsuitable qualifications	4
9. Affiliated to the anti-party groups (of Brandler and others)	4

At this moment, 12 out of 57 people who are slated to be removed are no longer working in the apparatus, among them:

1. In the Secretariats	1	person(s)
2. In the Translations Department	5	"
3. In the Cadres Department	1	"
4. ICC	1	"
5. Editorial Board of the *Kommunisticheskii Internatsional*	2	"
6. Propaganda Department	2	"

Several aspects of the report deserve comment. The commission directed its efforts at verifying the apparatus staff, not the Comintern leadership. Nor was it a verification of the ECCI members elected by the Seventh Comintern Congress, but rather of their paid employees. Apparently not all staff members were reviewed, because in early 1937 there were 606 people associated with the ECCI apparatus. How the 387 people reviewed were selected is unclear.[112] The staff of the ECCI apparatus paid the price for the leaders' vigilance. As the section on the reasons for removing people suggests, the goal of the commission was to remove anyone whose past political behaviors or associations raised doubts. People who had had or were alleged to have had ties to convicted "enemies," Trotskyists, or other oppositionists accounted for 63 percent of those removed. Political purity was of greater concern than competence, as the removal of only four people for incompetence suggests.

Although members of fraternal parties composed slightly less than half the staff reviewed by the Moskvin Commission, they accounted for 60 percent of those removed. This figure undoubtedly masks the true proportion of political émigrés removed, for many émigrés were VKP members. Departments (e.g., Translations and Publishing) that required the language skills that émigrés possessed were especially hard hit. The verification of the Moskvin Commission, like other verifications from 1935, had a decidedly antiforeign quality to it. Eighteen percent of all fraternal party members and 20 percent of the members of the German party who worked in the apparatus were removed. Their removal markedly changed the ethnic composition of the ECCI apparatus. Finally, the commission removed 15 percent of the staff members reviewed, a reasonably high proportion. But the rate was much higher in those departments, such as Translations, Publishing, and Propaganda, in which many émigrés worked and which were responsible for producing the materials that the Secretariat demanded for the anti-Trotskyist campaign. Stalin and the party leadership may have viewed vigilance and political education as complementary policies for improving the quality of cadres, but in this case, vigilance depleted those departments that were central to the educational mission. It bears noting, however, that removal from the ECCI apparatus in early 1937 did not necessarily result in arrest. In fact, many of those removed were not arrested, although full information on every person is not available.

As intriguing as Document 29 is, it is a summary and provides little insight into which specific types of political errors, other than political associations, warranted removal from the ECCI apparatus. Fortunately, there is evidence that sheds light on this issue. On 27–28 January, during the Pyatakov trial, the Moskvin Commission met to review its findings, make its final recommendations, and approve its final report. The commission organized its report by administrative units: the staffs of the Secretaries, the Propaganda Department, the Translation Department, the Cadres Department, and so forth. For each it listed the names and relevant biographical information about those people whose performance or political activities had raised concern. In the right-hand column of the report, the commission recorded its recommendations. The report presented the names and biographies of forty-seven people whom it recommended removing from their positions. Of these, it recommended that twenty-three be "removed from work in the ECCI apparat," that sixteen be "released from work in the ECCI apparat," that three be returned to their native countries, and that two be considered for internal transfers. The distinction between being removed and being released from work is unclear. Upon reviewing the report, Dimitrov approved all but four of the recommendations. In two cases, he overrode the recommendation to consider the people for internal transfer and wrote "remove" (*sniat'*); in one case, he wrote "review again" (*eshche raz proverit'*).[113] No one could accuse Dimitrov of lacking vigilance.

A few examples illustrate how the commission justified removing people. Consider the case of József Révai, a Hungarian who had worked in Ercoli's Secretariat as an analyst from November 1934. The son of an employee, Révai joined the Hungarian CP in 1918. During the short-lived Hungarian Soviet Republic of 1919, he was the editor of the party's theoretical journal. After the fall of the Republic, he made his way to Vienna, where he worked for the Hungarian party press. He returned to Hungary in 1926 as a member of the Central Committee Secretariat to conduct illegal party work. In December 1930 he was arrested; upon his release in January 1934 he went to the USSR and began work in the ECCI apparatus. His political credentials would appear to be impressive, but according to the commission, his political errors were as follows: "After the Sixth CI Congress, he joined in a bloc with the Sas-Barna group, and after breaking from this group, he did not carry out a consistent struggle against this group. Problems of philosophy separated [him from their] idealistic views. At the time of his arrest in 1930, he told the police that he had participated in the Second Congress of the party and that he had entered the USSR on a Soviet steamer. At the time of the struggle with Magyar, he took a position that comrade Smoliankii characterized as 'a daily game of cards.' He [Révai] confessed that Magyar cultivated him and that he did not rebuff Magyar."[114]

Révai's offenses, though relatively minor, were clear enough. He had deviated from the party line and had demonstrated a lack of vigilance toward Magyar, who had been expelled from the VKP and arrested in December 1934. His acknowledgment that he had given the Hungarian police some information, no matter how inconsequential, may well have caused the commission members to wonder what else he had told the police. Révai had on three occasions demonstrated a lack of vigilance and Bolshevik toughness. There was no room in the ECCI apparatus for those who wavered, hence the commission recommended that he be removed from work. Dimitrov's bold, handwritten lines next to the final paragraph suggest his support of the recommendation. Nonetheless, Révai survived the mass repression. From 1937 to 1939 he conducted underground party work in Prague, and then he returned to Moscow to work in the ECCI Press Department.

The case of Betty Shenfeld, who had belonged to the German CP for only nine months at some unspecified time and who had worked in the ECCI Translation Department from 1932 to October 1936, was straightforward. She arrived in the USSR in 1932 with her husband, "who in 1934 was arrested and convicted as a Trotskyist. She broke with him, but until recently had ties to the Trotskyists Vilenchuk, Berman-Yudin [Yurin], and others."[115] Personal connections to Trotskyists aroused serious suspicions among the commission members, so Betty Shenfield was removed.

Such was also the case with A. S. Belostotskaia, who was born in Poland and had family members there. Although she was not a party member, her husband had been expelled twice from the party as a Trotskyist. He had been expelled in 1924 but was readmitted in 1928. During the 1934 purge he was demoted to candidate status for his "low level of political literacy and poor party discipline." During the verification of party documents (1935) and the exchange of party documents (1936), he refused to denounce Trotskyists and Zinovievites allegedly known to him. Consequently, the Smolensk city party committee expelled him. Belostotskaia herself appears to have committed no political errors. But for her husband's consistent "oppositional activities" and her family ties to Poland, the commission recommended that she be released from work in the ECCI apparatus.[116]

The mere existence of the commission shows the seriousness with which the Secretariat viewed the need to have a staff of proven political reliability. Those who had previous contacts with former oppositionists or factionalists were natural suspects in an organization that touted the need for vigilance to its adherents throughout the world. The decisions of the Moskvin Commission reduced the size of the ECCI apparatus, but in so doing, the commission believed that the apparatus had been politically strengthened (one is reminded here of Lenin's aphorism "Better fewer, but better").[117] In the process of verifying staff, the files of the Cadres Department were augmented.

About the time the Moskvin Commission was completing its work, so, too, was the commission verifying the members of the Western Belorussian Communist Party who had emigrated from Poland to the USSR. Its report makes clear that the Western Belorussian comrades had vigilantly fulfilled their assigned task. On 1 March 1937 the commission had reached conclusions on 2,044 of the 2,164 party members in Soviet emigration. It recommended that 61 percent (1,247) of them be returned to Poland and that 80 percent of that group be denied contact with the party. The report noted that 151 people (7 percent) had already been arrested (five of them had been executed), that it had received "special orders" from the NKVD to keep 21 other people in the USSR, and that it had sent materials on 239 additional people (12 percent) to the NKVD. There was no indication that the NKVD had yet arrested any of the latter group. Although the commission recommended that slightly more than a quarter of the 2,044 people reviewed be allowed to remain in the USSR, almost 20 percent of that group was to live in "deep exile" in the "hinterlands."[118] According to the commission, "suspicious" and "dangerous" elements made up a substantial majority (69 percent) of those reviewed.

Unless one is to believe that "hostile elements" and "enemy agents" constituted two-thirds of Western Belorussian CP members living in the USSR, the recommendations suggest that the demands of party discipline, the desire of commission members to prove their vigilance, and the increasingly tense political atmosphere in the country profoundly influenced the deliberations and decisions of the commission. Party discipline and party identity proved more powerful than national identity and ethnic loyalties. The rationales of the commission members for making the decisions that they did remain a mystery. It is impossible to determine the extent to which the findings reflected their beliefs that their compatriots posed a potential threat to the USSR and the VKP or self-defense—that is, a decision to prove their personal vigilance by sacrificing others. Nor can we discount the possibility that Western Belorussian party members and émigrés used the verification to settle personal and political scores, to denounce each other to the commission or other agencies. Given the stresses that defined émigré life, such behavior is hardly improbable.[119] In all likelihood, party discipline, belief, fear, vigilance, self-defense, and pettiness all contributed to the results of the verification.

The report undoubtedly disturbed many in the ECCI and the Cadres Department. The commission concluded that more than two-thirds (69 percent) of the cases reviewed produced evidence sufficient to warrant arrest, investigation by the NKVD, or denial of the right to have any dealings with the party. The conclusions provided evidence to support those who believed that "enemies" had penetrated party organizations and that the vigilance to date had been insufficient. Nor was this the only such report.[120] It is unclear whether Stalin saw these reports. But by February 1937 he viewed the Comintern with increasing suspicion; he told Dimitrov: "All of you in the Comintern are working in the hands of the enemy."[121]

In the seven months following the July 1936 secret Central Committee letter, the political atmosphere and dynamics within the USSR, the ECCI, and the fraternal parties changed dramatically. The anti-Trotskyist and vigilance campaigns prior to July seem tame compared to what they had become by March 1937, and what they would soon become. It was not simply a case of those campaigns picking up momentum. Rather, the August and January trials and the results of the verifications of fraternal party members living in the USSR provided "evidence" that "proved" the correctness of and need for those campaigns. Each event provided "evidence" that lent credence to accusations that "enemies" were at work within the VKP and the USSR and that national security was at grave risk. Each provided "evidence" of the need for real as opposed to rhetorical vigilance. Each fostered the denunciations of "mutual suspicions" that Dimitrov had lamented but that his, the Secretariat's, and the ECCI's actions helped create.

The Cadres Department and ECCI party committee played crucial roles. The trials prompted both to compile lists of VKP members with "oppositional tendencies" and of "hostile elements" among émigrés. They forwarded those lists to the NKVD and ORPO. The verification commissions deemed substantial numbers of émigrés to be "suspicious" or "dangerous." The NKVD and ORPO received those lists, too. Such lists reinforced the deepening belief that there were many enemies within the gates.

For members of the ECCI and the fraternal parties, the political imperatives created by the trials and the reports of the verification commissions generated considerable political uncertainty and increased their vulnerability. Some surely entertained private doubts about the trials and the ensuing demands for greater vigilance. All behaved as though the trials were what they appeared to be—trials of conspirators who threatened the VKP and the USSR. Precisely because the dangers appeared so grave, whatever private doubts comrades harbored, they rallied more closely around the party, they demanded more vigilance, they suspected anyone who might threaten the institution that gave them identity, status, and power.

By 1936 the anti-Trotskyist campaign within the Comintern had been going on for more than a dozen years under the direction of several Comintern leaders—Zinoviev, Bukharin, Molotov, Pyatnitsky, and Dimitrov. The vigilance campaign was of even longer standing, although the "enemy" changed periodically. Those who may have doubted the veracity of the trials or the need for heightened vigilance found themselves (consciously or not) ensnared by their participation in these campaigns and the values, beliefs, and social norms that the campaigns instilled and reinforced. The demands of party discipline and political survival ensured their compliance. Many willingly complied, motivated by a sincere belief in the imminent danger. But these were not the only factors at work. As the ECCI leaders and members knew only too well, the world was a very dangerous place for Communists, and the prospects of war were very real. Those realities made it very difficult for Communists to deny the need for vigilance, especially in light of the "confessions" by the alleged conspirators. So long as vigilance and verifications were directed primarily against former oppositionists, lower-level staff, and foreigners, the dangers to "real Bolsheviks," Comintern leaders, and native-born Bolsheviks had seemed remote. What the August and January trials did was to make the danger much less remote for those groups. As the verification of the ECCI apparatus showed, one group—ECCI members—was not yet a target. To date, they had managed to deflect any suspicions or accusations. But as the political atmosphere deteriorated, the risks to all increased.

Although the number of people arrested mounted steadily from mid-1936, the mass repression, the Yezhovshchina, had not yet begun. Some groups had already become real or potential targets—former oppositionists and people associated with them, certain émigrés, and fraternal party members. Although they lived in an atmosphere of increasing anxiety and suspicion, most associated with the Comintern remained at liberty; most of those whose names appeared on the various lists went on with their lives. But the more lists were forwarded to the Central Committee and the NKVD, the more "evidence" Stalin and Yezhov had to buttress their argument that "enemies" threatened the party and the state.

Дорогой Николай Иванович!

Прошу Вас в ближайшие дни принять меня по вопросу о мероприятиях против проникновения под видом политэмигрантов и член братских компартий на территорию СССР шпионов и диверсантов.

Я бы хотел здесь вкратце определить круг тех вопросов, которые по моему подлежат обсуждению при нашей встрече:

о закрытии так называемых "зеленых" переправ, через границу не только для поляков, но и для финнов, латышей, литовцев, эстонцев, как партий, неблагополучных по провокации (у румынской партии "зеленой переправы" нев). Лишь в особо исключительных случаях допускать использование "зеленой переправы", в по специальному разрешению ЦК ВКП(б).

Ограничить приток политэмиграцию в СССР, политически обосновав это в братских компартиях. необходимостью борьбы против массового дезертирства с поля классовых боев и опасностью деконспирации партийных кадров. В этих целях необходимо

а) разрешать в'езд в СССР только тем лицам, которые лично известны ЦК соответствующей компартии и Коминтерну, имеют специальное разрешение и рекомендацию ЦК своей партии на от'езд в СССР и лишь в том случае, если этим лицам угрожает суровая репрессия в своей стране и преследования в других капиталистических странах. Исключение допускается лишь для больны товарищей, нуждающихся в специальном лечении и направляемых в СССР по ходатайству ЦК соответствующей компартии и с согласия ЦК ВКП(б) с тем, чтобы после окончания курса лечения товарищ немедленно вернулся в страну; б) см н. оборот

в) запретить международным организациям оставлять или содействовать оставлению на территории СССР интуристов по окончании срока их пребывания в СССР;

DOCUMENT 6. First page of the letter from Manuilsky to Yezhov regarding measures against "spies and saboteurs disguised as political émigrés," 3 January 1936

АНГЛИЯ

Trial gang Trotzky-Zinoviev unveils picture huge crime of these
mean degenerates stop ~~xxxxxxxxxx~~ These abominable traitors
of workingclass , ~~xxxxxxxxx~~ recognising all hope lost regards
failure socialist constuction, and having no support within country made terror to ~~their~~ chief method of their conterrevolutionary
activity step Now it has been clearly established that criminal murder of Kirov has been prepared and ~~xxxxxx~~ carried through according to direct ~~xxxxxxxxxxxx~~/Trotzky and Zinoviev, that accor-
                    instructions of
ding to their immediate ~~xxxxxxxx~~ instructions have been prepared
a serie of other terroristic actions against leaders of CPSU and
Soviet State, in first place against comrade Stalin stop New it has
been ascertained documentarily that they have established direct
collections with the fascist GESTAPO in order to carry through their
terroristic activity step RUNAG will inform fully about course of
                                              widely
trial step Point out newspapers necessity utilize/this material
~~xxxxxxxxxx~~ in order to tear off definitively mask ~~from~~ of mean
agent of fascism stop With facts in hands prove, that trotskism is
vanguard
/conterrevolutionary ~~xxxxxx~~ bourgeoisie, that he maintains open
connections with Hearst press in United States of America and so-
erate connections with fascist GESTAPO, that to-day he is endea-
       in Spain   most
vours/through criminal ~~xxx~~ game with/extremest slogans ~~fascist~~
to facilitate intervention ~~xx~~ of german and italian fascism and
                           fascist
playing into the hands of/rebels., that he is acting as ~~agent~~

DOCUMENT 13. First page of the telegram from the ECCI Secretariat to
the Communist Party of Great Britain on the lessons of Trotskyist
"counterrevolutionary activity" as revealed by the August 1936 trial,
20 August 1936

22

Сов.секретно.

С П Р А В К А

О ТРОЦКИСТАХ И ДРУГИХ ВРАЖДЕБНЫХ ЭЛЕМЕНТАХ В СОСТАВЕ ЭМИГРАЦИИ В К.П. ГЕРМАНИИ.

На территории СССР в числе немецкой эмиграции находятся люди, которые были известны в КПГ, как активные троцкисты и фракционеры вплоть до своего приезда в СССР:

1/ СОЛОМОН МУШИНСКИЙ /СЦАЛМОШ/ - член КПГ с 1921 г., активный соратник Рут Фишер - Маслова, участник Коршевской оппозиции, имевший за все время пребывания в партии тесную связь с исключенными из партии ультра-левыми и троцкистами. О нем еще в 1931г. в партии распространился слух, что его брат агент польской охранки, что он вместе со своим братом торговал в Хемнице кокаином и т.д. По заявлению немецкой секции, он постоянно домогался получать нагрузку, но ему, под разными предлогами, отказывали, не доверяя.

После ареста Бермана-Юрина, жена его, Соня Фихман рассказала Коска /члену КПГ/, что во время пребывания Коска в гостях на квартире Берман-Юрина последний разговаривал по телефону по-русски с Мушинским /Сцалмошом/. Этот факт свидетельствует о связи Мушинского с Берман-Юриным.

Мушинский приехал в СССР в 1931г. через торгпредство, где работал в Берлине. Исключен из ВКП/б/. Просил рекомендацию у Коска, который ему отказал.

Немецкое представительство 26 апреля 1936г. послало в Комиссию Партийного Контроля положительную характеристику, как члену КПГ, сославшись на хороший отзыв ячейки. Место его работы

DOCUMENT 17. Cadres Department memorandum "On Trotskyists and other hostile elements in the émigré community of the German CP," 2 September 1936

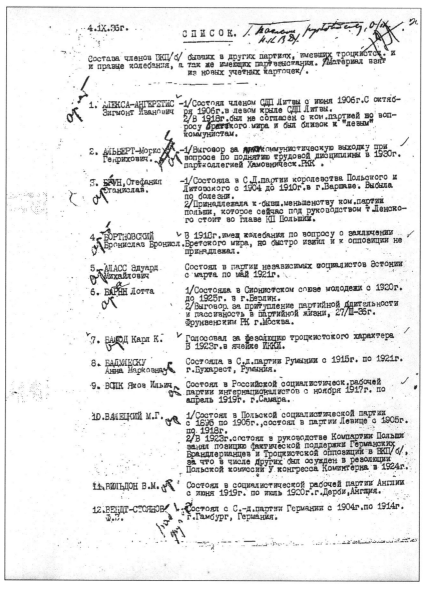

4.1Х.36г.

СПИСОК.

Состава членов ВКП/б/ бывших в других партиях, имевших троцкистск. и
и правые колебания, а так же имеющих партвзыскания. /Материал взят
из новых учетных карточек./

1. АЛЕКСА-АНГЕРЕТИС -1/Состоял членом СДП Литвы с июня 1906г.С октяб-
Зигмонт Иванович   ря 1906г.в левом крыле СДП Литвы.
                    2/В 1918г.был не согласен с ком.партией по воп-
                      росу Бретского мира и был близок к "левым"
                      коммунистам.

2. АЛЬБЕРТ-Морис   -1/Выговор за антикоммунистическую выходку при
Генрихович.   вопросе по поднятию трудовой дисциплины в 1930г.
                      партколлегией Хамовническ.РКК.

3. БРУН,Стефания   -1/Состояла в С.Д.партии королевства Польского и
Станислав.   Литовского с 1904 до 1910г. в г.Варшаве. Выбыла
                      по болезни.
                    2/Принадлежала к бывш.меньшенству ком.партии
                      польши, которое сейчас под руководством т.Ленско-
                      го стоит во главе КП Польши.

4. БОРТНОВСКИЙ   В 1918г.имел колебания по вопросу о заключении
Бронислав Бронисл.   Бретского мира, но быстро изжил и к оппозиции не
                     принадлежал.

5. АЛАСС Эдуард   Состоял в партии независимых социалистов Эстонии
Михайлович   с марта по май 1921г.

6. ВАРНН Лотта   1/Состояла в Сионистском союзе молодежи с 1920г.
                      до 1925г. в г.Берлин.
                    2/Выговор за притупление партийной бдительности
                      и пассивность в партийной жизни, 27/III-36г.
                      Фрунзенским РК г.Москва.

7. БАГОД Карл К.   Голосовал за резолюцию троцкистского характера
                     В 1923г.в ячейке ИККИ.

8. БАДУЛЕСКУ   Состояла в С.д.партии Румынии с 1915г. по 1921г.
Анна Марковна.   г.Бухарест, Румыния.

9. ВОЛК Яков Ильич   Состоял в Российской социалистическ.рабочей
                     партии интернационалистов с ноября 1917г. по
                     апрель 1919г. г.Самара.

10.ВАЛЕЦКИЙ М.Г.   1/Состоял в Польской социалистической партии
                      с 1895 по 1905г.,состоял в партии Левице с 1905г.
                      по 1918г.
                    2/В 1923г.состоял в руководстве Компартии Польши
                      занял позицию фактической поддержки Германских
                      Брандлерианцев и Троцкистской оппозиции в ВКП/б/,
                      за что в числе других был осужден в резолюции
                      Польской комиссии У конгресса Коминтерна в 1924г.

11.ВИЛЬДОН В.М.   Состоял в социалистической рабочей партии Англии
                     с июня 1919г. по июль 1920г.г.Дерби,Англия.

12.ВЕНДТ-СТОЯНОВ   Состоял с С.-д.партии Германии с 1904г.по 1914г.
Ф.В.   г.Гамбург, Германия.

DOCUMENT 18. First page of a list of VKP members "formerly in other
parties, having Trotskyist and Rightist tendencies," sent by F. Kotelnikov
to the NKVD, 4 September 1936

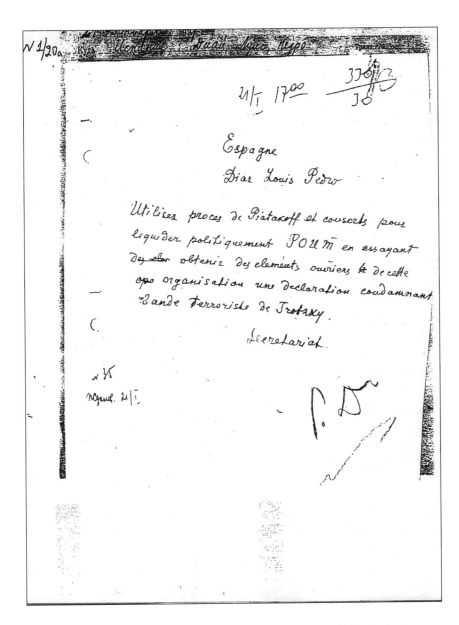

N 1/20a

21/I 17.00

Espagne
Diaz Louis Pedro

Utilisez procès de Piatakoff et consorts pour
liquider politiquement POUM en essayant
des obtenir des éléments ouvriers de cette
organisation une déclaration condamnant
bande terroriste de Trotzky.

Secrétariat

DOCUMENT 23. Telegram from the ECCI Secretariat to Díaz in Spain, 21 January 1937

Сов.секретно.

23

ДОКЛАДНАЯ ЗАПИСКА

О РЕЗУЛЬТАТАХ РАБОТЫ КОМИССИИ СЕКРЕТАРИАТА ИККИ ПО ПРОВЕРКЕ КВАЛИФИКАЦИИ АППАРАТА ИККИ.

Комиссия за период своей работы рассмотрела 387 дел со-трудников аппарата ИККИ и интернациональных организаций.

Рассмотренные дела по отдельным звеньям и секторам раз-биваются:

1. Работники Секретариатов 69
2. ИКК 2
3. Отдел Кадров 37
4. Бюро Секр-та 25
5. Отдел Переводов 60
6. Отдел Пропаганды 39
7. Издател.Сектор 15
8. Редакция "К.И." 20
9. Представители партий 26
10. Секции 32
11. Партком и местком 2
12. КИМ 1
13. Изд-во иностр.рабочих 11
14. Разные интернац.орг-ции . . . . . 48.

По партийному составу:

1. Членов ВКП(б) 107
2. Членов ВЛКСМ 25
3. Беспартийных 66
4. Членов братских компартий 189,

в том числе:

1. КП Германии 92
2. " Франции 7
3. " Англии 10
4. " США 9
5. " Австрии 9
6. " Румынии 3
7. " Югославии 3
8. " Венгрии 3
9. " Латвии 4

DOCUMENT 29. First page of the memorandum on the results of the work of the commission of the ECCI Secretariat to verify the qualifications of the ECCI apparatus, 5 February 1937

II-25

Г. Ежову.

Прилагаю заметки о различных делах,
касающихся следующих лиц:

1. Мельникова
2. Ганецкого
3. Наджанского (Бреслера)
4. Василевского
5. Брике
6. Млынецкого
7. Раскольникова
8. Карахана

18. V. 1937

[signature]

DOCUMENT 30. First page of the denunciations made by Walecki and sent to Yezhov, 18 May 1937

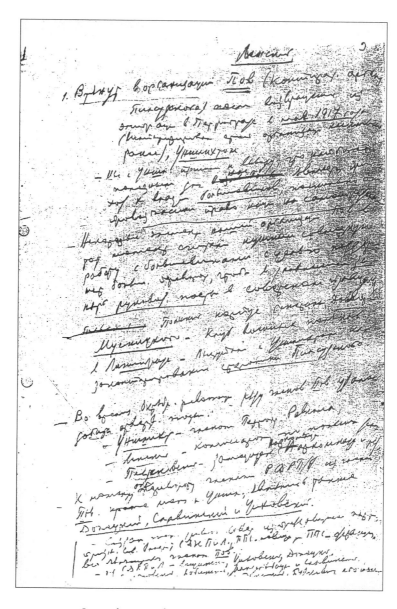

DOCUMENT 34. Second page of Dimitrov's handwritten notes from the investigation materials in the case of the Polish Communists, 1937

е/ 6/19.VII В архив дело личное прокофьево ЧЧ

Секретарю Исполкома Коминтерна

тов. МАНУИЛЬСКОМУ.-

Зав.Отделом Кадров Коминтерна

тов. БЕЛОВУ.-

Секретарю Парткома ИККИ

тов. КОТЕЛЬНИКОВУ.

В связи с указанием тов. Мануильского пишу следующие данные о моей политической биографии.

В 1924-25 году я был на областном совещании в Ленинграде, где враги народа Глебов-Авилов, Румянцев пытались протащить на троцкистско-зиновьевские позиции участников совещания, в частности по вопросу о середняке , о необходимости введения постоянных делегатских совещаний середняцкой молодежи — мы, псковская делега[ция] , в том числе и я , были активно против этой вылазки. Во время X1V с"езда партии я был секретарем Островского Укома комсомола Ленинградской области, как только стало известно о выступлении оппозиции на с"езде партии, я активно мобилизовал организацию на борьбу против оппозиции за линию партии. В Островскую организацию в тот период было прислано на комсомольскую работу три опп[о]зиционера (Магдариев, Кошин, Соколов) - все они были изгнаны из организации, как люди уже в то время активно разлагавшие рабо[ту] комсомола. В 1926 году в Ленинграде вместе с тов. Соболевым я выступал на собраниях актива комсомола Нарвского и Выбо[р]гского районов против открыто враждебных вылазок Румянцева, Толмазова и Суровал. В Выборгском районе дело дошло до физическо[го] столкновения с оппозиционерами, в котором я принимал участие.

Я по мере моих сил принимал активное участие в борьбе с правыми. В тот период я был секретарем Великолуцкого ОК комсомола, комсомольская организация этого округа, который я возглав-

DOCUMENT 35. First page of N. Prokofiev's "political biography,"
19 December 1937

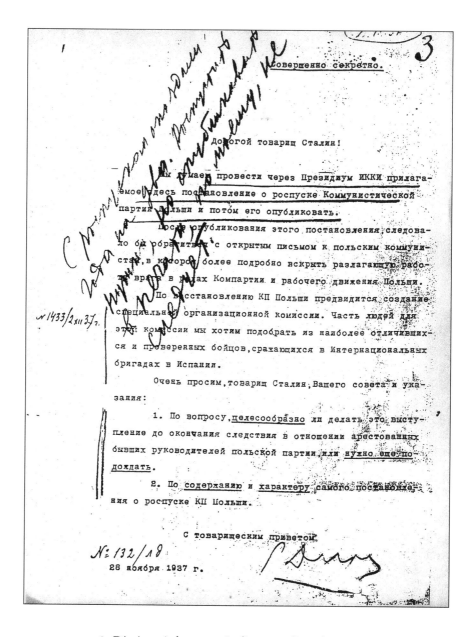

Совершенно секретно.

Дорогой товарищ Сталин!

Мы думаем провести через Президиум ИККИ прилага-
емое здесь постановление о роспуске Коммунистической
партии Польши и потом его опубликовать.

После опубликования этого постановления, следова-
ло бы обратиться с открытым письмом к польским коммуни-
стам, в котором более подробно вскрыть разлагающую работу врага в рядах Компартии и рабочего движения Польши.

По восстановлению КП Польши предвидится создание
специальной организационной комиссии. Часть людей для
этой комиссии мы хотим подобрать из наиболее отличивших-
ся и проверенных бойцов, сражающихся в Интернациональных
бригадах в Испании.

Очень просим, товарищ Сталин, Вашего совета и ука-
зания:

1. По вопросу, целесообразно ли делать это высту-
пление до окончания следствия в отношении арестованных
бывших руководителей польской партии или нужно еще по-
дождать.

2. По содержанию и характеру самого постановления о роспуске КП Польши.

С товарищеским приветом.

№ 132/18
28 ноября 1937 г.

DOCUMENT 38. Dimitrov's letter to Stalin regarding the ECCI resolution
on the dissolution of the Polish CP, with Stalin's handwritten reply,
28 November 1937

зкз.ас.
.УП-38г.

Сов.Секретно.

ПРОЕКТ ПОСТАНОВЛЕНИЯ

Об исключении из состава членов и кандидатов Исполкома Коминтерна
и членов Интернациональной Контрольной Комиссии, оказавшихся ~~Изме~~
~~и Изменами~~ врагами народа.

ПОСТАНОВИЛИ: Исключить из состава членов и кандидатов Исполкома Коминтерна и членов Интернациональной Контрольной Комиссии,
как врагов народа следующих лиц:

Члены Исполкома:

1. БРОНКОВСКОГО В.В.
2. КУНА Бела
3. ЛЕНСКОГО Ю.Е.
4. ЧАН-ГО-тао

Кандидаты Исполкома:

1. БЕЛЕВСКОГО Я.С.   6. ПОПОВ Н.Н.
2. ГОРКИЧА М.М.
3. КРУМИНА Я.М.
4. ПРУХНЯКА Э.
5. ЧЕМОДАНОВА В.Т.

Члены Интернациональной Контрольной Комиссии:

1. АНГАРЕТИСА З.И.
2. АНВЕЛЬТА Я.Я.
3. ВАЛЕЦКОГО М.Г.
4. ГРЖЕГОЖЕВСКОГО Ф.Я.
5. ИСКРОВА П.Х.
6. КРАЕВСКОГО А.П.
7. ЭВЕРЛЕЙНА Гуго

DOCUMENT 43. Draft resolution of the ECCI Presidium regarding the
expulsion of ECCI members and candidate members and ICC members
"who turned out to be enemies of the people," 3 July 1938

Генеральному Секретарю Исполкома Коминтерна
Г. М. Димитрову

Решением "Особого Совещания" от 17 января 1940г. я выслана на 3 года в Красноярский край с формулировкой "за участие в антисоветской организации". Это решение меня морально совсем убило, ибо оно непонятно мне и не по моей вине.

Георгий Михайлович, я вам подробно написала из тюрьмы в чем меня обвинили и что оклеветал меня Мюллер (Мельников) еще в мае 1937г. Для меня с первого дня ареста ясно было, что я оклеветана, что я ... клевета врагами, которые имея я работала в Секретариате, они прекрасно знали каким доверием я пользовалась, и конечно они значили быть иметь на этом участке работы своего человека и немудрено, что любой клеветой они решили от меня избавиться. 15½ месяцев я сижу оклеветанная в Бутырской тюрьме и, несмотря на мои физические недомогания я старалась морально себя поддерживать глубокой верой, что следствие разберется, что я буду реабилитирована и вернусь к семье, к работе к нормальной жизни. Тем сильнее был для меня удар, когда я получила решение "Осо". Для меня сейчас вопрос реабилитации себя является вопросом моей дальнейшей жизни, вопрос нормальной жизни моей семьи и его единственного ребенка, перед которым я действительно виновата отдавая себя целиком работе — очень часто не имея возможности уделять должного внимания ребенку.————————

Георгий Михайлович, ведь я хорошо знаю, что перед партией, перед Советской властью, перед руководством ИККИ у меня совесть чиста, также я хорошо и твердо знаю, что самые мои сознательные и лучшие годы жизни я провела в рядах партии и жила только интересами партии также хорошо я знаю, что все 19 лет моего пребывания в рядах партии где бы я не была, какую бы работу мне не поручали, на любом участке я всегда оставалась в первую очередь членом партии и в большинстве ... моя жизнь могла служить примером для многих и многих рядовых партийцев. Вопрос личной жизни всегда был у меня на последнем месте. Все это страшно легко проверить ведь есть.

Georgi Dimitrov

Dmitri Manuilsky

Osip Pyatnitsky

Ludwig Magyar
(Lajos Milgorf)

Georgi Safarov

Fyodor Kotelnikov

Nikolai Yezhov

Mikhail Moskvin
(Meer Trilisser)

Moisei B. Chenomordik

Béla Kun

Elena Valter

Anna Razumova-Khigerovich

Anni Etterer

Franz Guber

Comintern leaders, 1935: *front, from left*, André Marty, Georgi Dimitrov, Palmiro Togliatti, Wilhelm Florin, and Wang Ming; *back, from left*, Mikhail Moskvin, Otto Kuusinen, Klement Gottwald, Wilhelm Pieck, and Dmitri Manuilsky

The Victims of Vigilance

We will mercilessly destroy anyone who, by his deeds or thoughts—yes, his thoughts—threatens the unity of the socialist state. To the complete destruction of all enemies, them and their clans.

— JOSEPH STALIN

There is nothing I can add to what Com. Stalin has said about the merciless struggle against enemies . . . I myself will do everything in my power to ensure that it is taken into account in the ranks of the Comintern.

— GEORGI DIMITROV

FROM 23 FEBRUARY TO 4 MARCH 1937, the Central Committee of the VKP held a historic Plenum. The delegates' strident rhetoric and relentless demands for vigilance were to have a profound impact on the mass repression that erupted that spring. Two issues occupied their attention. The first was what to do about the "anti-party activities of Bukharin and Rykov"; the second centered on cadre policy.[1] During the August 1936 and January 1937 trials, Bukharin's and Rykov's names had been mentioned by defendants, and both were subjected to interrogation, although neither had yet been arrested or charged. Yezhov presented the main report against these two, who, in 1928–1929, had led the Right deviation that opposed Stalin's radical policies of collectivization and rapid industrialization. Since then, both had held responsible state positions and remained candidate Central Committee members. In a speech entitled "Lessons Flowing from the Harmful Activity, Diversion, and Espionage of the Japanese-German-Trotskyist Agents," Yezhov argued that the evidence available to the NKVD proved that Bukharin and Rykov knew of Trotskyist conspiracies. The two defended themselves before their comrades. Bukharin denied the charges and offered an impassioned defense in which he concurred with the widely shared belief that a conspiracy of spies and enemy agents existed, but he insisted that he was not one of them. The delegates were unconvinced. Speaker after speaker denounced the two whose activities "proved," they said, the need for heightened vigilance. Dimitrov described Bukharin's speech as a "disgusting and pathetic spectacle!"[2] The discussion occupied the delegates' attention for the better part of five days. No one present defended the two, and some delegates demanded blood. Stalin cautioned the delegates against violating the letter and spirit of party rules, and the final resolution reflected his counsel: "Expulsion from the Party; turn the case over to the NKVD" for further investigation.[3]

Although the Bukharin and Rykov case may have provided the most dramatic moments at the Plenum, the major debates centered on party cadre issues—the quality of party cadres and the relative roles of vigilance, education, and democracy in restoring the party to health. Solving them was anything but simple. Yezhov and Molotov advocated the radical position that stressed the need for greater vigilance in unmasking and removing former oppositionists and enemy agents, arguing that enemies had penetrated the party and some high-ranking state offices. To them, Pyatakov's conviction was proof of how thoroughly the enemy had penetrated the country and how essential vigilance was to national security. They advocated a similar position toward the party. No one publicly disputed the need for vigilance. The real issue was how much power to give to the NKVD.

Although vigilance might lead to unmasking enemies, it could not in and of itself improve the quality of party cadres. To achieve the latter goal, Andrei Zhdanov emphasized the need for improved education of party members and the strengthening of inner-party democracy.[4] He argued that only sustained party education would improve the quality of cadres and, in the process, lay the basis for enduring inner-party democracy. Like Yezhov and Molotov, Zhdanov called for vigilance and directed sharp attacks toward certain party officials, but he offered a different solution. Specifically, he advocated a return to secret-ballot party elections. He criticized the "intolerable practice" of the co-optation of party officials and the long-standing tradition of voting for party committees by lists. These practices had to be ended, he argued, and replaced by secret-ballot elections for individuals after party committees had openly revealed the shortcomings that afflicted their organization and leaders. Such inner-party democracy would enable the rank-and-file party members to remove those who had failed to properly or faithfully execute their duties and would thereby restore confidence in the party, confidence that ironically was eroded by the suspicions inherent in the continual calls for vigilance.

Stalin delivered two speeches to the Plenum. In the first, entitled "Deficiencies in Party Work and Methods for the Liquidation of the Trotskyists and Other Double-Dealers," he stressed the existence of widespread espionage and wrecking even among "responsible workers." He harshly criticized those who minimized the threats posed by "enemies" and who had "carelessly ignored the calls to improve political and organizational work and thus turn the party into an 'impregnable fortress.'"[5] His call for "vigilance against enemies" convinced the delegates to strengthen the powers and authority of the NKVD. Stalin stated bluntly that enemies had to "smashed," but he sidestepped defining who, other than the Trotskyists, constituted the "enemy." He said that there were only "about 12,000 party members who sympathized with Trotskyism to some extent or other. Here you see the total forces of the Trotskyist gentlemen." To Stalin, the ranks of the enemy constituted a small percentage of the 130,000 to 190,000 members who made up the "total command staff" of the party. "Enemies," not the party bureaucracy, not "real Bolsheviks," had to be "smashed." Although he stressed vigilance, he also underscored the importance of "giving ideological training to our party cadres."

In his second speech, the concluding speech of the Plenum, Stalin discussed how to balance vigilance, education, and party democracy. One historian has described it as "vintage Stalin—each point was treated as an attempt to find the mean between two extremes and pursue a pragmatic policy."[6] Given the relevance of Stalin's comments and cautions to what had already unfolded and would continue to unfold within the Comintern, it is worth examining them in some detail.

Stalin tempered somewhat his earlier call for vigilance against Trotskyists.

> But here is the question—how to carry out in practice the task of smashing and uprooting the German-Japanese agents of Trotskyism? Does this mean that we should strike and uproot not only the real Trotskyists, but also those who wavered at some time toward Trotskyism, and then long ago came away from Trotskyism; not only those who are really Trotskyist agents for wrecking, but also those who happened once upon a time to go along a street where some Trotskyist or other had once passed? At any rate such voices were heard at the plenum. Can we consider such an interpretation of the resolution to be correct? No, we can not consider it correct.
>
> On this question, as on all other questions, there must be an individual, differentiated approach. . . .

Among our responsible comrades, there are a certain number of former Trotskyists who left Trotskyism long ago, and now fight against Trotskyism not worse, but
better than some of our respected comrades who never chanced toward Trotskyism.
It would be foolish to vilify such comrades now.[7]

With such statements he apparently sought to moderate the more strident calls
for vigilance made by Yezhov, Molotov, and other "voices" and to warn party
leaders and members, like Kotelnikov, to prove their vigilance not by denouncing those who had "wavered at some time toward Trotskyism" but by
supporting those who "now fight against Trotskyism."

Stalin also joined Zhdanov in condemning violations of party democracy,
especially co-optation and "familyness"—that is the appointment to party offices of "personal friends, fellow townsmen, people who have shown personal
devotion." Familyness discouraged constructive criticism and self-criticism
and created conditions that provided family members with "a certain independence both of the local people and of the Central Committee of the
party."[8] To eliminate that practice and other problems that beset the party bureaucracy, Stalin advocated "still another kind of verification, the check-up
from below, in which the masses, the subordinates, verify the leaders, pointing
out their mistakes and showing the way to correct them. This kind of verification is one of the most effective methods of checking up on people."[9]

Stalin made a point of telling party leaders that their positions did not make
them omniscient and that they needed to heed the criticism and advice of the
party masses, of the "little people." He also condemned the "formal and
heartless bureaucratic attitude of some of our party comrades toward the fate
of individual party members" expelled from the party: "Only people who in
essence are profoundly anti-party can have such an approach to members of
the party."[10]

Taken together, Stalin's comments to the Plenum urged the party to greater
vigilance in unmasking enemies, demanded that party members be better educated, and condemned the time-honored tradition of co-optation and its inevitable consequence, familyness. For Stalin and others, vigilance, education,
and party democracy were complementary policies designed to achieve the
same goal—improving the quality of party cadres. What Stalin advocated was
steering a balanced course between the Scylla of root-and-branch vigilance
and the Charybdis of formalistic political leadership. While the "great helms-
man" might possess the strength and experience to steer such a course without
undue damage, not everyone did. Nor did everyone want to ignore the Sirens'

calls for vigilance. Over the next few months, the demands of the vigilance campaign overwhelmed efforts to improve party education.

Indeed, the calls by Stalin and the other Central Committee delegates to practice vigilance, smash enemies, and check up from below created considerable pressure on party members and non-party people alike to denounce what they deemed to be suspicious behaviors by their bosses, comrades, coworkers, rivals, and neighbors. Given the explicit assumption at the Plenum that "enemies" were within the gates, Stalin's measured call for an "individual, differentiated approach" to the verification of comrades was overwhelmed by the cacophony of calls for vigilance, for giving the NKVD increased powers, for smashing the enemy. His cautions may have tempered somewhat the resolution of the Plenum, but such nuances were drowned out by the rallying cries of the advocates of vigilance, comrades who believed that the August 1936 and January 1937 trials and other recent revelations proved that "enemies" threatened the party and national security. Of course, none of them believed that they themselves were "enemies."

In the months following the Plenum, the political atmosphere within the VKP and the ECCI apparatus became increasing uncertain and confusing. Denunciations, scapegoating, and demands for still more vigilance became common responses to the Plenum's challenge to root out "enemies." Arrests escalated notably during the spring. As they did, the lines between comrades and their denouncers, between comrades and "enemies," became increasingly blurred. In response, the members of the ECCI apparatus and party organization displayed two types of reactions. On the one hand, everyone conformed more strictly than ever to the rhetoric and behaviors expected of party members. On the other hand, subgroups of party members—leaders versus the rank and file, the native-born versus émigrés—crystallized, and each subgroup sought to prove its vigilance.

Dimitrov and Manuilsky both attended the February–March Plenum. Dimitrov described it as a "truly historic Plenum" and felt that Stalin's concluding speech contained "invaluable instructions."[11] Manuilsky voted with Yezhov and four other Central Committee members to expel Bukharin and Rykov from the VKP and "to transfer them to the court with application of the death penalty."[12] As the ECCI secretary responsible for cadres, Manuilsky sought to translate the Plenum's resolution and calls for vigilance into concrete policies. Given that he was responsible for cadre affairs, it is difficult to separate Manuilsky's personal views from his formal responsibilities or to ascertain when he was the enthusiastic initiator and when the loyal executioner of policies that stressed heightened vigilance. For almost three years Manuilsky had repeatedly called for vigilance, especially vis-à-vis Trotskyists and political émigrés. The Plenum reinforced his penchant for vigilance. But his was a vigilance shared by Dimitrov and Moskvin, as well as many others in the ECCI apparatus.

On 8 March 1937 a resolution of the ECCI Presidium and the ICC Bureau asserted that the penetration of "enemy agents" required still greater vigilance. It declared that fraternal party members who had joined the VKP and who were suspected of having abetted, even inadvertently, the "enemy" should be "unconditionally expelled from the party."[13]

On 1 April, Manuilsky drafted a letter on behalf of the ECCI Secretariat to Yezhov, Andreev, and Shkiriatov in which he expressed concerns about enemy penetration of the VKP. He wasted no time in stating that such penetration had occurred. The opening paragraph read: "The verification [1935] and exchange of party documents [1936] showed that the enemy uses a transfer to the VKP(b) to legalize its harmful activities and to cover its agents, Trotskyists, spies, and saboteurs with a party card. It is essential, therefore, to change the procedure for transferring members of the fraternal parties to the VKP(b) in order to protect the party from enemy penetration." Manuilsky expressed particular concern about the need to establish rigorous procedures for admitting members of fraternal parties to the VKP given that the party, which had halted admissions in 1933, was now ready to consider applications for admission. He noted that since 1933 more than ten thousand fraternal party members had taken up residence in the USSR and that half of them had already submitted applications for VKP membership.

Manuilsky viewed as unacceptable the previous method for transferring members of fraternal parties to the VKP. Before 1933 the Comintern leadership had relied on its section leaders to make recommendations. "The Comintern apparatus mechanically accepted the recommendations of the Comintern's responsible sections, and the commission for transfers within the CC VKP(b) accepted foreign Communists almost automatically into the VKP(b)." He then outlined the proposed guidelines of the ECCI Secretariat. Only those members of fraternal parties who had lived in the USSR for three years would be considered for admission to the VKP. Qualifying applicants needed recommendations and full biographical information from the Central Committee of their party. The Cadres Department of the ECCI would verify those documents. The applicants denied admission would be considered party sympathizers.

Such rules were to apply to all applicants except those from Poland. Manuilsky ended his letter, as he had his January 1936 letter to Yezhov, by expressing his deep concern about the Polish CP: "Finally, we recommend that in view of the penetration of agents of the class enemy in the Polish Communist Party that the transfer of members of the Polish Communist Party finding themselves on the territory of the USSR be temporarily suspended."[14] That was the least of the problems facing Polish Communists in the spring of 1937.

The Comintern's leaders devoted much of March to discussing how to translate the Plenum's decisions into policy. In early April those discussions began to bear fruit. On 9 April the Secretariat ordered all fraternal parties "to form Central Control Commissions," the chief tasks of which would be "to carefully examine and consider the cases of Party members who: a) Violate the unity and solidarity of the Party ranks; b) Violate Party discipline and rules of conspiracy; c) Reveal insufficient class vigilance; d) Do not show Bolshevik firmness in facing the class enemy; e) Conceal their anti-party position under the cloak of loyalty to the Party (double-dealers); f) Are agents of the class enemy who penetrated the ranks of the Party." The relation of the Control Commissions to their Central Committees was to be the same as that of the Central Control Commission to the Central Committee of the VKP.[15]

The same day, the ECCI Presidium and the Bureau of the ICC issued a resolution designed to end the "conciliatory attitude" among "leading Party members" toward "infringement of the rules of Party secrecy, [and] toward treachery and provocation." "Communists who betray the Party . . . are subject to unconditional expulsion," as were those "showing a conciliatory attitude toward the disclosure of secrecy [and] toward treachery and provocation." Such sanctions were hardly new. But then the resolution turned to the issue that so worried Manuilsky: "The I.C.C. must bring to strict Party accounting leading Party workers guilty of having recommended agents of the class enemy in their parties to the ranks of the leading sections of the Communist International"— that is, the VKP. Having announced the intention of continuing to pursue a vigilant policy toward "enemies" and their abettors, the resolution then echoed one of Stalin's "invaluable instructions." "Pitilessly expelling from the Party traitors, alien and hostile elements, double-dealers, degenerates, demoralized elements, crooks, incorrigible factionalists and people who systematically violate the rules of Party secrecy, the control commissions must, however, be lenient with those Party members who have made a mistake [but] are still capable of being good Party members and, realizing the incorrectness of their actions, honestly undertake by their future conduct to repair their guilt before the Party."[16]

Given the tone of the resolution, the conclusion that ECCI leaders appear to have drawn from the February–March Plenum was that vigilance was the most pressing task of the moment. Such a view was not unfounded.

The Plenum had addressed other issues, and the ECCI Secretariat sought to do the same. On 15 May 1937 a commission created by the Secretariat met to discuss a proposed resolution drafted by Manuilsky, its chair. Manuilsky's notes from the meeting and the transcript of the meeting reveal clearly that although the members spoke of the need for greater vigilance against Trotskyists, they viewed improved party education as essential to that struggle.[17] The draft resolution began by reiterating the Trotskyists' crimes, especially as they related to the international antiwar and labor movements. Trotskyists were the agents of "the darkest forces of reaction" (fascism, Japanese military imperialism, Hearst, etc.), who "disguise [their] undermining work here under the cover of 'Left' phrases." They acted as wreckers, provocateurs, and the "instigators of imperialist and counterrevolutionary war." The resolution stated that the "Presidium of the ECCI notes that many responsible workers of the Communist Parties in the capitalist countries, as well as workers in the Comintern, have not displayed adequate vigilance in relation to Trotskyism." This was cause for special concern because the "Trotskyists have been able to penetrate into such organizations as the Independent Labour Party, the Socialist Party of America," and, most critically, "the POUM in Spain . . . [where] they work freely in the rear of the Republican forces and organize counterrevolutionary uprisings at the request of the fascist command."[18]

In light of the "pernicious role of Trotskyism" and "the lessons of the Plenum of the CC CPSU," the ECCI Presidium proposed ten concrete measures to aid fraternal parties in their struggle. Half of them centered on how to heighten vigilance and expose Trotskyist penetration, half on improving party education and propaganda. Such a division faithfully reflected the major themes expressed at the February–March Plenum.

The suggestions designed to enhance vigilance were familiar: To use "the records of the trials" to expose Trotskyist activities, to remove "double-dealing Trotskyite elements . . . especially former Trotskyites who have . . . not shown that they sincerely abandoned Trotskyism," to have Central Committees "make a thorough examination of the entire illegal apparatus" to ensure that secrecy had not been compromised by hostile elements, and to "oblige the representatives of Communist Parties of the capitalist countries in the ECCI to carry through a serious campaign against Trotskyism among the Communist immigrants living in the USSR." There was, however, one new suggestion: "to audit all monetary records of Party property, paying particular attention to the detection of instances of embezzlement of Party funds by Trotskyite spies."

Complementing such recommendations were those that urged "extensive systematic propaganda work in all links of the Party." The resolution announced the ECCI's intention "to introduce into the curriculum of all Party schools and the people's universities under Communist influence a special course on the struggle against fascism and its Trotskyite agency." In these courses and in routine propaganda work, it noted the importance of using the "factual material on the spying and provocative work of the Trotskyites." "Realizing the importance of raising the ideological and political level of workers of the Comintern and its Sections in the interests of a successful struggle against Trotskyism," the Presidium further resolved to order the Cadres Department

> to organize work for raising the theoretical level of the representatives of the Communist Parties in the ECCI . . . [and] to organize for the Secretaries and members of the Politburos of the Communist Parties periodic three-month courses to work on the basic problems of world economics and politics, the world labor movement, Socialist construction in the USSR, and theoretical problems of interest to each of these comrades.
>
> To oblige the International Lenin School to organize one-year postgraduate courses and give editors of theoretical Party organs a higher ideological and political education.
>
> To oblige the Central Committees of the Communist Parties to raise to a higher level the study of the History of the [VKP].

Raising the ideological level of party members and strengthening the vigilance campaign were deeply intertwined in the commission members' comments on the draft. Dimitrov's comments exemplified their inseparability: "The struggle against Trotskyism should be argued theoretically, historically, politically. . . . We should proceed from [the assumption] that $9/10$ of the leading cadres of the Communist movement do not know the history of the Russian revolution and the history of the VKP(b), and [that] this has created fertile ground for the activities of the Trotskyists. . . . The serious study of Marxist-Leninist theory is necessary . . . to uncover the hidden Trotskyist enemies." The commission ended its deliberations by electing Manuilsky, Kuusinen, and Ercoli to compose the final resolution, to be entitled "On the Struggle with Trotskyism."[19]

In light of the firestorm of repression that was soon to engulf the Comintern apparatus and fraternal parties, the discussions over how to balance vigilance and education remind one of Francisco Goya's painting *Two Men Fighting in Quicksand*. Yet the discussion provides an important reminder that no one knew that mass repression was imminent, hence work proceeded as normal. It also allows us to reflect on some important points about how past Comintern behaviors set the stage for the Comintern's destruction.

Vigilance against critics of the VKP and the USSR was a long-standing tradition in the Comintern, which had once dubbed Social Democrats "social fascists." The anti-Trotskyist campaign was both its most enduring and its most recent manifestation. To Bolsheviks and the Comintern leaders, vigilance was a precondition of strength. The expulsions of the Safarovs, Magyars, dubious political émigrés, and others from late 1934 to early 1937 was consistent with the expulsions of Trotskyists, Brandlerites, Bukharinites, Lovestoneites, and all the rest in the 1920s.

Yet from 1935, vigilance had taken on an increasingly strident and anxious tone. Following Kirov's murder, the Trotskyist threat was presented as more sinister, more immediate. So, too, was the fascist threat and the fear of war. As anxieties about the foreign threat deepened in Moscow, foreign Communists, the raison d'être of the Comintern and people once proudly heralded as proof of Comintern successes, fell under suspicion. Although suspiciousness on the part of Stalin and other party leaders initiated this rising xenophobia, Nazi Germany's unchallenged military buildup and increasingly aggressive foreign policy, the Spanish Civil War, Italy's invasion of Ethiopia, Japan's military activities in East Asia, and the continual rebuffs to Soviet efforts to forge collective security agreements provided ample evidence to convince even the most skeptical that the threat posed by capitalist encirclement had increased alarmingly. The threat of a two-front war was a distinct possibility in mid-1937. That the defendants at the August 1936 and January 1937 trials, as well as others arrested from mid-1936, had "confessed" to being "enemy agents" convinced many in the USSR that there were enemies within the gates. The ECCI and its Cadres Department were quite convinced. The verification of the fraternal parties and émigrés had begun as a membership screening operation that reflected the fear of the Politburo and the ECCI that "enemy" agents disguised as émigrés might be operating within the USSR. The verification's findings that many émigrés warranted suspicion validated that fear, confirmed the need for greater vigilance, helped to justify the expansion of NKVD powers, and fueled the mounting spymania and xenophobia. The Comintern thus acted as both the agent and the instrument of its own eventual demise.

Although under Yezhov the NKVD dragnet widened markedly, Trotskyists remained the main enemy. The incessant calls for vigilance remained primarily calls to unmask Trotskyists. All of the crimes and threats from late 1934 to mid-1937 emanated from this minuscule and far-flung group, which, within the USSR, took on mythical proportions. They were the "spies," "wreckers," "provocateurs" in the service of the fascists, "nationalists," and the rest. The conspiratorial mindset is clear. In reality, the USSR and the international Communist movement faced multiple threats from multiple enemies and potential enemies. But to those who felt endangered, Trotskyism came to embody those threats; multiple threats emanated from one "enemy" who acted as the agent of all enemies, who used the language and logic of Bolshevism to destroy it. A host of perceived dangers had one name.

The culture of denunciation within the VKP and the Comintern facilitated the vigilance campaign. Denunciations of oppositional groups and tendencies, criticism and self-criticism, and the use of denunciations by comrades, both leaders and subordinates, to satisfy grievances and to settle personal and political scores meant that a tradition of denunciation, so essential to a successful vigilance campaign, existed. The calls for heightened vigilance were not calls to change behavior but calls to focus accepted behaviors on designated and familiar targets. That so many Cominternists had at one time or another denounced an oppositional group, a perceived deviationist, or a comrade made future denunciations easier, especially when the denunciations became a means of personal and political self-defense.

The ECCI leaders and apparatus were not sheep being led blindly to slaughter. Rather, they were the agents and instruments of their own downfall. They were people who believed in vigilance and conspiracies, who feared what Stalin feared and provided him with reasons for those fears, who dutifully acted on those fears to unmask perceived threats, who sought to prove their vigilance and loyalty by denouncing perceived enemies. Such acts put all of them at risk. Consider the case of the former Polish section.

As we have seen, the Communist Parties of Poland, Western Belorussia, and Western Ukraine, which made up the former Polish section, conducted the verification of their members in Soviet emigration with fervor and vigilance. The verification commissions "unmasked" large numbers of "suspicious elements" or "enemy agents." They sent their findings to the Cadres Department, which forwarded them to the NKVD. Yezhov, in his capacity as head of ORPO and later the NKVD, undoubtedly felt vindicated, and conveyed the information to Stalin. Until May 1937 the commissions themselves made the decisions about whom to expel and which names to forward to the NKVD. The commissions provided the evidence that confirmed the suspicions that émigrés from Poland posed a threat.

As the commissions' progress reports indicate, by spring 1937 hundreds of émigrés from Poland had been arrested. But most of the leaders of the CPP, CPWU, and CPWB remained free to urge their members on to greater vigilance. In the spring the leaders began to be arrested, a development that transformed party members' fear of enemy agents into fear for themselves. **Document 30** offers vivid evidence of that transformation. This document is a series of handwritten notes penned by Henryk Walecki, a founder of the CPP and, at the time of his arrest on 21 June 1937, a member of the ICC. Walecki addressed his notes to Yezhov. It is unclear whether he kept them in his desk or sent them to Yezhov. Walecki dated the notes 18 May 1937; the Cadres Department forwarded them to the NKVD five days after his arrest. It is also unclear what precipitated his denunciation of eight comrades, although the arrests of Brikke in April and Melnikov in early May suggest one reason—self-defense.

Document 30

Denunciations made by Walecki and sent to Yezhov, 18 May 1937. RGASPI, f. 495, op. 252, d. 510, ll. 1–10. Original in Russian. Handwritten. Walecki's original handwritten notes addressed to Yezhov were typed in the ECCI Cadres Department and sent to Yezhov by Belov (head of the department) on 26 June 1937. Copies of these notes were placed in the personal files of the people mentioned.

TO C. YEZHOV.

Enclosed are my notes about certain facts concerning the following individuals:

1. Melnikov [Müller]
2. Hanecki
3. Natanski (Bresler)
4. Wasilkowski
5. Brikke
6. Münzenberg
7. Raskolnikov
8. Karakhan.

18 May 1937

Walecki

About Melnikov. Several months ago, I informed the Polish section of the Comintern (c. Bronkowski) that Wasilkowski (currently the editor in chief of the [newspaper] *"Za industrializatsiiu"* [and] *a Polish Komsomol member until 1928) was an active Bukharinist in December 1928. The Polish section passed it on to the CC, which initiated an inquiry on Wasilkowski. Since then, I have never talked about Wasilkowski to anyone. In April of that year, during the party meeting, Melnikov approached me during the break and asked: "You have some material on Wasilkowski. Could you give* [it] *to me?" Without giving a direct answer, I asked Melnikov, on whose behalf he was asking me, and why me specifically. M*[elnikov] *replied incomprehensibly that* [he was asking] *supposedly on behalf of a certain "party organization" (later I learned that the Comintern party committee never gave him such a task). However, he did not insist and backed off.*

Now, remembering this incident, I think that the active interest that M[elnikov] *expressed toward the Wasilkowski case merits attention.*

18 May 1937

Walecki.

<u>About Hanecki</u>.

1) In late December 1923 (or early January 1924), at the Office of the Ambassador [Polpredstvo] [party] *cell meeting in Berlin that I attended, Hanecki (who was on a trip abroad at that time) gave a <u>passionate</u> speech in defense of Trotsky and against the CC.*

2) H[anecki] *has a number of more than suspicious relatives in Poland, with whom he maintains the closest relations. In particular, his nephew (sister's son) named <u>Gridiger</u> is a professional spy in the service of the Polish General Staff's Second Department. In 1923–24 (?), a trial took place in Warsaw of a group of our intelligence agents who had made contact with the Polish spies Lieutenant Skrudlik and Gridiger, who had been assigned for that purpose, with provocatorial intent, by the Polish General Staff's Second Department. Meanwhile, Gridiger and some other Polish spy who sneaked into Smolensk were exposed and arrested by our organs. Gridiger's partner was shot, while G*[ridiger], *after declaring that he had an uncle Hanecki, was transferred to Moscow. Here he had a meeting with Hanecki; he promised to work for us, was released, and went back to Poland, where he continued to work for the General Staff's Second Department.*

3) In the <u>whole</u> biography of Hanecki, there are a number of particular points requiring investigation.

I remembered all this after learning that H[anecki] *was elected a regional* [party] *committee member at the recent conference.*

Walecki.

18 May 1937

About Natanski (real name—Bresler).

Natanski, a VKP(b) member, transferred from the CP of Poland (or CP of Germany?) about ten years ago. Before 1935 he worked on a secret job at the Admin[istration] *of the Civil Air Fleet, then—in Glavlit,*[20] *and now is supposedly being sent to conduct Glavlit work in Ukraine.*

In 1922, N[atanski] *lived in Berlin on a <u>legal</u> Polish passport and worked with the Trade delegation. At that time, the trial against the Communist Party of Western Ukraine (the so-called St. Juri trial) was being prepared in Lvov. The chief provocateur at this trial was a certain Spiegel. Our* [organs] *managed to lure him to Berlin, where one of the embassy workers (either from the GPU or Razvedupr, I do not know) got certain information from Spiegel and, as a "proof" of his sincerity, Spiegel's Defenziwa* [Polish coun- terintelligence service] *agent badge (or medal). The party decided to pass this material evidence to the defense attorney at the trial in order to unmask the provocateur in open court. However, the defense attorney remarked that he would have to tell the court where he got that spy ID from. Then our* [peo- ple] *in Berlin told him to mention Bresler (currently Natanski), who lived in Berlin legally on a Polish passport and to whom Spiegel came to offer his services against the Polish okhranka.*[21] *Due to the rush, it could not be "agreed to" with Bresler himself (the messenger could not wait), and Bresler was informed after the fact. Bresler protested against such "arbitrariness" by the party that compromised his legal cover, and* [he] *ranted and raved. A couple of weeks later, the editorial board of the PPS's newspaper "Robot- nik" contacted our comrades in Warsaw and informed them that it had re- ceived by mail a letter from Berlin, from some Bresler, who was protesting against an attempt to point to him as the person who had passed on Spiegel's spy ID to the attorney, since he, Bresler, had never before seen Spiegel, etc. The "Robotnik" editorial board considered it inappropriate to publish such a letter stabbing a defense attorney at a political trial in the back, and passed that letter on to our* [people]. *When asked about this letter, Bresler confessed that he had written it, and explained this step as a natural reac- tion to the party's "arbitrariness" and abuse of his name.*

Some time ago, B[resler] *showed up in Moscow, raised the question of his transfer to the VKP(b), and asked me for a recommendation. I refused him, referring to the case of his letter to the "Robotnik."*

I do not know how, but he still managed to sneak into the party and [later] *worked top-secret jobs. B*[resler]*'s biography contains some dark spots, even before his arrival in Berlin.*

Walecki.

18 May 1937

About Wasilkowski.

I met Wasilkowski in the summer of 1928, during the Sixth Comintern Congress. He was a rabid <u>Polish</u> factionalist (he had just come from Po- land after spending several years in prison on a Komsomol case).

W[asilkowski] *was planning to return to underground work in Poland. In December 1928, in a conversation with me, W*[asilkowski] *took a radical Bukharinist position against the CC VKP(b). At the end of an agitated argument, I told him: "So you are planning to go to Poland to create rightist groups there?" W*[asilkowski] *answered: "Rightist—no, Bukharinist—yes." I told him then and there that I would inform the Polish section about this. I immediately made this declaration to the Representative of the CP of Poland, c. Purman, and W*[asilkowski] *was removed from the list of those to be sent abroad.*

Soon after that, W[asilkowski] *got a position on the "Pravda" editorial board.*[22]

Walecki.

18 May 1937

About Brikke.

I have known Brikke for a long time from his work in the Comintern. In 1923–24 he was [a member of] *the Trotskyist opposition and was rather active.*

His position in the fall of 1927 is of a crucial importance. It was in November, on the eve of the Fifteenth Party Congress.[23] *In conversations with many comrades that took place in his room in the* [Hotel] *Lux, B*[rikke] *harshly attacked the CC, in particular Trotsky's and Zinoviev's expulsion from the party, and expressed the conviction that when the delegates who were supposedly on their way came together, the situation would be cleared up,* [and] *the CC would have to change course.*

These pronouncements by B[rikke] *were very much influenced by his clashes with . . . , who at that time was the secretary of the West*[ern] *Siberian Krai* [region] *committee, where Br*[ikke] *worked temporarily as a Kraikom instructor. It is possible that the later unmasking of . . . , an obsessed right opportunist who was talking incessantly about forming a bloc with the leftists, made B*[rikke] *think that he was right in his struggle with . . . and* [right] *to conceal his Trotskyist activity of 1923–1927. In subsequent years, I hardly ever met B*[rikke], *and I do not know when and how he abandoned Trotskyism. I do not know if the party is aware of the many years of B*[rikke]*'s Trotskyist activity and vacillations.*

In 1927, B[rikke] *was in close contact with Varia Kasparova.*

Walecki.

18 May 1937

About Münzenberg.

In 1917–1918, Münzenberg was in prison in Switzerland (the only time in his life, I think). He used his free time to write a diary-memoir, and wrote quite openly about [his] *underground work during the war, mentioning specific people, etc. This diary "ended up in the hands" of the*

Swiss authorities and was used by them accordingly. M[ünzenberg] *explained this by his inexperience and thoughtlessness.*

Walecki.

18 May 1937

About Raskolnikov.
Recalling my meetings with R[askolnikov] *in 1925–1927 (in 1925–1926 he worked in the Comintern as an editor under the name of Petrov; in 1927–1928, it seems to me, he was an editor of "Novy Mir," but continued to live in the Lux until his appointment as the ambassador in Revel* [Estonia]*), I came to the conclusion, on the basis of different hints, anecdotes, etc., that R*[askolnikov] *was at that time an active Trotskyist and already a double-dealer. I am not an expert in literary currents, but I remember that his literary entourage (he was a napostovets)*[24] *consisted of people who now have been exposed as enemies and longtime double-dealers.*

Walecki.

May 1937

About Karakhan.
On 10 May 1937, I gave a lecture on the international situation to the activists in Factory No. 32. Among the questions submitted in writing was the question: "Why did they change the ambassador to Turkey?" [i.e., Karakhan]*. I enclose the original note.*[X] *It is important to locate the author of this note and to find out the motives for his odd interest in the changing of the ambassador to Turkey.*

Walecki.

18 May 1937

[X]*The original is being sent to you directly by the Moscow Committee.*

That Walecki recorded his denunciations on a single day suggests that he feared for himself as the attacks on the CPP were reaching their climax. He was right. In June he and many other CPP leaders were arrested. How many other such denunciations were sent to Yezhov is unknown. Only a few were required to produce multiple arrests.

If denunciations were lacking, other evidence of the alleged dangers posed by émigrés from Poland existed. The final report of the Western Belorussian verification commission was one such bit of evidence. Entitled "General Conclusions About Political Emigration from Western Belorussia," the "secret" report not only updated its earlier reports but drew ominous political conclusions.[25]

Glebov, the party representative in the ECCI, began the report by identifying the four groups that the verification commission targeted: people about
whom there were doubts, who could be returned to Poland; "suspicious elements" who might have been sent by the Polish police, whose cases were sent
to the NKVD; "dubious elements" to be removed (literally, "cleansed"
[ochistka]) from the USSR; and all Western Belorussian party members who
had been recommended to the VKP. In a clear example of the "heartless, bureaucratic" approach to cadres criticized by Stalin at the February–March
Plenum, Glebov reported that only eighty to ninety of the almost two thousand people reviewed were interviewed in person; decisions about all others
were made on the basis of personnel files (lichnye dela).

In Glebov's view, the verification was a success that produced disturbing results. On the one hand, it enabled the party to establish "a more accurate accounting . . . of each political émigré." But it also revealed a "colossal number
of suspicious and doubtful elements (30 percent of all émigrés)," many of
whom had been recommended to the VKP. The commission sent materials on
these people to the "responsible organs." Between 1920 and 1937 the CPWB
had sent 875 people to the USSR as political émigrés; another 1,124 arrived as
refugees. In the opinion of the commission, an "absolute majority" of the political émigrés and refugees emigrated without clear cause, which it defined as
justifiable fear of lengthy imprisonment in Poland. The vast majority of émigrés and refugees had entered the USSR between 1926 and 1932 because, Glebov opined, during those years Belorussian nationalists and police agents in
Poland had obstructed the party's work and, in the ensuing confusion, had
penetrated their agents and spies among those fleeing Poland for the USSR.

The commission paid special attention to those émigrés and refugees who
had joined the VKP. A significant number (386) of the 875 émigrés sent by the
party joined the VKP without receiving a careful review. The NKVD had already arrested an unspecified number of them, and the commission deemed
another 105 "doubtful." They were not the only people arrested by the
NKVD: 315 of the 875 émigrés (35 percent) and 274 of the 1,124 refugees (25
percent) were arrested. It is unclear whether those arrested were arrested before or after the commission sent materials on them to the NKVD.

Almost half of those whom the commission reviewed had been arrested in
Poland, although many of them were not sent to prison, a seeming anomaly
that caught the commission's collective eye. It concluded that "as a result of
terrorizing them, the police won over many. In many cases, the police arrested
or sent to prison their own agents to protect them within the ranks of the Com-

munist Party, creating for them an authority that they then used to be sent to the USSR." But not all of those arrested by the NKVD were Polish police agents; some were arrested as participants in "Belorussian nationalist, counterrevolutionary activities," others as Trotskyist spies, and still others as Polish nationalists engaged in counterrevolutionary activities.

In light of the above, the commission's general conclusions are hardly surprising. The first was that there existed "a very wide channel [*kanal*] through which hostile elements penetrated the Communist Party [VKP] and the USSR," a conclusion reminiscent of Krajewski's, Yezhov's, and Manuilsky's assertions in 1934–1935. Among those who used this channel, the "so-called 'Polish road,'" were "agents of Polish fascism and Belorussian nationalism" and "agents of Polish counterintelligence." Many of them had taken up "responsible posts in the BSSR [Belorussian SSR]." Second, many of those who had fled to the USSR after arrest in Poland had been "won over" by the Polish police and acted as their agents.

The commission's report to the Cadres Department was undoubtedly also sent to the NKVD. Its conclusion that a "so-called 'Polish road'" existed and was well traveled by Polish agents and Belorussian nationalists validated the correctness of the NKVD's earlier arrests of Belorussian émigrés and provided the pretext for further arrests.

One cannot help but wonder how the commission was able to discern from files alone that so many "enemy agents" existed among its constituents. One can imagine a NKVD investigator asking the same question, and other questions: Why did the leaders of the Polish section or the CPWB not detect these "suspicious" elements earlier? Did they not do so because they themselves had something to hide? Could the findings of the commission be trusted? Had its members condemned others in order to protect their own "hostile activities"? To the conspiratorial mindset, everything was potentially sinister.

In late May and early June 1937 arrests escalated sharply. The convergence of several factors accounted for this. Chief among them was the arrest and conviction of members of the military general staff in May and June. Those arrests electrified the country. If the "enemies'" conspiracies included senior Red Army officers, who could be trusted? National defense and self-defense, therefore, required even greater vigilance, a perspective that in turn gave rise to denunciations and arrests. Shortly after the arrests of the military leaders, the NKVD arrested many high-ranking VKP members.

Yezhov's belief that the Comintern had become a refuge for "enemy agents" put the ECCI apparatus and Cominternists at great risk. Acting on this assumption, in mid-May 1937 the NKVD began arresting members of the ECCI apparatus and fraternal parties. On 26 May, Dimitrov met with Yezhov to discuss the arrest of three important ECCI workers. Yezhov told him: "Major spies worked in the CI."[26] The arrest of ECCI personnel heightened the anxieties of all connected with the Comintern.

As the arrests proceeded, the ECCI continued to press the fraternal parties to be more vigilant and to challenge the increasing criticisms of the repression published abroad. The Comintern journal published articles that asserted the legitimacy of the show trials and charged that because "the majority of democratic newspapers were hostile to the USSR, their critiques of the trials served to facilitate fascist designs." The journal heralded the arrest of the military leaders as "a significant blow to the fascist warmongers" and published a resolution passed by the ECCI Presidium calling on Communist Parties "to purge double-dealing Trotskyist elements from party organizations" and demanding that they "discover and unmask the enemy" and intensify efforts to ascertain members' attitudes on "their relations to the USSR and VKP(b) leadership."[27]

The ECCI Secretariat had responded to the strident calls for vigilance at the February–March Plenum by ordering another verification of Comintern personnel.[28] The composition of this Special Commission to Verify Workers of the ECCI Apparatus differed from that of the Moskvin Commission, but its charge was much the same. As in the past, the Comintern leaders—Dimitrov, Manuilsky, and Moskvin—passed judgment on those who worked for them. As **Document 31** makes clear, the representatives of the fraternal parties in the ECCI warranted special consideration. Comintern rules gave the ECCI the right to review them, but from mid-May, the atmosphere in which this verification took place was fraught with anxiety. That the commission deemed only five of the twenty-five people that it reviewed worthy of retaining suggests that it had raised vigilance to a new level. Heightened vigilance, especially against foreigners, seemed the surest means of personal and institutional self-defense.

In and of itself, the report of the commission provides little insight into what motivated Dimitrov, Manuilsky, and Moskvin to remove 80 percent of the representatives in the ECCI. To remove so many implicitly raised doubts about the Secretariat's previous vigilance. We cannot rule out the possibility that, by removing the representatives, the Secretariat actually sought to protect them, because once freed of their responsibilities, they could be returned to their native countries. In fact, about half of those removed survived the repression by leaving the country in 1937. Nor can we rule out the other possibility—that the Secretariat sought to scapegoat the representatives for having failed to "unmask" "enemies" and "suspicious elements" among their charges. About half of those removed were arrested. Whatever the motives of Secretariat members, the results allowed them to claim that they had been vigilant and to deflect the consequences of their vigilance onto their staff.

Document 31

Protocol of the 1 June 1937 Special Commission to Verify Workers of the ECCI Apparatus, 21 June 1937. RGASPI, f. 495, op. 21, d. 52, ll. 63–64. Original in Russian. Typewritten.

[. . .]
21 June 1937

Top secret.

PROTOCOL No. 6
OF THE SESSION OF THE SPECIAL COMMISSION TO VERIFY WORKERS
OF THE ECCI APPARATUS
of 1 June 37.
PRESENT: members of the commission c.c.: Dimitrov, Manuilsky,
Moskvin,
workers of the Cadres Department c.c.: Belov and Tsirul.
RESOLVED:

a) about the parties' representatives:

1. KOLAROV (Bulgaria)	—keep.
2. SCHALKER (Holland)	—keep.
3. TOM (Czechoslovakia)	—keep.
4. DENGEL (Germany)	—leaving.
5. MORGAN (Canada)	—keep, but verify.
6. SALIM-ABUD (Arab countries)	—keep.
7. GALOEN (Norway)	—replace.
8. STEIN (Finland)	—replace.
9. WEIDEN (Austria)	—replace, send abroad.
10. ANGARETIS (Lithuania)	—consider desirable to replace, keep temporarily.
11. CHOBAN Maria (Romania)	—desirable to replace.
12. MUNK-PETERSEN (Denmark)	—desirable to replace.
13. LACERDA (Brazil)	—desirable to replace, keep temporarily.
14. MERING	—verify, desirable to replace.
15. ARNOT PAGE (England)	—verify thoroughly [his] connection with the arrested PETROVSKY.

16. COGNIOT	—verify thoroughly (served in the intelligence service).
17. MAYER (Switzerland)	—transferring to work in *Rundschau.*
18. ESCABEDO (Cuba)	—leaving.
19. FLEISCHER (Yugoslavia)	—suggest to the CC CP of Yugoslavia to nominate another candidate (moral disintegration, lack of vigilance, laziness).
20. FERDI (Turkey)	—wait for the results of the commission's work.
21. MARAT (Turkey)	—wait for the results of the commission's work.
22. FARKAS (Hungary)	—verify and admit [for work].
23. MASON (Australia)	—suggest to com. Marty [that he] examine his work.
24. KRUMIN-PILAT (Latvia)	—resolve the question together with the resolution of the issue of the party leadership.
25. FAN LING	—resolve separately.

b) ABOUT VITOL (secretary of com. Marty).

In view of the receipt of additional materials, relieve from work. (See protocol no. 2).[29]

MEMBERS OF THE COMMISSION: < . . . >

On 22 June 1937, of the VKP members and candidate members who worked in the offices of the ECCI Secretariat, 166 attended a closed party meeting. It was the first such meeting since the NKVD had begun arresting leading military, VKP, and Comintern members. **Document 32** presents portions of the stenographic report of that meeting, the atmosphere of which was tense. In the month before the meeting, the NKVD had arrested a number of prominent ECCI officials: Alikhanov and Chernomordik, two leaders of the Cadres Department; Müller, head of Communiciations; Walecki, a member of the ICC whose denunciation of others we have already read; Bronkowski, an ECCI member and head of the Polish section, and others. The meeting began with Moskvin's report on the political situation in the ECCI apparatus. Then Kotelnikov, secretary of the party committee, spoke on "exposing the enemies of the people who worked in the ECCI apparatus," and moved to expel from the party those who had already been arrested. To that point, the rituals that defined party meetings proceeded as always. But after Moskvin's report, rank-and-file members addressed their comrades. Some played their prescribed roles, but others, apparently emboldened by Stalin's call for a check-up from below by the "party masses," departed from the ritual and called some of their bosses and leaders to account. The transcript speaks for itself, but several themes deserve to be highlighted.

Based on Kotelnikov's report, the meeting passed a resolution to expel "enemies of the people Walecki, Chernomordik, Chernin, Bronkowski, and Grossman." Given that these five had already been arrested, what choice did the party committee have? Cause and effect were reversed. Theirs were not like other cases (e.g., Magyar's) in which the ECCI party committee expelled people before they were arrested. Nor would this be the last such instance. As on other occasions, Kotelnikov presented the arrest of "fifteen enemies [who] occupied important positions here" but whom "our party organization did not deal with" as evidence of "our weakness in raising the revolutionary vigilance of each of us." That the party organization had failed to unmask such "enemies" before the NKVD arrested them increased the risks for all in the organization. But as Moskvin implied when he stated that "it is still impossible today to say whether they [those removed by the verification commission] were enemies or not," these days no one was above suspicion. All party members, even "real Bolsheviks," were increasingly vulnerable; émigrés were even more vulnerable.

Moskvin made clear that the decimation of members of fraternal parties living in the USSR had begun. His own commission had expelled sixty-five members, and the NKVD had arrested seventeen of them. He noted in particular the arrest of leading members of the German and Polish parties; there were others whom he did not mention. Indeed, the mass repression of Germans and Poles was just then under way. Two days before this meeting, the Politburo passed a resolution permitting Yezhov to issue an immediate NKVD order to arrest all Germans working in defense plants and to exile some of those arrested from the country. It required him to send daily reports on the number of arrests to the Central Committee. Before and after passage of that resolution came arrests of the leaders of the CPP. By such acts, Stalin, Yezhov, and the Politburo pushed vigilance and xenophobia to their logical administrative conclusion; the pace at which foreigners were arrested picked up.

Many who spoke at the 22 June meeting conveyed a sense of shock about the recent arrests, which some stated were warranted. Many expressed the view that the party committee, and they themselves, had not appreciated that their arrested comrades had been "enemies." Shock melded indistinguishably with anxiety. Precisely because they had not "unmasked" those who had been arrested, they had reason to be fearful for themselves. Many went to considerable lengths to defend their personal failure in not detecting or "unmasking" their office mates' "hostile activities." Their statements convey various fears—fear for their own well-being, fear of "enemies," fear of the disorienting uncertainties created by the recent arrests. Some who sought to make sense of the new situation did so by claiming that conspiracies had existed among the arrested "enemies." As comrade Mingulin put it: "It is impossible [to believe] that there was nothing subversive in their work."

But their anxiety did not cripple them. One of the most distinguishing features of the meeting is the extent to which rank-and-file party members attacked or questioned the behavior not only of those arrested but also of the party committee leaders (especially Kotelnikov and Blagoeva) who presided over the meeting. Some speakers used Stalin's and Zhdanov's attacks on familyness to denounce such behavior within the Comintern apparatus. Others denounced their bosses' corruption and embezzlement. Still others criticized the inefficiency or incompetence of leading staff members. Many comments suggest that the ECCI apparatus and party committee suffered from their share of bureaucratic confusion and inefficiency, what Moskvin called "this idiotic disease, carelessness." These criticisms and attacks convey a sense of rank-and-file discontent and anger with their leaders, who heretofore had cajoled their subordinates to be more vigilant and to signal suspicious behaviors.

The dynamics of vigilance had shifted somewhat. Many of the incidents cited were not recent, which suggests that Stalin's call for check-up from below emboldened some people to settle grievances with their superiors and comrades. The shift heralded the arrival of a new cleavage within Comintern headquarters. Following Kirov's murder, the line was drawn between "real Bolsheviks" and some former oppositionists—later it was between "real Bolsheviks" and all former oppositionists and between native-born and foreign-born comrades. The rank-and-file members' criticism of their bosses and party leaders suggests that in mid-1937 they were seeking to redefine who the "real Bolsheviks" were. Document 32 provides an example of one of the underappreciated dimensions of the mass repression: its populist element, whereby the "party masses" attacked their bosses.

As was customary, self-criticism often tinged such attacks. Whether this self-criticism arose from people's anxieties for themselves or consisted of honest yet defensible admissions of past "mistakes" in an uncertain present or amounted to a parroting of Stalin's demand for criticism and self-criticism is impossible to ascertain. And what is the point of doing so? Each motive was powerful; one or all were present in those who spoke.

Finally, Kotelnikov referred to shortcomings of the party purge, verification, and exchange of party documents and to Alikhanov's and Chernomordik's nefarious use of their powers to issue party cards. From 1934 the issues of party accountability and party cards had concerned the party leadership. One concern was precisely what Kotelnikov alleged to have taken place—that "enemies" had secured positions that allowed them to issue party cards to other "enemies." There is no proof that Alikhanov and Chernomordik had misused their powers to this end. But the logic inherent in the accusation put party members in responsible positions at much greater risk than it did rank-and-file members.

Document 32

Protocol of the 22 June 1937 closed meeting of VKP members and candidate members in the ECCI Secretariat, 22 June 1937. RGASPI, f. 546, op. 1, d. 388, ll. 49–87. Original in Russian. Typewritten with signatures. In the transcript, several people refer to the comments of speakers who appeared after them but who clearly spoke before them during the meetings. The transcript has been reproduced as it appears in the archive.

PROTOCOL *No. 11*   OF THE CLOSED MEETING OF THE VKP(b) MEMBERS AND CANDIDATE MEMBERS IN THE ECCI SECRETARIAT of 22 JUNE 1937.
PRESENT: *166 VKP(b) members.*
PRESIDIUM: Moskvin, Blagoeva, Gopner, Kotelnikov, Angaretis.
Secretaries: Volk, Bialkovskaia, Smirnov, Paglina.

HEARD: Information by c. Kotelnikov about exposing the enemies of the people who worked in the ECCI apparatus.
RESOLVED: To ratify a decision by the party committee to expel from the party enemies of the people Walecki, Chernomordik, Chernin, Bronkowski, and Grossman.
HEARD: Report by c. Moskvin about the measures to improve the [political] health of the ECCI apparatus. [. . .]

REPORT BY com. MOSKVIN
Com. Stalin has stressed specifically what an unpleasant thing capitalist encirclement is. The recent trials have demonstrated to us what this capitalist encirclement means. Each of us has to thoroughly contemplate the question of how deeply the class enemy has penetrated into the very pores of our

Soviet system. There is hardly any sector of our construction where the enemy has not found ways to entrench himself and to attempt to undermine the fortress of our proletarian dictatorship from the outside.[30]

We are the organization that, more than any other, stands at the junction with the capitalist world. To our shame, one has to admit that our vigilance proved to be at a lower level than in the other organizations of the VKP(b). We see a picture of profound penetration by the enemy into the most important parts of our apparatus. The most affected are two such important sectors as communications and cadres. It turned out that both the old and the new leaderships were from the same camp. We watched cockfighting staged before us: Müller [B. N. Melnikov] against Abramov, etc. In reality, it is one and the same gang. One has to take this fact into consideration. It was a veil. If the next time one [person] exposes another before us, we should not take the side of one of them. It will be necessary to verify both of them, or else we may be tricked.

I have to admit my grave mistake that I committed in regard to Müller. I am responsible for it more than anybody else. Particular details that can justify this case are of no importance. The biggest mistake was that we [placed] too much trust in this sector and had little control over it. And when we felt that things were going wrong, we raised the question of removing Müller. I have to say that we could have removed him earlier. Incidental reasons delayed his removal. However, we failed to see the enemy in him, we failed to expose [him]. It turned out that he had been deceiving the party from almost 1919. Everybody knows that the OGPU leadership was saturated with enemies. This is why this scoundrel was exposed so late. He, like Abramov, could have been exposed many years earlier.

Of course, that does not mean that somebody [else] has to do our work. The organs of the proletarian dictatorship are doing their job and, under the leadership of com. Yezhov, will occupy their position of honor, a position that they should occupy. But that does not free any of us from the duty to be vigilant, to honestly serve the party in any sector of any work.

Look what happened. The most important sector—communications—turned out to be in the enemy's hands. The other most important organ—cadres—had been in the hands of the enemy for a number of years, since its creation. The enemies did not just enter them yesterday. I noticed that everybody was shocked by the arrest of Alikhanov. He seemed to be very much a party person. He managed to fool our whole collective, and the secret ballot [party election in spring 1937] gave him the majority of votes.

(GOPNER: In a situation when there was a lot of agitation in favor of his candidacy.)

It reflects the level of our organization.

The situation in some sections turned out to be very bad. In the German section, a number of people who used to work in our apparatus were arrested: Richter, Remmele, Neumann. In the Polish section: Bronkowski, Albert.[31]

And these two people controlled all the cadres of the Polish underground [party]. This is the reality.

It is hard to say where the limits of this treason are and what sort of miscreants are still to be exposed, are still hiding, etc. There are too many channels through which the enemy can sneak into our apparatus. That is why genuine Bolshevik vigilance is an essential condition for each of us. We have to expose, in a Bolshevik manner, everything that has hindered the organization of struggle against the enemies.

I wanted to draw the attention of [our] organization to one circumstance that I consider a great misfortune, [and did] even earlier. But I still do not have the concrete facts. I am referring to familyness. At our previous meetings we hardly even raised the question of familyness in the apparatus of the Communications Department. But tell me, was there not familyness in the old Cadres Department? Alikhanov and Chernomordik protected each other. And since they were members of the party committee, was there not familyness in the party committee, too? Yes, it was so, and it restrained the organization from exposing enemies.

In this connection, the ECCI Secretariat created a commission [the Moskvin Commission] to verify the apparatus. Socially, our apparatus is petit bourgeois. There are very few proletarian elements [who were] forged in the [class] struggle. Last year already, during a superficial verification, we learned that dozens of workers [of our apparatus], although they had worked here for years, had tarnished political reputations, as if it was supposed to be this way. A decision was taken to cleanse our apparatus of such people, about whom it is still impossible today to say whether they were enemies or not. This refers to each one personally, but altogether, when there are dozens of them in our apparatus and when they are entrenched in different sectors, it creates a very dangerous situation for our apparatus; i.e., an environment is created that enables the enemy to penetrate our apparatus. A spy does not necessarily have to sit in the apparatus (to our shame, there were such in the apparatus). He can do his work through higher-level and lower-level workers. We have to pay equal attention to each worker. Let us take a janitor. She comes to the office earlier than anybody else to clean up. She has to be an honest person, faithful to her fatherland. This is the [right] attitude when staffing the apparatus. First of all, we have to get rid of the politically unstable [workers] with dubious political ties. We do not need them in our apparatus. Let me take Siksoi as an example. We decided to remove her from our apparatus. You all know her. She spoke here. The general meeting rejected her. Do we need a person like Siksoi? The commission decided that we do not, and the Secretariat agreed. Or [take] Martha Morenz, or Borosh. First and foremost, we have to get rid of those elements with suspicious political ties and introduce new people in their places.

Then there is the group of people who had [committed] serious political mistakes, and who are also unsuitable for work in our apparatus. In general, since its creation the commission [to verify the ECCI apparatus] has removed from the apparatus sixty-five people so far, excluding those seventeen who were removed by NKVD organs. A special commission, created by the Secretariat, is working on verification of the workers of the Communications Department. In addition to that, a commission is working to verify the composition of the [apparatus] workers. In general, the reorganization spearheaded by the special troika (under the leadership of c. Dimitrov) will result in a radical reduction of the whole apparatus of the Communications Department and changes in its whole system. Besides that, a re-registration of our whole apparatus is necessary, because the personal files of most of our workers are in a chaotic state. And we have to know each worker in our apparatus.

Then the Secretariat considered it necessary to transfer a number of workers from one department to another. Here c. Dimitrov asked us especially not to treat the transferred comrades as suspicious but to create an atmosphere that is conducive for their work.

Finally, a series of measures have been planned to verify and staff our apparatus, etc.

In conclusion, I would like to speak to you about one thing. Recently I read in "Krokodil"[32] how one person learned about a state secret. He told it to his first-floor neighbor. [Eventually] this secret made its way to the seventh floor. The last person had no one to tell it to, so he went down to the first floor and told it to the person who first learned the secret. What I want to say is that one has to know how to keep his mouth shut because the enemy has big ears. Foreign counterintelligence is very interested in our apparatus. It is not advisable to babble about these arrests. The investigation is under way, and it is the duty of each of us to help it and not to babble. After the investigation is completed and we get the information, it will be possible to inform our collective about the details in order to draw conclusions and learn lessons.

We are making this announcement to you, and we expect from each of us and from everyone in our organization all possible help. Thanks to this idiotic disease, carelessness, spies were able to put down roots in our organization. We have to help our organization to rebuild itself and to make each of us so perceptive as to be able to expose our enemies. We have to roll up [our] sleeves and get down to work. I believe that we will salvage our apparatus from the poor state in which it finds itself today.

KOTELNIKOV. In his speech, com. Moskvin demonstrated the weakness of our party organization that failed to expose and remove in time the enemies who were later removed from our apparatus by NKVD organs. Fifteen enemies occupied important positions here. Until their arrest, our party organization did not deal with them. Some of them were exposed by NKVD organs without help from our party organization. It reveals our weakness in raising the revolutionary vigilance of each of us. The enemy proved to be more cunning than we were. Alikhanov and Müller—to our shame, we trusted them too much. Were there signals that should have caught our attention? Take

Müller: his grand lifestyle, throwing money around, winning [people] over with money, elements of moral degeneration about which some members of the party knew to some extent. None of this aroused the appropriate party suspiciousness, nor did it make any of us worry. It was known that in 1923–24, he was an active Trotskyist. The organs of the proletarian dictatorship have arrested him as a spy. But he could have been exposed earlier. It was not done, and our party organization bears responsibility for it. The leadership is also responsible.

Alikhanov—there had already been Zholdak's speech at the general meeting. It was a small signal, but nevertheless we had to pay attention to it. It was not done. Moreover, Alikhanov was taken under protection. In my speech I characterized him as a good party member. It reveals my blindness and stresses my responsibility before the party.

Chernomordik—we would have been able to expose him much earlier if we had not limited ourselves to trusting his reports, if we had not trusted his word. We did not check the documents, we did not ask questions with the appropriate party thoroughness. And in his sphere of work Chernomordik deceived the party organization and the leadership. One had only to dig into the materials and his true nature as an enemy of the people and of the party would have been exposed.

These three—Alikhanov, Chernomordik, Müller—were members of the party committee. You remember our discussion on the question of reprimanding the comrade who had lost his party card. Müller wanted to show himself as an extremely vigilant person, but behind that person was hiding an enemy, a spy from the very first years of our socialist state. The same with Alikhanov. This double-dealer has been deceiving the party organization for years. In any case, during my work with him directly in the party committee, I did not see his real face, I did not see through him. I was depending on the fact that the leadership trusted him, that he was a tested comrade, etc. [It is such] superficial tranquility that leads to political blindness. From this derives the responsibility of the party committee and me personally, as a secretary of the party committee.

Let us take the party group of the Communications Department. The largest number of enemies was arrested there. There were elements of moral degeneration there, but nobody reacted to it. Müller spent tens of thousands [of rubles] on parties, apartments, etc. < . . . > he tried to create for himself authority within the Communications Department.

Anikalchuk also spent < . . . > money [lavishly] here and there. The members of the party group did not help to expose these miscreants; the same was true in the Cadres Department. There is only one possible conclusion: lack of self-criticism, elements of familyness, the lack of a desire to raise principled questions, etc.

Our party organization now faces a task: to make every effort to liquidate the results of the enemies' work, of their counterrevolutionary activities in our apparatus. We heard a statement from one comrade who said that because I worked by his side and failed to expose him, I myself should leave. Comrades, this is an incorrect way to pose this question. To go or to stay, the collective, the party organization, the leadership, will decide this; we should not demobilize by ourselves. Each of us works in some sector, and each is required to help the leadership overcome the results of the enemies' counterrevolutionary activities here.

It is essential to study the enemy's methods of work, to study the materials and articles that are published now. This should be done by the experienced workers. The enemy sneaks into our apparatus thanks to our blindness and the lack of party vigilance. This demonstrates once again how right c. Stalin was when he emphasized the importance of capitalist encirclement. Our task is to raise party vigilance.

BLAGOEVA.

I am ashamed to face the party organization because for three months three enemies of the party worked alongside me in the party committee.

I was a party leader for more than a year, in a period when one enemy after another was relieved by the leadership. I failed to respond to the signals, to react in a timely manner. It is a shame, and it is very depressing, especially because of the one who skillfully played the role of a good party member. I trusted Alikhanov just as you did, but I had no right to do so, because I was also a cadres worker. I had to grasp those signals, I had to grasp the signal sent at the general party meeting (citations from his books, his speech at the meeting on the report of the party committee). I should have studied his biography more thoroughly.

It was not sufficient to satisfy ourselves with Chernomordik's statement about his Trotskyist error. We should have asked that party organization of which he was then a member, which we [only] did later. It was essential to restructure our work not in words but in deeds.

We had to investigate the friendship of Chernomordik and Alikhanov. Gopner's protest against their attitude toward her should also have served as a signal. Alikhanov knew how to dull vigilance; they charged me with the most secret tasks. He wormed his way into [people's] confidence everywhere, and into the party organization. The party group has the right to raise the question of whether I should remain a party leader, and the general meeting [to discuss] whether I should remain a member of the party committee.

No. 3. NUSBERG.

Com. Samsonov was right when he demanded a discussion of all of these issues.

I work in the Cadres Department. Familyness was not only between Alikhanov and Chernomordik. There was also friendship and familyness between Blagoeva, and Alikhanov and Chernomordik. And a very notable friendship existed between Razumova and Lebedeva, and Alikhanov and Chernomordik. Alikhanov tried to suppress self-criticism by referring to conspiracies. Com. Blagoeva failed to expose it. I know com. Gopner as an authoritative party member, but in our group she was pushed aside. The staffing of the Cadres Department was such that, even in the last months, undesirable individuals were admitted. A non-party member, Loganovskaia, whose husband turned out to be an enemy of the people, was entrusted with handling top-secret documents, which should be entrusted only to tested Communists. I told cc. Blagoeva, Tsirul, and Manuilsky about a number of people who turned out to be enemies. My mistake was not to report it to the party committee secretary. Once I went and spoke about my suspicions regarding Pataki, and I presented materials proving that he was a scoundrel. Nevertheless, he was removed only later, at the suggestion of the NKVD.

For some reason, references [*kharakteristiki*] for departing workers were given by the Cadres Department; the party committee and the social organizations were cut off.

It is not good when one person is in charge of the apparatus. The commission to verify the apparatus works slowly.

The fault of the party committee is that, knowing the bad [facts] in Krajewski's [and] Chernomordik's pasts, the party committee nevertheless made them speakers at the Moscow party committee; it did not verify these people's pasts.

[Tamara Akimovna] <u>VULFSON.</u>

I met Abramov in 1924, in the USSR embassy in Berlin, when the deceased c. Vulfson [her husband] and I went abroad for the first time.[33] Later we went to Italy, where Vulfson was a deputy trade representative, and after that to Vienna, where c. Vulfson was the trade representative, and I worked in the USSR consulate and later in the trade delegation. In <u>April</u> 1927 we returned to Moscow. In <u>June</u>, I started working in the Inotass [foreign news agency] as an intern. However, I failed my English test and had to leave. At that time, Vulfson was not in Moscow, and so I called Abramov and told him that I was looking for a job. He suggested that I come to him. I called on him the next day. After working in the OMS for a week or two, I said that it was difficult for me to deal with the <u>English language</u>. Then he recommended me to the Agitprop [Department]. In the fall of 1927, Vulfson returned from his business trip. Abramov and his wife visited us three times in two years (1927–1929), and we visited them twice. In 1929, c. Vulfson and I again went abroad. I returned to Moscow <u>alone</u>, because c. Vulfson died in a Berlin hospital on our way back to Moscow. I went to work for the ECCI for the second time, after talking with com. Tsirul. I never again saw Abramov at home, but I called him at work when I was hospitalized for five months in the Kremlin hospital. I asked him to come to see me and asked if he could get me a place in a sanatorium. It was <u>in August 1935</u>. He came, and I repeated my request. He promised [to fulfill it]. In the final account, I got a place [in a sanatorium] thanks to c. Gopner, who also knew how badly ill I was during these five months.

That was the last time I saw Abramov and called him on the phone.

I can say that in our publishing sector there were enough scandalous cases: the Chernin case and others. The party group has to know its members better. It is better to go too far, to commit mistakes when purging the apparatus, rather than to let the enemy stay. Each of us has to remain in his place. I promise to be vigilant; I will mobilize myself.

(NUSBERG: And what did you do in Kamenev's Secretariat?)

I had the archive of the Political Bureau of the CC VKP(b) in the cabinet there. But I do not remember an instance when I actually held those files. I translated from English some pamphlet by Lansbury. I was called upon to translate when the Presidium of the Moscow Soviet received foreigners.[34]

GOLUBTSOV.

I will give some examples of irresponsibility in our apparatus. In the Communications Department there worked one Yaschenko, Müller's shield bearer. She protected his office as if it were a sanctuary. No mortal could come to see him.

For a long time Loganovskaia worked in the apparatus. About a month ago I needed to see Alikhanov and ask him why leaving the doors open had become more frequent of late in the Cadres Department. She did not let me in to see Alikhanov. Yesterday she came again. Why did they let her inside the building? In the warden's office there is a reception room, but that room is not being used. In this regard, we lack vigilance. Such a system of controlling people is no good.

Take Walecki. At the party committee meeting, he behaved in such a way as to stress that he was an old party member and that, therefore, there could be no doubts about him.

Last year, when Kotelnikov was on vacation, Alikhanov replaced him. We had to solve the problem of assistance to low-paid workers. However, he showed no concern for people.

A new person, who did not know Müller, was hired. When that new person asked Müller for a pass, Müller replied, "Tell Davydov not to put anyone here without my consent," by which he meant that he wanted to secure [positions for] his people there, too. Abramov also threw a tantrum for us [when we] asked him to present his pass.

We received alarming signals from the warden's office: in the Cadres Department, they used to leave rooms open; once a fire happened; there were cases when the light was not switched off, etc. Nevertheless, the enemy, the former head of the Cadres Department, did not pay any attention to our signals from below.

Chernin weaseled around to prove his guiltlessness.

Com. Moskvin was right when he said in his speech that we need honest people on whom we can rely. The party groups have to undertake a serious verification of their groups, of their composition. It is essential to review the whole system of party education, since among the leaders of the study groups there were many enemies. We have to promote honest and devoted people to become leaders of the study groups.

LEVCHENKO.

I would like to focus on Müller's characteristics. Müller organized drinking bouts and spent tens of thousands [of rubles] to decorate offices; many Communists groveled before him. Kozhevnikov decorated rooms in the Rococo style and spent twenty-five thousand rubles on it.

When Müller was coming, Kozhevnikov set up dinners with the most exquisite wines and dishes.

I talked about this with party leader Yankov, but he only shrugged his shoulders.

Why did it take place? Because the party committee was removed from those sectors, it did not teach us vigilance. Bolshevik self-criticism is to be promoted regardless of the special character of our apparatus.

Kozhevnikov is a bureaucrat; it is necessary to purge such people.

One has to keep secrets but at the same time to watch so that the people with the party cards do not squander party money.

No. 7. MERING.

After the harsh words in c. Moskvin's report in which he demonstrated that we lack party vigilance, it is especially difficult to speak about myself. At the election meeting, I stood for Alikhanov; I had not seen any [evidence of] deviations by him since 1928, when I first met him.

There was a signal about Alikhanov at the election meeting. We should have paid attention to it. Alikhanov's speech contained a suppression of self-criticism, it contradicted the line of the Plenum.[35] We recognized his speech as incorrect but let him off easy. It was my mistake, too. I had no personal ties with Alikhanov; we were connected by work and study. And I failed to see through him. I am blameworthy for a significant lack of vigilance. In 1932–1933, I met with the double-dealer and enemy of the people Shatskin. I met him several times. We met because we were connected at work. I did not carry on political conversations with him. I never shared his anti-party views. We discussed only his departure from the opposition. When he asked, What's new in the Comintern? I answered that I did not know. I aggravated my mistake by not reporting my meetings with him to the party organization.

TSITOVICH.

We talk a lot about vigilance, but it was not we who exposed them, but the organs of the proletarian dictatorship. I think that the Central Committee and c. Stalin demand from us not the kind of criticism that we used to have. We repeatedly refer to the distinctiveness of our organization and talk about other practical considerations. If we raised all of the questions with complete party honesty, we would have exposed all the enemies much earlier. At the election meeting, when the discussion became very critical, Alikhanov raised the question about terminating the discussion. We talked about many wrongdoings, but we failed to notice the most important. Vulfson was wrong when she said here that it is no big deal if we go too far. No, it is necessary to hit the target, or else we will do our enemy a service speaking that way. This means that each small signal has to be investigated to the end. Obviously, it is not a pleasant thing to be investigated (I know it firsthand), but each party member and the entire party organization have to bring each undertaking to an end.

Müller's case is not clear to me. It turns out that in the past, Müller was a Trotskyist. I think that the party committee and the leadership have to investigate this case further. We do not have here a single comrade who knew about Müller's Trotskyist past. I think that the party committee has to investigate who knew about Müller's Trotskyist past and remained silent.

Regarding Alikhanov. There were signals. Ten months ago, com. Grishenin (he works in the Far Eastern regional party committee) conveyed that Alikhanov was a good friend of one miscreant, an enemy of the people who committed suicide, and that this person used to visit Alikhanov in his apartment. I reported it. Goldshtein reported the same thing. This case lasted for two to three months. We thought that our suspicions were not grounded. Then came the party committee elections. That evening, when Alikhanov's candidacy was discussed, I had been mobilized and was out of Moscow. Later I wondered if Alikhanov mentioned this fact in his biography. As it turned out, he did not. Goldshtein was ill at that time and in the hospital, but a number of comrades who knew about the case were present.

Later, a small group of [party] activists met. There I heard information about Müller for the first time. This information was given by the enemy of the people, Alikhanov. I spoke with c. Moskvin about this fact. I told him that this fact confused me a lot, and that I thought that the leadership should investigate whether the suspicions were groundless or whether they were serious.

(MOSKVIN—This fact was reported to the leadership, and Alikhanov did not conceal that he was close with Calzan.)

However, the [party] organization did not know about those ties. I think that it should have been brought up at the meeting when he was giving his autobiography. We often think that if one is a leading worker, this is sufficient.

Walecki, Bronkowski, and I worked on the editorial board of the "Kommunisticheskii Internatsional." I have to say that after Bronkowski and Walecki came to work on the board, the atmosphere there became very difficult. Kotelnikov was the only person with whom one could talk. In fact, a Polish faction, rather an enemy faction, was created in the "KI." I used to feel uneasy whenever I walked in there.

The organization knew Walecki well enough from his work in different sectors. It is typical of him to be concerned about money. As soon as he came to the board, he brought up the issue of raising his salary. Everybody knows Walecki's lifestyle, his looking down upon rank-and-file workers, often changing wives. It seems to me that we have to keep an eye on a person who is hungry for money.

Conclusion: we have to undergo a profound reorientation. Only then will our collective, which is quite qualified, be up to the tasks facing it.

SHOLOMOV.

The speeches by cc. Kotelnikov and Blagoeva are not quite sufficient. They criticized themselves enough, but in light of the newly discovered facts, the problems are now viewed differently, and therefore, we have to restructure our work on a new basis. Our vigilance is insufficient. It is essential to invent methods to restructure the work of our apparatus and to discuss in [party] groups all of the issues relating to this restructuring.

We have to study the methods of work of the enemy who operate in our apparatus. I realize that it is impossible to do now, but in the future, we must outline the methods of the enemies who are operating in our organization. For example, Alikhanov gained trust with his seeming straightforwardness.

Chernomordik and Alikhanov restrained criticism at the general meeting. Do not go too far, they said.

C. Kotelnikov has a formal approach, [and] he is not getting any deeper. Alikhanov and Chernomordik lorded over the party committee, in fact, they were the leaders of the party committee. Our party organization is not solid. [There are] bureaucratic struggles between the departments. It is necessary to raise self-criticism to a higher level. It is necessary to propagandize the good examples of the individual Communists who displayed vigilance, who managed to expose the enemy. Com. Kotelnikov raises the question of no confidence in the party committee. I think that we should not do it, we only have to restructure ourselves faster.

No. 10. KOZHEVNIKOV.

Levchenko was quite correct in his speech. They had been squandering resources, not tens of thousands, but millions, for many years. I reject the accusation that I am a bureaucrat. It was not I who squandered the money but those who were responsible for that money. I have been working in the apparatus for a little more than a year and did not understand the situation of the supposed struggle of Müller against the *Abramovshchina* [Abramov group]. How did my political blindness reveal itself? In the fact that I was never critical of what was going on around me. Thanks to that, subversive activities passed by me. There were signals, but the party committee, thanks to Alikhanov and Chernomordik, smoothed everything over. Here is one signal: One party member declared that he was going to give up his party card because wrongdoings were taking place around him and he was not able to put a halt to them. The party committee charged Müller and Chernomordik with investigating this case. There was a signal, and it faded. The same enemies used to come to our sector with party tasks. Once it was Kotelnikov, but even he was guarded so that he did not see, or, it is better to say, so that he could only see what was shown to him. [. . .]

I am at fault for trusting Müller. There were drinking and degeneration, and we failed to take those signals into consideration; we did not pursue them only because we considered that it would undermine his authority. [. . .]

NOVIKOV.

[. . .] The familyness in the Communications Department has no equal in other departments. Clashes between old and new workers took place. Self-criticism was not encouraged. Both Alikhanov and Chernomordik played leading roles in the party committee. [. . .]

SAMSONOV.

We are examining a very serious question. Com[rades] Stalin and Lenin said that capitalist encirclement of the USSR leads to confrontation between the capitalist elements and the USSR. It is essential to improve [our] study of the issue of the activities and methods of the bourgeois intelligence services that are struggling against us. How could it happen that the enemies Ali-khanov, Müller, and Chernomordik were "the heart and soul of the organiza-tion"? It is a slap in our face. The speeches by c.c. Kotelnikov and Blagoeva are completely incorrect. At two meetings, the enemies completely discred-ited me. As is known, the enemies are trying to buy off honest people. Last year, Alikhanov managed to get 100,000 rubles illegally from the Adminis-tration of Affairs Office through the party committee. [That money] was given to social organizations. At the meeting, they justly criticized me on some issues, but the enemies consciously tried to discredit me. I fought this gang from a position of principle. The argument centered on questions of principle (estimate, etc.). This gang discredited me for defending party posi-tions. Why did they work over c. Gopner at the party committee for saying that the enemy Chernomordik behaved in a Trotskyist way? I insisted that all those who had worked in Zinoviev's Secretariat should not work in the ap-paratus, but Chernomordik did not agree with this. Com. Drizul told me that Chernomordik was a dangerous person for our organization. Müller [and] Alikhanov discredited the Stalinist constitution[36] when, referring to "atten-tion to real people," they supported the enemies. I was absolutely right in my suppositions, and in my struggle I was not mistaken. When Alikhanov real-ized that I was struggling against him, he created his secret headquarters, which intercepted statements and spread rumors about me. I sent Alikhanov a statement regarding one party member. It became known to that person, probably from Alikhanov. Things are going badly in the Cadres Department. It was clear to me that personnel files were in danger. Facts and signals were not followed through on. C. Blagoeva said that everything was fine in the Cadres Department. Why did c. Blagoeva say nothing today about suppress-ing criticism[?] Where was com. Kotelnikov when I was unjustly criticized, and he himself permitted incorrect criticism[?] A rumor was intentionally spread that I had a "tail" of nineteen people. The verification showed that this was not true. Com. Kotelnikov does not have to cover me up. You have no such right, c. Kotelnikov. The party will set things straight and protect me. Influential members of the party committee, like Alikhanov, discredited me, and com. Kotelnikov did not straighten them out. Com. Kotelnikov, you worked in the Cadres Department yourself. Why was the "criticism" of fam-

ilyness not directed to the Cadres Department, to the OMS and other departments, but only to the Administration of Affairs Office? There is no answer
to this question. I am accused of suppressing Gurevich, supposedly because
he is a Jew; this comes from Alikhanov. The enemies bribed us. When I spoke
against bribes, Alikhanov said that I was slapping the organization across the
face. Regarding Pataki—there was a statement that he was a Trotskyist; nonetheless, he continues to work. Müller spoke at the meeting and said that he
was supposedly annoyed that they did not criticize him. This is the mask of
the enemy. I am not satisfied with the speeches by c. Kotelnikov and c. Blagoeva. At the last party committee [meeting] before the elections, com. Kotelnikov said that Samsonov ought to know how to behave, or else they would
criticize him. I stated that I felt bad at the party committee, because more
than half of them were Trotskyists. They said here that there were signals regarding some issues. We have to elect a commission to investigate how to
look into those signals. The party organization has to discuss whether or not
c. Kotelnikov and c. Blagoeva should continue to be members of the party
committee.

TSIRUL.

C. Samsonov spoke here regarding Pataki, that accusations against him
were unsupported. If Pataki is at large now, it does not mean that he will be at
large [in the future].

During the break, Samsonov remarked, Let us see how Tsirul will speak.
Comrades, I am not going to speak here as the accused. I had no personal
friendship or ties with any of these enemies. My great fault is that I had to
work together with three of these enemies for some time, and I failed to expose them. At the meeting I supported Alikhanov against Zholdak, although I
maintained closer relations with Zholdak.

I will speak individually about each of the five enemies who were removed
from our apparatus.

Müller—under him there existed an atmosphere of groveling and bribery,
which found its best expression during the New Year party; all the workers of
the Communications Department praised Müller and even awarded him a
prize for the best dance. Müller had a secret system of bonuses; one would go
directly to the accounting office to get his bonus. There was no political
essence in this issue.

Walecki—he had a different style, an artificial rudeness. You say one word,
he would say ten. He would yell [and] bang his cane. Once he wanted to beat
a chauffeur because he did not like the car that he was given.

Krajewski—I have worked with him occasionally since 1932. We thought
him to be a badly organized person, an artisan doing everything by himself, a
bad administrator. We criticized him hard for that. He was afraid to let other
people know about his work.

Chernomordik—basically the same unorganized person, lacking any system. He kept papers in his drawer for about six months and then wrote, to file,

without even writing down the date. Now I understand that that was his method of work in order to conceal everything.

Alikhanov—this one had a different method. First, he worked in the Organizational Department. He could do nothing well; everything went bad there. I asked him: Why do you hang around here, not knowing the languages, not knowing the situation in the countries? And he replied that he had a stomach ulcer and needed diet food and treatment; therefore, he had to stay in Moscow, that is why he remained in the Organizational Department apparatus. This happened in 1932. When I came to the ECCI again in 1937, I was stunned by Alikhanov's enormous authority within the party organization and the leadership. I used to know him as a bad worker. Alikhanov artificially created an authority for himself. For example, we, the workers of the apparatus, never addressed the leading comrades [familiarly] as *ty,* whereas he addressed both c. Moskvin and c. Manuilsky as *ty.*[37] He thus created a specific atmosphere of intimacy. I think that he artificially created his authority.

I can speak about Alikhanov more than about anyone else. Mering and I took classes on Marxism with Alikhanov. There, Alikhanov had a fight with Furschik. Furschik used to be a Menshevik. It was not politically correct to defend a Menshevik, but in fact he had to be defended.

After the classes were over, Alikhanov went to Baku. He left at the same time as Lominadze did. During the elections he said nothing about this in his biography. He was asked about Baku, and he replied that he was removed for [engaging in] an unprincipled group squabble. I remember, during the purge, Solts asked him a question: Do you always exit with a squabble?

Alikhanov raised before the leadership the question of Borosh, Shenfeld, and Brann, about helping them.

Once there was a need to give information about Krajewski to the leadership. The information was written but did not go anywhere because Alikhanov said that to send such information would mean that Krajewski would have to be removed.

Chernin—when he was expelled from the party, I thought that he was a bad Communist, but I never imagined that he was an enemy. We expelled Chernomordik. I thought that if he deceived the party, he should not be a member of the party, but again, I did not think that he was an enemy. To some extent, we failed to follow com. Stalin's principles of political verification and a businesslike approach. Here we frequently went to an extreme. For example, the party committee resolved to expel Walecki from the party, yet the commission headed by c. Moskvin decided to remove him from the "Kommunisticheskii Internatsional" but to continue to use him. Facts from Krajewski's past were known. (Moskvin: They were known.) Someone knew about Müller's Trotskyism. (Moskvin: As soon as the leadership learned about it, we immediately called a meeting and worked out a line [to use] for that type). Alikhanov worked under c. Moskvin, and from there he transferred to the Cadres Department. I think that c. Moskvin should have known Alikhanov's biography, should have known that he was in Leningrad during the Leningrad opposition and later was removed for [participating in] an unprincipled group struggle in Baku. If you approached the issue more carefully, everything could have been investigated.

No. 1. <u>VASILIEVA.</u>

The whole leadership of the Cadres Department was in the enemy's hands. The problem of the selection of workers to the Cadres Department was not approached in a satisfactory manner. There was labor turnover; during the past three years, forty-five people passed through the Cadres Department. The filing is still in bad condition. Com. Blagoeva did little to help expose the shortcomings and fight them. On the contrary, she sharply reacted to criticism, coming down on those who criticized [her] by using her authority as a party leader and a member of the party committee. It happened to me, too. In our department, enemies worked in such a way as to concentrate all activities in their hands while removing from leadership such worthy workers as c. Gopner. The enemies in our department sought to put their work under their own control. Alikhanov opposed planning in work.

In her work, com. Blagoeva was closely connected with the enemies who were in the leadership of the department, and it prevented her from hearing the voice of the party members. I do not think that it is right to put Blagoeva on a par with the enemies, but she has to admit honestly that she, just like all of us, overlooked the enemy and cannot get off with general phrases.

Secret.

<u>MINGULIN.</u> The party committee did not work well enough, but we know that Kotelnikov bore the bulk of work. In connection with the most recent events, our organization must draw conclusions for itself. Com. Moskvin was right when he said that the recent removals [of people] demonstrate that not everything is in order in our organization. It is essential to undertake a purge of all sectors of our organization.

Why did we overlook these enemies? We had people whom we knew as spotless, but after investigations, it turned out that they are not quite clean. There were signals, but we took them too lightly. Regarding some people, there were no indications at all. At this time, the organization faces the task of thoroughly investigating the political personality of each member of our organization, from the first to the last. Second, we have to thoroughly investigate each signal and to verify everything using all of the available documents. Third, we have to verify the work of each [member of the organization]. This is the conclusion we have to make.

We heard Blagoeva's and Tsirul's speeches, and what they actually said was that one enemy worked here, he was removed and exchanged for another, and that one for a third. And nobody noticed that they were enemies. It is impossible [to believe] that there was nothing subversive in their work. But the comrades are saying that secrecy made it impossible to detect everything.

The party organization needs assurance that you will investigate this side of the issue.

Com. Moskvin spoke about familyness, and these comrades mentioned two people. Two people do not constitute familyness. This means that to fool people, familyness must have been much more serious. Why did the comrades from the Cadres Department not disclose the methods of familyness to which com. Moskvin referred?

We face the task of making our party organization and our apparatus healthy again. We should not simply throw people out, but it is essential to investigate each case to the end. [. . .]

No. 5. <u>ANGARETIS.</u>

Why did the enemy find it so easy to work in our apparatus? Because many forget about real vigilance. Second, because many workers are working not as party members but as clerks. In the party group of the Propaganda Department, they investigated the case of Busch, whose father forged her party card and changed the date of her joining the party in order for her to be able to work in the CC CPG apparatus. And the party group in fact rehabilitated her, and party leader Zholdak attempted to gloss over the Busch case in the ICC. It was easy to expose her because she had left the USSR in 1929 as a Komsomol member and returned as a party member in 1928. Not just enemies but also other workers of the Cadres Department (Müller or others) are responsible for not exposing her. Another thing, when L.[38] came, there was information that he was a traitor, but he nevertheless was admitted to the Congress. Who is responsible for that? He had to go through the credentials committee. After that, with the help of the enemies of the people Ortega [S. Pestkowski], Chernomordik, and others, he sneaked into the apparatus. His case was studied by the ICC to decide whether it was possible to let him remain in the apparatus. The ICC raised a question about his membership in the party, and he was expelled from the party. Where were the other workers of the Cadres Department who handled this person? They have to give an answer.

Recently I found materials composed by com. Yakubovich, which lay idle for a long time and have not yet been sent to the NKVD. Such cases, when materials are not sent to the appropriate office, have to be revealed, and all those responsible have to give answers.

A number of enemies had not been arrested earlier because the Cadres Department failed to send materials that it possessed about these people to the leadership. The problem is that there is no real vigilance, [only] a formal approach to work.

<u>ROGOZHNIKOV.</u>

Com. Angaretis told us what the workers of the Cadres Department should have told us, in particular what c. Blagoeva should tell us in her second speech, about the methods of the enemy in our organization. It is necessary to hold a political [information] day in accordance with the decision of the Moscow party committee.[39] Com. Stalin said that it is essential to learn how to work from the rank and file, but Blagoeva did not pay attention to the workers' signals. Our leadership has to take that into account. I do not understand why they did not let Kotelnikov go to the centers.[40] Com. Kotelnikov cannot entrust that to others. How could the party committee have allowed workers from the centers not to be permitted to [attend] our general meetings? It is the party committee's fault. [. . .]

Martynov wanted to accuse c. Tsirul of Trotskyism, basing [his accusations] only on c. Tsirul's speech.

(MARTYNOV FROM THE AUDIENCE: I do not consider Tsirul a Trotskyist, but he defended Alikhanov. I have no other information, but during the elections to the party committee, c. Tsirul gave a positive reference to Alikhanov.)

(FROM THE AUDIENCE: Afonina also gave Chernomordik a positive reference when he was elected to the party committee.) [. . .]

MOSKVIN.

It seems to me that the discussion has gone off in the wrong direction. We will have to return over and over again to the question of how the enemy penetrated us, especially since today we do not have a complete picture of the enemies' work. We will have to wait for the results of the ongoing investigation, which obliges us not to babble too much.

We are very weakly protected from external enemies. And I want to refer to a fact that com. Krylova told me about. The administrative decisions of the ECCI apparatus are already making their way to the fascist press. Consider this fact, and learn how to keep [your] mouths shut. Do not babble about what was discussed at the party meetings.

Each of us will have to talk about [his] mistakes in more detail. We need vigilance, not in words but in deeds. It is essential to put an end to this idiotic disease—carelessness. Lack of control and entrusting work [to others] facilitated the enemies' work.

At the closed meeting of the Secretariat, we thoroughly exposed the shortcomings and mistakes present in our work. We planned a series of practical measures in this regard. I repeatedly spoke about my blindness toward Müller. But it is not enough to talk. We have to mobilize ourselves and to work to rectify our mistakes. I think that the party committee will have to conduct the mobilization into this affair. Work discipline has deteriorated lately. It is necessary to improve it. For example, our papers are in terrible condition. God knows who has access to them. There is a certain sense of confusion among the workers of the apparatus. This is absolutely inadmissible, because panic will only favor the enemy. In order to unite ourselves in a Bolshevik way, it is essential to lead the whole apparatus on to the broad Bolshevik road.

Now about the discussion. There are reasons to criticize the party committee. We now have the right to demand more from it. But that does not mean that we can raise the question of dissolving the party committee. I spoke about familyness in the apparatus, the carriers of which were Alikhanov and

Chernomordik. But it would be incorrect to heap the blame on others, for example, on com. Blagoeva. We cannot lump together those miscreants and honest comrades. We have to help Blagoeva to learn this lesson.

In his speech, com. Samsonov correctly pointed out several issues. He made clear that it was no accident that Alikhanov and Chernomordik tried to target the Administration of Affairs [Department], tried to attract attention to it. They wanted to distract attention from other sectors. However, Samsonov's idea that all party work revolves around these two issues is incorrect. Therefore, his originally correct idea became unconvincing. He did not keep a sense of proportion.

We have not felt the presence of the party committee lately. Rogozhnikov is right when he says that throughout the [Soviet] Union, the mobilization of party and non-party Bolsheviks to study methods to fight the enemy is under way, but we have failed to organize this. This [situation] has to be rectified quickly.

The Secretariat planned a series of measures to clean up the apparatus, in particular, the Communications Department. Com. Anvelt, who is currently reviewing the work of the Communications Department, is coming to the conclusion that the existing system impedes the [proper] development of work there.

I believe that the party committee will be up to its tasks, but all of us will have to help it. Each of you can come to the leadership to talk about the shortcomings that you notice in your work.

As for those who are leaving, it is important that they do not leave us as enemies. If they are not the enemies, why not use them in the publishing house, why not provide them with jobs? We decided to move some comrades to other departments, from one sector to another. But the attitude toward these comrades has to be friendly. It will be necessary to thoroughly purge the apparatus. By the way, the KIM helped us a lot with cadres.

KOTELNIKOV.

I agree with Samsonov that the party committee and I, when criticizing Samsonov, failed to expose even worse facts in the Communications Department and in the Cadres Department. It was our political mistake. However, one cannot agree with Samsonov when he says that it is necessary to liquidate *Alikhanovschina* [Alikhanov group]. The task of the whole party organization, including Samsonov, is to study, expose, and cleanse our party organization. Here the role of each individual party member has to be greater than [it has been] until now.

We talked here about familyness and mentioned Alikhanov and Chernomordik. It is a fact that Alikhanov and Chernomordik always supported each other at party committee meetings. On the Chernin question, Alikhanov defended his point of view; he was against expelling Chernin from the party. We expelled Chernin despite Alikhanov's resistance. In the case of Eisenberger, Alikhanov also offered resistance.

Alikhanov is an experienced enemy and double-dealer. He understood the situation in the organization well; he utilized every fact to deceive us.

During the exchange of party documents, Alikhanov concluded his speech by stating that [the members of] our entire organization, one and all, will come with new party cards. Did he not deceive the party organization when he raised a question about lifting the reprimand from Chernin? Alikhanov was an experienced enemy.

In its work the party committee has guided itself by the decisions of the CC [and] by the directives of the Moscow party committee and the district committee. We made mistakes. We failed to promptly expose these enemies.

There were voices here in favor of reelecting the party committee. It is the business of the party collective. It is difficult for me to discuss this because I am the party committee secretary. However, I think that we now need to strengthen the party committee. New comrades will help to overcome difficulties and shortcomings. If the general meeting agrees, we will raise the question in the district committee to let us supplement the party committee [with new members].

Political studies have weakened lately. The network of the party schools must be restructured. It may be necessary to replace some study group leaders. A series of comrades are retiring. It will be necessary to complete this work in the next few days.

You can blame the party committee for only now raising the issue of the arrest of several enemies in our apparatus. We did not raise it, not because we wanted to conceal it from the organization, [but rather] we did it in the interest of the cause. I do not think that a party crime was committed.

I suggest electing a commission that, together with the party activists and based on this discussion, will put together suggestions. Our collective will undertake the task of overcoming the current difficulties in a united, Bolshevik manner.

RESOLVED: To take the report into consideration. To charge the party committee, together with the party activists, to work out measures in connection with the lessons deriving from the latest arrests and removals from our organizations, to liquidate the results of sabotage and to further mobilize the organization to struggle against the remnants of the enemies' subversive activities. Second, [to work out measures] to mobilize the party organization to study Bolshevism. And third, to charge the party committee to suggest in the higher party organs of the Moscow organization that the election of additional members to the party committee be permitted.

TSIRUL.

Martynov accused me here of being a Trotskyist. I do not know what motivated him, but I request that if there are any reasons to accuse me of Trotskyism, they be investigated. If not, I request that this comrade be held responsible for this.

The majority in the party organization have known my work for several years. I was elected chairman of the purge commission, and there have never been any accusations against me. I am asking Martynov to state on what basis he called me a Trotskyist. He has no right to offend me, and the party meeting has to react to this. I have been struggling for the revolution for all these years and will not permit [him] to offend me.

KOTELNIKOV.

As far I as understand it, Martynov referred to Tsirul's speech because when the meeting asked Martynov to repeat [his statement], he immediately rejected his formulation. Therefore, Martynov probably had no other basis for it except the speech by Tsirul.

MARTYNOV.

I have never considered, and do not consider him a Trotskyist.

VOICE. Before you speak, you must think.

KOTELNIKOV.

I see no reasons for passing any decision on this matter.

POLINOV.

Martynov is not well educated, so he blurted [this] out.

KOTELNIKOV.

I think that the party meeting will take into consideration Martynov's declaration that he had no reason to accuse Tsirul of Trotskyism. And second, the party meeting considers Martynov's statement irresponsible and not serious.

DEDKOV.

During the elections, Tsirul positively characterized Alikhanov; [he said] that he knew him well. I think that he then referred to him as a valuable worker. In this case, it is insincerity.

DEDKOV'S SUGGESTION IS PASSED.

KOTELNIKOV.

I believe that no one deduced from c. Tsirul's speech that c. Tsirul is a Trotskyist.

A suggestion is made to compare the two speeches by c. Tsirul about Alikhanov: [the speech] at the time of electing Alikhanov to the party committee, and [the speech] at the present meeting.

(Suggestion passed.)

BLAGOEVA.

The party meeting should know the following fact: Kotelnikov and I have long been collecting and studying materials against Chernomordik. This fact must be taken into consideration in connection with the statement that Blagoeva joined this group. I also want to add that under the leadership of Kotelnikov, I initiated the request of materials from the Irkutsk organization that exposed Chernomordik, though too late.

Second note: com. Angaretis cited facts about the poor work of the Cadres Department. Comrades have to know that secrecy was treated as the most important principle, and I was unaware of the facts cited by com. Angaretis. The new leadership of the Cadres Department will have to study this question.

Third note: I think that the party organization heard from me how I evaluate my responsibility, my grave error of trusting, along with the whole party organization and the leadership, the enemy Alikhanov.

We will discuss the elections when we are able to summarize the results of the subversive work that the enemies conducted here. [. . .]

Chairman: F. Kotelnikov
Secretary: Volk.

Defense and denunciation dominated the remarks of the participants in the 22 June meeting. Although a few people's comments (e.g., Vulfson's and Mering's) were of a purely defensive nature and designed to render innocuous previous contacts with arrested enemies, most who spoke blended defense and denunciation. The standard line of defense was that although one worked with an arrested enemy, so skillful was the enemy that one did not detect the enemy's methods. This defense was most common when people spoke of Alikhanov. Judging from some people's comments, Alikhanov had been well respected because he was honest and straightforward. Those people viewed his arrest with incredulity. Kotelnikov's concluding comment that Alikhanov was "an experienced enemy" served, therefore, to absolve those who had not suspected Alikhanov. Others, in particular Sholomov, transformed Alikhanov's virtue into an enemy's ruse—"Alikhanov gained trust with his seeming straightforwardness"—and in so doing not only conveyed the logic of the conspiratorial mindset but also cast doubt over all behaviors.

Given the wave of arrests of ECCI officials in May and June, defensive comments are hardly surprising, nor are denunciations of arrested "enemies." However, the denunciations leveled by the rank and file against the party committee's leaders, Kotelnikov and Blagoeva, suggest that some speakers took advantage of Stalin's call for a check-up from below to settle grievances with their leaders and to defend themselves against becoming scapegoats for their leaders' shortcomings, mistakes, or wrath.[41] Rogozhnikov was quite explicit on this last point: "Com. Stalin said that it is essential to learn how to work from the rank and file, but Blagoeva did not pay attention to the workers' signals." That there were "voices" in favor of reelecting the party committee makes clear that some rank-and-file members had defied the ritual of party meetings, choosing instead to augment their attacks on arrested "enemies" with attacks on their superiors. Those attacks had political and personal roots. Sholomov took a slightly different tack when he stated that the arrested enemies Alikhanov and Chernomordik were the leaders of the party committee, thereby implying that Kotelnikov, the party committee secretary, did the "enemies'" bidding. To Sholomov, one of Chernomordik's and Alikhanov's, and implicitly Kotelnikov's and Blagoeva's, major offenses was that they "restrained criticism" at the general party meeting. "Do not go too far, they said." Novikov expressed the same sentiment, but gave it a twist: "We are responsible for not criticizing high-ranking workers. One cannot take refuge in the fact that these people had authority."[42]

By denouncing the alleged misuse of ECCI funds by arrested "enemies" (and their former bosses) to support their purportedly lavish lifestyles, several speakers expressed resentment of their leaders' material comfort. Given that there existed within the ECCI a "problem of assistance to low-paid workers," such attacks probably found some support. Nor were such attacks confined to those already arrested. Levchenko denounced Kozhevnikov for spending twenty-five thousand rubles to decorate rooms in the Rococo style and for having dinners with the "most exquisite wines and dishes." "Kozhevnikov is a bureaucrat," he asserted, and "it is necessary to purge such people." Kozhevnikov rejected the accusation and, in time-honored fashion, defended himself by appealing to his comrades' frustration with their leaders: "It was not I who squandered the money but those who were responsible for that money."

It was Samsonov who articulated most forcefully the sense that the arrested enemies "completely discredited" and "are trying to buy off honest people" like himself. He cast himself as an "honest" party member, who "fought this gang from a position of principle." Nor were the arrested enemies the only objects of his frustration. He, too, railed against Kotelnikov and Blagoeva, who did not defend him when he was "unjustly criticized." He went so far as to suggest that Kotelnikov and Blagoeva be removed as members of the party committee. Although Samsonov's denunciations may have expressed the feelings of some at the meeting, he did not become the spokesman for the discontented, probably because he displayed signs of instability: "[Alikhanov] created his secret headquarters, which intercepted statements and spread rumors about me," and "more than half" of the party committee members were Trotskyists. But in the atmosphere of mid-1937 people like Samsonov had the right to speak their mind, and they did.

Such incipient rebellion by the rank and file alarmed Moskvin, whom Tsirul had criticized for his lack of vigilance toward arrested "enemies" Walecki, Müller, Krajewski, and Alikhanov. "It seems to me that the discussion has gone off in the wrong direction," Moskvin asserted before defending Bla-goeva, criticizing Samsonov ("He did not keep a sense of proportion"), and announcing that the Secretariat, that is, the leadership, "planned a series of measures to clean up the apparatus," that is, the rank and file. The views enun-ciated by the leadership (Moskvin, Kotelnikov, and Blagoeva) prevailed. The meeting also passed a resolution that expelled seven rank-and-file members from the party. But on one point, rank-and-file demands to reelect the party committee, the leaders responded by agreeing to seek permission to elect addi-tional members to the party committee. With artful compromise, Kotelnikov endorsed the view that "new comrades will help to overcome difficulties and shortcomings." Familyness seems to have ensured the victory of the party committee leaders.

Another factor suggests that the party committee leaders cooperated to stem rank-and-file attacks on them. In September 1936, Kotelnikov had included Blagoeva's name on the list of VKP(b) members, "formerly in other parties, having Trotskyist and Rightist tendencies" (Document 18). Yet at the meeting, the ever-vigilant Kotelnikov gave no hint that she might have such tendencies. His silence suggests that he appreciated that he and the other party committee leaders had more to lose than to gain by raising the issue.

The security organs by whatever their name—Cheka, OGPU, GPU, NKVD—had played a prominent role in Soviet politics and history before 1937. The Politburo authorized a dramatic expansion of NKVD powers in 1937–1938, transforming the police into an exceedingly powerful institu-tion, one that rivaled even the party. As we have seen, the ECCI apparatus routinely cooperated with the police on a range of issues and over people with police backgrounds, such as Moskvin. Yet never before had the Com-intern or its party committee felt obliged to pay public homage to the head of the police. Then again, never before had the head of the police been an ECCI member. But in July 1937 such homage was wise. **Document 33** is the letter sent by the party committee of the ECCI apparatus to Yezhov congratulating him on receiving the Order of Lenin. Although Yezhov was an ECCI mem-ber, given his belief that major spies worked in the Comintern and given that the NKVD had begun to round up leaders of the ECCI apparatus, there is reason to doubt the seemingly boundless appreciation expressed in the telegram. Fear and self-preservation probably account for its sycophantic tone. But as the vigilance campaign suggests, one should not dismiss the "sincere congratulations" of the party committee nor its promise to hunt down shared "enemies."

Document 33

Letter of congratulations from the ECCI party organization to Yezhov upon his receiving the Order of Lenin, 21 July 1937. RGASPI, f. 546, op. 1, d. 388, l. 98. Original in Russian. Typewritten.

<u>To Com. Yezhov.</u>
(Adopted at the general closed meeting of the party organization of the ECCI apparatus of 21 July 1937.)

The party organization of the ECCI apparatus sends you, com. Yezhov, the faithful disciple and comrade-in-arms of the great Stalin, the renowned NKVD leader, an ardent greeting and sincere congratulations on the occasion of [your] being awarded the Order of Lenin.[43] The entire Soviet nation, all the honest workers of the world, are enthusiastically watching the crushing blows that our NKVD, under your leadership, delivers to the fascist spies, the saboteurs, [and] the Trotskyist-Zinovievite-Bukharinist rascals.

Our collective is particularly thankful to the NKVD and to you, com. Yezhov, for that great assistance rendered to us in rooting out the vilest enemies—Trotskyists [and] spies—who have sneaked into and have cunningly disguised themselves in the apparatus of the headquarters of the world revolution.

We promise to strain every nerve to stop the fascist rascals, to help the NKVD to defend the USSR by [our] deeds, [and] to purge the VKP(b) and the Comintern of the enemies of the party and the people.

In early July 1937, Stalin authorized the mass arrests of selected "anti-Soviet elements." Soon after, the NKVD issued operational orders that identified the "groups subject to punitive measures" and set regional quotas for punishments.[44] The arrests of political émigrés and members of the ECCI apparatus accelerated. The arrests quickly decimated the ranks of the CPP leaders and of Polish émigrés living in the USSR. On 9 August, after Yezhov had reported that members of the Central Committee of the CPP had confessed to participating in an anti-Soviet conspiracy, the Politburo authorized the NKVD to arrest suspected Polish spies and Polish Military Organization members. That Politburo resolution provided the basis of NKVD Order No. 00485, which unleashed the "Polish operation," the purpose of which was to rid the USSR of any and all Poles and Polish émigrés who allegedly posed a threat to the USSR. The Polish operation was but one of many NKVD operations directed against national and ethnic groups.[45] To the ECCI leaders, the fate of the CPP became a serious concern as the arrest of its leaders became implicit proof of their guilt. Jan Bielewski, the CPP representative in the ECCI, conveyed this belief in his 31 August letter to Moskvin:

> Regarding the existing situation in the CP Poland, I arrive at the following conclusions:
>
> 1. The arrest by NKVD organs of a series of CPP members, and especially of members of the CC CPP, indicates the existence of agents of the class enemy, particularly Pilsudskyites and Trotskyists, in the ranks of the CPP and its CC.
> 2. It is beyond doubt that the agents active in the party leadership had their own branches among party activists and in the party apparatus. In view of this, it is essential to start a careful selection of party workers in order to single out the healthy and reliable elements and to reveal and dismiss all enemies of the party and all of the rotten and undesirable.[46]

On 4 September, Bielewski wrote a "top secret" document entitled "On the Issue of the Crisis of the Leadership of the CPP" that focused on the dangers posed by fascists, reactionaries, and their agents, especially the Trotskyists.[47] In light of the alleged dangers, he asserted that the destruction of these counterrevolutionary elements by the "NKVD under the direction of comrade Yezhov is a necessary act of self-defense." According to Bielewski, the arrested leaders of the CPP pursued an emigration policy designed to penetrate agents of the Polish Military Organization into the USSR. After listing and decrying the party leadership's errors, which dated back to 1919, and its repeated failure to promote workers' causes, he recommended that the "healthy elements" carry out a complete reorganization of the party and its leadership and enhance its ties to the masses.[48]

As fantastic as this conspiratorial explanation seems, it was the assumption upon which Yezhov's NKVD built its case against present and former leaders of the CPP, including Bielewski, who was arrested a week after writing his report. The NKVD's assumption became the ECCI's conclusion.

Document 34 reflects precisely the allegations and suspicions found in NKVD Order No. 00485. They are, in fact, symbiotic documents. The document is a reproduction of part of the handwritten notes made by Dimitrov, who was allowed to read the "confessions" of nine members and candidate members of the Central Committee of the CPP: Lenski, Bronkowski, Slawinski, Henrykowski, Skulski, Bertynski, Rylski, Stoliarski, and Walecki. Only Lenski's "confession" is reproduced below. From whom Dimitrov received the "confessions" is unclear, but surely Stalin and Yezhov approved giving them to him. Dimitrov did not date his notes, although internal evidence suggests that he made them no sooner than early September 1937, that is, about the same

time that Bielewski wrote his report. Each of the nine men was accused of being a POW agent. That organization was formed in 1914 and engaged in sabotage against the Russian, Austrian, and German armies that occupied Poland
during the war. After the war the POW played an important role in the Pilsudski regime and engaged in efforts to destabilize radical Polish parties and the
political situation in Russia, Ukraine, and Belorussia. Around these kernels of
truth, Yezhov and his NKVD interrogators devised a conspiracy so ubiqui-
tous, so fantastic, that as a description of historical reality, it deserves to be dismissed. But to do so before pondering the conspiratorial mindset that gave
birth to it would be ill advised, for Dimitrov's notes on the "confessions" tell
us more about the interrogators' worldview than they do about those CPP
leaders who had played such an important role in Comintern history.

Because the "confessions" grossly distort the historical realities and the behaviors of the accused, it is essential to bear in mind that NKVD interrogators
used a variety of tortures, ranging from continuous interrogation over the
course of days to vicious beatings. (For some of the kinds of torture used, see
the cases of Razumova-Khigerovich and Terziev in Chapter 7.) Such inhumane
treatment explains not only the "confessions" but also the inconsistencies
among them. One example will suffice. According to Lenski's "confession,"
four members of the Politburo of the CPP elected at the Sixth Congress and 90
percent of the delegates were POW agents. Yet according to Slawinski's confession, all of the Politburo members elected at the Fifth Congress were POW
members. NKVD interrogators apparently never pondered why the POW
would relinquish absolute control of the Politburo.

But focusing on inconsistencies in the evidence misses the point. Yezhov was
not after the truth. He knew the truth—"Polish spies . . . had infiltrated all departments of the organs of the Cheka [NKVD]" as well as the ranks of the VKP,
the state bureaucracy, and the Comintern—and he demanded that his subordinates share his assumptions and act on them.[49] The confessions, therefore, reflected the interrogators' beliefs, not the victims' activities. M. P. Frinovsky, head
of the NKVD's Main Administration of State Security (GUGB) and a man who
shared many of Yezhov's views, testified after his own arrest that "often interrogators themselves gave the testimony and not those under investigation. Did
the leadership of the People's Commissariat, that is, Yezhov and I, know about
this? They knew and they encouraged it. How did we react to it? I, honestly,
didn't react at all, and Yezhov encouraged it."[50] Other testimony supports
Frinovskii's admission. Shneidman, an NKVD interrogator under Yezhov, testified that "Yezhov's authority in the NKVD was so high that I, like other em-

ployees, did not doubt the guilt of the individuals who were arrested on his direct orders even when the investigator did not have any materials which compromised the given individual. I was convinced of the guilt of such an individual
even before the interrogation and then, during the interrogation, tried to obtain
a confession from that individual using all possible means."[51]

Many NKVD agents shared Yezhov's conspiratorial worldview. The more
fervently they did so and the more enemies they unmasked, the more Yezhov
rewarded them. To such people, inconsistent testimonies were trifling details
created by participants in an "omnipresent conspiracy" that the NKVD was
committed to smashing.[52]

An equally disturbing aspect of the "confessions" is that they contain the
names of Poles and others who had not yet been arrested but who were arrested soon thereafter because they had been implicated in the "confessions."
Dimitrov's complete notes contain a numbing array of names of people who
would be arrested. One small example of this all-too-common practice is Stoliarski's confession. Stoliarski was arrested on 25 July 1936 and sentenced to
five years of hard labor on 20 May 1937 for espionage. Precisely when during
that ten-month period of incarceration he confessed is unclear. Among those
whom Stoliarski implicated as POW agents were his fellow Poles, Lenski and
Skulski, and the German, Heckert, all of whom were then prominent Comintern officials. Based on Stoliarski's "confession," those three and others
were arrested. Walecki, in his "confession," named thirty-four people. In this
way, the scale of the repression widened at an exponential rate. One "confession" implicated people who had to be arrested and made to sign "confessions," which in turn contained the names of still more people whom the
NKVD arrested. The ranks of Cominternists and émigrés shrank quickly.

Document 34

Dimitrov's notes from the investigation materials in the case of the Polish Communists,
undated, 1937.[53] RGASPI, f. 495, op. 74, d. 411, ll. 1–62. Original in Russian. Handwritten.

Polish files.
CC CPP—1930

—*Knorin*
—*Lenski*
—*Bronkowski*

—*Slawinski*
—*Bur*
—*Bratkowski*
—*Henrykowski*
—*Marek*
—*Korczyk*
—*Próchniak*

Candidates:

—*Ryng*
—*Grzegorzewski*
—*Skulski*
—*Bertynski*
—*Rwal and oth*[ers].

<u>Lenski</u>

1. **Drawn into the <u>POW organization</u>** *(Pilsudski's conspiratorial organization) after his return from emigration in Petrograd in <u>May 1917</u> (sympathized with this organization sometime earlier) by <u>Unszlicht</u>.*

—*Unszlicht and I came to the conclusion that the <u>Bolsheviks</u> coming to power would be most useful to us since they proclaimed <u>the right of nations to self-determination</u>.*

—*Some elements in our POW organization considered joint work with the Bolsheviks necessary at that moment in order to support the Bolshevik coup so as in the future to <u>occupy leading positions</u> in the Soviet government.*

The Polish corps of the General <u>Dowbor-Musnicki</u>—Polish military clubs in <u>Leningrad</u>—worked with Unszlicht as secret <u>supporters of Pilsudski</u>.

At the time of the October revolution, a number of the POW members managed to get important positions:

—<u>*Unszlicht*</u>—*member of the Petrograd rev*[olutionary] *committee;*

—<u>*Lenski*</u>—*commissar for Polish affairs;*

—<u>*Pestkowski*</u>—*deputy people's commissar People's Commissariat for Nationalities.*

By the time of the October coup, members of the POW were also RSDRP(b) [Russian Social Democratic Workers' Party] *members; besides me and Unszlicht, there were <u>Dolecki, Slawinski, and Cichowski</u>. The Polish revolutionary council was created from representatives of parties recognizing the Soviet power: SDPKPiL* [Social Democratic Party of the Kingdom of Poland and Lithuania], *PPS* [Polish Socialist Party]-*Lewica, PPS-fraction*[54] —*all were POW members:*

—*from the SDPKPiL—Leszszynski, Cichowski, Dolecki, Bortnowski, Bobinski, Mandelbaum, and Slawinski.*

—*from the PPS-Lewica—Lapinski, Budkiewicz, his wife, Longwa,*[55] *Muklewicz, Matuszewski, Fabierkiewicz.*

—from the PPS-fraction—Sibin, Krahelski, Krahelska, Puzak, Makowski, Plawski, Żarski(??), and Kochelok < . . . >.

The section of the Polish commissariat existed in a number of cities: for example, in Orel—Kwapinski, in Minsk—Slawinski, in Moscow—Próchniak, etc.

—Creation of an additional military force for Pilsudski in the USSR.

—In 1918, a conference [held] in Moscow with Pilsudski's envoy, Długoszowski-Wieniawa (the Warsaw POW center representative); present— Unszlicht, Pestkowski, Leszszynski, Longwa, and Budkiewicz.

—A number of positions were worked out to accelerate the formation of a reserve infantry division.

—Against the Brest peace[56]—connection with the left SRs[57] to overthrow the Soviet government, arrest Lenin, and form a new government on the basis of a bloc of the left SRs and "left" Communists,[58] because the members of our POW organization were affiliated with the latter.

—I know from Pestkowski that on behalf of our organization [he] maintained a connection with the representative of French intelligence in Moscow; together they sought to subvert the Brest peace and involve Russia in continuing the war with Germany.

—The surrender of Vilno was made by the POW people—Unszlicht et al.

—During the Polish-Soviet war (1919–1920), almost all members of our organization on the western front occupied important positions and conducted propaganda work.

—Passing Soviet military plans and information about Soviet troops to the Polish high command.

—Setting the peasants on the territory under Red Army control against Soviet power.

—Failure to destroy bridges and passages when the Red Army was in retreat.

—The activities of Polish saboteurs in the Red Army was facilitated in every way possible.

In the fall of 1920, I was recalled from the southwestern front to Moscow, where the CC RKP(b) sent me to Riga as a political consultant to the Soviet peace delegation negotiating with Poland. Miller, another member of the POW, was there, too. Exploiting the difficulties of the peace process, we sought to gain the greatest possible concessions to Poland from the Soviet government.

This resulted in:

a) The forfeiting of Soviet Russian valuables to Poland.

b) The payment of a considerable war indemnity to Poland, although the payment was not justified by the real state of affairs.

c) The Lithuanian borders were set in such a way as to completely sepa-

*rate Lithuania from Soviet Russia, which makes it much easier for Poland
to carry out its aggressive plans against Lithuania.*

*Pilsudski attached great importance to the latter Polish achievement
during the peace negotiations with Soviet Russia. During a face-to-face
confrontation with me, <u>Pestkowski</u> correctly stated that Pilsudski had actually instructed <u>Koc</u>*[59] *to convey his thanks, via Pestkowski, <u>to me and
Miller</u>.*

*As early as <u>1918</u>, during <u>Długoszewski-Wieniawa's</u> stay in Moscow, we
discussed the <u>necessity of my going to work in the Polish Communist Party,
for the POW's benefit</u>.*

*In <u>1921</u>, the CC RKP(b) appointed me to work in the CC's Polish Bu-
reau.*[60] *There I worked along with the POW member, <u>Makowski;</u>* [we were]
*trying to infiltrate the Polish Communist Party. I also took an active part in
discussions of the problems and training of cadres in the Polish Communist Party school in Moscow.*

*By planting its agents in the Polish Communist Party, the POW sought to
<u>take over</u> the CPP leadership and subordinate it to the pilsudchiks' inter-
ests in order to <u>destroy the</u> party as a revolutionary force while <u>capitaliz-
ing</u> on its influence.*

—The POW worked to:

*a) Paralyze the activities of the CPP as the vanguard of the Polish revo-
lutionary workers' movement and thus to hamper or bring to naught the
entire mass revolutionary movement in Poland.*

*b) Use the Polish Communist Party in the interests of pilsudchiks in a fu-
ture Polish war against the USSR, similar to the way the Polish Communist
Party was used by the pilsudchiks during the so-called coup of May 1926.*

*c) Use the Polish Communist Party and the Polish section of the ECCI as
channels for the massive transfer of POW members and agents of the official institutions of Polish intelligence, disguised as political émigrés, to the
USSR to conduct sabotage and intelligence work.*

"The end justifies the means":

*—Promoting the members of our organization to the leading positions in
the CPP by arresting and isolating in prisons the Communists who stood in
our way; disseminating provocative rumors; direct tampering with facts
that raise suspicions of the Defenziwa's relations with those Communists;
hindering the work of the CPP by members of our organization; direct
physical elimination of Communists who stood in our way; artificially stir-
ring up factional struggles inside the CPP; systematic, persistent, and
variable inculcation of the pilsudchik-style nationalist ideology in the CPP
ranks—these are examples of the successful means used by the members
of our organization to achieve their goals in the <u>Polish</u> Communist Party.*

—Taking into consideration the fact that the <u>Walecki, Warski, and Kostrzewa</u> group, which then (in 1923) had taken over the party leadership, was compromised by open support from Trotsky, I spearheaded a struggle against this group at the Fifth Comintern Congress, accusing it of <u>Trotskyism</u>. At the same time, in accordance with the decision of the Polish commission at the Fifth Congress, I was sent to Poland to prepare for the next CPP congress.

—In order to <u>enhance</u> my popularity, my arrest in the Dombrowski region in <u>1925</u>, as well as my subsequent escape from prison, was staged.

—In January <u>1926</u>—IV CPP party conference[61]*—the leading group in the CC—<u>Warski, Próchniak, and I</u>!*

Before the IV conference—the POW members of Walecki's group—personal friction, disorder.

—<u>IV</u> party conference was attended almost exclusively by Poles [who were] *members of different <u>POW</u> groups:*

a) the <u>Malecki</u> group (Lauer, Wojtkiewicz, Wrublewski, Krajewski, <u>Rylski</u>, Próchniak, Bogucki, <u>Cichowski</u>, <u>Walecki</u>, who headed the group connected to Lapinski).

b) the Żarski (??) group (Klara [Maria Kaminska], *Bertynski Albert).*

c) the <u>Domski</u> group (Osinska, Markowski)—Domski was known as a Trotskyist and was expelled from the party.

The <u>unification</u> of these groups did not occur at the <u>IV</u> conference because of the continuing argument about which group <u>was to head the CPP leadership</u>.

At the conference, prominent POW members were also present: Leszszynski (my namesake), <u>Aronsztam</u>, and <u>Korczyk</u>.

—The <u>POW's</u> line at the IV conference was defined by a directive from the POW Warsaw center that Żarski received in <u>1925</u> from Colonel <u>Koc</u>.

—The direct result and a substantial achievement of our activity in that period was the open support offered by the Polish Communist Party to Pilsudski during the so-called coup of May 1926, when the CPP press was entirely in the hands of the POW members, who eulogized Pilsudski as a national hero, claimed his action to be revolutionary, and called on workers to support Pilsudski's actions.

The delegation of the Sejm [parliament] *deputies—"Communists" (Warski, Sochacki (??) and others) had friendly discussions with General <u>Skladkowski</u> about how to undermine the movement for the* [rights of] *<u>political prisoners</u>.*

Of course, I contributed in every possible way to the implementation of this position with my <u>articles</u> from Danzig as well as by <u>positioning people</u>. In Poland, <u>Rylski</u> and <u>Henrykowski</u> (POW member since 1916) headed the CC Secretariat.

—Wojewódzki became a [theorist] *of the "peasant question"* [and was] *sent to the CPP by the* Second Department *of the Polish General Staff. On orders from Defenziwa, he created the Independent Peasant Party.*

—In order to divest ourselves of the responsibility for becoming traitors to working-class interests, on the one hand, we promoted the "May mistakes theory," and, on the other, in order to divert Communists from opposing a policy that strengthened the pilsudchiks, on orders from the representative of the POW center, we artificially unleashed fractional struggle in the CPP *by breaking into two groups—*the majority and the minority.

[In] 1929, *the entire CC leadership joined the former minority group under my leadership.*

V CPP congress *(Fall 1929)*[62]*—"renewal of the leadership."*

The congress's decisions devoted little attention to the forms of struggle that could stir the masses, but instead prematurely stressed the forms of struggle that were isolating the party from the masses. *Regarding the war—the major emphasis was not on how to prevent it with the help of mass movements but on the general deliberations about what is to be done in case the war breaks out.*

—The CC Military Department, which was under surveillance by both the okhranka and the Second Department of the Pol[ish] *Gen*[eral] *St*[aff], *was destroyed by systematic arrests; the POW hampered its work.*

—Thanks to the efforts of us POWists, the experience of the CPP military schools, which existed in 1929–30–31 in the USSR, yielded negative results. Those graduating from these schools were not prepared for the current conditions of struggle in Poland [and] *occupied themselves with somewhat mechanical discussions about how to transfer examples from the underground work to Poland, rather than how to win the army over to the people's side, thereby losing sight of the urgent tasks of the antiwar struggle.* Those coming [to Poland] after graduation were promptly exposed by us, and the energetic antiwar work in the army quickly collapsed thanks to us.

(pg. 23!)

—In discussions with Koc [about] *the question of the POW's tasks in the CPP within Poland itself, we agreed that it is important to continue hindering the mass revolutionary movement in Poland and to prepare for political diversion in case of war against the USSR. For example, we discussed how, in case a new Polish war against the USSR breaks out, it would be essential to issue, in the name of the Communist Party, an appeal to the Polish working masses calling on them to stand up for the defense of Poland, demonstrating that the Soviet Union is the aggressor.*

—[We] *also agreed on using Cichowski, Bielewski, Redens* [Mieczyslaw Bernstein]*, and Maksymowski. We used the first three and planted* [them] *in the Comintern. Maksymowski was placed on the editorial board of "Trybuna Radziecka."*

In 1932—VI CPP congress.

—90 percent of the delegates [were] *POW members.*

—Characteristic of our work at this Congress was not the resolutions but rather the behind-the-scenes instructions to the POW delegates by me, Bortnowski, and Henrykowski.

—In order to infiltrate the CPP, we set for POW members the task of taking military studies courses at the pilsudchik Rifleman,[63] *which they had to join under the pretext of conducting Communist work in this organization.*

Another task [was] *the complete takeover of the CPP's territorial and regional committees, of which POW members already constituted 50% by the time of the Sixth congress.*

—The previous main task remained in force.

—At the sixth congress, four POW members were planted in the Political Bureau: Próchniak, Henrykowski, Korczyk, and me. We worked in this capacity for almost three years. The secretaries in the country were also the POW members—Nowak (??) ("Marek"), Starewicz ("Edwin"), and "Metek."

—"Metek" was killed by the Polish Defenziwa.

—Both Nowak and "Metek" were POW members. While working in the Polish Komsomol, they were constantly at odds with each other. Since "Metek" continued to attack Nowak, they were both arrested by the Defenziwa in the summer of 1933. Of course, Nowak was put in jail and convicted so as to later be sent to the USSR. As for "Metek," he vanished without a trace. The Polish police announced the discovery near Warsaw of a corpse that looked like "Metek."

—In 1934–35, we established continual cooperation with the POW elements from the PPS and later with the Peasant Party, disguising it as United Front tactics in order to jointly hinder the United Front movement.

—In 1936, we were facing big problems in further planting our cadres. The arrest of Stasiak and Kopecki[64] *in Kiev prompted the Comintern to concern itself with the CPP's organizational affairs. At the Comintern's insistence, the verification of activists was launched.*

I suggested appointing the following individuals, who were the POW members, to the verification commission: Próchniak, Skulski, Bielewski, Bortnowski, Krajewski.

The composition of the commission, suggested by me, was approved, but I myself was also made a member.

(pg. 28)

—As a result of this "purge," we managed to safeguard our organization from more or less significant failures; however, we had to sacrifice two POW members—Henrykowski and Korczyk.

—Henrykowski was removed from the CC; Korczyk was handed over to the NKVD.

Soon experienced <u>POW</u> members such as <u>Makowski, Landy, and Sosnowski</u> were arrested. [. . .]

Lenski's and the others' "confessions" were a surreal blend of facts embedded in a conspiratorial fantasy that transformed these men's actual political activities into sinister plots by the Polish police and intelligence services. Their confessions "proved" to Soviet satisfaction that Polish intelligence had planted spies and saboteurs within the CPP and among Polish émigrés and that these agents had wreaked havoc in the economy, Comintern, Profintern, and VKP. Taken together, they provided "evidence" that a vast Polish conspiracy existed and that that conspiracy, rather than historical contingency or inherent flaws in the Soviet system, explained the problems that frustrated the USSR, VKP, and the CPP: the Russo-Polish war of 1920, the peace treaty that ended the war, the deep divisions within the CPP, the failure of the CPP to gain worker and peasant support, opposition to the Popular Front, and so on. Coupled with the results of the verification of CPP members living in the USSR, the "confessions" provided the NKVD with the "evidence" it needed to order a dragnet of CPP members and Polish émigrés. At least thirty of the thirty-seven members of the CPP's Central Committee were arrested. How many other CPP members and Polish émigrés were arrested, were executed, or perished in 1937–1938 is still unknown. The available evidence indicates that almost 140,000 people were convicted during the Polish operation between August 1937 and November 1938 and that more than 111,000 of them were executed.[65]

Precisely because the supposed espionage network was so vast, the "confessions" force us to reflect on the worldview of its NKVD creators. And they were its creators: men who by torture, relentless interrogation, and sleep deprivation extracted from their prisoners all the nuances and details that explained the CPP's failure to foment revolution in Poland and the problems that affected the USSR; men who by their sheer persistence and addled sense of history and politics melded fact and fear into "confessions"—which they often wrote themselves—which distorted beyond recognition the sincerity and sacrifices of hundreds of Polish Communists and which destroyed their life's work and lives. Sadly, the Poles were not the only foreigners ensnared in the web of perceived conspiracies.

The NKVD's distorted sense of history and politics is succinctly exemplified in the fact that all who confessed claimed to be POW agents. Yet by 1930 the

POW was a defunct organization. Only Lenski and Walecki claimed to be agents of the Second Department of the Polish General Staff, the agency responsible for foreign intelligence and espionage. Why did the NKVD interrogators insist that those who confessed claim to be agents of a moribund organization and not of Poland's major intelligence agency? In the absence of reliable evidence, any hypothesis is mere speculation.

As surreal as the "confessions" were, we should not conclude that the Polish government (or any other government) did not engage in espionage within the USSR, that it did not have agents within the CPP, that it did not infiltrate agents into the USSR under the guise of émigrés. In an era when intelligence and espionage were essential to the national defense of all Eurasian countries, to believe that there were no agents in the CPP nor Polish spies in the USSR is as naive as believing that there were no Soviet spies in Poland or that the "confessions" should be taken at face value.[66] Delineating fact from fiction required a judicious investigation, but what occurred was a witch hunt.

Two details in the Poles' "confessions" are worth noting, for they reveal the temporal limits of the mass repression. All of the men listed on the first page of Dimitrov's notes on the confession had been arrested except for Marek [Adolf Lampe], who was in prison in Poland at the time. Lenski, Slawinski, and Rylski had accused Lampe of being a POW agent. Yet when Lampe arrived in the USSR in 1939 after his release, he was not arrested, and nothing untoward happened to him. Being in a Polish prison also spared his comrade Martsel Nowotko, whom Rylski had denounced as a POW agent. Upon being released, Nowotko, too, went to the USSR. Not only was he not arrested, but he and a group sent to Poland from Moscow in late 1941 became the first leaders of the underground Polish Workers Party, which, after World War II, became Poland's ruling party. Yezhov's removal from the NKVD in December 1938 appears to have marked the end of the imagined Polish threat.

The repression of CPP leaders sheds light on Dimitrov's roles during this period. Until mid-1937 the Dimitrov who emerges from the available documents was a true believer, a man willing to carry out Stalin's and the VKP's policies because he believed them to be correct. His repeated calls for vigilance against Trotskyists and "enemy agents," his role in the verification of the ECCI apparatus, his belief that the accused at the August 1936 and January 1937 trials were guilty, his belief in Bukharin's guilt and his scornful disdain of Bukharin's defense at the February–March 1937 Central Committee Plenum—all suggest a man who shared the assumptions, beliefs, and logic that defined the period before the onset of mass repression in June 1937. He had had doubts about certain inconsistencies and anomalies; for example, he wondered why, if Trotskyism had been "destroyed," it was necessary to press the anti-Trotskyist campaign. But those doubts do not diminish his role in the vigilance campaign and verification of émigrés.

In fact, Dimitrov helped to secure the arrest of some of the CPP leaders. The Politburo of the CPP was headquartered in Paris. On 21 May 1937, Dimitrov and Moskvin sent a telegram to Lenski in Paris: "We request you to come [to Moscow] soon for the settlement of a series of urgent issues." Three weeks later Dimitrov sent another telegram: "Urgently convey to Lenski that a visa for him and his wife has been sent."[67] Dimitrov recorded in his diary the parade of Polish Politburo members to the NKVD: "Lenski arrived. Rylski, Skulski, and Prukhin also summoned"; "L[enski] to Yezhov's"; "Walecki too"; "Prukhin arrived at Yezhov's."[68] On 10 July, Dimtrov signed a telegram sent to Albacete, headquarters of the International Brigades in Spain: "Kautsky [José Díaz]. We ask you to send Tsikhovski [commissar of an International Brigade] here to report on his work." A 17 September telegram to Díaz stated: "Send Rwal, the representative of the Polish party, here."[69] We can only wonder what Dimitrov thought of his role in the arrests of those whose "confessions" he had read.

In this respect, Dimitrov exemplifies many in the ECCI and the VKP during the period, people who by their beliefs, rhetoric, behavior, fulfillment of orders, denunciations, or silence at various important political junctures supported, and thereby validated, the policies and behaviors that created the political conditions and mindset that made the mass repression possible or served to accelerate it. Of course, for Dimitrov to have openly opposed the arrests or refused to send the telegrams abroad would have been tantamount to admitting he was an "enemy agent." In mid-1937 party discipline and conforming to Stalinist norms were essential to political survival. But Dimitrov's behaviors prior to that time do not suggest that he blindly followed orders. Even prior to mid-1937 he had enthusiastically acted as the agent and instrument of VKP leaders.

Dimitrov was a "real Bolshevik" who wholeheartedly supported the general line of the VKP and its assumptions and values. Yet as the weeding of the Comintern's ranks continued and increasing numbers of comrades whom he had believed to be honest Communists were arrested, he apparently began to have doubts. He did not express them publicly, nor did he confide them to his diary. But the ways he quietly worked to right injustices and defend some of the Comintern members and workers suggest that he had developed reservations about the excesses of, and perhaps the necessity for, mass repression. One example shall suffice for now (for others see the case studies in Chapter 7). In his confession, Rylski claimed that Blagoi Popov, Dimitrov's codefendant at the Leipzig trial of 1933, was a Bulgarian police agent and that he had betrayed Dimitrov. Yet after Popov's arrest, Dimitrov appealed on his behalf.

Not everyone had reservations. The arrest of fraternal party leaders, ECCI members, and staff of the ECCI apparatus was enabled in part by denunciations from comrades, coworkers, or subordinates. The precise role of denunciations in the selection of those arrested deserves closer study. But as the case of Nikolai Prokofiev, former head of the Cadres Department of the Executive Committee of the KIM and, from 1935 to late 1937, a secretary of that Executive Committee, suggests, denunciations contributed to the dynamics of the repression and the selection of victims.[70]

On 19 September 1937, Prokofiev had a "conversation" with the three leaders of the ECCI party committee—Kotelnikov, Blagoeva, and Krylova.[71] Who initiated the conversation is unclear. What *is* clear was the reason for it: the arrest on 15 September of Vasili Chemodanov, the secretary of the Executive Committee of the KIM from 1930 until his arrest and Prokofiev's comrade and coworker. In the course of the conversation, Prokofiev criticized or cast suspicion on many aspects of Chemodanov's party and professional work, as well as his personal life.

He began by attacking Chemodanov's unwillingness to address and resolve problems relating to KIM cadres abroad, an issue that related directly to both men's work. He criticized Chemodanov's alleged refusal to address problems affecting fraternal parties in half a dozen countries. His comments on the German party are typical: "We spoke [with Chemodanov] about Germany several times, but he never carried the business to its conclusion. For this reason, today we don't have reliable and verified people [there]." He also cast suspicions on Chemodanov's relations with people who had already been arrested—for example, Lenski ("It seems that Chemodanov had many relations, and not [simply] formal ones, with Albert Lenski") and Pyatnitsky ("He was very well connected with Pyatnitsky . . . Pyatnitsky always showed him a special sympathy . . . I don't know how many times Chemodanov talked with Pyatnitsky, but undoubtedly he cried on his shoulder").[72] Prokofiev also bluntly criticized Chemodanov's attitudes toward his political responsibilities—"he didn't like to go to meetings of the ECCI Secretariat and stubbornly ignored these meetings"—and his "anti-party talk against the leadership." According to Prokofiev, "It was clear to us [that] Chemodanov is a bureaucrat" who lacked proper party consciousness.[73]

Prokoviev was particularly loquacious about Chemodanov's personal life and self-indulgences. He claimed that in 1935 "Chemodanov announced a new theory, that it was necessary to support himself better, to live life better." Prokofiev then expounded on what he thought of as Chemodanov's womanizing and the exorbitant amounts of money that he had spent renovating his apartment.[74]

Although Prokofiev spoke for himself, he frequently made his allegations as if he were repeating those of coworkers and comrades: "We spoke time and again with Chemodanov"; "It was clear to us"; "We had the impression that he was hostile" to certain comrades. Whether Prokofiev deployed the technique consciously or subconsciously, it served to universalize and justify his allegations.

During the course of the conversation, Prokofiev indicated that in the past, he had denounced no fewer than a dozen other comrades. It was perhaps this aspect of the conversation that prompted Manuilsky, to whom a copy of the transcript of the conversation was sent, to ask Prokofiev to write his "political biography." **Document 35** is what Prokofiev sent to Manuilsky.

Document 35

N. Prokofiev's "political biography," 19 December 1937. RGASPI, f. 495, op. 10a, d. 395, ll. 31–38. Original in Russian. Typewritten with signature and handwritten additions.

19 December [1937]

*To the archive, the
personal file of Prokofiev*

To
Secretary of the Executive Committee of the Comintern,
comrade <u>MANUILSKY</u>,
Head of the Cadres Department of the Comintern,
com. BELOV,
Secretary of the ECCI Party committee,
com. KOTELNIKOV

In response to com. Manuilsky's request, I write the following information about my political biography.

In 1924–25, I was at an oblast [party] meeting in Leningrad where the enemies of the people Glebov-Avilov [and] Rumiantsev tried to insinuate a

Trotskyist-Zinovievite position into the meeting, in particular concerning the issue of the middle peasant [*seredniak*] [and] the necessity of introducing standing delegates into meetings of middle-peasant youth. We, the Pskov delegation, and I, in particular, were actively opposed to this effort. At the time of the Fourteenth Party Congress [1925], I was the secretary of the Komsomol committee for Ostrovskii *uezd* [district] in Leningrad oblast. Since only at the party Congress did the position of the opposition become known, I actively mobilized the organization in the fight against the opposition [and] for the party line. In the Ostrovskii organization at that time, three oppositionists (Magdariev, Koshin, Sokolov) had been sent [to do] Komsomol work. They were all expelled from the organization as people who, already at that time, were actively undermining the work of the Komsomol. In Leningrad in 1926, at a meeting of Komsomol activists from the Narva and Vyborg districts, along with com. Sobolev, I came out against the openly hostile efforts of Rumiantsev, Tolmazov, and Surovag. In the Vyborg district [*raion*], it came to physical clashes with the oppositionists, in which I participated.

For my part, I actively participated in the struggle against the Rights. In that period [1928–1929], I was secretary of the Komsomol of the Velikolutsky OC [oblast committee]. The Komsomol organization in this region, which I headed, was the first organization in Leningrad oblast to turn out for the introduction of collectivization.

In 1930, when I was secretary of the Komsomol of the Volodarskii RK [district committee] in Leningrad, on my initiative we broke up (without the NKVD's intervention) an illegal meeting of young Zinovievite oppositionists who were meeting in the cemetery of the Alexander Nevsky monastery in connection with the anniversary of the death of the Trotskyist Kankin (former secretary of the Komsomol collective of Krasnyi Putilov [factory]).

Also in 1930, I addressed the oblast party conference (S. M. Kirov gave the introductory remarks), at which I clearly depicted the hypocrisy (of the repentance) of the Zinovievites [and] stated that this serpent [*zmeya*] was again creeping into the party ranks and carrying a grudge against the party.

In 1930, I happened to participate in the struggle with the former secretary of the Komsomol of the Leningrad OC, R. Vladimirov. In the fall of that year, Vladimirov began spreading the Trotskyist-Bukharinist theory about the futility and hopelessness of the Komsomol. In this struggle against Vladimirov, I gave active support to the Komsomol CC, in particular to com. Kosarev. Not working in the Komsomol at that time, my service was that the Volodarsky district [party committee] turned out in support of the CC's crushing defeat of the *Vladimirovshchina.* After that, when the foul murder of com. Kirov had been committed, com. Kosarev, together with com. Yezhov, on the instructions of the CC VKP(b), went to Leningrad to purge it of hostile party elements. I went personally to com. Kosarev and pointed out to him that Vladimirov (who at that time was the second secretary of the district party committee in Moskovskii district) was a former Trotskyist. As a result of com. Kosarev's investigation, Vladimirov was removed from the party. In the summer of 1937, fearing exposure, Vladimirov shot himself.

In 1931, at com. Kosarev's suggestion and in accordance with the decision of the Orgburo CC VKP(b), I was sent to work in the EC KIM.

In spring 1932, I was abroad with the leaders of the VEB.[75] My activity focused primarily on the struggle against the Neumann-Remmele group, that is, against Müller, Hiller, Valter, and others. In this struggle I relied on the advice of com. Dimitrov (who was in Berlin at that time and with whom I had several meetings) and com. Sher and Thälmann, with whom I also met. For my active struggle against this group, Neumann and Müller, with Knorin's help, wanted to remove me, but they did not succeed in doing so, because at the Twelfth ECCI Plenum they were smashed politically, and the Comintern's and Thälmann's line triumphed.

In 1932, while working in Berlin, twice I had to deal with the situation in the Spanish union [i.e., Komsomol]. As a result, the Trotskyist Vega (former secretary of the CC of the Spanish Komsomol) and his followers were thrown out of the leadership.

In 1933, I raised the question of the mistaken [political] line of the Polish [youth] union in its struggle with the Trotskyists (several districts in Warsaw and Lodz had fallen into the Trotskyists' hands). As a result, there was a change in the union's line, [and] Stefak-Rudy was removed from the leadership. He has now been expelled from the party ranks. I struggled for the Comintern's line on the Bulgarian question. On my initiative, acting in concert with the Foreign Bureau of the CPB[ulgaria], Rumenov, Tsetkov (arrested), and Popov (arrested) were dismissed from work in the KIM apparatus.

On my initiative, special tasks were enacted for purging the leaderships of the youth unions of Trotskyist elements within the Komsomols of Greece, Czechoslovakia, [and] Austria. On my initiative, the question of replacing and expelling San Fuentos, secretary of the Chilean [youth] union, was put forward, [as was the case of] Forslued [who worked for] the Agitprop [department] of the CC of the Canadian Komsomol and [was] the second secretary of the Swedish [youth] union.

On my initiative, during the last two years [1936–1937], the following people were purged for not inspiring political confidence:

Polit[ical] workers [in the EC KIM apparatus]:

Gaft, Chevalier, Douglas, Viktorovich, Panteleev, Fritz Balder, Arno, Landver (arrested), Inka (deported from the Soviet Union), Dolly Verner, Nowak, Vera Nowak, Tsetkov, Rumenov, Gary Wilde (arrested), Kocheryants, Vintsel, Steiger Karl (reportedly arrested), Karl Müller, Baum, Verbenov, Petrova, Yonkers, Darnitskaya, Bergman, Shtorm, Maisky.

Technical Workers:

László Sály, Rozenberg, Fainshtein, Zvonkin, Marto, Ketner L., Donets, Kalinin, Rokovitz, Klinger, Hennesey, Furboten.

If I noticed someone doing something hostile to the party, I immediately notified the leaders of the Comintern and the NKVD. Among such people were the following:

1. Wasilkowski—former editor of the newspaper "Za industrializatsiiu." I sent material on him to the NKVD and the CC VKP(b). At the last CC VKLSM [Komsomol] plenum, com. Tal told me that this had helped him to unmask Wasilkowski as an enemy.

2. Gonchev (Alexandrov), Bulgarian. I sent materials about him to the NKVD and the Cadres Department—he has been arrested.

3. Tsetkov (Bulgaria). I sent materials about him to the NKVD and the Cadres Department—he has been arrested.

4. Khitarov (former general secretary of the KIM), second secretary of the Cheliabinsk Obkom [oblast committee] VKP(b). I personally collected compromising materials about him and sent [them] to com. Dimitrov, to the NKVD, and to com. Kosarev. Since the material was very serious, com. Kosarev sent it to com. Andreev—rumor has it that Khitarov has been arrested.

5. Krajewski (information reached me that he had close ties to Valter [Communications Department]). I sent this material to com. Manuilsky and the NKVD.

6. Tsoi Shenu. I personally collected materials about him on the basis of which he was expelled from the party. I sent those materials to the NKVD, and com. Lanfang (KRO)[76] told me that these materials helped them to identify Tsoi Shenu as an enemy.

7. Baronchini. I sent to the NKVD materials about his ties to Trotskyists (in Odessa, in Nikolaev) and about his being in a fascist organization and behaving treacherously during his arrest in Italy.

8. Khodorova—a former KIM worker, she was sent to the Executive Committee by Molchanov (NKVD) personally. I personally removed her from work and sent materials on her to the NKVD—she has been arrested.

9. Krumin—I informed com. Moskvin and Kotelnikov and the NKVD about his close and very suspicious ties to Rudzutak.

10. Nazarov—the former head of the Org[anizational] Department in the CC VLKSM, recently he was the secretary of the Saratov Kraikom [district committee] of the Komsomol. In spring 1936, I placed before the CC VLKSM (com. Kosarev) and the NKVD the question of his being a former Trotskyist who is actively, illegally struggling against the party—now Nazarov has been unmasked.

11. Davidovich—former secretary of one of the Komsomol district committees in Moscow. I placed before com. Kosarev and the MC [Moscow Committee] of the Komsomol the question of her participation in factionalist groups in the Polish party and her suspicious entry into the country (through Western Belorussia). She has been arrested.

12. Poliakov—former secretary of the Kiev district committee of the Komsomol. I placed before the CC and the MC of the Komsomol the question of his suspicious ties to Ozrin. Unmasked.

13. Frumkin—twice I placed before the NKVD the question about him, giving specific facts. On the basis of the materials gathered by me and forwarded by our party com[mittee] and party organization, to which he belonged, Frumkin was expelled from the VKP(b).

14. Asmarova—a worker in the CC VKP(b). While on vacation in Sochi, I accidentally learned about her long-standing ties to Alikhanov [and] brought this to the attention of the NKVD.

15. Shubin. In 1936, his non-party attitude toward com. Stalin became known to me. I immediately brought this to the attention of com. Manuilsky.

16. Mira Poliakova—a former KIM worker, of late she has been working in the organs of the People's Commissariat of Defense. I brought [the fact] that she was connected with Abramov, Kurella, Saltanov, and Antipov to the attention of the leaders of this organization.

17. Alekseev—a former KIM worker, he now works in the same place as Poliakova. I raised the question of his ties to Saltanov, Ptukhoi, Yerofitsky, and Khapchenko with the leaders of this organization.

18. Dvorina—a former KIM worker. I placed before the Kiev district committee of the party the question of her close ties to enemies of the people Listovsky, Demchug, and others.

19. Buyanov—a former KIM worker. I raised the question of his close ties to Saltanov and his Trotskyist past with the organs of the NKVD.

20. Saltanov—when the suicide of a chauffeur in Saltanov's apartment became known to me and Krasnov, it was decided [to ask] com. Kosarev to investigate this fact, since we then suspected that Saltanov has homosexual traits [u Saltanova elementy muzhelozhstva].

21. Kharchenko. I learned that Kharchenko personally had large sums of foreign currency at his disposal. Krasnov and I then placed this question before Chemodanov so that the issue would be brought to Kosarev's attention.

22. Lukianov. At the opening of the Tenth Congress of the VLKSM, I learned by chance that Vasiliev had held a meeting in [his] apartment regarding factional organizational issues. Lukianov, Saltanov, Cherna, [and] Vasiliev [attended]. I immediately communicated this fact to com. Kosarev.

23. Listovsky—former secretary of the Far Eastern district committee of the Komsomol. Being the envoy to the Komsomol's Far Eastern conference [and] being acquainted with the state of affairs in the organization, even before the opening of the conference, I sent an encoded telegram to com. Kosarev about removing Listovsky from the leadership. But the answer was such that this issue was not decided locally. After the Tenth Congress, in the Bureau of the CC, where Listovsky presented his report on the FEC [Far Eastern Committee] of the Komsomol, I came out with a harsh criticism of the condition of the organization. Listovsky was freed from work in the FEC but remained the secretary of the Northern Caucasus district committee of the Komsomol.

24. Regarding Finnish cadres. I sent to com. Dimitrov and Moskvin a reporting memo on the beginnings of decomposition [o nalichii razlozheniia]

among the Finnish party cadres. Com. Dimitrov approved of my raising this issue, of saying this is a very important political issue. A special commission was created to investigate the materials that I had collected. As a result, a group of people were released from work and received party reprimands.

25. Regarding Polish cadres. Upon receiving permission from com. Manuilsky, [and] making good use of Poles working in the KIM, I collected compromising materials on a series of leaders of the Polish party, among them Lenski, Bronkowski, Bielewski, and sent these materials to comrades Dimitrov, Manuilsky, Moskvin, and to the NKVD.

26. Regarding Austrian cadres. In connection with the unmasking of the Trotskyist group in the Austrian Komsomol, I collected, in addition [to materials on] the youth, materials that demanded the investigation of specific party workers, in particular Konrad. All these materials I sent to c. Dimitrov and Manuilsky and to the NKVD.

In addition to the aforementioned facts, which describe my specific activity in unmasking enemies, it was possible [for me] to cite another ten families, foreigners on the whole, who provoke doubts or suspicions. Materials on these [families] were forwarded to the organs of the NKVD.

N. Prokofiev
N. Prokofiev

19 December 1937

Prokofiev was clearly quite proud of his vigilance and the role he had played in denouncing more than sixty people, many of whom were subsequently arrested. To Prokofiev, vigilance and denunciations were proper behaviors expected of any "real Bolshevik." Party discipline demanded nothing less. For his vigilance in the late 1920s and 1930, in 1931 the Orgburo had promoted him to the apparatus of the Executive Committee of the KIM. Later the Central Committee Secretariat appointed him a secretary of the Executive Committee of the KIM. The tone of his statement suggests that he was no mere careerist but rather a true believer in the party line, a man who brooked no opposition to that line and who viewed any perceived deviance as "enemy" activity. His vigilance did not save him, however. On 19 February 1938, two months after penning his political biography, Prokofiev was arrested as an "enemy of the people and the party."

Prokofiev's remarks about the CPP imply intriguingly that Manuilsky, who had a long-standing distrust of that party, had authorized him to ferret out compromising materials on CPP leaders from among its rank and file. He reported his findings to Manuilsky, the NKVD, and Dimitrov, who ordered Lenski and others to return to Moscow to face arrest. Prokofiev's statement suggests that the role played by denunciations in the mass repression should not be underestimated.

The Poles were but one of many groups arrested in large numbers from 1937. Fraternal party members and émigrés living in the USSR, members of the ECCI apparatus, VKP members, and others were rounded up by the NKVD. The mass arrests could not have come at a worse time for the Comintern. The active role of the USSR in defending the Popular Front government in Spain and channeling the mounting international concerns about Germany's remilitarization and aggressive foreign policy had provided the Comintern with growing international support for its anti-fascist and Popular Front policies. Yet by October 1937 not only was international criticism of the repression increasing, but the arrests of members of the ECCI apparatus was seriously affecting its ability to function, let alone take advantage of its recent international success. On 10 October 1937, Dimitrov and Manuilsky sent the following letter to Yezhov, Zhdanov, and Andreev in their capacity as Central Committee secretaries, outlining the impact of mass arrests on the ECCI's ability to function and requesting the Central Committee to help them alleviate the personnel crisis that was crippling the ECCI apparatus.

Document 36

Letter from Dimitrov and Manuilsky to Yezhov, Zhdanov, and Andreev on the effects of the arrests on the ECCI apparatus, 10 October 1937. RGASPI, f. 495, op. 73, d. 50, ll. 25–26. Original in Russian. Typewritten.

<u>SECRET</u>

To: cc. YEZHOV, ZHDANOV, ANDREEV.

People's Commissariat for Internal Affairs [NKVD] organs have recently exposed a number of enemies of the people, and a wide-ranging espionage organization in the Comintern apparatus has been revealed. The Communications Service, the most important department in the Comintern apparatus, turned out to be the one most saturated. It is now necessary to completely abolish this [Communications Service] and to proceed without delay to organize this department anew with fresh, carefully selected and verified workers. Other units of the Comintern apparatus also proved to be saturated, although to a lesser degree: the Cadres Department, political assistants to the ECCI secretaries, analysts, translators, etc.

In addition, the Comintern leadership conducted a verification of the whole apparatus that resulted in the firing of about one hundred people as individuals who were not sufficiently trustworthy politically.

In the past, the Comintern apparatus was usually staffed with the cadres from foreign, especially illegal Communist Parties who made up the large émigré reserves in the USSR. Experience has shown that such a method of staffing the Comintern apparatus is, in the current conditions, dangerous and harmful, because a number of CI sections—for example, the Polish—turned out to be completely taken over by the enemy. Therefore, we will not be able to overcome this serious crisis without the help of the CC VKP(b). We ask the CC VKP(b) to help us with cadres, members of the VKP(b), a request that we have presented to c. Malenkov. The most urgent and pressing need is for CC VKP(b) help in staffing the Communications Service, since the suspension of its work has completely cut us off from abroad. In light of this, we request a Polit[ical] Bureau resolution to satisfy the request [that we] sent to com. Malenkov.

per order of <u>Dimitrov</u>.
<u>Manuilsky</u>.

10 October 1937
N1/3/ld.

Two points in **Document 36** deserve note. The first is that, in less than a year, the Moskvin Commission and its successor, the Special Commission to Verify Workers of the ECCI Apparatus, had already removed about a hundred workers from the apparatus. The fate of every one of these people is unknown: some were arrested; some were not. Second, the arrest of all or virtually all the workers in the Communications Department, which played an integral role in illegal operations abroad, seriously hamstrung the Comintern's ability to engage in clandestine and anti-fascist activities at a time when the fascist threat loomed ever larger. The arrests seriously weakened the Comintern. The agent and instrument of the Politburo had become its victim. By October 1937 the ECCI apparatus was virtually moribund.

In this context, Dimitrov's letter to Yezhov dated 11 October 1937, the day after he sent Document 36, warrants mention. Dimitrov wrote that in recent years, the Comintern archive had provided the NKVD with "documents, letters, and other materials having historical value" from Zinoviev, Radek, Bukharin, Béla Kun, Pyatnitsky, Knorin, and others. Despite repeated requests, the NKVD had refused to return these materials. His letter was but one more futile effort to have them returned.[77] For our purposes, the value of his letter rests in the light that it sheds on the NKVD's thorough efforts to cull from internal Comintern documents evidence to prove its assumption that those arrested had engaged in anti-Soviet conspiracies. Because those documents are still not available to historians, it is impossible to reconstruct the types of evidence that interrogators might have used to script "confessions" from their victims.

Dimitrov's efforts in defense of the Comintern's institutional interests did not diminish his role in the ongoing vigilance campaign. At a party celebrating the twentieth anniversary of the Bolshevik revolution, at which Yezhov and Dimitrov were present, Stalin made clear his views on how to handle enemies: "We will mercilessly destroy anyone who, by his deeds or his thoughts—yes, his thoughts—threatens the unity of the socialist state. To the complete destruction of all enemies, them and their clans!" Whatever doubts Dimitrov may have harbored about the repression, on that night he kept them to himself. In his toast to Stalin, he stated: "There is nothing I can add to what Com. Stalin has said about the merciless struggle against enemies. That will be taken into account in the Party, and I myself will do everything in my power to ensure that it is taken into account in the ranks of the Comintern as well."[78] Four days later, Stalin told Dimitrov that for the ECCI to repeatedly resolve to "intensify the struggle against Trotskyists using all means" was "not enough." According to Stalin, "Trotskyists must be hunted down, shot, destroyed. They are worldwide provocateurs, fascism's most vicious agents."[79]

There is no need to dissect Stalin's comments, which served as marching orders for Yezhov and his minions and which put those who might challenge such views on the defensive. The Comintern, which had zealously directed the anti-Trotskyist campaign and provided lists of names of those engaged in "suspicious" activities, thereby validating Stalin's and Yezhov's views, became the victim of its own vigilance.

The speed with which the NKVD arrested people associated with the ECCI not only hampered its ability to function but also appears to have overwhelmed the ability of ECCI members to react to events. There is a Kafkaesque quality to **Document 37**, which conveys the decision by half of the ICC members to expel from their respective parties the other half, who were, by that time, either dead or languishing in a prison or labor camp.

Document 37

Protocol of the 22 November 1937 session of the ICC on the question of five members: Grzegorzewski, Iskrov, Krajewski, Walecki, and Eberlein. RGASPI, f. 505, op. 1, d. 51, l. 88. Original in Russian. Typewritten.

To c. Moskvin   <u>Top secret</u>

lm. 12 cop[ies]

PROTOCOL No. 1
of the ICC Session of 22 November 1937
Attended by members of the ICC: cc. Anvelt, Angaretis, Dengel,
Tu Houxin, and Tskhakaia.
<u>Agenda:</u>

1. About ICC members: Grzegorzewski, Iskrov, Krajewski, Walecki, and Eberlein.[80]

<u>HEARD</u>: 1. ICC members Grzegorzewski, Iskrov, Krajewski, Walecki, and Eberlein have been expelled from [their] Communist Parties as enemies of the people and have been arrested by the organs of Soviet power.

<u>RESOLVED</u>: To remove from the ICC the following members arrested by the organs of Soviet power and expelled from [their] Communist Parties as enemies of the people: Grzegorzewski, Iskrov, Krajewski, Walecki, and Eberlein.

ICC Secretary

Anvelt
Ya. Anvelt

The expulsion of Grzegorzewski, Krajewski, and Walecki, three Poles arrested as "enemies of the people," symbolized the fate of many Poles then living in the USSR. As the previous discussion has made clear, of all of the émigrés living there, the Poles aroused the greatest suspicion; Germans, Japanese, and Balts were also arrested in large numbers. The arrest of the CPP leaders and many rank-and-file members in 1937–1938 decimated the party. On 28 November 1937 the ECCI passed a resolution to dissolve the CPP, a decision that had been reached five days earlier by Dimitrov, Manuilsky, Kuusinen, Moskvin, and Pieck.[81] The Communist Parties of Western Ukraine and Western Belorussia were dissolved at the same time. The regrettably familiar political justifications for the decision can be found in **Document 38**.

On the same day that the ECCI passed the resolution to dissolve the Polish party, Dimitrov sent Stalin a copy of the resolution and a letter requesting his "advice and directives" on two issues: "the contents and the character of the resolution" and when it should be issued. Stalin responded by writing across the letter: "The dissolution is about two years late. It is necessary to dissolve [the party], but, in my opinion, [this] should not be published in the press." Dimitrov's letter to Stalin is included in Document 38.

Document 38

The ECCI resolution on the dissolution of the Polish CP and the accompanying letter from Dimitrov to Stalin about the resolution, 28 November 1937. RGASPI, f. 495, op. 74, d. 402, ll. 2–6. Original in Russian. Typewritten.

<u>Top Secret.</u>
<u>RESOLUTION OF THE EXECUTIVE COMMITTEE OF THE COMMUNIST INTERNATIONAL.</u>[82]

Polish fascism, unable to resist the growing mass revolutionary movement by means of open terror alone, has made espionage, sabotage, and provocation the major tool of its struggle against the workers' movement, against all of the anti-fascist, democratic forces, [and has] poisoned all political and social life in Poland with this foul system. For many years it has been planting its spies and agents among all the workers' and peasants' democratic organizations. However, the pilsudchiks made a special effort to infiltrate the Communist movement, which represents the major threat to Polish fascism.

The Executive Committee of the Communist International has established, on the basis of irrefutable documented evidence, that for a number of years there have been enemies, agents of Polish fascism, within the leadership structures of the Polish Communist Party. By organizing splits, usually fictitious, within the workers', national-democratic, [and] petit bourgeois organizations, the pilsudchiks poured their spies and provocateurs into the Communist Party disguised as the oppositional elements coming over to the ranks of the Communist movement (the PPS group headed by Sochachki-Bratkowski, the Poalei Zion group headed by Henrykowski and Lampe, the Ukrainian SD group, the UVO group of Wasyłkiw-Turianowski, Korchiks group of Belorussian SRs, the Wyzwolenie group of Wojewódzki). By arranging the arrests in such a way as to remove the most loyal elements from the Communist ranks, the Polish Defenziwa gradually planted its agents in leading positions in the Communist Party. At the same time, in order to give its agents provocateurs and spies authority among the workers and members of the Communist Party, after staging mock trials fascism often subjected its own agents to imprisonment so that later they could be liberated, at the earliest convenience, by organizing escapes or exchanges for spies and saboteurs [later] caught red-handed in the USSR. With the help of their agents in the leading organs of the party, the pilsudchiks promoted their people (for example, Żarski, Sochachki, Dombal) to the Communist faction of the Sejm during the elections to the Sejm and instructed them to deliver provocative speeches, which the fascists used [as justification] to attack the Soviet Union and for the bloody repression of the [Polish] workers' and peasants' movement.

A gang of spies and provocateurs entrenched in the leadership of the Polish

Communist Party, having, in turn, planted agents in the periphery of the party organization, has been systematically betraying the best sons of the working class to the class enemy. By organizing failures, [they were] destroying, year after year, party organizations in the Polish heartland, as well as in Western Belorussia and Western Ukraine. [This gang] has been systematically perverting the political line of the party in order to weaken the influence of communism among the masses, in order for the party to become increasingly alien and hostile to the Communist International. For its disintegrating work, Polish fascism widely used the Trotskyist-Bukharinist reprobates, [who] already were, or willingly became, the agents of the Polish Defenziwa by virtue of having a common political purpose with fascism. The Polish Defenziwa kindled the factional struggle in the party through its agents in the Kosheva-Warski group and in the Lenski-Henrykowski group and used both factions to disorganize the party and its work among the masses and to separate the workers from the Communist Party.

However, the most ignoble role that this espionage agency played in relation to the USSR was following the directives of fascist intelligence. Playing on the nationalist prejudices of the most backward masses among the Polish people, it sought to create obstacles to the rapprochement of the peoples of Poland and the peoples of the USSR and, in the interests of the fascist warmongers, to wreck the cause of peace that is selflessly defended by the great country of the Soviets. At the same time, this network of the class enemy, [made up of people] disguised as political émigrés, was transferred by Polish fascism to the USSR in order to conduct espionage, sabotage, and wrecking activities.

All attempts to purge the agents of Polish fascism from the ranks of the Communist movement while retaining the current organization of the Polish Communist Party have proven to be futile because the central party organs were in the hands of spies and provocateurs who used the difficult situation of the underground party to remain in its leadership.

Based on all this and in order to give honest Polish Communists a chance to rebuild the party, the Executive Committee of the Communist International, in accord with the statutes and the decisions of the Congresses of the Communist International, resolved:

1. To dissolve the Communist Party of Poland, owing to its saturation with spies and provocateurs.

2. To recommend that, until the re-creation of the Polish Communist Party, all the honest Communists shift the emphasis of their work to those mass organizations where there are workers and toilers, while fighting to establish the unity of the workers' movement and to create in Poland a popular antifascist front.

At the same time, the ECCI warns the Communists and the Polish workers against any attempt by Polish fascism and its Trotskyist-Bukharinist espionage network to create a new organization of espionage and provocation, under the guise of a pseudo Communist Party of Poland, to demoralize the Communist movement.

The Communist International knows that thousands of Polish workers sacrifice themselves and their lives to serve and protect the vital interests of the toiling masses; it knows that the heroic Polish proletariat has had, in its glorious revolutionary past, many remarkable moments in its struggle against the tsarist and Austro-Hungarian monarchies, against Polish fascism. It knows about the heroic deeds of the Dombrowski battalions sent by the Polish proletariat to defend the Spanish people. It is convinced that the Polish proletariat will [again] have a Communist Party, purged of the foul agents of the class enemy, which will indeed lead the struggle of the Polish toiling masses to their liberation.

<u>Top secret.</u>[83]

Dear comrade Stalin!

We are thinking of <u>passing, within the ECCI Presidium, the attached resolution on the dissolution of the Polish Communist Party and then to publish it</u>.

After publishing this resolution, we would send an open letter to the Polish Communists that reveals in greater detail the enemy's demoralizing activities within the ranks of the Communist Party and the Polish workers' movement.

To re-create the CP Poland, the formation of a special organizational commission has been suggested. We plan to select some of the members of this commission from the most distinguished and tested fighters from the International brigades in Spain.

We entreat you, comrade Stalin, to give your advice and directives:

1. regarding this issue, whether this announcement will be <u>expedient</u> before the investigation of the arrested former Polish party leaders is completed, or <u>should we wait longer</u>.

2. regarding the <u>contents</u> and the <u>character</u> of the resolution on the dissolution of the CP Poland itself.

With fraternal greetings
G. Dimitrov

No. 132/ld
28 November 1937.
[Across the letter Stalin wrote: ***The dissolution is about two years late. It is necessary to dissolve*** [the party]***, but, in my opinion,*** [this] ***should not be published in the press.***]

Not until 16 August 1938, nine months after Stalin approved the ECCI resolution, did the ECCI Presidium pass a resolution that formalized the dissolution of the defunct CPP.[84]

The reliability of political émigrés had concerned the ECCI and VKP leaderships from at least 1935.[85] The verifications of members living in the USSR conducted by each fraternal party had resulted in "evidence" that fomented those concerns and that was used to justify mass arrests. But an administrative solution to the problems posed by political emigration remained elusive. By December 1937 the ECCI leadership had concluded that MOPR, the organization responsible for émigré affairs, was incapable of solving the problem. In early January 1938 the ECCI Secretariat announced the removal of Elena Stasova, head of MOPR, and appointed a commission to investigate how to solve the problems posed by political émigrés in the USSR.[86]

The assertion by the ECCI that MOPR was unable to solve the problems relating to emigration and its decision to replace Stasova made political sense in a period of xenophobic mass repression. Such acts allowed the ECCI to demonstrate its vigilance. We can wonder why the decision was not made earlier. Two years earlier, Manuilsky had written to Yezhov recommending replacing "the current MOPR leadership for not coping with its tasks and . . . [for creating] a secretariat composed of a number of foreign comrades."[87] Why had it taken the ECCI two years to implement its own recommendation? The available evidence does not provide a ready answer.

The appointment of a commission by the ECCI Secretariat to investigate how to solve the problems posed by political emigration appears Sisyphean in light of the Politburo resolution passed on 31 January 1938. That resolution ordered the NKVD to arrest suspected spies and wreckers from designated ethnic groups—Poles, Letts, Germans, Estonians, Finns, Greeks, Iranians, Kharbinites,[88] Chinese, Romanians, Bulgarians, and Macedonians—whether they were Soviet citizens or foreign nationals. It gave the NKVD until 15 April to do so. A 26 May Politburo resolution extended the 15 April deadline to 1 August; the deadline for those suspected of espionage, wrecking, terrorism, and other anti-Soviet activities was extended yet again, until mid-November 1938.[89] Xenophobia and vigilance, the perspectives of the fearful, had reached their terrifying logical conclusion.

Each of the nationalities designated by the Politburo had a sizable number of émigrés living in the USSR. Their native lands, save for those of the Germans, Bulgarians, and Greeks, bordered on the USSR. A deep-seated belief in capitalist encirclement and the fascist threat apparently played a role in the selection of nationalities. So, too, did the belief that the "enemy" was within the gates. But the list was selective; not all foreigners were slated for arrest. Except for the Chinese, the designated foreigners came from countries where the

Communist Party was illegal. The Politburo's anxieties about the threat posed by these "suspect" nationalities is evident in its 1 February 1938 decision relating to security in the Far East. It instructed the NKVD to evict from the region "all foreigners possessing neither Soviet nor foreign passports" and, in an effort to reduce the foreign population in gulag camps there, to execute "persons of Japanese, Korean, German, Polish, Latvian, Estonian, and Finnish nationality as well as residents of Kharbin" sentenced to camps in the region.[90]

Between the Kirov murder in December 1934 and the onset of the mass repression in spring 1937, the ECCI, its Secretariat, its apparatus, its party organization, and many fraternal party members living in the USSR participated in the anti-Trotskyist campaign, the vigilance campaign, the verifications of the ECCI apparatus and of foreigners living in the USSR, denunciations of comrades, and the dissemination of propaganda to popularize the verdicts of the August 1936 and January 1937 trials. At each particular moment, doing so made sense to those who participated. According to the official investigation into the Kirov murder, Trotskyist conspirators had helped to orchestrate the murder, an allegation that underscored the need for intensifying the anti-Trotskyist and vigilance campaigns. The VKP leadership announced that the 1935 verification of its ranks had revealed that "suspicious" elements, including foreigners, had secured party cards and infiltrated the VKP. That finding and Manuilsky's report to the December 1935 Central Committee Plenum justified the need for the verification of the fraternal party members living in the USSR. The defendants at the three Moscow show trials (and others) confessed to participating in a "Trotskyist-fascist" "anti-Soviet conspiracy" and thereby "proved" to their audience that "enemies" had infiltrated the highest reaches of the VKP and the Soviet government. We today know that there is still no evidence of a Trotskyist-fascist conspiracy, that the allegations reflected anxieties, fears, and pathologies, not reality. But to those who believed that the allegations and "confessions" were true, that party leaders would do nothing to harm the party, vigilance, verifications, and denunciations of "suspicious" behavior were essential.

Each response flowed logically from the belief that each revelation was legitimate, from the logic of a particular political moment, from the need to protect the group, from the desire not to violate group norms. For those who may have harbored doubts, party discipline ensured compliance in words or in deeds. As the "evidence" accumulated, the perception of the threats deepened. Perceived threats validated the assumption that conspiracies existed. As enemies and conspiracies were uncovered, the political influence of the advocates of heightened vigilance, such as Yezhov, grew. Yezhov's power obviously increased markedly after he became the head of the NKVD and was able to extract "confessions" that "proved" his belief that conspirators honeycombed the VKP, the state bureacracy, the ECCI apparatus, and the émigré communities. The "confessions," together with the results of the verifications of émigrés and the escalating denunciations, provided Stalin and the Politburo with the "evidence" that if the USSR was to survive, "the complete destruction of all enemies" was imperative. Some in the leadership needed little convincing by early 1937.

To appreciate the Comintern's role in this process, it is important to realize that it was an agent, instrument, and, ultimately, victim of the repression. The behaviors and beliefs of its leaders and members contributed to the repression, and they suffered as a consequence. Various motives, in varying degrees, accounted for their individual and collective behaviors. Consider the case of Skulski, a CPP member from 1921 and a member of its Politburo from 1935. In 1936–1937 he served on the commission to verify CPP members living in the USSR. Despite his occasional expressions of frustration with the ECCI leaders, he carried out his assignment with Bolshevik vigilance, seemingly convinced that doing so was essential to the well-being of the VKP and the CPP and that "enemies" threatened both parties and the USSR. He and his fellow commission members deemed a substantial percentage of their fellow Poles to be suspicious enough to warrant isolating them from the party or sending their dossiers to the NKVD. For Skulski, being a "real Bolshevik" was apparently more important than being Polish. But to the NKVD, his being Polish cast doubts on his Communist credentials. In mid-1937, based on denunciations extorted from his comrades by NKVD interrogators, he was arrested; in mid-September, he was sentenced to death.

The Consequences of Vigilance

A week ago, my son comes from school and says that all the boys are preparing a pogrom and will beat up all the other nations, the Poles, Latvians, Germans, because all their parents are spies.

— M. SIMENOVA

Guided by Stalin's compass, raising our revolutionary vigilance and relentlessness toward the enemies of the people, working energetically to verify our organization and the workers of its apparatus, we exposed many enemies of the people in the ECCI apparatus . . . we did not stand on the sidelines during this most important political undertaking.

— F. KOTELNIKOV

THE LAST OF THE MOSCOW SHOW TRIALS was held from 2 March to 13 March 1938. The trial of the "Right-Trotskyist Bloc" brought together in the docket an unlikely group of supposed conspirators: Bukharin and Rykov, the leaders of the Right deviation in 1928–1929, who since that time had served the party well; Khristian Rakovsky and Arkady Rozengolts, former leading Trotskyists; Genrikh Yagoda, Yezhov's predecessor as head of the NKVD, and others. The defendants confessed to belonging to a Trotskyist-fascist conspiracy that carried out sabotage and espionage on behalf of Germany, Poland, and Japan and sought to provoke a military attack on the USSR, its dismemberment, and the restoration of capitalism. All were either executed or died in confinement.[1]

As for the 1936 and 1937 trials, the ECCI issued a series of directives after the March 1938 trial designed to properly direct this most recent phase of the international anti-Trotskyist, anti-fascist campaign. **Document 39** below is the

ECCI directive to fraternal parties on how to conduct that campaign. In many ways, it is a familiar document. But the familiar aspects should not divert attention from the "central point" of the campaign: "the explanation of the fact that there is a <u>world</u> conspiracy of reaction and fascism directed immediately against the Land of Socialism." As odd as the concept of a Bloc of Rights and Trotskyites may seem, it paled in comparison to a "world conspiracy": "There exists a conspiracy, inspirated [*sic*] by the espionage centres of Hitler's Germany and Japan and carried out with the participation of the remnants of all anti-Soviet groupings: The Trotskyites, Rights, Zinovievites, Bourgeois-Nationalists, Mensheviks and S.R.s" and the "leading circles of the Second International." "Trotskyist" had become an elastic, shorthand term for all of the USSR's perceived enemies. It was a vast conspiracy indeed, encompassing political groups that had long fought with each other, whose conception suggests more about the party leaders who produced it than about the realities of contemporary socialist and émigré politics.

The underlying belief in a world conspiracy reflected the deepening anxiety within the USSR about the imminence of war. By March 1938 there was ample reason for Soviet leaders to fear war. Japanese aggression in the Soviet Far East and in China, the Spanish fascists' victories over the army of the Spanish Republic and the International Brigades, Germany's increasingly menacing policies and its occupation of Austria, and the anemic reaction of Western powers to these events and their reticence in supporting Soviet collective security efforts provided sufficient cause for concern in Moscow. Yet such realities differ immensely from a world conspiracy. Document 39 vividly conveys the anxieties that preceded the anticipated war: "With the occupation of Austria, Hitler begins direct military operations in Central Europe. All forces of peace must be rallied . . . to curb the blood-thirsty onslaught of fascism and save universal peace."

The tone is very defensive. Not only did its ECCI authors seek to use "the abundance of facts in connection with the trial" to prove the existence of a world conspiracy, but they urged, almost pleaded, with the fraternal parties to "effectively refute the various hypocritical and slanderous arguments" used by the outside world and "the enemy" to condemn the trial and the repression. The Kremlin and the ECCI Secretariat were quite aware that the mass repression of the enemies of the party and the people had undermined its antiwar efforts, hence this directive urging fraternal parties to tell workers "the truth about the trial and its significance," to have them counter international criticisms of the trial by pointing out that "the accused were caught red-handed" and that they admitted "their guilt." It is, in fact, the juxtaposition of fear with the familiar that gives Document 39 its force. The usual assignment of tasks and routine attacks on critics of the USSR seem designed to convey a sense of normalcy within the Comintern when, in fact, it was being gutted by arrests.

Document 39

ECCI directive on the campaign of enlightenment in connection with the trial of the "Bloc of Rights and Trotskyites," 22 March 1938. RGASPI, f. 495, op. 18, d. 1238, ll. 29–33. Original in English with handwritten notes.

ECCI Secretariat
22.III.38

[. . .]
rc/Trans. Russ. M.L.
17.5.38   <u>Confidential</u>

ON CARRYING OUT A CAMPAIGN OF ENLIGHTENMENT
IN CONNECTION WITH THE TRIAL OF THE "BLOC OF
RIGHTS AND TROTSKYITES".

1. The central point of the campaign in connection with the trial of the "Bloc of Rights and Trotskyites" must be the explanation of the fact that there is a <u>world</u> conspiracy of reaction and fascism directed immediately against the Land of Socialism, but also against the peace and liberty of all peoples. There exists a conspiracy, inspired [*sic*] by the espionage centres of Hitler's Germany and Japan and carried out with the participation of the remnants of all anti-Soviet groupings: The Trotskyites, Rights, Zinovievites, Bourgeois-Nationalists, Mensheviks and S.R.s,[2] as agents of the fascist war incendiaries. Therefore, the disclosure and crushing of this conspiracy is a great service rendered to all of peace-seeking humanity.

2. On the basis of the military aggression of the fascist powers in Spain and China and especially on the basis of the occupation of Austria by Hitler Germany [on 11 March], it is necessary to show that the same reactionary forces are operating here, which with the help of their Right-Trotskyite agency are organizing an attack against the Soviet Union. Consequently, he who defends the Trotskyite accomplices of fascism is acting in favour of the fascist murderers of the Spanish, Chinese and Austrian peoples.

3. With the occupation of Austria, Hitler begins direct military operations in Central Europe. All forces of peace must be rallied and exerted to the utmost in order to curb the blood-thirsty onslaught of fascism and save universal peace. Consequently, he who uses the extermination of the fascist Trotskyite agents in the Soviet Union as a pretext for deepening the split in the

working class and for slander against the Soviet Union, weakens the forces of peace and clears the road for the fascist aggression.

4. It has been proven that the Mensheviks were connected with the Right-Trotskyite criminals. The leading circles of the Second International, who on their part conduct a particularly furious campaign against the trial, have come out in their defense. An energetic repulse must be offered against this attack and the masses of Social-Democratic workers must be told the truth about the trial and its significance. This is necessary in the interests of working-class unity in the struggle against war and fascism.

5. We must effectively refute the various hypocritical and slanderous arguments of the enemy. For example, we should point out that the liquidation of the fascist agency is a sign of the strength of the Soviet Union. If, for example, France took the same action with regard to the Cagoulards,[3] then the French people would feel themselves much more at ease in the face of reaction at home and Hitler fascism. Facts of people who occupied important posts in the past turning traitors are known both at the present time and in the history of all countries. But in the Soviet Union such people are punished independent of the position they once occupied, whereas in capitalist countries they often remain free. With regard to the reasons which prompted the accused to admit their guilt, on this point it is necessary to show that on the one hand the accused were caught red-handed, and on the other hand, the admittance of their guilt was facilitated by their isolation from the masses of people and by the fact that no social forces in the country stood behind them.

6. The abundance of facts in connection with the trial makes it easier to conduct a successful struggle against the slanderous campaign of the enemy and to go over to the offensive. We must analyze and refute the enemy's arguments, basing ourselves on the concrete conditions of each specific country. We must especially convince the wide masses of the criminal character of Trotskyism.

7. With regard to practical measures in the further carrying out of the campaign, the following is decided upon:

a) Leading comrades of the individual Parties must deal with the trial in the press and at meetings, basing themselves upon the specific interests of the working masses in their country.

b) The comrades who were personally present at the trial must, on their return to their respective countries, especially speak at meetings giving information on the trial.

c) A protest must be registered at all meetings, factories and organizations, against the anti-Soviet slander initiated by the enemy in connection with the trial. Special attention should be devoted to having Social-Democrat[ic] and trade union workers refute the anti-Soviet slander of their leaders and newspapers and demonstrate this by protest resolutions, telegrams and deputations to various organs.

d) The full report of the court proceedings is to be published in English,

French and German languages and must be circulated not later than March 20, 1938.

e) An <u>abridged</u> report of the court proceedings in the form of a book in the Spanish, Italian, Czech, Hungarian, Dutch, Danish, Swedish, Norwegian, Finnish, and Croat languages should be published not later than March 25, 1938.

Special attention must be devoted to circulating the report of the court proceedings among Social-Democratic and trade union functionaries and among functionaries of other anti-fascist organizations.

f) Apart from this, the same material will be published in a special edition of the "Rundschau" with an enlarged circulation in the following languages: German, English, French, Spanish, Czech, Hungarian and Swedish.

g) The following pamphlets on the trial will be published here:

<u>Gottwald</u>, general pamphlet on the trial.

<u>Ponomarev</u>, material on the trial.

<u>Arnot & Tim Buck</u>, pamphlet for Anglo-Saxon countries.

<u>Cognoit</u>, pamphlet for France and Belgium.

<u>Šmerel</u>, pamphlet for Czechoslovakia.

<u>Dengel</u>, pamphlet for Germany.

<u>Lager</u> [Fritiof], pamphlet for Scandanavian countries.

<u>Willard</u>, pamphlet dealing with the trial from the juridical point of view.

<u>Freidrich</u>, reports from the courtroom.

<u>Garlin</u>, an American reporter at the trial.

<u>Koltsov</u>,[4] on Gorky.[5]

The manuscripts of these pamphlets must be submitted not later than March 20, 1938. The pamphlets to be published not later than March 30, 1938. Besides this, a pamphlet should be prepared dealing with the provocative activities of the Trotskyites in the ranks of the labour movement in capitalist countries.

h) The Radio Commission must make it its duty to see to the further enlightenment on the trial over the radio, especially in connection with the enemy's slanderous campaign.

i) All Party representatives and referents [analysts] are instructed to cooperate in dealing with the trial in the press of their countries as well as over the radio.

j) The Information Bulletin (Kellerman) is instructed to supply regular information regarding both the campaign of the enemy and the counter-campaign of our Parties.

k) The Press Department is instructed to increase the supply of our press with materials on the positive sides of Soviet life (for example, the return of the Papanin expedition).[6]

8. We must especially demand that in the explanatory campaign in connection with the trial, the most thorough use be made of fact[ual] material contained in the trial report (by using it in the press, pamphlets, at meetings,

etc.). All our assertions and conclusions must be sustained by facts in order to make our campaign more convincing and give it a more driving force.

9. A Commission consisting of Comrades Gottwald, Ponomarev and Freidrich is responsible for conducting this campaign. The Commission is instructed to submit to the Secretariat by April 1, 1938 a summary report of the campaign in connection with the trial.

The year 1937 had begun with the VKP leadership, NKVD, and ECCI gripped by an escalating spymania. By late 1937 the mass arrests of Soviet citizens and émigrés living in the USSR who were charged with being foreign agents had transformed that spymania into full-blown xenophobia. The Politburo resolutions ordering the arrests of people by nationality reflected and deepened the distrust of foreigners. Newspaper and radio announcements of the arrests of spies as well as the information on arrests passed by word of mouth stimulated both the xenophobia among Soviet citizens and foreigners' fear of being arrested. The VKP leadership and the press urged citizens to be vigilant and to report suspicious activities. And people did.

The line between spymania and xenophobia is always a rhetorical one. Even in periods of social and political frenzy, some people see clearly the excesses of such campaigns and are willing to take a principled stand against them. One such person was Eugen (Jenő) Varga, the Hungarian economist and longtime party member who was a consultant to Stalin and an ECCI member. In late March 1938, Varga wrote a "strictly secret" letter to Stalin (with copies to Dimitrov and Yezhov) on the "problem of the cadres of illegal parties and of mass arrests." He told Stalin that "foreigners are indiscriminately viewed as spies; foreign children in school are cursed as fascists, etc." He attributed such attitudes not only to the "mass arrests of foreigners" but also to "capitalist encirclement, the danger of war, and the remnants of a Great Russian nationalism from tsarist times." The mass arrests flowed, in part, from what he viewed as a belief that it was better "to arrest two innocent people than to not catch one spy!" Varga recognized the need for the USSR to defend itself and realized that innocent people might be arrested. But the result of mass arrests was the "demoralization of the cadres of the Communist Parties of fascist countries. . . . This demoralization grips the majority of Comintern workers and extends right up to specific members of the ECCI Secretariat."

To Varga, "the main reason for this demoralization is the feeling of complete helplessness in the matter concerning the arrests of political émigrés." In his view, the presence of "many new NKVD workers ill informed about the history of fraternal parties" accounted for the use of "false denunciations to secure the arrest of honest revolutionaries from underground parties." Faced with increasing numbers of arrests, foreigners did not know whom to trust or what to believe in. For them, fear of arrest was constant: "Each evening many foreigners gather their things in anticipation of possible arrest."[7]

Varga asserted that this situation demoralized underground Communists in fascist countries, who learned of the mass arrests from letters, the bourgeois press, and "through Trotskyists." He illustrated his point by noting the anxieties among Hungarian Communists who were confused by the arrests of their party leaders in Moscow and of "several hundred Hungarian workers at the bench [production workers], political émigrés." What were they to believe? he asked. "That the Hungarian proletarian revolution [of 1919] was undertaken by enemies of the working class?" Were they to believe the "Trotskyist slander" that these honest Hungarian Communists were arrested "because they are revolutionaries?" Each arrested Hungarian had friends and relatives in Hungary who knew of the arrests, so the Hungarian party found its work increasingly difficult. Varga ended his letter by calling for a "thorough, deliberate review [proverka] of the arrests of foreigners" and for informing "foreign comrades in the Soviet Union and in fascist countries" of this review.[8]

Varga's letter vividly captures some of the effects that the mass arrests had on foreigners in the USSR, be they ECCI personnel or political émigrés, and the politically destructive consequences of the repression abroad. He was not arrested, perhaps because of the political line that he took.[9] He condemned the adverse political consequences created by the arrest of foreigners and attributed the unjust arrests to the ignorance of some NKVD workers (a less than subtle criticism of Yezhov), the dire international situation, and the intrusion of prerevolutionary values. He did not challenge Stalin's line, nor did he challenge the notion that spies and enemies existed. He presented himself as a "real Bolshevik" who was concerned with the well-being of the party and the USSR. That tactic and his position enabled him to protest strongly against the xenophobia and the maelstrom of violence.

Dimitrov, too, tried to curtail the excesses. His efforts in 1938 were not as dramatic as Varga's, but they were honest efforts. Two examples will suffice. One effort addressed administrative problems that bedeviled émigrés. As a result of changes in the procedures for issuing Soviet visas, a change that reflected the prevailing political atmosphere, many émigrés found themselves ensnared in a bureaucratic Catch-22.[10] In **Document 40** Dimitrov discusses their predicament. He sent the letter to M. Frinovsky, head of the NKVD's Main Administration of State Security, and urged him to "resolve this problem." By so doing, Dimitrov moved incrementally to limit the arbitrariness that the xenophobia engendered.

Document 40

Letter from Dimitrov to M. Frinovsky about the conditions of political émigrés in the USSR seeking to secure residency permits, 2 March 1938. RGASPI, f. 495, op. 73, d. 60, l. 24. Original in Russian. Typewritten.

<u>Top secret.</u>

To comrade <u>FRINOVSKY.</u>

Recently, when issuing residence permits to foreigners, the Department of Visas and Registration of Foreigners has been requiring that they present [their] national passports. As a result, a significant number of political émigrés are unable to obtain documents to stay in the USSR. Without Soviet documents, the political émigrés lose their jobs and apartments: they are fired from work and denied registration in the houses where they dwell. Thus, they find themselves in an extremely difficult situation.

The majority of the political émigrés came illegally, without national passports. Others had national passports, but they have expired.

Until now, the political émigrés, who have not taken Soviet citizenship and who had no national passports, received residence permits through the CC MOPR of the USSR and through the ECCI.

As is known, the ECCI Secretariat firmly carries out the policy of returning the political émigrés to their countries or sending them to other countries abroad. However, since it requires time and significant preparation, it is essential during this period to secure legal residence in the USSR for these political émigrés. There are also political émigrés who cannot be sent abroad without risking their lives due to their health situation or given the character of their sentences (i.e., capital punishment).

Based on the above facts, we ask you to resolve this problem in such a way as to retain the policy of issuing documents for political émigrés that existed until recently, i.e., to issue residence permits to those political émigrés without national passports for whom an appeal would be filed by the CC MOPR of the USSR and the Cadres Department of the ECCI.

G. DIMITROV

2 March 1938
No. 168/ld.

Dimitrov also sought to alter the widespread view that all members of certain ethnic groups were "enemies." In April 1938, he wrote to Andrei Zhdanov protesting the characterization published in a Soviet-financed French-language newspaper that all Japanese living abroad were spies and all Germans were Gestapo agents. That letter, reproduced below as **Document 41**, was far milder and more politically circumspect than Varga's. By calling attention to "this clearly erroneous and politically harmful characterization," Dimitrov apparently hoped to combat the stereotyping that made the ECCI apparatus and the émigrés so vulnerable and to influence Politburo policies.

Document 41

Letter from Dimitrov to Zhdanov regarding *Le Journal de Moscou*, 26 April 1938. RGASPI, f. 495, op. 73, d. 61, ll. 24–25. Original in Russian. Typewritten with handwritten additions.

<u>Secret</u>

CC VKP(b) To com. <u>Zhdanov A. A.</u>

Dear comrade Zhdanov!

The lead article of the French-language newspaper "Journal de Moscou"[11] of 11 April this year contains the following statement: "Every Japanese living abroad is a spy, just as every German citizen living abroad is a Gestapo agent."

Letters expressing surprise and protest against such a formulation have been coming in connection with this clearly erroneous and politically harmful characterization of all the Germans living abroad, including the political émigrés persecuted by German fascism.

In my opinion, it would be expedient to mention in the press, in *Pravda,* or in any other convenient form, the erroneousness and harmfulness of this statement by "Journal de Moscou."

With fraternal greetings

G. Dimitrov

26 <u>April</u> 1938.

[Attachment:]

Translation from the French

"In fact, all the Japanese residents abroad participate in anti-Soviet espionage. It is not an exaggeration to say that every Japanese living abroad is a spy, just as every German citizen living abroad is a Gestapo agent."

The newspaper and the translation are attached to the letter to c. Zhdanov.

Varga and Dimitrov were not the only ones to express dismay over the dimensions and consequences of the rampant xenophobia. In early 1938 the ECCI received a letter from a Hellen Piteliia, who lived in Petrozavodsk, Karelia, a region with a substantial Finnish community. Piteliia asked if there had not been some "mistakes" committed by leaders in Karelia. In their struggle against "bourgeois nationalism," she wrote, local leaders had shut down the only Finnish-language newspaper. She thought that such an act violated the Constitution and might be used by "enemies" to weaken Soviet power among the local Finnish-speaking residents because, since the closing down of the newspaper, only "White" Finnish newspapers circulated. She went on to complain that workers were being arrested while "more dangerous" elements remained free. She was particularly upset that American workers, former members of the CPUSA, had been arrested: they "came to build socialism, not to sit in prison." She suggested that the situation, and the Karelian leaders, be investigated.[12]

M. Simenova, a Muscovite factory worker, was another citizen offended by the virulent antiforeign sentiment and willing to say so. In May 1938 she sent the following letter to Dimitrov, who forwarded it to Zhdanov.

Document 42

Letter from M. Simenova to Dimitrov about popular attitudes toward foreigners, 13 May 1938. RGASPI, f. 495, op. 73, d. 61, ll. 17–18. Original in Russian. Typewritten from a handwritten original.

Copy
Dear comrade Zhdanov!

I am sending you the enclosed letter for your consideration.

If [the information] expounded in the letter conforms to reality, then corresponding measures should possibly be taken.

With fraternal greetings,

G. Dimitrov

13 <u>March</u> [*sic*] 1938

<u>Moscow, 10 May 1938</u>.

Comrade Dimitriev [*sic*]!

You might be surprised that I am writing to you, and not to com. Stalin. I also wrote several letters to him, but it seems they do not transmit to him letters from such humble and illiterate [people], and this is wrong, under Soviet power we have learned how to read and write. He himself called on us to signal about disorders, which are still plentiful, but the truth about the current situation is being [concealed] from him. I am working at a factory, I am a Stakhanovite, and sympathize with the party. Last *piatidnevka*,[13] a week ago, my son comes from school and says that all the boys are preparing a pogrom and will beat up all the other nations, the Poles, Latvians, Germans, because all their parents are spies. When I tried to find out who said this, he says that one boy's brother is a Komsomol member and works in the NKVD, and said that soon all the foreign spies who lived in Moscow would be put on trial, and their families [in the apartments][14] and children at school would be beaten up as Yids [Jews] were under the tsar. I went to the school to see the director, but he says that it is all the parents' fault and that he could not track down every rumor. Today again, I saw a group of women at our factory discussing the sign "Kill the Latvians, the Poles" [that appeared] on the wall in the morning. It is a bad deal. I also wrote to com. Stalin, and other women suggested informing you too because one can hear this kind of talk every day. Even the party members are all scared, but still there is talk in private about whether the children and women are guilty, [and] that they would be beaten up and thrown out of their apartments.

M. Iv. Simenova

Received 11 May [1938]

The implications of several aspects of Simenova's letter are as disturbing as the social attitudes that she conveys. Calls for beating up or killing "Poles, Latvians, Germans," had become common in late 1937 and 1938. Protests against this were futile. Equally disturbing is the expressed belief that "all their parents are spies." We can only wonder about the conversations and advice that native-born schoolchildren heard at home. Given that the media whipped up antiforeign sentiments, which had precedents in Russian culture, it is tragic but not surprising that some people spoke of pogroms.

Simenova's statement that "the party members are scared" succinctly conveys the atmosphere in 1938. Yet she also expressed another view common in the society. She had written to Stalin, "but it seems they do not transmit . . . letters." "They" concealed "the truth about the current situation" from Stalin. If only Stalin knew, it was widely thought, then justice would prevail.[15] Of course, Stalin did know. Without his approval, the mass arrests by nationality would have been impossible. Implicit in the popular belief was another—that "they" conspired to keep the "truth" from Stalin, that "they" were engaged in a conspiracy. The idea of Stalin as the just leader echoes the prerevolutionary belief in the "good tsar." Then and now, many citizens believed that those who served and advised the leader conspired to keep the truth from him.[16] Simenova's juxtaposition of Stalin and "they" conveys implicitly a popular belief that conspiracies existed within the ruling caste and that Stalin's advisers suppressed that information. The show trials and arrests had provided "evidence" to validate that belief.

Dimitrov sent a copy of Simenova's letter to Zhdanov, thereby registering again his protest against the crude characterizations of foreigners. There were good institutional (and personal) reasons for him to do so: by mid-1938 the repression had taken a very heavy toll on the Comintern leadership. **Document 43** is a draft resolution to exclude from the ECCI or the ICC those members, virtually all of whom were foreigners, who had been arrested as "enemies of the people." The resolution was passed by a voice vote the same day, 3 July 1938.

Document 43

Draft resolution of the ECCI Presidium regarding the expulsion of ECCI members and candidate members and ICC members "who turned out to be enemies of the people," 3 July 1938. RGASPI, f. 495, op. 2, d. 264, l. 211. Original in Russian. Typewritten with signatures.

Top secret.

Copy ac.
3 July 1938.

DRAFT RESOLUTION
On the expulsion of members and candidate members of the Executive Committee of the Comintern and members of the International Control Commission who turned out to be enemies of the people.

RESOLVED: To expel from the Executive Committee of the Comintern and the International Control Commission the following members and candidate members:

Members of the Executive Committee:
1. BRONKOWSKI, B. B.
2. KUN, Béla
3. LENSKI, J. E.
4. ZHANG, Guotao
   Candidate members of the Executive Committee:
1. BIELEWSKI, Ya. S.
2. GORKIĆ, M. M.

3. KRUMIN, Ya. M.
4. PRÓCHNIAK, E.
5. CHEMODANOV, V. T.
6. POPOV, N. N.
   Members of the International Control Commission:
1. ANGARETIS, Z. I.
2. ANVELT, Ya. Ya.
3. WALECKI, M. G.
4. GRZEGORZEWSKI, F. Ya.
5. ISKROV, P. Kh.
6. KRAJEWSKI, A. P.
7. EBERLEIN, Hugo

Dimitrov
Manuilsky
Florin
Kuusinen.

Although many on the list were VKP members and had lived for many years in the USSR, all but two (Chemodanov and Popov) were foreign-born and had risen to prominence in the Communist movement in their native countries. Six of the seventeen were Poles (Bronkowski, Lenski, Bielewski, Walecki, Grzegorzewski, Próchniak, and Krajewski). Germans, Hungarians, Chinese, Balts, and Bulgarians made up the remaining foreigners. Save for Zhang, all were arrested and either were executed or died in confinement.

There is an odd quality to the resolution, because most of the former comrades "who turned out to be enemies of the people" had been arrested in 1937, and several of them had already been expelled. Why had the ECCI waited so long to resolve such a politically important issue? Given the charged atmosphere, bureaucratic sloth seems an unlikely explanation; the lives of those serving on the ECCI were at stake. The available evidence sheds no light on this issue. However, we cannot exclude the possibility that Dimitrov and his colleagues hoped that the repression, or at least specific arrests, might be reversed and that they would not have to explain to their followers abroad why internationally renowned Communists had been arrested as "enemies of the people." Having to explain such allegations could only undermine further the already damaged credibility of the Comintern and the USSR at a crucial time in the anti-fascist struggle abroad.

Document 43 also illustrates that prominent political rank and reputation offered little protection from arrest. On the contrary, in 1937–1938 they were often liabilities. Before 1935, during the verifications of the fraternal parties and of the ECCI apparatus, the leaders of those organizations had passed judgment on their subordinates. Within the Comintern, prominence and high rank had generally offered protection from expulsion from the party and arrest in those years.[17] Such was not the case in 1937–1938.

In late 1938 the repression even penetrated the leading body of the ECCI, its Secretariat. On 23 November 1938, Dimitrov confided to his diary: "M [Moskvin] was called to the NKVD. He hasn't come back!" The next day he wrote: "At Yezhov's (his dacha). M. [Moskvin] was closely tied to all of that crowd. It will have to be determined to what extent he had those ties in recent years. It will also be determined whether he was entrapped by any foreign intelligence service that was pressuring him." Precisely who constituted "that crowd" is unclear.[18]

Though opaque, the language that Dimitrov used to record Moskvin's arrest suggests considerable anxiety. The arrest of a member of the Secretariat meant that Dimitrov himself, the only foreigner in the body, might be vulnerable, even though he socialized with Stalin and Yezhov. Yet his wording is such that we cannot dismiss the possibility that Dimitrov believed that Moskvin might have been "entrapped" by the "enemy." At that moment, he may not have known what to believe. What is certain is that "on assignment from Stalin" he had to again verify Comintern personnel.[19]

As Moskvin's arrest indicates, the repression continued into late 1938. But within the Politburo, pressure to curb the NKVD's excesses and temper the mass arrests gradually mounted. In April 1938, Yezhov was appointed People's Commissar of Water Transport. His appointment made some sense given the NKVD's use of forced labor to build canals. But that Yagoda, his predecessor in the NKVD, had been appointed to the same post prior to his arrest, made the appointment portentous. Beginning in the summer of 1938 a coalition of Politburo members, reportedly consisting of Zhdanov, Andreev, Kaganovich, Mikoyan, and Molotov, worked to limit Yezhov's and the NKVD's powers. In August, Lavrenti P. Beria was appointed deputy people's commissar of the NKVD without Yezhov's consent. During the fall, the Politburo restricted the NKVD's powers somewhat and appointed a series of commissions to investigate NKVD operations, arrest procedures, and Yezhov's performance. The most dramatic move came on 17 November 1938, when it criticized aspects of the NKVD's work, abolished its troikas that had summarily sentenced so many to death or hard labor, and condemned its excesses. On 23 November 1938, Yezhov submitted his resignation as NKVD chief to Stalin.

The Politburo accepted it and replaced him with Beria. Yezhov retained his other party and state positions until he was arrested in April 1939. He was executed on 4 February 1940. Although the repression did not end after Yezhov's removal, its scope diminished. Some cases were dropped, some were reviewed, and a "partial amnesty" resulted in the release of some who were under arrest.[20]

After Yezhov's removal, Dimitrov and those who remained in the ECCI tried to repair the damage done to their organization and remedy the injustices dealt to trusted comrades who were serving time in labor camps and prisons. As **Document 44** suggests, that damage was significant. So thorough had the NKVD been in arresting Poles and people from the Baltic states that there was not "a single reliable comrade from these parties here in Moscow." Echoing Varga's comments in his letter to Stalin, Dimitrov noted that the mass arrests had left "sincere Communists in those countries . . . disoriented." The lack of foreign-born comrades with appropriate language skills made it impossible for the Comintern to reestablish contact and credibility in those countries. Similar problems afflicted other fraternal parties. The ECCI apparatus was a dead man walking.

Document 44

Letter from Dimitrov to Andreev requesting help in identifying Baltic and Polish comrades for Comintern work, 3 January 1939. RGASPI, f. 495, op. 74, d. 625, l. 1. Original in Russian. Typewritten with handwritten additions.

TO THE SECRETARY OF THE CC VKP(B)
Com. ANDREEV A. A.

After the arrest of the former leaders and representatives of the Communist Parties of Lithuania, Latvia, and Estonia in Moscow as enemies of the people, sincere Communists in those countries have been left disoriented and with no connections to the Comintern. We do not now have a single reliable comrade from these parties here *in Moscow* on whom we could count to establish connections with or eventually send to the country.

Meanwhile, there no doubt are in the USSR a number of tested Lithuanian, Latvian, Estonian, and Polish Communists, members of the VKP(b), who could be used to rebuild the leading organs of the corresponding parties and to renew party work [there].

In view of this, the ECCI Secretariat asks the CC VKP(b) to select a group of comrades to be used for work in the Communist Parties of Lithuania, Latvia,

Estonia, and Poland—Lithuanians, Latvians, Estonians, Poles, two–three of each—[they should be] VKP(b) members.

All these comrades have to be fluent in the native language.

General Secretary of the ECCI

G. DIMITROV

3. 1. 39.

Sent under number 1.

In addition to seeking to repair the damage done to the ECCI apparatus, Dimitrov and other ECCI members sought to redress the injustices done to comrades whom they believed innocent of the crimes for which they had been convicted. The case studies in Chapter 7 provide specific examples of such appeals, but they are not the only ones. From early 1939 into the war years, Dimitrov wrote to leading VKP and judicial officials asking them to review cases of specific individuals. Sometimes he did so on his own initiative; in most cases, however, he did so at the behest of the convicted person or his or her relatives. Dimitrov was especially diligent in requesting reviews of the cases of convicted fellow Bulgarians, either as a group or as individuals. But other incarcerated comrades also received his attention. In each case, he requested evidence from the ECCI Cadres Department that there were good reasons or evidence to warrant an appeal. He was but one of many officials who requested that certain cases be reviewed. Consequently, the review process proceeded at a very slow pace. Dimitrov frequently had to send inquiries and reminders to the review boards.[21]

Yezhov's removal should not be interpreted to mean that arrests were halted, nor that the xenophobia prompting the arrest of foreigners had ceased to exist. Once unleashed and legitimized, prejudices are not easily restrained. Nor did the VKP leaders make serious efforts to do so.

In July 1939, Dimitrov wrote a letter to Georgi Malenkov, a Central Committee secretary, that indicates clearly the persistence of suspicions of foreigners within Soviet society and his own belief that "hostile elements" continued to operate within the USSR. In some respects, his letter to Malenkov echoes that sent to Frinovsky the previous year. He opened by stating that "despite a series of measures, the position of political émigrés in the USSR remains unfavorable in the areas of political-enlightenment work and also in the area of material and daily life [*material'no-bytovykh*] issues." "A significant proportion of the [foreign] comrades" were having difficulties securing work and were omitted from important aspects of party life. The inability of émigrés to participate in political and productive work resulted from a fear of foreigners and created a self-fulfilling prophesy that, Dimitrov claimed, "assisted the demoralization of the ranks of political émigrés by hostile elements, and also the recruitment from their ranks of spies and provocateurs." Such prejudices extended even to the most recent émigrés, the anti-fascist soldiers from Spain and Czechoslovakia. He warned Malenkov that to avoid future "enemy" penetration of the ranks of these recent émigrés, "it is essential to improve decisively" their material conditions and political work among them.[22] Despite the anti-fascist credentials of the Spanish and Czechoslovak émigrés, fear of imminent war, the legacies of party propaganda, and cultural traditions sustained many leaders' and citizens' suspicions of foreigners.

While the ECCI leadership sought to undo some of the damage done by the mass repression, in fall 1939 the ECCI party organization took stock of its depleted ranks and responded to queries about its political behavior during 1937–1938. **Document 45** is a memo from Kotelnikov, secretary of the ECCI Party Bureau, to Guliaev, head of the ECCI Cadres Department. The eight-page memo consists of the names of ninety-five former members and candidate members of the VKP(b) of the ECCI apparatus party organization who were arrested in 1937–1938.[23]

Document 45

Lists of arrested former members and candidate members of the party organization of the ECCI apparatus, 11 September 1939. RGASPI, f. 546, op. 1, d. 434, ll. 25–32. Original in Russian. Typewritten with handwritten additions and signature.

157/I

11 September 1939   Top secret.
CADRES DEPARTMENT OF THE ECCI.

To com. Guliaev.

We are forwarding [to you] lists of the arrested former members and candidate members of the VKP(b) party organization of the ECCI apparatus for 1937–1938.

    1. List No. 1 those arrested whose cases were not reviewed by the party committee.

    2. List No. 2 those arrested who were only members of the party organization [and did not work in the apparatus at the time of their arrest].

3. List No. 3 those arrested after being expelled [from the party] by the party committee.

4. List No. 4 those arrested after receiving a party punishment and after sending their cases to NKVD organs.

5. List No. 5 those arrested after being removed from work and expelled from the ECCI party organization for political reasons.

6. List No. 6 those arrested by country.

7. List No. 7 those arrested by department.

SECRETARY OF THE PARTY BUREAU: *F. Kotelnikov*
Kotelnikov
Received by Ya<...>ova
11/IX-39.

9 September 1939   Top secret.
Sent on 10/IX of this year <...>
to <...> c. Guliaev.
F. Kotelnikov   LIST No. 1
THOSE ARRESTED IN 1937–1938 WHOSE CASES WERE NOT REVIEWED
by the party committee.

1. MÜLLER B. N.
2. KRAJEWSKI
3. ALIKHANOV
4. ROZENFELD
5. BARTNOVSKY
6. GROSSMAN
7. KATSEV
8. FORMEISTER
9. VOLK
10. MINGUNIN
11. MÜLLER Lucia
12. SMIRNOV A. (KIM)
13. DOBROVOLSKAIA
14. ALASS
15. ALASS
16. BRIGADER
17. KASHIN
18. ORBELIANI
19. TETSEN
20. LEVCHENKO A.
21. FRED [Manfred Stern]
22. VALTER
23. MÜLLER (Cadres Department)
24. M*oskvin.*

Secretary of the Party committee: Kotelnikov

2 copies   <u>Top secret.</u>
9 September 1939.
t. t.
<u>LIST No. 2.</u>
THOSE ARRESTED IN 1937–1938 WHO WERE ONLY MEMBERS OF THE
PARTY ORGANIZATION [and did not work in the apparatus at the time of
their arrest].
    1. YEZERSKAIA
    2. LIPMANOV
    3. MERTENS [Stanislaw Mertens (Skulski)]
    4. JANKOWSKA
    5. PAPENCHEV
    6. YANSON.

                                                            <u>Top secret.</u>

2 copies
9 September 1939.
t. t.
<u>LIST No. 3.</u>
THOSE ARRESTED IN 1937–1938 AFTER BEING EXPELLED [from the party]
BY THE PARTY COMMITTEE.
    1. ORSKY
    2. CHERNIN
    3. EISENBERGER
    4. BARTELS
    5. WALECKI
    6. BADULESKO
    7. BOROWSKI
    8. HARTMANN BENZ
    9. GRZEGORZEWSKI
  10. ISKROV
  11. KOKER
  12. MERTENS [Skulski]
  13. SHUBIN
  14. TSOI SHENU
  15. GREGOR
  16. REDIKO
  17. SHOK
  18. SALNA
  19. KHEIMO
  20. KRUMIN
  21. SHOLOMOV
  22. BALOD Anna
  23. BRANN LOTTA

24. SCHWARZSTEIN
25. ZMIJEWSKI
26. PAGLINA
27. STEIN
28. SUVOROV.

Top secret.

2 copies
9 September 1939.
t. t.
LIST No. 4.
THOSE ARRESTED AFTER RECEIVING A PARTY PUNISHMENT AND AFTER SENDING THEIR CASES TO NKVD ORGANS.
1. SEREGIN
2. MILTER Fritz
3. SMIRNOV (SS [Communications Department])
4. FISCHER Anna
5. ZONBERG
6. KRUSTYN
7. MENIS
8. GURISH [Gerish]
9. CHERNOMORDIK
10. TSIRUL
11. ORTEGA [Pestkowski]
12. CHEMODANOV
13. BALOD Karl
14. MERING
15. ANVELD [Anvelt]
16. PROKOFIEV
17. TÖRÖK
18. VIRTA
19. MILTER Filipp
20. RAZUMOVA
21. ANGARETIS
22. PETERMAN V.
23. PETERMAN E.
24. SUKHACHEV
25. ALEKSEEV
26. KRASNOV
27. KOZHEVNIKOV

Top secret.

2 copies
9 September 1939.
t. t.

LIST No. 5
THOSE ARRESTED IN 1937–1938 AFTER BEING REMOVED FROM WORK
AND EXPELLED FROM THE PARTY ORGANIZATION OF THE ECCI APPA-
RATUS FOR POLITICAL REASONS.

1. ALBERT [Zyltowski]
2. WHEELDON
3. GENIS
4. KAMRAN
5. SIKSOI
6. SHTANGE
7. SHTORM
8. ULREIKH
9. KHAZANKIN
10. VILGELMSON
11. VOLODIN.

Top secret.

2 copies
9 September 1939.
t. t.
LIST No. *6*
COMPOSITION OF THOSE ARRESTED BY COUNTRY FOR 1937–1938.
POLAND

1. Orsky
2. Krajewski
3. Dobrovolsky
4. Formeister
5. Ortega [Pestkowski]
6. Bronkowski
7. Grossman
8. Walecki
9. Borowski
10. Mertens [Skulski]
11. Rediko
12. Grzegorzewski
13. Sholomov
14. Fischer A.
15. Yankovskaia
16. Yezerskaia
17. Ulreikh
18. Zmijewski
19. Paglina

GERMANY

1. Genis
2. Eisenberger

   3. Rozenfeld
   4. Bartels
   5. Müller, Lucia
   6. Mertens [Edna; Margarete Wilde]
   7. Hartmann, Benz
   8. Brann
   9. Wheeldon [he was not German but British]
  10. Peterman
  11. Peterman, E.
  12. Muller
AMERICA
   1. Gerish
   2. Brigader
ROMANIA
   1. Badulesku
   2. Schwartzshtein
FINLAND
   1. Heimo
   2. Virta
   3. Stein
HUNGARY
   1. Schock
   2. Török
   3. Stern
FRANCE
   1. Albert
MOSCOW
   1. Chernin
   2. Katsev
   3. Müller, B.
   4. Menis
   5. Alikhanov
   6. Chernomordik
   7. Shubin
   8. Volk
   9. Smirnov, A.
  10. Smirnov
  11. Kashin
  12. Mingulin
  13. Chemodanov
  14. Seregin
  15. Lipmanov
  16. Orbeliani
  17. Khazankin
  18. Prokofiev

19. Krasnov
20. Suvorov
21. Razumova
22. Sukhachev
23. Alekseev
24. Levchenko, A.
25. Valter
26. Moskvin
27. ***Kozhevnikov***

ESTONIA
1. Mering
2. Anvelt
3. Zonberg
4. Alass
5. Alass

LATVIA
1. Shtange
2. Milter, Fritz
3. Milter, F.
4. Koker
5. Balod, K.
6. Salna
7. Krumin
8. Tsirul
9. Krustyn
10. Shtorm
11. Balod, A.
12. Tetsen
13. Yanson
14. [left blank]

BULGARIA
1. Iskrov
2. Papenchev
3. Volodin

LITHUANIA
1. Angaretis

PERSIA
1. Kamran

YUGOSLAVIA
1. Gregor

1. Tsoi Shenu—a Korean.

<u>Top secret.</u>

2 copies
9 September 1939.

t.t.

LIST No. *7*

COMPOSITION OF THOSE ARRESTED BY DEPARTMENT.

Communications Department

1. Müller B.
2. Anvelt
3. Ulreikh
4. Genis
5. Khazankin
6. Balod K.
7. Balod A.
8. Smirnov
9. Orsky
10. Katsev
11. Lipmanov
12. Rozenfeld
13. Menis
14. Formeister
15. Shok
16. Grosman
17. Gregor
18. Milter Fritz
19. Hartmann Benz
20. Kashin
21. Seregin
22. Papenchev
23. Zmijewski
24. Suvorov
25. Sukhachev
26. Milter Filipp
27. Yanson
28. Levchenko
29. Kozhevnikov

CADRES DEPARTMENT

1. Krajewski
2. Alikhanov
3. Chernomordik
4. Mertens [Edna]
5. Brigader
6. Kheimo
7. Tsirul
8. Zonberg
9. Muller
10. Török

POLISH SECTION
    1. Bronkowski
    2. Grzegorzewski
    3. Borowski
    4. Yankovskaia
    5. Yezerskaia

LATIN SECTION
    1. Salna
    2. Krumin
    3. Krustyn
    4. Virta

KIM
    1. Chemodanov
    2. Smirnov A.
    3. Prokofiev
    4. Krasnov
    5. Shtorm

TRANSLATIONS DEPARTMENT
    1. Eisenberger
    2. Bartels
    3. Wheeldon
    4. Brann
    5. Albert

ARCHIVE
    1. Badulescu
    2. Shwartshtein

PROPAGANDA DEPARTMENT
    1. Chernin
    2. Shubin

EDITORIAL BOARD OF "COMMUNIST INTERNATIONAL"
    1. Walecki
    2. Orbelioni

Bulgarian section
    1. Iskrov

ESTONIAN section
    1. Alass
    2. Alass

Administration of Affairs
    1. Tetsen

SECRETARIATS
    1. Koker
    2. Dobrovolskaia
    3. Sholomov
    4. Fischer A.

   5. Gerish
   6. Müller Lucia
   7. Tsoi Shenu
   8. Volk
   9. Kamran
  10. Mingulin
  11. Mering
  12. Siksoi
  13. Fred-Stern
  14. Valter
  15. Peterman V.
  16. Peterman E.
  17. Alekseev
  18. Razumova

Latin American
   1. Ortega [Pestkowski]

ICC
   1. Rediko

MEMBERS OF THE ICC
   1. Anvelt
   2. Grzegorzewski
   3. Walecki
   4. Krajewski
   5. Iskrov
   6. Angaretis

Despite the depressing simplicity of Document 45, it deserves some comment. First, a detail—Kotelnikov's seventh list omits Hugo Eberlein, a German member of the ICC; the number of ICC members arrested in 1937–1938 was eight, not seven. Second, and perhaps most important—Kotelnikov's lists contain only the names of party members arrested in 1937–1938. By confining himself to those two years, Kotelnikov (or whoever requested the memo) made it clear that he viewed the Yezhovshchina as a distinct period with distinct characteristics. Party members in the ECCI organization had been arrested earlier (for example, Safarov and Magyar in December 1934), but their names do not appear on the list. Nor do the names of others expelled and arrested before 1937. Taken together, the ninety-five people arrested in 1937–1938 constituted about 20 percent of the party organization in early 1935, but the proportion of party organization members arrested from early 1935 to late 1939 was in fact higher.[24]

As Kotelnikov's sixth list indicates, among ECCI apparatus staff the repression fell most heavily on native-born citizens ("Moscow"), Poles, Latvians,[25] and Germans. Soviet citizens were a sizable plurality of the ECCI party organization, and their prominence among those arrested is not surprising. Few people from countries where the Communist Party was legal and free to operate (e.g., France, Holland, Great Britain, and the United States) were arrested. No single factor explains the ethnic breakdown of the victims, but the most likely explanation is by now familiar: Stalin, Yezhov, NKVD agents, and members of ECCI organizations believed that the police and intelligence services in those countries that had outlawed Communist Parties had infiltrated their agents into the ranks of émigrés to the USSR. List 7 provides the details to substantiate Dimitrov's claims in late 1937 and late 1938 that arrests had decimated the ranks of the working bureaucracy of the ECCI, especially the Communications Department.

The criteria according to which Kotelnikov organized the first five lists require explanation. As Document 46 will make clear, one reason, perhaps *the* reason, for Kotelnikov's memo was to explain and justify the behavior of the ECCI party committee in 1937–1938. That is why his lists make precise distinctions as to whether expulsion from the party preceded arrest or vice versa. List 3 contains the names of those arrested after they had been expelled from the party, whereas list 1 contains the names of those comrades who had not been reviewed by the party committee before they were arrested. The distinction was of considerable importance to both the party committee and those who appealed for a review of their cases. Although the decision of the party committee to expel a member before arrest provided proof that the committee had been vigilant, its failure to expel members before their arrest was a double-edged sword after 1938. On the one hand, it could be interpreted as evidence of lack of vigilance; on the other, it could be used to substantiate charges that the NKVD had arrested innocent comrades. How it was interpreted depended on who interpreted it in the context of 1939.

Those who had been expelled from the party before their arrest had much less chance of having their case reviewed because the party organization had already decided that the person's actions or associations had raised sufficient doubt as to warrant expulsion. Only after expulsion was the person's name sent to the NKVD. Expulsion had resulted from Bolshevik vigilance, and to those processing appeals the subsequent arrest may, therefore, have had merit, whereas those people arrested before being expelled from the party were possibly, in the eyes of the review boards, reliable party members who had been the victims of NKVD excess or arbitrariness or baseless denunciations. For these reasons, Kotelnikov's precise accounting of the order of arrest and expulsion was of considerable political importance.

As informative as Kotelnikov's lists are, they identify only ninety-five former members and candidate members of the ECCI party organization who had been arrested.[26] Yet between 20 January 1936 and 1 April 1938, the size of that organization shrank from 394 members to 171, a reduction of 223 members, 128 more members than appear on Kotelnikov's lists.[27] Some of the 128 were removed from work by the Moskvin Commission, some were expelled from the party during the 1936 exchange of party documents (see Document 46 below), some were transferred to other work, some returned to their native countries, and a few may possibly have been arrested without Kotelnikov's knowledge. The arrest of ninety-five people sharply reduced the size of the party committee, but that does not appear to have been the primary reason for the declining number of cadres. Whatever their fate, the effect on the apparatus and its party organization was devastating and, as Document 45 indicates, crippled the ability of many ECCI departments to function.

In October 1939, Kotelnikov sent to the Rostokinskii district party committee, to which the ECCI party organization was formally subordinate, a report summarizing the activities of the ECCI party organization in "purg-[ing] it of politically suspicious individuals, double-dealers, [political] degenerates, provocateurs, spies, and saboteurs" from its ranks. **Document 46** is that report. Though reasonably straightforward, certain aspects deserve comment. The report conveys an implicit sense of closure, an assumption that the mass repression had ended. It also conveys succinctly what Kotelnikov and other party members viewed as the distinct subperiods during the years 1934–1939 and the role of the party organization in unmasking "hostile elements" in each subperiod.

Kotelnikov did not view the years 1934–1939 as a seamless period of terror, but rather as composed of separate yet related events, campaigns, or policies. The first event was Kirov's murder in December 1934, which "shook us out of our philistine lethargy . . . and showed [us] what had to be done." The second was the Seventh Comintern Congress in July–August 1935. The review of the credentials of potential delegates to the Congress and the behavior of certain delegates alerted the party organization to "suspicious" elements. The 1935 verification, the 1936 exchange of party documents within the VKP, and the 1936 verification of fraternal parties defined a third subperiod. The final subperiod began in spring 1937 and lasted through 1938. Although each subperiod was discrete, according to Kotelnikov, each event or policy aided the party organization in its efforts to cleanse its ranks. Implicit in Kotelnikov's account is the sense that, with the "unmasking" and expulsion of each person, the party organization became increasingly concerned about the presence of "enemies" in its midst. In short, his characterization of the subperiods of 1934–1938 conveys his view that the "unmasking" of alleged enemies was an evolutionary process, each phase of which grew naturally out of its predecessor.

It is also possible to interpret his subperiods as phases in a scripted drama of which Kotelnikov was unaware and in which he was a pliant actor. Some students of the 1930s view the period from December 1934 to 1939 as one in which Stalin orchestrated events according to a preconceived plan.[28] To date, there is no evidence to prove that argument, which is based on assumptions about Stalin's intentions. Kotelnikov's report is of no value in assessing Stalin's intentions. Rather it is the report of a historical actor, a participant in a drama not of his making, but a drama in which he played an active role and which he and his party organization significantly affected.

His report also conveys clearly the conspiratorial mindset so prevalent at the time, one that, as we have seen, he himself had expressed over the years. He asserts that "enemies," many of whom had been "selected by the now exposed worst enemies of the people—Zinoviev, Trotsky, Bukharin, Pyatnitsky, Knorin, and many other enemies"—"had been working for years" within the Comintern. Blaming the presence of "enemies" within the ECCI apparatus on "exposed . . . enemies" also served a political purpose: it absolved the present "vigilant" leadership of responsibility.

Kotelnikov's report indicates that the "cleansing" of the ECCI party organization was a layered phenomenon. Prior to spring 1937, the organization aimed at unmasking "suspicious" elements who worked in the lower and middle levels of the ECCI bureaucracy. Only in spring 1937 were Dimitrov and Manuilsky (and Moskvin, a convicted "enemy of the people" conveniently omitted from the report) forced to turn their attention to the ECCI leadership. As we know, the ECCI leaders examined themselves only after the arrest of Polish comrades who held prominent positions, an event that Kotelnikov refers to only obliquely: "On direct orders from com. Dimitrov and c. Manuilsky, it became a routine . . . that the party committee reviewed personal cases of the former members of the International Control Commission."

Document 46

Letter from F. Kotelnikov to the Rostokinskii district committee of the VKP about the role of the ECCI party committee in the struggle against "politically suspicious individuals, . . . provocateurs, spies," 13 October 1939. RGASPI, f. 546, op. 1, d. 434, ll. 38–42. Original in Russian. Typewritten with signature.

Secret.

13 October 1939.
TO THE ROSTOKINSKII DISTRICT COMMITTEE OF THE VKP(b).[29]
com. Perutskaia.

You asked me about the role of the Party Bureau and previously the party committee in helping the Comintern Executive Committee leadership to verify the workers of the ECCI apparatus and to purge it of politically suspicious individuals, double-dealers, [political] degenerates, provocateurs, spies, and saboteurs. I briefly informed you about what we had done in this area. You asked me to give [you] a written [report], which I am doing.

First of all, I have to note that I have worked without interruption as a leader of the party organization—deputy secretary after 1934 and secretary after May 1935—until now. Therefore, I am responsible for the situation in the organization, its purging of enemies of the people, of agents of Trotsky-ist-Zinovievite and Bukharinist bandits, and saboteurs, and you have the right to ask what I, the Party Committee and the Party Bureau have done in this area. Before answering your question, it is necessary to remind [you] that the workers of the Comintern apparatus were, at some point, selected by the now exposed worst enemies of the people—Zinoviev, Trotsky, Bukharin, Pyatnitsky, Knorin, and many other enemies. The assassination of Sergei Mironovich Kirov, [who was] beloved by the people, by the ignoble scum of society [and] the appeal by our Leninist-Stalinist CC VKP(b) and the leader of our party, com. Stalin, to raise revolutionary vigilance, to examine our ranks, and to purge them of double-dealers shook us out of our philistine lethargy, from our blind trust, and showed [us] what had to be done. There was a lot to be seriously done in our organization. Enemies who had been working for years cleverly disguised themselves and played a double game, occupied the most responsible positions, protected the conspirators, and supported each other. Under these conditions, work was extremely difficult, but we did not lose our heads when faced with these challenges. Guided by Stalin's compass, raising our revolutionary vigilance and relentlessness toward the enemies of the people, working energetically to verify our organization and the workers of its apparatus, we exposed many enemies of the people in the ECCI apparatus. I do not mean to claim that we managed to expose everybody and that we made no mistakes. We did make mistakes, and we were far from exposing everybody. Many were arrested with party cards in their pockets. However, it would not be an exaggeration to say that great cleansing work has been done. Who conducted it? The members of our organization who to the end remained faithful to the cause of our party, to com. Stalin, led by the party committee—Kotelnikov, Blagoeva, Reshetov, Krylova, Miller, with the assistance of cc. Dimitrov and Manuilsky.

In order to be specific, let us look at the facts that prove that we conducted serious work to purge our party organization and the ECCI apparatus of many enemies of the people.

1. MAGYAR—an experienced double-dealer and a vicious enemy of the people was exposed by us and arrested by the NKVD organs. See my reports on the party organization of the former Eastern Secretariat of December 1934 and of the general party meeting of 28 December 1934 (there is a verbatim report), where Magyar was exposed and expelled from the party. Based on my report, the district party committee confirmed his expulsion, and he was arrested while leaving [the building].

2. SINANI—(Saklava) [Georgy Borisovich Sinani (Skalov)] a White Guard officer, an organizer of terrorist groups composed of White officers [who sought] to murder the leaders of the party and the government. We exposed him and he was arrested by NKVD organs in 1935 before the Seventh [Comintern] Congress. See the materials of the party committee and the general party meeting. This enemy had been decorated with a medal and, according to the position which he then occupied, he would have been placed near the Presidium at the Seventh Congress. However, he was exposed before he could realize his foul plans.

3. Fritz David—(he was not a VKP(b) member). A base agent of the bandits Trotsky, Zinoviev, Kamenev, Bukharin, whose bloody hands were stretching toward the heart and the brain of the party, the working class, toward the Central Committee of our party and its leader, com. Stalin. He worked in the ECCI apparatus, preparing himself and waiting for the moment to carry out his bloody, ignoble plan.

On 9 July 1935, on the eve of the Seventh Congress, I interrogated this bandit for more than two hours, and everything was documented. It was revealed then that this active Menshevik was arrested in 1919 by the ChK [Cheka], and in 1926, he left for Germany in order to infiltrate the Communist Party and from there to begin his career. He succeeded in this. The stenographic reports were sent to the Secretariat and to the NKVD. Thus we helped the NKVD organs to expose him.

4. HEINRICH (SÜSSKIND) (a non-VKP(b) member)—by a resolution of the party committee of 11 January 1935, we exposed him as a double-dealer and secured his expulsion from the ranks of the fraternal Communist Party of Germany, his removal from the apparatus, and, later, his arrest by NKVD organs.

5. During the verification and the exchange of party documents, with our active participation [the following] were purged from the party and later ar-

rested (as can be seen from the documents): Mironov, Kuchumov, Brann Lotta, Racyborski, Liao, Kim Semen, Li Wangshu, Badulescu, Berger.

6. During the same period in 1935 and in 1936, the party committee examined several cases of former members of fraternal Communist Parties as they were exposed, and thus we helped the NKVD organs to purge them from the apparatus, and they were arrested: Ander, Zaurland, Schroeder, Martha-Moritz, Licht, Yugenfeld [Betty Schenfeld], Veil, Kalzan. (The materials can be seen here and in the NKVD.) This is still not a complete list.

7. All the work of the party committee and the party organization to verify its ranks and purge them of enemies of the people during the verification and the exchange of party documents did not suffice to expose many double-dealers, provocateurs, and subversives, who still remained in the ranks of our party organization even after the verification and the exchange of party documents.

Beginning in spring 1937 and in 1938 the party committee and the party organization began to actively verify their ranks and purge them of enemies of the people. We failed to expose many who had been arrested with party cards. Here are some results of the purging of the party organization in this period:

a) former party members arrested by the NKVD whose cases were not reviewed by the party committee—24.

b) Arrested after their expulsion from the party ranks—28.

c) Arrested after incurring party penalties and [our] giving materials to NKVD organs—27.

1. On direct orders from com. Dimitrov and c. Manuilsky, it became a routine in the apparatus of the Comintern Executive Committee that the party committee reviewed personal cases of the former members of the International Control Commission and representatives of some Communist Parties.

We dealt with the cases of the former members of the ICC—Walecki, Grzegorzewski, Iskrov. They were expelled from the party and later arrested. We gave our recommendations to the ECCI leadership and the NKVD about the former ICC members—Angaretis and Anvelt—[and] about their removal from their jobs. They were arrested.

We dealt with the cases of the former representatives of the Communist Parties—Saln [Salna], Krumin, Stein—and expelled them from the party. They were later arrested.

On c. Dimitrov's direct orders, we reviewed the cases of the former KIM secretaries Yanitsky and Massie. We gave our materials to the leadership of the ECCI and the NKVD, they were removed from [their] jobs, and Yanitsky was later arrested.

We based our decisions on the facts, and we realized the tremendous responsibility. We did not try to protect ourselves, but at the same time we did not always recognize and expose the double-dealers.

In this document I am not dwelling on the work of the party committee (now the party bureau) in that period, on how we helped the ECCI leadership in selecting workers for the ECCI apparatus and in verifying and removing certain workers for political reasons or their performance. I suppose that what is shown here is sufficient to say that we did not stand on the sidelines during this most important political undertaking.

SECRETARY OF THE PARTY BUREAU OF THE PARTY
ORGANIZATION OF THE ECCI APPARATUS:

F. Kotelnikov
Kotelnikov

13 October 1939.

CHAPTER SEVEN

Case Studies

You know, it is good to be a Communist.

— ANNI ETTERER

SO FAR WE have explored how and why the mass repression unfolded within the ECCI apparatus and its party organization, as well as among fraternal parties in the USSR. Now the focus shifts to individuals who fell victim to the repression. Although no modest collection of case studies can be representative, examining at least a few allows us to appreciate how the repression engulfed individuals, how those who were arrested made sense of what befell them, what roles individuals played in the repression, and to what extent individuals internalized the values and worldview that defined public discourse.

The case studies here are of two types. The first three concern members of the ECCI and its apparatus (Béla Kun, Elena Valter, and Anna Razumova). The remainder concern political émigrés (Béla Szántó, Anni Etterer and Franz Guber, Petko Petkov, Iordan Terziev, and Karl Kurshner). Taken together, they provide additional insights into the personal experiences and the political dynamics of the period.

The Case of Béla Kun

On 4 September 1936, less than two weeks after the trial and the executions of Zinoviev, Kamenev, Fritz David, and the others, the ECCI Secretariat voted to remove from the ECCI Béla Kun, leader of the Hungarian Soviet Republic of 1919, leader of the Hungarian CP (CPH), and an internationally recognized leader of the Comintern, and to deny him the right to participate in CPH and Comintern affairs. Given the timing of the decision, we might be tempted to view Kun's fall from power as linked to that trial and the subsequent arrests. Such was not the case. Rather, Kun's downfall resulted from political and personal divisions and intrigues within the ECCI and the CPH that antedated the mass repression. Kun was not arrested until 28 June 1937, when he was charged with "creating a counterrevolutionary organization of Hungarian political émigrés, inspired by the Hungarian espionage organs," and helping to create a "so-called anti-Comintern organization existing inside the Comintern."[1] There is no evidence to support that accusation.[2]

Because the ECCI Secretariat removed Kun for his political and personal activities rather than for criminal behavior, his case illuminates the political and personal divisions that riddled the ECCI and its fraternal parties and the decisive, albeit shadowy part that these divisions played in the downfall and arrest of other Cominternists. Kun's case also suggests that some of the ECCI members who were repressed were sacrificed by other ECCI members in order to protect themselves from a NKVD convinced that political émigrés in the ECCI apparatus were actively engaged in anti-Soviet activities. There is no representative model for how and why ECCI members were repressed. Because Kun's case is one of the few for which there are sufficient materials to reconstruct most of the case, the insights it provides into Comintern politics are intriguing.[3]

The Kun affair began to unfold in December 1935 as evidence mounted regarding the refusal of the Hungarian CP to implement the policies adopted by the Seventh Comintern Congress in July–August 1935. That Congress had called on Communist Parties to create a Popular Front by cooperating with Social Democratic parties and labor movements to stem the rising tide of fascism. Even though Comintern policies were binding on fraternal parties, as of December 1935 the CPH had done little to implement the directives. The reluctance of the CPH Central Committee to implement the new Comintern line stemmed primarily from Kun's opposition to the Popular Front and the strained relations that developed between Kun and Dimitrov, and Manuilsky, and Kun and the supporters of the policy.[4]

This inaction divided and created confusion within the CPH. While Kun was away from Moscow on vacation, some members of the Central Committee of the CPH and their supporters met with ECCI officials and accused Kun of refusing to implement the new Comintern line. Upon learning of the accusation, Kun wrote a letter to the Central Committee in which he admitted some mistakes and proposed a meeting to discuss the issues involved. That letter is reproduced as **Document 47**. In practice, the ECCI had followed an unwritten rule that when one of its members erred, that person could write a letter acknowledging his or her mistake. In short, someone in error engaged in self-criticism. Doing so was often sufficient to put an end to the affair—but not in Kun's case.

Document 47

Letter from Béla Kun to the Central Committee of the CPH recognizing his erroneous attitude toward the new Comintern policy and leadership, 14 December 1935. RGASPI, f. 495, op. 18, d. 1038, ll. 241–243. Original in Russian, translated from the German. Typewritten with handwritten additions. The German original in the RGASPI was altered: part of the text from pages 1 and 3 was cut out, including Kun's signature.

11855 (a) from the German
Kup. la.
14 December 1935.   Secret.
A LETTER FROM COM. BÉLA KUN TO THE CC CP HUNGARY.
Dear comrades,

I am rushing to write this short letter immediately upon my return from vacation without having looked at the materials that have arrived in my absence. Such haste is caused by the following two reasons:

1. Two leading comrades in the CI informed me during a discussion about my future work that my position before and during the Congress (as well as com. Gross's behavior during the Congress) has caused doubts within the CI leadership as to whether the proper attitude of the CC CP Hungary toward the new CI leadership has been guaranteed. Naturally, from this follows the suspicion that an incorrect attitude by the party leadership toward the new CI leadership [provides] no guarantee of consistent implementation of the Seventh Congress line in the party and its work.

2. Comrade B. [Imre Komor][5] informed me that a certain member of the delegation to the Congress,[6] whom he had talked to in person, did not fully understand the line of the Congress and the political and organizational aspects of the resolution regarding the work of the CP of Hungary. He also informed me that all of the other delegation members were also dissatisfied with the work of the delegation and with the failure of the delegation leadership to adequately apply the Congress line in practice to the situation in Hungary and to the work of the CP of Hungary.

These two factors, which compelled me to write this letter, are closely related. The reservations that the CI leaders have about the future work of the party leadership and the dissatisfaction of the comrades who have recently arrived from the country with the performance of the delegation undoubtedly have the same roots. My attitude toward the new CI leadership, before and during the Congress, prevented **us** from discussing all the [relevant] issues with the delegation at the time of the Congress. We also failed to properly inform the CC members, so that the party, by implementing the correct political line, would promptly accomplish the turn that is consistent with the Congress resolution and, in particular, with com. Dimitrov's report. Neither the written report of the delegation nor the prompt delivery of the minutes of the Congress to the [party] organizations can [by themselves] guarantee the turn in party policy and organizational work that, according to the resolutions of the Seventh Congress, is necessary in Hungary as well. Suggestions regarding negotiations in Prague and the creation of the Popular Front that were sent from here are just preparatory steps.[7] They are not yet sufficient to assure [proper] understanding by the party members of the necessity of a radical political turn nor to explain the historical significance of the resolutions of the Seventh Congress either to the party members or to all Hungarian workers.

Any attempt to base relations between the party CC and the CI leadership on the recent mistakes that I committed while in the CI, which caused my erroneous attitude toward the new CI leadership, would cause immeasurable harm to the party.

I most firmly declare that only that leadership which has been formed from the best representatives of the Communist Parties of capitalist countries, with com. Dimitrov at its head, and which fully enjoys and deserves the confidence of all Communist Parties, especially of the VKP(b), can guarantee the implementation of the line of the Seventh Congress. In general, the CC CP of Hungary has not contradicted, before, during, or after the Congress, the new CI leadership or the policy initiated at the Congress by com. Dimitrov. My erroneous attitude toward the new CI leadership formed independently of the CC as a whole, without its knowledge, and, no doubt, in defiance of its line.

Wishing to avoid, at any cost, further harm to the party as a result of my mistake (of which the comrades have been informed), I make the following suggestion. If, within a month, we are not able to call a broader meeting, we call an enlarged plenum of the CC with the participation of several comrades who occupy the most important positions in the leadership. At this meeting we will discuss the question of making even more concrete the resolutions of the Seventh Congress. The plenum should also express its opinion regarding the performance of the delegation and criticize my behavior, which led to the well-founded doubts of the CI leadership about the party leadership. Be assured that neither personal relations in the CC nor my work as the party representative will be affected by even the harshest criticism, but, on the contrary, will only benefit from it.

Greetings,

[Béla Kun].

At Ercoli's (Togliatti's) suggestion, Kun presented his letter at a meeting of the ECCI Secretariat held on 16 December to discuss the Hungarian question. The meeting was attended by representatives of the ECCI and its Secretariat (Manuilsky, Moskvin, Ercoli, and Kuusinen) and representatives of the CPH (Béla Kun, Béla Szántó, Imre Komor, and Shwarz). They harshly criticized him for underestimating the leading role of the VKP delegation in the ECCI, for trying to counterpose the delegations of the fraternal parties to that of the VKP, and for failing to properly implement the Popular Front policy within the CPH. The Secretariat ordered the Hungarian Central Committee to send to Moscow a delegation composed of Central Committee members and local party leaders to review the situation within their party.

The attack on Kun precipitated heated and deeply divisive debates within the CPH. On 4 January 1936 members of the anti-Kun faction announced the formation of the "temporary leadership of the CP Hungary" (whether on its own or at the behest of the ECCI Secretariat is unclear) and issued a position paper entitled "On the Application by the Communist Party of Hungary of the Line of the Seventh World Congress of the C.I.: Resolution of the Temporary Leadership of the CP Hungary."[8] That document denounced certain of the Central Committee members, particularly Kun and Gross, for their sectarian political behavior, their failure to implement the new Comintern line, and the negative effects that their actions had had on the party. It also charged that the shortcomings of the Central Committee had resulted in the party's becoming isolated from the masses, "internally disorganized," and "corrupted by provocateurs working for the class enemy." This "temporary leadership" announced its intention to overcome these problems, the significance of which intensified with the arrest in January 1936 of more than a dozen key party officials in Hungary.[9]

Not until late March 1936 did the Hungarian delegation convene in Moscow for its meeting with the Secretariat. Ercoli (Togliatti) chaired the meeting, which he described as "rather excruciating." Although Kun and Gross engaged in a limited degree of self-criticism and acknowledged that they had not ensured the correct implementation of the new Comintern line, their reports did nothing to defuse the situation. Supporters of the temporary leadership charged that Kun, Gross, and their supporters on the Central Committee had engaged in incessant petty personal squabbles among themselves (and in Gross's case, also with Manuilsky), that they had dismissed the new Comintern policies as irrelevant to the Hungarian situation, and that they had been duplicitous in implementing those policies. As a result, sectarianism and factional struggles permeated the party, which was increasingly alienated from the masses. Such sectarianism, they argued, had enabled police agents and provocateurs to enter the party, which had resulted in the periodic arrests of key party members and the disruption of party work. In short, Kun's critics charged that he had sabotaged the CPH's work and the Comintern's policies.[10]

In April the ECCI Secretariat established a special commission, chaired by Yan Anvelt, the ICC secretary, to investigate the situation within the CPH, as well as those of its Central Committee members who displayed "tendencies hostile to the Comintern or revealed an anti-party tendency against the Comintern."[11] In early May the ECCI Secretariat formally dissolved the Central Committee of the CPH and replaced it with a provisional Secretariat.[12] From May until September the ECCI Secretariat carefully monitored that investigation and the Hungarian question.[13] Based on Anvelt's ongoing investigation, in June the ECCI Secretariat issued a "top secret" resolution on the Hungarian question that condemned the former Central Committee for refusing to implement the decisions of the Seventh Congress and charged that such behavior continued "even after" the decision of the ECCI Secretariat in December 1935. It described the leadership style of the Central Committee under Kun and Gross as "stupid sectarianism" and recommended removing Gross from the party leadership and investigating whether to allow Kun to continue to work in the ECCI apparatus.[14]

During his investigation, Anvelt collected sworn declarations from various Hungarian comrades. Among them was the declaration of Zoltán Szántó, which is presented as **Document 48**.[15]

Document 48

Statement of Zoltán Szántó about Béla Kun's "double-dealing," 29 June 1936. RGASPI, f. 495, op. 74, d. 101, ll. 38–42. Copy in Russian. Typewritten with handwritten additions. Quotation marks are as in the original.

TOP SECRET

Statement of com. Z. Szántó.[16]

A particular feature of Béla Kun's behavior is that he supports different positions at the Comintern meetings on the Hungarian questions than he does during private conversations with us. At the meetings with com. Ercoli[17] and in the Secretariat, he declared that he supported the line of the Seventh Comintern Congress, that the CC CP of Hungary had made mistakes in implementing the Seventh Congress's decisions, and that he was ready to assume partial responsibility for it.

Outside those meetings, he expressed reservations regarding political mistakes committed by the CC CP of Hungary. His opinion was that Gross, who wanted to discontinue his work in the Hungarian Communist Party, had to be relieved of the work in the CC, and that instead of him, Szántó had to be co-opted, and then everything would be all right. He was of the opinion that the Comintern is not always fair toward the CP of Hungary, since other parties (in particular, in the Balkan countries) had accomplished much less than the CP of Hungary. "Ercoli in particular has no right to criticize [our party], because the CP of Italy did nothing to prevent the Abyssinian war."[18] When Soviet newspapers published the news about the electoral victory of the Popular Front in France[19] and we were discussing it, com. Kun said that it was too early to celebrate. [He said that] the victory of the Popular Front was very profitable for Hitler. When asked what he meant by that, he explained that the Popular Front government would pursue an antiwar policy, and that was exactly what Hitler needed.

At the 7 May meeting of the Secretariat, Kun declared that he would work honestly for the Communist Party of Hungary and that he would support the new leadership as much as he could. Several days later, however, he was saying something very different. He told [us] that he had been received by com. Kaganovich, that he had informed com. Kaganovich that he had been without work for eight months, that the Comintern did not give him any work, that he was badgered in the Comintern, that com. Manuilsky was **opposed to his being** sent as a speaker to party meetings. According to him, com. Kaganovich was very indignant at this, promised to find him an appropriate job in the party, and called the Moscow Party Committee and suggested that com. Kun again be sent as a speaker.

The next day he told me that he had been received by com. Stalin in the presence of com. Molotov, Mikoyan, Andreev.

According to him, he told com. Stalin that he was being badgered in the Comintern as the "result of squabbles." Nobody could point out any of his political mistakes or prove them in writing. For eight months he had been promised a job, but these promises had not been fulfilled. It was Manuilsky who took a particularly unjust position toward him. He badgered him, but when he saw him (Kun) after his illness, he smothered him with kisses. "What kind of a kiss was that?" asked Stalin. "A kiss of Judas," I [Kun] replied. "Then I told [him] that they told me that I was a publicist. This was said by the people who could never write a decent article." Everyone laughed a lot when I said that a former Trotskyist was accusing me of demonstrations against the ECCI. They asked me, What were these demonstrations. I said that it was when I did not stand up when Manuilsky appeared [on the podium at the Comintern Congress] and did not applaud him. This caused great laughter, but I added that later this accusation was directed against only one *other* CPH member." "Then Stalin asked me if it was possible to *again settle my problems* with the Comintern. I answered that under no conditions would I like to remain in the Comintern and that I wanted to work in the VKP(b). Then Stalin ordered that I speak with Yezhov."

"Yezhov was empowered to *say* that the CC had nothing against me." "I told Yezhov that I was feeling as if I had been born again by finally having an opportunity to speak with real Bolsheviks. I told him that now, when I did not belong to the ECCI apparatus anymore, I felt like a man who had stepped out of a dirty closet into a forest of pine trees."

"You will see that in a while I will again be occupying a leading position in the Comintern. And it will happen very soon. Zinoviev also sent me to the Urals, but I came back."[20]

"When Pyatnitsky and I refused to let Zinoviev into the *building* at a time when Zinoviev was *still* the *Comintern* President, Ercoli, who was *then* at the head of the French and Italians, *made* a fuss."

"The ECCI apparatus is saturated with suspicious elements. I frequently told this to Manuilsky. His and Kuusinen's milieu is not free of such people."

The Paris émigré newspaper "Khabud Kho" / "Libre Parol" published several reports about com. Kun's trip to Spain, which supposedly did not take place. When we discussed it and said that the article had a White Guard scent, Kun told us that it had been initiated by Manuilsky. "How dare you say such things about Manuilsky?" I [Szántó] said. "No, I do not mean that Manuilsky wrote it himself, but it was someone from his circle," replied Kun. "Maybe you think that it was Gerő?" I asked. "No, I am not saying that it was Gerő exactly. There are others," he replied.

The next time I had to go see Kun, Gross was with him. They were talking about Moskvin. Kun said that the reason that Moskvin had come to the Comintern was that they could not give him another job. Then Gross added that com. Moskvin had been removed from the GPU because he had engaged in "self-criticism" there. "Moskvin did not understand that the GPU was not an organ where one could engage in 'self-criticism.'" Béla Kun jeered at the Comintern leaders' inability. When I pointed out to him that he was mistaken, that foolish people could not make good policies and that the Comintern policy is correct, that there had been achievements, he replied by laughing [and stating] that Comintern policy originates from Stalin. I told him that he should not tell me that Stalin was consciously *selecting* foolish people to promote his policy. "Not *selecting*," said Kun, "but Stalin cannot appoint able people to all positions, either."

He told me that the CC VKP had appointed Gross to do a very important job. "You see, the Comintern removes him, and the CC gives him an important, responsible, and very secret job, which it would not give to either Moskvin or Chernomordik." "So you think that Gross is more reliable than Moskvin?" I asked. "No, I do not think so," replied Kun. "Moskvin is *reliable*, but he lacks adequate abilities. But Chernomordik is not so reliable, because he is a former Trotskyist."

He said that one could do nothing to Gross. The ICC cannot make short work of him [simply] because he did not applaud Manuilsky.

At that moment the telephone rang. Com. Kun picked up the phone. He asked the person who was calling: "Did they summon you to the ICC too because you did not applaud?" "Yes, I think that you were questioned again today because you did not applaud for Manuilsky." When he finished the conversation, he told me that he had spoken with Gross. Gross was already gossiping all around the city that he was being summoned to the ICC only because he did not applaud Manuilsky. I told him what com. <u>Rudas</u> had told me about Gross. (I have already orally informed com. Anvelt about this.)

Com. Kun accused me of "blabbing out" the resolutions and the content of conversations of the Secretariat, of conducting a campaign against him, and of arguing with him. He told me that I was acting the same way as Sas did. When I took exception to these ***unheard-of*** accusations by saying that he would not be able to accuse me of provocation, he said that, in his opinion, I was an honest man who acted according to sincere convictions.

29 June 1936.

Signed: Z. Szántó.

<u>Translated from German</u>.
True to the original:

p.p. <u>Ya. Anvelt</u>

21 August 1936. I made three copies and sent them personally to com. Manuilsky.

E. Valter.

< . . . >

Szántó's allegation that Kun was a double-dealer who had publicly supported Comintern policies while privately criticizing them was very serious. Szántó's version of Kun's complaints to Stalin, Kaganovich, and Yezhov about the ECCI Secretariat's treatment of him, of Kun's attacks on Manuilsky, Moskvin, and Chernomordik, and of Kun's allegations that "suspicious elements" obstructed the ECCI not only confirmed the allegations of his Hungarian comrades about his petty political intrigues but also understandably angered Dimitrov, Manuilsky, and Moskvin. Nor did Kun's attacks on the ECCI leaders stop there. In a declaration to Anvelt, E. D. Andich stated that a Hungarian comrade, Béla Landór, claimed that Kun had told Stalin, Kaganovich, and Yezhov that Manuilsky was a "poor dictator but a good intriguer" and that Manuilsky's wife had lived in "White emigration," had been married to a

"White émigré," and maintained ties to the Whites.[21] In light of his opposition to and refusal to carry out Comintern policies, Kun's personal attacks on the ECCI leaders and staff sealed his political fate.

On 5 July, Anvelt sent a copy of Szántó's decalaration to Dimitrov, who sent it and other materials to Yezhov.[22] Dimitrov also wrote a long letter to Politburo member Lazar Kaganovich in which he charged that Kun, Pyatnitsky, and Knorin, each of whom had opposed the adoption of the Popular Front, had "used every appropriate occasion to discredit the [Comintern] leadership." The three men had been the core of an anti-Popular Front group in the Comintern. Dimitrov informed Kaganovich that Kun admitted opposing the line and leadership of the Comintern, and reminded him of Kun's New Year's Eve meeting with Kamenev eight years earlier. He then opined that Szántó's declaration implied that Kun might be in league with "hostile elements." After noting that Stalin had given permission for Kun to be the chief editor of the Foreign Workers' Publishing House, he suggested that, given the evidence, Kun should not be allowed to stay "either in the ECCI or in Moscow," and asked Kaganovich for a quick resolution of this matter.[23] On 28 August the Politburo considered the question of "the subversive work of Kun" and endorsed Dimitrov's recommendation.[24]

Armed with Politburo support, on 4 September 1936 the ECCI Secretariat approved two resolutions related to the Kun affair. The first was a resolution of the temporary leadership of the CPH declaring its intention to carry out the "line of the Seventh World Congress of the C.I."[25] The second was the resolution of the ECCI Secretariat regarding Béla Kun. That resolution is reproduced as **Document 49**. Though not a member of the Anvelt commission, Manuilsky, against whom Kun had made a series of serious accusations, wrote the resolution, which Dimitrov signed.[26]

Document 49

Resolution of the ECCI Secretariat on the Béla Kun question, 4 September 1936. RGASPI, f. 495, op. 18, d. 1112, l. 46. Original in Russian with the title written in German. Typewritten with handwritten signature.

Top secret.
MK / 3 /
Conclusions of the Commission on com. BÉLA KUN.[27]
Having examined all the available materials in the case of com. BÉLA

KUN's campaign against the new leadership of the CP of Hungary, the Comintern line and the ECCI leadership and having carefully examined the explanations of com. KUN, the commission found that this campaign is a continuation of com. BÉLA KUN's destructive work in the Communist Party of Hungary and among the Hungarian émigrés in the USSR.

Having conducted an unscrupulous, factionalist policy for a number of years, com. BÉLA KUN selected cadres exclusively on the basis of his group's interests [and] discredited and removed from party work all those who did not want to reconcile themselves to his factionalist methods of leadership. As a result of this factionalist policy, com. KUN overlooked the saturation of the party by provocative elements, which destroyed the best party activists and undermined the faith of the masses in the party. An ambiguous speech by BÉLA KUN at the party meeting at the time of Magyar's expulsion from the party was another example of the dulling of [his] Bolshevik vigilance.

After the [Seventh Comintern] Congress, in defiance of a special directive from the ECCI Secretariat, com. BÉLA KUN, along with certain other members of the CC CPH (Gross and others), actually sabotaged the implementation of the line of the Seventh Congress in the Communist Party of Hungary by persistently pursuing his sectarian aims and by inculcating into the CC of the Communist Party of Hungary hostility toward the line and the new Comintern leadership.

To [sustain] the disorganizing work against the new ECCI leadership, com. BÉLA KUN also employed absolutely inadmissible methods to discredit the leading workers of the ECCI by spreading slanders about them.

Having established the destructive work of com. BÉLA KUN against the leadership of the C.P.H. and the leadership of the ECCI, the commission considers completely impossible any [further] participation by com. BÉLA KUN in the work of the CP of Hungary or using him as a worker in the ECCI apparatus.

G. Dimitrov.

Although strongly worded, Document 49 is notably free of the vitriolic rhetoric regarding spies, enemy agents, and Trotskyists that punctuated ECCI resolutions and directives to the fraternal parties during and after the recently concluded August 1936 trial. The rhetoric and substantive points make clear that the Secretariat removed Kun as part of its ongoing efforts to strengthen the Comintern and fraternal parties by removing those people who refused to conform to the Comintern line and who sowed dissension within the movement.[28] Kun's behavior was all the more egregious because it continued after repeated warnings from the ECCI and allegedly "destroyed the best party activists and undermined the faith of the masses in the party." That Kun repeatedly spread "slanders" to discredit Manuilsky and other ECCI personnel added a powerful personal dimension to Dimitrov's efforts to neutralize or remove those who opposed the new Comintern line.

Kun's case demonstrates that personal and political relations within the ECCI staff and the émigré communities were often contentious and strained.[29] Such a working environment created conditions in which even petty differences contributed to denunciations and accusations that, in 1937–1938, often led to tragic consequences. His case illustrates the ways personal and political conflicts were tightly intertwined and reminds us that political documents often masked personal struggles. It also indicates that, despite the strident rhetoric of public pronouncements against Trotskyists and other enemies, the ECCI did not always use that rhetoric in September 1936 to settle high-level internal political struggles. And in this case, it was not necessary.

On 5 September the ECCI Secretariat met and informed Kun of its decision. **Document 50** is a transcript of that meeting.

Document 50

Stenographic report of the ECCI Secretariat's meeting to discuss the results of the work of the commission to investigate the case of Béla Kun, 7 September 1936. RGASPI, f. 495, op. 18, d. 1112, ll. 52–55. Original in Russian. Typewritten.

Top secret.
EK/2 copies
7 September 1936.
STENOGRAPHIC REPORT
OF THE SECRETARIAT'S MEETING of 5 September 1936.[30]
Regarding Béla Kun.
Béla Kun: Comrades, it is difficult for me to speak because this blow is the hardest blow for me. But I think that it will also be a lesson for me.

[This] blow is particularly hard because it makes impossible my [giving] further assistance to the party that I took part in creating.

I think that the conclusion that all of my work and assistance are harmful is unfair.

However, comrades, I realize that a situation has been created in which it will be better if I no longer participate in the work of the CP of Hungary and, even better, if I am completely separated from the Hungarian emigration. I have thought this over seriously, and I am asking the appropriate VKP(b) organs to send me to work in some province far from Moscow.

A situation has been created in which, whether or not I wanted it, I became some sort of point around which the disgruntled elements of the Hungarian [party] gathered.

Therefore, I consider unfair the formulation that my work is considered harmful. At the same time, in contrast to what I used to write three–four months ago or even a month ago, I have come to the conclusion that it would be better if I leave the leadership of the Hungarian CP. I also consider the conclusion that it is impossible to use me in the ECCI apparatus any more to be correct. Why? I think that it is not because of political considerations, nor because I was resented, but because, owing to my nasty, nervous nature, I did not develop the correct attitude toward the leadership. Despite all this, as I have written, I consider the Comintern policy to be absolutely correct, and I think that this leadership is in order.

Now, regarding specific issues. It is correct that I overlooked the contamination of the party, not just now but also in the past. It is correct that frequently I approached the selection of leading cadres on the basis of factionalist principles. And in doing so, I committed a double mistake. On the one hand, I would promote my friends; on the other, I would promote [people] from other factions, thinking that by doing so, I would liquidate the factionalist atmosphere. I told com. Révai at [the meeting of] the Secretariat of com. Ercoli[31] that the majority of the members of the CC [CP of] Hungary were not from my group but from other factions. But the factions remained there, and it was therefore impossible to work in an appropriate way.

I overlooked the contamination of the party by provocative elements precisely because, while working here in the Comintern, I was loosely connected with the party's work.

As to Magyar, I think that my speech was incorrect, inappropriate.[32] Regarding Magyar, I have to say the following. After I delivered this speech, I warned some comrades about Magyar's bad attitude. Of course, I did not know that he was connected with that counterrevolutionary gang of Zinoviev, Kamenev et al. I had an impression that he was not loyal to the party: writing and saying one thing and thinking another. I warned comrades, if not at that very time, at least while he was still in our apparatus.

I also had a mistaken attitude toward certain comrades. This was a result of that situation to which I have already referred.

I am finishing, comrades.

I ask you to believe me [when I say] that in [whatever] work that I undertake, I will gain your confidence, and you will return me to Hungarian work and to international work.

I do not think that I am a person who cannot be trusted. But if there are [people] who do not trust me, I will prove by my work that I deserve to be trusted and that it will be possible to return me to work in the CP of Hungary and to the Comintern.

DIMITROV: The commission has unanimously adopted the resolution. I think that Béla Kun's statement is known to everyone and that we should not open a discussion on this question.

To take into consideration the commission's conclusion and to relieve com. Béla Kun from work in the Hungarian party and in the Comintern apparatus.

BÉLA KUN: I am asking only to change [some] formulations:

1) Regarding considering my work harmful. I ask [you] to replace this formulation with another.

2) Regarding Magyar. I consider this decision unfair. To be exact, I warned Knorin about Magyar when they wanted to send him to work. However, Magyar was then included in the commission to work out the draft of the first point.[33]

It would have been double-dealing if I considered it [this decision] fair.

MANUILSKY: In order to give [Kun] a chance to work in the VKP(b), we will have to soften this formulation.

ANVELT: I consider [it] impossible [to do so] because this is the minimal [version of] what we have written. We did not write down the speech at the purge [commission] when Magyar was found trustworthy on the basis of com. Béla Kun's speech.

BÉLA KUN: I recognized this mistake before, and I do it now.

ANVELT: As a member of the commission, I consider it impossible to suppress this fact, particularly in such a serious situation.

DIMITROV: I think that we can do the following. To agree with the commission's decision regarding Magyar and regarding the "harmful work," say: to consider inappropriate Béla Kun's work in the Comintern, as well as using him as a worker in the Comintern apparatus.

Who is for softening [the formulation]? (Adopted unanimously.)

Consider using com. Béla Kun in the Comintern apparatus [to be] impossible.

The softening of the resolution was a Pyrrhic victory for Kun. Kotelnikov had already included Kun's name on his 5 September 1936 list of those deemed to have Rightist or Trotskyist tendencies (see Document 18), a list he sent to the NKVD. On 27 November 1936, Kun's name was removed from the list of members of the ECCI party organization.[34] Although his political and personal intrigues had precipitated his downfall, it is worth noting the devastating impact that the Secretariat's decision had on Kun. Here was a man who had devoted much of his adult life to the revolutionary struggle. That struggle defined him, his stature, his worldview, his world. Faced with the collapse of that world, his self-criticism was probably sincere. "To work in some province far from Moscow" was to start life anew.

And that is what Kun had to do, at least until June 1937, when he returned to face an ECCI meeting at which Manuilsky charged him with insulting Stalin and having maintained contacts with the Hungarian secret police since 1919, charges that resulted in his arrest on 28 June 1937.[35] But those charges did not exhaust the bill of particular against Kun. On 1 May 1937 the ECCI Secretariat sent to Yezhov a packet of materials to support those charges as well as charges that linked him to "enemies of the people" Zinoviev, Kamenev, and Pyatnitsky.[36] The ECCI's decision to sacrifice a discredited former member to the widening hunt for "enemies" was a way to defend itself from further police scrutiny. But back in September 1936, Kun faced a more pedestrian future. In fact, he had a future precisely because his errors were just that, errors, not crimes. They became "crimes" in spring 1937.

The ways political and personal conflicts within the ECCI and the Hungarian émigré community were intertwined are further illustrated by **Document 51**, a declaration made by Irina Kun, Béla Kun's sister, regarding a fellow Hungarian's denunciation of her. Although the declaration contains accusations against her, it was included in Béla Kun's file.

Document 51

Statement by Irina Kun (Béla Kun's sister) about György Benedek, 2 September 1936. RGASPI, f. 495, op. 199, d. 977, ll. 2–2ob. Original in Russian. Typewritten copy. The author's style is retained unaltered.

STATEMENT[37]

On 29 August, György Benedek (residing: Moscow, Starosadsky per[eulok], [dom] 4, kv[artira] 59) called me on the phone and, his voice trembling, said that he had something to tell me but had "no heart to do it at that moment." Then he hung up. An hour later, he called again and said the following: "A great misfortune has happened, I have committed a crime against you, I have compromised you, but I still have no heart to tell you." When he called me again an hour and a half later, he told me the following. Several months ago he started to record facts that could compromise me. Thus, in April, he made a note of seeing me talking in the doorway to a certain Trotskyist. He asked a girl who had stepped inside the doorway to get out of the rain to sign that note.

Benedek explained to the girl that he needed that note as evidence for divorce purposes. After that, according to Benedek, he recorded another case. Once, after he had read me one of Stalin's speeches, I supposedly wondered about Trotsky's opinion on the peasant question. Benedek put all this on paper and hid it among his books. At that point, I asked him what his motive was. He replied: "I myself have no idea. I did not intend to hurt you. I wanted to use these materials later, but not against you." "Against whom?" I asked. "You must have [already] guessed," he replied. When I repeated my question, Against whom? he said nothing. He reiterated, however, that someone had stolen his note recently, that it was missing from among the books where he had left it. "The person who stole the note," he continued, "evidently has already submitted it." (He did not specify to whom, but implied that he meant the NKVD.) He, Benedek, had already been interrogated twice, and they would interrogate me, he declared. I said, "Fine," and hung up.

[The day of] 30 August was a weekend, so I could do nothing. On 31 [August], I went to our party secretary, c. Stoianov, and told him everything about this affair. I also went to M. Ya. Frumkina and told her everything. At 2 PM, Benedek approached me at the tram stop with the words: "I don't know what I have done to you, but I have certainly messed up my VKP(b) re-registration." I did not answer, but he continued, very agitated: "You know, don't tell your brother about all this, you may run into trouble. Anyway, there is a struggle going on in my mind. I don't know what will happen to me, but I'd like to be ten thousand miles away from here." I asked: "Why did you do it, what was the purpose?" This time his reply was explicit and cynical: "I did it because I already know you and your brother. I wanted to show this note to your brother because at one of the meetings, he called on us to be vigilant. I planned to demonstrate my vigilance and see what he would say when he saw this record of a conversation by his sister." I said: "But you yourself admit that whatever is in it is not correct; it is a lie." He responded: "I am not saying that it's incorrect any more, and I advise you, too, to confess that the note's contents are accurate. You kept repeating 'yes, yes, I am listening' over the phone. Thus, you have admitted everything. Don't think that I alone heard you. There were witnesses who heard you saying 'yes, yes.'"

I could not stand that any longer and went to the district NKVD department, where I declared what had happened.

I have known Benedek for three years; we live in the same building. He studied at the VKU [actually, KUNMZ], where I was working. I always knew that he was mentally unsound. But I would never have suspected him of being so mean until, according to his own words, c. Béla Kun refused to give him a recommendation to the KUNMZ graduate school in June–August 1935. After that, he started telling me and c. E. Nagy things that aroused my suspicions that Benedek was either crazy or an agent provocateur.

Of all that he wrote down (and told me) only one thing corresponds to the facts. I have known Lazutov since the session of a board of which we were members. In April 1936, I was standing in the doorway waiting for the rain to stop, since I planned to go shopping. Lazutov walked in and asked me how I was feeling. I answered: "Good." He started lamenting: "Your life is good, and mine is bad. I was expelled from the party, removed from my job. Comrades said that I was a Trotskyist, but I am as pure as gold." I said that if he believed himself to be innocent and if comrades had indeed slandered him, he should appeal. The party does not expel useful and needed members.

He wanted to add something, but seeing that I had started reading a newspaper, he left. He extended his hand to me, but I pretended not to see him. This is all.

I know nothing more about Lazutov. Neither he nor I have [ever] visited each other.

Irina Kun.

2 September 1936.

Irina Kun's declaration speaks for itself. But three points deserve note. In August 1936, Benedek sent a declaration about Irina and Béla Kun to the Central Committee Secretariat.[38] Andreev, the Central Committee secretary to whom Benedek sent the letter, forwarded it to the NKVD. Only after he had sent the letter did Benedek call Irina Kun. His claim that someone stole the letter was a lie. The second point is that petty jealousies and intrigues were common within the Hungarian émigré community living in the USSR. Benedek's denunciation provides but one example of these conflicts and how they later fed into the repression. Finally, Benedek sought revenge upon Béla Kun. Yet he accused Irina Kun, not Béla Kun, of having ties to Trotskyists. The Hungarian émigré community in Moscow was well aware of Béla Kun's gradual fall from power. Benedek could have easily demonstrated his vigilance and satisfied his desire for revenge by accusing Kun himself of ties to Trotskyists. That he chose not to do so suggests that, however complex and petty the dynamics within the émigré community were, accusations by the rank and file against the powerful and prominent were not the norm in August and September 1936. But by 1937 the atmosphere had begun to change. In January 1937, Benedek sent a letter to Dimitrov in which he wrote that he had facts concerning Béla Kun that he wanted to give to Dimitrov. What those facts were and whether or not Benedek delivered them are unknown; there are no materials on this in the open archives.

The available materials in the archives do not allow us to reconstruct precisely how and when Kun's errors became "crimes."[39] But a few documents written in 1938 by Hungarian émigrés suggest that Kun had falsified the personnel records of several Hungarians in the Cadres Department files while he was an ECCI member. Those whose records Kun allegedly falsified were ar-

rested in 1937–1938.[40] Whether Kun falsified these records or whether his accusers adopted this tactic to defend their arrested comrades is impossible to
determine.

The Kun affair sheds light on three important issues. The first is that there
existed a complex matrix of personal and political differences and struggles
within the ECCI and the fraternal parties. Kun's case aside, precisely how and
in what ways those divisions affected who was repressed and why remains
murky. But any explanation of the dynamics of the repression must somehow
take these realities into account. The second is that we should not assume that
the strident rhetoric of the Comintern's directives to its members to unmask
Trotskyists and other nefarious elements always determined the behavior of
the leaders behind closed doors. In September 1936, Kun fell from grace for
understandable political reasons. In June 1937, the ECCI offered him up as a
sacrificial lamb to the NKVD. Precisely how and why the ECCI arrived at that
decision remain unclear. What is clear is that the political atmosphere, not
Kun's errors, led to it.

Finally, Kun was one of several Comintern leaders who opposed the adoption of the Popular Front policy. Pyatnitsky and Knorin also opposed it. Before, during, and after the Comintern Congress, Dimitrov succeeded in removing his political opponents from the ECCI or its apparatus; prior to 1937,
that was a sufficient political victory. But as his letter to Kaganovich suggests,
as political tensions and repression mounted, linking the leaders of the anti–
Popular Front group to "enemies" enabled Dimitrov to ensure his rivals'
defeat and to prove his own vigilance. In this way, policy debates and disagreements that had occurred prior to 1937 were, in 1937, transformed into
repressive retribution.

The Case of Elena Valter

In mid-October 1938, Elena Osipovna Valter was vacationing in Kislovodsk,
the resort spa and sanatorium where Dimitrov, her boss, received periodic
treatments for his chronic medical problems. Born in Minsk in 1898, Valter
had joined the Bolsheviks in 1919, and from that time had proven herself to be
a dedicated party member and a true believer. She began work in the ECCI apparatus in October 1931 and in September 1934 became Dimitrov's personal
secretary and trusted assistant.[41] Although she believed herself to be a "completely clean" Bolshevik and had a powerful boss, her vacation in Kislovodsk
ended in Moscow's Butyrka prison. Her case provides insight into the *menta-*

lité and beliefs of dedicated Stalinists and illustrates how even powerful leaders like Dimitrov, who had access to Stalin, Yezhov, and the Politburo, were unable to free their most trusted aides from the NKVD's clutches. Although no single person can be considered representative of those who staffed the ECCI apparatus, Valter's position, work experience, and dedication to the cause make her an appropriate example.

Dimitrov, too, was vacationing in Kislovodsk when he received a telegram from Moskvin informing him that Elena Valter had been removed from her position. He immediately sent the following telegram to Moskvin.

Document 52

Telegram from Dimitrov to Moskvin regarding Dimitrov's secretary, 16 October 1938. RGASPI, f. 495, op. 184, d. 8, outgoing telegrams for 1938 from Kislovodsk to Moscow, l. 70. Original handwritten in Russian. Typewritten copy.

---

16 October 1938.

To com. Moskvin.

Since my secretary [E. Valter] has been relieved [of work], let her pass on to Krylova, in the presence and under the supervision of Andreev, all the registered files. It should be explained to her that the issue [at hand] is the necessity of renewing the apparatus.

Since we have relieved her from work, she also has to be offered an appropriate salary.

Dimitrov.

Dimitrov's formulation "we have relieved her from work" suggests his internalization of party discipline and his willingness to accept without protest the firing of his assistant in his absence. He no doubt feared the worst, a fear confirmed two days later, when he received the following telegram from Moskvin informing him of Valter's arrest ("an appropriate solution").

Document 53

Telegram from Moskvin to Dimitrov regarding the firing of Dimitrov's secretary, 18 October 1938. RGASPI, f. 495, op. 184, d. 7, outgoing telegrams for 1938 from Moscow to Kislovodsk, l. 40. Original in Russian. Handwritten decoded text.

---

18 October 1938
To c. Dimitrov.
**The inventory of the files will have to be conducted without the partici-
pation of the former secretary, whose case found an appropriate solution
the day before yesterday.**
Moskvin.
G.D.[42]

Precisely what Dimitrov did or tried to do for Valter over the next twenty
months is unknown, for no written materials in the archive shed light on this
issue. We do not know, therefore, whether he made any efforts on her behalf
before June 1940, when Valter wrote to Dimitrov asking him to support her
appeal. That month Dimitrov and Manuilsky wrote to Beria asking him to review her case on the grounds that "a mistake has been committed." Attached
to their letter they sent a copy of Valter's letter to Dimitrov. Both letters are reproduced in **Document 54.**

Document 54

Letter from Dimitrov and Manuilsky to People's Commissar of Internal Affairs L. Beria
requesting a review of E. O. Valter's case, with enclosed letter from Valter, 25 June
1940.[43] RGASPI, f. 495, op. 73, d. 107, ll. 5–7. Original in Russian. Dimitrov and Manuilsky's letter is typewritten with handwritten notations and signatures. Valter's letter, sent
from exile, is handwritten in violet ink.

Top secret.
Dear Comrade Beria,
In October 1938, Valter, Elena Osipovna, a worker in the Secretariat of the
general secretary of the ECCI, was arrested by NKVD organs.
She had worked in the ECCI apparatus for four years, from the time the Secretariat was formed. [She] invested a lot of work and energy in coordinating
and organizing the work of the newly created Secretariat. During her time on
the job, she showed herself to be a conscientious worker and loyal to the
cause of the party and Soviet power.
Considering that a mistake has been committed regarding Valter, E. O., we
ask [you] to reexamine her case.
Enclosure: Copy of a letter from Valter, E. O.
Information from the ECCI Cadres Department about Valter.
c. Dimitrov
c. Manuilsky

Moscow, 25 June 1940.
Sent on 25/6—40
in parcel No. 125
Stern.

Enclosure: The letter from the arrested ECCI worker E. O. Valter to G. Dimitrov asking to reexamine her case.

[25 June 1940]

To the General Secretary of the Executive Committee of the Comintern G. M. Dimitrov.

By the decision of the "Special Council [OSO][44] *of 17 January 1940," I was exiled for three years to Krasnoiarsk region* [in accordance] *with the formulation "For participating in an anti-Soviet organization." This decision completely devastated me because it is incomprehensible to me to this day.*

Georgy Mikhailovich, I have written you from jail in detail about what I was accused of and that in May 1937 I was slandered by Müller (Melnikov). From the very first day of my arrest, it was clear to me that I was slandered, that I was slandered by enemies to whom I was a hindrance in y[our] *Secretariat. They knew perfectly well what kind of confidence I enjoyed, and of course they were interested in having their own person in that job. No wonder they decided to get rid of me by using whatever slander possible. For fifteen and a half months I sat defamed in the Butyrskaia prison. However, despite my physical indisposition, I tried to keep up my morale with the deep belief that the investigation would uncover the truth, that I would be rehabilitated and would return to family, to work, and to a normal life. So much harder for me was the blow when I learned about the "Oso" decision. Today the question of rehabilitating myself is the question of my future life, the question of a normal life for my family and my only child, before whom I am really guilty because I was giving all of myself to work and very often it was not possible to give the required attention to the child.*

Georgy Mikhailovich, I know for sure that before the party, before Soviet power, before the ECCI leadership, my conscience is clear. I also know and firmly believe that I spent the best and most conscious years of my life in the ranks of the party and lived exclusively for the interests of the party. I also know for sure that throughout all the nineteen years of my membership in the party, wherever I was, whatever work was assigned to me, I always remained, first of all, a party member, and that my private life could serve as an example for many, many rank-and-file party members. My private life has always been of the least importance to me. All this is extremely easy to verify: there are real people, honest people; and I need only the truth. Only the truth is needed to reestablish my good name. I want to return to the trust of the party because I do not know why was I de-

prived of all that I cherished, of all what I was proud of, of all I lived for. I do not know why I brought tragedy to my family, to my child who, in his eleven years, has known so much grief. [I do not know] *why my life is so ruined. I do want and I am trying to understand why have I been, though temporarily, deprived of trust, and for what. But no matter how long I think about it, I feel no* [guilt]. *Therefore only sharp pain is left, and it grows from day to day.*

Throughout the investigation, nothing specific was said about the anti-Soviet organization of <u>which</u> I was presumably a part, nor about my activities in this organization. I have not seen anyone but the investigators, although I wrote to the head of the investigation department and to the prosecutor overseeing my case asking [them] *to inform me about the essence of the accusations. On 8 July, at the time of signing* [the papers] *concluding the investigation, I looked through my case. There was nothing but the <u>indirect</u> statement of what he heard <u>from Abramov</u>, nothing but the slanders of the bandit Müller; there could be nothing but the enemies' slanders. My grief can only make happy my "well-wishers," who are probably still plentiful in the apparatus and who hated to know that I had an opportunity to signal you personally about detected abnormalities in the apparatus, which I did* [as I] *considered it my duty, the duty of a party member. And, in my opinion, there were plenty of abnormalities. I know perfectly well that <u>Mikhail Abramovich</u>* [Moskvin] *and <u>Andreev</u>, and undoubtedly others, disliked me for this. No matter how hard it is for me, I still deeply believe in and wait for the question of my innocence to be reexamined soon and for my being rehabilitated, since I have never been a part of an anti-Soviet organization and never knew about the existence of such an organization in the ECCI apparatus. Only the investigative organs can help me in my rehabilitation; therefore, first of all, I sent People's Commissar L. P. Beria a statement on 20 March. During the investigation, I did not want to bother him with my case, and only a year later did I request* [information] *about my child, and received a prompt reply. Now I consider it my duty to address him first, because this was the decision of the NKVD's Special Council. I also wrote to the State Procurator. It is very important now for me to establish the fact of my losing the keys to the safe in 1936, because this served as the basis for Müller's slander. But you knew about this fact, as did the commissars and the former warden Davydov, who received orders to call* [repairmen] *from the factory to fix the lock. For those fifteen–twenty minutes when I was in the Kremlin cafeteria, <u>Bashmakov M. Z.</u> occupied my desk. Immediately after that, the loss of the keys was discovered. I took the second set of keys from you and moved the documents to another safe. In the lower drawer there were greeting cards sent to you during the Leipzig trial, but there was nothing secret in them. It is very easy to examine all of my work in your Secretariat during the entire four years, since I left everything in exemplary order. I tried to and did work ef-*

ficiently all the time before leaving for vacation in Kislovodsk, although I did not know that I would never return to work and that in my absence some of my "friends" would do me such a "favor." It is easy to examine my work in the Cadres Department, since I came there when there was no department yet, there was [only] a sector with a few workers. There are still people who remember me from then. I have rendered no special services to the revolution, and the only thing that can rehabilitate me is the truth about me, about my work and life as a party member.

In the final account, I will be rehabilitated completely, even if it happens after my death. I need it for my child, for my family; but I, too, want to live, to work as loyally for the party as I have worked, I want to bring up my child myself. No temporary moral blows will change me for the worse. I was, I am, and I will be, until the end of my life, the same loyal party member that I have always been, that the party brought me up to be. Enemies can slander me, but nobody will ever be able to make an enemy of me. I know this as surely as I know that my conscience is clear.

E. Valter.

Valter's moving letter speaks for itself. Yet it is worth exploring her belief that there were "enemies" at work within the ECCI apparatus, "enemies" whom she believed conspired to impede its work and to place "their own" people in trusted positions. After more than fifteen months in NKVD custody, she believed that "enemies" were "still plentiful in the apparatus." To achieve their goals, these "enemies" had slandered her, a "real Bolshevik," who "lived exclusively for the interests of the party." "Enemies can slander me, but nobody will ever be able to make an enemy of me." She was undoubtedly a true believer. But by 1938, being such meant more than being a dedicated Marxist-Leninist and a devoted follower of Stalin. It also meant sharing and propagating the belief that "enemies" had infiltrated the party and state. It meant "signal[ing] . . . abnormalities," which she did because it was "my duty, the duty of a party member." Such vigilance created personal enemies. Precisely because she was a true believer—and remained such even after twenty months in prison and the gulag—she explained her tragic fate as the result of a conspiracy of "enemies" and continued to fulfill her "duty" by denouncing people whom she suspected had conspired to get her arrested. For true believers like her, the only explanation consistent with her worldview was that "enemies" and conspirators had slandered her and had caused her arrest as part of their nefarious mission. And it was true believers like Valter who no doubt denounced other "real Bolsheviks" and created for them the nightmare through which she had to live. What makes Valter's fate tragically ironic is that it resulted from fervently held beliefs that she and her jailers shared.

Dimitrov and Manuilsky's appeal to Beria on Valter's behalf was met with silence. Several months passed before Dimitrov learned from three prosecutors (Yakunin, Kurov, and Gitman) that the Procurator's Office of the Moscow Military District was collecting materials and reviewing cases of people who had been falsely convicted and that there were disputes between the NKVD and that office regarding the cases of political émigrés. Armed with this information, Dimitrov moved decisively. On 7 February 1941 he wrote to Andreev and Zhdanov, both Politburo members and Central Committee secretaries, requesting a review of the cases of repressed Bulgarian political émigrés. "It is beyond doubt," he wrote, "that among the ranks of the arrested political émigrés there are other nationalities (Germans, Austrians, [people from the] Balkans, and others) a considerable number [of whom] are honest and devoted Communists whose cases deserve to be reviewed, and the mistakes committed against these people [deserve to be] corrected." He then suggested that Andreev and Zhdanov speak with Yakunin, Kurov, and Gitman, "who maintain that their work to clear up cases of political émigrés does not lead to practical results. Even after exposing completely groundless accusations, it makes no difference. In the majority of instances, the cases are not closed, and those wrongly convicted are not set free."[45]

On 10 February, Dimitrov received a copy of an Orgburo resolution that established a commission consisting of Merkulov (deputy people's commissar of the NKVD), Bochkov (the USSR procurator), and Shkiriatov (deputy chairman of the Party Control Commission) and charged it with reviewing the materials sent by Dimitrov. After this, Dimitrov sent to the commission new lists of arrested people whose cases deserved review. One such list included Valter, Razumova (both native-born workers in the ECCI apparatus), and seventeen political émigrés. He did not succeed in gaining Valter's release, although the commission did release a modest number of people who had been arrested.

The appeal on behalf of Valter constitutes only a small part of that list, reproduced here as **Document 55**, nor are all of the appeals in the original document included. The appeal for Valter is representative of many such appeals sent by the ECCI on behalf of repressed workers in the ECCI apparatus and of political émigrés.[46] The appeals presented here provide snapshots of aspects of the period; taken together, they illuminate the repression's dynamics and impact on individuals. The cases of Khigerovich (Razumova) and Kurshner, both of whom are included in Document 55, are discussed more fully later in this chapter.

Document 55

Letter from Dimitrov to Merkulov requesting a review of the cases of E. O. Valter, A. L. Khigerovich (Razumova), K. F. Kurshner, and other arrested political émigrés, 28 February 1941. RGASPI, f. 495, op. 73, d. 107, ll. 23–24, 27–34, 36, 41–56. Original in Russian. Typewritten.

TO COMRADE MERKULOV.

(To the commission of cc. Merkulov, Bochkov, Shkiriatov.)

Dear comrade Merkulov,

I entreat you to have the commission review, along with the list of arrested political émigrés submitted by me, the cases of <u>Valter</u>, Elena Osipovna, and <u>Khigerovich</u>, Anna Lazarevna (Razumova). Both are former ECCI workers. [Please review] as well the case of <u>Drenowski</u>, Emil Dragovich (he was a commander in the International Brigade in Spain), and <u>Cavalli</u>, Adolf (an Italian political émigré, former member of the CP of Italy).

Attached to this letter please find information on sixteen [*sic*] more political émigrés, whose cases should be reviewed based on what we know about them.

With comradely greetings,

G. DIMITROV

28 February 1941.

71

Enclosure: 1) Information about Valter, E. O., Khigerovich [Anna Razumova], A. L., Drenowski, E. D., and Cavalli, A.

2) Information on 15 arrested political émigrés.

<u>VALTER, Elena Osipovna</u>.[47]

(maiden name—BRAVERMAN).

Born in 1898 in Minsk, she is a white-collar worker. She joined the VKP(b) in 1919. Between 1919 and 1922, she worked as a chief clerk in the Gubrevkom,[48] the headquarters of the Sixteenth Army, the Political Department of the Western Front, and in the NKID [People's Commissariat of Foreign Affairs]. Between 1922 and 1930, she stayed abroad with her husband. From 1931 to October 1938, she worked in the ECCI, including four years in the Secretariat of the ECCI general secretary.

She was arrested by NKVD organs in October 1938. On 17 January 1940, she was sentenced by the Special Council of the NKVD of the USSR and exiled for three years to the Krasnoiarsk region.

On 25 June 1940, c.c. G. DIMITROV and D. MANUILSKY forwarded Valter's letter to c. BERIA and petitioned for a review of her case. There has been no reply.

Secret.

INFORMATION.

KHIGEROVICH, Anna Lazarevna (RAZUMOVA)[49] She was born in 1899 in Minsk into the family of a military conductor (he died in 1932 while holding this position in the RKKA [Worker-Peasant Red Army]), Jewish, a white-collar worker. She graduated from high school in 1917. In 1929–1930, she attended courses of Marxism. She joined the VKP(b) in 1918.

WORK EXPERIENCE:

In 1917 and early 1918, she was a librarian in the Society for Spreading Enlightenment among the Jews in Leningrad. She was fired for refusing to boycott the October socialist revolution.

In 1918–1919, she was a head of the Agitation and Recruitment Department of the Gatchina military commissariat. After the merging of Gatchina with Detskoe Selo, she was head of the Department of Agitation and Education of the Political Department of the Gatchina zone of the Northwest RR [railroad]. Before the liquidation of the Yudenich front, she was an intelligence officer for the special detachment of the Sixth Division, Seventh Army. She was a member of the bureau of the railroad party cell of the Gatchina goods yard, later of the repair shops of the Gatchina-Warsaw [line].

In 1920–1921, she was in Leningrad as the head of the Cultural Department of the local committee of the Railroad Workers' Union of the Northwestern RR, a member of the revolutionary committee during the Kronstadt rebellion,[50] [and] a member of the bureau of the [party] cell of the Petrograd railway repair shops (the Warsaw RR).

In 1921–1922, she worked as an instructor and later as a head of the Cultural Department of the Railroad Workers' Union of the Northwestern Railway in Leningrad.

In 1922–1923, she was elected a member of the local committee of the Railroad Workers' Union in Rybinsk and sent to Rybinsk as a head of the Cultural Department. At the Provincial Congress of Soviets, she was elected a member of the Provincial Executive Committee and the deputy chair of the commission to fight famine. Later she was named head of the Provincial Women's Department, where she worked until the liquidation of Rybinsk province.

In 1923–1924, she worked in Orel as the head of the Cult[ural] Department of the provincial union and the Union of Educational Workers. She was elected a member of the Provincial Council of the Educational Workers' Union, and later elected a member of the Regional Committee of the VKP(b) and named the head of its Agitation and Propaganda Department [and] a member of the Regional Committee's bureau. At the same time, she was a member of the bureau of the [party] cell of the twine factory.

In 1924–1925, she worked in Ufa as a deputy head of the Agitation and Propaganda Department of the VKP(b) oblast committee, a member of the oblast committee, a member of the bureau of the [party] cell of the Ufa RR repair shops. She was elected a member of the purge commission for the [party] cells of the service railroad.

In 1925–1926, she worked in Moscow as a head of the Political Department for schools in the Agitation and Propaganda Department of the Sokolnicheskii district committee of the VKP(b). At the same time, she was a member of the bureau and later secretary of the SONO[51] [party] cell.

In 1926–1927, she worked in Tashkent as a deputy head of the APO [Agitprop Department] for the Propaganda [Department] of the Central Asian Bureau of the CC VKP(b) [and was] a member of the bureau of the railroad [party] cell.

In 1927–1928, she worked in China on assignments for the International Women's Secretariat of the ECCI[52] as an instructor on women's work.

July 1928–1931, she worked in Moscow as an analyst in the ECCI apparatus, first in the International Women's Secretariat, later as an organizational analyst in the Eastern Secretariat. She was a member of the bureau of the [party] cell, a women's activist, [and] the chair of the Inspection Commission.

June 1931–February 1936, she was in France on assignment for the ECCI.

March 1936–November 1936, she worked in Moscow in the ECCI as an analyst in the Secretariat of com. Manuilsky and conducted work in the KUTV [Communist University for Toilers of the East] in two national groups.

November 1936–April 1937, she was in France and Spain on assignment for the ECCI.

May–September 1937, she worked in Moscow in the ECCI apparatus as a political assistant in the Secretariat of com. Manuilsky. She also conducted party propaganda work.

October 1937–April 1938, she was a secretary of the editorial board of the "Kommunisticheskii Internatsional" magazine.

She conducted work on the liquidation of the SRs in Rybinsk in 1922–1923. She struggled actively against the Trotskyist opposition in Orel in 1923–1924, against the Leningrad opposition in Moscow in 1925–1926, [and] against the Trotskyists and the rightists in the ECCI apparatus in 1929.

In 1937, her former husband (in the years 1923–1925), RAZUMOV, M. O., who was a former secretary of the East-Siberian oblast committee of the VKP(b), was arrested by NKVD organs. In connection with this, the VKP(b) party committee of the ECCI apparatus reviewed the case of KHIGEROVICH, A. L., and in August 1937 resolved that there was no evidence that she had been connected to or shared the Trotskyist ideas of the now exposed and arrested enemies of the party.

In its decision, the party committee, basing itself on the unverified information that ABUROV was a Trotskyist and was arrested by NKVD organs, resolved that KHIGEROVICH, A. L., while having intimate relations with him in China in 1928 and in the USSR, failed to assist in the unmasking of ABUROV.

Later it turned out that this information was incorrect and that ABUROV, a VKP(b) member, was still a propaganda worker in the Rostokino district committee of the VKP(b) in Moscow.

In late December 1937, KHIGEROVICH, A. L., wrote a statement to the VKP(b) party committee of the ECCI apparatus regarding her relations with MITKEVICH, O. A. (a former member of the party committee, and later director of Plant No. 22), who was arrested by the NKVD. She got to know her in 1928, during their work in China, and later, in March 1936–May 1937, she lived in her apartment in the government house. She also informed [the party committee] that in late 1937, her brother's wife was arrested by the NKVD for allegedly crossing the border illegally.

All her brothers and sisters are still members of the VKP(b) and the Komsomol.

KHIGEROVICH, A. L., was arrested by the NKVD in April 1938.

DEPUTY HEAD OF THE ECCI's CADRES DEPARTMENT:
                                        Belov BELOV

"27" February 1941
3 copies ak.
< . . . > *Blagoev* < . . . >

Secret
INFORMATION.
DRENOWSKI, Emil Dragovich (Iovanovich, Yanko Pavlov; Uroshevich, Dushan; Daskal; Yankovich; Dragutin)[53] was born in 1901 in Serbia in the family of an artisan (village blacksmith), a Serb by nationality. He has a higher education, graduated from the Higher Pedagogical School in Yugoslavia, studied for one year in the KUNMZ graduate school, and for several months in the MLSh. He joined the CP of Yugoslavia [CPYu] in 1922. From 1919, he was a member of the Komsomol of Yugoslavia.

The ECCI Cadres Department possesses the following information about the work of Drenowski, E. D., in the CP of Yugoslavia.

From 1919 to 1922, he worked in student organizations in Yugoslavia and distributed flyers and other revolutionary literature for the Young Communist League.

In 1922, being a schoolteacher, he joined the CPYu and worked among teachers and peasants in the countryside.

Between 1923 and 1925, [because he had] a high school education, he served in the Yugoslav army in the school of the reserve officers. After six months, he was expelled from this school for a lack of discipline and was transferred to a mounted regiment as a rank-and-file soldier. In the army he continued his work as a Communist, although he did not maintain connections with the party.

Between 1925 and 1927, he worked as a teacher in the countryside and disseminated Communist literature among teachers and the peasantry. In 1927, he was removed from teaching [after being] accused of insulting the king and of antigovernmental activities. He was not tried for lack of evidence.

Between 1928 and 1935, he was reestablished in a teacher's position (after an appeal) and worked to rebuild the party organization in the countryside. He was a party organizer, secretary of the regional [party] committee, member of the district [okrug] committee (in the towns of Bogatich and Shabats).

In 1935, he went underground and was sent to study in the USSR. Going underground and coming to the USSR were caused by the exposure of the party organization in Shabats and Bogatich. This exposure resulted from him (Drenowski) passing on [information about] addresses and secret meeting places to a person who was later arrested. [He did this] with the sanction of the party organization while in Belgrade in 1933.

In 1932, Drenowski, E. D., met with S. Markovich (from the group of rightists in the CPYu, arrested by the NKVD) [and] received from him materials on the agrarian and national question for distribution. Drenowski, E. D., explains that he did not know that, at that time, S. Markovich had already been working against the CPYu, [and that] he thought that he had connections with the CC CPYu.

Com. Shpiner (currently working in the International Publishing House) confirmed that the CC CPYu was aware of this fact, but nobody accused Drenowski of being tied to Sima Markovich.

Between 1935 and 1936, Drenowski studied in the USSR. He received a positive reference from the KUNMZ.

In late 1936 (in October), he was assigned to group "A."[54] In Spain, he was a commander of the Slovenian company, participated in battles, was injured and lost his right arm.

He received a positive reference from Spain. In 1937, on 16 May, Drenowski, E. D., returned to the USSR, where he worked in the ECCI Cadres Department and later in the International Publishing House.

In 1938, Dragachevaz (expelled from the CPYu and arrested by the NKVD) sent a statement to the ICC accusing Drenowski of sympathizing with the former rightists in the CPYu and, in particular, of friendly relations with Kreschich [and] Sandanskij ([both] arrested by the NKVD). Drenowski declared this statement by Dragachevaz [to be] slander. Belich Milan and Shpiner also confirmed that this was a slander. Regarding this statement, the latter wrote the following to the ECCI Cadres Department: "The statement of Dragachevaz against Drenowski reflects the dissatisfaction of Dragachevaz himself, as well as that of Berger and Richter, with their situation (both were expelled from the CPYu and arrested by the NKVD), which they, for some reason, relate to Drenowski. Second, it reflects the continuing factional struggle in the CPYu, whose center is represented by Andrej [Stejepan Stjepan] (also arrested by the NKVD)."

In 1938, Drenowski, E. D., was arrested by the NKVD.[55]

DEPUTY HEAD OF THE ECCI CADRES DEPARTMENT:
Vilkov VILKOV
HEAD OF THE BALKAN COUNTRIES GROUP:
Vladimirov VLADIMIROV
"21" February 1941
2 copies gm.

Secret.
INFORMATION.
CAVALLI, Gaetano (aka Partelli, Adolfo Domenico, Gino Spartaco)[56] was born in 1898 in Vallstania, Vichenza province (Italy), in a worker's family. He himself was a mason.

From 1919, he was a member of the Socialist Party of Italy.

In 1921, he joined the CP of Italy.

In 1922, he emigrated to France for economic reasons. In Meurthe et Moselle [Department], he was a leader of the group of Italian political émigrés.

In 1924, he went to Switzerland for economic reasons. There he also conducted work among the political émigrés.

In 1927, he returned to France, from which he was expelled in 1929 for revolutionary activities. After that he lived in Belgium for some time, and in 1931, he went to Luxembourg, from which he was also expelled. In 1932, he lived for seven months, until his departure for the USSR, in Zurich, Basel, and Germany.

In November 1933, with the consent of the CP of Italy, he went to the USSR and was sent to conduct work in the Crimea. In the Crimea, he worked in the kolkhoz Sacco and Vanzetti. During his work in the kolkhoz, he received bonuses several times. In [his] personnel file there is a recommendation by c. Gallo [Luigi Longo] for his transferal to the VKP(b).

In July 1938, Cavalli was arrested by NKVD organs.[57]

SOURCE: MATERIALS FROM THE PERSONNEL FILE.
                    BLAGOEVA
                    BOGOMOLOVA
_____ February 1941.

KURSHNER, Karl Filippovich (GARAI, Karl).

He was born in 1899, a Hungarian, a Soviet citizen, an economist-journalist by trade.

He joined the CP of Hungary in 1918. Between 1921 and 1923, he was a member of the CP of Czechoslovakia; between 1923 and 1929, he was a member of the CP of Germany. After 1929, again a member of the CP of Hungary.

Until 1923, he conducted Komsomol work. Between 1923 and 1929, he worked in the Berlin embassy. In 1929, he was sent to conduct work in the country [Hungary]. In July 1929, he was arrested and sentenced to two years and two months in prison. After being released, he conducted underground work as a secretary of the Budapest committee of the CP of Hungary and, later, as a member of the Secretariat of the CC CP of Hungary. In 1932, he went to the USSR with the party's consent.

While in Moscow, he worked in the Institute of the World Economy and as an editor in chief of the <u>DZZ</u> [*Deutsche Zentral-Zeitung*].[58]

Com. GERŐ has given him a positive reference.

In February 1938, he was arrested by NKVD organs and accused of being part of the counterrevolutionary organization of <u>E. VARGA</u> (a candidate ECCI member and a member of the Academy of Sciences).

In March 1940, the procurator of the <u>Moscow Military District</u> closed the case for lack of evidence, and Kurshner was released. However, in July 1940, he was arrested again, since the procurator of the USSR annulled the decision of the procurator of the MMD [Moscow Military District] and reopened the old case.[59] In September 1940, the Special Department of the NKVD of the USSR sentenced Kurshner to eight years in a corrective labor camp. The indictment again mentions participation in the counterrevolutionary organization of E. Varga.

[. . .]

<u>Rudnitsky, Kalman Noevich</u>.

He was born in 1904 in Latvia. He is a Jew, a worker. He was a member of the Russian Komsomol between 1918 and 1920, a member of the CP of Latvia from 1929. In 1920, he and his family moved to Latvia. He was arrested two times for his Communist activities. He spent four years in prison.

In 1934, he returned to the USSR. He worked in the auto plant in Gorky.

In 1937, he was arrested by NKVD organs and condemned to the supreme penalty. In his letter, No. 42434 of 31 August 1940, the deputy procurator, in response to the letter from Dimitrov's Secretariat, No. 110 of 23 February 1940, conveyed that "he was sentenced on the basis of unverified and unconfirmed information." The Office of the Procurator of the USSR sent the case of Rudnitsky to the Latvian SSR for verification. There has been no answer.

[. . .]

<u>VÁGI, Stefan Frantsevich</u>.

He was born in 1883 in Hungary. A Hungarian, he is a construction worker. He joined the SD Party between 1902 and 1924. A member of the CP of Hungary from 1925.

[He was] an active participant in the Hungarian revolutionary movement.

During [the period of] Soviet power in Hungary, he was a member of the directorate and a political commissar in the Red Army. He was arrested several times for his revolutionary activities and spent seven and a half years in prison altogether.

He came to the USSR in 1932. He worked in the Profintern until its reorganization.

The representative of the CP of Hungary in the ECCI, c. Gerö, wrote in his reference of 18 January 1940 that "Stefan Vági is a prominent figure in the Hungarian workers' movement. He played an especially prominent role in the years following the fall of Soviet power in Hungary. . . . He was a leader of the Hungarian workers' movement . . . Vági is still one of the most popular figures in the Hungarian workers' movement, the most popular after com. Rakosi. B. Kun hated Vági and persecuted and badgered him. It is not impossible that Vági became a victim of B. Kun's intrigues."

Vági, Stefan, was arrested on 21 March 1938 by NKVD organs and convicted.[60]

On 31 February 1939, we forwarded a letter from Vági's wife, along with information from the Cadres Department, to the procurator of the USSR.

Given the existence of a number of positive references for Vági, com. DIMITROV addressed the procurator of the USSR on 4 February 1940 asking for a review of the case of Vági, Stefan.

In a letter of 25 July 1940, under No. 4–55382, the procurator of the USSR communicated that "the case of Vági, S. F., has been reviewed. Vági pleaded guilty. Besides, his guilt is confirmed by the evidence [given] by Rakowitch and Koroli-Mat. I find no grounds to review the case."

SEIKELI, Ludwig Mikhailovich[61]

He was born in 1901 in Hungary. He was a member of the SD Party between 1917 and 1919. In 1919, he joined the CP of Hungary and, in 1927, the VKP(b). He is a worker-shoemaker. He worked most recently in the Foreign Censorship Department in Glavlit.

C. Gerö, the representative of the CP of Hungary in the ECCI, knows Seikeli from his work in Hungary and, in his reference of March 1940, wrote that Seikeli worked actively, that there was no reason to doubt his personal and political honesty, and that at that time, he accomplished several party assignments in which he could be tested. He [Gerö] knows nothing about his work in the USSR.

In the files of the Cadres Department, there is a positive reference [for Seikeli] written by the secretary of the Glavlit party committee on 21 May 1937.

In March 1938, Seikeli was arrested by NKVD organs, accused of counter-revolutionary activities, and sentenced to five years in a labor camp.[62]

On 17 February 1939, on orders from c. DIMITROV, a letter from Seikeli's wife, along with information from the Cadres Department, was forwarded to

c. Vyshinsky. On 5 September 1939, a reply was received from the procurator of the USSR, c. Pankratiev, stating that Seikeli had been exposed by the testimony of witnesses, and that there was no reason for reviewing his case.

On 15 March 1940, a letter from Seikeli, L. M., was received, in which he writes about his innocence and [says] that he signed the examination record after being subjected to physical methods of pressure.

In connection with this statement, a letter signed by c. DIMITROV was sent to the procurator of the USSR asking [him] to review the case of Seikeli again. In his reply of 12 December 1940, com. Bochkov informed [him] that the case had been reviewed again and that he had found no reason to contest the OSO decision. He based it [his decision] on the fact that Seikeli had connections to foreigners, most of whom were later arrested, and that he was repeatedly engaged in anti-Soviet conversations.

[. . . .]

KOMOR-KATSBURG, Imre Maksimovich.[63]

He was born in Hungary. He is a Soviet citizen, a journalist. He was a member of the CP of Hungary between 1918 and 1925, a member of the VKP(b) between 1925 and 1933, and a member of the CP of Hungary in 1933–1935.

In the country [Hungary], he conducted active revolutionary work. He was arrested several times and, in 1922, was sentenced to twelve years in prison. In 1924, he came to the USSR after an exchange [of political prisoners].

Between 1926 and 1927, Komor worked for the Foreign Committee of the CC CP of Hungary in Moscow. In 1927–33, Komor again worked in Moscow.

In 1933–1935, Komor worked for the CC CP of Hungary, which was dissolved in 1936 by a decision of the ECCI Secretariat for sabotaging the implementation of the decisions of the Seventh Comintern Congress, for gross violation of the rules of conspiracy, for clamping down on self-criticism, and for the presence of Hungarian police agents in the CC.

However, it is clear from ECCI apparatus documents that when KOMOR learned about the behavior of the Hungarian delegation (Kun and Gross) at the Seventh Congress and about [their] sabotage in implementing the decisions of the Seventh Congress, he informed the ECCI leadership about it.[64]

The representative of the CP of Hungary in the ECCI thinks that "Komor has serious shortcomings, that he is a rather light-minded and somewhat superficial man . . . but an honest Communist and a talented person. . . . He conducted a decisive struggle against the Trotskyist-Bukharinist gang."

He was arrested in July 1937[65] by NKVD organs, and on 23 October 1939, the Special NKVD Council sentenced him to eight years in a corrective labor camp for participating in the rightist-Trotskyist organization.

For more than two years, the case of Komor-Katsburg was under investigation. The Military Board of the Supreme Court of the USSR heard this case three times, and each time it remitted it for further inquiry. As stated in the letter from the deputy procurator of the USSR of 19 September 1940, No.

61419, Komor-Katsburg "has been exposed by the testimony of <u>Kreichi</u>, Béla Kun, <u>Ersh</u>,[66] <u>Magyar</u>, and others."

The reference letter from the Cadres Department of 15 April 1940 points out that Komor-Katsburg "in his speeches at the sessions of the CC CP of Hungary in December 1935, and at the meetings with c. Ercoli in March 1936, criticized the sectarian policies of <u>Kun</u> and Gross in the CP of Hungary and their unscrupulous behavior at the Seventh ECCI Congress."

We sent exhaustive information about Komor-Katsburg on 14 November 1939, 21 November 1939, and 17 April 1940 under No. 991.

In his reply of 19 December 1940, No. 61419, the deputy procurator of the USSR indicated that there was no reason to review the case, and the complaint remained unresolved.[67]

KUTLU, Ali-Geidar Yusufovich (EROL)[68]

He was born in 1909 in Turkey; he is a worker. Between 1927 and 1935, he lived in the USSR. A member of the CP of Turkey from 1935. In 1937, the party leadership sent him again to the USSR.

In his letter of 16 May 1940, the representative of the CP of Turkey in the ECCI characterized Kutlu as a good conspirator and as an honest person devoted to the proletariat's revolutionary cause.

In 1937, he was arrested by NKVD organs, and on 20 May 1938, sentenced by the Military Tribunal of the Transcaucasian Military District to twenty years in a corrective labor camp.

In our letter of 4 June 1940, No. 448, to the procurator of the USSR, we raised the question of the possibility of reviewing the case of Kutlu, A. G.[69]

The procurator of the USSR, in a letter, No. 52671, of 30 October 1940, communicated that after the protest by the Office of the Procurator, the Plenum of the Supreme Court of the USSR reversed the verdict of the Transcaucasian Military District and closed the case. However, despite this decision, Kutlu still remains in prison.

Several aspects of Document 55 deserve note. The first is that the form and formulations of this appeal were representative of others sent by Dimitrov. Each contained brief biographical information, a summary (in varying degrees of detail) of the person's political and work experiences, information that raised questions about the conviction, the date of arrest, and testimony from appropriate party leaders on the victim's personal and political qualities. Because review commissions had the right to summon all materials relevant to a case, such appeals, however terse, were sufficient to initiate a review.

The willingness of prominent members of the fraternal parties (for example,

Varga, Gerő, and Gottwald) to vouch for their imprisoned comrades in 1941 indicates how much the political climate had changed since 1937–1938, when vigilance frequently destroyed the bonds of trust, and few were willing to risk themselves to vouch for others.

That change should not obscure the familiar themes that punctuate Document 55. The cases of Rudnitsky, who "was sentenced on the basis of unverified and unconfirmed information," of Kutlu, whose verdict had been overturned but who "still remains in prison," of Kurshner, who was convicted of belonging to "the counterrevolutionary organization of E. Varga," who remained at liberty, and of Komor, whose case was three times "remitted . . . for further inquiry" illustrate the arbitrariness of the repression. The cases of Vági, Komor, and Drenkowski, each of whom Dimitrov believed to be the victim of intraparty intrigues, serve as reminders of the important but shadowy roles played by political and personal conflicts within the fraternal parties.

All of the cases testify implicitly to the crucial role played by xenophobia during the mass repression.[70] None does so as explicitly as Seikeli's.[71] Although his case had been reviewed, Bochkov, the USSR procurator, "found no reason to contest the OSO decision. He based it [his decision] on the fact that Seikeli had connections to foreigners, most of whom were later arrested." That Seikeli, a foreigner, "had connections to other foreigners" is hardly surprising. Nor is it surprising that, given the Politburo's directives to arrest people based on nationality, many of his acquaintances were arrested. Bochkov's circular reasoning was common in 1937–1938 and was obviously still alive and well in 1941: the arrest and conviction of foreigners "proved" their guilt, and foreigners who "had connections to foreigners, most of whom were later arrested," must also be guilty.

The fact that Bochkov sat on the review commission to which Dimitrov sent the appeals did not augur well for a successful appeal. Nor did his presence on the review commission augur well for people like Vági who had pleaded guilty, albeit probably after being tortured. Given their confessions, we might wonder why Dimitrov even bothered appealing on their behalf. The most likely reason is that he knew that they had been tortured to confess. Even though the judicial branch denied an appeal, a party commission might force a conviction to be overturned. To succeed, one had to exhaust all of the bureaucratic options. Only by such persistence might justice prevail. But Dimitrov's appeals were, by and large, fruitless. Only Kutlu, whose sentence had already been overturned, was released. Apparently unbeknownst to Dimitrov, three of those on his list, Drenkowski, Rudnitsky and Vági, had already been executed.

Valter, Razumova, Seikeli, and Komor were not released until after the war. The others apparently perished in the gulag.

The Case of Anna Razumova-Khigerovich

We have already met Anna Razumova-Khigerovich, better known as Anna Razumova, who in 1936 had worked in the Secretariat of Manuilsky. At the age of eighteen Razumova broke with her father, a White Army officer, and joined the Bolsheviks.[72] As her political biography in Document 55 indicates, Razumova repeatedly proved her dedication to the party and her willingness to put her life on the line for it. In the late 1920s she conducted undercover work in China; during the 1930s she engaged in similar work in France and Spain. Throughout her career she supported the struggles against Socialist Revolutionaries, Trotskyists, Rightists, anyone who challenged the party line. Following the August 1936 show trial, Razumova implored her comrades to be "vigilant in deeds, not in words" (see Document 15). At a party meeting in October of that year, she announced that "among us there are still comrades who have not communicated to the party organization their own ties to those arrested and shot following the [August] trial of the Trotskyists."[73] In short, Razumova appears to have been a model Stalinist, a "real Bolshevik," who had actively supported the vigilance campaign within the ECCI apparatus.

But many a model Stalinist fell under suspicion and was arrested in these years. During the August 1936 party committee meeting, which she chaired and at which she implored comrades to be "vigilant in deeds," Kotelnikov, the party secretary, announced the existence of the "Razumova affair," which centered on her past acquaintances with arrested "enemies of the people." The bill of particulars noted that her former husband (Razumov) had been "exposed and arrested as an enemy of the party and people" and that when she worked in China, she had been "acquainted with Neumann, Tarakhanov, Lominadze, [and] Magyar," all of whom had been arrested.[74] The party committee investigated her case and concluded that "there is no evidence that Razumova was tied politically to the Trotskyist views of the exposed enemies of the party and people (Razumov, Magyar, Neumann, Tarakhanov, Lominadze); [in fact,] she had separated herself" from them. Nonetheless, the party committee resolved to send the information to the party leadership to determine whether Razumova should continue "at work in the ECCI apparatus."[75] She was permitted to do so, but she received a party reprimand.

After receiving the reprimand, Razumova wrote a letter to Manuilsky in which she declared herself to be politically pure and expressed her views on guilt by association: "I have always maintained that it is impossible to accuse a person because through no choice of his own, he worked in a place with an enemy of the people, [especially] when the people and work were not of your choice."[76] When a longtime friend and comrade (O. A. Mitkevich) was arrested in late 1937, Razumova dutifully submitted a declaration about their friendship saying that she knew of Mitkevich's work activities.[77] Her political behavior conformed to that expected by VKP leaders. Nonetheless, some party members viewed her and her familyness with arrested "enemies of the people" (see Document 32) with suspicion. So did the NKVD. On 7 April 1938 she was arrested.

Dimitrov's 1941 effort (see Document 55) to have Razumova's case reviewed failed: "Review of case denied."[78] In 1945 the NKVD forwarded to Dimitrov a letter that Razumova had written to him in his capacity as a member of the USSR Supreme Soviet requesting that her case be reviewed. She was not optimistic: "I have little faith that it [the review] will be successful, but maybe our procurator and the Supreme Court will be able to investigate all these problems better than before the war." Document 56 includes the NKVD's cover letter to Dimitrov, Razumova's letter to him, and the enclosed letter of reference for Razumova written by the commandant of the gulag camp where she had worked since 1939.

Document 56

Letter from Razumova to Dimitrov requesting a review of her case, with cover letter and attachment, May–July 1945.[79] RGASPI, f. 495, op. 65a, d. 8364, ll. 192–199. Original in Russian. Typewritten with handwritten additions.

<u>Secret.</u>

vkh-2 in[coming] No. 284108
USSR
PEOPLE'S COMMISSARIAT
OF INTERNAL AFFAIRS
First special department
"16" July 1945
No. 8/13–*103342*
Moscow.
C.C. of the VKP(B).
<u>to com. DIMITROV, G. M.</u>

Enclosed please find a sealed file from the prisoner <u>RAZUMOVA-KHIGEROVICH</u>, Anna Lazarevna addressed to you, with the reference information on her.

<u>ENCLOSURE:</u> as described.

DEPUTY HEAD OF THE SPECIAL DEPARTMENT OF THE NKVD USSR
Piadyshev Piadyshev
HEAD OF THE Thirteenth DEPARTMENT
Ko<...>in
Ko<...>in.

[Across the text:]
To c. Mirov
Investigate and report.
20. 7. 45 GD
A letter sent to com.
Merkulov, V. N.
To archive.
Ya. Mirov.
7. 9. 45 <...>

COPY.
TO THE MEMBER OF THE SUPREME SOVIET OF THE USSR
GEORGY MIKHAILOVICH DIMITROV.
From the prisoner RAZUMOVA-KHIGEROVICH, A. L.
In the Ukhta women's corrective labor camp, Komi ASSR
Ukhta, OLP 7.
<u>Petition to review the case.</u>

On <u>7 April 1938,</u> I was arrested in Moscow by NKVD organs and, thirteen months later, on <u>5 May 1939,</u> I was sentenced by the Military Board of the Supreme Court of the USSR to fifteen years in a corrective labor camp under articles 58-II, 6, 7, 8 or 9 (I do not remember) over 17. I <u>did not plead guilty</u> during the trial. To the question of the chairman of the trial, What was correct in the indictment? I replied: "I consider correct only the names of people who worked in the ECCI apparatus and whom I could not but know, since I have worked in that apparatus for eleven years in a row." I learned specifically about what I was charged with only on 30 April 1939, five days before the trial. During the thirteen months in prison and in the course of daily interrogations, I was not charged with anything. They only <u>suggested</u> that I write a statement in Yezhov's name admitting my "crimes." Since I have never committed any crimes, in deed or even in thought, it is clear that I could not sign such a statement. These "suggestions" were accompanied by daily beatings, insults, and mockery. The interrogations lasted: one for eleven days in a row; others for three days with fifteen–twenty-minute breaks to eat. During all these interrogations, I had to <u>stand on my feet without any sleep.</u> I suffered from hallucinations, and my feet swelled so much that I was unable to move them. However, all the physical torture could not break me. The moral suffering was the hardest. I was afraid to mention any name because whatever person I could refer to, it was said about him that he was a well-known spy, etc. I mentioned a number of facts that proved my genuine attitude toward work. In particular, I mentioned all the documents that I had sent from abroad that dealt with shortcomings in the work of our apparatus. I was sure that all these materials were held in the Cadres Department or in the Eastern Secretariat. To name a few: my reports on the colonial affairs (about provocation in Indochina with photographs of the provocateurs; about provocation in the Arab Communist Parties in Syria, Algeria, Tunisia, Egypt, Palestine; references for the colonial workers sent to me in Paris, indicating the inadmissibility of sending such people); reports on the Trotskyists in Spain, about the volunteers from the French and other Communist Parties; reports on the inefficient work of the OMS, about poorly written documents, etc. Finally, a series of reports sent to you personally about the inefficient work of some of the workers in the apparatus that could negatively affect all our work. I said that during eleven years of work in the ECCI apparatus (among them, eight years abroad working in the underground), there was not a single failure of any person that I worked with, or of my own. You know about the nature of my trips and of the assignments that I fulfilled. You know that if I had practiced treason in any form, the results of it would have been terrible, and it would have been impossible not to know about it. To all my attempts to defend myself, they responded that I was lying and that the materials to which I was referring did not exist in the ECCI, that the Cadres Department had supposedly informed [them] that they had received nothing from me. These conversations and everything that was going on provoked strange thoughts in my mind: as if there were indeed, in the ECCI apparatus, some enemies who were destroying all of the carefully collected materials that had helped us to restructure [our] work and get rid of provocateurs and Trotskyist elements. It seemed to me that it was essential to remember, to reconstruct, [in order to] to inform the NKVD and the Comintern. Having refused to write a statement to Yezhov, I asked for paper to write about everything. They told me that they would give me paper if I would write a statement to Yezhov as though I knew something about being a member of a counterrevolutionary organization within the Comintern. They even dictated to me the text of such a statement. I again refused to write it, and the investigator again slapped me and threw a stone paperweight at me. After that I <u>stood for eleven days without sleep</u>, was mocked during the day, and was regularly beaten at night. They beat me with the armrests of a chair and punched me in the chest, and then let me stay for one night in my cell. Then these terrible interrogations resumed. My only wish was to commit suicide so as not to remember that I was in a Soviet prison, that I was being tortured and accused of betraying my motherland, which I love more than anything else and to which I have been faithful despite everything. After lengthy consideration, I decided that it was necessary to somehow inform the Comintern and the NKVD about what they supposedly did not know. I decided to obtain paper by writing the statement to Yezhov and later to write another statement to Yezhov from my cell stating that if it was necessary to sacrifice myself in order to reveal what I had to tell, I was ready to do it. I thought that they would shoot me, that I alone would suffer, but [at least] the NKVD would learn how badly prepared for the war our apparatus is, how saturated our apparatus abroad is (in short, everything that I informed about after each trip abroad). And so I did. I wrote the statement dictated by the investigator and got the paper that I had tried so hard to obtain. I started writing. [However,] they ripped up my testimony and instead gave me a plan to follow in which I had to describe everything from the viewpoint of a member of a counterrevolutionary organization within the ECCI. In reply to the question of who sent me to China, France, Spain, etc., they would put, not some ECCI workers, but a member of a counterrevolutionary organization within the ECCI; all the documents and travel money I received [came] not from the appropriate ECCI workers but from the members of a counterrevolutionary organization. In general, all my work ties, relations, and assignments were portrayed as ties and relations within a counterrevolutionary organization. It was reflected in the examination record as follows:

"Q.—Who provided you with money to travel?"

"Ans.—Melnikov and Gregor [Grgur Vujović]." (The examination record: "Money for counterrevolutionary activities received from the members of Melnikov's counterrevolutionary organization, etc."). Could I go abroad without money, without documents? Who but the responsible workers of the ECCI apparatus could have provided me with all this? Thus, all my work, all my life, all my connections—all of it became counterrevolutionary, although I have never been a member of a counterrevolutionary organization and never even suspected its existence in the ECCI system.

However, despite the totally inadmissible methods of interrogation, I still believed those NKVD officials because I thought it impossible that within the NKVD there were entrenched enemies of the people who were interested in perverting the truth. If that had been the case, I would have behaved differently during the interrogations. I had gotten used to being mentally ready to be captured by fascists, and I knew how to behave at a fascist trial. But here I treated my investigators as comrades whom I had to help to cleanse the party and the country of all sorts of garbage. I could not even think about meeting insult with insult or defending myself when I was beaten, or yelling and cursing the way they did. Only on 30 April 1939, five days before the trial, was I able to read the indictment. I demanded to see the prosecutor for an explanation. They promised me [a meeting], but they never fulfilled that promise. The indictment states that I was recruited into the counterrevolutionary organization by Fokin, that I spied for all the [capitalist] countries, that I plotted something against Manuilsky, etc. I do not remember the details because I

only read that rubbish once and was indignant at this material that had nothing to do with me. I never read the verdict, I listened to it as something unre-
lated to me personally, I did not even remember the article under which I was
accused. My file contains testimony by Fokin, Brigader, Melnikov, Rylsky,
and some Korean (I do not remember his name)—I think this is it.

Fokin says that he recruited [me] into the counterrevolutionary organization in order to obtain information about colonial work. According to him, I
was supposed to pass that information over to Grant. I have never had either
revolutionary or counterrevolutionary ties to Fokin. I knew him only because
he worked in the KIM and later in the Eastern Department of the Profintern,
and I attended the same meetings of the Eastern Secretariat that he attended,
and lived in the [Hotel] Lux as he did. Grant was an analyst in the Eastern Secretariat of the Profintern specializing in Indochina, and we used to exchange
newspapers from Indochina since we subscribed to different newspapers to
save money. This was before my trip to France, which means in 1930. From
1931 to [my] arrest, i.e., for eight years, I neither heard of nor saw those people.

Also, Brigader testified that he had heard from somebody that Arnot had recruited me to spy for England. I have never talked with Brigader or with Arnot
about anything but work. I informed you about Brigader shortly before he was
arrested. He had provided the NKVD with incorrect information about the
American Negro Haiswood, having concealed that the latter was a member of
the Lovestone group.

Melnikov testified that he had given me money for trips abroad. Rylsky informed [the court] that he had provided me with a passport, and so on. Both
these facts are correct. These people were in charge of providing money and
passports, and I received everything necessary from them, not as the members
of a counterrevolutionary organization but as workers of the ECCI apparatus.
The examination record contains my answers to the question What goals did
the counterrevolutionary, rightist-Trotskyist bloc set for itself? All of the Soviet
people knew about it, and I knew about it. I described the tasks of the counterrevolutionary organization in the Comintern the way it was depicted at party
meetings and at meetings of the ECCI Political Secretariat. It was known to
every [Comintern] worker because it was discussed at our meetings.

I implore you to request this examination record for review in order to satisfy yourself of the mythical quality [*legendarnost*] of the whole case. For example, I was held responsible for the fact that the students who were expelled
from the Chinese University were sent, in accordance with the decision of the
Orgburo of the CC VKP(b) (after the purge), to work in the factories of Moscow, Vladivostok, and other cities. Of course, you realize that I played no role
in that decision. I was accused of surrounding myself with provocateurs in
France while I was writing protests against the people being sent to me from
Moscow. Besides, being in France, I could not send back people [coming]
from Moscow.[80] In general, everything that I wrote, everything that I did to

correct the inflexibility of the Eastern Secretariat of the ECCI was turned against me. You remember my confrontation with the Arabs at the Seventh CI Congress and how you yourself dealt with it. That conflict is clear proof that I was fighting for the ECCI line, not for them.

I cannot lay out in sufficient detail everything that I was charged with. Since then, seven years have passed, and I have neither the verdict nor the indictment, and I was interrogated round the clock daily for thirteen months. If I had indeed committed some crime, I would have clearly remembered what it consisted of. However, since I did nothing [wrong], I could not remember this myth.

I know that Moskvin is to blame for my arrest. I stated it at the session of the trial by the Military Board, and it is written down in the minutes. Moskvin several times (jokingly) threatened me with arrest.

I ask you to initiate a petition to review my case. I have little faith that it will be successful, but maybe our procurator and the Supreme Court will be able to investigate all these problems better than before the war. In any case, whatever the result of this appeal may be, nothing can possibly change my attitude toward the party and the Soviet government. I have been, and will be, loyal to them until the end of my days. Unfortunately, I cannot prove my devotion with anything but my work. Therefore, despite repeated offers to change my work assignment, I continue to perform hard physical labor [as I have done] for all these seven years, dedicating the last of my strength to it. Even in dying, I will be able to say to myself that, even under the worst circumstances, I glorified the party and Soviet power, and gave all my efforts to them.

A. RAZUMOVA.

4 March 1945.

Copy.

REFERENCE FOR THE PRISONER.

The prisoner RAZUMOVA-KHIGEROVICH, Anna Lazarevna, came to the NKVD's Ukhta women's corrective labor camp on 29 June 1939. She is in custody in OLP No. 7—Vetlosian and works on the milling machine in the joiner shop. At work she has shown herself to be an efficient and enterprising worker, systematically overfulfilling her tasks by 200 percent and higher. She has rewards for her good work. Her personal life is exemplary. She has never incurred an administrative penalty.

Provisional head of the OURZ Ukhta

of the NKVD Izhemsky camp: Tarasevich

Senior inspector of the ORUZ: Skriabina.

25 June 1945.

Razumova's letter, like that of Elena Valter, illustrates the belief held by many within the ECCI apparatus that "enemies" had infiltrated the country and apparatus, a belief that remained unshaken even after being tortured and falsely convicted. Like Valter, Razumova maintained her faith in the NKVD: "I treated my investigators as comrades whom I had to help cleanse the party and the country of all sorts of garbage."

As revealing as her belief in the existence of "enemy" conspiracies is, her letter provides even more valuable insight into the NKVD. Her interrogators interpreted denunciations of her extracted from other prisoners and her official clandestine trips abroad as evidence of her membership in a counterrevolutionary organization. Her interrogators distorted strands of truth to weave a tapestry of lies. When she appealed to them to let her write to Yezhov to "inform the Comintern and the NKVD about what they supposedly did not know," they denied her paper. Only when she agreed to name the people involved in her mythical counterrevolutionary organization did she receive permission to write to Yezhov, whom she was convinced would rectify the situation. But having "confessed," she became guilty, and no one, least of all Yezhov, would have believed her protestations.

Perhaps Razumova's most tantalizing, though unsubstantiated, accusation is her belief that "Moskvin is to blame for my arrest." It may well have been the case, but more likely is the possibility that the nature of Razumova's and Moskvin's work involving clandestine activities abroad elicited the NKVD's suspicions. As head of the OMS, Moskvin had directed the clandestine trips abroad of Razumova and others like her, a fact that she undoubtedly told her interrogators. As one who spent many years in police and intelligence work, Moskvin no doubt had engaged in activities that could be misinterpreted as service to a foreign intelligence service.[81] Whatever occasioned Moskvin's arrest, Razumova's and Valter's letters suggest that some in the ECCI apparatus disliked and even feared him.

Razumova paid dearly for her letter to Yezhov. Having "confessed," she in essence forfeited her right to appeal. She was not released from the gulag until January 1955, after serving sixteen years of a fifteen-year sentence. She died in Moscow on 5 October 1973.

The Case of Béla Szántó

The previous case studies have been of people who worked in the ECCI apparatus. Although many ECCI staff members fell victim to the repression, even more political émigrés did so. How many foreigners living in the USSR were arrested is still unknown and will remain so until the opening of the archive of the security organs. What is known is that émigrés from border states and countries where the Communist Party was illegal—Germany, Poland, the Baltic states, Hungary, Bulgaria, Finland, and Romania—were frequent targets for arrest. At even greater risk were émigrés who had become VKP members. They were at risk for several reasons. Stalin and the VKP leadership, the NKVD, and the ECCI believed that agents from these countries disguised themselves as émigrés fleeing political prosecution. Based on this assumption, in 1937 and 1938 the Politburo ordered the arrest of people based on nationality. That their home governments offered them little or no extraterritorial protection made them even more vulnerable.

Here we examine the fates of five political émigrés. The Comintern archive contains materials on many émigrés who fell victim to the NKVD; these five have been selected because the available materials are sufficient to convey some nuances of their cases.

Although the orders to arrest foreigners came from the Politburo and the NKVD leadership, which individuals within a given émigré community were arrested sometimes seems arbitrary. At other times, as the case of Béla Szántó indicates, the choice of who was arrested had a bizarre logic to it, a logic rooted in the personal and political relations between those under arrest and those who remained free. The deep divisions within the Hungarian CP and Szántó's efforts in 1935–1936 to remove Kun from the CPH leadership seem to have played a significant role in Szántó's arrest, even though he had opposed Kun.

Béla Szántó was a lifelong revolutionary. Born in 1881, he joined the Social Democratic Party of Hungary at age nineteen. At the founding congress of the CPH, in November 1918, he was elected to the Central Committee, a post he held until 1921 and again from 1926 to 1929. During the short-lived Hungarian Soviet Republic of 1919, Szántó served as the people's commissar of defense. After the collapse of the republic, he emigrated to Vienna, where, from 1921 to 1926, he was the ECCI representative for the countries of southeastern Europe. In April 1926 he emigrated to the USSR and joined the VKP. From 1928 to 1931 he sat on the central council of the Profintern. From 1931 to December 1937 he worked for the Supreme Council of the National Economy (VSNKh) and then as director of the Scientific Library of the People's Commissariat of Heavy Industry (NKTP). During the 1935–1936 struggles within the CPH, Szántó actively opposed Kun and supported the temporary leadership that first challenged and then replaced Kun and Gross. But on 25 December 1937, Béla Szántó was expelled from the VKP, and his—and his family's—troubles began.

On 24 January 1938, Zoltán Szántó, secretary of the CPH Central Committee and Béla Szántó's brother, wrote the following letter to Dimitrov.

Document 57

Letter from Z. Szántó to Dimitrov about the arrest of his relatives and the expulsion of his brother, Béla Szántó, from the VKP, 24 January 1938. RGASPI, f. 495, op. 73, d. 57, l. 28. Original in German. Typewritten with handwritten notations and signatures.

The materials read by:
com. Manuilsky *Manuilsky*
com. Moskvin *Moskvin*
com. Gottwald *Gottwald*

Top secret.
24 January 1938
Dear comrade Dimitrov,
Upon my arrival in Moscow, I learned that:
1) My brother Béla Szántó[82] was expelled from the VKP(b);
2) The husband of my sister Elza, György Szamuely, was arrested by organs of the Commissariat for Internal Affairs along with the anti-party group of Béla Kun;
3) Stefan Natonek, the husband of my sister Rosa, with whom my daughter lives, was arrested by organs of the Commissariat for Internal Affairs.
By informing you about these facts, I ask you to explore whether these circumstances will impede my work in the Communist Party of Hungary.
24 January 1938.
With Communist greetings,
                    Zoltán Szántó
                    Z. Szántó.
Show to cc. Manuilsky, Moskvin and Gottwald.
G. D[imitrov].
25 January 1938.[83]

Zoltán's letter served the formal purpose of informing the ECCI leadership that members of his family had been arrested. Party members were expected to report to their superiors whenever family members or close acquaintances ran afoul of the law or the party. The letter fulfilled that obligation. Understandably, he asked Dimitrov if these events would affect his leadership of the Hungarian party. The letter also served a defensive purpose: to avoid being accused of consciously hiding information about ties to enemies. His letter raises a series of questions that cannot be easily answered. Zoltán's brother was expelled from the party, and his two brothers-in-law were arrested, yet he remained at liberty. Given that the Szántó family had struggled against Béla Kun, one wonders what precipitated the arrest of the brothers-in-law but not him or his brother. Given that Kun had, during his interrogation, denounced the Szántós, who had supported the attack against him in 1935–1936, why weren't all of the Szántó males arrested? Regrettably, the available evidence is too fragmentary to to explain NKVD logic.

What occasioned Béla Szántó's expulsion from the VKP was his authorship of a 1920 brochure entitled "The Class Struggle and the Dictatorship of the Proletariat in Hungary," which featured an introduction by Karl Radek, who along with Pyatakov, was a defendant at the January 1937 show trial. People with more tenuous ties to convicted "enemies" were arrested in this period, yet temporarily Béla Szántó remained free.

On 7 February 1937, Zoltán Szántó again wrote to Dimitrov, this time to announce that the "accusations that led to the expulsion of my brother Béla Szántó from the VKP(b) proved to be slander. The Molotovskii district VKP(b) committee refuted all accusations and readmitted [him] to the party without any party reprimand."[84] Because there is no evidence that Dimitrov intervened on Béla Szántó's behalf, his reinstatement most probably resulted from the January 1938 resolution of the VKP Central Committee calling on party organizations to review those members who had been unjustly expelled during the hunt for enemies in 1937.[85] But Béla Szántó had little time to savor his victory; he was arrested on 24 February 1938. In hindsight, this is hardly a surprise. When a party committee expelled a member, it routinely notified the NKVD (whether his party committee notified the NKVD of Szántó's reinstatement is unknown). In 1937–1938 expulsion from the party was sufficient to arouse the NKVD's suspicion and often prompt it into action.

Five days after Béla Szántó's arrest, his wife wrote to Dimitrov seeking his help in her appeal for her husband. Hers is typical of the many letters received by Dimitrov from relatives of those arrested.

Document 58

M. G. Szántó's letter to Dimitrov regarding the arrest of her husband, Béla Szántó, 29 February 1938. RGASPI, f. 495, op. 199, d. 184(II), l. 67. Original in Russian. Handwritten.

Comrade Dimitrov,

I have learned from the procurator that the case of my husband Szántó,
**Béla Aleksandrovich, arrested by the NKVD on 24 February 1938, has
been transferred to the Military Board of the Supreme Court.**

I know [my] *husband, and I have worked with him for thirty-four years,
and I am convinced that he is an honest fighter of the Bolshevik Party.*

*I know that you, comrade Dimitrov, are a very busy person and yet I am
asking you very, very much to find time to read my letter to the Military
Board in which I described the struggle of* [my] *husband against Béla Kun,
and also to review the attached materials*[86] *in order to satisfy yourself that
my belief in my husband's honesty is well grounded.*

*For ten years my husband has been conducting underground work for
the Comintern and the Profintern. Therefore, I believe, com. Dimitrov, that
your opinion will make a difference in evaluating my husband's case. I
beg you to take an interest in my husband's case and, if you find it possible,
to say some words on his behalf.*

Moscow, 29 February 1938.

Szántó M. G.

*5 Kaluzhskaia, Vystavochnyi pereulok 16/a, kvartira 55, Szántó Maria
Germanovna.*

Though written on 29 February, Dimitrov's office did not record receiving
the letter until 29 June.[87] What accounted for the delay is unclear. Perhaps it
is an indication of the extent to which the decimated ECCI bureaucracy was
unable to cope with its workload. Or perhaps the timing has nothing to do
with workload but rather with the fact that Dimitrov, who spent much of
mid-1938 in Kislovodsk tending to his health, made no effort to appeal on
Béla Szántó's behalf. Not until November 1939, almost a year after Yezhov's
fall, did Dimitrov order materials be prepared for such an appeal. Those materials show the extent to which personal and political conflicts contributed
to arrest. **Documents 59 and 60** are two of the documents prepared for the
appeal.

Document 59

József Révai's reference for Béla Szántó, written for the Cadres Department of the ECCI in
connection with Dimitrov's inquiry regarding Szántó's arrest, 11 November 1939.
RGASPI, f. 495, op. 199, d. 184(II), l. 73. Copy in Russian. Typewritten translation made
in the ECCI.

Secret.

11 November 1939

I copy a.k.

Trans. from Hungarian yes.

ABOUT SZÁNTÓ Béla.

He was one of the founders of the CP of Hungary. During the imperialist war, he was the chairman of the trade union of private employees and was one of the leaders of the left opposition in the Socialist Party of Hungary against the war.

He was a member of the CC of the CP of Hungary, and <u>after the declaration of the proletarian dictatorship, he was people's commissar for defense</u>. As far as I know, he worked well.

In emigration, he was a member of the CC of the CP of Hungary from the time of the reorganization of the CP of Hungary.

At the outset of the factional struggle [of 1928–30], he behaved insincerely and was double-faced. At first, he signed a protest adopted by the majority of the CC against the factional activities of Kun, and then he joined Kun's faction without any notice. During the factional struggle, he supported Kun to the end.

He dissociated himself from Kun only in the last years. <u>He wrote a book about the history of the Hungarian workers' movement</u>, which is undoubtedly a book with anti-Kun tendencies.[88] Among other things, in his book he criticizes the role of the repatriated prisoners of war in the creation of the CP of Hungary. The book correctly criticizes the left radicalism of this group of Béla Kun, but, as far as I remember, this book contained an incorrect, opportunistic evaluation of the history of Hungarian Social Democrats and an overestimation of the left opposition's role in the Socialist Party at the time of the war and the creation of the CP of Hungary.

When I analyze the reasons for Béla Szántó's taking anti-Kun positions [in 1935–1936] (although he followed him for almost ten years), I come to the following conclusions: there are objective and personal reasons.

1) The objective reason is the fact that, in 1929/1930, Szántó was indeed against the "left" policies of Béla Kun. This opposition was partially correct, because Szántó took a stance against the vacillations, against the personality, and against the dictatorial attitude of Béla Kun. But it would be wrong to assume that Béla Szántó's line was in many cases right-opportunist. He could not forgive Béla Kun for turning his back on him during the intraparty debates in 1929, when Szántó occupied a right-opportunist position (Szántó's point of view was opportunely characterized as right-opportunist in an <u>open letter from the ECCI to CPH</u>).[89]

2) The second reason is personal. I think that Szántó's opposition to Béla Kun started because he thought that Kun had betrayed him and his supporters, left him out, removed him from the CP of Hungary, etc. Kun was, indeed, "ungrateful" to his supporters when it was in his personal interests. For a

long time (1926–1928) Kun struggled to co-opt Szántó into the CC CP of Hungary; Kun protected Szántó <u>when harsh personal conflicts between Szántó and Alpari began (1928)</u>. Kun protected Szántó when the ICC forbade him to conduct responsible work in the CP of Hungary following [his] slanders against Alpari.[90] In 1928/1929, Kun took a conciliatory position toward the right-opportunist views of Szántó in order to deflect attacks against him. But when Kun saw that Szántó's situation in the party was becoming unbearable and that his support of Szántó could be harmful to him, he turned his back on Szántó, as, for example, in the Moscow Club [incident].[91]

Béla Szántó is a man with much political experience. I consider him a politically conscientious person, meaning that those questions with which he deals, he studies very scrupulously and carefully.

As far as I know, he is also very conscientious about organizational issues. At the time, he had a deep, practical knowledge of the Hungarian workers' movement, mainly in the trade union movement, and this old experience has been a strong asset for him. However, it is also a source of his weakness: administrative pettiness, overestimation of Social Democrats, etc. He always had deviations [prejudices?] against young party cadres who had not passed through the school of old Social Democracy. In the party and in emigration, he was not liked because he always gave himself airs and had a very high opinion about his former leading role. His main mistake was that he was prone to squabbles. His conflict with Alpari (who in 1928 protested his co-optation on to the CC and his transfer to work in the country [Hungary] based on his lack of ability) was a real squabble (I do not remember the details).

For a long time, he conducted international work, but I am not aware of details of this work, nor do I know anything about his work in the USSR and in the VKP(b), but I do not think that he belonged to any opposition. I never noticed in him any hostility toward the Comintern or the VKP(b) leadership. I think that he was unable to commit any hostile act. In connection with his squabbles, he was able to maintain personal relations with hostile elements, but I consider it very unlikely that he could consciously support the enemy or that he was an enemy himself.

RÉVAI, JÓZSEF

10 November 1939.

Document 60

Zoltán Szántó's statement about his brother Béla Szántó's ties with Béla Kun, written for the ECCI Organizational Committee regarding Béla Szántó's arrest, an inquiry begun at Dimitrov's request, 16 November 1939. RGASPI, f. 495, op. 199, d. 184(II), l. 76. Copy in Russian. Typewritten translation with handwritten additions made at the ECCI.

<u>Secret.</u>

16 November 1939.

1 copy ak.

Trans. from German yes.

<u>About Béla Szántó's ties with Béla Kun.</u>

From 1919 to 1928, Béla Szántó belonged to Béla Kun's narrow circle of friends. In Béla Kun, he saw a leader of Bolsheviks, a VKP(b) representative. This relationship continued until approximately 1928.

Béla Szántó committed mistakes in the CP of Hungary and was criticized for it. Kun refused to support him. *As a result,* relations between them cooled.

In studying the history of the Hungarian workers' movement and the history of the CP of Hungary, Béla Szántó came to the conclusion that the party's policy under Béla Kun's leadership, before and after the proletarian dictatorship in Hungary, was incorrect and un-Bolshevik. <u>Béla Szántó wrote a book about the history of the Hungarian revolution, in which he criticized Béla Kun</u>. This sharpened disagreements between Béla Szántó and Béla Kun and hostile *relations* developed. Kun stood in the way of *publishing this* [book].

When I came to Moscow in 1935, Béla Szántó told me about his conflicts with Béla Kun. He talked about the "fatal" role of Kun in the CP of Hungary. I had no reason to doubt Béla Szántó's sincerity.

In <u>1935</u>, Béla Szántó gave a report, "<u>Remembering the Hungarian Revolution,</u>" at the <u>Hungarian Club in Moscow</u>. In his speech, Béla Szántó criticized the foreign policy and military policy (strategy) of the Hungarian Soviet Republic, i.e., Béla Kun. Kun and some of his supporters harshly and rudely attacked Béla Szántó, but *this* speech was not *considered* "Trotskyist" and had nothing to do with Trotskyism.

Zoltán Szántó

Several features of these two documents deserve note. They address only political and personal squabbles between Béla Szántó and Kun. There is no mention of an anti-Comintern conspiracy or a counterrevolutionary organization of Hungarian émigrés, which were both adduced to justify Kun's arrest. This focus suggests strongly that the ECCI had determined that the best defense would be to provide evidence that Szántó and Kun were former allies turned antagonists and were, therefore, unlikely co-conspirators. The focus of the documents conveys the authors' implicit belief that personal and political reasons led to Szántó's arrest and that setting the record straight would aid in Szántó's release. Also noteworthy is the absence of strident, sectarian rhetoric. Only once, near the end of Zoltán Szántó's statement, is Trotskyism even mentioned, and then only to distance his brother from that charge. Rather, what is striking about these two documents is what they imply about the debates within the Hungarian party over intraparty and Comintern policies and the personal squabbles and political struggles that often divided its members in emigration. Such divisions, which also riddled other émigré communities, no doubt played a role in the arrest of other émigrés.[92]

While the materials for Béla Szántó's appeal were being gathered, Dimitrov received a letter from Béla Szántó himself in which he protested his innocence and asked Dimitrov to appeal on his behalf. On 26 February 1940, Dimitrov sent to the USSR procurator, Pankratov, a letter requesting a review of Béla Szántó's case: "I ask you to take all appropriate measures for a speedy review of the case."[93] He enclosed Révai's and Z. Szántó's statements and other relevant materials compiled by the Cadres Department. Dimitrov's appeal on Béla Szántó's behalf had its desired affect. In March 1940 the military procurator for the Moscow Military District sent the ECCI a series of questions germane to the review of Szántó's case. **Document 66** reproduces that letter. It was the office of the military procurator that, in the course of reviewing appeals, at times clashed with the NKVD over the reasons for the arrests of some émigrés.

Document 61

Inquiry from the military procurator of the Moscow Military District to the ECCI regarding the case of Béla Szántó, 9 March 1940. RGASPI, f. 495, op. 199, d. 184 (II), ll. 82–82ob. Original in Russian, on letterhead. Typewritten with handwritten additions.

TOP SECRET Copy No.*1*

9/10 March 1940 No. *01629*

Please refer to our number when responding.

TO THE EXECUTIVE COMMITTEE OF THE COMMUNIST INTERNATIONAL.

In connection with the case of the for[mer] member of the Communist Party of Hungary (former People's Commissar for the Military Affairs of the Hungarian Soviet Republic) SZÁNTÓ Béla Aleksandrovich, which was forwarded to the Office of Military Procurator of the Moscow Military District for evaluation, in order to ensure the most complete and thorough inquiry in the case, I ask you to communicate [answers to] the following: [In margin: *To c. Privorotskaia / Prepare the answer / 13/III Guliaev.*]

1) Whether, since 1927, SZÁNTÓ has had differences with the rest of the CC CP of Hungary regarding questions of party work. [What was] the essence of these differences?

2) Whether the condemnation of SZÁNTÓ's line on this issue by the Politi-

cal Secretariat of the Comintern in November 1929 and by the Second Congress of the CP of Hungary was a result of the CC having incorrect information about his actual position at that time.

3) Whether that CC of the CP of Hungary was exposed and dissolved by the decision of the Comintern.

4) [What was] the essence of the differences between SZÁNTÓ, Béla, and Béla KUN in 1935?

5) [What was] the decision of the International Control Commission about SZÁNTÓ regarding his differences with the CC of the CP of Hungary in 1935?

6) Whether the CC of the CP of Hungary was dissolved in 1936 and what the reason was for its dissolution.

7) Whether after the Seventh Comintern Congress the newly elected CC ordered SZÁNTÓ Béla to write a book on the history of the Hungarian revolution.

MILITARY PROCURATOR OF THE MVO [Moscow Military District]
JURIST OF THE MILITARY DIVISION

Ankudinov
ANKUDINOV

[. . .]

Strikingly, what concerned the judicial review board were neither legal nor procedural issues; rather, it addressed political issues relating to struggles within the CPH and Szántó's personal and political relations with Kun. In fact, these questions were very relevant. To prove that he was not a part of Kun's alleged counterrevolutionary organization, Szántó needed to prove that he and Kun disliked each other and viewed politics rather differently. Under Yezhov, such logical arguments had little influence; but in the post-Yezhov era, they could not be entirely ignored.

Dimitrov forwarded Andukinov's letter, received on 11 March 1940, to the Cadres Department and ordered its staff to prepare answers. Two weeks later, the head of the Cadres Department, Guliaev, sent the following report to Andukinov. Guliaev clearly relied heavily on Révai's and Zoltán Szántó's evaluations (Documents 59 and 60) in writing this report.

Document 62

Reply from the head of the ECCI Cadres Department, P. Guliaev, to the military procurator regarding Béla Szántó, 27 March 1940. RGASPI, f. 495, op. 199, d. 184 (II), ll. 85–87. Copy in Russian. Typewritten with handwritten additions.[94]

Hungary
27 January 1940 Szántó Béla   Top secret.
TO THE MILITARY PROCURATOR OF THE MOSCOW MILITARY DISTRICT.

c. ANKUDINOV.

Moscow, Arbat 37.

In response to your request No. 01629 of 10 January 1940 regarding BÉLA SZÁNTÓ, based on the materials available to us, we inform you of the following:

During the time when Béla Szántó was a member of the CC and one of the leaders of the Hungarian Communist Party (1926–1929), he displayed opportunistic views toward the Hungarian workers' movement. The 1929 open letter from the ECCI about Szántó's views read: "Szántó fell into opportunism [by] overlooking the decisions of the Fourth Profintern Congress, the Sixth Comintern World Congress, and all of the Third Period. This misunderstanding of the character of the Third Period [was] the most dangerous deviation of the present moment. Szántó denied the leftward movement of the working class in Hungary, confused the situation in the workers' movement with the situation in the increasingly fascist trade unions, and promoted in the Foreign Committee absolutely baseless pessimistic views on the prospects for the revolutionary movement in Hungary. He went so far in his petit bourgeois evaluation of the mood of and the situation within the working class that he considered large groups of the working class lost for the revolutionary movement and developed a 'theory' about the decomposition of the workers' movement."

These opportunistic views of Szántó's were condemned by the ECCI Political Secretariat and by the Second Congress of the CP of Hungary. The condemnation of Szántó's line was not the result of incorrect information by the CC of the CP of Hungary at the time but was a result of mistakes committed by him, which he himself admitted, as the ECCI's open letter also pointed out. It is true that that CC also committed serious political and organizational mistakes, which were sharply criticized in the ECCI's open letter. However, that CC was not dissolved.

At the time of factional struggle in the CP of Hungary, approximately 1928–1929, Béla Szántó was a supporter of Béla Kun and belonged to his narrow circle of friends. Later Kun's attitude toward Szántó changed and became hostile. This was due to the fact that Béla Szántó wrote a book about the history of the Hungarian revolution, in which he criticized Béla Kun's activities in that period. They disagreed mainly over the evaluation of foreign policy during the proletarian dictatorship in Hungary and of the Hungarian working class.

In 1935, Szántó gave a speech about the history of the Hungarian revolution and the Hungarian Red Army in the Hungarian Club for political émigrés. In the discussion that followed, Béla Kun's supporters accused Szántó of Trotskyist deviations. Regarding this, Szántó Zoltán (brother of Béla Szántó) reports that Béla Szántó's speech at that time was basically correct and "had nothing to do with Trotskyism."

This question was not reviewed in the ICC in 1935, and, in general, the question about him was not raised. In 1936, Szántó Béla appealed to the ICC to lift the party penalty (a harsh reprimand with a <u>warning, which was imposed on him in 1928 for slanders against a certain comrade</u> [Alpari]). The NKTP party committee (at that time Szántó worked as a director of the library in the NKTP) gave him then a positive reference and supported his appeal to lift the part[y] penalty, but there was no ICC decision on this question.

On [the basis of] the resolution of the ECCI Secretariat, the CC of the CP of Hungary was dissolved in 1936 for sabotaging the decisions of the Seventh Congress of the Comintern, for gross violations of the rules of secrecy, for suppressing self-criticism, and because among the CC members were agents of the Hungarian police. The majority of the members of that CC have been arrested by the NKVD.

In 1937–1938, Szántó Béla appealed to the ECCI Secretariat regarding publication of his book, but this question remained under deliberation.

HEAD OF THE CADRES DEPARTMENT
OF THE ECCI

GULIAEV

No. **6476**
"27" March 1940
[. . .]

One month later Szántó was released from custody and readmitted to the VKP. After more than two years in prison, he rejoined what remained of his family. In 1945 he returned to Hungary.

Béla Szántó's case illustrates several aspects of the repression that deserve further research. Personal and political differences were often intertwined factors that contributed to an arrest. Directly or indirectly, his arrest was bound up with Kun's political behavior and arrest. The second is that, although the political struggles within émigré communities in the USSR played a role in determining who was arrested and who was not, being an émigré was of overriding importance in 1937–1938, when the NKVD arrested people based on their nationality. Third, following Yezhov's fall, cases could be and were successfully appealed. Although the review process moved slowly and the criteria for what constituted convincing evidence remained intensely political, some of those who had been unjustly arrested were released and their good names restored. During the Yezhovshchina, justice was arbitrary. Béla Szántó survived and regained his freedom; his brothers-in-law were executed.

The Cases of Anni Etterer and Franz Guber

At meetings of the ECCI party organization from 1935 on, Dimitrov and other ECCI leaders expressed their frustration with political émigrés who worked for the Comintern but refused to learn Russian and to participate fully in Soviet political life. Their concern was understandable. Many émigrés learned only enough Russian to get by. As is often the case in immigrant communities throughout the world, they socialized with people who spoke their native language and frequented ethnic clubs. Anni Etterer was such a person.

Born into a German working-class family in 1913, Anni Etterer joined the German Communist Party in 1931. She and her husband, Franz Guber, worked as party activists until she was arrested in Germany in 1933. After her release from prison in late 1934, she emigrated to Prague and then to the USSR, where she joined her husband, who had arrived in 1933. Although Etterer had lived in the USSR for three years at the time of her arrest in March 1938, she spoke virtually no Russian; Guber spoke some Russian. At her job in the International Agrarian Institute she spoke German; at home she spoke German; with her friends she spoke German. Hers was a German-speaking world. But the security that that world had provided proved to be her downfall.

After Etterer's arrest in March 1938, Guber was expelled from the German CP. Although his situation was very tenuous, Guber behaved courageously. He appealed to the ICC for reinstatement to the party and was finally reinstated in the fall of 1939. From the moment of his wife's arrest, he worked persistently to secure her release. He appealed on her behalf to Dimitrov, to the ICC, and to the German CP representative in the ECCI. Florin, the ICC Secretary, supported Guber's efforts and wrote to Dimitrov requesting a review of Etterer's case.

Document 63 includes the packet of materials that comprised the ECCI's 1939 appeal on behalf of Anni Etterer. It has four parts—a cover letter sent by Tatarenko, Dimitrov's assistant, to A. A. Andreev, a Politburo member who served on a commission to review cases of unjust repression; a letter from Florin, the ICC secretary, to Dimitrov requesting a review of Etterer's case; and two letters written by Franz Guber on his wife's behalf.

Document 63

Materials relating to a request for a review of the case of Anni Etterer, 13 December 1938–8 January 1939.[95] RGASPI, f. 495, op. 74, d. 133a, ll. 5–17. Original in Russian. Typewritten with handwritten additions.

TO THE SECRETARY OF THE CC VKP(B)
com. ANDREEV.
On the orders from com. G. DIMITROV. we are forwarding to you a letter from the ICC and the materials on Anni Etterer and Franz Guber for your review.
We also inform you that the ICC's letter and [other] materials have been sent to com. BERIA, L. P.
SECRETARIAT OF com. DIMITROV:
Tatarenko
[. . .]
Sent in package No. 18
11 January 1939. Stern.

No. 62
[Written across page by Dimitrov:]
Send to c. Beria.
Besides, send to c. Andreev (CC) separately, indicating that the ICC's letter and the materials were sent to c. Beria.
G.D.
9.1.39.

Top secret.

TO THE GENERAL SECRETARY OF THE COMINTERN
Com. DIMITROV, G. M.
Franz Guber, a member of the CP of Germany from 1926, has appealed to the ICC with a statement in which he asks for a complete reinstatement into the party.[96] The German party expelled him in connection with the arrest of his wife, Anni ETTERER, by NKVD organs on 9 March 1938.
In his statement, Guber says that he has always considered his wife to be an honest Communist and that the letters that he has received from her from exile only strengthen his conviction.
The ICC material on Anni Etterer and Franz Guber can be reduced to the following.
Anni Etterer was born in 1913; her parents were workers. She worked as a clerk and received a professional education in 1930. A member of the CP of Germany from 1931, she conducted work among women in the construction workers' trade union in Bavaria. In 1933 she was arrested in Munich and spent one year in prison as a hostage for her husband, Franz Guber. Between

her release in March 1934 and December 1934 she was a party instructor in a district committee. Following a decision by the party, she emigrated to Prague, from where, at her husband's request and with the consent of the party, she came to the USSR.

Franz GUBER was born in 1910. His parents were workers (his father was an old S.D., a member of the CPG from 1920 or 1921. After Hitler came to power, he was put in a concentration camp, where he spent more than four years. His mother spent three years in a concentration camp as a hostage for her son). He is a plasterer by trade. Between 1923 and 1926 he was a Pioneer. In 1926 he became a Komsomol member and, in the same year, a member of the CPG. He was a delegate to the Gotha Conference of the children's Communist groups in 1924 [and] a delegate to the Eleventh Komsomol Congress, where he was elected a candidate member of the Komsomol CC. He was a delegate to the Party Congress in Wedding in 1929 and worked as a party worker until Hitler came to power. In the underground period (until September 1933) he was the organizational secretary of the South-Bavarian committee of the CPG. In September 1933, in accordance with the party's decision, he emigrated to the USSR.

Regarding their work in Germany and their behavior before the class enemy, both Anni Etterer and Franz Guber have good references.

In the USSR, Anni Etterer worked as a typist in the International Agrarian Institute, and Franz Guber studied in the MLSh, where he received a party reprimand for mistakes regarding school discipline and for lack of self-control.

Here are some abstracts from Anni Etterer's letters cited by **Guber**:

"I cannot understand a thing. I have spent four and a half months in prison. . . . I think and think, but I cannot find an explanation. I was interviewed once by an investigator. As far as I could understand (without an interpreter), he was asking me about my biography. I answered in my really bad Russian. I signed everything, although I could not read it . . . because until now I have not lost faith in my own comrades, in our Soviet power. When I came to the investigator the second time, he told me so I could understand him (in Russian): [I have] finished [the investigation], [you] are not guilty, you are not a spy, everything is good with you. . . . However, I received quite a shock when, on 16 July, I was sentenced to five years in a labor camp for counterrevolutionary activities.[97] I want to tell you that what supports me is that I have always acted as a class-conscious Communist, that I am imprisoned here, innocent. . . ."

Franz Guber outlined his ideas about the possible reasons that led to the arrest of his wife.

Among the most important of them are:

A. In the Agrarian Institute, Anni Etterer used to type materials in languages unknown to her, on orders from her boss, who was [later] arrested by the NKVD;

B. Guber's neighbor, in his opinion, has a suspicious lifestyle and may have slandered [Etterer]. (This neighbor is using the room as a reserve while living in a different place. In this room, she is visited by a man of unclear origin, and she is typing something all the time.)

We consider it appropriate to raise the question of reviewing the materials on Anni Etterer with the appropriate state organs.

ENCL.—16 pages.[98]

SECRETARY OF THE ICC:

FLORIN

8 January 1939.

TO THE INTERNATIONAL CONTROL COMMISSION OF THE ECCI.

Dear comrades!

Here are my considerations regarding the arrest of my wife, Anni Etterer. After I thoroughly thought over all the events, I singled out the following facts, which might have led to my wife's arrest.

1. The International Agrarian Institute [MAI] (where my wife worked).

For three–four months before my wife's arrest, there were arrests among the leading administrative workers and among researchers. Among them was the deputy director of MAI, a Pole, who spoke German well. My wife *got a job* as a German typist with the help of com. Weber, who at that time (1936) was the representative of the German party in the ECCI. My wife told me that this deputy director once called her to his office and asked [her] to maintain secrecy. [He told her] that she had no right to talk about it with anybody, including myself. I found it to be quite right given current conditions, especially since the MAI was a party institute.

In early 1937 (I do not remember when exactly), my wife boasted jokingly after work that she knew "several languages" since she was typing in different languages. Thus, she told me that she was typing manuscripts probably in Polish, as well as in one of the Balkan languages, and in Russian. That she *typed* letter after letter when copying from handwritten manuscripts. Although there was a Russian typist in the Agrarian Institute, she was frequently ill. I do not now know whether or not she reported to work in that period.

Therefore, it could have happened that my wife could have been involved, without her knowledge, in a counterrevolutionary activity. What kind of documents were those? My wife could not know that, because she does not know a word in languages other than her native one. Until her arrest, she knew in Russian only what was necessary to know in a tram or in a grocery store. She worked in the Agrarian Institute, [but] dealt only in the German language, with German comrades, and spoke only in German.

When my wife learned about the arrest of the director, she told me: "You see, we have not yet learned how to recognize the enemy. That is why this person was so kind and attentive to his staff. You see, here, too, one has to be on guard!"

Thus, this could be one factor that could be crucial for her arrest. Another thing is whether there were sufficient grounds for such a decision, such as what happened to my wife. First, my wife followed her boss's orders. Second, she did not know the contents of the documents that she was typing in different languages. She was sure that they were somehow related to scientific agrarian problems. When she told me about it, I did not think it bad, either. However, a thorough investigation by NKVD organs could easily have clarified these things. Therefore, if this did take place, then my wife was an unwilling victim of the class enemy. But my wife did not even mention this [aspect of the] case, because she was not asked about **anything** like that.

My wife would have never been able to commit, on her own initiative, an act hostile to the [working] class or to the party. I also want to note that I have a very strong influence on my wife and that she would have never done anything that might be harmful to me. I met my wife when she was seventeen, at the age of puberty. For many young people, this is an emotionally difficult period, and she **too had problems** then. Her mother, a hysterical woman, tormented her so much that my wife, who is very sensitive, tried to take poison. However, her mother noticed this and after that was a little kinder to her. Then I met my wife and educated her in a Communist spirit. This explains my wife's attitude toward me.

2. Our neighbor, a Russian named Glinkina.

The room next to our apartment is occupied by citizen Glinkina. She claims to be a Narkomzdrav [People's Commissariat of Health] inspector. This is what happened to this person.

1. This so-called permanent apartment of hers here in the Oktiabrskoe pole (VLIEM building, site No. 1, dom 1, kvartira 7) must be her reserve apartment. Sometimes she does not show up for weeks. She does not sleep there more than four–six times in the course of a month. For the most part, she is here on weekends, but inconsistently. Sometimes she spends three–four days here, and then she is not seen for fourteen days or even a whole month.

2. On rare occasions (once every half a year or more), a man comes to visit her and stays for a week. She claims that he is her husband. In these periods, she is always at home. Naturally, a question arises, Where and how does this woman spend her time? Why is she away from home the rest of the time? Where does she sleep the other days? What if he is not her husband and uses this room only as a secret meeting place?

3. When she is in her room, she types all the **time**. Then she regularly types until 2 a.m., and sometimes for the whole day. The typewriter is always in her room. (She has been typing hard since this [past] summer.)

4. In August or September 1937 her friend lived with her for about two months. This woman gave us the impression that she lived there illegally. It is worth mentioning that they never left the apartment together, but always ten–fifteen minutes apart from each other. Then, too, the neighbor was not at

home for a whole week, and [her] friend stayed alone in the room. We think that she lived there without being registered.

5. Already in late 1937 my wife and I thought this visit by the man, and the friend's living there illegally, and the strange use of the room (at the time of a great need for apartments) to be suspicious. My suspicions were especially heightened by the continual typing. That is why (after my wife's arrest) I frequently tried to disturb her when she was typing in order to see her reaction, and I must say that each time she was very frightened. Once I wanted to send my wife a package of food, but I did not have paper. I went to the neighbor and asked for some paper. She gave me different kinds of typing paper. The used parts had already been cut off, but still she looked through the paper once again, smiled, and said that it is important that there was nothing written on the paper, because there (i.e., in the camp) everything is being checked.

6. In November or December 1937 another Russian woman with a child, **her** mother-in-law, and a nurse moved in with our neighbor. That woman worked somewhere as a typist. In late February the following happened: one evening, an NKVD worker in civilian clothes, accompanied by one witness, came to our apartment and inquired about this Russian [who had] recently moved in. He [also] asked about some particular typist (I no longer remember the name). He entered our room and asked whether my wife could type on a Russian typewriter and what her name was. I replied by giving my wife's name and by stating that she could not type in Russian. At that point, the [NKVD] worker said that the last name was different, and went to the neighbor.

Their nurse later told us that they were very upset, pale, and were crying. She could only hear how the [NKVD] worker was asking where certain things were—a piano, etc. After that, they sent her out [of the room].

Maybe here one could find a possible explanation. Those people may have been class enemies. That woman with a child, mother-in-law, and nurse moved out of here in late April of that year.

Maybe that inspector wrote a denunciation in order to protect herself. In any case, it seems to me that that woman has provided sufficient grounds to suspect her. My wife writes me about it from the camp:

"Is that neighbor still living there with her relatives? The idea that she had a hand in this case nags me. Do you remember that civilian visitor, in late February? I wish them nothing good."

Maybe it is a prejudice on my wife's and my part, but this phrase indicates that, in the final account, my wife has no idea why she is imprisoned [or] in what kind of counterrevolutionary activity she engaged. Because otherwise, she might have guessed where the denunciation came from.

Thus, if my wife and I knew who the accuser was, it would have been very easy to clarify [the case] by direct confrontation. Whether or not my guess is correct, I still think that something is wrong with my Russian neighbor. I also spoke about this to Walter Dittbender, before my wife was arrested. Walter Dittbender worked then in the German delegation. He told me not to conduct an investigation [and said] that I should not interfere in this case, since it was the Russians' problem. That is why I made no further use of this incident.

Eight days after the visit of the NKVD worker, my wife was arrested.

It is possible that the NKVD worker wanted to verify, among other things, whether my wife could type on a Russian typewriter; maybe his visit was related to the documents in the Agrarian Institute, but it would have been a strange inquiry. Anyway, my wife was not asked about this.

3. <u>Correspondence abroad</u>.

My wife and I maintained correspondence only with our parents. We used a transfer address in Prague and one address in Stockholm. Corresponding with these friends was limited only to forwarding letters to our parents in Germany. We received one letter from, and sent one letter to, Spain, where a Bavarian comrade, Joseph Wimmer, is fighting. By the way, all the correspondence was received under my name and at my address. Therefore, I should have been held responsible.

4. <u>Our personal ties in the USSR</u>.

My wife had no ties other than those that I had. The party knows about all of our acquaintances. I cannot imagine that my wife could have been arrested because of any of these ties. It is possible that one of the arrested denounced her, but it is very unlikely.

This is all that I wanted and had to say in this regard. I stress once again that a thorough investigation might be able to clarify everything.

With Communist greetings

F. Guber

13 December 1938.
Translation correct.
11. I. 1939 < . . . >

<u>TO THE INTERNATIONAL CONTROL COMMISSION OF THE ECCI.</u>

Dear comrades, I have just received, for the first time in two months, a letter from [my] wife. I definitely want to familiarize you with the most important sections of this letter. [My] wife writes:

"25 November 1938. My dear, beloved Franz. Regarding my case, I have to tell you the following: I could not send you the draft [of my appeal]; all petitions and statements are being forwarded from here. I have already written to the procurator of the USSR, Vyshinsky. In the coming days, I will write to the Party Control Commission. I have already written to you <u>that I did not appear before any court, only the Special Council</u> (OSO) (underlined by me—F.G.), which sentenced me to five years in a labor camp for counterrevolutionary activities. <u>I was interrogated only once, and they asked me about [the facts of] my biography. Despite repeated requests, I was not given an interpreter</u> (underlined by me—F.G.). On 7 April 1938 the questioning was finished, and the investigator told me, as best as I could understand, that the investigation was over, that I was not a spy, that I was innocent, and that I was a good person.

"I was not given any materials or charged with anything. I signed the entire examination record although I understood nothing in it, since I thought that it was normal; besides, I trusted the Soviet organs of justice completely. (underlined by me—F.G.). The power of attorney for my money is not needed, since it will be sent directly from here to the institute. I will follow your other advice; i.e., I will write to a deputy of the Supreme Soviet. Thus, if you will do something on my behalf, what I have written to you today will be sufficient.

"You are right [when you say] that it is necessary to be strong-willed, but everything has its limits. I cannot tell you in what state I sometimes find myself. You know, it is good to be a Communist, but because I always act in such a way, I can achieve very little. It is impossible to forget what kind of people surround us here. I have been working in the forest for two months, and it is very hard for me. I have enough exercise while working in the forest. I have lost most of my [sense of] humor already, but I will regain it when I am with you.

"In general, I am healthy, and I do not lose courage. Of course, I will follow your advice and will retain my will power. At least I am not losing hope."

Dear comrades, let me nevertheless note that I absolutely do not know what else to add here. At this point, I will not refer to Marxism-Leninism. [I wonder] if the class enemy had a hand in this case in order to undermine Socialism for honest Communists and to turn friends of the USSR into the enemies of the USSR. If this is not so, then I do not understand the program, strategy, and tactics of Communism anymore. In any case, it is obvious that this is an unprecedented enemy sortie against Soviet democracy. By such means, it is thus possible to create misfortune for any honest person [simply] by not giving him a chance to defend himself.

I reiterate my request for a thorough investigation of my wife's case. This investigation might produce other useful results for Soviet power. It is necessary to thoroughly question my wife via interpreter, [to let her] confront the slanderers with translations of the examination records, which she will have to sign, to let her write an explanation.

With Communist greetings,

Franz Guber.

Moscow, 10 February 1938.
Translation correct < . . .>
11.I.1939.

Although émigrés suffered heavily during the Yezhovshchina, not all émigrés were arrested. Fortunately for Etterer, her husband remained free to plead her case. Her ignorance of Russian (and other languages) appears to have been her undoing. She spoke German at work and typed materials in languages that she did not understand for her Polish boss. One can only imagine how poorly educated, overzealous NKVD agents, who probably spoke only Russian, interpreted the activities within a Soviet institution (the International Agrarian Institute) in which Russian was rarely spoken and "suspicious elements" (Poles and Germans) prepared materials in foreign languages. Etterer also signed whatever documents her NKVD interrogators put before her. In this case, however, her ignorance of Russian may have been her saving grace. Her arbitrary treatment by the NKVD and the court worked to her long-term advantage. People who confessed to crimes, whether they were guilty or not, usually forfeited their right to appeal. In Etterer's case, her ignorance of Russian provided a reasonable basis for her appeal.

The way Guber constructed his wife's appeal is intriguing. Besides playing heavily on his wife's ignorance of Russian, he cast suspicion on their neighbor, whose role, if any, in Etterer's arrest is unclear. He portrayed the neighbor not only as the possible accuser but also as a potential class enemy who had two apartments at a time when housing was extremely scarce and as a suspicious woman who entertained a man whom Guber doubted was her husband. Consciously or unconsciously, Guber sought to defend his wife by casting suspicion on others and used the political rhetoric of the day to do so. In his hands, what may have been an amorous affair became suspicious behavior by potential "enemies." Denouncing and casting suspicion on others was a common behavior of the period.

Thanks to her husband's and the ECCI's efforts, Etterer won her freedom in March 1940, three years before her scheduled release. Soon after, she was reinstated in the German CP and received a Soviet passport. Guber had been restored to the German CP in September 1939. But the couple's troubles were not over. On 11 September 1941, after the war with Germany had begun, the NKVD arrested Guber "as a socially dangerous element." Following his arrest, Etterer and their daughter were exiled to Karaganda oblast. In February 1946 she returned to Germany.

Regrettably, Etterer's tragic story did not end there. In the summer of 1962 a man arrived at the motor pool of the All-Union Institute of Experimental Medicine, where, from 1938 until his arrest, Guber had worked as a chauffeur. The man, a German political émigré who had been a chauffeur there before the war, chatted with the workers. He told them that he had been arrested before the war, was living in Tomsk oblast, and was on his way to Riga for a rest. He asked them about his wife, who had also been arrested. When the KGB heard of this, it began a search for Guber, but without success. KGB officials came to the conclusion that Guber had taken advantage of another man's death, exchanged documents, and left the gulag under an assumed name.

The following year, Etterer arrived in Moscow from Berlin. After visiting the institute where her husband had worked and being told by the motor pool workers that Guber had been there the year before, she requested East German officials to press the KGB to reopen the search for Guber.

On 24 April 1964, *Izvestiia* ran an article entitled "Two Lives" that recounted Etterer's story and her search for Guber. The article produced an unexpected ending. It turned out that before the war, a German political émigré named Mark Karlinsky had worked with Guber at the motor pool. Both men were arrested about the same time, as was Karlinsky's wife. The motor pool workers in 1962 mistakenly took Karlinsky for Guber, who had died in 1942, eight months after his arrest. In a letter to Etterer, Karlinsky wrote: "Fate has played tricks on all of us. But this final trick, this unfortunate muddle, is the most terrible of tricks."[99]

The Case of Petko Petkov

After Kirov's murder in December 1934, Stalin, the Central Committee, and the ECCI urged all Communists to be vigilant and to signal the appropriate authorities about any "suspicious" activity of which they were aware. Denunciations became a measure of proof of one's vigilance, of being a "real Bolshevik." Denunciations of comrades by comrades, of citizens by citizens, were common during the Stalin era. Fervently held beliefs, party discipline, xenophobia, ignorance, petty jealousies, and mean-spiritedness were but some of the reasons that people denounced others. We have already seen examples of denunciations.[100] But the case of Petko Petkov deserves special note because it suggests how difficult it is for historians to attribute motives to those who denounced others. As **Document 64** indicates, between 1934 and 1937, Petkov denounced "a large number of . . . Bulgarian Trotskyists and spies" and other "Trotskyist bandit-spies." He explained these denunciations as resulting from party discipline: "I only fulfilled my duty to the party and workers." His declaration that "I feel very uncomfortable talking with you about it, but I was compelled to," implies that the demands of party discipline left him no choice but to denounce some of his comrades. Using Yezhov as a personal reference implies that he believed his behavior to be correct. But Dimitrov's assertion that at least one of Petkov's denunciations was "a stupid insinuation and slander" raises questions about why Petkov did what he did.

Born in 1906, Petkov joined the Bulgarian Komsomol in 1918 and the Bulgarian CP in 1924. In 1928, after serving a two-year prison sentence for political crimes in Bulgaria, he emigrated to Vienna, where he took courses and worked as an intelligence operative for the Fourth Department of the Red Army Staff. He emigrated to the USSR in 1932 and two years later began work for the Comintern, first in Moscow and then in Alma-Ata. In 1937 he was arrested and sentenced to fifteen years of hard labor. In 1940, Petkov appealed his conviction.

Central to his appeal was his argument that his denunciations of "Trotskyist bandit-spies" proved his Communist credentials and loyalty to the party. The Comintern archive contains several documents relating to his appeal, two of which are reproduced in Document 64. The first is a 1940 letter of inquiry about Petkov from Bochkov, the USSR procurator; the second is Dimitrov's response to that inquiry. Although Dimitrov offered no comments about those arrested as a result of Petkov's denunciations, his contention that there was no basis for Petkov's slanderous denunciation of a comrade who remained free suggests Dimitrov's disdain for Petkov's action. But in this period of persistent calls for vigilance, the Petkovs of the world could and did denounce others. Whatever Dimitrov's opinion of Petkov's actions, given Dimitrov's own repeated calls for vigilance, he was in no position to condemn Petkov for carrying out his orders.

Document 64

Inquiry from the procurator of the USSR, Bochkov, to Dimitrov regarding Petko N. Petkov, and Dimitrov's reply, 13 October 1940–21 January 1941. RGASPI, f. 495, op. 73, d. 122, ll. 7–10. Original in Russian. Typewritten on letterhead with handwritten notations.

[Written by Dimitrov: *To c. Bogdanov, c. Belov. Prepare an answer. 19.11.40 G.D.*]

TOP SECRET
"13" October 1940[101]
No. 55373

TO THE GENERAL SECRETARY OF THE EXECUTIVE COMMITTEE OF THE COMINTERN

com. DIMITROV

[In response] to your No. 377 of 17 July 1940.[102]

Due to a need that has arisen in connection with the continuing verification of the case of PETKOV, Petko Nikolov (aka YANTAROV, Ognian), please provide the information that you have about <u>PETKOV's signals regarding the un-</u><u>masking of individuals with counterrevolutionary moods</u>.

In his declarations and testimony, Petkov states that between 1934 and 1937 he wrote multiple declarations exposing a number of individuals as enemies of the party, in particular:

In late 1934 or early 1935, [he] sent a statement to the Foreign Bureau of the CPBul [Bulgarian CP] and <u>to the International Control Commission</u> in which he outlined the anti-party actions of <u>GENCHEV, Khristo</u>.

In August 1937, [he] sent a statement to the Bulgarian section of the ECCI regarding the anti-party moods of the former worker of the CC VKP(b) <u>YUR-DAN-MARIN</u>.[103] <u>In an August 1937 statement sent to you, he informed [you]</u> <u>about the anti-Soviet, Trotskyist declarations of</u> PAPENCHEV (ATANASOV), Boyan Ivanovich, who was his predecessor at work. <u>In August 1937 [he sent]</u> <u>to the Foreign Bureau of the CPBul a statement exposing the anti-Soviet</u> <u>moods of certain individuals</u>. If PETKOV indeed sent such statements, please send copies of them.

In addition to this, please send a copy of PETKOV's 1937 statement <u>in</u> <u>which he condemns the factional policy</u> of the former sectarian leadership (ISKROV-BOIKOV-ROSSEN, etc.)[104] and criticizes himself for failing to actively participate in exposing the promoters of this line.

PROCURATOR OF THE USSR

BOCHKOV

[Dimitrov's reply:]
Sent on 21.I.41 in package No. 11
Tatarenko

<u>Top secret.</u>

TO THE PROCURATOR OF THE USSR
<u>COM. BOCHKOV.</u>

[In response] to No. 55373 of 13 November 1940, I inform you that in his letter of 22 August to the CPB[ul] delegation in the ECCI, PETKOV, Petko Nikolov, wrote:

"In order to clearly present my political essence, I consider it necessary, although to the detriment of secrecy, to convey to you the following regarding my activities, if I can call it such, to unmask counterrevolutionary, Trotskyist bandit-spies.

1. I exposed the Trotskyist spy Boyan Ivanovich Papenchev (Atanasov) to NKVD organs. I exposed him in such a way that, through him, a large number of our other Bulgarian Trotskyists and spies were exposed. I had already declared everything in my statement to the NKVD on 20 May 1936, i.e., before the Kamenev and Zinoviev trial. He was a scoundrel who got in with our leaders and did nasty things behind their backs.

2. Georgy,[105] if I am not mistaken, was a carpenter from Plevna, a Trotskyist double-dealer, the same kind of a scoundrel. I exposed him already in late

1934 or early 1935. I sent [my] statement to c. Iskrov through Yankov. He was put on trial a long time ago, and it is known to c. Boian Bolgarinov.

3. In my statement of 20 May 1936 about Papanchev, I pointed out evidence against Pyatnitsky, which helped guide the NKVD to the final unmasking of Pyatnitsky.

4. With my statement [sent] to the party collegium (com. Katchenko), I exposed the former SR Kenig, director of the party house.

I consider it unnecessary to write about those people whom I have already exposed, but I am not sure whether they have been arrested or are still being investigated by NKVD organs.

Comrades, by telling you some of what I have done to expose the Trotskyist bandit-spies I am far from boasting before you, and I do not think that I did something heroic. I only fulfilled my duty to the party and workers. I feel very uncomfortable talking with you about it, but I was compelled to . . . .

Ask the following comrades:

1. Andreev, the former deputy people's commissar of the NKVD in Kazakhstan, currently head of the Sixth NKVD Department in Moscow.

2. People's Commissar of the Internal Affairs c. Yezhov.

3. Katchenko, member of the party collegium in Alma-Ata."

Since PETKOV stated in his letter that he had exposed Papanchev and others directly to NKVD organs, the delegation considered it unnecessary to forward PETKOV's statements anywhere.

In addition, the representative [to the ECCI] received PETKOV's letter of 26 August 1937, in which he accused c. Yurdan Tutundzhiev of supposedly counterrevolutionary declarations, about which he learned from Papanchev (aka Atanasov) and from someone else, whom Petkov did not remember.

The representative did not forward the statement about Yurdan Tutundzhiev anywhere because the contents of this statement are a stupid insinuation and slander by the already arrested Papanchev against c. Tutundzhiev. The CPBul delegation in the ECCI knows c. Tutundzhiev well and considers the statements attributed to Tutundzhiev by Papanchev to be impossible.

The delegation received two letters from PETKOV, on 28 January 1935 and on 11 June 1935, in which he accuses Khr. Genchev of "desertion (he had left Bulgaria supposedly without the party's permission), careerism, and moral degeneration." These letters by PETKOV were sent to the International Control Commission.

PETKOV wrote about himself in a letter of 26 August 1937, a copy of which is enclosed.

ENCLOSURE: Copy of a letter from PETKOV of 26 August 1937.[106] *(for the addressee only)*

p/p DIMITROV, G. M.

"21" January 1941.

No. 579.

From these two letters, it is difficult to ascertain with any degree of confidence Petkov's motives for denouncing comrades and Dimitrov's opinion of Petkov's motives. Whatever Dimitrov's opinion, in 1941 and again in 1944 he submitted several appeals for a review of Petkov's conviction. His 1941 appeal failed,[107] but his September 1944 appeal to Merkulov, the people's commissar of state security, proved successful.[108]

Petkov was but one of many repressed political émigrés for whom Dimitrov supported appeals for review. The cases in this book represent but a small sampling of his efforts to undo the injustices that befell many. Those efforts began almost immediately after Beria replaced Yezhov as head of the NKVD. A few examples of appeals submitted on behalf of arrested Bulgarians will suffice to convey Dimitrov's efforts for his fellow countrymen in the years following Yezhov's removal.[109]

On 7 December 1938, Dimitrov sent Beria the names of 131 arrested Bulgarians and requested that he "speed up" the investigation of these cases.[110] That appeal seems to have been largely unsuccessful, for many of the same names appear on a list of 122 people that he sent to Malenkov, a Central Committee secretary, on 3 July 1940. In a letter to Malenkov, Dimitrov wrote: "Among the arrested Bulgarian political émigrés are quite a large group of people about whom it is impossible to believe that they are enemies of the people and spies. I know quite a few of them to be irreproachable Communists."[111] On 7 February 1941, Dimitrov sent to Andreev a list of 132 people, many of whose names had appeared in the two aforementioned lists, requesting that their cases be reviewed. Although the appeal process was very slow and often involved submitting appeals to various state and party commissions, Dimitrov's efforts to get his Bulgarian comrades released yielded some results. Attached to his November 1943 letter to Merkulov was a list of 40 people for whom Dimitrov was submitting appeals: "We consider them to be the victims of slander. We are convinced of this by a thorough and systematic study and through knowledge of our cadres. Prior to fascist Germany's vile invasion of the Soviet Union, reviews of the cases of arrested members of the CP of Bulgaria had begun at our request. More than 150 people were freed."[112]

That Dimitrov included Petkov, who had denounced Bulgarian and Soviet comrades, in his appeals suggests that Dimitrov, whose repeated calls for vigilance and the unmasking of enemies and whose expressed willingness to aid Stalin and Yezhov in any way possible, may have realized his role in inspiring the Petkovs of the time to denounce and "slander" innocent people. Like many other ECCI and VKP leaders, Dimitrov had helped to create and legitimize a political climate and culture in which the repression could flourish. Having done so, he could not halt the process, nor could he protect his comrades from the horrors that befell comrades like I. T. Terziev, whose case we examine next.

The Case of Iordan T. Terziev

The tragic experience of I. T. Terziev at the hands of the NKVD was all too common during this period. Yet his case warrants attention for what it conveys not only about the horrors experienced by those arrested, but also about the NKVD interrogators' mindset.

Document 65

Letter from I. Terziev to Dimitrov and Kolarov describing his arrest and the methods of investigation, 5 August 1939.[113] RGASPI, f. 17, op. 121, d. 19, ll. 115–119. Original in Russian, translated from the handwritten Bulgarian letter. Typewritten with handwritten additions.

To the leader of the Comintern and the Bulgarian Communist Party
—Georgy Dimitrov and Vasil Kolarov.
From Terziev, I. T. (Yanko Atanasov).
Dear comrades,

On 6 February 1938, I was arrested for no reason by NKVD organs and, after **spending** fifteen months in the Ashkhabad prison, was released on 25 April 1939. After my release, I learned that almost all of the Bulgarian émigrés had been arrested and were still held in prisons and camps. I do not know whether you are aware of all the reasons that led the [Bulgarian] émigrés to this tragic situation; therefore, I will tell you everything that happened to me. Because, even if it is not typical for all the arrested émigrés, it is typical for the comrades whom I got to know during the investigation: those comrades who are still in prisons and camps.

In Ashkhabad (Turkmenia), I worked along with Ivan Piperkov and Piotr Stanev. We were instructors in the CC of the Communist Party of Turkmenia, sent personally by Yezhov. Georgy Tsanev worked as a woodworker, and I [worked] as head of a section of the social sciences in an institute. I was sent there in accordance with a directive of the CC VKP(b), which was signed personally by A. A. Andreev.

Our party papers and travel documents indicated that we were important party members. However, in early November 1937, Iv. Piperkov and Georgy Tsanev were arrested. Twenty days later, Piotr Stanev was also arrested. Immediately after their arrest, I wrote to the section [CPBul delegation in the ECCI], via c. Anton Ivanov, describing everything that had happened, and a month after their arrest, I went to the Turkmenian NKVD to inquire about the reasons for arresting the comrades in question. I was received by an investigator named Erastenko, to whom I described all the activities of the comrades in Bulgaria and expressed my opinion that the NKVD had made a mistake by arresting them. In addition, I presented written references for the comrades with whom I worked in Bulgaria, and declared that I was only fulfilling my party duty and wanted to assist the organs in clarifying the question of Bulgarians in Turkmenia. Erastenko told me that I was vouching for them in vain, since they had already confessed of espionage . . . .

Soon after that, I was also arrested and sent to the Ashkhabad prison. There I met many party activists, soldiers, doctors, etc. When I said that I was Bulgarian, those arrested told me: "You, com. Terziev, will be a Bulgarian spy, and if you want to save your skin, [you have to] recruit as many accessories as you can and confess immediately. Otherwise, you are dead." The slogan "Recruit as many as you can" was promoted by the Turkmenian Trotskyists, in particular by the old Trotskyist Rubinstein, a member of the CC of the party and the director of a chemical plant in Kara-Bugas, Tol. Around this slogan, a sharp ideological struggle went on between the Trotskyists and the loyal party members. Using this slogan, the Trotskyists managed to deliver a heavy blow both to the party and to the NKVD, since many of the arrested gave in to this provocation, and [gave in] especially to the prosecutors. As a result of this provocation, one arrested [person] dragged down with him dozens of innocent and honest party members and non-party Bolsheviks. I simply cannot describe this issue more specifically, but I urge you to pay special attention to it because the roots of the problem are in Moscow—this slogan was implemented in an organized manner everywhere.

My case was investigated by Lieutenant Kovalevsky. On 9 February he called me in for interrogation. His first question was, "<u>By whom, when, and how were you recruited [to work] for foreign intelligence?</u>" Then he continued: "<u>The prosecution possesses reliable information that you are an IKR spy</u>. Confess on your own, because voluntary confession will lighten your penalty. Your fate was sealed before your arrest, and keep in mind that if you do not confess, you will be shot." I told him that I had no idea about this work. He then made me sit on a <u>stool</u>, which it was absolutely impossible to sit on. I spent three days, unable to move, on this stool; my limbs swelled, and I felt particularly strong, dull pains in my legs. Along with the physical suffering, I was insulted with refined obscenities. Not only was my honor as a Communist and a man outraged, but so was the honor of my deceased parents. On 13 February 1939 they started beating me. I was beaten by the investigator Kovalevsky and his assistant who, in addition to regular beatings, struck me several times on the back of my head. I do not remember what they did to me afterward, but when I recovered, I felt a <u>strong pain in the eyes. As a result of the shock, my eyes hemorrhaged</u>. At present, treatment can <u>only localize the disease, but, as doctors told me, I will never regain normal sight</u>.

After these physical and moral treatments, and after a long "rest," the investigator again summoned me to an interrogation and subjected me to new tortures. I was kneeling with my hands raised while the investigator opened a book and read a number of Bulgarian names, of which I remember Grancharov, Dr. Maksimov, Novakov, Nikolov, etc. He characterized them as Trotskyists and asked if I knew them. I answered that I knew them as loyal Communists. After that I was beaten again.

It is hard to describe what I lived through in those days, but I felt that I was fading away, that I would die in an NKVD dungeon. A person commits suicide only under extreme psychological conditions, which I reached twice. However, the investigators must have been watching my feelings and intentions. They used to guard me particularly closely so that I could not approach the window or the stairs. I decided to break my head against the wall, but when I started doing it, I was caught by two investigators. They must have been frightened by my terrible act and started to calm me down, saying that I should not torment myself, that there was a way out, I only had to agree to write something. I objected, saying that I could not invent crimes and attribute them to myself because that would mean misleading the party and the government and thus actually help the enemies. Kovalevsky told me several times: "Regarding the truthfulness of the testimony, we warn only the witnesses. But remember that you have to provide the testimony of a spy."

I could not kneel anymore, and I asked [them] to give me some rest, after which I would testify. With a bloody head and tormented body, I was returned to the prison [cell] for a rest. After several hours, I was again taken for interrogation. I decided to ruin myself, but not to permit additional victims, and if I could not hold this line, to mention comrades who were not in the Soviet Union or who had already been arrested.

I started to write a confession that I was an agent of French intelligence, but my investigator, after reading it, told me that it was no good, that I had to write something more intelligent if I wanted to avoid torture.

They made me kneel again, but this time they put six-sided pencils under my knees. One can only stand [the pain] for a maximum of four to five hours, after which he passes out. After this procedure, the following day I became a German spy. My confession, in short, consisted of the following:

I supposedly had met through a comrade a woman who, in turn, led me to a worker in the German embassy, for whom: 1. I provided information about the political émigrés [and] the moods among them, about who was coming to the USSR and who was going back; 2. On his orders, following special plans, I prepared to sabotage factories in case of a war. In this confession, I included, as the members of the espionage group, Dustabanov, Kiskinov, and Iv. Sterev. In late February I signed the final examination record. However, the next day, during the night, I was brought [back] to my investigator and the head of the NKVD's Third Department, [a man] named Bolshakov, *who* started to swear at me and said: "We will liquidate all of you political émigrés." He was dissatis-

fied with my confession because I had recruited too few people. He ordered
the physical torture to continue. Then I declared to him that being a foreigner,
I could give valuable testimony but, for several reasons, could do so only before the people's commissar, and they, in the interests of the investigation,
would have to let me see him. He agreed.

Three or four days after this conversation, in early March, I was called for
questioning. My investigator repeated again a series of physical tortures, this
time in a more disgusting form. I could not stand it and started to write a new
confession, this time as an agent of Bulgarian counterintelligence. I decided
to involve in the espionage organization people who had been compromised
in the movement or those representing no special interest [to the movement].
My confession can be reduced to the following: 1. That in 1925, Dustabanov
accidentally introduced me to P. Topalov, to whom I expressed my disillu-
sionment with the revolution. Topalov promised me rehabilitation by the
Bulgarian government if I agreed to provide information about the émigrés. 2.
[That] Topalov and I supposedly named those émigrés who returned to Bulgaria and who later were shot by the Bulgarian government. 3. That we engaged in provocation in Constantinople throughout the whole period. 4.
That, through Todor Lukanov and Georgy Popov, we conducted sabotage activities in the People's Commissariat of Foreign Trade and in the Central
Council of Consumer Societies. 5. That Topalov and I stole some central
archive [Tsentro-Arkhiv] documents that compromised a number of bourgeois parties in Bulgaria.

I signed this confession on 21 March 1938. In early April 1938, I was again
interrogated and made to sign a new examination record, which included, besides those first records, the following paragraphs:

1. That I was supposedly connected with the Popov-Tanev group,[114] and
that I rehabilitated them in the émigré circles, and that we supposedly carried
on a struggle against c.c. G. Dimitrov and V. Kolarov.

2. That Topalov supposedly told me that the minister plenipotentiary in
Moscow, Antonov, was connected with German counterintelligence.

Having signed this confession, I waited every night for five months for
them to shoot me.

I retracted my confession on 20 September 1938 and again on 19 October.
The last time, my retraction was documented, and the conditions under
which this confession was given were noted. I repeated this retraction in front
of other investigators.

Five more months passed, and not until 1 April was I summoned for questioning by my first investigator, Kovalevsky. He composed a detailed examination record, refuting the records of 21 March and 5 April 1938. After that I
was called three times to the military procurator, who questioned me in detail
about the methods of investigation and what I knew about the escape from St.
Anastasia.[115] I answered that c. G. Dimitrov had characterized this escape as
a CPBul affair. On 25 April 1939, I was summoned to a commission where

they asked me who in the Comintern knew me. After that, they told me that I was free and could appeal to the Comintern or CC VKP(b).

As to the other Ashkhabad comrades, I learned that <u>Georgy Tsanev</u> confessed to being a <u>member of some terrorist</u> group that sought to murder c. G. Dimitrov. He was sentenced to eight years and exiled.

In October 1938, Professor Dziakovsky from the Medical Institute <u>was transferred to my cell. He told me that Ivan Piperkov had been subjected to a terrible beating. He confessed to being an agent provocateur. After he recovered, he was transferred from a common cell to solitary confinement.</u>

On 1 April 1939, during the interrogation, investigator Kovalevsky let me read <u>one page from Iv. Piperkov's testimony. It said that in Odessa in 1926, Iv. Piperkov had organized a counterrevolutionary group consisting of Iv. Piperkov, Boyan Atanasov, Vasili Ivanov, Yakim Ivanov, Terziev, V. Novakov, Stoenchev, K. Nikolov, Stareishinsky, Dr. Maksimov, and a number of other comrades. I thoroughly refuted that statement</u> in order to rehabilitate the comrades. Judging from the investigator's behavior, I understood that Piperkov was alive.

<u>I could not learn anything specific about Peter Stanev. In prison they said that he had been shot.</u>

I have described to you, very objectively, the procedures and methods of the investigation of my case. <u>I declare before you that I have never been a member of any oppositional groups, never shared anti-party views, but in spite of this, they attempted to turn me into an enemy of the party and a fascist hero.</u>

The opinion of some comrades who think that the <u>NKVD does not arrest those not guilty</u> is wrong. <u>In prisons, I met many innocent comrades.</u>

<u>Besides the Boikovtsevs, Zlatorovtsevs, and some other types, Bulgarian political émigrés, and the political émigrés in the USSR in general, are the victims of a planned and broad provocation undertaken by Trotskyists and [agents of] foreign counterintelligence in the NKVD apparatus. It would be interesting to know about the role played here by the Bulgarian Trotskyists and sectarians, many of whom worked for the NKVD officially or unofficially.</u>

<u>These arrests had as a goal the political degeneration of the émigrés and the compromising of the CC VKP(b) and c. Stalin personally, [as well as of] the Comintern and c. Dimitrov personally. Many of the arrested shared the opinion that everything that was going on in the country was sanctioned by c.c. Stalin and Dimitrov.</u>

In addition, there was created in the party a certain psychosis against foreigners. The word "vigilance" became synonymous with "mistrust," which has nothing to do with revolutionary vigilance. As a result of this psychosis and the false denunciations, many political émigrés were imprisoned.

Bulgarian political émigrés were educated ideologically in Bulgaria under your direct guidance. Under your guidance, these émigrés offered examples of selflessness and heroism. [Events in] Spain have once again verified the remarkable qualities of Bulgarian Communists.

Ideologically, our émigrés have never been with the Boikovtsy[116] and Iskrovtsy,[117] except for a few petit bourgeois types and comrades who incidentally lost their way. The Bulgarian political emigration has a great respect for the party's past and for its founders.

You have to do everything possible to save the people, because without your active involvement in this question, the émigrés will not be freed and will vanish in the camps. The cadres whom you have been creating for decades will vanish.

Nalchik,

5 August 1939.

With fraternal greetings,
P. Terziev (Ya. Atanasov).

Translation correct.

Terziev's graphic description of his brutal treatment in prison requires no comment. His portrayal of the rampant xenophobia in the local NKVD was succinctly expressed by the head of its Third Department: "We will liquidate all of you political émigrés." The result of the NKVD's obsession with ferreting out "enemy" conspiracies, which, he correctly asserted, the country's leaders had "created in the party," was that "the word 'vigilance' became synonomous with 'mistrust.'" To local NKVD officials, who were implementing central directives, Terziev's nationality was sufficient reason to arrest him. So convinced were they of his guilt that their only dilemma was determining which invented conspiracy to assign him to.

Whereas Valter and Razumova believed that Stalin, Dimitrov, and even Yezhov were unaware of what NKVD interrogators were doing, Terziev and some fellow inmates concluded that Stalin and Dimitrov had sanctioned the arrest of émigrés. We can only wonder how Dimitrov reacted to Terziev's statement that "many of the arrested shared the opinion that everything that was going on in the country was sanctioned by c.c. Stalin and Dimitrov." Despite the tortures he had endured, Terziev explained that many of his prison mates denounced others not as a result of their treatment but rather as a Trotskyist provocation. He viewed the work of "Trotskyists and [agents of] foreign counterintelligence in the NKVD" as compromising the VKP Central Committee, the Comintern, Dimitrov, and "Stalin personally." His cynicism aside, Terziev persisted in explaining events in terms of "enemy" conspiracies.

One of the more surprising aspects of Terziev's letter is his recounting of his sudden release and being advised of his right of appeal. Given that many others (e.g., Valter and Razumova) languished in captivity for years, Terziev's abrupt release seems unusual. The available evidence does not allow us to decide whether his release was due to efforts to rein in the police after Yezhov's fall or due to Dimitrov's appeal on Terziev's behalf.[118] Whatever the reason, his release was the exception rather than the rule.

The Case of Karl F. Kurshner

The preceding case studies illustrate somewhat different aspects of the repression, but all share certain features. Among those is the fact that each person was convicted of belonging to a conspiratorial organization of which he or she had no knowledge, but whose leaders had been arrested. As Kafkaesque as their experiences were, they pale in comparison to those of Karl Kurshner, who was twice arrested and once convicted of belonging to a counterrevolutionary organization headed by the economist and ECCI member Jenő Varga. Varga was Kurshner's boss. While Kurshner began serving eight years at hard labor, Varga went as usual to his job as director of the Institute of World Economy and World Economics of the Academy of Sciences and continued to act as a consultant to Stalin. Although Varga had written to Stalin protesting the persecution of émigrés, he remained a free man. Kurshner's case suggests that Varga came close to being arrested. We may wonder whether Varga was aware of his situation and whether he experienced the fear that his letter to Stalin so eloquently described. Why Varga was not arrested, who protected him, and why he was protected are unclear.

Kurshner's troubles began in early 1938. In January, Dimitrov had received from Florin, secretary of the ICC, a report on the 1932 arrests and executions in Hungary of two Communists (Sallai and Furst). Florin wrote that "in the leadership of the CP of Hungary sat, alongside good comrades, enemies and agents of the Hungarian police, and that the arrest of Sallai and Furst was the result of betrayal." In Florin's opinion, Kurshner was probably the traitor. On 19 January 1938, Dimitrov sent Florin's report to Beria and suggested that he "take an interest in this affair."[119] Kurshner was arrested in February.

Given Dimitrov's role in Kurshner's arrest, it might seem that he would show no interest in Kurshner. Such was not the case. In January 1940, even before Kurshner had been convicted, Dimitrov appealed on his behalf. Kurov, the assistant military procurator of the Moscow Military District, who reviewed the case, concluded that Kurshner had been arrested "without clear cause" and ordered him released because he had been unjustly denounced by Hungarian comrades (Kun, Vágó, and Kreichi) who had "something against Kurshner." Kurshner's release did not end his troubles. In fact, his ordeal had only begun. The chief of administration of the NKVD protested to Beria and USSR Procurator Pankratov about Kurshner's release, claiming that Kurov had "ignored evidence that Kurshner belonged to a Brandlerite organization that was preparing a terrorist act against the leader of the people, com. Stalin."[120] That argument convinced the NKVD to arrest Kurshner a second time in July 1940. In September he was convicted of "participating in a right-Trotskyist counterrevolutionary organization" and sentenced to eight years of hard labor. **Document 66** is Kurshner's letter to Dimitrov requesting a review of his conviction.

The bizarre nature of Kurshner's case should not overshadow other of its notable aspects. Kurshner's (and Kurov's) belief that Béla Kun and people from Kun's narrow circle "slandered me" reminds us yet again of the role that intraparty struggles and personal squabbles played in people's arrests. Many Hungarians, Kun's friends and enemies, rode his coattails into the gulag. Linking alleged Hungarian counterrevolutionaries to Kun seems to have been standard NKVD fare. And what was true for Hungarians was true for other groups.

Although the crime Kurshner was accused of makes his case somewhat unique, like all others who appealed for a review of their conviction, Kurshner believed that a full review of his case would reveal the baselessness of the charges. Given his experiences, how could he cling to that belief? But then, what other choice did he have?

Document 66

Letter from K. F. Kurshner to Dimitrov requesting a review of his case, 22 January 1941. RGASPI, f. 495, op. 73, d. 107, ll. 37–40. Original in Russian. Typewritten.

To the General Secretary of the Executive Committee
of the Communist International,
Deputy of the Supreme Soviet of the USSR
G. Dimitrov.
From prisoner Kurshner, Karl Filippovich
Vetlag of the NKVD l/p No. 11.

On 10 September 1940, the Special Council [OSO] of the People's Commissariat of Internal Affairs of the USSR sentenced me to eight years in a corrective labor camp for "participating in a right-Trotskyist counterrevolutionary organization."

To which organization does it refer? Supposedly, the organization headed by the ECCI member academician Jenő Varga.

You and everyone know that, in fact, Varga is not a counterrevolutionary, that he has never been arrested by NKVD organs, and that he is not now arrested. How could non-counterrevolutionary Varga have recruited me into a counterrevolutionary organization? What kind of counterrevolutionary am I, to which [counterrevolutionary] organization do I belong? The answer is as clear as the slanderous character of the accusation: J. Varga is not a counterrevolutionary, and I am not a counterrevolutionary. Neither Varga nor anybody else has ever recruited me into any counterrevolutionary organization anywhere, especially into a nonexisting organization. Such are the facts. But it is also a fact that I am in the camp, that I am imprisoned for eight years.

The explanation is that for the investigating organ of the NKVD that handled my case, papers proved to be more important than obvious, well-known facts. The charges are formally based on the testimony of Béla Vágó of 22 December 1938 and in part on the testimony of Béla Kun and A. Kreichi of December 1937 and January 1938. If there is testimony, there should be indictment. But if the indictment contradicts facts, well, too bad for the facts: this is the position of the investigation in my case.

I was sentenced by the OSO in 1940, after the procurator of the Moscow Military District [MVO] had closed my case in March 1940, and I was released after spending twenty-six months in prison.[121]

After my release, I was already working as an editor of Hungarian broadcasts at the All-Union Radio Committee in Moscow, when, on 10 July 1940, I was again arrested, [and] the closed case was reopened because the procurator of the USSR, in his resolution of 5 June, overturned the decision of the MVO procurator.

The new decision to arrest [me] reiterates the accusation related to the counterrevolutionary organization headed by J. Varga! (See case No. 1444 of the NKVD for the Moscow region.) A special resolution of the investigations department confirms the reopening of the old case. (Even the no. of the old case was brought back.) In reality, since my second arrest, there has not been any investigation besides some formal procedures required by the Criminal Law Procedure Code of the RSFSR [Russian Republic]. The question arises once again: What is going on here? In March 1940 the procurator of the MVO satisfied himself that Varga's counterrevolutionary organization was a myth. Has anything changed since then? Of course not. What did take place was an obvious mistake on the part of the procurator of the [Soviet] Union.

On what is this accusation in general based? [It is based] on the testimony by Béla Vágó of 22 December 1938. Members of the Hungarian Communist Party and you personally know well enough about the activities of B. Vágó before his arrest: following Béla Kun's political orders, for many years he slandered those members of the CP of Hungary who struggled against Béla Kun and his group. This is also known to E. Gerő, the CPH representative in the ECCI. It is also known in the ECCI Cadres Department.

Even after his arrest, Béla Vágó continued his anti-party activity aimed at destroying honest party cadres [and] trying to mislead NKVD organs. Béla Kun and A. Kreichi acted in the same way. To evaluate their testimonies, it is sufficient to contrast them.

Béla Vágó claims that he learned from Béla Kun (in another section [of the testimony] he, Vágó, told it to Kun) that there existed a counterrevolutionary organization [led by] Varga, and that I was a member. Kun knows nothing about it; he connects me to some German organization—to be exact, he claims that I supposedly distributed Brandlerite flyers in Moscow (though not mentioning to whom, when, and what kind [of flyers]). A. Kreichi, for his part, claims that I was a member of Béla Kun's organization, about which Béla Kun again knows nothing.

Like Kun, people from Kun's narrow circle, such as Vágó, Kreichi, and Fodor, slandered me, and only they [did]! The reason for this slander is revealed by the ECCI document of 19 January 1940, which was sent to the NKVD on my behalf. In this ECCI document it was stressed that Béla Kun had badgered me for many years. My "case" is nothing else but a result of this badgering. The Soviet organs may not be well aware of the struggle that was going on within the CP of Hungary, so they might easily have committed a mistake. That is why I am asking that you intervene in my case. In support of my request [for a review], I am asking you to raise the question of a review of my case with the procurator of the [Soviet] Union and before the people's commissar of internal affairs of the USSR. I also request you:

1. to give the ECCI member academician J. Varga a chance to address the procurator of the [Soviet] Union regarding this case;

2. to give members of the CP of Hungary, including E. Gerő, György Lukács, Zoltán Szántó, and J. Révai, a chance to write references for me and send them to the procurator of the [Soviet] Union.

I have not a slightest doubt that an unbiased, careful review of my case will clearly determine the obviously false [and] slanderous character of the accusations that were cast on me, and will lead to my full rehabilitation.

Viatlag, 11 lagpunkt, 22 January 1941.

K. F. Kurshner.

Dimitrov had included Kurshner along with Valter and Razumova in his 28 February 1941 appeal on behalf of a number of arrested Cominternists (see Document 55). The appeal was denied. Kurshner died in the gulag on 20 March 1942. Jenő Varga died a natural death in 1964.

CHAPTER EIGHT

Fear, Obedience, Belief, and Repression

If you believe certain words, you believe their hidden arguments. When you believe something is right or wrong, true or false, you believe the assumptions in the words which express the arguments. Such assumptions are often full of holes but remain most precious to the convinced.

— FRANK HERBERT

Ideological justification is vital in obtaining willing obedience, for it permits the person to see his behavior as serving a desirable end.

— STANLEY MILGRAM

MOST PEOPLE viewing Francisco Goya's disturbing masterpiece *Colossus* for the first time assume that the panicked people in the foreground are fleeing the enormous Colossus, whose clenched fists and snarling expression convey his rage. The sense of fear and panic is visceral. But upon closer examination, viewers realize that the Colossus is not approaching the fleeing crowd. He is partially facing away, not even looking at it, eyeing instead something that we cannot see, something so implicitly horrible that even he is gripped by fear, and the people are fleeing at the mere hint of its arrival. Viewed from this perspective, Colossus appears to be the people's protector, the last line of defense between them and an unknown but terrible fate. Yet even after this realization, viewers cannot shake the image of Colossus as a threat of inhuman proportions, capable of quickly turning and, with a sweep of his clenched fist, destroying the fearful crowd.

Colossus provides us with an analogy when pondering what we know about the Stalinist mass repression. Many scholars present Stalin as a threatening Colossus who, with a single word or stroke of a pen, could destroy people's lives. This view has merit. Stalin was larger than life, and he used his immense power to destroy. But, as with the interpretation of Colossus as a threat, it is inadequate. Soviet realities in the 1930s were complex and ambiguous.

There can be no doubt of Stalin's direct role in and political and moral culpability for the mass repression. He clearly feared that individuals and groups threatened his power or Soviet power. He believed that conspirators ranged widely in Soviet society. His use of the NKVD and the party to repress many is beyond dispute. He demanded that the VKP expel "Trotskyists" and "suspicious" and "hostile elements." He authorized the NKVD to arrest and execute "anti-Soviet elements," "enemies," "spies," "wreckers," "saboteurs." He ordered the NKVD to arrest members of certain ethnic groups and to conduct mass operations against certain social groups. To view Stalin as the threatening Colossus is understandable and reasonable.

But, as the documents presented in this book indicate, Stalin may have set the tone of the period and set the repressive policies in motion, but he did not act alone. Politburo and Central Committee members, Comintern leaders and staff, party secretaries and rank-and-file party members, and political émigrés and ordinary citizens endorsed, implemented, legitimized, and validated those policies. Many members of the Comintern and its party organization shared his views and provided evidence that not only legitimized them but helped push them beyond reasonable limits. They did so for a variety of reasons—party discipline, fervent belief, careerism, fear of disputing the party that protected their privileges, fear of perceived enemies, revenge, mean-spiritedness. Many did so because they believed that Stalin and the VKP leaders articulated the strategies and tactics necessary to overcome obstacles that obstructed the realization of a shared vision. Although that belief proved to be misplaced, the results do not impugn the motive. Reflecting briefly on some of the major themes in this book allows us to ponder the complexities of the period. Whether Stalin, like Colossus, was seen as a threat or a defender depended on the beholder.

The connections between Kirov's murder in December 1934 and the mass repression of 1937–1938 were indirect. The period from the murder through 1938 consisted of discrete yet related events, campaigns, and procedures that, in hindsight, contributed to the mass repression. Yet the evidence presented here provides no indication that there was a master plan. On the contrary, the path from vigilance to mass repression was blazed in response to revelations and events that contemporaries viewed as demanding action.

After expelling several comrades and calling for heightened vigilance in De-

cember 1934 and early 1935, the ECCI party organization expressed a clear
sense of accomplishment and closure. It had done its job well, or so it thought.
In 1935 it and the ECCI apparatus devoted their energies to other tasks that
seemingly bore no relation to repression: verifying comrades' political credentials, preparing for the Comintern Congress of 1935, implementing the Popular Front, restructuring the ECCI apparatus. For most of 1935 the threats
posed by Kirov's murder receded. Only at year's end did a new threat emerge
—"spies" "disguised as political émigrés." To ward off that threat, the ECCI
leaders ordered the formation of commissions to verify the members of fraternal parties. During 1936 and early 1937 those commissions carried out their
work and generated lists of "suspicious" comrades. Their purpose and goal
were to expose threats to their parties, the Comintern, the VKP, and Soviet national security.

The August 1936 trial provided startling "proof" that "enemies"—foreign
and domestic—posed a serious threat and justified the sending of lists of "suspicious elements," "Trotskyists," and those with "oppositional tendencies" to
the Central Committee or the NKVD. The January 1937 trial and the February–March 1937 Central Committee Plenum deepened the fears that "enemies" were within the gates and heightened the need for vigilance. At the time,
no one in the Comintern envisioned that the NKVD would be unleashed on society. The sending of lists to the Central Committee or the NKVD, the purging
of the ECCI apparatus, the verification of foreigners, and the increasingly strident calls for vigilance were understandable reactions to perceived threats.
Even to those who reacted this way, the onset of the mass repression in May–
June 1937 came as a shock.

In hindsight, the connections between the discrete activities that preceded
the NKVD's assault on the party and society in 1937 are clear. But as Kotelnikov's report on the activities of the ECCI party organization from December
1934 through 1938 (Document 46) indicate, those who participated in them
did not view them as leading to mass repression. Each campaign, each activity,
was rooted in the logic of a particular political moment. To contemporaries,
there was no evidence of a master plan for repression, yet compelling reasons
for expulsions and arrests did arise.

Whether or not Stalin had a master plan that guided the repression is unknown. This book is a case study of how the mass repression unfolded within
and affected the headquarters of the Comintern. As such, it sheds little light on
Stalin's private intentions. It does, however, reaffirm the critical roles that he
and other party and state leaders played, as well as confirm the findings of

other studies of this tragic period. As in the Central Committee and in the Smolensk party organization,[1] politics in the Comintern headquarters prior to spring 1937 consisted of a series of political actions, campaigns, and struggles that centered on specific political and bureaucratic activities but that later contributed to the dynamics and contours of the repression. As we saw, public political behavior and the internalization of the VKP's political values played a decisive role; the conspiratorial mindset was particularly important in shaping the repression.[2] Like several other studies, this one underscores the crucial part that the deteriorating international situation played in legitimizing the need for vigilance, expanding the definition of "enemy," and rendering ethnicity a threat.[3]

The documents presented here that confirm these findings enrich our understanding in ways that few other studies can. We saw how the leaders and staff at the Comintern headquarters interpreted and implemented central directives and reacted to specific short-term political events and campaigns, contributing thereby to the mass repression. We saw how and why long-standing anxieties about "spies" and "enemy agents" were transformed into xenophobia. Perhaps most important, we can now appreciate the complex multiple roles played by the Comintern leaders, staff, and workers.

The Comintern was agent, instrument, and victim of the mass repression. Within the Comintern headquarters and abroad, the ECCI leaders, departments, and party organization implemented the anti-Trotskyist and vigilance campaigns initiated by Stalin and the Central Committee. The ECCI leaders and Cadres Department oversaw the verification of fraternal party members living in the USSR, a process mandated by the Central Committee. The ECCI party organization periodically verified and purged its ranks in accordance with Central Committee directives. There can be no doubt that the Comintern acted as the agent of the VKP.

That role was intertwined with another—being the instrument of VKP policies. The ECCI leaders, staff, and party committee may not have decided what the policies of the moment were, but they did have some leeway in how to implement them. Given Zinoviev's and Safarov's arrests after Kirov's murder, scapegoating Magyar was an obvious decision. Less obvious today is why others expelled or reprimanded in early 1935 were selected. The Cadres Department staff responded to orders when they compiled lists of "suspicious" or "hostile elements," but they determined whose names were included or omitted from the lists. Kotelnikov, the party committee secretary, made similar judgments in compiling his list of VKP members who had oppositional tendencies. The commissions that reviewed émigrés did so under orders, but their members, too, decided who was or was not reliable. The Moskvin Commission did the same. In each case and in others, those bodies acted as the instrument of VKP policies. But the members had discretionary powers to apply policies in ways that they deemed appropriate.

The decisions of the party organization to expel members, the verification of fraternal party members living in the USSR, the verification of workers in the ECCI apparatus, the sending of dossiers on "suspicious" or "hostile elements" to the Central Committee or the NKVD—all were done in accordance with established bureaucratic procedures. Appreciating how party and state bureaucracies implemented central directives is essential to understanding how discrete political campaigns provided the materials to justify and unleash the mass repression. Following Kirov's murder, leaders of the ECCI party organization identified and expelled certain comrades. In 1935 and 1936 they conducted the verification and exchange of party documents and, in the process, expelled more comrades. Both times they adhered to prescribed guidelines and rituals; both reviews resulted in the sending of names to the Central Committee or the NKVD. The verification of foreign comrades living in the USSR also followed mandated guidelines and resulted in the accumulation of new lists of "suspicious" people. In accordance with time-honored practice, the leaders of the ECCI Cadres Department and the party committee routinely forwarded names and materials to the appropriate higher organs. Each such act was a response to a specific charge, but the cumulative effect was substantial—and deadly for many. What facilitated the Comintern's role as an instrument of repression was the incremental, bureaucratic way it generated lists of "suspicious" and "hostile" elements over time.

The Comintern's role as victim is also obvious. Not only did the mass repression result in the arrests and deaths of many of its charges (not to mention the dissolution of the Polish, Western Ukrainian, and Western Belorussian parties), it also crippled the ECCI apparatus. The precise number of victims may remain in doubt, but many affiliated with the Comintern were victims of the mass repression.

To understand why many in the Comintern's headquarters played the roles of agent and instrument, it is important to appreciate that, by the time of Kirov's murder, they had internalized the party mindset, a mindset forged and tempered in a conspiratorial underground party before 1917, in the horrific battles and suffering of the Civil War, in the internecine struggles with oppositionists in the 1920s, in the pitched struggles with kulaks during collectivization, by the realization that Nazi Germany viewed Slavs as potential slave labor and Communism as a boil on the body politic. For émigrés residing in the USSR, who did not share the same formative experiences as their Soviet comrades, there were others that were rooted in their experiences as members of parties often persecuted in their native lands, as members of organizations the ranks of which were frequently rounded up by police and denounced by agents provocateurs, as idealists whose dreams of socialist revolution were crushed by the armed might of the state. Whether Soviet citizens or political émigrés, those who acted as agents and instruments of VKP policies had complex identities forged in cauldrons of political idealism and desperation, identities that they sought to maintain by interpreting their failures and frustrations as the result of the machinations of sinister forces. Stalin had no monopoly on the conspiratorial mindset.

Living as they did in a country isolated from the rest of the world, a country whose government conveyed a simplified version of complex realities, a country where adulation of Stalin and the VKP had become the social norm, citizens and émigrés alike accepted the use of force as a legitimate way to ward off threats. After all, force had been a key instrument in the Soviet successes—and failures—to date.

Given the absence of evidence of Stalin's direct complicity in Kirov's murder, historians will continue to argue about his role. Doing so should not divert attention from the more enduring legacy of that murder—the VKP's interpretation of it, which fostered the belief that foreign and domestic "enemies" had conspired to kill a prominent Soviet leader. This belief enabled VKP leaders to later accept the existence of more widespread conspiracies and the need for all party members to be ever vigilant.

To Cominternists, the rhetoric and often the reality of political vigilance was familiar. The incessant struggles against Social Democrats, "social fascists," Trotskyists, Bukharinites, Brandlerites, Lovestoneites, and other enemies had conditioned them to use the strident rhetoric of vigilance with daunting facility. Vigilance had become the accepted means of political and personal defense. It had become a routine. But as political anxieties deepened, "'vigilance' became synonymous with 'mistrust.'"

The VKP's and Comintern's campaign against Trotsky and Trotskyism came easily. From 1923, VKP and Comintern stalwarts had attacked Trotskyists' oppositional behavior within the USSR and the fraternal parties. In exile, Trotsky became even more threatening because he was beyond the reach of party discipline and state power. The VKP leaders viewed Trotskyists as a serious

threat, not only because they used Bolshevik rhetoric and Leninist logic to critique the USSR and Comintern but also because they were willing to take their
views directly to workers and rank-and-file Communists. Given the hardships
that Soviet and other workers endured during the 1930s, any Trotskyist success among workers threatened to weaken Soviet and Comintern influence
within that class, upon which both relied for political legitimacy.

Although the demands of party discipline help to explain the Comintern's
vigilance campaign, to appreciate the vehemence it is essential to remember
that political instability and uncertainty riddled the USSR and Europe in the
1930s. Cominternists understood how unstable the world was and how high
were the political and personal stakes. Those who endorsed and promoted the
vigilance campaign were intelligent human beings. As the case studies suggest,
they did not deny the need for vigilance or the existence of "enemies." What
they came to lament were the excesses and injustices of the campaign.

At the core of the vigilance campaign—and a key aspect of Stalinist political
culture—was the assumption that clandestine conspiracies existed within the
USSR, the VKP, and the international Communist movement. That assumption was the link between political vigilance and the mass repression. Having
accepted the premise that conspirators operated within the party, how could
one distinguish between "Trotskyist" conspirators and honest comrades,
given that both used the same rhetoric and political logic? NKVD interrogators obviously could not distinguish "comrades" from "enemies." Yet so fervent was their belief that conspiracies existed that nothing short of a "confession" was acceptable, because it proved that their assumptions and brutal
behavior were correct. As the documents in this book make clear, many VKP
members believed that if the VKP or the NKVD had enough "evidence" to arrest a person, then that person must be guilty. Even some of those who were repressed continued to believe that "enemies" existed. In fact, they attributed
their unjust fate to "enemy" machinations and believed that if only Stalin or
Yezhov knew the facts of their case, Soviet justice would prevail, and they
would be set free. But Stalin and Yezhov did know. We should not judge the
victims too harshly for their beliefs. Who among us is willing to admit to ourselves that assumptions upon which we have built our lives, careers, even faiths,
might be flawed?

A key assumption about the USSR in the 1930s is that its borders were impregnable, for such was a precondition for totalitarian control. In fact, the
borders were somewhat porous. From the revolution into the 1930s, the Soviet government welcomed foreign Communists and workers who sought

refuge from repression in their native countries. Until the mid-1930s those people stood as symbols of the USSR as shield and safe haven for those fighting for social justice and socialist revolution. They were welcomed into the country, and often into the VKP, precisely because they and the Bolsheviks had a common enemy. Every Pole, German, Japanese, Hungarian, Bulgarian, Balt, and Finn who sought refuge in the USSR was living proof of the justice of Soviet socialism and the injustice of capitalism. But as the international situation grew more tense after Hitler's ascension to power and increased Japanese military activity, VKP leaders came to view the émigrés in a different light.

It was not simply the shifting international climate or Stalin's paranoia, or that of the Politburo, that prompted this change. Domestic realities were crucial. The VKP's membership screenings in 1933–1935 provided "evidence"— real or perceived—that "enemy agents" posing as émigrés had infiltrated the USSR and the party. The possibility that a fifth column existed within the VKP prompted a shift in party attitudes toward foreign comrades. From that assumption flowed the concern that "enemy agents" "masked" as students and political émigrés had infiltrated party schools, factories, and other Soviet institutions.

The party's decision to verify every foreigner in the country and the ways that process unfolded suggest how complex the political dynamics of the period were and how intertwined were the actions of the leaders and their followers. Manuilsky, the Central Committee representative in the ECCI, gave the report that provided a justification for the December 1935 Central Committee Plenum to order a verification of foreigners. His report came almost six months after Yezhov's declaration that foreign intelligence services used émigrés in the USSR to obtain party cards, a conclusion that Krajewski of the ECCI Cadres Department had reached in the fall of 1934. It was Manuilsky who drafted the guidelines for how the review should be implemented. The available evidence offers no insight into whether Stalin or someone else in the Politburo told Manuilsky how to draft his report and those guidelines. There may have been no need for anyone to do so, for Manuilsky was a "real Bolshevik" who had internalized VKP assumptions and values. What is known is that Manuilsky and the ECCI feared that "suspicious" and "hostile elements" existed within the émigré community and took seriously the need to verify foreigners.

Stalin and the ECCI were most concerned about émigrés from Poland— Poles, Western Ukrainians, and Western Belorussians. For this reason, those who carried out the verification of those parties did so with pronounced vigilance. Either in their zeal to prove that they personally were above reproach or in their concern about the reliability of émigrés, those who implemented the verification of the Polish section deemed a significant proportion of their members to be "suspicious elements" or "proven enemies." Their reports provided "proof" to justify Stalin's and Yezhov's suspicions, to dissolve the parties, to expand the repression.

Stalin's long-standing suspicions of Poles might lead us to conclude that he had orchestrated this outcome. But even a casual perusal of the stacks of lists and notes generated by the Polish verification commission makes clear that more complex processes were at work. To assume that there were no suspicious elements among the Polish émigrés is baseless. To explain why those who reviewed their compatriots' files concluded that so many were "suspicious" forces one to ruminate about their unspoken assumptions, beliefs, anxieties, and motives. Their own experiences in Poland had convinced them that the police routinely infiltrated radical groups. They viewed the Polish government's repression of Communists as proof of its reactionary intentions, they remembered vividly that the struggle with Trotskyists in the 1920s had divided their party, and recalled which comrades had been on which side of that struggle, they had risen to their positions in the Comintern and their adopted party, the VKP, precisely because they had been vigilant and had accepted the values and logic of Stalinism. In short, their personal histories had predisposed them to share the suspicions of the VKP leaders about their fellow Poles and to view the verification as an opportunity to cast out all who threatened what they had struggled so hard to achieve and what they held sacred. In the process, they became the instruments of their comrades' and their own demise.

The fate of many Hungarian émigrés reminds us that, within fraternal parties, personal and political disputes quite distinct from disputes within the VKP influenced their fates. Such shadowy realities may well have had a comparable effect in other émigré groups. Future efforts to explain why certain émigré groups became victims must take the intraparty divisions into account.

In seeking to understand the origins of the Soviet leadership's distrust of foreigners, it would be prudent not to dismiss out of hand the possibility that foreign intelligence agencies had sent spies into the USSR and that Soviet intelligence agencies had learned of their existence. The Soviet government and the Comintern supported a wide espionage network abroad and believed that other countries did the same within the USSR.[4] To believe that there were no spies in the USSR would be as naive as it is mad to believe that all foreigners were potential spies. As the U.S. policy of incarcerating Japanese Americans

during World War II and many other examples indicate, the Soviet government was not the only one to fear that spies lurked within the ranks of émigré
communities. The archival materials that might reveal what Soviet intelligence
and Stalin knew, or believed they knew, about spies have yet to be examined.
But Soviet leaders clearly believed that spies posed a threat to national security.

At the core of xenophobia is a fear of what is foreign. The émigré communities in the USSR had, by the mid-1930s, become the objects of suspicion, even
fear. Given that many émigrés staffed the Comintern bureaucracy, the Comintern itself became the object of suspicion. By 1937, Stalin and Yezhov believed it to be a "nest of spies." Their suspicions were fantastic, but that should
not lead us to dismiss the underlying fear. They were not the only fearful members of Soviet society. As document after document has shown, many people
acted on the basis of fear. The consequences of that fear were tragic in ways
that defy facile description. As the scale of the repression points up so pain-
fully, no one is more brutal and irrational than fearful people willing to use all
means to extinguish their fears. For all the power and armed might that the
VKP leaders brought to bear on their "enemies," theirs were the actions of
people who believed themselves to be vulnerable.

This leads us back to the ambiguity of Goya's *Colossus*. Like Colossus, Stalin was abnormally powerful yet hauntingly fearful of something that we cannot see. In Goya's painting, the masses are fleeing—but from whom or what?
What makes them flee in such panic that they crush each other in their efforts
to be safe? The answer lies in the unseen. We see only their reactions.

Likewise, the documents in this volume allow us to view only our subjects'
reactions. Those reactions are revealing for what they convey not only about
the political dynamics of the period but also about the very human behaviors
of the people themselves. Existing studies of the mass repression have interpreted it as a Stalinist phenomenon. It was unquestionably that. Yet the behaviors of the Comled
haviors of the Cominternists examined here provide ample evidence that although they lived in a specific political culture, their behaviors were basic
human behaviors. They deserve to be treated as such. One advantage of a case
study is that it allows us to examine how people acted, individually and collectively, within a shared environment. It seems reasonable, therefore, to maxi-
mize that advantage by exploring the human and social reasons for why the
people in the Comintern behaved as they did. Doing so allows us to appreciate
the extent to which their behaviors were specifically Stalinist and universally
human.

Party discipline was one of the VKP's central characteristics, which its members and most Communists had internalized. When Stalin, Dimitrov, or another party authority urged comrades to be vigilant, they obeyed. Some, like Razumova, used the rhetoric of vigilance. Some, like Valter, signaled their bosses about suspected improprieties. They engaged in what Stanley Milgram has called signal conformity—conveying information requested by legitimate authorities. Others engaged in action conformity, which produced tangible results.[5] People like Prokofiev and Petkov obeyed orders to be vigilant by denouncing comrades to party authorities or the NKVD. Others, like Kotelnikov, Chernomordik, Moskvin, and Manuilsky and other Cadres Department officials, compiled and reviewed lists, assembled dossiers, and refined policy implementation. They were, in short, bureaucrats who obeyed orders. They were "just doing their jobs" and trying to do them well. Their behaviors evoke Hannah Arendt's description of Adolf Eichmann, whom she dubbed the quintessential example of "the banality of evil."[6] Regardless of their precise role, the Razumovas, the Prokofievs, the Kotelnikovs, the Manuilskys, the Dimitrovs had internalized the basis of their obedience; it was not simply imposed upon them.[7]

Despite any private reservations, despite the personal stress their behavior might have induced, despite the various animosities within the ECCI apparatus, the comrades obeyed their leaders. They were not inherently malicious. On the contrary, many were selfless, idealistic people who had sacrificed much in hopes of creating a better world, people who behaved the way they did because they believed that their leaders would never have done anything to harm the party, because they were "real Bolsheviks." Like people everywhere, they had a strong "propensity to accept definitions provided by legitimate authority."[8] They shared their leaders' definitions; they did what they did because what they held sacred appeared to be threatened. Like the organization for which they worked, they aspired to be the agents and instruments of their leaders' policies.[9]

The strident rhetoric associated with the vigilance campaign should not divert us from its success in eliciting the very human propensity to obey legitimate authority. Like the members of German police battalions who executed thousands of Polish Jews, or U.S. soldiers who gunned down women and children in My Lai, many Cominternists who participated in the vigilance campaign willingly followed orders that they believed were designed to achieve shared goals. Those beliefs made obedience a duty and an honor. They were proud of their obedience. Carrying out orders well, performing one's duty, even if it produces suffering in others, contributes to one's sense of self-worth and produces a sense of honor.[10] Party loyalty and discipline served the needs of the party hierarchy, but they were also personal imperatives for individual party members, as Prokofiev's political biography and Razumova's and Valter's letters to Dimitrov indicate.

The presence of prominent and powerful Bolsheviks and international Communist leaders within the Comintern headquarters meant that political authority was immediate and omnipresent. The immediacy of authority made the desire to please superiors a powerful drive and at the same time made the possibility of disobedience slim.[11] Like soldiers in a military unit, Comintern-ists operated in a world circumscribed by hierarchy and authority. It is possible that disobedience was never seriously contemplated.

While the people examined here acted as individuals, they also acted collectively. Conformity was a powerful factor in ensuring compliance. Within the VKP and the Comintern, pressures to conform were intense. Individuals' social status, economic well-being, careers—their self-worth and social identity—depended on their conformity to party norms. To challenge or disobey those norms was to run the almost certain risk of rejection and criticism, and the possible risk of expulsion from the party. That comrades who had transgressed policies and norms were subjected to public criticisms and censure by their peers reinforced conformity. As the political situation became more uncertain from mid-1936 and arrests mounted, conformity became an essential means of self-defense and an affirmation that one belonged to the group.[12]

Several other factors made obedience and conformity normal, proper, and desirable behaviors for Cominternists. The leaders of the ECCI party committee made the December 1934 decision to expel Magyar. But Magyar himself legitimized that decision by admitting that his errors warranted expulsion, that he was not a "real Bolshevik." Who attending that meeting could have doubted that expelling him was the correct course of action? Who could have thought even fleetingly that party authorities had erred? The VKP's practice of self-criticism was both a means by which the accused sought absolution and forgiveness and a means of demonstrating that the norms and values of the party were proper and fair. In Magyar's case, demonstrating the fairness of party norms and values was of paramount importance. The defendants at the three major show trials (August 1936, January 1937, and March 1938) "confessed" to their "crimes." In light of their "confessions," who would contemplate disobeying the subsequent calls for vigilance against "enemies"? Self-criticisms and confessions enabled comrades to believe or rationalize that vigilance was essential. VKP members and many fraternal party members believed that their leaders and the NKVD wielded their authority justly. They assumed that the VKP leaders would not label someone an "enemy" without good cause and that the NKVD would not arrest Communists without good cause. Even after being tortured, Razumova, Valter, and Terziev did not believe the NKVD as an organization to be at fault. Rather, they believed that "Trotskyists" and "enemies" had infiltrated its ranks. Self-criticisms, "confessions," and the belief that the authorities were just facilitated conformity.

One of the more striking features of the documents presented here is the absence of any sense of personal responsibility. Prokofiev expressed pride in having denounced many comrades. Petkov evoked duty to justify his denunciations. Kotelnikov took credit for the role he had played in the "unmasking" of "enemies." The examples are many. The absence of expressions of personal responsibility is due in part to the nature of the documents and in part to the belief that such actions were proper. But the abrogation of personal responsibility is also a common consequence of obedience.[13] Like soldiers, bureaucrats, and workers in any hierarchical organization, those in the Comintern headquarters carried out their leaders' orders and, in doing so, shifted responsibility for their actions to their leaders.

Two other factors contributed to the denial of personal responsibility. People tend to believe that victims bring punishment upon themselves. Such was the common perception as to why Safarov, Magyar, David, and others were arrested and why the defendants at the trials were punished. The tendency to blame the victim extended to others as well and was bolstered by self-criticisms and confessions. The second is that the consequences of denunciations were usually far removed from the denouncers. The Prokofievs and Petkovs of the time did not have to face those whom they denounced; quite the reverse: they were praised by their peers or superiors for their actions.

The recurrent calls for vigilance made vigilance, obedience, and conformity routine behaviors. Routinization validates not only the repeated behaviors but also the assumptions, values, and perceptions implicit in the behaviors. The more people repeat an action—going to school, doing a job, or denouncing "enemies"—the easier it is to repeat it and to justify it in terms of some higher goal or good.[14] So routine had vigilance, obedience, and conformity become to Cominternists that they were second nature, a part of who they were.

Although party discipline may have been a specifically Bolshevik trait, party members' willingness to obey and their desire to conform are normal human behaviors. The policies and historical context were specifically Stalinist, but the behaviors were universal. We all have a limited capacity to extricate ourselves from our social environment and a limited ability to imagine what the future holds. We all have a capacity to rationalize our behavior as serving a higher purpose.

Obedience and conformity were but two common human behaviors in evidence in these documents. Other common behaviors help us to understand why obedience and conformity were socially desirable.[15] The men and women who staffed the Comintern headquarters and who belonged to its party organization shared a powerful identity—they were Communists, "real Bolsheviks." Some were VKP members, others belonged to fraternal parties, but all were committed to shared assumptions, values, and goals. They had internalized a worldview that provided them with standards of judgment and frames of reference that enabled them to interpret their world, to reduce uncertainty, and to give meaning to their existence. To be a Communist in the USSR was to be a part of a small, privileged social group the members of which had social status, power, and material benefits. To be a Communist provided powerful personal and group identities that were tightly intertwined.

From Kirov's murder on, Stalin, VKP leaders, and Comintern leaders repeatedly told their followers that "Trotskyists" and "enemies" threatened the party. With each passing year the dimensions and seriousness of that threat purportedly grew. Why Stalin and other VKP leaders chose to frame politics in terms of enemy conspiracies is beyond the scope of this book. But its effect was to threaten party identity. The allegation that party members were complicit in Kirov's murder and other threatening activities required that "real Bolsheviks" ferret out the "enemies" in their midst. The allegations against Trotskyists and Zinovievites, past or present, real or alleged, provided the criteria by which "real Bolsheviks" could define the Other, by which the in-group could define an out-group. Magyar's "confession," Safarov's arrest, and Zinoviev's conviction validated the creation of an out-group.

That process was not an easy one, and it evolved over time. First the threat came from Trotskyists and Zinovievites, then from "enemy agents" disguised as émigrés, then from those who displayed "oppositional tendencies," and then from those who, as Stalin put it, "by his deeds or thoughts . . . threatens the unity of the socialist state." By 1938 the threat came from a world conspiracy. Transforming certain comrades into an out-group required delving into past actions and associations, politicizing personal relationships and styles of work, and interpreting benign behaviors in a sinister light. Doing so required categorizing some members of the in-group into threats to the group. The process of recategorizing comrades required that they be depersonalized

first by defining them as members of an out-group—Trotskyists, Zinovievites
—rather than as individuals and then dehumanizing these groups by giving
them labels like "hostile elements," "enemies," "spies," "murderers," "scum."
Stalin and other VKP leaders defined the terms. But accepting the process provided "real Bolsheviks" in the Comintern headquarters with the psychological
distancing and the personal justifications that allowed them to denounce others and to rationalize their victims' fates.[16]

Scapegoating Trotskyists, Zinovievites, and other perceived "enemies" served
other psychological needs. Those labels were easy to conceptualize, and their
historical associations within the VKP gave them resonance. They offered simple answers to more complex problems that bedeviled the party and its members and supporters. That the anti-Trotskyist campaign had, by 1936, been going on for more than a decade gave it a routine, ritualistic quality that created
binding pressures to participate.[17] Having accepted the initial assumptions
made rejecting more elaborate "explanations" very difficult.

Depersonalizing and dehumanizing threats to the VKP not only solidified
the identity of the in-group, of "real Bolsheviks," but intensified the demands
for group loyalty. The criteria that members used to describe Trotskyists were
the antithesis of the qualities of "real Bolsheviks"—they lacked party discipline, they lacked sufficient vigilance, they "wavered" about party policies,
they placed their personal interests above those of the party. In short, they es-
chewed the norms in which "real Bolsheviks" took pride and which made
"real Bolsheviks" "better than others."[18] To remain an in-group member
meant adhering strictly to VKP values, social norms, and practices.

Implicit in these criteria was the message that the in-group of "real Bolsheviks" was good, and the out-group, "the enemy," was incorrigibly evil. Had
"enemies" not killed Kirov? Did they not plan to kill Stalin? Did they not betray their comrades? Did they not serve the Gestapo? From being an out-
group, the enemy became the "demonic Other."[19] No "real Bolshevik" wanted
to associate with demonic enemies. Consequently, obedience and conformity
intensified for all, especially for those who had once supported but later rejected political opposition groups. Quite a few such people staffed the ECCI
apparatus or lived within the émigré communities.

Although the hunt for accomplices in Kirov's murder abated in 1935, the
vigilance campaign continued. Late that year, the VKP and ECCI leaders announced a new threat—"secret agents" "under the guise of émigrés." That announcement created a new out-group, a new Other, whose members had to be
identified. Given the increasingly tense international situation, the transfor-

mation of émigrés, an ethnic out-group, into the Other was relatively easy. During the verification of émigrés living in the USSR, the power of party identity became clear. Foreign-born VKP members and prominent fraternal party members staffed the verification commissions. To prove their vigilance and their adherence to the in-group, commission members appear to have signaled any suspicions to their superiors.[20] Their behavior, like that of Petkov and other émigrés who submitted denunciations, bound them psychologically to the in-group, even as their ethnicity was becoming a political liability.

The August 1936 trial not only ratcheted up the demands for vigilance but (with the January 1937 trial) welded the two existing out-groups into a single group of conspirators, a single Other. The arrest and conviction of former Comintern workers created a bewildering and critical situation among its staff. As fantastic as the explanations for the arrests might seem to us, they provided answers that resonated with the values and traditions of "real Bolsheviks." They provided meaning. The VKP leaders demanded that their followers identify any potential enemy. The Cadres Department and the party committee compiled lists of those with oppositional pasts and tendencies, as well as lists of "suspicious" people, thereby expanding the ranks of the out-group, which in turn fanned the anxieties of the party leaders. In this uncertain situation, the members of the ECCI apparatus responded in a variety of ways. The rhetoric of vigilance and the demands for compliance intensified. Some comrades, out of conviction, careerism, or fear, denounced other comrades. The defense of the in-group and one's membership in it required proving that one possessed the attributes prized by the group.

Denouncing comrades, transforming comrades into an Other, were acts of personal and group defense. "Real Bolsheviks" viewed their personal interests and those of the in-group as identical. The defense of the group was a defense of its members—their ideals, status, self-worth, and all that they had struggled to achieve. Identification with the group provided its members with personal stability, however illusory that may have proven to be in 1937–1938.[21] As we have seen, actions carried out to defend the group and its members actually put those who worked in the Comintern headquarters, in the "nest of spies," at increased risk. When Stalin unleashed the mass repression in spring 1937, the ranks of those affiliated with the Comintern—its staff and émigrés residing in the USSR, "real Bolsheviks," and those with alleged oppositional tendencies alike—were quickly thinned.

The stresses associated with the onset of the mass repression created significant strains among all associated with the Comintern, even among the self-proclaimed "real Bolsheviks." Some, like Walecki, denounced his comrades. Others took a different tack. As the June 1937 party meeting suggests, subgroups of "real Bolsheviks," in this case the rank and file, sought to redefine the criteria of "real Bolshevism" in an effort to gain safe ground in a struggle that exposed the fissures hidden under party discipline and rhetorical homogeneity.

It is tempting to view the tragedy that unfolded within the Comintern from late 1934 to 1939 in strictly Soviet or Stalinist terms. The phenomenon was undoubtedly a Stalinist one. Stalin, the Politburo, the Central Committee, and the NKVD orchestrated and executed the mass repression. The Soviet state, which implemented party policies, had no restraints save for the party itself; it had no capacity to restrain the repression. But the behaviors—individual and collective—of those in the Comintern apparatus were not uniquely Soviet. Just as tragic as the senseless deaths and incarcerations, as the deformation of the human spirit, was that normal human behaviors produced inhumane consequences. What makes any study of the Stalinist or any other mass repression so disturbing is not the capacity and willingness of a state to repress its citizens—that is, sadly, a tale as old as history—but the capacity of citizens to participate in the repression.

Using theories about obedience, authority, and group behaviors provides a way to help understand the complex political and human dynamics of the 1930s. They cannot explain everything. The available evidence is of limited utility in revealing people's private thoughts and motives or even their unrecorded actions. And it sheds only dim light on the extent to which individuals lived in fear of denunciation or arrest and the extent to which their public behaviors were hypocritical. Such are the limitations imposed by the sources. As with Goya's *Colossus,* we can only interpret what we can see. As important as knowing private thoughts is to enhancing our understanding of the period, the fact remains that what validated the vigilance campaign among Cominternists, what fueled the repression, what resulted in some people being arrested and others remaining free, were the public acts taken by groups and individuals in the name of the group. Finding methods to interpret those actions enhances our appreciation of the human history of Stalinism.

The twentieth century had more than its share of state-sponsored repression: Soviet collectivization, the Stalinist mass repression, Nazi and fascist mass repression, the Holocaust, the Great Proletarian Cultural Revolution in China, the Armenian genocide, McCarthyism, the killing fields of the Khmer Rouge, genocide in Rwanda and the former Yugoslavia, the "disappearing" of citizens in several South and Central American countries—and the list could go on. Neither Communists nor fascists, neither nationalists nor generals, have a monopoly on crimes against their fellow human beings. Brutality in service of a higher good is ideologically neutral. The capacity of governments, especially dictatorial governments, to unleash murderous policies is hardly a revelation. If we are to learn from the past, we need to learn more about those basic human propensities and behaviors that, under certain conditions, make human beings capable of behaving inhumanely.

Notes

Introduction

1. On the founding and early activities and expectations of the Comintern, see Chapter 1; Edward Hallett Carr, *The Bolshevik Revolution, 1917–1923*, 3 vols. (London, 1973), vol. 3; Julius Braunthal, *History of the International, 1914–1943* (London, 1967), 1–255 passim; Kevin McDermott and Jeremy Agnew, *The Comintern: A History of International Communism from Lenin to Stalin* (New York, 1997); R. Craig Nation, *War on War: Lenin, the Zimmerwald Left, and the Origins of International Communism* (Durham, N.C., 1989); C. L. R. James, *World Revolution, 1917–1936* (Atlantic Highlands, N.J., 1993). For collections of Comintern documents relating to this period, see Jane Degras, ed., *The Communist International, 1919–1943: Documents*, 3 vols. (London, 1965); J. Riddell, ed., *Founding the Communist International: Proceedings and Documents of the First Congress, March 1919* (New York, 1987); J. Riddell, ed., *Workers of the World and Oppressed People, Unite! Proceedings and Documents of the Second Congress*, 2 vols. (New York, 1991).

2. Although somewhat dated, the best English-language discussion and taxonomy of the literature relevant to the mass repression can be found in Chris Ward, *Stalin's Russia* (London, 1993), chapter 4. No single footnote can do justice to the substantial literature on the mass repression. But among the most influential English-language works written before the opening of Soviet archives are John Armstrong, *The Politics of Totalitarianism: The Communist Party of the Soviet Union from 1934 to the Present* (New York, 1961); Zbigniew Brzezinski, *The Permanent Purge: Politics in Soviet Totalitarianism* (Cambridge, Mass., 1956); Robert Conquest, *The Great Terror: A Reassessment* (New York, 1990); Robert Conquest, *Stalin and the Kirov Murder* (New York, 1989); Issac Deutscher, *Stalin: A Political Biography* (New York, 1967); J. Arch Getty, *The Origins of the Great*

Purges: The Soviet Communist Party Reconsidered, 1933–1938 (New York, 1985); Roberta T. Manning, "Government in the Soviet Countryside in the Stalinist Thirties: The Case of Belyi Raion in 1937," *The Carl Beck Papers in Russian and East European Studies,* no. 301 (1983); Robert McNeal, *Stalin: Man and Ruler* (New York, 1988); Roy Medvedev, *Let History Judge: The Origins and Consequences of Stalinism,* trans. Colleen Taylor, ed. David Joravsky and Georges Haupt (New York, 1972); Gábor T. Rittersporn, *Stalinist Simplifications and Soviet Complications: Social Tensions and Political Conflicts in the USSR, 1933–1953* (Chur, Switzerland, 1991); Robert Tucker, *Stalin in Power: The Revolution from Above, 1928–1941* (New York, 1990); Adam Ulam, *Stalin: The Man and His Era* (New York, 1973); and the essays in J. Arch Getty and Roberta T. Manning, eds., *Stalinist Terror: New Perspectives* (New York, 1993), but especially Gábor Rittersporn, "The Omnipresent Conspiracy: On Soviet Imagery of Politics and Social Relations in the 1930s," 99–115; J. Arch Getty and William J. Chase, "Patterns of Repression Among the Soviet Elite in the Late 1930s: A Biographical Approach," 225–246; Sheila Fitzpatrick, "The Impact of the Great Purges on Soviet Elites: A Case Study of Moscow and Leningrad Telephone Directories of the 1930s," 247–260.

With the publication of documents during *glasnost,* students of the history of the Stalin period have begun to rethink their interpretations. For a discussion of Soviet scholars' early rewriting of Soviet history, see R. W. Davies, *Soviet History in the Gorbachev Revolution* (London, 1989). See also Takayuki Ito, ed., *Facing Up to the Past: Soviet Historiography Under Perestroika* (Sapporo, 1989).

For recent studies based on formerly closed archives, see Oleg Khlevniuk, *1937: Stalin, NKVD i sovetskoe obshchestvo* (Moscow, 1992) and *Politbiuro: Mekhanizmy politicheskoi vlasti v 1930-e gody* (Moscow, 1996); Peter H. Solomon, Jr., *Soviet Criminal Justice Under Stalin* (Cambridge, Mass., 1996); Robert W. Thurston, *Life and Terror in Stalin's Russia, 1934–1941* (New Haven, 1996); Dmitrii Volkogonov, *Stalin: Triumph and Tragedy,* ed. and trans. Harold Shukman (New York, 1991); J. Arch Getty and Oleg V. Naumov, *The Road to Terror: Stalin and the Self-Destruction of the Bolsheviks, 1932–1939* (New Haven, 1999); Edvard Radzinsky, *Stalin,* trans. H. T. Willetts (New York, 1996).

3. The only party archive open to scholars prior to the collapse of the USSR was the Smolensk Archive. For a history of the forced migration of the Smolensk Archive from Smolensk to Washington, see Patricia Kennedy Grimsted, "The Odyssey of the Smolensk Archive: Plundered Communist Records for the Service of Anti-Communism," *The Carl Beck Papers in Russian and East European Studies,* no. 1201 (1995). For a discussion of the Smolensk Archive as a source, see J. Arch Getty, "The Smolensk Archive," in Sheila Fitzpatrick and Lynne Viola, eds., *A Researcher's Guide to Sources in Soviet Social History in the 1930s* (New York, 1990).

4. Case studies that relate to the mass repression are relatively few. For examples, see Merle Fainsod, *Smolensk Under Soviet Rule* (Cambridge, Mass., 1958); Getty, *Origins;* Getty and Naumov, *Road to Terror;* Manning, "Government in the Soviet Countryside"; Roberta T. Manning, "The Great Purges in a Rural District: Belyi Raion Revisited," in Getty and Manning, *Stalinist Terror,* 168–197; Roger R. Reese, "The Red Army and the Great Purges," in ibid., 198–214; David Hoffman, "The Great Terror on the Local Level: Purges in Moscow Factories," in ibid.,

163–167; Hiroaki Kuromiya, "Stalinist Terror in the Donbas: A Note," in ibid., 214–222; James R. Harris, *The Great Urals: Regionalism and the Evolution of the Soviet System, 1917–1939* (Ithaca, N.Y., 1999); Hiroaki Kuromiya, *Freedom and Terror in the Donbas: A Ukrainian-Russian Borderland, 1870s-1990s* (New York, 1998), esp. 201–250. Fainsod's and Manning's works, as well as Getty, *Origins,* focus on the Smolensk party organization.

5. Although the name of the Bolshevik Party changed during 1917–1939, I will use the abbreviation VKP to identify it. Its official name during the 1930s was the All-Union Communist Party (Bolshevik), and the common abbreviation used was VKP(b). The shortened abbreviation VKP will be used in the narrative text. However, VKP(b) is used in the documents of the period, including many quoted in part or in full in this book.

6. I draw on theories of social psychology that relate to obedience, conformity, group identity, and group behavior to explain the behaviors manifested during this period. The theories utilized are summarized at the end of Chapter 1, and the behaviors are analyzed in Chapter 8.

7. The name and bureaucratic location of the state security organ were changed often during the Soviet period, from Cheka (All-Russian Extraordinary Commission for Combating Counterrevolution and Sabotage, 1917–1922), to GPU (State Political Administration, 1922–1923), to OGPU (Unified State Political Administration, 1923–1934), to NKVD (People's Commissariat for Internal Affairs, 1934–1943), to NKGB (People's Commissariat for State Security, 1943–46), to MGB (Ministry for State Security, 1946–1953), to MVD (Ministry for Internal Affairs, 1953–1954), to KGB (Committee for State Security, 1954–1991). In 1934 the OGPU and the NKVD were merged; however, the state security section (the former OGPU) retained much of its autonomy within the NKVD.

8. Jonathan Haslam, *The Soviet Union and the Struggle for Collective Security, 1933–1939* (New York, 1984); Oleg Ken, *Collective Security or Isolation? Soviet Foreign Policy and Poland, 1930–1935* (St. Petersburg, 1996); O. N. Ken and A. I. Rupasov, *Politbiuro TsK VKP(b) i otnosheniia SSSR s zapadnymi sosednimi gosudarstvami. (konets 1920–1930-x gg.)* (St. Petersburg, 2000). Émigrés from the Scandinavian countries, Western Europe (especially Austria and Italy), Asia (especially Korea and China), and the Americas also resided in the USSR. Many of them were political refugees.

9. See the 27 May 1937 entry in *The Diary of Georgi Dimitrov,* ed. Ivo Banac and F. I. Firsov (New Haven, forthcoming).

10. Figures on the number of ECCI party organization members who were arrested, as well as materials on the effect of mass arrests on certain ECCI departments, are discussed in Chapter 6. For efforts to ascertain the precise number of Comintern officials and members repressed, see Mikhail Panteleiev, "La terreur stalinienne au Komintern en 1937–1938: Les chiffres et les causes," *Communisme: Revue du Centre d'etude d'histoire et de sociologie du communisme,* 40–41 (1994–1995), 37–53; Branko Lazitch, "Stalin's Massacre of Foreign Communist Leaders," in Milorad M. Drachkovitch and Branko Lazitch, eds., *The Comintern: Historical Highlights, Essays, Recollections and Documents* (New York, 1966).

11. See Rittersporn, "Omnipresent Conspiracy."

12. "Tragediia RKKA.: M. N. Tukhachevskii i 'Voenno-fashistskii zagovor,'" *Voenno-istoricheskii arkhiv,* no. 2 (1997), 3–42.

13. A. K. Sokolov, *Lektsii po sovetskoi istorii, 1917–1940* (Moscow, 1995), 229–242.

Chapter 1. The Comintern

1. For discussions of Lenin's views on the Second International and the need for a Third International, see Nation; Braunthal; McDermott. For examples of Lenin's writings on these issues, see his 1915 pamphlet *The Collapse of the Second International* (Moscow, 1969) and his 1918 pamphlet *The Proletarian Revolution and the Renegade Kautsky* (Moscow, 1967).

2. As quoted in "Ustav Kommunisticheskogo Internatsionala," in *Vtoroi kongress Kominterna, Iiul'-avgust 1920g.* (Moscow, 1934), 536. On the First Congress, see Riddell, *Founding the Communist International.*

3. Historians have accepted that the Twenty-One Points were written by Lenin and Zinoviev; but nowhere, other than in secondary works, is joint authorship attributed. A draft of the Twenty-One Points was published as a brochure under Zinoviev's name: *Theses to the Second Congress of the Communist International* (Petrograd, 1920), 75–83. The Comintern journal *Kommunisticheskii Internatsional*, 12 (1920), published the draft and gave authorship to the ECCI. In 1934 the Twenty-One Points were published in Lenin's *Collected Works* as a document written by Lenin, but there were obvious political reasons for doing so.

4. For the Twenty-One Points, see Braunthal, 537–542.

5. The quotation is from "Platforma Kommunisticheskogo Internatsionala," in E. Korotky, B. Kun, and O. Pyatnitsky, eds., *Pervyi Kongress Kominterna, Mart 1919g.* (Moscow, 1933), 179.

6. For the proceedings and decisions of the Second Congress, see Riddell, *Workers of the World.*

7. *Kommunisticheskii Internatsional v dokumentakh: Resheniia, tezisy i vossvaniia kongressov Kominterna i plenumov IKKI, 1919–1932*, ed. Béla Kun (Moscow, 1933), 407–408.

8. Ibid., 782, 880.

9. For discussions, see Braunthal; McDermott; Issac Deutscher, *The Prophet Unarmed: Trotsky, 1921–1929* (New York, 1980); Stephen Cohen, *Bukharin and the Bolshevik Revolution: A Political Biography, 1888–1938* (New York, 1975), 243–336 passim.

10. For a discussion, see McDermott; Braunthal; Julian Jackson, *The Popular Front: Defending Democracy, 1934–38* (New York, 1988), 17–51.

11. On Dimitrov's questioning of Third Period tactics, see *Stalin and Dimitrov,* 7–22.

12. *Tsentralnyi partinii arkhiv* (Sofia), f. 146, op. 2, a.e. 317, l. 11. My thanks to Fridrikh Firsov for sharing this material with me.

13. "Platforma Kommunisticheskogo Internatsionala," 179.

14. For example, at the Sixth Comintern Congress in 1928, eight VKP members were elected to the fifty-eight member ECCI: Bukharin, Stalin, Molotov, Rykov, Manuilsky, Pyatnitsky, Lozovsky, and Skrypnik. Seven VKP members were elected to the ECCI Presidium : Bukharin, Stalin, Molotov, Manuilsky, Pyatnitsky, Khitarov (from the Communist Youth International), and Lozovsky (from the Trade Union International). Bukharin, Molotov, and Pyatnitsky were elected members of

the ECCI Political Secretariat; Manuilsky, Khitarov, and Lozovsky were candidate members. For a list of ECCI members and candidate members elected at the Sixth Comintern Congress, see G. M. Adibekov, E. N. Shakhnazarova, and K. K. Shirinia, *Organizatsionaia struktura Kominterna, 1919–1943* (Moscow, 1997), 140–143. At the Seventh Comintern Congress, the VKP delegation in the forty-six member ECCI consisted of five members: Yezhov, Manuilsky, Stalin, Moskvin, Zhdanov. Ibid., 182–185. Although as a rule, fraternal parties had only one representative each on the ECCI, the most important parties were exceptions. For example, in 1929 Thälmann and Remmele of the German CP were members of the ECCI Presidium; Alfredo Ercoli (Palmiro Togliatti) and Serra of the Italian CP were members; Lenski and Bronkowski of the Polish CP were member and candidate member, respectively; and Pierre Semard and Henri Barbé of the French CP were likewise member and candidate member, respectively.

15. For example, at its 14 May 1929 meeting, held in Stalin's office, the VKP delegation to the ECCI adopted the following resolution regarding the CPP: "To consider as essential the lowering of the number of members of the PB [Politburo] CP Poland so that in the PB [there will be]: two [members] of the former majority, two [members] from the former minority, and c. Sokolik [aka V. Knorin]. This decision should be introduced by c. Sokolik [Knorin] at the plenum of the CC CP Poland. Note: . . . this decision should not be communicated to anyone among the Polish comrades." Regarding the CPUSA, the delegation resolved: "To abolish the post of general secretary in the CP USA. The Secretariat to be comprised of five comrades: two from the majority, Foster, Wainstein, and the ECCI representative. To give the ECCI representative the right to veto Politburo decisions if they contradict ECCI decisions." F. 508, op. 1, d. 83, l. 1. The VKP delegation that reached these decisions consisted of Stalin, Molotov, Lozovsky, Gusev, Khitarov, Knorin, and N. N. Popov.

16. See *Diary of Georgi Dimitrov.* On 10 August 1935 the Politburo transferred Pyatnitsky to work outside the Comintern.

17. F. 495, op. 1, d. 274, ll. 117–118. Kotelnikov was the second party secretary of the ECCI party organization, from December 1934 until he became the first secretary in May 1935.

18. The ECCI's partkom reported to the Rostokinsky district committee (*raikom*), which itself reported to the Moscow city committee (*gorkom*).

19. While this generally held true within the higher levels of the Comintern, the extent of Bolshevization varied somewhat within the fraternal parties, both in and outside the USSR.

20. *Archives de Jules Humbert-Droz,* vol. 3: *Parti communistes et l'international communiste dans les annes 1928–1932* (Dordrecht, 1988), 165. On this attitude, see also Fischer.

21. It should be pointed out that such campaigns were not confined to "deviant" VKP members and groups. Instigated by such VKP campaigns, the ECCI conducted campaigns against members of its fraternal parties who supported oppositionists (e.g., against Brandlerists in Germany, Lovestoneites in the United States).

22. For a discussion of the history and evolution of the Comintern bureaucracy, see Adibekov, Shakhnazarova, and Shirinia.

23. In August 1939, after the signing of the Nazi-Soviet non-aggression pact,

the ECCI unilaterally changed a fundamental Comintern policy for the first time when it abandoned the anti-fascist Popular Front and defined the mission of fraternal party members as to struggle first and foremost against imperialism.

24. The ECCI Presidium existed without interruption from July 1919 until the dissolution of the Comintern in June 1943, although between July and September 1919 it was called the Small Bureau of the ECCI (Maloe biuro IKKI).

25. The Political Commission of the Political Secretariat was the highest executive organ of the ECCI in 1929–1935. In January 1935 its members were Dimitrov, Wang Ming, Fritz Heckert, Klement Gottwald, Otto Kuusinen, Manuilsky, Pyatnitsky, and Ercoli (Togliatti); Bronislav Bronkowski and Knorin were candidate members.

26. The Comintern Congresses elected the members and candidate members of the ECCI and the International Control Commission. The elections to the ECCI Presidium and Secretariat took place at an ECCI plenum following the Congress. For a discussion of the reorganization, see Adibekov, Shakhnazarova, Shirinia, 186–187.

27. F. 495, op. 2, d. 64, l. 214. For the groupings of the various Communist Parties into Lendersecretariats (also referred to as Ländersecretariats) or Secretariats, see Adibekov, Shakhnazarova, Shirinia, 152–156; Getty and Kozlov, eds., *Kratkii putevoditel'*, 74–83.

28. F. 495, op. 18, d. 1073, l. 3, 65–66. See also Adibekov, Shakhnazarova, Shirinia, 203–206. Although some larger CPs, such as the German CP, had their own representatives, smaller parties, like those in Latin America, shared a single representative. Large parties, such as the German CP, also had their own section, the head of which was the representative. Other parties were grouped into sections based on geographic proximity. For example, the Polish section included the representatives of the Polish, Western Ukrainian, and Western Belorussian parties. The representative of such combined sections was usually the representative of the largest party.

29. For a discussion of the OMS and Communications Department, see Adibekov, Shakhnazarova, Shirinia, 199–201. After the Seventh Comintern Congress in 1935, the leading members of the Cadres Department were A. Krajewski, M. Chernomordik, A. Andreev, and P. Guliaev. For a discussion, see ibid., 193–196.

30. Very often the leaders of fraternal parties sent to the ECCI Cadres Department information on members and others they deemed worthy of note by the Comintern. For one example, see f. 495, op. 74, d. 128, l. 1, a letter from Belov of the Cadres Department to Manuilsky informing him that the German CP had sent to the Cadres Department "sixty-seven documents containing 257 pages. Their contents include materials on the verification of [German] political émigrés in Holland, reports from political émigrés concerning their work in the country, and information on the activities of Trotskyists in other countries (a list of addresses)." Belov attached "Notes from materials on Trotskyists." See ibid., ll. 19–20.

31. F. 495, op. 21, d. 28, l. 34. For a similar list compiled between December 1932 and May 1934, see ibid., l. 28. My thanks to Fridrikh Firsov for sharing these materials with me.

32. MOPR is the abbreviation for Mezhdunarodnaia organizatsiia pomoschi bortsam revoliutsii, also known as the International Red Aid. It was created in 1922 on the initiative of the Fourth Comintern Congress. Its tasks were to provide legal and material support to political prisoners and their families. It was com-

posed of national sections with individual and collective members. Among the émigrés and refugees were Communist Party members affiliated with the Comintern. The ECCI assigned officials to direct the work of Communist factions among MOPR's charges and took special interest in MOPR's activities. In 1928, B. Šmeral, an ECCI Presidium member, was responsible for relations with MOPR; in 1935 that responsibility fell to André Marty. See Adibekov, Shakhnazarova, Shirina, 166, 189. MOPR was dissolved in 1938.

33. The names of the various organs responsible for state security changed over time. For a discussion, see *Lubianka, 1917–1960 gg. Spravochnik* (Moscow, 1997).

34. F. 495, op. 21, d. 47, ll. 1–3. For example, on 9 May 1939, Guliaev, an official in the Cadres Department, wrote to Smorodinskii, head of the Third Department of GUGB: "I ask that you quickly verify the following [eight] Hungarian comrades for leadership work." Ibid., d. 66, l. 5. Similar letters were sent seeking verification for members of other fraternal Communist Parties and workers in the ECCI apparatus. Ibid., ll. 1–3, 4, 6, 8–11, 13. My thanks to Fridrikh Firsov for sharing these materials with me.

35. F. 495, op. 175, d. 101, l. 105. See also ibid., l. 107. My thanks to Fridrikh Firsov for sharing these materials with me.

36. But as Aino Kuusinen who worked for the ECCI in the 1920s and 1930s and was the wife of Otto Kuusinen, an ECCI member, noted, such routines did not mean the absence of friction between the two organizations. Aino Kuusinen, *The Rings of Destiny: Inside Soviet Russia from Lenin to Brezhnev,* trans. Paul Stevenson (New York, 1974), 40.

37. F. 495, op. 21, d. 24, l. 26. My thanks to Fridrikh Firsov for sharing these materials with me.

38. As we shall see, the expansion of police powers in 1937–1938 occurred with the Politburo's approval and as a result of its initiative. See Chapter 6; and Getty and Naumov, *Road to Terror.*

39. The VKP party organization within the Comintern conducted a purge in 1921, a verification in 1924, a purge in 1929, a purge in July–August 1933 and another in September–November 1933, a supplemental purge of selected party organizations within the ECCI (e.g., OMS) in 1935, a verification in 1935, and an exchange of party documents (*obmen partdokumentov*) in the summer of 1936. On each occasion, the CC VKP had ordered a purge or verification for the entire party; supplemental purges (e.g., of OMS in 1935) resulted when a party organization failed for some reason to properly conduct what the CC viewed as a routine membership screening. For a discussion of these screenings within the VKP in the 1930s, see T. H. Rigby, *Communist Party Membership in the USSR, 1917–1967* (Princeton, 1968); Fainsod, *Smolensk*; Getty, *Origins,* 38–136 passim.

40. F. 495, op. 19, d. 342, l. 3. Military intelligence (Razvedupr) was later renamed the Fourth Department of the Red Army Staff and then the Main Intelligence Directorate (Glavnaia razvedovatel'naia upraleniia) within the USSR Ministry of Defense. My thanks to Fridrikh Firsov for sharing these materials with me.

41. Ibid., d. 362a, ll. 167–168. My thanks to Fridrikh Firsov for sharing these materials with me.

42. For example, see f. 495, op. 19, d. 362a, ll. 167–168.

43. The ties and relations among the Comintern, Soviet security organs, and fraternal parties abroad were multifaceted and complex. This was especially the

case in such areas as China and Japanese-occupied Manchuria from the early 1930s and Spain in 1936–1939 where military operations took place. Such activities deserve special attention, but are beyond the scope of this book.

44. Stalin suggested appointing Moskvin to the ECCI. In 1923–1924, Moskvin had worked briefly for the Comintern as a leading member of its Illegal Commission. For materials relating to Moskvin's work for that commission, which directed the types and nature of illegal work which fraternal parties were to carry out in their native countries, see f. 495, op. 27, d. 1, ll. 1, 38. My thanks to Fridrikh Firsov for sharing this material with me.

45. Other ECCI personnel who worked in the Red Army's Fourth Department included Alexander Mirov (aka Jacob Abramov), Richard Sorge, and Aino Kuusinen. Kuusinen, 40–41, 112–148.

46. See the entries for 1934–1936 passim in *The Diary of Georgi Dimitrov* for his belief in the progress and promises of the Soviet experiment.

47. F. 546, op. 1, d. 274, l. 293.

48. On the blend of these emotions in individuals, see Richard Crossman, ed., *The God That Failed* (New York, 1965); Pavel Sudaplatov and Anatoli Sudaplatov with Jerold L. and Leona P. Schecter, *Special Tasks: The Memoirs of an Unwanted Witness—A Soviet Spymaster* (Boston, 1994); Kuusinen; Feliks Ivanovich Chuev, *Molotov Remembers: Inside Kremlin Politics—Conversations with Felix Chuev* (Chicago, 1993). Robert Thurston, in *Life and Terror,* makes an effort to explore personal values during the 1930s. The recent publication of private diaries from the 1930s allows readers to explore the complexities of personal values. For examples, see Veronique Garros, Natalia Korenevskaya, and Thomas Lahusen, eds., *Intimacy and Terror: Soviet Diaries of the 1930s* (New York, 1995); Jochem Hellbeck, "Fashioning the Stalinist Soul: The Diary of Stepan Podlubny (1931–1939)," *Jahrbücher für Geschichte Osteuropas,* 44 (1996), 344–373.

49. Stanley Migram, *Obedience to Authority: An Experimental View* (New York, 1974). For a different perspective, see Arthur G. Miller, *The Obedience Experiments: A Case Study of Controversy in Social Science* (New York, 1986). For the application of Milgram's findings to a historical phenomenon, see Christopher R. Browning, *Ordinary Men: Reserve Police Battalion 101 and the Final Solution in Poland* (New York, 1998).

50. For a discussion of the influence of peer pressure and peer conformity on people's tendency to obedience, see Stanley Milgram, "Group Pressure and Action Against a Person," *Journal of Abnormal and Social Psychology,* 69, no. 2 (1964), 137–143.

51. For examples of this internalization among Communists outside the USSR, see Crossman, *God That Failed,* esp. the essays by Koestler, Silone, and Wright.

52. Hadley Cantril, *The Psychology of Social Movements* (New York, 1941), 28, 38. On adopting norms and rules, see Cantril, *Psychology of Social Movements,* 15, 38. On social groups and social identity, see Henri Tajfel, ed., *Differentiation Between Social Groups: Studies in the Social Psychology of Intergroup Relations* (London, 1978); Tajfel, *Human Groups and Social Categories: Studies in Social Psychology* (New York, 1981); W. Peter Robinson, ed., *Social Groups and Identities: Developing the Legacy of Henri Tajfel* (Oxford, 1996).

53. See Viktor E. Frankl, *Man's Search for Meaning: An Introduction to Logotherapy* (New York, 1963).

54. See Tajfel, *Differentiation;* Tajfel, *Human Groups;* Robinson; Michael Hogg and Dominic Abrams, "Toward a Single-Process Uncertainty Reduction Model of Social Motivation in Groups," in Hogg and Abrams, eds., *Group Motivation: Social Psychological Perspectives* (New York, 1993).

55. Cantril, *Social Movements,* 64.

56. On this, see Gordon W. Allport and Leo J. Postman, "The Basic Psychology of Rumor," in *Readings in Social Psychology,* 3d ed. (New York, 1958), 54–65; Hadley Cantril, "The Invasion from Mars," in ibid., 291–300; Tamotsu Shibutani, *Improvised News: A Sociological Study of Rumor* (New York, 1966), 1–62 passim; , Cantril, *Social Movements,* 57–58.

57. For an intriguing view of the power of conspiracy theories as a means of framing reality during this period, see Rittersporn, "Omnipresent Conspiracy."

58. See Tajfel, *Human Groups,* 254–259.

59. V. I. Lenin, *"Left-Wing" Communism: An Infantile Disorder* (Moscow, 1968).

60. For discussions, see Michal Reiman, *The Birth of Stalinism: The USSR on the Eve of the "Second Revolution,"* trans. George Saunders (Bloomington, Ind., 1987); Ruth Fischer, *Stalin and German Communism: A Study in the Origins of the State Party* (New Brunswick, N.J.,1982); *Stalin's Letters to Molotov,* ed. Lars T. Lih, Oleg V. Naumov, and Oleg V. Khlevniuk (New Haven, 1995); Catherine Merridale, *Moscow Politics and the Rise of Stalin: The Communist Party in the Capital, 1925–32* (New York, 1990).

61. This is not to imply that the Stalinist leadership viewed the Rightists as a lesser danger in 1928–1929. On the contrary, Stalin and Molotov viewed the possibility of a reformist victory with great alarm. For example, see *Stalin's Letters to Molotov,* 148–169; Merridale; Reiman.

Chapter 2. The Kirov Murder and the Call for Vigilance

1. For examples of differing viewpoints, see Conquest, *Great Terror;* Robert Conquest, *Stalin and the Kirov Murder* (New York, 1989); Tucker, *Stalin in Power;* Medvedev, *Let History Judge;* Ulam; Getty, *Origins;* Getty and Naumov, *Road to Terror,* chapter 4; Alla Kirilina, *Rikoshet, ili skol'ko chelovek bylo ubito vystrelom v Smol'nom* (St. Petersburg, 1993); Amy Knight, *Who Killed Kirov? The Kremlin's Greatest Mystery* (New York, 1999).

2. On 2 December 1934 the Military Board of the Supreme Court of the USSR considered the cases of the "recently arrested White Guards charged with organizing terrorist acts against the representatives of the Soviet power." On 5 December, thirty-seven people in Leningrad and twenty-nine in Moscow were shot on the basis of this charge. On 11 December, nine people accused of terrorism were shot in Minsk, and on 15 December, twenty-eight were shot in Kiev.

3. The political cost of trying the White Guardists in a closed court and of executing them was clearly expressed by a professor at Edinburgh University who wrote to the CC VKP that "when people read in the newspapers that the case of these criminals was tried in a secret court and that as a result 117 were executed, they are horrified. Newspapers including those which up to now were sympathetic to strengthening relations with the USSR call this the beginning of a new epoch of terror." F. 17, op. 120, d. 205, l. 21. My thanks to Fridrikh Firsov for sharing this material with me.

4. By February 1935, according to Yezhov, who oversaw the CC's investigation into the Kirov murder, more than one thousand former Leningrad oppositionists had been rounded up. Some three hundred were arrested; the remainder were exiled from the city. In addition, several thousand "former people" (nobles, former bourgeois, etc.) were exiled from the city. See the discussion in Getty and Naumov, *Road to Terror*, chapter 4; Conquest, *Kirov Murder*; Conquest, *Great Terror*, chapter 2.

5. For an example of such a telegram from the ECCI, see f. 495, op. 184, d. 21, outgoing 1935 to London, dated 11 January 1935.

6. KIM (Kommunisticheskii internatsional molodezhi) was also known as the Young Communist International (YCI). It was founded in November 1919 at the first congress of Communist and left socialist union of youth in Berlin. In 1921 the Executive Committee of the KIM moved to Moscow, where it became a section of the Comintern. It was dissolved on 1 June 1943 along with the Comintern. On the KIM, see Richard Cornell, *Revolutionary Vanguard* (Ithaca, N.Y., 1982).

7. Signatures at the bottom of the telegram indicate that Vasili T. Chemodanov, secretary of the Executive Committee of the KIM from 1930 to 1937, and Alexander L. Abramov, who headed the OMS from 1926 and was deputy head of the Communications Department from 1935, approved the text. Chemodanov (1903–1937) joined the VKP in 1924. He was arrested by the NKVD on the evening of 15–16 September 1937 and sentenced to be shot on 27 November 1937. Abramov (pseudonym Mirov; 1895–1937) joined the Bolsheviks in 1916. He was arrested in 1937 and executed on 26 November 1937.

8. The quotations in the text come from the "top secret" telegram from the Scandanavian Lendersecretariat of the ECCI to the CC of the Swedish CP dated 2 January 1935. The telegram was written in German and signed by Abramov and one other person, whose signature is illegible. F. 495, op. 184, d. 47, outgoing telegrams for 1935.

9. See, e.g., ibid.; and the telegram dated 3 January 1935 sent to the CC of the Swiss CP: f. 495, op. 184, d. 50, outgoing for 1935 to Switzerland, dated 3 January 1935 and signed by Knorin and Abramov; the original is handwritten in Russian.

10. Another telegram that told fraternal parties how to respond to Western doubts about the judicial activities following the Kirov murder can be found in f. 495, op. 184, d. 21, outgoing 1935 to London, dated 11 January 1935.

11. The German original was signed by Gottwald, Manuilsky, Pyatnitsky, Knorin, Gerish, and two others, whose signatures are illegible.

12. *Lo Stato Operaio* was the theoretical journal of the Italian CP. It was published legally in Paris from 1927 to 1939; it was published in New York from 1940 to 1943. The telegram refers to the article entitled "On the Leningrad Attempt" ("Dopo l'attentato di Leningrado") in the January 1935 issue.

13. For reactions to the Kirov murder within the Smolensk party organization, see Getty, *Origins*, 113–116; Fainsod, 56–57, 222–223. For the reactions to it among Leningrad residents, see Leslie Rimmel, "Another Kind of Fear: The Kirov Murder and the End of Bread Rationing in Leningrad," *Slavic Review*, 56, no. 3 (Fall 1997), 481–499.

14. On Safarov's oppositional views and activities in 1927, see Fischer, *Stalin and German Communism*, 586–604 passim. Fischer claims that Safarov advo-

cated the arrest of Stalin and a few hundred party leaders as a means of revitalizing party democracy. The trial of the Leningrad Counterrevolutionary Zinovievite Group of Safarov, Zalutsky, and others resulted in the seventy-seven defendants being sentenced to four to five years in prison, the gulag, or exile. *Izvestiia TsK KPSS,* no. 1 (1990), 38–58. For the June 1935 order to remove Safarov's books from libraries, see Getty and Naumov, *Road to Terror,* document 45.

15. On the role and importance of "speaking Bolshevik," see Stephen Kotkin, *Magnetic Mountain: Stalinism as Civilization* (Berkeley, 1995).

16. Consider the case of F. I. Mordukhovich, a worker in the ECCI archive, who was expelled from the party in late 1932 "for active propaganda, counterrevolutionary viewpoints, [and] duplicity and dishonesty before the party." What occasioned her expulsion was her telling a coworker that the party and its leaders "probably did not see the real situation [in the country] and to what this might lead." F. 546, op. 1, d. 190, ll. 181–184. That such a seemingly minor infraction could lead to expulsion illustrates the punitive use of party discipline. For an example of five members of the German CP expelled for criticizing their party leaders in private conversations, see ibid., d. 209, l. 77. My thanks to Fridrikh Firsov for sharing this material with me.

17. On oppositional activities in the early 1930s, see Getty and Naumov, *Road to Terror,* chapter 2.

18. On the war scare, see Alfred Meyer, "The War Scare of 1927," *Soviet Union/Union Sovetique,* 5, no. 1 (1978), 1–25; Reiman, 12–36. See Sheila Fitzpatrick, "The Foreign Threat During the First Five-Year Plan," *Soviet Union/Union Sovetique,* 5, no. 1 (1978), 26–35. These events led many young people who believed that "the Fatherland is in danger!" to volunteer for the Far Eastern Army.

19. The Shakhty trial of May 1928, the Industrial Party trial of October 1930, and the Metro-Vickers trial of April 1933 are the most notable.

20. Stalin, quoted in Fitzpatrick, "Foreign Threat," 27. His 1931 declaration that "we are fifty to one hundred years behind the advanced countries. We must cover this distance in ten years. Either we do this or they will crush us" injected a renewed sense of urgency into defense preparations and further stoked the fear of war. I. V. Stalin, *Sochineniia,* 13 vols. (Moscow, 1946–1951), vol. 13, pp. 38–39.

21. For examples, see *Stalin's Letters to Molotov,* 208–210; Reiman, 12–13.

22. On the regular anxieties of the Soviet leadership regarding the threat of war, see Reiman; Jonathan Haslam, *Soviet Foreign Policy, 1930–1933: The Impact of the Depression* (New York, 1983); Haslam, *Soviet Union and the Struggle for Collective Security;* Ken.

23. Questioned, for example, during the 1927 war scare; see Meyer, "War Scare of 1927."

24. Examples of calls for vigilance within the ECCI apparatus prior to Kirov's murder are numerous, see, e.g., f. 546, op. 1, d. 105, l. 5 (an April 1929 party committee resolution); ibid., l. 36 (a June 1929 party committee resolution); ibid., d. 191, l. 256 (a 16 September 1932 party committee resolution); ibid., d. 211, l. 13 (a 15 January 1933 party committee resolution); ibid., d. 214, l. 88 (a 4 September 1933 party committee resolution).

25. F. 495, op. 21, d. 22, l. 1. My thanks to Fridrikh Firsov for sharing this material with me.

26. On this, see V. N. Kaustov, "Iz predystorii massovykh repressii protiv poliakov: Seredina, 1930-x gg.," in A. E. Gurianov, ed., *Repressii protiv poliakov i polskikh grazhdan* (Moscow, 1997), 10–21; V. Kaustov, "Repressii protiv sovetskikh nemtsev do nachala massovoi operatsii 1937g.," in I. L. Shcherbakova, ed., *Repressii protiv rossiskikh nemtsev. Nakazannyi narod* (Moscow, 1999), 75–83; Terry Martin, "The Origins of Soviet Ethnic Cleansing," *Journal of Modern History,* 70, no. 4 (December 1998), 846–858.

27. For examples, see Antikainev's 16 February 1934 report "On questions concerning Finnish émigrés," in which he cites reports from VKP party committees in Magnitogorsk and Sviestroi. Antikainev worked for the Foreign Bureau of the Finnish CP. F. 17, op. 120, d. 131, ll. 39–54. See his report to the Organizational Department of the CC VKP dated 20 October 1933; ibid., d. 98, ll. 164–175. See also the discussion in Chapter 1 of denunciations sent to the Cadres Department.

28. F. 495, op. 21, d. 23, ll. 6, 23, 9. My thanks to Fridrikh Firsov for sharing this material with me.

29. The protocol of the meeting can be found in f. 546, op. 1, d. 269, ll. 70–71ob. The Cooperative Publishing House for Foreign Workers, located in Moscow on the 25-letia Oktiabria (now Nikolskaia) Street, was financed by the Comintern.

30. The VKP leaders' insistence on raising political vigilance antedated Kirov's murder, but that event provided a significant political justification, with which few VKP members could argue, for intensifying the vigilance campaign. For an example of an admission that vigilance was not as intense as party leaders wanted, see Akulov's comments to the January 1933 CC Plenum in f. 17, op. 2, d. 571, ll. 205–214, quoted in Getty and Naumov, *Road to Terror,* document 9.

31. Two Rakows were associated with the Comintern: Paul Rakow (aka Paul Heinz) and Werner Rakow (aka Felix Wolf). They were not related. It is uncertain which Rakow attended this meeting, but it was probably Paul Rakow (Heinz).

32. Borowskii's name later appeared on a September 1937 list of VKP members "having Trotskyist and Rightist tendencies." F. 546, op. 1, d. 378, ll. 30–36. See Document 18. He was arrested in 1938.

33. F. 546, op. 1, d. 269, ll. 78–81. In January 1935, Budzynska's husband, Vujović, had been arrested.

34. On the psychological dynamics of lynch mobs, see Cantril, 78–122.

35. Magyar was not the only VKP member to be accused of acting like a lawyer. At the December 1936 CC Plenum, Molotov hurled the same insult at Bukharin, who, like Magyar, protested certain "facts" used to support accusations against him. F. 17, op. 2, d. 575, ll. 122–126, cited in Getty and Naumov, *Road to Terror,* document 97.

36. On people internalizing standards, frames of reference, and attitudes and identifying with the group that espouses them, see Cantril, 35; and Tajfel, *Human Groups,* 254–259.

37. Sinani himself was expelled from the VKP in spring 1935. See the resolution found in Document 4 for details. For a 29 February 1937 unsigned denunciation of Sinani's alleged planting of Trotskyist conceptions among the Latin American Communist Parties, see f. 495, op. 17, d. 7, ll. 12–13.

38. At the 14 May 1929 meeting of the VKP delegation to the ECCI held in Stalin's office, those in attendance not only resolved to authorize the GPU to take appropriate measures to counteract the influence of police agents supposedly

within the CPP but also changed the composition of the CPP's leadership. F. 508, op. 1, d. 83, ll. 1, 10.

39. For a discussion of these arrests and of the Polish CP and the Comintern, see F. I. Firsov and S. Iazhborovskaia, "Komintern i Kommunisticheskaia partiia Pol'sha," *Voprosy istorii*, 11–12 (1988), 1–32.

40. F. 495, op. 12, d. 30, ll. 12–16.

41. On 29 December, the day after the meeting, the leadership of the party committee met to attend to issues raised at the meeting: writing the final resolution to present to the party organization for approval and initiating investigations into several comrades. The protocol of that meeting precedes the resolution on Magyar's expulsion passed by the party committee.

42. Refers to D. Manuilsky's speech "About the Counterrevolutionary Group of the Zinovievite-Trotskyist Bloc," delivered on 23 December 1934 at the closed meeting of the ECCI party organization.

43. The Eastern Secretariat of the ECCI was created in 1920. In 1921–1922 it was called the Far Eastern Department; in 1923–1926, the Eastern Department; and after 1927, the Eastern Secretariat. In the fall of 1935 it was renamed the Secretariat of O. Kuusinen.

44. *Bolshevik*—a theoretical and political journal of the CC VKP(b) published from 1924 to 1952, when it was renamed *Kommunist*. G. Zinoviev was on its editorial board from 1933 until his arrest on 16 December 1934.

45. The Fifteenth VKP Congress, which took place on 2–19 December 1927, declared "belonging to the Trotskyist opposition and propagandizing its views incompatible with membership in the Bolshevik Party." The congress expelled seventy-five leading members of the Trotskyist-Zinovievite bloc from the VKP.

46. *Bezvozhdentsy*—refers to a group of left oppositionists in the VKP(b). It was formed in late 1927 by former supporters of Zinoviev who were dissatisfied with his rupture with Trotsky on the eve of the Fifteenth Party Congress. By 1930 this group had ceased to exist.

47. Abbreviation of Mezhdunarodny Agrarny Institut, the International Agrarian Institute, created in January 1925 under the auspices of the Krestintern (Peasants' International). It studied agrarian and peasant questions in different countries. MAI was dissolved in 1940.

48. Mensheviks—originally the moderate wing of the RSDRP; it became an autonomous group with the Russian Social Democratic Workers' Party (RSDRP) after the Second Party Congress in 1903. After 1912 it was an independent party, though retaining the RSDRP name. It existed legally in Russia until 1922.

49. I. I. Fainberg. He and his wife, Eta Rubinovna Fainberg, worked in the ECCI apparatus.

50. Miklos Horthy de Nagybanyai (1868–1957). An admiral, he was the leader of Hungary from 1920 to 1944. In 1919 he led the crushing of the Hungarian revolutionary movement. In October 1944, he was interned by the Germans. After 1949 he lived in Portugal.

51. Refers to a thesis proclaimed by Zinoviev at the Sixth Enlarged ECCI Plenum which read that the Comintern should be ready for the outbreak of the world revolution in the coming three to five years, as well as for its delay until some undefined time.

52. Refers to the letter from Zinoviev to Rumiantsev of 30 June 1928. This let-

ter was used to prove Zinoviev's double-dealing. As a CC member, Knorin was privy to various materials on former oppositionists, materials he quoted from in his speech.

53. Conciliators—a group in the German CP that occupied a centrist buffer position between the party's Right wing (Brandler, Thalheimer) and the supporters of the party chairman E. Thälmann, who sided with Stalin.

54. The movie *Chapaev* (directed by Sergey and Georgy Vasiliev) was made in 1934. It was based on the story of the Red Army military commander during the Civil War.

55. The text is blacked out. (Trans.)

56. On 7 November 1927, supporters of Trotsky and Zinoviev organized counter demonstrations in Moscow and Leningrad, which were dispersed by the police and voluntary patrols.

57. For example, see the case of Sinani in f. 546, op. 1, d. 272, l. 1.

58. For example, see the case of Heinrich (Züsskind), who was allegedly "tied to the counterrevolutionary Magyar," expelled, and later arrested. F. 546, op. 1, d. 272, ll. 72, 90.

59. F. 546, op. 1, d. 300, l. 20.

60. The resolution of the 20 June 1929 party meeting that discussed the purge of that year had called for precisely that. F. 546, op. 1, d. 105, l. 36.

61. F. 546, op. 1, d. 215, l. 214.

62. For the 18 January 1935 CC letter, see Getty and Naumov, *Road to Terror*, document 28.

63. Shortly after the Seventh Congress, which adopted the Popular Front policy, Stalin endorsed Dimitrov and Manuilsky's recommendation that Pyatnitsky, who opposed that policy, be transferred from the ECCI to "other work." He was appointed to head the Administration of Affairs Department of the CC VKP. On Pyatnitsky's and others' opposition to the Popular Front, see f. 495, op. 73, d. 15, ll. 37–40; B. M. Leibzon and L. K. Shirinia, *Povorot v istorii Kominterna* (Moscow, 1975), 93–102 passim; E. H. Carr, *The Twilight of the Comintern, 1930–1935* (New York, 1982), 123–146; J. Haslam, "The Comintern and the Origins of the Popular Front, 1934–1935," *Historical Journal*, 3 (1979), 673–691.

64. The closed general meeting of the ECCI party organization on 20 February 1935 continued the discussion of the report by Kotelnikov "On the Work of the Party Committee During the Last Two Months," which he had presented to the 16 February 1935 meeting of the ECCI party organization.

65. Alfred Kurella was removed from work in the ECCI for participating in the meeting of the so-called KIM veterans in late November 1934, in connection with the fifteenth anniversary of the creation of the KIM. The meeting was considered to be a factionalist gathering. In early 1935, A. Guralsky "repented" for having concealed from the leadership his meetings with G. Zinoviev and L. Kamenev after their readmission to the party and for not helping to expose the "conciliators" in the German CP.

66. Mokhovaia—the street in Moscow where the central apparatus of the ECCI was located.

67. Pyatnitsky's comments can be found in f. 546, op. 1, d. 274, ll. 99–115.

68. Ibid., l. 112.

69. On 8 June 1935 the ECCI party organization passed a resolution that or-

dered the Cadres Department to conduct a verification of the ECCI apparatus: "The goal of this verification is to cleanse from the apparatus dangerous and class enemy elements." F. 546, op. 1, d. 273, l. 178. My thanks to Fridrikh Firsov for sharing this material with me.

70. In a letter to Manuilsky in 1926, Dimitrov described the Left Opposition as a "serious disease of the entire Comintern," which required that they resort to "methods of party surgery." "It will be necessary to cut off the rotten [*gnilye*] members of the VKP(b) and other sections of the Comintern in a timely fashion, so that the entire organism does not become infected." TsPA (Sofia) F. 146, op. 2, a.e. 1740, ll. 4–5, quoted in *Stalin and Dimitrov,* 10.

71. On this, see Getty, *Origins,* 92–136 passim.

72. F. 456, op. 1, d. 274, ll. 117–121.

73. The five people arrested in 1935 were Safarov, Magyar, Abramovich, Sinani, and Vujović. Although the resolution mentions Shatskin, who was arrested on 10 January 1935, he is not included in these calculations because he was working for Gosplan in Central Asia at the time.

74. According to Getty and Naumov, in *Road to Terror,* chapter 4, in addition to the seventy-seven convicted members of the so-called Leningrad Counterrevolutionary Zinovievist Group of Safarov, Zalutsky, and others, 843 former Zinovievites in Leningrad were arrested.

Chapter 3. The Search for "Hostile Elements" and "Suspicious" Foreigners

1. The Comintern referred to the new policy as the United Front, but the term Popular Front, which is widely used in the West, will be used in the text to distinguish it from earlier Comintern policies.

2. For discussions, see Julian Jackson, *Popular Front;* Gabriel Jackson, *The Spanish Republic and the Civil War, 1931–1939* (Princeton, 1972); Braunthal; McDermott.

3. "Tragediia RKKA," no. 2, pp. 3–42 passim.

4. For examples, see Kaustov, "Iz predystorii," 10–13; Kaustov, "Repressi," 75–83.

5. F. 17, op.120, d. 179, ll. 34–77, quoted in Getty and Naumov, *Road to Terror,* document 54.

6. Ibid.

7. For a discussion, see Getty, *Origins,* 58–91.

8. F. 17, op. 162, d. 19, l. 4. My thanks to Arch Getty for sharing this material with me.

9. The ECCI Secretariat labeled the draft resolution, dated 15 December 1935, "top secret." At several points in the text, Dimitrov wrote comments and questions about aspects of the proposal. F. 495, op. 18, d. 1039, ll. 22a–22d.

10. The concerns expressed in the report about the reliability of party organizations to properly document who their members were and which members had joined the VKP mirrored those expressed by party leaders following the 1935 verification of the VKP. Manuilsky appears to have believed that the verification had revealed the existence of "dangerous" elements in the party. His handwritten notes on the results of this operation in the Kiev oblast party organization state that "class alien" and "enemy elements" and "double-dealers and secret agents of the

class enemy" held party cards. So, too, did "agents of foreign capitalist states" and anti-Soviet nationalist parties, including Ukrainian Socialist Revolutionaries, Social Democrats, Bundists, and members of Poalei Zion. F. 523, op. 1, d. 108, ll. 1–22 passim.

11. In 1933 the CC had ordered all party organizations to conduct a purge (*chistka*) of its members. The purge was an administrative measure taken by the party to assess its members. But in the eyes of Politburo members, local party committees bungled the operation, which dragged on for a year longer than it was supposed to. Dissatisfied with the way the purge had been conducted the CC ordered a verification (*proverka*) of all party members in 1935. That operation also suffered from shortcomings. Even more distressing was the revelation that thousands of party cards were missing and that hostile elements from abroad had penetrated the party's ranks. The December 1935 CC Plenum passed a resolution ordering that an exchange of party documents (*obmen partdokumentov*) be conducted in 1936. The ECCI party committee, like all other party committees, conducted the purge, verification, and exchange of party documents.

12. The resolution, entitled "Results of the Verification of Party Documents," noted the penetration into the party of enemies—in particular, agents of foreign intelligence services—in the guise of political émigrés and members of foreign parties. The Plenum, held from 21 to 25 December 1935, passed a resolution calling for the exchange of party documents. See *KPSS v rezoliutsiiakh i resheniiakh s"ezdov, konferentsii i plenumov TsK.*, vol. 6 (Moscow, 1985), pp. 295–304.

13. F. 495, op. 18, d. 71039, l. 9a. The 29–30 December 1935 resolution of the ECCI Secretariat addressed issues relating to the transfer of fraternal party members to the VKP. It warned that the transfer of members of Communist Parties in capitalist countries to the VKP could not be made without permission from the CC of the fraternal party; the CC had to say that the member was allowed to leave the country and recommend that the member be transferred to the VKP. The resolution called for investigating those party representatives who recommended hostile elements, spies, and subversives for admission to the VKP.

14. Manuilsky's letter in RGASPI is dated 3 January 1936. It is typed with handwritten corrections and additions. According to Kaustov, "Iz predystorii," 12, the version that Yezhov received, which is housed in the Presidential Archive, is dated 19 January 1936.

15. The green passages were networks maintained by the VKP and the Soviet security organs that allowed for safe, undetected passage across international borders.

16. KUNZ is incorrect. Manuilsky is referring here to the KUNMZ—Kommunisticheskii Universitet Natsionalnykh Menshinstv Zapada (Communist University of the National Minorities of the West). KUNMZ was created by a 28 November 1921 decree of the Council of People's Commissars and charged with training party cadres from the western regions of Russia and the Volga Germans. In 1929–1930 it began to admit representatives of the Communist Parties of the Central European, Scandinavian, and Balkan countries, as well as Italy. KUNMZ was dissolved following the decision of the ECCI Secretariat of 7–8 May 1936.

17. Less than two weeks later, Yezhov's assistant acknowledged Manuilsky's letter and asked him "to order the Cadres Department and the archive [of the ECCI] to send to SEP CC all materials characterizing the party membership [his-

tory] of former members of the fraternal Communist Parties transferred as members and candidates of the VKP(b)." See Vasiliev to Manuilsky, dated 15 January 1936, f. 495, op. 18, d. 1147a, l. 41. Vasiliev was the head of the SEP in the ORPO. The letter was designated "secret." Handwritten comments on the letter indicate that Manuilsky ordered those offices to comply with Yezhov's request.

18. Manuilsky's concern about the quality of émigrés who had transferred to the VKP was shared by the ECCI Presidium, which, on 19 February 1936, drafted a resolution that called on the ICC to conduct an investigation into the "criminally careless attitude on the part of the representatives of the brother parties in the ECCI, toward the giving of recommendation for transfers to the [VKP] . . . with the object of bringing to party responsibility all those representatives of various parties and persons who recommended or helped in transferring the abovementioned elements to the [VKP]." "Facts" revealed during the verification of 1935 provided the basis for these concerns. F. 495, op. 18, d. 1039, l. 14.

19. For a discussion of these policies, see Getty, *Origins*, 92–136 passim; and Rittersporn, *Stalinist Simplifications*, 30–112 passim.

20. See f. 17, op. 120, d. 260, ll. 1–13, for Manuilsky's letter to Andreev. For other documents relating to these issues, see ibid., ll. 24–29, 32–33, 45–46, 48–55. On Manuilsky's concern about the infiltration of hostile elements from abroad into party schools, see f. 495, op. 18, d. 1147a, ll. 75–95. This document provides a detailed discussion of the alleged penetration of "alien party elements" into the VKP and the various party schools. For an unsigned denunciation of Trotskyists, most of whom were CPP members, in a party school, see f. 495, op. 74, d. 398, ll. 98–99.

21. F. 495, op. 21, d. 34, l. 2. My thanks to Fridrikh Firsov for sharing this material with me.

22. F. 495, op. 21, d. 21, l. 20. My thanks to Fridrikh Firsov for sharing this material with me.

23. Kaustov, "Iz predystorii," 13–14.

24. F. 495, op. 74, d. 369, ll. 1–8. On the first page, Angaretis wrote "*To Moskvin.*"

25. Handwritten by Angaretis.

26. *Starosta*—the head or elected representative selected by a group of workers. (Trans.)

27. MLSh, abbreviation for Mezhdunarodnaia Leninskaia Shkola (International Lenin School), the political school of the Comintern, opened in 1926. Until 1928 it was called Mezhdunarodnye Leninskye Kursy (Course). The leading cadres of the Communist Parties were trained there. The deans were Nikolai Bukharin (1926–1930), K. I. Kirsanov (1930–1931, 1933–1937), Wilhelm Pieck (1932), and P. Chervenkov (1937–1938). The school was closed in 1938.

28. Okhranka is a contraction of Okhrannoe Otdelenie, the police department in tsarist Russia.

29. See also the 3 February 1936 proposal from Smolianskii of the Cadres Department to Manuilsky on why and how to review foreign cadres from Austria, Germany, Hungary, Czechoslovakia, Switzerland, and Holland. F. 495, op. 20, d. 812, ll. 10–36.

30. F. 495, op. 18, d. 1071, l. 64. The resolution, which cited the December 1935 CC resolution on the verification of party documents and the December

1935 resolution of the ECCI Secretariat on the transfer of fraternal party members to the VKP (see f. 495, op. 18, d. 71039, l. 9a), was signed by Dimitrov, Manuilsky, Ercoli, Wang Ming, M. Moskvin, Gottwald, and Florin.

31. F. 495, op. 18, d. 1039, l. 14.

32. On the repression of Poles and Polish citizens, see *Repressii protiv poliakov i pol'skikh grazhdan* (Moscow, 1997).

33. Stalin, *Sochineniia*, vol. 6, p. 266.

34. SDPKPiL—Social Democratic Party of the Kingdom of Poland and Lithuania (Socialdemokracja Krolestwa Polskiego i Litwy), created in July 1893 as a result of merging of the Union of the Polish Workers and the Proletariat-2 Party. In 1900, at the Second Congress of the party, it united with the left elements of the Lithuanian workers' movement. In April 1906 it joined the RSDRP but retained its factional independence. In December 1911 the SDPKPiL split into two parts: the *zazhondovtsy* (those supporting the Main Directorate) and the *razlomovtsy* (those cooperating with the Bolsheviks). In 1916, however, both wings reunited. In December 1918, at the unification congress of the SDPKPiL and the PPS-Lewica, the Polish Communist Party was formed.

35. For a discussion of the formation and growth of the CPP, see M. K. Dziewanowski, *The Communist Party of Poland* (Cambridge, Mass., 1959), 55–96; Gabriele Simoncini, *The Communist Party of Poland, 1918–1929: A Study in Political Ideology* (Lewiston, N.Y., 1993).

36. Kommunisticheskaia Partiia Zapadnoi Ukrainy—the Communist Party of Western Ukraine (CPWU). Until 1923 it was named the Communist Party of Eastern Galicia. The party was formed in October 1921 in Lvov. The CPWU was a regional autonomous organization of the CPP. The mistakes of the party leadership on the national question were used by the Comintern to accuse the CPWU leadership—I. Krilyk (Wasilkiw) and R. Kuzma (Turianski)—of nationalism and treason. Most of the leaders were branded as fascist agents. In 1933 the same charge was presented to the new party leaders, headed by M. T. Zaiachkowski (Kosar) and G. V. Ivanenko (Baraba). In 1938 the CPWU was disbanded along with the CPP and its leadership was repressed.

37. Kommunisticheskaia Partiia Zapadnoi Belorussii (CPWB)—the Communist Party of Western Belorussia. It was created in 1923 as an integral part of the CPP. In 1938, after the dissolution of the CPP, the CPWB ceased to exist, and its leaders and many workers repressed.

38. See *Stalin's Letters to Molotov*, 208–209.

39. For a discussion, see Haslam, *Collective Security*; Ken. Finally, it should be remembered that Poland had one of the most effective espionage organizations in Europe; it was the first to capture the German Enigma machine. Popular opinion had it that its agents had infiltrated the CPP.

40. On 11 August 1932, Stalin confided to Kaganovich that "in the Ukrainian Communist party, [among the] 500,000 members . . . are more than a few rotten elements, conscious or unconscious Petliurists, ultimately direct agents of Pilsudsky." F. 81, op. 3, d. 99, ll. 147–148. See also, ibid., l. 36. My thanks to Gabor Rittersporn for sharing this material with me.

41. F. 508, op. 1, d. 83, l. 1, 10. My thanks to Fridrikh Firsov for sharing this material with me.

42. "Tragediia RKKA," no. 2, pp. 33–38.

43. F. 495, op. 19, d. 248, l. 191. My thanks to Fridrikh Firsov for sharing this material with me.

44. POW—Polska Organizacja Wojskowa, a secret paramilitary organization created in October 1914 on the initiative and with the participation of Pilsudski in Poland. During World War I it conducted subversive activities against tsarist Russia; some of the POW members joined Pilsudski's legions. The POW collaborated with the Polish nationalist organizations and conducted activities against the German and Austrian invaders. By the end of the war it took part in military action. The POW formed the core of the armed forces of the first Polish government. The POW organizations acted on the territory of Russia, Ukraine, and Belorussia, where they conducted an anti-Soviet campaign. In the 1920s the POW played an important role in establishment of the Pilsudski dictatorship in Poland.

45. Soviet security organs were concerned not only about Poles who were POW agents, but also those who were agents of the Ukrainian Military Organization (for more on this, see below). Arrests of émigrés charged with being agents of either group mounted from 1933. See also the discussion in Kautsov, "Iz predystorii," 10–15.

46. F. 495, op. 73, d. 212, l. 7.

47. For another example of a Pole arrested in Ukraine, see the appeal written to Dimitrov by the wife of Ivan Lipinski, a longtime CPP member who was arrested in early 1936. She wrote: "I realize that many turned out to be traitors (Sochacki), but not everybody is dregs." F. 495, op. 17, d. 216, ll. 99–102.

48. *Pilsudshchina*—a derisive name used by the Communists to describe the policy of the Polish government under Marshal Pilsudski and a generic term used to describe his followers. Josef Pilsudski (1867–1935) was a leader of the right wing of the Polish Socialist Party. In 1918 he was the war minister; between 22 November 1918 and 1922, head of state. In May 1926 he staged a coup d'état and established a regime of "sanitation." After May 1926 he was the war minister. Between October 1926 and June 1928 he was the prime minister; later he was the war minister again and the inspector general of the Polish armed forces.

49. F. 495, op. 74, d. 398, l. 1. The resolution appears to have been prepared by the Cadres Department. My thanks to Fridrikh Firsov for sharing this material with me.

50. The extent to which the dangers posed by the CPP were viewed with special alarm is clear from the ECCI Secretariat's evaluations of other fraternal parties. See, e.g., its more positive "Decision" regarding the Bulgarian CP, f. 495, op. 20, d. 170, ll. 15–19.

51. Handwritten by G. Dimitrov.

52. Lenski's report on behalf of the CC CPP was presented at the ECCI Secretariat session on 28 January 1936. The draft of the resolution suggested by the CPP leadership was declined in favor of Dimitrov's draft. A commission composed of Dimitrov, Moskvin, Ercoli, and the CC CPP representatives was charged with completing the draft of the resolution. The final text was approved by the ECCI secretaries on 31 January 1936.

53. Handwritten by G. Dimitrov.

54. On 5 March 1936 the ECCI Secretariat heard the report of J. Lenski on the results of the CC CPP plenum. The Secretariat approved in principle its political and organizational decisions.

55. Just because Trotsky published articles in a Hearst newspaper did not mean that the two men shared a political perspective, although they did share a common enemy—Stalin. In fact, Trotsky viewed Hearst as a reactionary. Why, then, did he publish his articles in the *New York American?* The answer is simple—money. Trotsky lived off the income that he received from publishing his books and articles and from the contributions of individuals. And Hearst paid well. To Trotsky, using the class enemy to help spread the revolution, which was how Trotsky viewed his writings, was a time-honored Bolshevik tradition. But Moscow viewed Trotsky's anti-Soviet attacks in the Hearst press as a counterrevolutionary, not a revolutionary, act. The campaign against Trotsky and Trotskyism abroad and the vigilance campaign within the fraternal parties were complementary policies in the struggle against counterrevolution.

56. An undated "Proposed Position Regarding the Cadres Department," which was designated "Top Secret," is in f. 495, op. 18, d. 1147a, ll. 49–52. For other drafts relating to reforming the Cadres Department, see f. 495, op. 20, d. 812, ll. 1–4, 6–36. An English translation of the approved regulations is in f. 495, op. 20, d. 811, ll. 51–55. According to both versions, Krajewski was responsible for the parties of Western Europe, the Baltic states, Poland, England and its colonies, and North America; Chernomordik was responsible for the parties in Central Europe, the Balkans, Scandinavia, Japan, China, and Latin America.

57. For example, see the proposed "Decision of the Secretariat on Strengthening the Roles and Raising the Responsibilities of the ECCI Secretariat and Representatives of the Parties in the Realization of Cadre Policy." F. 495, op. 18, d. 1147a, ll. 43–44, 53–55.

58. See the ECCI Secretariat's "Position on the Work of the Representatives of Parties Under the ECCI." F. 495, op. 18, d. 1236, ll. 63a, 72–73.

59. At the end of this document was typed: "To whom to send:
    1) CC of the parties,
    2) Representatives of the parties,
    3) Secretaries and their assistants,
    4) Analysts [*referenty*] and the Cadres Department's sector heads."
That distribution list was crossed out and next to it someone wrote: "*one copy to the Secretaries in each language.*" That person also wrote the names **Kirsanov** and **Stasova.**

60. The evidence from this document, and surely from others, was sufficient for the ECCI to order a more thorough verification of the staffs and students of party schools as part of the verification of political émigrés. Manuilsky had recommended that these party schools be disbanded and re-created only after reliable staffs and students could be found. See his 2 January 1936 letter to A. A. Andreev in f. 17, op. 120, d. 260, ll. 1–13. On this issue, see also ibid., ll. 17–18, 24, 25–29, 32–33, 45–46, 48–55.

61. F. 495, op. 21, d. 166, l. 31; ibid., ll. 38–39. See also ibid., ll. 36, 69, 73. My thanks to Fridrikh Firsov for sharing this material with me.

62. The secret report, signed by Krajewski, head of the Cadres Department, and Anvelt, secretary of the ICC, and dated 19 February 1936, was sent to the ECCI Secretariat. F. 495, op. 18, d. 1039, ll. 24–25.

63. On MOPR's receipt of 314 requests, see f. 17, op. 120, d. 262, l. 2. For correspondence between MOPR and Yezhov's office, and between the ECCI and his

office relating to visas for foreigners, see f. 17, op. 120, d. 261 and 262. My thanks to Arch Getty for calling these materials to my attention.

64. F. 495, op. 175, d. 105, l. 9. Of the 201 names, forty-four were recorded in 1933, fifty-five in 1934, fifty-nine in 1935, and twenty-seven in the first half of 1936. My thanks to Fridrikh Firsov for sharing this material with me.

65. For a discussion, see Getty and Naumov, *Road to Terror,* chapter 7 and document 72.

66. Based on Alexander Orlov's memoirs, *The Secret History of Stalin's Crimes* (New York, 1953), Robert Conquest argues that Olberg was a NKVD agent charged with penetrating Trotskyist circles and that the NKVD arrested him and urged him to confess as a party assignment in order to frame others for the August 1936 trial. Conquest, *Great Terror,* 80–81. Other than Orlov's account, there is no evidence to support this hypothesis. But even if it was true, surely neither the German comrades who denounced Olberg nor the Cadres Department knew of it. Rather, they operated on the basis of evidence that they possessed.

67. The results of the commission's work are discussed in the next chapter. Members of the ICC and the ECCI Cadres and Administration of Affairs Departments served on the commission.

68. F. 495, op. 74, d. 398, ll. 20–21.

69. "Statistical information on the verification of émigrés in the CPP" is in f. 495, op. 74, d. 399, ll. 5–6. Skulski's cover letter is in ibid., ll. 9–10. The documents relating to the final assessments reached by the verification commission are in f. 495, op. 123, d. 247, ll. 1–103.

70. For a discussion of the letter, see Getty, *Origins,* 121–123; Getty and Naumov, *Road to Terror,* document 73. The quotations in the text come from Getty.

71. The verification and exchange of party documents of the members of the ECCI apparatus party organization was undertaken in June 1936 as a part of an all-party campaign.

72. It refers to the secret letter from the CC VKP "About the Terrorist Activities of the Trotskyist-Zinovievite Counterrevolutionary Bloc" of 29 July 1936 and to *Pravda* editorial "Bolshevik Vigilance in Every Sphere of Activity" of 9 August 1936.

73. E. N. Nikolaeva's first husband, I. K. Traubenberg, whom she divorced in 1922, had been arrested for "wrecking" by the OGPU collegium on 22 October 1933.

74. Refers to the Seventh Comintern Congress, which took place from 25 July to 20 August 1935.

75. Trotsky was one of the leaders of the interdistrict (*mezhduraionnyi*) committee in 1917.

76. Kotelnikov's report on Fritz David may have played a role in Pyatnitsky's subsequent arrest. During the June 1937 CC Plenum, Pyatnitsky opposed several of Yezhov's proposals; Yezhov countered that Pyatnitsky was a provocateur who infiltrated "counterrevolutionary Trotskyist agents into the Comintern and party and Soviet organs." Shortly thereafter, Pyatnitsky was arrested. Boris A. Starkov, "The Trial That Was Not Held," *Europe-Asia Studies,* 46, no. 8 (1994), 1297–1315; see esp. p. 1299.

77. Getty, in *Origins,* argues that the purge, verification, and exchange of party documents were not witch hunts for former oppositionists. Conquest, in *Great*

Terror, maintains that they were aimed primarily at identifying and removing former oppositionists.

78. No other information is available.

Chapter 4. Campaigns Converge, Anxieties Deepen

1. There was some truth to one of the charges, namely that in 1932, E. S. Goltsman, a Soviet official and former Trotskyist, had met with Trotsky's son, Sedov, and had given him information on Soviet economic performance. He also gave Sedov a proposal from Ivan Smirnov, a former Trotskyist and a defendant at the August trial, to form a united bloc of former oppositionists within the USSR. During 1932, Trotsky had tried to rebuild an organization of former oppositionists, including Smirnov and Zinoviev, in order to challenge Stalin. Sedov later informed his father that the bloc had been formed but regrettably some of its key leaders had been arrested. Yet there is no evidence to suggest that Trotsky or his supporters in the USSR ever contemplated using terrorism. The OGPU smashed this embryonic bloc. But on this grain of truth, Stalin and others constructed a conspiracy of significant dimensions and sinister intentions, although what caused them to do so in the summer of 1936 and not in 1932 or 1934 remains unclear. For a discussion, see Getty and Naumov, *Road to Terror*, chapter 1; Getty, *Origins*, 119–122. See also Pierre Broué, "Trotsky et le bloc des oppositions de 1932," *Cahiers de Leon Trotsky*, no. 5 (January–March 1980), pp. 5–37, for a different perspective. In 1932, Olberg's contacts with oppositionists in the USSR were also exposed. Olberg was among the defendants at the trial. On this, see Chapter 3.

2. Among those who did so was Dimitrov, who found it incomprehensible that the accused had committed such crimes, that they had admitted their guilt knowing they would be executed, and that no convincing evidence other than their confessions had been introduced. In his opinion, the trial was "atrociously conducted." But it is interesting to note that Dimitrov expressed these doubts in his entry of 18 December 1936, three months after the trial. What accounts for this delay is unclear, although it may be that in the intervening period Dimitrov had had time to reflect on the serious doubts cast on the trial in the Western press. As we shall see, in the aftermath of the trial, Dimitrov behaved as if the trial were valid, and demanded that Comintern members draw the proper conclusions from the trial. See *Diary of Georgi Dimitrov*, entry of 18 December 1936.

3. RUNAG was the informational agency (Rundschau) created by the Comintern in 1933.

4. Refers to the event on the evening of 4–5 August 1936, when a group from the Norwegian fascist party (National Association), dressed in police uniforms, broke into the house where Trotsky was living in Norway.

5. For one measure of the importance of the Spanish Civil War, see *Diary of Georgi Dimitrov*, entries from August 1936 to early 1939, passim; and the coverage given the war in *Kommunisticheskii Internatsional*.

6. Radek's article, "The Trotskyist-Zinovievite Fascist Band and Its Hetman, Trotsky," was published in *Izvestiia* on 21 August 1936.

7. Pyatakov's article, "Ruthlessly Destroy the Despicable Murderers and Traitors," was published in *Pravda* on 21 August 1936.

8. Rakovsky's article, "There Should Be No Mercy," was published in *Pravda* on 21 August 1936.

9. Founded in 1924, *Daily Worker* was the official newspaper of the CC CPUSA.

10. Toward this end, on 25 August 1936, Mikhail Kreps, head of the ECCI Editorial and Publishing Department, sent to Dimitrov a memorandum proposing a series of "publications dealing with the [recently] concluded trial." F. 495, op. 78, d. 141, l. 104.

11. F. 495, op. 184, d. 33, outgoing for 1936 to Kaunas, l. 53. Though dated 26 August, the telegram was not sent until 14 September. My thanks to Fridrikh Firsov for sharing this material with me.

12. *Kommunisticheskii Internatsional*, 15 (1936), 33. The entire report is in ibid., 31–45.

13. This was not the only such meeting. For the protocol of the 2 September 1936 closed meeting of the Communications Department of the ECCI Secretariat, see f. 546, op. 1, d. 356, ll. 35–36.

14. Despite the strictures imposed on her as the rapporteur, Razumova believed strongly in the necessity for vigilance. See "The Case of Anna Razumova-Khigerovich" in Chapter 7.

15. Abbreviation of Mezhdunarodny Yunoshesky Den (International Youth Day), celebrated annually after 1915 on 1 September both in the USSR and by the Left abroad.

16. In this context, observing the rules of conspiracy refers to people acting to ensure that unauthorized people would not have access to confidential information.

17. Refers to the group led by Henri Barbé (1902–1966) and Pierre Celor (1902–1957), a leftist faction in the French CP that actually controlled the party leadership in 1929 and early 1930. In December 1931, Barbé and Celor were removed from the leadership of the party.

18. Georgette Fabre (born in 1908) was C. Servet's wife. She was a member of the French CP from 1933. In 1933–1936 she worked as a copyeditor for the Foreign Workers' Publishing House in the USSR, and later she worked for Foreign Radio, also in the USSR. On 2 June 1936 she left for France.

19. Workers in the ECCI apparatus and the Comintern lived in the Hotel Soiuznaia in Moscow.

20. According to the press, 600,000 people took part in the demonstration in connection with the International Youth Day on 1 September 1936.

21. The Brussels Peace Congress took place between 3 and 6 September 1936. It was organized in Paris by the International Bureau for the Preparation of the Congress for Universal Peace.

22. The German Reichstag was set on fire on 27 February 1933. A former CP Holland member Marinus van der Lubbe was accused of setting the fire. Dimitrov was among those tried for complicity in the fire.

23. The French Socialist Party was officially called the French Section of the Workers' International, or SFIO (French abbreviation). The party was created in 1905.

24. *Volkischer Beobachter*—newspaper of the Nazi party.

25. Croix de Feu (Cross of Fire) was the largest fascist group in France. It emerged in 1927 as an organization of veterans. In 1935 it was renamed the

French Socialist Movement of the Cross of Fire. It was disbanded by a government decree of 18 June 1936.

26. This article by G. Dimitrov was published in the August 1936 issue of the *Kommunisticheskii Internatsional.*

27. Second International—International Union of Socialist Parties, formed in 1889. It almost ceased to exist after the outbreak of World War I but was recreated in 1919 as a union of Social Democratic parties. In 1923, after merging with the so-called Second and a Half International, it was reorganized as the Labor and Socialist International.

28. On 13 February 1936 members of the Royal Youth and of the youth wing of the extreme right-wing movement Action Français attacked Léon Blum as he was driving home from the Parliament.

29. F. 495, op. 184, d. 73, outgoing telegram for 1936, l. 78. My thanks to Fridrikh Firsov for sharing this material with me.

30. *Kommunisticheskii Internatsional,* 14 (1936), 4–6.

31. See *Diary of Georgi Dimitrov,* entry of 18 December 1936.

32. F. 495, op. 10a, d. 39, l. 49.

33. F. 495, op. 21, d. 34, l. 210.

34. Handwritten by Dimitrov.

35. Stsalmosh is incorrect. Muschinski's real name was Franz Samusch. Solomon Muschinski (Franz Samusch; 1897–1936) was arrested in May 1936 and condemned to face the firing squad.

36. The Korsch opposition was an ultra-Left oppositional group in the CPG that was led by Karl Korsch in 1925–1926. Korsch (1889–1961), a theoretician of the German ultra-Leftists, was one of the founders of the oppositional magazine *Kommunistische Politik.* In 1926 the ECCI expelled him from the party.

37. Probably Ryndhorn Gerszel (Mindsigorski).

38. Brandlerian—a supporter of Henrich Brandler (1881–1967), the German CP leader in 1922–1924, a leader of the right wing of the party, who was expelled from the party in December 1928.

39. The Wedding opposition was an ultra-Leftist group in the German CP, led by Max Reise, that had its base in the Wedding workers' district of Berlin. Reise was expelled from the German CP in 1928.

40. The *Deutsche Zentral-Zeitung* (German Central Newspaper) was published in German in Moscow between 1927 and 1938.

41. Mostremass—Moscow State Trust for Mass Production, which supervised the luxury goods plants and factories.

42. Refers to the ECCI commission, headed by Béla Kun, that directed antiwar campaigns from 1932 to 1935.

43. IMEL—Institute of Marx-Engels-Lenin of the CC VKP, a party research institution, created in 1934 by merging the Institute of K. Marx and F. Engels of the CC VKP(b) with the Institute of Lenin, which was created in the early 1920s. IMEL staff worked on publishing the works of Marx, Engels, and Lenin, researching the problems of the Marxist-Leninist theory, and studying the history of the workers' and Communist movement. The institute was closed in 1991.

44. *Za industrializatsiiu*—the newspaper of the People's Commissariat for Ferrous Metallurgy, published in Moscow between 5 September 1937 and 29 September 1940.

45. Robert Hauschild (Rudolf Haus) was arrested on 31 August 1936; on 28 May 1937 he was sentenced to five years in prison.

46. Probably Herbert Fichtenberg, a German YCL worker suspected of provocation because of his prompt release after he was arrested by Gestapo in March 1933.

47. Probably Faibish Newijashevski (Paul Wiezenfeld).

48. Some of the individuals named below do not appear in this abridged document.

49. During the August trial, Kamenev had mentioned Bukharin. Soon thereafter, Vyshinsky announced his intention to investigate Bukharin, Rykov, and Tomsky, the leaders of the 1928–1929 Right deviation. This no doubt explains why the list included former rightists (e.g., supporters of Brandler). This probably also explains Razumova's call to unmask former Rightists; see Document 15. For Kamenev's mention of Bukharin, see *Report of Court Proceedings: The Case of the Trotskyite-Zinovievite Terrorist Centre* (Moscow, 1939), 68. On 10 September 1936, six days after Chernomordik's report, *Pravda* reported Vyshinsky's announcement that the investigations into Bukharin and the other former Rightists were being dropped.

50. For a discussion of the transformation of accusations into proof by including them in official documents, see Vladimir A. Kozlov, "Denunciations and Its Function in Soviet Governance: A Study of Denunciations and Their Bureaucratic Handling from Soviet Police Archives, 1944–1953," in Sheila Fitzpatrick and Robert Gellately, eds., *Accusatory Practices: Denunciations in Modern European History, 1789–1989* (Chicago, 1997), 121–152. See also Sheila Fitzpatrick, "Signals from Below: Soviet Letters of Denunciation in the 1930s," in ibid., 85–120.

51. F. 495, op. 175, d. 105, ll. 55–60; ibid., d. 116, ll. 17–21. My thanks to Fridrikh Firsov for sharing this material with me. Greta Wilde also helped to compile the January 1937 list of Gestapo agents and anti-Soviet elements.

52. The ECCI party committee and Cadres Department were not the only organizations to compile such lists. For example, from the late 1920s at least, ORPO maintained lists of VKP members who had at one time or another supported an opposition. For examples, see f. 17, op. 71, ed. khr. 17, ll. 1–409 (3,737 signatories to the 1927 "Platform of the Eighty-Three"); ed. khr. 31, ll. 1–24 (dated 26 October 1932); ed. khr. 20, ll. 1–9 (a 1936 list of former oppositionists); ed. khr. 37, ll. 1–158 (February 1937 lists of former oppositionists); ed. khr. 41, ll. 1–138 (20 June 1937 list of former oppositionists excluded from work in 1937).

53. For an example, see Shkiriatov's speech to the VKP CC Plenum of 7–12 January 1933. F. 17, op. 2, d. 511, ll. 168–178, cited in Getty and Naumov, *Road to Terror*, document 10.

54. Béla Kun was removed from the Hungarian CP and from Comintern work on 5 September 1936, the day after the date on Document 18, but his fall from power had been more than nine months in the making. See his case study in Chapter 7.

55. Those listed in Document 18 represent only a portion of the members of the ECCI party organization who were repressed. The precise number is unclear, but we do know that between January 1936 and April 1938 the number of members in that organization shrank from 394 to 171. Repression was the primary, but not the only, reason for this drastic decline. Fridrikh I. Firsov, "Samouvichtozhenie Kom-

interna," unpublished manuscript, p. 36, citing f. 546, op. 1, d. 376, ll. 17–37; ibid., d. 437, l. 43. By early 1937 some 3,500 VKP members had been expelled as "enemies." *Voprosii istorii*, no. 10 (1995), 8. Lists like Kotelnikov's no doubt played a role in their expulsion.

56. Handwritten by F. Kotelnikov in black ink. Other handwritten notes in the margins are made with red pencil. (Trans.)

57. "New party registration forms" refers to the files compiled during the 1936 verification and exchange of party documents (*obmen partdokumentov*).

58. Probably a typographical error. He may be referring to Sovet Rabochikh, Krestianskikh i Soldatskikh Deputatov—Soviet of Workers', Peasants', and Soldiers' Deputies. (Trans.)

59. Morriens left the USSR for Belgium in 1936.

60. *Narodovoltsy*—members or followers of the Narodnaia Volia, an organization of radical populists in late nineteenth-century Russia. (Trans.)

61. Numbers 86 and 87 appear as they do in the original; the information relates to Eisenberger.

62. In 1938 membership in Trotskyist parties adhering to the Fourth International numbered 5,485, of which 2,500 belonged to the Socialist Workers Party in the United States. These figures are probably optimistic. See *Documents of the Fourth International: The Formative Years (1933–40)* (New York, 1973), 289; Christopher Z. Dobson and Ronald D. Tabor, *Trotskyism and the Dilemma of Socialism* (Westport, Conn., 1988), 89–94.

63. On the size of the opposition and Stalin's and the leadership's fear that it posed a threat even after its dissolution, see Reiman. On Trotsky's views after 1929 and his views of Stalin's and Soviet policies, see Issac Deutscher, *The Prophet Outcast: Trotsky, 1929–1940* (New York, 1977).

64. Getty, *Origins*, 125. For a brief discussion of the changing meanings of Trotskyism in the USSR in the 1930s, see ibid., 119–128.

65. F. 17, op. 3, d. 981, ll. 58, cited in Getty and Naumov, *Road to Terror*, document 80. See also *Izvestiia TsK KPSS*, no. 5 (1989), 72. For the number of Trotskyists expelled from the VKP in late 1936 and early 1937, see Getty and Naumov, *Road to Terror*, table 4.

66. F. 495, op. 184, d. 3, outgoing telegram to Kislovodsk, 1936, l. 75; ibid., d. 47a, incoming 20 October 1936, l. 85. Trotsky's suit was halted by the Norwegian government, which obtained a royal decree stating that an interned foreigner could not be a plaintiff in the royal court without the consent of the Ministry of Justice. The Ministry of Justice forbade the court to hear Trotsky's case. Trotsky had been placed under virtual house arrest on 26 August 1936. His situation remained unchanged until he left Norway for Mexico in late December.

67. Starkov, "Narkom Yezhov," in Getty and Manning, 24.

68. On this, see Getty and Naumov, *Road to Terror*, document 50.

69. Starkov, "Narkom Yezhov," 24–26.

70. Ibid., 25.

71. Ibid., 25–26.

72. Detailed materials on the verification of the Polish party, including lists of all party members reviewed, are in f. 495, op. 123, d. 224, 225, and 233.

73. For examples of such lists, see ibid., d. 233, ll. 1–63.

74. For an example, see ibid., d. 224, ll. 1–16 passim.

75. Ibid., op. 123, d. 225, ll. 129–130.

76. Ibid., ll. 165–166.

77. See, e.g., ibid., l. 111.

78. Prior arrests in Poland and associations with people deemed suspicious warranted inclusion. For example, see ibid., ll. 107–109.

79. For examples, see ibid., d. 224, ll. 42–45.

80. For an example, see ibid., d. 225, ll. 135–139.

81. F. 495, op. 74, d. 398, ll. 67–72.

82. The stenographic record of Lenski's report is in f. 495, op. 18, d. 1129, ll. 1–57; see especially ll. 1–7, 35–36, 55.

83. The quotation comes from the authorized English translation of the report, in f. 495, op. 20, d. 466, l. 13. The full report is in ibid., ll. 10–13. The original Russian-language text is in ibid., ll. 5a–5d.

84. See *Diary of Georgi Dimitrov,* entry for 20 December 1936; underlining in the original. According to that entry, the commission consisted of Dimitrov, Lenski, Kolarov, Moskvin, Ercoli, and Lozovsky. But the entry for 22 December 1936 lists the members as Dimitrov, Manuilsky, Moskvin, Lenski, Bronkowski, and Skulski.

85. See *Diary of Georgi Dimitrov,* entry for 4 December 1936; underlining in the original.

86. Ibid., entry for 16 December 1936.

87. See ibid., entry for 11 January 1937. The full text of that entry reads: "Read the testimony of Radek and Ust.—Bukharin's guilt is beyond doubt."

88. F. 495, op. 184, d. 16, outgoing telegram 1937, l. 19, directives to the leadership of the Lithuanian CP dated 21 January 1937; f. 495, op. 184, d. 21, l. 40, directives to the CC of the CPP dated 21 January 1937; f. 495, op. 184, d. 26, l. 17, directives to the leadership of the Estonian CP dated 23 January 1937.

89. Handwritten in Russian by Togliatti. (Trans.) My thanks to Fridrikh Firsov for sharing this material with me.

90. That same day the Secretariat informed Earl Browder, head of the CPUSA, that "during coming trial Radek-Piatakoff, Daily Worker [the CPUSA newspaper] to be considered as main instrument our campaign" in the Americas. F. 495, op. 184, d. 17, outgoing telegrams for 1937 to New York, 17 January 1937.

91. Handwritten in Russian by Ercoli (Togliatti). (Trans.)

92. *L'Humanité*—French daily newspaper founded in 1904. After 1910 it was the newspaper of the Socialist Party; after December 1920, the newspaper of the Socialists-Internationalists; from 8 February 1923, the official newspaper of the French CP.

93. F. 495, op. 184, d. 23, outgoing telegrams for 1937 to Paris, l. 57. The original was in French, approved by Dimitrov and signed by Ercoli (Togliatti).

94. F. 495, op. 21, d. 47, ll. 1–3. Ercoli (Togliatti) was the ECCI member responsible for the foreign correspondents who attended the trial and for coordinating the international press campaign. One of the three translators was Anna L. Razumova, who, in August 1936, urged members of the Secretariat party group to be more vigilant "in deeds, not in words." On 23 January 1937, the day the trial began, Dimitrov sent a "top secret" request to Yezhov for passes to the trial for another seven people who would attend as observers and correspondents. F. 495, op. 73, d. 50, l. 3.

95. For example, a 21 January 1937 telegram from Dimitrov and Ercoli (Togliatti) to Mario Roncoli and Ruggero Garlandi (members of the CC and Politburo of the Italian CP) stated: "The anti-Trotsky struggle in the émigré press is extremely weak. It is necessary for you to guarantee, during the trial, two pages in "Grido del popolo" [a weekly party newspaper]. . . . Make a Politburo member responsible for the publications and the campaign." F. 495, op. 184, d. 23, outgoing telegrams for 1937 to Paris, l. 76

96. Pritt wrote a number of articles defending the legitimacy of the Moscow trials. On 3 February, after the trial, Harry Pollitt, the secretary of the British CP telegraphed Arnot, the party representative in Moscow, to inform him that the party had published a "full report trial with preface by Pritt and Collard." F. 495, op. 184, d. 7, incoming for 1937g., l. 13.

97. *Manchester Guardian,* founded in 1821, was and remains England's most prominent liberal newspaper.

98. F. 495, op. 184, d. 24, incoming telegram for 1937, l. 97, received from Stockholm. The telegram was signed by Levlien and Grabe, leaders of the Norwegian CP. My thanks to Fridrikh Firsov for sharing this material with me.

99. F. 495, op. 184, d. 12, incoming telegram for 1937, l. 185. The telegram was sent via Julius (Gyula Alpari) in Paris. My thanks to Fridrikh Firsov for sharing this material with me.

100. For a discussion of the POUM, see Victor Alba and Stephen Schwartz, *Spanish Marxism Versus Soviet Communism: A History of the P.O.U.M.* (New Brunswick, N.J., 1988).

101. On 15 October 1938, while vacationing in Kislovodsk, Dimitrov sent the following telegram to Manuilsky and Moskvin: "I hope that you have taken all responsible measures in connection with the trial of the POUMists in order to: 1. Unmask publicly in the best way possible the counterrevolutionary crimes of the Spanish and foreign trotskyists and their role as agents of fascism. 2. Depict their protectors from the Second International, in particular the English Independents and the French Pivertists, as collaborators. 3. [Have] the press and other media use this trial of the international general staff for the purpose of expelling Trotskyists from the ranks of the workers' movement." F. 495, op. 184, d. 9, incoming for 1938, l. 51. My thanks to Fridrikh Firsov for sharing this material with me.

102. For a discussion of efforts to find asylum for Trotsky and his stay in Mexico, see William Chase, "Trotskii v Mekcike: K istorii ego neglasnykh kontaktov s praviltel'stvom SShA (1937–1940)," *Otechestvennaia istoriia,* 4 (July–August 1995), 76–102. On the role played by Andrés Nin through his representative Bartomeu Costa-Amic, see Bartomeu Costa-Amic, *Leon Trotsky y Andreu Nin: Dos Asesinatos del Stalinismo (Aclarando La Historia)* (Mexico City, 1994), 9–35.

103. According to *The Diary of Georgi Dimitrov,* plans for the campaign began on 20 January, and the troika was appointed on 23 January.

104. Ibid., entries for 31 January and 1 February 1937

105. Dimitrov wrote in his *Diary* on 2 February 1937: "On the trial: 1) Diversionary actions, espionage, terror—proved; 2) Also proved: that Trotsky inspired and directed."

106. Ibid.

107. The quotations in the text come from the authorized English-language translation of the resolution. That version is in f. 495, op.20, d. 752, ll. 37–45. The

original Russian version is in f. 495, op. 2, d. 246, ll. 35–43. The underlined text exists in both versions.

108. *Diary of Georgi Dimitrov,* entry of 11 February 1937. On 16 February, Dimitrov noted: "Edited the final text of the letter on the Trotskyite Center trial at home." The next day he wrote: "Sent Stalin the draft letter." An English-language translation of the letter, entitled "Letter to the Sections of the Communist International and to All Workers' Organizations. Lessons of the Trial of the Anti-Soviet Trotskyite Centre," is dated 18 February 1937. F. 495, op. 20, d. 753, ll. 47–68. The letter drew verbatim from sections of the resolutions "The results of the trial of the Trotskyists" (f. 495, op. 2, d. 246, ll. 35–43) and "On carrying out the campaign against Trotskyism" (Document 26).

109. "Letter to the Sections of the Communist International and to All Workers' Organizations. Lessons of the Trial of the Anti-Soviet Trotskyite Centre" is dated 18 February 1937. F. 495, op. 20, d. 753, ll. 47–68.

110. Its members included Moskvin (the chair), Ya. Anvelt (an ICC member), V. Florin (an ICC member), T. Samsonov (head of the ECCI Administrative Affairs Department), M. Filimonov (Moskvin's political assistant), and M. Chernomordik and G. Alikhanov (of the Cadres Department).

111. The numbers presented in the report do not always add up to the totals presented. The problem is in the document, not the translation.

112. For materials relating to the Moskvin Commission, see f. 495, op. 21, d. 52, ll. 4–25.

113. The report, "Protocol No. 17: The Meeting of the Secretariat's Commission for the Verification of the Apparat," 27–28 January 1937, was designated "top secret." F. 495, op. 21, d. 52, ll. 4–22.

114. Ibid., ll. 4–5.

115. Ibid., l. 14.

116. Ibid., l. 16

117. According to Adibekov, Shakhnazarova, and Shirinia, 191, the size of the ECCI apparatus shrank from 606 to 504 people during the first seven months of 1937.

118. There are two reports of the results of the CPWB's verification. The first, an unsigned report, is dated 29 December 1936 and presents data on 2,038 cases and specifies the number executed. F. 495, op. 123, d. 233, l. 95. The second report, from which the figures in the text were taken, is dated 1 March 1937, signed by Bronkowski, and designated "top secret." It details the decisions in 2,044 cases and reports that 120 were still being reviewed. F. 495, op. 123, d. 248, l. 1.

119. For an engaging study of German writers in emigration, the stresses that emigration produced, and their resultant behaviors, see David Pike, *German Writers in Soviet Exile, 1933–1945* (Chapel Hill, N.C., 1982).

120. For example, see the commission created to verify Italian émigrés living in the USSR, which reviewed 307 people; 98 of them were arrested in 1936–1938. F. 495, op. 21, d. 125, l. 126. A different list entitled "Italians Arrested by the NKVD, 1935–1938" puts the number arrested in those years at 108. F. 513, op. 2, d. 69 (Italiani arresati dall' NKVD. 1935–1938.). See also f. 513, op. 2, d. 65, l. 99. Ercoli (Togliatti) knew of these lists. My thanks to Fridrikh Firsov for sharing this material with me.

121. *Diary of Georgi Dimitrov,* entry for 11 February 1937.

Chapter 5. The Victims of Vigilance

1. For partial transcripts of Bukharin's and Rykov's speeches to the Plenum, see Getty and Naumov, *Road to Terror,* chapter 10.

2. See *Diary of Georgi Dimitrov,* entry of 23 February 1937.

3. Ibid., entry of 27 February 1937; Getty and Naumov, *Road to Terror,* document 141 and chapter 10.

4. Getty, *Origins,* 141 and 137–149 passim. Translations of the quotations from Stalin's speeches are from Getty.

5. Ibid., 139.

6. Ibid., 143.

7. Quoted in ibid., 144–145.

8. Quoted in ibid., 145. On familyness, see Harris, *Great Urals.*

9. Quoted in Getty, *Origins,* 146.

10. Quoted in ibid., 145.

11. *Diary of Georgi Dimitrov,* entry of 4 March 1937.

12. See f. 17, op. 2, d. 577, ll. 30–33; Getty and Naumov, *Road to Terror,* document 143. On 5 April 1937, Manuilsky gave the report on the February–March Plenum at the meeting of the ECCI Secretariat. F. 495, op. 18, d. 1192, ll. 1–36, esp. ll. 1–5.

13. F. 495, op. 20, d. 756, ll. 36–37.

14. F. 523, op. 1, d. 66, ll. 28–31. This letter is a typed draft with handwritten additions and corrections. Handwritten notes on the letter suggest that it was sent as edited.

15. The translations in the text are taken from the authorized English-language translation, dated 10 April 1937, in f. 495, op. 20, d. 756, ll. 46–47. Given the Comintern's long-standing sectarian tradition and recent demands for heightened vigilance, we may wonder why the ECCI had not ordered the creation of party control commissions before 1937.

16. The translations in the text are taken from the authorized English-language translation, in f. 495, op. 20, d. 756, ll. 45–46. The Russian version is in ibid., ll. 36–37.

17. Manuilsky's notes are in f. 523, op. 1, d. 66, ll. 1–27. The transcript of the meeting is in f. 495, op. 18, d. 1198, ll. 1–6. The commission members were Manuilsky (chair), Florin, Bogdanov, Kuusinen, Wang Ming, Marty, Ercoli (Trogliatti), Kone, Anvelt, Arnot, Moskvin, Bronkowski, Weiden, Dimitrov, Kirsanova, and Chemodanov. Manuilsky's draft resolution, dated 14 May 1937, is in f. 495, op. 20, d. 751, ll. 7–11. An English translation of the draft prepared for Arnot is in ibid., ll. 84–89.

18. On the Trotskyist penetration of the Socialist Party of America, see M. S. Venkataramani, "Leon Trotsky's Adventure in American Radical Politics, 1935–7," *International Relations of Social History,* 9, no. 1 (1964), 1–46; Constance Ashton Meyers, *The Prophet's Army: The History of American Trotskyism* (New York, 1972). The reference to the counterrevolutionary uprising in Spain is to the POUM uprising in Barcelona, which began in May 1937. On this, see Alva and Schwartz; Gabriel Jackson, *Spanish Civil War;* George Orwell, *Homage to Catalonia* (London, 1951).

19. The final resolution is dated 31 May 1937. The English-language version is

in f. 495, op. 73, d. 15, ll. 88–94. The resolution incorporated the suggestions made by the commission but is not notably different from the draft. Underlining in the original.

20. Glavlit—Central Directorate for the Literature and Publications of the USSR. This office acted as the state's main censor in order to prevent publishing state secrets.

21. Comintern members often used *okhranka*, the popular name of the police department in tsarist Russia, to describe the Polish police.

22. Until April 1929, Bukharin was the editor of *Pravda*. In making a point of Wasilkowski's securing a position on the *Pravda* editorial board, Walecki implies that Bukharin was protecting Wasilkowski. Given that Bukharin was under arrest at the time Walecki wrote these notes, this was a very serious implication.

23. The Fifteenth VKP Congress was held on 2–19 December 1927. It adopted the directives to develop the First Five-Year Plan. After discussing the opposition, the Congress stressed that the Trotskyist-Zinovievite oppositionists had broken away from Leninism and become an instrument of class enemies in their struggle against the party and Soviet power. Belonging to the opposition and propagandizing its views were declared incompatible with membership in the party. The Congress approved Trotsky's and Zinoviev's expulsion from the party and expelled many other members of the opposition.

24. *Napostovtsy*—members of the Na postu (On Post) literary group (1923–1925), who took a negative view of classical literature and any "nonproletarian" art in general. They advocated the hegemony of proletarian literature.

25. The report, dated 26 June 1937, is in f. 495, op. 123, d. 248, ll. 2–14.

26. Dimitrov, in his *Diary* entry for 25 May, notes the arrest of Müller, Alikhanov, and Dobrich. Dimitrov recorded Yezhov's statement in his entry for 26 May 1937.

27. *Kommunisticheskii Internatsional,* 2 (1937), 95–100; ibid., no. 6 (1937), 4–8; ibid., 101.

28. *Diary of Georgi Dimitrov,* entry for 27 May 1937. Dimitrov recorded "checking the apparatus."

29. Regarding Vitol, Protocol No. 2 of the 27 May 1937 meeting of the special commission to verify the workers of the ECCI apparatus reads: "verify additionally at the moment of the exchange [of party documents]."

30. Probably should read "from within." (Trans.)

31. Albert—alias of Albert Zyltowski (aka Wiktor Bertynski).

32. *Krokodil*—a satirical magazine, published from 1922.

33. Semyon Davydovich Vulfson was deputy head of the trade delegation in Italy in 1924–1925, head of the trade delegation in Austria in 1925–1927, deputy chairman of Exportkhleb (Bread Export) in 1927–1928, and a foreign director of Exportkhleb in Rotterdam in 1929–1930. He died in March 1932.

34. In 1918–1924, L. B. Kamenev was the chairman of the Moscow City Soviet.

35. Refers to the VKP CC Plenum that took place between 23 February and 5 March 1937.

36. Refers to the Constitution of the USSR adopted by the Eighth Extraordinary Congress of Soviets of the USSR in November 1936.

37. *Ty* is a familiar, friendly way to address a person, as opposed to *Vy*, a more formal address. (Trans.)

38. Probably refers to F. Likhte (R. Vujović).

39. The 29 May 1937 resolution of the Fourth Moscow City Conference of the VKP read: "The Conference suggests that the Moscow city committee of the VKP work out measures to introduce Communists to the goals and aims, practice and techniques, of the sabotage, subversive, and espionage activities of the foreign espionage organs in order to teach every Communist how to precisely and promptly recognize and smash the enemies of the people."

40. Refers to the centers of communications in the ECCI apparatus, most of which were located in the Moscow suburbs.

41. This was not the only occasion on which Kotelnikov's political credentials were challenged. In June 1939 he penned two letters—one to Dimitrov and Manuilsky, the other to Dimitrov and Pugovkin in the CC—in which he defended himself against allegations that when he worked in the Eastern Secretariat, he had knowledge of Trotskyist conversations and activities there. For the letters, see f. 546, op. 1, d. 434, ll. 9–21.

42. RGASPI, f. 546, op. 1, d. 388, l. 68.

43. On 17 July 1937 the Politburo directed the Central Executive Committee of the USSR to award Yezhov the Order of Lenin. For the Politburo resolution, see f. 17, op. 3, d. 989, l. 60, cited in Getty and Naumov, *Road to Terror,* document 158.

44. For Stalin's order, see Getty and Naumov, *Road to Terror,* document 169. For a NKVD operational order, see ibid., document 170. On 31 July 1937 the Politburo established a timetable for these operations. The orders were extended in January 1938. See ibid., document 182.

45. For discussions of these and other national operations, see N. V. Petrov and A. B. Roginskii, "'Polskaia operatsiia' NKVD, 1937–1938gg.," in Gurianov, 22–34; N. Okhotin and A. B. Roginskii, "Iz istorii 'nemetskoi operatsii' NKVD, 1937–1938gg.," in Shcherbakova, 35–75. NKVD Order No. 00485 is reproduced in full in Yuri Shapoval, Volodymyr Prystaiko, and Vadym Zolotariov, *ChK-GPU-NKVD v Ukraini: Osobi, fakti, dokumenti* (Kiev, 1997), 350–376. Two weeks earlier, on 27 July 1937, the Politburo ordered the dismissal of the leaders of the CC of the Communist Party of Belorussia (KP[b]B) for failing to liquidate "the effects of sabotage committed by Polish spies." F. 17, op. 3, d. 989, l. 76, cited in Getty and Naumov, *Road to Terror,* document 160.

46. F. 495, op. 74, d. 400, l. 87. My thanks to Fridrikh Firsov for sharing this document with me.

47. F. 495. op. 74, d. 400, ll. 94–98

48. Bielewski's recommendation that the party's "healthy elements" clean out "all the rotten and undesirable" was not new. It faithfully reflected a resolution issued by the Secretariat in 1936. He himself had drafted a similar resolution in September 1933; see Chapter 3.

49. Yezhov made his assertion regarding "Polish spies" in his 3 February 1940 statement before a secret judicial session of the Military Collegium of the Supreme Court of the USSR following his arrest for being an agent of Polish and British intelligence. That statement is reproduced in Getty and Naumov, *Road to Terror,* document 199.

50. Quoted in Starkov, "Narkom Yezhov," 33.

51. Quoted in ibid., 33. Shneidman's statement that he "was convinced of the [accused's] guilt" echoes that of a NKVD officer captured by the Germans in 1941.

In 1937–1938 he had been assigned to monitor Comintern officials and foreigners residing in Moscow. The agent told his incredulous German interrogators of a "profession of conspiracies" and "even presented a chart of the complicated relations among secret organizations of 'leftist' and 'rightist' groups that included . . . leading officials of the Komintern and NKVD." Rittersporn, "Omnipresent Conspiracy," 99.

52. For a discussion, see Rittersporn, "Omnipresent Conspiracy," 99; and Starkov, "Narkom Yezhov," 29–33. For examples of NKVD interrogators' conspiratorial view of the world, see the case studies in Chapter 7.

53. Most of Dimitrov's notes are written in the past tense, but at times he used the present tense. To make this document easier to read and to render it consistent, I have changed present tense verbs to the past tense when the latter was more appropriate (Trans.)

54. PPS—Polish Socialist Party (Polska Partia Socijalistyczna), formed in 1893. It had as its programmatic goal to rebuild the Polish state. The left wing stood for the armed insurrection of the Polish proletariat, together with the Russian working class, against tsarism. The Ninth PPS Congress (1906) expelled the PPS leader, J. Pilsudski, and his supporters from the party. The left wing, known as the PPS-Lewica, adopted a revolutionary program and, in December 1918, united with the SDPKPiL, thus creating the Polish Communist Workers Party. After being expelled from the party, Pilsudski's supporters created a new organization, the PPS-Revolutionary Faction (from 1919, PPS). This party helped create the independent Polish state and, in July 1920, entered the coalitional government of W. Witas. In May 1926 the PPS supported Pilsudski's coup d'état. In November 1926 the PPS refused to cooperate with the regime of "sanitation" and shifted to the opposition.

55. Probably Roman Lagwa.

56. The Brest peace—peace treaty between Soviet Russia and Germany, Austria-Hungary, Bulgaria, and Turkey signed on 3 March 1918 in the city of Brest-Litovsk (now Brest). It was ratified by the Fourth Extraordinary Congress of Soviets on 15 March 1918. On 13 November 1918, after the defeat of these countries in World War I, the Brest peace was repealed by the VTsIK decree.

57. Left SRs—the Russian Party of Left Socialist Revolutionaries, 1917–1921. It emerged as an oppositional movement in the SR Party. Along with the Bolsheviks, the Left SRs formed part of the Military Revolutionary Committees, participated in the 1917 October revolution and in the work of the Second All-Russia Congress of Soviets, and were elected to the VTsIK. In December 1917, at their first congress, the Left SRs formed an organizationally independent party. At the same time, seven Left SRs joined the Council of People's Commissars (SNK). Tensions between the Left SRs and the Bolsheviks were aggravated during negotiations for the Brest peace treaty, which the Left SRs opposed. After the ratification of the treaty, they left the SNK and turned to open struggle against Lenin's policy by organizing an uprising against Soviet power. After the defeat of the uprising, some of the Left SRs were expelled from the soviets, and the active participants in the rebellion were convicted. The party ceased to exist in the early 1920s.

58. Left Communists—a group of RKP(b) members that emerged in January 1918 and supported the continuation of the revolutionary war in order to promote world revolution. The leaders of the group were N. Bukharin, A. Bubnov, A. Lomov (G. Oppokov), N. Osinsky (V. Obolensky), E. Preobrazhensky, G. Piatakov,

and K. Radek. In May–June 1918, not having received support from any party organization, the group ceased to exist. On the Left Communists, see Ronald Kowalski, *The Bolshevik Party in Conflict: The Left Communist Opposition of 1918* (Pittsburgh, 1991).

59. Adam Koc—an army colonel and a member of Beck's ruling group in the Polish government in the late 1930s.

60. The Polish Bureau of Agitation and Propaganda of the CC RKP(b) was created in 1919 to direct the political and cultural work among Russia's Polish population. Independent party groups were created in different cities of the USSR. Following the decision of the Eighth RKP(b) Congress (1919), all revolutionary organizations of the Polish proletariat were integrated into the Bolshevik Party. The Polish bureau had its departments in the local RKP(b) committees. The bureau ceased to exist in the early 1930s.

61. The Fourth CPP conference took place between 24 November and 23 December 1925. The major result of the conference was the dissociation of the party from the ultra-Leftist course of the L. Domski group. No representatives of the ultra-Left group were elected to the new party leadership.

62. The Fifth CPP Congress took place on 16–29 August 1930 in Petergof, near Leningrad. Lenski read the report of the CC CPP. The congress recognized the growth of the revolutionary situation in Poland and sharply criticized the position of the "majority," characterizing it as a Right deviation. Only "minority" members were elected to the CC and the Political Bureau. J. Lenski was elected general secretary.

63. Union of Riflemen—a paramilitary organization of Polish youth led by Polish army officers; it was closely connected with the ruling circles of the Pilsudski regime.

64. Probably Josef Konecki (real name—Leon Rozin).

65. The most reliable figures on the "Polish operation" can be found in Petrov and Roginskii, 40. The figures on the number of CC members purged come from F. I. Firsov and S. Yazhborovskaia, "Komintern in Kommunisticheskaia partiia Polshii," *Voprosy istorii*, nos. 11–12 (1988), 40–55. Walter Laqueur estimates that approximately 5,000 CPP members were arrested and killed in mid-1937. Laqueur, *The Glasnost Revelations* (London, 1990), 108. Another author claims that as many as 50,000 Poles residing in the USSR were executed prior to 1939. Ex-Insider, "The Party That Vanished," *Soviet Survey*, no. 33 (1960), 105. Hiroaki Kuromiya, in *Freedom and Terror*, 231, argues that "nearly 50,000 Soviet Poles" were repressed, as were more than 25,000 Germans and many Latvians. Based on a review of archival materials, Barry McLoughlin asserts: "During the 'Polish operation,' for instance, 140,000 prisoners were sentenced, 110,000 of them to death, between November 1937 and November 1938." McLoughlin, "Documenting the Death Toll: Research into the Mass Murder of Foreigners in Moscow, 1937–38," *AHA Perspectives* (May 1999), 30. For a brief discussion of the estimates of arrests and deaths among the Polish and other émigré communities in the USSR, see McDermott, 147–148.

66. Examples of Soviet espionage activities abroad are numerous. Pavel Sudaplatov's recent memoir, *Special Tasks*, provides insight into such activities on the USSR's western borders and into the mindset of Soviet intelligence agents. Unfor-

tunately, scholarly research into whether there were Polish intelligence networks in the USSR has been nil.

67. F. 495, op. 184, d. 11, outgoing telegram for 1937, ll. 17, 42. My thanks to Fridrikh Firsov for sharing this material with me.

68. *Diary of Georgi Dimitrov,* entries for 17 June 1937, 20 June 1937, 21 June 1937, and 7 July 1937.

69. F. 495, op. 184, d. 4, outgoing telegram for 1937, ll. 32, 53. My thanks to Fridrikh Firsov for sharing this material with me.

70. For other examples of denunciations, see "The Case of Petko Petkov" in Chapter 7; see also f. 495, op. 10a, d. 395, ll. 12–14; op. 73, d. 50, l. 22; op. 74, d. 398, ll. 98–99; op. 65a, d. 8364, l. 39.

71. For the transcript of that conversation, see f. 495, op. 109, d. 395, ll. 1–8.

72. F. 495, op. 109, d. 395, l. 1; ibid., l. 2; ibid., ll. 3–4.

73. Ibid., l. 4.

74. Ibid., ll. 5–8.

75. As in the text, but it appears to be a mistake. He is probably referring to the West European Bureau (Zapadnoevropeiskoe Biuro—ZEB) because he mentions meeting Dimitrov in Berlin. At that time, Dimitrov headed the ZEB and lived in Berlin.

76. What the abbreviation KRO represents is unclear, possibly the Counterrevolutionary Department of the NKVD.

77. F. 495, op. 73, d. 58, l. 27. Dimitrov deemed the letter a "top secret" document.

78. See *Diary of Georgi Dimitrov,* entry for 7 November 1937.

79. See ibid., entry for 11 November 1937.

80. Aino Kuusinen met Eberlein in the gulag and, in her memoirs, writes of his final days. See Kuusinen, 156–157.

81. Dimitrov mentions this meeting in his *Diary,* entry for 23 November 1937.

82. This resolution was adopted by a vote by the members of the ECCI Presidium on 16 August 1938, under the title "Resolution of the ECCI Presidium." F. 495, op. 2, d. 264, ll. 198, 202–205.

83. Document 38 reproduces the resolution and letter to Stalin in the order that they appear in the archive. This resolution was first published in *Voprosy istorii KPSS,* no. 12 (1988), 52.

84. F. 495, op. 2, d. 264, l. 211. During late 1937, the newspaper of the Polish Socialist Party (PPS), *Robotnik,* published a series of articles publicizing and criticizing the repression of Poles in the USSR. Shortly thereafter, the journal of the Comintern published an article under Swentsitski's byline, which harshly criticized the CPP and asserted that its former leaders "strove for the ideo-political separation of the Communist Party of Poland from the Communist International and subjected the CPP to the criminal designs of the Pilsudshchina." *Kommunisticheskii Internatsional,* 1 (1938), 93. True to Stalin's advice, the article made no mention of the dissolution of the CPP, which had taken place by then. That article was not the only effort to justify the Poles' arrests. In January 1938 someone in the ECCI apparatus prepared a letter from a nonexistent "old PPS member" criticizing the PPS for slandering the USSR. The letter directly addressed its criticisms: "To me these continual cries in *Robotnik* about the executions in the USSR

are becoming stronger. Why are they executing [people] there? For treason, for espionage in the service of a fascist state, for wrecking and sabotage, for contaminating bread and drinking water, for organizing railroad accidents, for fires in mines, etc. To me as a worker, I think that the executions of these people are nothing bad. How else to defend oneself from such enemies, especially when the Soviet Union is surrounded by hostile capitalist states?" The letter was dated 14 January 1937, although it was written in January 1938. The ECCI never published the letter. But that it was prepared at all is remarkable and suggests how anxious the ECCI's leaders were about international criticisms of the repression. F. 495, op. 10, d. 273, ll. 5–6. My thanks to Fridrikh Firsov for sharing this material with me. For a discussion of the issues relating to the dissolution of the CPP, see Firsov and Iazhborovskaia.

85. According to Hiroaki Kuromiya, anxieties about émigrés in Ukraine dated from late 1934. In December 1934 "anti-Soviet elements" were ordered removed from border zones. In 1935–1936 hundreds of Poles and Germans were deported from border regions and/or arrested. In December 1935, Postyshev, the VKP leader in Ukraine, asserted that 90 percent of Polish émigrés were enemy agents. Kuromiya, *Freedom and Terror*, 207–208.

86. For materials relating to the Secretariat's discussion of MOPR on 17 December 1938, see f. 495, op. 18, d. 1229, ll. 24–30. Wilhelm Pieck replaced Stasova, who was not arrested. For the announcement that Pieck was replacing Stasova, see ibid., ll. 34–35. For the resolution announcing the composition of the commission, see ibid., ll. 36–37.

87. See Document 5.

88. Kharbinites were residents of the Manchurian city of Kharbin (Harbin), which was returned to the USSR with the Soviet government's sale of the Northern Chinese Railroad in 1935.

89. For a discussion of the various national operations and deadline extensions, see Okhotin and Roginskii; Petrov and Roginskii.

90. For this decision, see Getty and Naumov, *Road to Terror*, document 184.

Chapter 6. The Consequences of Vigilance

1. For the trial transcript, see Narodnyi Kommissariat Iustitsii SSSR, *Sudebnyi otchet po delu antisovetskogo "Pravo-Trotskistskogo bloka"* (Moscow, 1938).

2. SRs—abbreviation for the Party of Socialist Revolutionaries, which was created in 1901 as a left radical party representing the interests of peasants. The party stood for democratic political reforms and for the liquidation of private ownership of land. Among its methods of struggle were the organization of mass movements as well as individual terrorist acts. In August 1917 the left wing broke away and formed an independent party, the Left SRs. Between late November 1917 and March 1918 several Left SRs held ministerial portfolios in the Soviet government. They quit to protest the terms of the Brest-Litovsk treaty and conducted an active anti-Bolshevik struggle. It ceased to exist as a legal party in the USSR after 1923.

3. Cagoulards (from the French word *cagoule*, "a hood")—members of the French Social Movement for Revolutionary Action, headed by the Secret Committee for Revolutionary Action. It was an illegal, extreme right-wing organization.

The members attending the Secret Committee sessions reportedly wore hoods to conceal their identities.

4. In 1938 the State Publishing House (Gosizdat) published Mikhail E. Koltsov's pamphlet *A Thunderbird: The Life and Death of Maxim Gorky.*

5. Maxim Gorky (real name—Aleksei Peshkov; 1868–1936). A Russian and Soviet writer, he was the organizer and the chairman of the first All-Union Congress of Soviet Writers in 1934. The indictment of the procurator of the USSR and the verdict of the Military Board of the Supreme Court of the USSR in the case of the Right-Trotskyist bloc stated that the accused were responsible for Gorky's death.

6. Refers to the successful 1938 expedition to rescue four Soviet explorers, led by Ivan Papanin, who were stranded on an ice floe that broke off the Arctic ice shelf.

7. The NKVD's dragnet of émigrés left many comrades, friends, and family members wondering about the fate of those arrested, and prompted them to request that Dimitrov appeal on their behalf. On this, see below, especially Chapter 7. In some cases, the representative of a fraternal party initiated the appeal process by requesting that Dimitrov ascertain what had happened to arrested people. For an example, see W. Pieck's April 1938 letter to Dimitrov asking him to inquire about the fates of fifteen arrested Germans, eight of whom, according to Pieck, had "had no ties to hostile anti-Soviet elements" and for whom "the Cadres Department has no compromising material." F. 495, op. 73, d. 60, ll. 23–36.

8. F. 495, op. 73, d. 48, ll. 96–99. This letter is not reproduced in full here because it has already been published. See *Problemy mira i sotsializma,* 7 (1989), 90. The underlined sections are as in the original. For a discussion of the arrest of some Hungarian party leaders, see the case studies of Béla Kun and Béla Szántó in Chapter 7. Varga was not the first person to protest the mass arrest of foreigners. For another example, this time addressed to Yezhov and dated 10 January 1938, see f. 495, op. 73, d. 60, ll. 1–5. The copy in the Comintern collection is unsigned. The author wrote to Yezhov to protest the arrest of leaders of the CP of Finland, whom the author believed to be honest and efficient leaders. He or she also noted that there were suspicious elements within that party and among Finnish émigrés.

9. As "The Case of Karl F. Kurshner" in Chapter 7 indicates, although Varga was not arrested, some Hungarian émigrés living in the USSR were arrested for belonging to an alleged counterrevolutionary group headed by Varga.

10. In November 1937, Elena Stasova, then the head of MOPR, wrote to the VKP Party Control Commission asking it to clarify MOPR's legal role in helping the spouses and family members of arrested émigrés to find work. F. 356, op. 2, d. 30, ll. 1–3, cited in Getty and Naumov, *Road to Terror,* document 174.

11. *Le Journal de Moscou* was a political, economic, and literary weekly published in Moscow in French from 1934 to 1939.

12. F. 495, op. 73, d. 61, ll. 14–16. Piteliia wrote her letter in Finnish; it was translated into Russian by ECCI translators. Both Kuusinen and Dimitrov read it. Kuusinen wrote on it "Who to arrest?" and recommended sending it to the CC. On 3 March 1938, Dimitrov sent the translated letter to CC Secretary Andreev.

13. Five-day week. (Trans.)

14. The typed letter reads "*po kvarty(?),*" suggesting that the person who typed the letter could not read this phrase in the original handwritten letter. The original could not be found. (Trans.)

15. For examples, see the case studies in Chapter 7. For a fictional account written in 1939–1941 that conveys this assumption, see Lydia Chudovskaya, *Sofia Petrovna,* trans. Aline Werth (Evanston, Ill., 1990).

16. For an example, see Daniel Field, *Rebels in the Name of the Tsar* (Winchester, Mass., 1989).

17. On the importance of rank as an explanatory factor in the repression, see J. Arch Getty and William Chase, "Patterns of Repression Among the Soviet Elite in the Late 1930s: A Biographical Approach," in Getty and Manning, 225–246.

18. See *Diary of Georgi Dimitrov,* entries for 23 and 24 November 1938.

19. On 25 November 1938, Dimitrov wrote in his *Diary* that "Nikolaev's an agent of several intelligence services at once; Volin's a German agent; Polyachek's a Polish spy!—A number of cases will have to be re-examined. New instructions, on assignment from Stalin, to work up instructions regarding arrests."

20. For a discussion of the events leading up to and following the ouster of Yezhov, see Getty and Naumov, *Road to Terror,* chapter 12, esp. documents 189–192; Starkov, "Narkom Yezhov," 37–39. The quotations are from Starkov, "Narkom Yezhov," 38, 39. According to Starkov, "Yezhov's primary crime, however, consisted in the fact that he had not informed Stalin of his actions." For an example of someone released after Yezhov's removal, see "The Case of Iordan T. Terziev" in Chapter 7; for an example of someone for whom Yezhov's removal made no difference, see "The Case of Karl F. Kurshner" in Chapter 7.

21. For a list of appeals submitted by Dimitrov for the first six months of 1940, see f. 495, op. 73, d. 88, ll. 186–189. That list contains the name of the individual on whose behalf the appeal was filed, when and to whom it was sent (e.g., USSR procurator, chief military procurator, NKVD, oblast procurator, Beria), and the answer received. Of the sixty-six people on the list, only two had been freed at the time the list was compiled, two had been shot, one had died, and the remaining cases were either pending or the first appeal had been denied. For examples of appeals made by Dimitrov on behalf of Bulgarians (whom he described as "irreproachable Communists"), see f. 495, op. 74, d. 77, ll. 7–8 ; f. 495, op. 73, d. 88, ll. 1, 6, 56, 73–78, 91, 100; see also the discussion in "The Case of Petko Petrov" in Chapter 7. For examples of appeals filed on behalf of Hungarians, see f. 495, op. 73, d. 88, ll. 8–13, 165–168, 177–180, 185; ibid., d. 72, ll. 42–43; f. 495, op. 74, d. 101, ll. 3–20. For examples of appeals on behalf of Germans, see f. 495, op. 73, d. 88, ll. 43, 94–95. For examples of appeals on behalf of Letts, see ibid., d. 72, ll. 29–31, 33–34. For examples of appeals on behalf of Austrians, see ibid., d. 88, ll. 63–70.

22. F. 495, op. 73, d. 71, ll. 15–16 (dated 21 July 1939 and deemed "top secret").

23. In compiling the list, Kotelnikov no doubt drew on other lists, such as lists of members expelled from the party organization of the ECCI apparatus. For examples of such lists, see f. 546, op. 1, d. 408, ll. 6–11 (dated 1 February 1937); ll. 12–13 (dated 23 October 1937); ll. 19–24 (dated 9 December 1937).

24. On the size of the party committee in 1935, see Dimitrov's comments in Document 4.

25. That so many Latvians were arrested reflects a belief among some VKP leaders that there existed a "National Latvian Center" in Moscow and within the "Latvian Section of the Comintern." In 1937 Yezhov ordered the arrest of "no less than

1,600–2,000" Latvians residing in the USSR. Nikita Ilkevich, "Rasstrrelnianyi v Viaz'me: Novoe o M. N. Goretskom," *Krai Smolenskii,* nos. 1–2 (1994), 129–144, esp. 138. My thanks to Roberta Manning for sharing this material with me.

26. Mikhail Panteleiev, in "La Terreur stalienne au Komintern en 1937–1938: Les chiffres et les causes," *Communisme,* nos. 40–41 (1995), 38–40, has calculated that 113 workers in the ECCI apparatus were arrested in 1937–1938.

27. These figures come from Fridrikh I. Firsov, "Samounichtozhenie Kominterna," unpublished manuscript, 36. Firsov cites f. 546, op. 1, d. 37, ll. 7–37, for the 1936 figures and ibid., d. 437, l. 43, for the 1938 figures. On 21 January 1937 there were 338 members of the party organization. F. 546, op. 1, d. 407, ll. 85–95. My thanks to Fridrikh Firsov for sharing this material with me.

28. See, e.g., Conquest, *Great Terror.*

29. After March 1938 the ECCI party organization was part of the Rostokinskii district VKP organization and was subordinate to the Rostokinskii district party committee.

Chapter 7. Case Studies

1. Boris A. Starkov, "The Trial That Was Not Held," *Europe-Asia Studies,* 46, no. 8 (1994), 1301. Starkov argues that Kun was one of a group of former Comintern leaders, among them Pyatnitsky and Knorin, who were slated for a fourth Moscow show trial. Although the evidence presented in his article does show how confessions were extracted and cases compiled, the evidence that a trial of those engaged in an anti-Comintern conspiracy was planned is circumstantial. But as we shall see, Kun's, Pyatnitsky's, and Knorin's opposition to the Popular Front policy and Dimitrov's leadership played a significant role in their arrests.

2. Kun was rehabilitated in an article that appeared in *Pravda* on 21 February 1956.

3. In most other cases, the NKVD took possession of the relevant documents. For examples, see f. 495, op. 73, d. 58, l. 27; and Chapter 5.

4. The available archival evidence supports E. H. Carr's and Jonathan Haslam's hypothesis that Kun, Pyatnitsky, and Knorin were among those ECCI leaders who opposed the adoption of the Popular Front prior to the Seventh Comintern Congress. Carr, *Twilight of the Comintern;* Haslam, "Origins of the Popular Front." The three men formed the core of what Starkov believes was to be an anti-Comintern show trial. See Starkov, "Trial That Was Not Held."

5. Known also as Imre Komor-Katsburg Bácskai.

6. The Hungarian CP delegation to the Seventh Comintern Congress consisted of six people. Five had deciding votes: János (Z. Szántó), Róbert Györi, Karoly Kovács, Béla Kun, and János Nagy (Gross). Éva Lakatos had a consultative vote.

7. In December 1934 the CC CPH suggested to the leadership of the Social Democratic Party (SDP) and the Trade Union Council in Hungary that they cooperate in common action and common struggle in defense of the trade unions with the goal of broadening democratic rights and freedoms and that they unify forces to support the activities of the SDP. The CC CPH invited the SDP leadership to speak out in support of common action with the then illegal CPH. The SDP leadership declined these suggestions. In spring 1935 the CC CPH suggested conducting a meeting with the SDP leadership. The SDP leadership again refused.

8. F. 495, op. 18, d. 1097, ll. 21–25. This unsigned, typed document was designated "top secret" and written in Russian. It is unclear whether it was originally written in Russian or whether it was translated from the Hungarian.

9. For a discussion of these arrests and their consequences for the CPH see Gross's letter of 12 February 1936 to Dimitrov, Manuilsky, and Ercoli in f. 495, op. 20, d. 823, ll. 1–7.

10. See the stenographic record of the 29 March 1936 meeting of Ercoli's Secretariat on the Hungarian question. F. 495, op. 12, d. 10, ll. 2–90. Ercoli chaired the meeting, which was attended by Béla Kun, Gross, B. Szántó, Révai, Kover, Smoliansky, Komor, Chernomordik, and Sorkin. This was not the first time that divisions between Kun's faction and other members of the Hungarian CP necessitated ECCI intervention. For example, see f. 495, op. 19, d. 261, l. 1.

11. The members of the commission were Anvelt, Wang Ming, André Marty, Ercoli, and Raimon (real name Rodolfo Ghiodi).

12. At the 7–8 May 1936 meeting of the ECCI Secretariat, a decision was taken to dissolve the CC CPH and to create a provisional Secretariat headed by S. Szántó. This new provisional leading organ of the CPH worked in Prague until late 1938. Kun was not among the new CPH leadership, but, in accordance with the ECCI Secretariat's decision and party discipline, he had to support it. Not until 26 June did the ECCI Secretariat formally approve the provisional Secretariat for the Hungarian party, and authorize it to devise and implement policies to undo the damage done by Kun, Gross, and the CC. Zoltán Szántó was appointed to head the provisional Secretariat. The resolution is in f. 495, op. 12, d. 30, ll. 25–26. In fact, the provisional Secretariat had been operating since the announcement of the "temporary leadership" in early 1936. One reason for appointing Szántó to head the provisional Secretariat was that, because he had only recently been released from prison, he had not been compromised by the political and petty intrigues of the former party leaders. At the March meeting Révai asked: "Who would be able to live up to the requirements necessary to ensure the healing process in the party leadership? Maybe only comrade Szántó, who spent eight years in prison. (Interjection: In this respect, it proves an advantage for him.)" F. 495, op. 18, d. 1047, l. 85.

13. The ECCI Secretariat met on 7 May to discuss "the state of the Hungarian CP" and "concluded that the CP of Hungary is in a very difficult crisis." It met again on 23 June to consider the policies proposed by that party's provisional Secretariat. See the stenographic report of the June meeting: F. 495, op. 18, d. 1047, ll. 1–25. Anvelt kept Dimitrov and the Secretariat informed of his committee's work; see, e.g., f. 495, op. 74, d. 101, l. 27.

14. F. 495, op. 12, d. 30, ll. 25–26. For Anvelt's views on and proposal regarding the Hungarian party, see f. 495, op. 18, d. 1097, ll. 19–20. In June 1936 the ECCI expelled him from the CC of the party. Gross's expulsion from the CPH came after his political position and behavior at the Seventh Comintern Congress were discussed at the 27 May 1936 ECCI meeting. Gross was accused of disrupting organizational work and violations of the rules of secrecy (in connection with the discovery and arrest of the party printing press in Hungary), of sabotaging the implementation of the decisions of the Congress, and of a hostile attitude toward ECCI members. Gross allegedly expressed his hostility by failing to stand up when the audience gave standing ovations to Dimitrov and Manuilsky, who had been elected to the ECCI Presidium. Gross explained his action by the fact that the Hun-

garian delegation was denied the right to nominate Béla Kun to be a member of the ECCI Presidium. In October 1937 the ECCI reviewed Gross's case. At that time, he had already been arrested. The ECCI decided to expel him from the party as an enemy of the people.

15. Dimitrov sent a copy of Szántó's declaration to Yezhov (in ORPO) and the ICC on 19 July 1936. F. 495, op. 74, d. 101, l. 33–37.

16. Z. Szántó's statement was forwarded to the ICC as part of the gathering of materials for a session of the special commission on the B. Kun case. Anvelt, the ICC secretary, sent a copy of the statement, written in German, to Dimitrov on 5 July 1936. He sent a copy of the translation to the CC VKP for Yezhov's information, on 19 July 1936.

17. The meetings of Ercoli's Secretariat devoted to intraparty and cadres questions concerning the CP of Hungary took place on 10 and 29 March 1936.

18. Refers to the war unleashed by Italy against Abyssinia (Ethiopia), which lasted from October 1935 to May 1936 and resulted in the occupation of Ethiopia.

19. During the parliamentary elections of 26 April–3 May 1936 in France, the French CP, French Socialist Party (SFIO), and the Radical Party supported a common Popular Front platform worked out in January 1936. The Socialist, Communist, and Radical coalition received an absolute majority in the National Assembly (380 seats). Léon Blum, the SFIO leader, formed and headed a Socialist-Radical government.

20. Kun was referring to the events in May 1921 when, following Lenin's criticism of Kun's role in the March Action in Germany, Kun was sent to work for the Urals regional committee of the RCP(b). The March Action was an abortive uprising by the German CP and was inspired by Zinoviev and Kun.

21. Declaration of E. D. Andich dated 22 August 1936, f. 495, op. 18, d. 1113, ll. 73–74. Another Hungarian, S. F. Timar, declared that he had been told, by yet another Hungarian, that Kun had been removed from work because "he was very liberal toward Trotskyists." Declaration of S. F. Timar dated 25 August 1936, f. 495, op. 18, d. 1113, l. 78.

22. Dimitrov sent the materials to Yezhov on 19 July 1936. F. 495, op. 74, d. 101, l. 105.

23. F. 495, op. 73, d. 15, l. 37–40.

24. See *Diary of Georgi Dimitrov,* entry for 28 August 1936.

25. For this resolution, see f. 495, op. 12, d. 20, ll. 32–36.

26. F. 495, op. 74, d. 101, ll. 117–118.

27. German title: <u>Schlußfolgerungen der eingesetzten Kommission betr. Gen. BÉLA KUN.</u>

28. At the Seventeenth VKP Congress in 1934, such behavior was explicitly forbidden within that party and, by extension, in those parties that belonged to the Comintern. The resolution passed by that Congress noted that the VKP would not tolerate attempts by "an insignificant minority to impose its will on the vast majority of the party, nor to attempt to form factional groups, destroying party unity, nor to attempt to create a schism." Robert H. McNeal, ed., *Resolutions and Decisions of the Communist Party of the Soviet Union,* vol. 3: *The Stalin Years: 1929–1953* (Toronto, 1974), 151.

29. On the tensions that riddled the German community in Soviet emigration, see Pike.

30. At the 5 September 1936 meeting of the ECCI Secretariat, Anvelt presented the report of the Secretariat's commission "On the Behavior of Béla Kun." Anvelt chaired the commission. The materials collected by the commission were presented at the meeting and, along with the commission's report, formed the basis of discussion. Document 50 is a typewritten fragment of the stenographic report containing Béla Kun's speech. The report of the Anvelt commission is missing from the files of the ECCI Secretariat.

31. Kun is referring to either the 10 March or 29 March 1936 meetings of Ercoli's Secretariat on issues relating to cadres and other affairs of the CP of Hungary. Révai attended those meetings.

32. Refers to B. Kun's speech at the 21 November 1933 meeting of the purge commission of the ECCI party organization. In that speech, Kun gave a positive evaluation of Magyar.

33. Refers to the commission headed by Kuusinen to work out the first point (the report on the ECCI's activities) on the agenda of the Seventh Comintern Congress. On 3 June 1934 the ECCI Political Secretariat appointed Magyar to serve on this commission. Other members were Pieck, Knorin, Wang Ming, Manuilsky, Pyatnitsky, Dimitrov, Varga, S. Lozovsky, Kun, Bronkowski (Bortnowski), A. Vassart, R. Makilom, P. Shubin, G. Lorenz (S. E. Schukin), and Sinani (G. Skalov). Ercoli (Togliatti) and Heckert also participated in the work of the commission.

34. F. 546, op. 1, 329, l. 129. My thanks to Fridrikh Firsov for sharing this material with me.

35. For a discussion, see *Ogonek*, no. 45 (1988); Arvo Tuominen, *The Bells of the Kremlin* (Hanover, N.H., 1983); György Borsányi, *The Life of a Communist Revolutionary: Béla Kun,* trans. Mario D. Fenyo (Highland Lakes, N.J., 1993). On 9 September 1938, Dimitrov sent to Yezhov the conclusions of the Anvelt commission and the ECCI Secretariat's 4 September 1936 resolution. Dimitrov knew of Kun's arrest, but he may not have known that Kun had been executed on 29 August 1938.

36. F. 495, op. 199, d. 6810, ll. 160–167, 192–193.

37. The statement by Irina Kun was probably sent to the ECCI Cadres Department.

38. On 27 January 1937, Benedek also wrote a letter to Dimitrov asking to receive him so that he could convey certain facts regarding Béla Kun.

39. The available evidence provides no evidence to support or negate the accusations that he tried to create an "anti-Comintern organization . . . inside the Comintern." See Starkov, "Trial That Was Not Held," 301. Stalin reportedly told Dimitrov in November 1937, five months after Kun's arrest, that "Kun has acted with the Trotskyists against the party. In all likelihood, he is also mixed up in espionage." A. G. Latyshev, "Riadom so Stalinym," *Sovershenno sekretno*, no. 12 (1990), 19.

40. See Varga's 21 January 1938 letter to Manuilsky, Moskvin, and Belov in f. 495, op. 74, d. 104, l. 1. See also Szántó's 11 July 1938 letter to Dimitrov, Manuilsky, and Moskvin in f. 495, op. 74, d. 104, l. 17. See other related materials in f. 495, op. 74, d. 104, ll. 7–15 and 19–20.

41. For a more complete biography of Valter, see Documents 55 and 56.

42. When Dimitrov's initials were affixed is unclear, but they apparently indicate that he had received the telegram.

43. The letter was sent on 25 June 1940, according to a handwritten note on the letter by Dimitrov's secretary, A. Stern.

44. OSO—Russian abbreviation of Osoboe soveschanie, Special Council of the NKVD, an extra-judicial organ that existed in the NKVD between 10 July 1934 and 1 September 1953. The OSO had the power to sentence people to corrective labor camps and to exile and deport individuals considered "socially dangerous." The OSO was chaired by the people's commissar; its members consisted of his deputies, the head of the NKVD of the Russian Federation, the head of the Main Board of the Worker-Peasant Militia (police), and the people's commissar of internal affairs of the republic in which the criminal case was originated. The state prosecutor of the USSR or his deputy had to be present at OSO meetings.

45. F. 495, op. 74, d. 81, l. 1.

46. Many of the people listed in Document 55 also appeared in a list of appeals submitted by Dimitrov during the first half of 1941: f. 495, op. 73, d. 88, ll. 186–189.

47. This reference was written, at Dimitrov's request, by the ECCI's Cadres Department, and was sent, along with E. Valter's letter, to L. Beria on 25 June 1940.

48. Gubrevkom—abbreviation of Gubernskii revolutsionnyi komitet (Provincial Revolutionary Committee). (Trans.)

49. Information about A. Khigerovich (Razumova) was prepared, at Dimitrov's request, by the ECCI Cadres Department in three copies. Two copies were sent to the Secretariat to be sent to V. Merkulov. For more on the case of Anna Razumova, see below.

50. Refers to the early 1921 anti-Bolshevik rebellion led by sailors at the Kronstadt naval base.

51. SONO—probably Sokolnicheskii otdel narodnogo obrazovaniia (Sokolnicheskii District Department of Education). Sokolnicheskii was a district of Moscow. (Trans.)

52. International Women's Secretariat (renamed the ECCI Women's Department on 15 May 1925) existed between 1920 and November 1935.

53. Information about Drenowski was prepared, at Dimitrov's request, by Vladimirov (V. Chervenkov), the ECCI Cadres Department's analyst for the Balkan countries, and was sent to Dimitrov's Secretariat.

54. Comintern-sponsored training and transit to Spain of political émigrés from different countries who served in the International Brigades that defended the government of the Spanish Republic during the Spanish Civil War.

55. Drenowski was arrested on 3 November 1938. On 19 April 1939, the Military Board of the Supreme Court of the USSR sentenced him to be shot. He was executed the same day.

56. Information about Gaetano Cavalli was prepared by Blagoeva and Bogomolova, workers of the ECCI Organizational Committee and sent to Dimitrov's secretary, A. Stern, on 21 February 1941. A letter from Cavalli to Stalin dated 25 July 1940 is stored along with this document in the files of Dimitrov's Secretariat. The letter states that Cavalli was arrested on the basis of an accusation that he was engaged in espionage. He was sentenced, on 20 July 1940, by the OSO of the

Crimean Board of State Security, to five years in the labor camp. Also discussed in the letter are the NKVD's methods of investigation and interrogation.

57. Cavalli was arrested (according to his letter) on 22 June 1938, not in July 1938.

58. *Deutsche Zentral-Zeitung* was the daily newspaper of the Central Bureau of the German section in the CC VKP. It was published in Moscow by the Mezhdunarodnaia Kniga Publishing House from 1926 to 12 July 1939. Between 1926 and 1927 it was published as *Deutsche Zentral-Zeitung für Stadt und Land;* in 1931 and 1933–1938, as *DZZ;* and in 1939, as *Deutsche Zeitung.*

59. On 14 January 1941 the military procurator of the Moscow Military District sent a request to the ECCI Cadres Department in connection with the second verification of K. Kurshner. In that letter he asked about the relations between B. Vágó, A. Kreichi, and J. Fodor. The reply by the head of the Cadres Department, Guliaev, was sent to the Office of the Procurator on 19 February 1941. Kurshner died on 20 March 1942.

60. On 29 July 1938, Vági was sentenced to be executed.

61. Seikeli is probably a Russified version of Székely, but all references are to Seikeli.

62. On 21 June 1938, the OSO sentenced Seikeli to five years in a corrective labor camp. Between 1938 and July 1946 he was held in the Karlag labor camp in Ertsevo, Arkhangelsk region.

63. Information about Komor-Katsburg was provided at Dimitrov's request by the ECCI Cadres Department on 5 January 1939. Although his real name is Imre Komor, many documents in the archive refer to him as Komor-Katsburg and some as Komor-Katsburg Bácksai.

64. Though not present at the Seventh Comintern Congress, Komor wrote a statement to the ICC in which he condemned the behavior of the Hungarian delegation as the "rebellion of Gross and Kun against the Comintern leadership."

65. He was arrested on 23 July 1937.

66. Probably Iosif Ershov.

67. Between 1937 and 1947, Komor stayed in a corrective labor camp. After 1947 he worked at a metallurgical plant in Temir-Tau, Karaganda region.

68. According to Guliaev, head of the ECCI Cadres Department, Kutlu was arrested when he was crossing the Soviet border after being sent by the party to study in the USSR. After his arrest, he was kept in Orlovskaia prison. In May 1940 he wrote a letter to Dimitrov asking for a review of his case.

69. In reply to Dimitrov's letter, the procurator of the USSR, Bochkov, communicated that Kutlu had been released on 3 March 1941 and that his case had been closed. After March 1941, Kutlu lived in Moscow. In 1942 he left for Turkey.

70. The distribution of known dates of arrest for those listed in the full version of Document 55 begs for attention. Twelve of the sixteen people for whom arrest dates are known were arrested in 1938, three were arrested in 1937, and one was arrested in 1936. This list is by no means a representative sample, so we can draw only limited inferences from it, given that we know that many foreigners were arrested in 1937. But it suggests an area worthy of exploration. Given the CC's January 1938 criticism of the unjust arrests of party members, we may well wonder whether the ever vigilant NKVD turned more of its energies to political émigrés than to citizens.

71. For other correspondence relating to Seikeli's case, see f. 495, op. 78, d. 88, ll. 177–180.

72. For information on Razumova's family background, see f. 546, op. 1, d. 11, l. 145.

73. F. 546, op. 1, d. 340, l. 59. My thanks to Fridrikh Firsov for sharing this material with me.

74. On the June 1937 allegation that Razumov was a leader of a "united Trotskyist-'rightist' counter-revolutionary organization," see Getty and Naumov, *Road to Terror*, document 162.

75. F. 546, op. 1, d. 384, ll. 53–54. My thanks to Fridrikh Firsov for sharing this material with me. For Razumova's declaration regarding the affair, see f. 495, op. 65a, d. 8364, ll. 91–97. This *delo* contains materials relating to the Razumov affair.

76. F. 546, op. 1, d. 406, l. 55. My thanks to Fridrikh Firsov for sharing this material with me.

77. Razumova's undated declaration was addressed to Dimitrov and Manuilsky and submitted to the ECCI party committee in late December 1937. The declaration is in f. 495, op. 109, d. 395, l. 53.

78. Arkhiv Glavnoi voennoi prokuratory, d. 9872–39, l. 27. My thanks to Fridrikh Firsov for sharing this material with me.

79. This document was received in the CC VKP on 18 July 1945. On 22 April 1953, the personal file of A. Razumova-Khigerovich, which had been held by the Fifth Sector of the General Department of the CC CPSU, along with the enclosure, was transferred to storage. The cover note, addressed to E. Golubeva, a worker in the Sector, read: "After finding out whether Razumova is still in prison, send a copy of this document to the Minister." A. Razumova-Khigerovich was released and rehabilitated in January 1955.

80. Another way to read this sentence: "I could not myself select people from Moscow." (Trans.).

81. When Dimitrov asked Yezhov about Moskvin's arrest, Yezhov reportedly told him that Moskvin "was closely tied to all of that crowd. It will have to be determined to what extent he had those ties in recent years. It will also be determined whether he was entrapped by any foreign intelligence service that was pressuring him." See *Diary of Georgi Dimitrov*, entry for 24 November 1938.

82. On 25 December 1937, Béla Szántó was expelled from the VKP. One of the reasons for his expulsion was his pamphlet "The Class Struggle and the Dictatorship of the Proletariat in Hungary," written in 1919 and published in 1920 by the Comintern with a foreword written by Karl Radek. On 4 February 1938 he was readmitted to the party. On 24 February 1938 he was arrested. In spring 1940 he was released and rehabilitated. In 1945 he left the USSR for Hungary.

83. This letter from Z. Szántó was received by Dimitrov's Secretariat on 24 January 1938, on the same day it was written. Dimitrov read the letter the next day. The document is stored in the files of the Secretariat.

84. F. 495, op. 73, d. 57, l. 29. The Molotovskii district VKP committee in Moscow readmitted Béla Szántó to the party on 4 February 1938.

85. For a discussion of the January 1938 CC Plenum that passed this resolution, see Getty, *Origins*, 185–190.

86. The materials referred to in the letter have not been found.

87. On 24 June, M. Szántó sent a letter to the chairman of the Military Board of the Supreme Court of the USSR regarding her husband's arrest. The handwritten original of this letter is also located in the RGASPI collection.

88. On 12 February 1938, Béla Szántó sent Dimitrov a letter in which he suggested publishing in *Kommunisticheskii Internatsional* a series of articles written by him on the Hungarian revolution and the reasons for the collapse of Soviet power in Hungary; the purpose would be to reveal Béla Kun's anti-Bolshevik, sectarian, and counterrevolutionary character and his supporters' activities. No other information about such a publication is available.

89. The text of the "Open Letter of the ECCI" to the CPH was discussed at the meeting of the ECCI Political Secretariat of 26 October 1929. In this letter, "Robert" (B. Szántó) was criticized for opportunism and his pessimistic view of the collapse of the revolutionary movement. But, it was noted, he had recognized his mistakes.

90. In 1928, Béla Szántó wrote a letter to G. Alpari that contained a series of accusations. He sent copies of this letter to several people in Berlin, Paris, and Moscow. Alpari sent an appeal to the ICC, which met on 2 April 1928, to hear the case. The ICC harshly reprimanded Szántó and decided to temporarily relieve him of all leading positions in the CPH. On 29 January 1929 the ICC revoked the ban on Szántó's holding any leadership positions in the CPH, but the reprimand was not formally lifted.

91. On 8 March 1935 a meeting of the Hungarian section of the International Club of Political Émigrés, dedicated to the 1919 Hungarian revolution, took place. At this meeting, Szántó gave a speech about the Hungarian Red Army. The discussion between Szántó and Béla Kun's supporters that followed took the form of mutual accusations of Trotskyism.

92. For an engaging discussion of the divisions and squabbles within the German émigré community, see Pike.

93. F. 495, op. 73, d. 88, l. 19

94. The letter was prepared by the Cadres Department's analyst E. Privorotova and typed in two copies. The original was sent to the addressee.

95. The letter with enclosures was received in the Secretariat of G. Dimitrov on 8 January 1939. On 11 January it was forwarded to A. Andreev and to L. Beria.

96. Franz Guber appealed to the ICC on 21 November 1938. He also sent a letter to G. Dimitrov. On 10 August 1939 a session of the ICC took place with the participation of F. Guber, Lukanov, the ECCI Organizational Committee analyst E. Privorotskaia, the ICC secretary W. Florin, and W. Ulbricht. In the informational letter about Guber written for the meeting, Lukanov stated that "there is no reason not to trust his party honesty." In September 1939 the commission of the CC of the German CP readmitted Guber to the party. On 11 September 1941 he was arrested by the NKVD as a "socially dangerous element." He died on 4 June 1942 in the NKVD prison in Chistopol, Tatar ASSR. The OSO convicted him posthumously on 13 June 1942.

97. Anni Etterer was sentenced to five years in prison on 26 May 1938 by the OSO. On 27 February 1940 she was released; the OSO had decided to close her case in light of the absence of evidence of a crime. Until 19 March 1940 she was held in the NKVD labor camp in Kargopol, Arkhangelsk region. On 17 April 1940 she was readmitted to the German CP and received a Soviet passport. After the ar-

rest of her husband, Franz Guber, Etterer was exiled to the Karaganda region. On 14 February 1946 she left for Germany.

98. Enclosed were three typewritten copies of Franz Guber's letters to the ICC, translated from the German. On each of the letters there is a handwritten note (probably made by the party investigator Lukanov), dated 11 January 1939, confirming the accuracy of the translation. Guber's seven-page appeal of 21 November 1938 in connection with his expulsion from the German CP is not reproduced here. Its essentials are presented in Florin's letter to G. Dimitrov and in the two letters in the text that follow his letter. The originals can be found in Guber's personal file. The letters here are published in the order they were sent as enclosures in the letter from Florin to Dimitrov, A. Andreev, and L. Beria.

99. See also f. 495, op. 205, d. 793. My thanks to Fridrikh Firsov for alerting me to this article.

100. For other examples of denunciations within the ECCI apparatus, see the discussion of N. Prokofiev in Chapter 6; and f. 495, op. 109, d. 395, ll.1–8, 12–14, 31–400b., 40–470b.

101. The letter was received in Dimitrov's Secretariat on 16 November 1940.

102. On 11 July 1940, Dimitrov sent a letter to the procurator of the USSR, M. Pankratov, in response to his 16 June 1940 request for information about Petkov. That letter contained a brief biography of Petkov and a letter of reference from the delegation of the Bulgarian CP in the ECCI. It stressed that the delegation did not believe that Petkov could commit an "anti-Soviet or anti-party act." Mikhail Ivanovich Pankratov was the procurator of the USSR in 1939–1940. On 7 August 1940, Viktor Mikhailovich Bochkov was named the procurator of the USSR. Bochkov must have made a mistake when he referred to Dimitrov's letter. Dimitrov's letter to Pankratov (No. 377) was dated 11 July 1940 and sent on that day. Three copies were made; two of them are stored in Dimitrov Secretariat's file.

103. Presumably Yurdan T. Tutundzhiev, who is discussed below.

104. The case of the so-called factionalist, left-sectarian group of Iskrov, Boikov, Rassen, B. Popov, B. Tanev, and other Bulgarians who were members of the VKP was falsified by the NKVD. In 1941 the Military Board of the Supreme Court of the USSR convicted the former head of the Sixth Department of the Main Board of State Security of the NKVD, V. S. Bril, for falsifying this case.

105. Probably Georgy Tsanev.

106. The original of this letter could not be found.

107. See f. 495, op. 73, d. 88, l. 111; ibid., d. 122, l. 7.

108. F. 495, op. 282, d. 104, ll. 112–117.

109. For a "List of Appeals Submitted to the Procurator and NKVD" in Dimitrov's name in early 1939, see f. 495, op. 73, d. 72, ll. 93–101. That list is dated 7 July 1939.

110. F. 495, op. 74, d. 71, l. 40.

111. F. 495, op. 74, d. 77, ll. 77, 7–76.

112. F. 495, op. 74, d. 92, ll. 62–63; d. 81, ll. 1–52. On 25 September 1944, Dimitrov sent a letter to the people's commissar of state security, G. B. Merkulov, asking him to review Petkov's case and inform him of the results.

113. The letter from I. Terziev to Dimitrov and V. Kolarov was received in Dimitrov's Secretariat on 10 August 1939. The letter and its translation into Russian were sent to the CC VKP secretary, G. Malenkov, on 14 December 1939 "for con-

sideration." The letter was sent to the Organizational Bureau of the CC VKP for storage and is preserved in the CC VKP collection at RGASPI.

114. The so-called Popov-Tanev group never existed.

115. In 1925, forty-three (from other sources—ninety-three) prisoners managed to escape from the Island of St. Anastasia prison after disarming the guards. The escape was organized by the local Bulgarian CP organization. Among the escapees were members of that party who later emigrated to the USSR: Ivan Piperkov, Ivan Sterev, Vasili Novan, Konstantin Nikolov, and others.

116. Refers to the leaders of the Bulgarian CP in the late 1920–1930s, who were deposed in 1934 and later repressed.

117. Refers to the so-called left-sectarian group of Iskrov.

118. On 16 February 1939, Dimitrov forwarded to Merkulov a letter from Terziev's wife requesting that her husband's case be reviewed. F. 495, op. 73, d. 71, l. 94. Less than two months later, Dimitrov received word that "the case has been closed" and that Terziev had been released. F. 495, op. 74, d. 71, l. 71. For a discussion of the special troikas created in September 1938 to review the "remaining unconsidered cases" of arrested émigrés and foreign nationals, see Okhotin and Roginskii, 61–62.

119. F. 495, op. 74, d. 105, l. 3, 5. My thanks to Fridrikh Firsov for sharing this material with me.

120. Arkhiv Glavnoi voennoi prokuratory, d. 6158–39, l. 15, 3. My thanks to Fridrikh Firsov for sharing this material with me.

121. Kurshner stayed in Butyrskaia prison between 22 February 1938 and 14 March 1940. He was released after his case was closed.

Chapter 8. Fear, Obedience, Belief, and Repression

1. For examples, see Getty and Naumov, *Road to Terror*, and Getty, *Origins*; Rittersporn, *Stalinist Simplifications*.

2. For examples, see Kotkin, *Magnetic Mountain*; Kuromiya, *Freedom and Terror*; Rittersporn, "Omnipresent Conspiracy."

3. For examples, see Deutscher, *Stalin*; Kuromiya, *Freedom and Terror*.

4. That the USSR had spies in Poland and among the Western Ukrainians and Western Belorussians is well known. For example, see Sudaplatov, *Secret Tasks*. For a discussion of Soviet intelligence activities in Estonia during the interwar years, see Silva P. Forgus, "Soviet Subversive Activities in Independent Estonia (1918–1940)," *Journal of Baltic Studies*, 23, no. 1 (Spring 1992), 29–46. For a recent discussion of other Soviet intelligence activities, see John Costello and Oleg Tsarev, *Deadly Illusions* (New York, 1993). For a discussion of these operations in the late war years and early postwar years, see Jeffrey Burds, "*Agentura*: Soviet Informants' Networks and the Ukrainian Underground in Galicia, 1944–1948," *East European Politics and Societies*, vol. 11, no. 1 (Winter 1997), pp. 89–130.

5. On signal and action conformity, see Stanley Milgram, "Group Pressure and Action Against a Person," *Journal of Abnormal and Social Psychology*, 69, no. 2 (1964), 137–143.

6. Hannah Arendt, *Eichmann in Jerusalem: A Report on the Banality of Evil* (New York, 1964).

7. On the internalization and imposition of obedience, see Milgram, *Obedience and Authority,* 141.

8. Ibid., 145. On the absence of disobedience when groups share a definition of a situation, see ibid., 150–151; and E. Goffman, *The Presentation of Self in Everyday Life* (New York, 1959).

9. Milgram, in *Obedience and Authority,* 133–134, stresses that a central feature of obedience is that people enter an "agentic state," which he defines as "the condition a person is in when he sees himself as an agent for carrying out another person's wishes . . . [and] as an instrument for carrying out the wishes of others."

10. For a discussion of this, see ibid., 186; Fred E. Katz, *Ordinary People and Extraordinary Evil: A Report on the Beguilings of Evil* (Albany, N.Y., 1993).

11. Milgram, in *Obedience and Authority,* 62, argues that "the physical presence of an authority was an important contributing factor contributing to the subjects' obedience or defiance."

12. Milgram, in ibid., 152, notes that people who "attempt to alter the defined structure" often view their actions as "moral transgression," which evokes "anxiety, shame, embarrassment and diminishes feelings of self-worth."

13. Ibid., 160.

14. For a compelling example of the impact of routinization on behavior, in this case the execution of thousands of Polish Jews, see Christopher R. Browning, *Ordinary Men: Reserve Police Battalion 101 and the Final Solution in Poland* (New York, 1992).

15. The ensuing discussion draws on findings from the following studies: Tajfel, *Human Groups;* Tajfel, *Differentiation Between Social Groups;* Frankl, *Man's Search for Meaning;* Robinson, *Social Groups and Identities;* Hogg and Abrams; Allport and Postman; Goffman; Cantril, "Invasion from Mars"; Shibutani.

16. On categorization, depersonalization, and dehumanization by social groups, see Tajfel, *Human Groups,* 127–142, 146–161.

17. On binding pressures, see Milgram, *Obedience and Authority,* 148.

18. On groups needing to define themselves as "better than others," see Cantril, *Social Movements,* 9.

19. For a discussion of the juxtaposition of good and evil in stereotypes, see John W. Dower, *War Without Mercy: Race and Power in the Pacific War* (New York, 1986), esp. 16–53, 94–117, 234–261.

20. We should also keep in mind that there were differences between groups within the émigré communities and fraternal party organizations in exile in the USSR, which no doubt contributed to assessments by members of the verification commissions that certain individuals or groups of individuals were suspicious.

21. For a discussion of personal stability and group identification, see Cantril, *Social Movements,* 21–38.

Biographical Sketches

Names are listed as they appear in the text. If they are pseudonyms, the real name is also given.

Alikhanov, Gevork Sarkisovich (1897–1938). Held responsible positions in the ECCI Cadres Department from 1935 until his arrest in July 1937. Served as a member of the Moskvin Commission to verify workers in the ECCI apparatus in 1936–1937.

Alpari, Gyula (aka Julius) (1882–1944). Member of the CP of Hungary after 1918. Deputy people's commissar of foreign affairs in the Hungarian Socialist Republic, 1919. Editor of the Comintern journals *Inprecorr* and *Rundschau*, 1936–1937. In 1940 he was captured by Gestapo agents; he was killed in the Sachsenhausen concentration camp.

Andreev, Andrei Andreevich (1895–1971). Member of the Bolshevik Party from 1914; member of its CC in 1920–1921 and 1922–1961; member of the Politburo in 1932–1952; secretary of the CC VKP in 1924–1925 and 1935–1946.

Angaretis, Zigmas (real name, Aleksa) (1882–1940). Member of the Bolshevik Party from 1906. Member of the Petersburg Committee of the Russian Social Democratic Workers' Party (Bolshevik), or RSDRP(b), in 1917. People's commissar of internal affairs in Soviet Lithuania, 1918–1919. One of the founders of the CP of Lithuania; a member of its CC from 1918; a secretary of its Foreign Bureau after 1920; and the representative of the Lithuanian CP in the ECCI from 1921. After 1924, he was a member and the secretary (1926) of the ICC. Arrested in 1937. Repressed.

Berman-Yurin, Konon (Hans Stauer) (1901–1936). Born in Kurland (Latvia). Member of the Latvian CP from 1921. In 1923 he went to Germany without the party's permission and was expelled from the party as a deserter. In 1923 he joined the German CP, was a member of its regional directorate, and conducted propaganda and organization work. In March 1933 he went to the USSR and worked for the newspaper *Za industrializatsiiu* in Moscow. On 22 May 1936 he was arrested. One of the accused at the trial of the so-called Anti-Soviet United Trotskyist-Zinovievite Center, he was convicted and sentenced to death; he was shot on 25 August 1936.

Bertynski, Wiktor (real name, Albert Zyltowski) (1900–1937). A member of the Polish CP (CPP) from 1920, one of the leaders of the Lodz party organization and a member of the CPP regional committee. Imprisoned between 1921 and 1924, he went to the USSR in 1925 and transferred to the VKP. Between 1926 and 1928 he worked as an assistant to the head of an OGPU department. He was a delegate at the Third, Fourth, and Fifth CPP Congresses; in 1930 he was elected a candidate member of the CC CPP, becoming a full CC member in 1935. Between 1933 and 1936 he was a deputy party representative in the ECCI. Bertynski was arrested in 1937. On 3 November 1937 the Military Board of the Supreme Court of the USSR sentenced him to be shot.

Bielewski, Jan (real name, Paszyn). Member of the Social Democratic Party of the Kingdom of Poland and Lithuania (SDPKPiL) from 1913 and of the CPP from 1918. Member of the Warsaw city committee of the Polish CP in 1919–1925; member of the CC CPP after 1925; member of its Politburo in 1926–1930 and 1932–1937. In 1932 he went to Moscow after an exchange of political prisoners and was the party representative in the ECCI. At the Seventh Comintern Congress, he was elected a candidate member of the ECCI. Arrested on 11 September 1937, he was sentenced to be shot by the Military Board of the Supreme Court of the USSR.

Blagoeva, Stella (1887–1954). Member of the Bulgarian Social Democratic Party (SDP) from 1919, member of the CC of the Bulgarian CP in 1926 and 1950–1954, candidate member of the CC of the Bulgarian CP in 1948–1950, and member of the VKP from 1926. She worked as an analyst in the ECCI apparatus in Moscow in 1927–1929 and 1931–1943. In 1946 she left for Bulgaria.

Blum, Léon (1872–1950). Leader of the SFIO and, as such, head of the first (4 June 1936–21 June 1937) and fourth (13 March–8 April 1938) Popular Front governments in France.

Bochkov, Viktor Mikhailovich (1900–1981). Head of the OSO, 1938–1941. Procurator of the USSR, 1940–1943. Head of the Directorate for the Convoy Troops of the NKVD, 1944–1951. Deputy head of the USSR Ministry of Internal Affairs after 1951. He retired in 1959 at the rank of lieutenant general.

Borowskii, Noah Isaakovich (1885–1944). A translator and editor on a number of VKP editorial boards, he translated Lenin's works into German. While working in the Foreign Workers' Publishing House in Moscow, he translated Popov's book *The Outline History of the All-Union Communist Party (Bolshevik)* (Moscow, 1932) into German. In the commentaries for the German edition, he allegedly smoothed over the political criticisms of the opposition. As a result, he was fired. On 10 February 1933 the ICC resolved to consider Borowskii a non-party member from 1929; that is, it disallowed his restoration to the party in 1933. Between 1935 and 1937 he worked in the Turkstroi trust. In 1938 he was arrested. Later he worked in Alma-Ata, where he died.

Brikke, Semyon Karlovoch (1898–1937). Member of Poalei Zion in 1916–1918 and of the RKP(b) from 1918. Served in the Red Army in 1918–1919. Conducted underground work in Tiraspol in 1919–1920. Worked in the ECCI in 1922–1926, heading its Eastern Department in 1923–1924. Worked later for the Moscow party committee and the CC VKP. Served on the Party Control Commission of the CC VKP after 1934. Arrested on 30 April 1937 and was sentenced to be shot by the Military Board of the USSR Supreme Court on 29 October.

Bronkowski, Bronislaw (alias of Bronislav Bortnovski) (1894–1937). He was born in Warsaw. A member of the SDPKPiL from 1912, he belonged to the *rozlamovtsy* faction. He was arrested in 1914 and released in 1915. In 1917 he was a member of the Red Guard unit in Saratov. In December 1917 he went to Petrograd and worked as a secretary of the editorial board of the newspaper *Trybuna,* organ of the SDPKPiL in Russia, and, later, as secretary of the Polish Secretariat in the People's Commissariat for Nationalities. After 1918 he worked in the Cheka; in 1919–1920, in the Intelligence Department of the Western Front; later, in the Intelligence Department of the Red Army. After 1929 he worked in the CPP and was a member of the minority faction. In 1929–1930 and 1932–1934 he was a CPP representative on the ECCI. After December 1934 he was a head of the Polish-PriBaltic Lendersecretariat of the ECCI. In 1935 he was elected an ECCI member and a candidate member of the ECCI Presidium, Political Secretariat, and Political Commission. Bronkowski was arrested on 10 June 1937 and condemned to death and executed on 3 November.

Browder, Earl (1891–1973). Member of the Socialist Party of America in 1906–1912 and 1918–1920; member of the CPUSA and its CC from 1921 to 1946. Member of the Secretariat and the Politburo of the CPUSA from 1929. General secretary of the CC CPUSA, 1930–1944. Chairman of the Communist Political Association, 1944–1945. In 1946 he was expelled from the party. Between 1931 and 1943 he was a candidate member and then a full member of the ECCI; in 1933–1935 he was a member of its Political Secretariat.

Budzynska, Regina (1897–1937). A member of the SDPKPiL from 1914, she joined the Polish CP in 1918. In 1920 she arrived in the USSR after an exchange of political prisoners and joined the VKP. She worked in the KUNMZ. She actively participated in the Zinovievite opposition in 1926–1927 and was repeatedly expelled from the party. In 1935 she was expelled from the party and arrested; that March she was sentenced to five years in prison. She was re-sentenced on 11 November 1936 to ten years' loss of personal freedom. On 9 October 1937 a troika of the Leningrad oblast NKVD condemned her to execution. She was shot on 2 November 1937.

Bulak-Balakhovich, Stanislav Nikolaevich (1883–1940). In February–November 1918 he was a regimental commander in the Red Army, but he later defected to the White Army. From August 1918 he worked for the Estonian and, later, Polish governments. After the Soviet-Polish war, he formed a people's volunteer army, which was defeated by Soviet troops.

Bur, Stanislaw (real name, Burzynski) (1892–1937). Born in Warsaw. Member of the CPP from 1921. Elected a member of the Warsaw party committee in 1924. Worked in the trade union department of the CC CPP, 1927–1930. Served as a delegate to the Fourth (1928) and Fifth (1930) Profintern Congresses and the Seventh Comintern Congress (1935) in Moscow. Served as a member of the CC CPP from 1929 and of its Politburo from 1930. Was a Sejm deputy, 1930–1932. Facing arrest, he emigrated to the USSR in 1932, where he worked in the Executive Bureau of the Profintern as a secretary of the Polish-PriBaltic section. The Fourth Plenum of the CC CPP (February 1936) expelled Bur from the Politburo and from its CC. He was arrested in 1937, and the Military Board of the Supreme Court of the USSR sentenced him to be shot.

Cachin, Marcel (1869–1958). Member of the French Workers' Party in 1891–1901, the French Socialist Party in 1901–1905, and the SFIO in 1905–1920. Member of the Permanent Administrative Commission of SFIO, 1906–1912. Member of the French CP and its CC after 1920; member of the Politburo after 1923. Editor of *L'Humanité*, 1912–1918, and its director, 1918–1958. Member of the ECCI Presidium, 1923–1943.

Calzan, Claude-Joseph (1876–1959). Member of the French Socialist Party from 1905 to 1920; member of the French CP from 1920. Member of the CC and candidate member of the Politburo of the French CP, 1924–1926. In 1933–1936 he worked as an editor in the Press and Propaganda Department of the ECCI. In March 1936 he returned to France. On 9 November 1936 he was expelled from the French party for "not meriting confidence."

Cavalli, Gaetano. *See* Document 55.

Chemodanov, Vasili T. (1903–1937). He joined the VKP in 1924. From 1930 to 1937 he was secretary of the Executive Committee of KIM and a candidate member of the ECCI. He was executed on 26 November 1937.

Chernomordik, Moisei Borisovich (1889–1937). Born in Dnepropetrovsk. Member of the Bolshevik Party from May 1917. A professional party worker after 1921. Deputy head of the ECCI Cadres Department, 1931–1937. Arrested on 14 June 1937 and shot on 14 September.

David, Fritz (real name, Ilya Krugliansky) (1897–1936). Born in Novozybkovo. He went to Germany in 1926, joined the German CP, and worked on the editorial board of *Die Rote Fahne*. After 1929 he worked on the CC and published several books. In 1933 he returned to the USSR and worked on the editorial board of *Kommunisticheskii Internatsional*. In 1936 he was arrested in connection with the case of the Trotskyist-Zinovievite center. He was convicted and sentenced to be shot on 24 August 1936 and executed the next day.

Denikin, Anton Ivanovich (1827–1947). A Russian general, he was one of the leaders of the White (émigré) movement. He was commander in chief of the Armed Forces of the Russian South and deputy supreme governor of Russia. He lived in emigration after 1920.

Díaz Ramos, José (1895–1942). Member of the Spanish CP from 1927; member of the CC and general secretary of the party from 1932. An ECCI member after 1935. In February 1939 he emigrated to the USSR. The same year he was elected an ECCI secretary.

Dimitrov, Georgi (1882–1949). Born in Bulgaria, he joined the Bulgarian Social Democratic (SD) movement in 1902 and became a member of the Tesniak faction (often considered the Bulgarian equivalent to the Bolsheviks) following a split in the movement. He was elected to the Tesniak CC in 1909. In 1913 he was elected to the Bulgarian Parliament. He was arrested in 1918 on charges of undermining military discipline but was released at the end of World War I, whereupon he joined the recently formed Bulgarian CP. After the abortive party insurrection in 1923, Dimitrov was sentenced to death in absentia for his role in it. In 1924 he was elected a candidate member of the ECCI; in 1926, a candidate member of its Presidium and Secretariat. He became secretary of the Balkan Communist Federation in 1926 and head of the West European Bureau of the ECCI in Berlin in 1929. He was arrested in Germany in March 1933 and charged with participating in the burning of the Reichstag. During the trial Dimitrov challenged the allegations and, in so doing, won considerable admiration among Communists and anti-fascist non-Communists. The court found Dimitrov not guilty, and in February 1934 the Soviet government granted Soviet citizenship to him and the two other Bulgarian defendants (Blagoi Popov and Vasil Tanev). In April 1934, Stalin suggested that Dimitrov join the Comintern leadership. At the Seventh Comintern Congress in July–August 1935, Dimitrov was elected general secretary of the Comintern, a post he held until its dissolution in 1943. The resolution of the VKP Politburo selecting Dimitrov to be general secretary was passed on 10 August 1935, prior to the vote of the Seventh Congress.

Doriot, Jacques (1898–1945). Member of the French Socialist Party, 1915–1918. Joined the French CP in 1921 and was a member of its CC and its Politburo after 1924. Secretary of the KIM Executive Committee, 1922–1923. Candidate member of the ECCI, 1924–1932. Expelled from the party in June 1934. On 28 July 1936 he announced the creation of the French People's Party. During World War II he collaborated with the occupying German forces.

Drenkowski, Emil Dragovich. *See* Document 55.

Ercoli (real name, Palmiro Togliatti) (1893–1964). Member of the Italian Socialist Party, 1914–1920. Member of the Italian CP after 1921; member of its CC from 1922 and of its Executive Committee after 1923. Political secretary of the Italian CP in 1926 and 1928–1943. Member of the ECCI Political Secretariat in 1926–1927 and 1931–1935. ECCI secretary, 1935–1943. Minister without portfolio, minister of justice, and deputy prime minister of the Italian government, 1944–1946.

Etterer, Anni. *See* her case study in Chapter 7.

Fischer, Ruth (real name, Elfrieda Eisler) (1895–1961). Member of the Austrian CP from 1918. In 1919 she moved to Berlin and became an active worker in the German CP. Together with Arkady Maslow, she headed the Left Opposition in the party. In 1924 she took a leading position in the party and was elected a Reichstag deputy. At the Fifth Comintern Congress she was elected a candidate member of the ECCI. In fall 1925 the ECCI removed her for helping to found the oppositional group Leninbund, but soon thereafter she broke from it. In 1933 she moved to Paris and helped organize the Gruppe Internationale. She worked until 1936 in the Secretariat of the

International Communist League. After 1940 she lived in the United States and engaged in scholarly work.

Franco, Francisco (1892–1975). A Spanish general from 1926. Head of the general staff, 1932–1936. Military governor of the Canary Islands. A key member of the Military Junta Executive that organized the rebellion against the Popular Front government in 1936. Head of the "Spanish State" and commander in chief of the rebel armies. After 1939 he was the Spanish head of state and the leader of the Spanish Falange Party for life.

Frinovsky, Mikhail (1898–1940). Deputy people's commissar of internal affairs from October 1936 and, until April 1937, head of the Main Board of Frontier and Internal Guards of the NKVD. He was Yezhov's associate in organizing the mass repression. On 3 February 1940 he was convicted and shot.

Gerish, Grigory Moiseevich (1895–1937). Member of the Socialist Party of America, 1915–1919. Member of the CPUSA, 1919–1921. Worked in the ECCI, 1922–1937. Arrested by the NKVD on 14 September 1937; sentenced on 14 October to be shot.

Gerö, Ernö (real name, Singer) (1898–1980). A member of the Hungarian CP from 1918, he emigrated to the USSR in 1925 and worked in the ECCI apparatus. From 1945 he was a member of the CC and the Politburo of the Hungarian CP. Between 1953 and 1954 he was Hungarian minister of internal affairs. In 1962 he was expelled from the party.

Golubtsov, Pavel Aleksandrovich (born in 1905). Joined the VKP in 1931. Worked in the ECCI apparatus as a warden in the Administrative Office and as an analyst's assistant and, later, analyst in the Cadres Department from 1932 to 1941. After that, chaired the local trade union organization in the ECCI apparatus.

Gottwald, Klement (1896–1953). Member of the SDP of Czechoslovakia until 1921. Member of the CP of Czechoslovakia in 1921; member of its CC and Politburo from 1925; general secretary of the party from 1929; president of the party, 1945–1953. Member of the ECCI after 1929; member of the Political Commission of the Political Secretariat of the ECCI after 1934; ECCI secretary, 1935–1943. Head of the government of the Czechoslovak Republic, 1946–1948; president of the republic from 1948 until 1953.

Green, Gilbert (born in 1906). Joined the CPUSA in 1925. Elected to the ECCI at the Seventh Congress of the Comintern (1935). Served as secretary of the National Committee of the CPUSA from 1967.

Gross, Franz (real name, Ferenc Huszti; aka János Nagy) (1893–1937). A lawyer by profession, he joined the SDP of Hungary in 1912 and the Hungarian CP in 1918. In the Soviet Republic in Hungary, he was a prosecutor in a city revolutionary tribunal. In August 1919 he was arrested, and held in prison until September 1920, when he escaped to Czechoslovakia. In 1923 he emigrated to the USSR. He was a member of the VKP in 1923–1931. He worked in the People's Commissariat of Justice and, in February 1923, was sent to the city of Engels, where he was chairman of the city court. In 1925 he was second secretary of the VKP city committee in Saratov. He was a member of the All-Union Central Executive Committee, a delegate to the Eleventh and Sixteenth VKP Congresses, and a delegate to the Sixth and Seventh Comintern Congresses. Between 1931 and 1936 he was a secretary of the CC of the Hungarian CP, a member of the Foreign Committee of the party, and the party representative in the ECCI. He worked illegally in Vienna, Prague, Paris, and other European cities. On 10 December 1937 the Military Board of the Supreme Court of the USSR sentenced him to be shot.

Grzegorzewski, Marcin (real name, Franciszek Grzelszczak) (1881–1937). Born in Warsaw, he was a member of the SDPKPiL from 1904. At the Second All-Russian Congress of Soviets (November 1917), he was elected member of the VTsIK Presidium. In early 1918 he returned to Warsaw. He was a delegate to the First, Second, Third, Fifth, and Sixth Polish CP Congresses and a member of the party CC in 1918–1927 and 1932–1937. He was an ECCI member in 1924–1928 and was elected a member of the ICC in 1935. He was imprisoned in Poland in 1919, 1921, and 1925–1928. He went to the USSR in 1928, after the exchange of political prisoners, and worked in the Central Control Commission of the VKP; he was also the Polish CP representative in the ECCI. In the summer of 1937, Grzegorzewski was arrested; on 22 December the Military Board of the USSR Supreme Court sentenced him to be shot.

Guber, Franz. *See* Document 63.

Hanecki, Jakób (real name, Fürstenberg) (1879–1937). A longtime participant in the Russian and Polish Socialist Democratic movements and a delegate to the Second, Fourth, and Fifth RSDRP Congresses. A member of the CC RSDRP from 1907 and a member of the General Directorate of the SDPKPiL. After 1917 he worked in the People's Commissariat for Finance of the Russian Soviet republic. In 1923–1929 he was a member of the Collegium of the Commissariat for Trade. After 1929 he occupied prominent positions in the USSR state apparatus. Arrested on 26 November 1937, he was sentenced to be shot by the Military Board of the USSR Supreme Court.

Heckert, Fritz (1881–1936). Member of the German CP and its CC from 1919; member of its Politburo after 1925. Representative of the German CP in the ECCI, 1932–1935. Secretary of the Profintern after January 1935.

Member of the Political Secretariat and Political Commission of the Political Secretariat of the ECCI between 1933 and 1935. Repressed.

Heinz, Paul (Paul Rakow) (1901–1937). Born in Neibekum, Westphalia. A German CP member from 1919, he conducted party work in Berlin and Hanover until 1928, when he worked in the ECCI apparatus. After that, he was sent to China. He studied in KUNMZ in 1931–1934. Between 1934 and 1937 he worked as an instructor of the foreign workers in the Donets Basin. He was arrested on 15 April 1937. On 19 September 1937 the Military Board of the Supreme Court of the USSR sentenced him to death. He was shot on 20 December 1937.

Henrykowski, Henryk (real name, Saul Amsterdam) (1898–1937). A member of the Poalei Zion from 1918; a member of the Polish CP from 1921. During the internal struggle in the party, he was part of the minority faction. In 1930 he was elected a member of the party CC and candidate member of the Politburo. He was a delegate at the Fourth, Fifth, Sixth, and Seventh Comintern Congresses. In January 1935, following an ECCI decision, he was removed from party work and sent to the USSR. In mid-1936 he was removed from the CC. On 5 April 1937 he was arrested; on 1 November 1937 the Military Board of the Supreme Court of the USSR sentenced him to be shot.

Iskrov, Petr Khristov (1891–1938). Member of the Bulgarian Social Democratic Workers' Party (Tesniak) from 1914; member of the Bulgarian CP from 1919. Member of the CC of the Komsomol, 1919–1925; its secretary, 1920–1922. Member of the CC of the Bulgarian CP after 1923 and a member of its Foreign Bureau from 1925. Member of the ICC after 1928. Joined the VKP in 1931. Representative of the Bulgarian CP in the ECCI, 1931–1935. Head of the Bulgarian section of the Foreign Workers' Publishing House after November 1936. Expelled from the VKP on 16 August 1937, later arrested, and, on 10 January 1938, sentenced to be shot.

Julius. *See* Alpari, Gyula.

Kaganovich, Lazar Moiseevich (1893–1991). Member of the Bolshevik Party from 1911; member of the CC from 1924; and member of the Politburo (and later Presidium) of the CC VKP/CPSU between 1930 and 1957. People's commissar for communications in 1935–1937, 1938–1942, and 1943–1944. People's commissar for heavy industry, 1937–1939. Deputy chairman of the Council of People's Commissars (Council of Ministers) of the USSR, 1938–1947. Removed from the Presidium of the CC and from the CC in 1957 for factional activities. Expelled from the CPSU in December 1961.

Kamenev, Lev Borisovich (real name, Rosenfeld) (1883–1936). A member of the RSDRP from 1901, of the CC RSDRP(b) in 1917–1927, and of the

Politburo in 1919–1925. Chairman of the Moscow City Soviet, 1918–1926. Deputy chairman of the Supreme Council of the National Economy (VSNKh) and the Council of Labor and Defense (STO) after 1922. First deputy chairman of the VSNKh after 1923 and chairman of the STO between 1924 and 1925. Director of the Lenin Institute, 1923–1926. A leader of the New Opposition within the VKP(b) in 1925–1926. He was expelled from the party three times—in 1927, in 1932, and in 1934. He was convicted at the August 1936 show trial and executed.

Karakhan (Karakhanian), Lev Mikhailovich (1889–1937). Member of the RSDRP(b) from 1917. Member of the Military Revolutionary Council in October 1917. Secretary of the Soviet delegation at the Brest-Litovsk peace talks. Deputy people's commissar for foreign affairs, 1918–1920 and 1927–1934. Soviet ambassador to Poland, 1921; to China, 1923–1926; and to Turkey, after 1934. Arrested and executed in 1937.

Kirov, Sergei Mironovich (real name, Kostrikov) (1886–1934). Joined the Bolsheviks in 1904. Became a candidate member of the CC VKP in 1921, a full member in 1923, a member of the Politburo in 1930, and secretary of the CC from 1934. Succeeded Zinoviev as first secretary of the Leningrad city and provincial committees in 1926. Assassinated on 1 December 1934.

Kolchak, Aleksandr Vasilievich (1873–1920). Russian admiral; monarchist; a leader of the White movement. During the Civil War, he was proclaimed the Supreme Governor of the Russian State. The Irkutsk Revolutionary Committee sentenced him to be shot.

Koltsov, Mikhail Efimovich (1898–1942). A Soviet writer and journalist, he was the secretary of the Foreign Commission of the Union of Soviet Writers. He was arrested by the NKVD on 12 December 1938 and later shot.

Komor-Katsburg, Imre Maksimovich (real name, Imre Komor). *See* Document 55.

Kon Sin (real name, Kang Sheng) (1901–1975). Born in China, he was a member of the Communist Party of China (CPC) from 1925. In 1931 he was elected to the CPC Politburo and became head of the Orgburo. In 1933 he was elected to the ECCI Presidium and, in 1935, became a candidate member of the ECCI Presidium. He returned to China in 1937. In 1945 he was elected to the CC CPC and, again, to the Politburo, becoming a member of its Standing Committee in 1966. After the 1949 Chinese Revolution, he held various leadership positions in the CPC, specializing in issues relating to organization, cadres, security, and relations with foreign CPs. In 1980 he was expelled retroactively from the CPC for his alleged complicity with Mao Zedong's widow, Jiang Qing.

Kosarev, Aleksandr Vasilevich (1903–1939). Joined the Komsomol in 1918; became a party member in 1919. Served in the Red Army. Secretary of the Baumanskii district Komsomol committee in Moscow, 1921; of the Penza provincial Komsomol committee, 1924–1926; of the Moscow-Narva district Komsomol committee in Leningrad, 1926; and of the CC of the All-Union Komsomol, 1927–1928. General secretary of the last in 1929. Candidate member of the Orgburo of the CC VKP, 1930–1934, then a full member. Candidate member of the CC from 1930. Elected to the Supreme Soviet in 1938.

Kostrzewa, Maria (real name, Koszutska) (1879–1939). A member of the Polish Socialist Party from 1902, she conducted underground work in Poland, Austria, and Russia and helped found the Polish CP in 1918. She was a member of the party CC in 1918–1922 and the party representative in the ECCI after the Fifth Comintern Congress. At the time of the factional struggle, she headed the majority faction. Together with Warski, she was relieved of party leadership for "Rightist" mistakes. In 1930 she emigrated to the USSR, with party permission. In August 1937 she was arrested by the NKVD and in October condemned to ten years in prison.

Kotelnikov, Fyodor Semenovich (1893–1972). A member of the Bolshevik Party from 1919, he worked in the ECCI apparatus from 1931 to 1940. In 1934 he was deputy head (in charge of the cadres) of the Eastern Lendersecretariat. Between 1935 and 1936 he was secretary of the party committee of the VKP Cadres Department; in 1936–1939, secretary of the VKP party committee of the ECCI apparatus. In 1940 he transferred to work in the Rostokino Moscow district committee of the VKP.

Kotolynov, Ivan Ivanovich (1901–1934). In the mid-1920s he was secretary of the Leningrad Provincial Komsomol Committee and a member of the Komsomol Central Committee. In 1927 he was expelled from the VKP but was later readmitted. On 3 December 1934 he was arrested in connection with the Kirov murder, and on 29 December the Military Board of the Supreme Court of the USSR sentenced him to be shot.

Kozhevnikov, Ilya Abramovich (real name, Kozhevnik) (born in 1898). Joined the RKP(b) in 1918. Between 25 February 1936 and 1 April 1938, worked as head of the radio center of the ECCI Communications Department. Arrested on 22 March 1938; expelled from the VKP as "the enemy of the party and the people" on 16 May. Released from prison on 12 October 1946.

Krajewski, Anton (real name, Wladyslaw Stein) (1886–1937). A member of the SDPKPiL from 1904, he was a delegate to the Fourth RSDRP(b) Congress in 1907 and took part in the work of the Kienthal Socialist conference (1916). He was one of the organizers of the Polish CP in 1918 and was elected a member of its CC in 1920. In 1930 he worked in the Lenin Institute in Moscow. He worked in executive positions in the ECCI apparatus after 1931 and was a leading official in the Cadres Department between 1932 and 1937. At the Seventh Comintern Congress (1935) he was elected a member of the ICC. He was arrested on 26 June 1937 and repressed.

Krasnov, Emil Vladimirovich (born in 1906). Joined the VKP in 1925. Between 1 December 1930 and 16 November 1937, he worked in the Executive Committee of the KIM apparatus as head of the Press Department, head of the Central European Secretariat, and head of the Propaganda Department. He was elected member of the KIM Presidium. On 17 September 1937 he was expelled from the VKP for "failing to expose the enemy of the party and the people, Frumkin." Repressed.

Kreichi, August (real name, Ágoston Krejcsi) (1893–1938). An economist and a member of the Hungarian CP from 1918, he emigrated to Prague in 1922 and later to Berlin. From 1923 to 1929 he was a member of the German CP. Between 1922 and 1928 he worked as an analyst in the Soviet embassy in Berlin and, between 1930 and 1933, in the Soviet trade delegation. In August 1933 he was deported from Germany and went to the USSR. In 1934 he joined the VKP. Between 1934 and 1935 he worked in the ECCI apparatus. In 1937 he was arrested and, on 8 April 1938, sentenced to be shot.

Kreps, Mikhail Yevseyevich (1895–1937). VKP member from 1919. Worker in the ECCI apparatus, 1921–1936. Head of the Editorial-Publishing Department of the ECCI, 1922–1936, and, later, chairman of the Editorial Board of the Foreign Workers' Publishing House. Arrested in 1937; shot on 26 October 1937.

Kun, Béla (1886–1938). Born into a Hungarian Jewish family in Transylvania, he studied law at the University of Kolozvar and then in Budapest. He was drafted into the Austro-Hungarian army in 1914 and later taken prisoner on the Russian front. After the February 1917 revolution, he joined the Bolshevik Party in Tomsk. In November 1918 he returned to Hungary and was elected to head the newly formed Hungarian CP. He was the leader of the party and its CC from 1918 to September 1936. During the Hungarian Soviet Republic of 1919, he was the commissar of foreign affairs and the de facto head of the government. Arrested in Austria after the fall of the Hungarian Republic, he was released in mid-1920 and went to Soviet Russia, where he was a member of the ICC for many years and a member of the ECCI from 1921 to 1922 and from 1926 to September 1936. He was on the ECCI Presidium in 1921–1922 and 1928–1935, a candidate member of that body in 1926–1928, and head of the ECCI commission, known as the Kun commission, which directed antiwar campaigns, from 1932 to 1935.

From December 1935, Kun was under investigation by the ECCI, which, in September 1936, barred him from working for the Hungarian CP or the Comintern. In June 1937 the ECCI accused him of insulting Stalin and having worked for the Hungarian secret police. He was arrested on 28 June 1937 and executed on 29 August 1938.

Kurshner, Karl Filippovich. *See* Document 55 and his case study in Chapter 7.

Kutlu, Ali-Geidar Yusufovich. *See* Document 55.

Kuusinen, Otto Wilhelm (1881–1964). Member of the Finnish SD Party from 1904; president of the Executive Committee of the party, 1911–1917. Member of the Council of the People's Representatives of the government of the Finnish Workers' Republic, January–April 1918. A founder of the CP of Finland, 1918. Secretary of the ECCI, 1921–1939; general secretary of the ECCI, December 1921–December 1922; member of the ECCI Presidium after that. Head of the so-called government of the Finnish Democratic Republic, December 1939. President of the Presidium of the Supreme Soviet of the Karelo-Finnish Soviet Socialist Republic and deputy president of the Supreme Soviet of the USSR, 1940–1958. Member of the CC VKP after 1941. Member and secretary of the Presidium of the CC CPSU from June 1957.

Lansbury, George (1859–1940). A member of the British Social Democratic Federation in 1892–1906, he joined the Labour Party in 1906. He was a member of its Executive Committee after 1922 and party chairman between 1927 and 1928. In 1929–1931 he was the British minister of public works.

Lenski, Julian (real name, Leszszynski) (1889–1937). Member of the SDP-KPiL from 1905; member of the RKP(b) after 1917. A CC member from 1925. A member of the Politburo of the Polish CP from 1926 and, from June 1929, the elected general secretary of the party CC. A member of the ECCI from 1928 and, from 1935, a member of its Presidium. On 20 June 1937 he was arrested. On 21 September 1937 the Military Board of the Supreme Court of the USSR condemned him to be shot.

Levchenko, Andrei Andreevich. Between 1936 and 1938 he worked as a warden in the Communications Department of the ECCI. On 15 June 1938 he was arrested; on 20 June he was expelled from the VKP as "the enemy of the party and the people," and later he was repressed.

Lominadze, Vissarion Vissarionovich (1897–1935). A member of the Bolshevik Party from 1917. Secretary of the CC of the CP of Georgia, 1922–1924. Secretary of the KIM Executive Committee, 1925–1926. Member of the ECCI Presidium, 1926–1927. Secretary of the Trans-Caucasian regional VKP committee, 1930. Member of the CC VKP after 1930. In 1934 he was expelled from the party. He later committed suicide.

Lovestone, Jay (real name, Jacob Liebstein) (1898–1990). Born in Lithuania, he and his parents emigrated to the United States when he was nine years old. In 1917 he was a member of the Socialist Club of the City College of New York. At the founding congress of the CPUSA in September 1919, he was elected to the Central Executive Committee, and in October he was elected party secretary. In March 1925 he was a member of the American delegation to the enlarged ECCI plenum. In 1924 he was named general secretary of the CPUSA. At the Sixth Comintern Congress (1928), he was elected a member of the ECCI. In May 1929 he was recalled by the Comintern to Moscow and relieved from the position of general secretary. After his return to the United States, he left the CPUSA and formed an oppositional CP, which, until 1933, was called the Independent Workers' League of America. After its dissolution in 1940, Lovestone was one of the leaders of the American Federation of Labor until 1974.

Lukács, György (1885–1971). He joined the Hungarian CP in 1918 and, during the 1919 Hungarian Soviet Republic, was a political commissar in the Fifth Division of the army. Following the collapse of the republic, he fled to Vienna, where he lived until 1929. As early as 1921, Lukács opposed Kun during factional struggles in the party, yet he was a CC member at various times in the 1920s. From 1929 to 1931 he worked at the Marx-Engels Institute in Moscow. He lived in Berlin from 1931 to 1933 but returned to Moscow to do scientific work. In 1945 he returned to Hungary, where he taught. A supporter of the 1956 Hungarian revolution, he was expelled from the Hungarian CP and exiled to Romania. He returned to Budapest in 1957 and was readmitted to the Hungarian CP in 1967.

Lurye, Jlse Koigen (born in 1900). Wife of Nathan Lurye. Member of the German CP from 1926. Between 1923 and 1926 she worked at Foreign Radio in Moscow. In August 1936 she was expelled from the German CP for "connections with hostile elements and lack of vigilance," and she was later repressed.

Lurye, Moise Ilyich (Alexander Emel) (1897–1936). Born in Belorussia, he was a professional historian and, from 1922, a member of the CP of Germany (CPG). In 1922–1927 he lived in the USSR and taught history in the KUNMZ. A supporter of Zinoviev's New Opposition, he was expelled from the VKP in 1927; in 1928, he was readmitted. Later he worked in the Department of Agitation and Propaganda of the CC CPG and for *Die Rote Fahne* and *Imprekorr*. In March 1933, on the decision of the CC CPG, he emigrated to the USSR and taught at Moscow State University. Between March 1933 and July 1934 he worked as an analyst for the ECCI Editorial and Publishing Committee. Lurye was one of the accused at the trial of the

"Anti-Soviet United Trotskyist-Zinovievite Center." On 24 August 1936 he was sentenced to be shot by the Military Board of the Supreme Court of the USSR.

Lurye, Nathan (Hans Wolf) (1901–1936). Born in Latvia, he was a physician who became a member of the German CP in 1925. In 1932 he emigrated to the USSR, where he worked in Cheliabinsk. One of the defendants at the trial of Zinoviev and Kamenev, he was convicted and executed on 25 August 1936. He was the husband of Jlse Koigen Lurye.

Macsschalek, Willem (born in 1886). He was a member of the Democratic Party of Belgium until 1920, when he joined the Belgian CP. From 1928 to 1931 he was a member of that party's CC and Politburo. From 1934 he worked as a translator for the Foreign Workers' Publishing House.

Magyar, Ludwig (real name, Lajos Milgorf) (1891–1937). A member of the Hungarian CP from 1919, he was sentenced by Hungarian authorities to ten years in prison for participating in the Hungarian Soviet Republic. In 1922, arriving in the USSR after an exchange of political prisoners, he joined the VKP. Between 1924 and 1934 he worked in the ECCI apparatus and was a deputy head of the Eastern Department of the ECCI. In 1925 he supported the New Opposition; in July 1928 he made a statement dissociating himself from the Left Opposition. He was arrested on 29 December 1934, a day after being expelled from the party. On 2 November 1937 the Military Board of the Supreme Court of the USSR sentenced him to be shot.

Manuilsky, Dmitri (1883–1959). Member of the RSDRP from 1903 and the Bolshevik Party from 1917. Conducted clandestine work in France, 1917–1920, and in Italy and Germany, 1923–31. Secretary of the Ukrainian CP, 1921–1922; member of the CC VKP, 1923–1952. Delegate to Third–Seventh Comintern Congresses. Member of the ECCI Secretariat, 1926–1943; CC representative in the ECCI and ECCI secretary in charge of cadres, from 1935. Deputy prime minister and foreign minister of the Ukrainian government, 1944. Attended the founding conference for the United Nations in San Francisco in 1945. Member of the Soviet delegation to the Paris peace conference in 1946.

Marek, Nowak (real name, Adolf Lampe) (1900–1943). A member of the CP of Poland from 1921, he was imprisoned in Poland between 1922 and 1926. From 1929 to 1930 he was a member of the Politburo of the CC CPP, as well as a member of the Foreign Secretariat of the Politburo in Berlin. The representative of the CPP in the Executive Committee of the Profintern between 1932 and 1933, in 1933 he was sent to conduct party work in Poland, where he was arrested and sentenced to fifteen years in prison. Liberated in September 1939, he emigrated to the USSR.

Maslow, Arkady (real name, Isaak Chemerinsky) (1891–1941). Originally from Russia, he was a member of the German CP from 1918, one of the theoreticians of the left wing. Together with Ruth Fischer, he headed the party from April 1924. In fall 1925 the ECCI removed him from the leadership; in August 1926 he was expelled from the German CP. He was one of the founders of the Leninbund. In 1939 he moved to Paris, where, together with Fischer, he founded the Gruppe Internationale, which later joined the International Communist League. In 1940 he went to Cuba, where he died.

Melnikov, Boris Nikolaevich (Müller) (1895–1938). A member of the RSDRP(b) from 1916, he graduated from the Mikhailovsky Artillery School in 1917. He later became head of a military garrison, a member of the Far Eastern Military Council, and a member of the Revolutionary Military Council of the Eastern Front. In 1923–1924 he was in China. In 1924–1928 he was a department head in the People's Commissariat of Foreign Affairs. In 1928–1931 he was the general counsel in Harbin; in 1931, chargé d'affaires in Japan. In 1932–1933 he was deputy head of the Intelligence Department of the Worker-Peasant Red Army (RKKA). Between 1933–1934 he was the People's Commissariat of Foreign Affairs representative in the Far East. After October 1935 he was head of communications for the ECCI Secretariat. He was arrested in May 1937, sentenced to execution on 25 November, and shot on 28 July 1938.

Menis, Boris Yakovlevich (1904–1937). Member of the VKP from 1920. Worked in the ECCI apparatus, 1930–1936. Headed the Editorial and Publishing Department and was deputy director of the Publishing House for Foreign Workers from July 1934 to November 1935 and was then director. Headed the Eastern Sector of the Communications Department of the ECCI, February 1936–November 1937. Arrested on 10 May 1937; sentenced to be shot on 9 September 1937.

Merkulov, Sevolold Nikolaevich (1895–1953). Member of the VKP from 1925; of its CC, 1939–1952. People's commissar of state security from February 1941. First deputy people's commissar of internal affairs and head of the Main Administration of State Security (GUGB) from July 1941. People's commissar of state security, April 1943–May 1946. He was arrested on 23 December 1953, following Beria's fall, and sentenced to death by the Special Board of the Supreme Court of the USSR.

Mertens, Edna (real name, Margarete Wilde) (1904–1943). Member of the German CP from 1921 and of the VKP from 1928. She worked in the ECCI apparatus in 1922–1923 and 1935–1937 and, later, as an analyst in the Cadres Department. On 4 August 1937 she was expelled from the party. In October she was arrested and repressed.

Mif, Pavel Aleksandrovich (real name, Mikhail Aleksandrovich Fortus) (1901–1938). A member of the Bolshevik Party from 1917, he worked in the ECCI apparatus between 1928 and 1938. From 1931 to 1935 he was deputy head of the Eastern Secretariat; in 1935–1936, a political assistant on China in Dimitrov's Secretariat. In December 1938 he was sentenced to be shot.

Mola, Emilio (1887–1937). A Spanish general, he was the head of the Spanish Military Union from 1932. On the eve of the mutiny against the Popular Front government he was the military governor of Navarre. He was a member of the Junta of National Salvation (July–September 1936), the first government of the Spanish rebels, and commander of the rebels' Army of the North. He died in a plane crash in 1937.

Molchanov, Georgi Aleksandrovich (died in 1937). A longtime worker in Soviet security organs, he was head of the Secret Political Department of the GUGB in 1935–1937. In that capacity, he played a central role in the interrogation of defendants in the August 1936 and January 1937 show trials. In 1935 he was elected to the All-Union Central Executive Committee. In very late 1936 or January 1937 he was appointed to head the Belorussian NKVD. In February 1937 he was arrested; later he was shot.

Morriens, Franz (1901–1945). A member of the Belgian SDP from 1916 to 1919, he was one of the founders of the Belgian CP in 1921, a member of its CC in 1925–1930, and a member of its Politburo in 1927–1930. He worked in the USSR in 1930–1936, heading the Roman section of the ECCI and working as an analyst in the Foreign Workers' Publishing House in 1933–1936. In 1936 he returned to Belgium to do party work. He was arrested in 1943 and died in a German concentration camp.

Moskvin, Mikhail Abramovich (real name, Meer Abramovich Trilisser) (1883–1941). Member of the Bolshevik Party from 1901. Worked for state security—the Cheka and GPU—after 1921. Deputy GPU chairman after 1926. Deputy people's commissar of the Workers and Peasants Inspectorate (RKI), 1930–1934. ECCI member and a candidate member of the ECCI Secretariat, 1935–1938. Arrested on 23 November 1938; sentenced to be executed on 1 February 1940; shot on 2 February 1941.

Müller. *See* B. N. Melnikov.

Münzenberg, Willi (1889–1940). A member of the German CP from its founding; a member of its CC, 1927–1938. He organized the Workers' International Relief (Mezhrabpom) and its many publications. After 1933 he worked in Paris as a publisher and as coordinator of the Comintern's Popular Front campaigns. In 1939 he was expelled from the German CP. In October 1940 his body was found hanged in a forest near the French town of St. Marcellin.

Nusberg, Liubov Genrikhovna (born in 1904). She joined the VKP in 1924. Between 4 October 1936 and 16 March 1938 she worked as an assistant analyst in the ECCI Cadres Department. She retired on disability.

Perutskaia, Agafia Mefodievna (born in 1899). Member of the RKP(b) from 1922. Deputy head of the Cadres Department of the Rostokinskii district VKP committee in Moscow and head of its Organizational and Instructional Department in 1938–1939; head of the district Agitprop Department from late November 1939 to December 1941.

Petkov, Petko Nikolov (real name, Ognian Yantarov) (born in 1906). A construction worker, he joined the Bulgarian Komsomol in 1918, working in its apparatus between 1919 and 1921, and the Bulgarian CP in 1924. He was arrested and in prison in Sofia from 1926 to 1928. In 1928–1930 he studied in Austria and Czechoslovakia and worked for the Fourth Department of the General Headquarters of the Red Army. In 1932 he emigrated to the USSR, where he studied in a special school. He worked in the ECCI apparatus between 1934 and 1937—in Alma-Ata after 1935. There he was arrested and sentenced to fifteen years in a corrective labor camp in Vorkuta, Komi Autonomous Soviet Socialist Region.

Pieck, Wilhelm (1876–1960). A member of the German SD Party from 1895. A leader of Die Internationale (later known as the Spartacus League), during World War I. A member of the German CP and its CC from 1918 and a political leader of the Berlin party organization between 1926 and 1929. Reichstag deputy, 1928–1933. Member of the ECCI Presidium after 1928 and of the ECCI Secretariat after 1935. Chairman of the German Democratic Republic, 1949–1960.

Popov, Blagoi (1902–1968). A Bulgarian CP member, he participated in the September 1923 insurrection in Bulgaria. After October 1924 he was in emigration and conducted underground work in Bulgaria. Member of the Politburo of the Bulgarian party CC, 1931–1932. The ECCI sent him to Berlin in late 1932. On 9 March 1933 he was arrested along with Dimitrov and V. Tanev, and was one of the defendants at the Leipzig trial. After 1934 he lived in the USSR. He was arrested and convicted in 1938 and released in 1954, whereupon he returned to Bulgaria.

Pritt, Dennis (1887–1972). Pritt, an English jurist and social activist, was a member of Parliament from 1935 to 1950. From 1937 to 1940 he was a member of the executive committee of the Labour Party; later he became head of the parliamentary group Independent Labourites. After he attended the August 1936 show trial of Zinoviev and Kamenev, he wrote a pamphlet entitled "The Zinoviev Trial."

Próchniak, Edward (1888–1937). Born in Pulawy, Poland. Member of the

SDPKPiL between 1903 and 1917; member of the Polish CP from 1918; and member of the RKP(b) in 1917–1918 and 1920–1926. First commissar in the People's Commissariat for Nationalities, 1918. Member of the Provisional Polish Revolutionary Committee, 1921. Elected a member of the party CC, 1923; was a candidate member of the Politburo, 1931–1937. During the factional struggle in the Polish party (1926–1929), he played an important role in the majority faction. Member of the ECCI, 1922–1924; member of the ICC, 1924–1928. At the Sixth Comintern Congress (1928), he was elected an ECCI member, and he served on the ECCI Presidium. At the Seventh Congress (1935), he was elected a candidate ECCI member. He was arrested by the NKVD on 7 July 1937 and, in accordance with the verdict of the Military Board of the Supreme Court of the USSR, executed on 21 August.

Prokofiev, Nikolai Fyodorovich (1905–1938). A member of the VKP from 1925, he worked as head of the Cadres Department of the Executive Committee of the KIM between February 1931 and 1935 and was Executive Committee secretary between 1935 and December 1937. He was arrested; on 19 February 1938 he was expelled from the VKP as "the enemy of the party and the people," and he was later repressed.

Purman (Porai), Leon (1892–1933). A member of the Polish CP from 1918 and a secretary of the Warsaw party organization; after 1924, a member of the CC CPP. In early 1925 he was arrested by Polish police and sentenced to six years in prison. At the end of 1925, the CC CPP organized his escape from the Paviak prison. After the Fourth CPP Congress (1927), he was the representative of the party in the ECCI. At the Sixth Comintern Congress he was elected a candidate member of the ECCI and its Presidium, and in 1931–1933 he served as the ECCI representative to the CP of Spain, where he worked under the name Andres. He committed suicide in Moscow in late 1933.

Pyatakov, Georgi (Yuri) Leonidovich (1890–1937). Member of the Bolshevik Party from 1910; candidate member of the CC VKP, 1921–1923; member of the CC, 1923–1927 and 1930–1936. He was expelled from the party in 1927 for participating in the Left Opposition, readmitted in 1928, and expelled again in 1936 following his arrest on 12 September. From 1932 until his arrest he was deputy people's commissar of heavy industry. He was sentenced to death at the January 1937 trial.

Radek, Karl (born Sobelson) (1885–1939). A participant in the Social Democratic movement in Galicia, Poland, and Germany, he joined the Bolshevik Party in 1917; he was a member of its CC, 1917–1924. He was a member of the ECCI, 1920–1924; of the ECCI Presidium, 1921–1924; and ECCI secretary, 1920. He participated in the Left Opposition from 1923 to 1928 and was expelled from the VKP in 1927, then readmitted in 1929, and expelled again in 1936, following his arrest on 16 September. At the January 1937 trial he was convicted and sentenced to ten years in prison, where he died.

Rakovsky, Khristian (1873–1941). A longtime activist in the Social Democratic movement, he joined the Bolsheviks in 1917 and was a member of its CC from 1919 to 1927. He was an ECCI member in 1922; chairman of the Ukrainian Council of People's Commissars, 1918 to 1923; Soviet ambassador to England, 1923–1925; and Soviet ambassador to France, 1925–1927. A leader of the Left Opposition from its inception in 1923, he was expelled from the VKP in 1927, readmitted in 1935, and arrested on 27 January 1937. At the March 1938 trial of the "Anti-Soviet Right-Trotskyist Bloc," he was sentenced to twenty years in prison, where he died on 11 September 1941.

Rakow, Paul. *See* Heinz, Paul.

Rakow, Werner (aka Felix Wolf) (born in 1893). Born in Latvia, he grew up in Russia in the family of a German factory foreman. In 1918 he was secretary of the German workers' and soldiers' deputies Soviet in Moscow, then went to Germany and took part in the founding congress of the German CP. Expelled from the party in 1933, he was readmitted in 1934. The NKVD arrested him in August 1937.

Raskolnikov, Fyodor Fyodorovich (1892–1939). A member of the RSDRP(b) from 1910. After the February 1917 revolution he was elected deputy chairman of the Kronstadt Soviet. Deputy people's commissar for the navy, 1918; commander of the Caspian Sea flotilla, 1919; and commander of the Baltic Fleet, 1920. After the Civil War, he did diplomatic work, serving as the diplomatic representative to Afghanistan, Estonia, Denmark, and Bulgaria. On 17 August 1939 he wrote an "open letter to Stalin" in which he condemned Stalin for establishing a regime of personal power, violence, and terror. He died in Nice.

Razumova-Khigerovich, Anna Lazarevna. *See* Document 55 and her case study in Chapter 7.

Redyko, Matek (aka Metek, alias of Mieczyslaw Muetzenmacher) (born in 1903). Member of the Young Communist League of Poland from 1920, of its CC from 1925; secretary of the CC after 1926. He was arrested in 1926, spent two years under investigation, and was sentenced to five years of hard labor. During that time he collaborated with the Polish Defenziwa. He was released in early 1931. After liberation, he headed the Dombrowski organization of the Polish CP. After being taken into J. Lenski's confidence, he started planting suspicions about the leading Polish cadres and organized the downfall of A. Lampe and other Communists. After that, the police hid Redyko and circulated a rumor that he had been killed. The party CC believed that rumor and put his assassination down to the Polish police. In 1934, Redyko, under the pen name J. Regul, published a book in Warsaw about CPP activities in which he cited facts that compromised the CPP and its leaders. During the occupation, Redyko served as a Gestapo agent; he was not exposed until 1947.

Reich, Wilhelm (1897–1957). A psychoanalyst who specialized in the problems of sex and sexual education, he joined the German CP in 1930 and was expelled in 1934.

Révai, József (real name, Lederer) (1898–1959). Member of the Hungarian CP, 1918–1948. Member of the Budapest Soviet and of the Executive Committee of the Central Soviet of the Workers' Deputies of the Hungarian Soviet Republic, 1919. Member of the Foreign Bureau of the party CC in Austria, 1919–1926. Member of the underground Secretariat of the CC and editor in chief of the party newspaper, 1926–1929. In 1930 he was arrested by the Hungarian police and sentenced to four years in prison. He emigrated to the USSR in 1934 and served as an analyst in the Central European Lendersecretariat of the ECCI and then as a lecturer at the International Lenin School until 1937. He conducted illegal work in Prague in 1937–1939 and then returned to the USSR, where he worked in the ECCI Press Department and was a member of the Western Bureau (ZB) of the CC of the Hungarian CP. In 1944 he returned to Hungary, where he served in high party and state posts.

Rudnitsky, Kalman Noevich. *See* Document 55.

Rudzutak, Yan Ernestovich (1887–1938). Bolshevik Party member from 1905. Active in trade union and economic affairs, 1917–1922. CC member, 1920–1937; CC secretary and candidate member of the Orgburo, 1920–1937; member of the Politburo, 1926–1932, and, from 1934, a candidate member of that body. People's commissar for means of communication, 1924–1930. Deputy chairman of the Sovnarkom and Council of Labor and Defense, 1927–1937. Arrested in 1937; died in prison, 29 July 1938.

Rumiantsev, Vladimir Vasilievich (1902–1934). A member of the RKP(b) from 1920, he was an active member of the Zinovievite opposition. In 1925 he was secretary of the Leningrad Komsomol provincial committee. In 1927 he was expelled from the VKP, but he was readmitted in 1928. In December 1934 the Military Board of the Supreme Court of the USSR sentenced him to be shot for "participating in a counterrevolutionary terrorist group and committing a terrorist act against S. M. Kirov."

Rwal, Gustaw (real name, Reicher) (1900–1938). Born in Lodz, he was a member of the SDPKPiL from 1917 and a member of the Polish CP from 1919. He worked in the Dombrowski basin. In 1919–1920 he was imprisoned, and in fall 1920 he started working in the Communist movements of Poland and Germany; he was political secretary of the German CP organization in the Ruhr. In May 1925 he was arrested in Poland and sentenced to six years of hard labor; in 1928, after the exchange of political prisoners, he went to the USSR, where he was sent to work in the ECCI (1928–1929). In 1930–1937 he was a candidate member of the CC of the Polish CP; in 1932 he was a member of the CC of the Communist Party of Western Belorussia. He taught at the International Lenin School between 1933 and 1934. In 1937 he was in Spain as a commissar of the Dombrowski International Brigade. Recalled to Moscow by the ECCI, Rwal was arrested and, on 17 September 1938, sentenced to be shot.

Ryng, Jerzy (real name, Heryng) (1886–1938). A member of the Polish CP from 1919, he was on the editorial boards of several party newspapers and journals. For many years he was the editor of the party's theoretical magazine *Nowy Pzzeglad* (New Review). In August 1924 he was arrested and convicted. After his liberation in April 1925, he again worked as an editor. He was a delegate to the Sixth and Seventh Comintern Congresses. Ryng was recalled to Moscow in early 1937; there he was arrested by the NKVD. He was later convicted and shot.

Safarov, Georgi Ivanovich (1891–1942). A member of the Bolshevik Party from 1908, he was a candidate member of the CC VKP in 1921–1925. In 1925 he became a member of the New Opposition led by Zinoviev, and joined the United Opposition in 1926. In 1927 he was expelled from the party. He was readmitted in 1928 and expelled again on 23 December 1934 following his arrest. Between 1922 and 1923 he was an ECCI secretary. He worked in the ECCI apparatus again in 1929–1934, first as deputy head of the Anglo-American Lendersecretariat and later as deputy head of the Eastern Secretariat. After his arrest, the OSO sentenced him to five years in prison, although he remained incarcerated until 1942, when the OSO sentenced him to be executed. He was shot on 27 June.

Sas. *See* Serényi-Sas, Sandor.

Sedov, Lev Lvovich (1906–1938). The eldest son of Leon Trotsky and the editor in chief of the *Bulletin of the Opposition*, the Trotskyist newspaper, from June 1929 until his death in February 1938.

Serényi-Sas, Sandor (born in 1905). Born in Budapest, he was a secretary of the CC of the Hungarian CP in 1929–1931 but was removed by the ECCI from leading positions in the party for factional struggle (he was in the so-called Sas-Barna group). In 1933 he was arrested by the GPU for allegedly provocative activities in the Hungarian CP and repressed.

Servet, Claude (real name, David Rechitsky) (born in 1904). An analyst in the Secretariat of Manuilsky in 1935–1937, he left for France in March 1937.

Shkiriatov, Matvei Fyodorovich (1883–1954). Member of the RSDRP from 1906. Secretary of the CC of the sewers' union after 1918. Member of the Presidium of the Central Control Commission of the VKP from 1923 to 1934 and, from 1930, secretary of its Party Board. Member of the CC VKP after 1939 and deputy chairman—after 1952, chairman—of the Party Control Committee of the CC CPSU.

Sholomov, Evsei Idkovich (1906–1938). A member of the VKP from 1926, he became a member of the Communist Party of Western Belorussia in 1932; he became a member of its CC and its Secretariat in June 1935. He was the party representative in Minsk after December 1935 and worked in the ECCI apparatus in Moscow as a political analyst for Moskvin after 25 November 1936. He was expelled from the party on 2 November 1937 and arrested soon after. On 25 September 1938 the OSO sentenced him to be shot for espionage.

Skulski, Stefan (real name, Stanislaw Mertens) (1892–1937). Born in Lodz, he was a member of the SDPKPiL from 1910 and of the Polish CP from 1921—he was elected a member of its CC in 1923. After the Third Congress of the Polish CP (1925), he was arrested along with the other CC members. In 1928, after an exchange of political prisoners between the USSR and Poland, he went to the USSR. There he studied at the Institute of Red Professors and later worked as a propagandist at the Kuibyshev regional VKP committee. After 1931 he was head of the Central European Secretariat of the Profintern. In 1935 he was made a member of the Politburo of the Polish CP. In 1936–1937 he headed the commission to verify party members in Soviet emigration. He was recalled to Moscow from Paris in 1937 and arrested. On 21 September the Military Board of the Supreme Court of the USSR sentenced him to be shot.

Slawinski, Adam (real name, Kaczorowski) (1890–1937). Member of the RSDRP(b) from 1914; member of the Minsk RSDRP(b) committee. Head of the Minsk police and head of the provincial Commissariat of Internal Affairs after 1917. People's commissar of agriculture in the Belorussian SSR, 1921–1924. Representative of the CP of Western Belorussia in the ECCI, 1924–1928. Secretary of the Minsk regional party committee of the Bolshevik Party of Belorussia, 1928–1930. Sent to conduct party work in Poland, 1930–1931. Representative of the Polish CP in the ECCI, 1931–1933. Secretary of the party collegium and head of the political department of the Moscow-Belorussian railroad, 1933–1936. Worked in the People's Commissariat for Railways, March 1936 to July 1937. He was arrested on 9 July 1937 and sentenced to be shot by the Military Board of the Supreme Court of the USSR on 3 November 1937.

Šmeral, Bogumir (1880–1941). Member of the Czech SDP in 1897–1920. A founder of the Czech CP in 1921 and a member of its CC in 1921–1929 and 1936–1941. Member of the ECCI in 1922–1935; of the ECCI Presidium, 1922–1931; of the ECCI Political Secretariat, 1926–1929. Member of the ICC, 1935 and 1941. Worked in Paris in the Universal Unification for Peace (Rassemblement universel la paix), 1936–1938.

Sochacki-Bratkowski, Jerzy (Czeszejko, aka J. Bratowski) (1892–1933). A member of the Polish Socialist Party from 1915, he was elected to its Executive Committee in 1919 and later became its general secretary. He belonged to the left wing of the party. He became a Polish CP member in 1921. He was elected to the CC in 1923, to the Politburo in 1929, and to the CC Secretariat in 1933. In 1923 he was elected to the Polish Sejm. He supported the majority faction in the party leadership. From 1931 he served as the Polish party representative in the ECCI. At the Eleventh ECCI Plenum he was elected a candidate member of the ECCI. He was arrested by the NKVD in 1933 and committed suicide on 4 September.

Solts, Aron Aleksandrovich (1872–1945). One of the leading legal theorists in the USSR in the 1920s and 1930s. Member of the RSDRP from 1898. Member of the Central Control Commission of the VKP in 1920–1934 and, after 1923, of its Presidium. Member of the ICC, 1924–1934. Chairman of the commission created to purge the party organization of the ECCI apparatus, September–November 1933.

Souvarine, Boris (real name, Lipshitz) (1895–1984). Member of the French CP from 1920; its representative in the ECCI and a member of the ECCI and its Secretariat between 1921 and 1924. In 1924 he was expelled from the party for supporting Trotsky and creating a faction in the French party.

Süsskind, Lew (born in 1898). Born in Poland, he was a member of the German CP from 1930. He was arrested by the NKVD in 1937.

Szamuely, György (born in 1899). Born in Hungary, he joined the Hungarian CP in 1918 and the VKP in 1922. He was deputy chairman of the Moscow city Soviet between July 1935 and 1937 and later worked in its institute, Mosgoroformleniie. He also worked for the Comintern on special assignments. In 1937 he was arrested and sentenced to be shot.

Szántó, Bela. *See* his case study in Chapter 7.

Szántó, Maria (Kramer) (born in 1883). Born in Hungary, she graduated from Budapest University as a teacher of physics and mathematics. She was a member of the SD Party of Hungary in 1903–1918 and joined the Hungarian CP in 1918. After the fall of the Hungarian Socialist Republic, she emigrated to Germany, where she was a member of the German CP between 1921 and 1926. She emigrated to the USSR in 1926, joined the VKP, and worked in the Institute of Marx-Engels-Lenin, retiring in March 1932. On 28 August 1945 she and her husband left the USSR for Hungary.

Szántó, Rosa (born in 1896). A physician. Member of the SD Party of Hungary, 1917–1918; member of the Hungarian CP (and the VKP) from 1918. In the Soviet Republic in Hungary she worked as an analyst in the People's Commissariat for Social Security. In 1922 she arrived in the USSR after being exchanged for prisoners of war. She took Soviet citizenship in 1931, was expelled from the VKP in connection with the arrest of her husband, S. Natonek, and, on 8 October 1949, left the USSR for Hungary.

Szántó, Zoltán (aka János Sallai, Elek) (born in 1893). Member of the SD Party of Hungary, 1908–1918. Joined the Hungarian CP, 1918. Deputy head of the Political Department of the Hungarian Red Army Main Command, 1919. Headed the secret apparatus of the Foreign Bureau of the Hungarian CP. Hungarian party representative in the Comintern, 1935–1936 and 1938–1939. Left the USSR for Hungary, 1945.

Szántó-Szamuely, Elza (born in 1886). A Soviet citizen but not a party member, she worked in a library in Tomsk. After World War II she left the USSR for Hungary.

Terziev, Iordan (real name, Yanko Dimov Atanasov) (born in 1900). Born in Bulgaria, he was a member of the Bulgarian CP in 1922–1926 and, later, of the CP of Argentina. In 1930 he emigrated to the USSR, where he attended the Institute of Red Professors and then became a professor in the Agrarian Institute in Ashkhabad, Turkmenia, in 1936–1938. On 6 February 1938 he was arrested by the NKVD, only to be released in 1939 and his case closed.

Tetsen, Karl Tenisovich (born in 1894). After 1921 he worked in the ECCI apparatus as a bursar in the Administration of Affairs. He joined the VKP in 1924. He was arrested and, on 31 March 1938, expelled from the VKP as "the enemy of the party and the people"; he was later repressed.

Tsitovich, Yakov Iosifovich (real name, Lev Davydovich Khasin) (born in 1901). Joined the RKP(b) in 1919. Ambassador in Vladivostok for the Executive Committee of KIM, January 1923–June 1924. An analyst and a member of the editorial board of *Kommunisticheskii Internatsional*, 1933–1937. Editor in the Publishing House for Foreign-Language Literature after May 1937. On 19 September 1937 he was expelled from the VKP; he was readmitted in February 1938.

Unszlicht, Jozef (1879–1938). Member of the Bolshevik Party from 1900. Member of the Military Revolutionary Committee in Petrograd, October

1917. People's commissar for military affairs of the Lithuanian-Belorussian SSR and a member of the Revolutionary Council of the Sixteenth Army and the Western Front during the Civil War. Deputy chairman of the GPU after 1921. Member of the Military Revolutionary Council of the Russian Soviet republic and head of the Supplies Department of the Red Army after 1921. Deputy chairman of the Revolutionary Military Council of the USSR and deputy head of the People's Commissariat for the Navy, 1925–1930. Deputy chairman of the Supreme Council of the National Economy, 1930–1933. Head of the Main Board of the Civil Air Fleet, 1933–1935. Secretary of the All-Union Soviet of the Central Executive Committee of the USSR after 1935. In June 1937 he was arrested and repressed.

Vági, Stefan [Istvan] Frantsevich. *See* Document 55.

Vágó, Béla (1881–1939). A member of the SD Party of Hungary from 1900, he was a founder of the Hungarian CP and a member of its first CC (November 1918). On 21 March 1919 he was named people's commissar of internal affairs of the Hungarian Soviet Republic. After the collapse of Soviet power in Hungary, he emigrated to Austria and later to Germany. Between 1925 and 1928 he worked in the Soviet trade delegation in Berlin and on the board of *Die Rote Fahne* newspaper. In 1933 he emigrated to the USSR, where he worked as head of the Hungarian section of the Foreign Workers Publishing House. He was arrested in 1938; on 10 March 1939 the Military Board of the Supreme Court of the USSR sentenced him to be shot.

Valter, Arthur Yakovlevich (real name, Khavkin; aka Khavkin-Valter) (1898–1936?). He belonged to the RSDRP (Internationalists) in 1918–1920. He joined the VKP in 1920, was expelled in 1921, and rejoined in 1927. From 1932 to 1936 he worked for the OMS. He was arrested in 1936.

Valter, Elena Osipovna. *See* Document 55 and her case study in Chapter 7.

Varga, Eugen (Jenő) (1879–1964). Member of the Hungarian SD Party from 1906. Joined the Hungarian CP in 1919. People's commissar of finance in the Hungarian Soviet Republic. Joined the RKP(b) in 1920 and worked in the Comintern apparatus. Headed the Statistical-Informational Institute of the ECCI, 1921–1927. Elected candidate ECCI member at the Second, Third, and Seventh Comintern Congresses. Director of the Institute of the World Economy, Academy of Sciences, 1927–1947; academician at the academy after 1939.

Vasilieva, Vera Yakovlevna (born in 1900). Joined the RKP(b) in 1918. Worked as an analyst in Manuilsky's Secretariat, July 1934–September 1936, and was a senior analyst in the Cadres Department of the ECCI, September 1936–September 1939.

Vulfson, Tamara Akimovna (born in 1889). Joined the RKP(b) in November

1918. Worked in the secret archive in Kamenev's Secretariat, January 1921–April 1922. Worked in the ECCI as a technical secretary in the Organizational Department, 1927–1929; as a translator in the Translations Department, 1932–1935; and as a translator in the Press Department, 1936–1939.

Vyshinsky, Andrei Yanuarovich (1883–1954). Member of the Menshevik party, 1903–1920. Member of the RKP(b) after 1920. Deputy general procurator of the USSR, 1933–1935, and general procurator, 1935–1939. Chief state procurator at the three Moscow show trials (August 1936, January 1937, March 1938).

Walecki, Henryk (real name, Maksymiliam Horowitz) (1877–1937). A leader of the left wing of the Polish Socialist movement, he took part in the creation of the Polish CP in 1918. At its first congress, he was elected a member of its CC. He was the Polish party representative in the ECCI from 1921 to 1924. After 1925 he worked in the ECCI and as the editor in chief of the *Kommunisticheskii Internatsional*. At the Seventh Comintern Congress he was elected a member of the ICC. Arrested on 21 June 1937, he was sentenced to death by the Military Board of the Supreme Court of the USSR; he was shot on 20 September 1937.

Warski, Adolf (real name, Warczawski) (1868–1937). Member of the main directorate of the SDPKPiL from the time of the party's founding. Member of the CC RSDRP after 1906. A leader of the Warsaw Workers' Soviet, 1918–1919. Member of the CC of the Polish CP, 1919–1929, and participant in the Third, Fourth, and Fifth Comintern Congresses. Member of the Polish Sejm, 1925–1929. After 1930, Warski lived in the USSR and conducted research at the Marx-Engels-Lenin Institute. He was arrested and died in 1937.

Wasilkowski, Henryk (1903–1938). He went to Russia from Poland in 1921 and joined the Russian Komsomol. He was the editor of the Komsomol newspaper *Yunosheskaia Pravda* in 1922–1923. In 1928 he left to conduct underground work in Poland; he was elected a member of the CC of the Young Communist League of Poland and a secretary of the Łodzinsk and Dombrowski regional committees. He was imprisoned in 1925–1928, then returned to the USSR, where he worked on the newspaper *Komsomolskaia Pravda* and was head of the Economics Department of *Pravda*. After 1935 he was editor in chief of the newspaper *Za industrializatsiiu*. He was arrested on 19 February 1938 and sentenced to be shot by the Military Board of the Supreme Court of the USSR.

Weber, Fritz (real name, Heinrich Wiatrek) (born in 1886). Member of the German CP from 1922; member of the Upper Silesia district committee, 1928–1932; member of the party CC after 1935. Delegate at the Seventh

Comintern Congress. Student at the International Lenin School, 1932–1934. CPG representative in the ECCI, 1935–1937; CPG representative in Denmark, 1937–1941. He was arrested by the Gestapo in Denmark in 1941 and, in 1946, lived in the British occupied zone in Germany.

Willard, Marcel (1889–1956). A lawyer, he joined the SFIO in 1919 and the French CP in 1923. He was a member of the French section of the MOPR and a member of the International Committee against War and Fascism. In 1944 he was secretary general of the French Ministry of Justice.

Wojewódzki, Sylwester (1892–1938). Born in Pskov. Served in the legions in World War II and in the Second Department of the headquarters of the Lithuanian-Belorussian front after 1918. Member of the Polish populist party Wyzwolenie (Liberation) and a Sejm deputy, 1922–1924. A founder and deputy chairman of the CC of the Independent Peasant Party after November 1924. Member of the Polish CP after 1928. Lived in emigration in Germany and later in the USSR. On 16 March 1933 the OGPU Collegium sentenced him to ten years in prison on the charge of espionage. On 28 April 1938 the Military Board of the Supreme Court of the USSR sentenced him to be shot.

Żarski, Tadeusz (1896–1934). Member of the Polish Socialist Party from 1912; member of the Polish CP after 1921. During the factional struggle in the party, he was in the minority faction and, in 1925, supported the ultra-Leftist group. Polish police arrested him several times. In 1930 he was condemned for his membership on the party CC and sentenced to eight years of hard labor, as well as six years in prison for "shooting at police." After spending two and a half years in prison, he was released during the exchange of political prisoners in September 1932 and sent to the USSR. He worked at the Institute of World Economy and World Politics as a researcher. He was arrested in 1934, and on 16 June, the OGPU Collegium sentenced him to be shot.

Zhdanov, Andrei Andreevich (1896–1948). Member of the VKP from 1915. CC secretary and secretary of the Leningrad city and regional party committees in 1934. Member of the Politburo of the CC VKP after 1939.

Index of Documents

Chapter 4. Campaigns Converge, Anxieties Deepen

Chapter 5. The Victims of Vigilance

Index

Abramov: attacks on, 241

Agranov, Ya.: 119; on Yezhov, 187

Alikhanov, Gevork: on Magyar, 81–83; on Zinovievites, 82–83; on visas, 194; arrest of, 237; attacks on, 241–261 passim; biography, 473; mentioned, 56

All-Union Communist Party (VKP): influence within Comintern, 17–18; expulsions from, 100

—Central Committee (CC): verification of party documents, 103, 104, 141; Plenum (1935), 103–105; exchange of party documents, 104, 141; purge (1933–1934), 104; delegation to ECCI, 119; secret letter (July 1936), 137, 187; ORPO, 163, 178; Plenum (1936), 191–192; Plenum (1937), 217–221, 406; on quality of party cadres, 218–221; review of expelled members, 371

—ECCI party committee: and vigilance campaign, 215; rank-and-file attacks on, 239, 260–261; behavior during repression, 319

—ECCI party organization: 18; composition of, 29; party meeting in Publishing House for Foreign Workers, 48–51; meeting of December 1934, 59–94; verification of party documents, 138; members arrested, 309–318; reduction of, 320

—Party discipline: 29–30, 44, 56, 157, 205, 214, 389, 413; within Comintern, 16; and social norms, 31; and party identity, 36; and Popular Front, 127; and anti-Trotskyist campaign, 127–128; and verification of émigrés, 145

—Party identity: 417, 418, 419; and ethnic identity, 214

—Party membership: and psychological needs, 32

—Party mindset: 408–409

—Politburo: resolution on Germans, 238; resolutions on arrest by ethnicity, 290–

291; anti-Yezhov coalition, 306; on Kun, 335

Alpari, Gyula (Julius): 191, 193, 374; biography, 473

Andreev, Andrei A.: 108, 393; biography, 473

Angaretis, Zigmas: memo on cadres, 109–115; as Old Bolshevik, 116–117; political past, 179; report by, 255; biography, 473–474

Anti-Trotskyist campaign: 38–42, 147–149, 157–158, 215–216, 409–410

Anvelt, Yan: 331, 335

Balod, Karl: allegations against, 179

Barbé-Celor group: 153, 154

Belostotskaia, A. S.: allegations against, 212–213

Benedek, Gyögy: 340–342

Berg, Bronislaw: letter to Dimitrov, 120

Beria, Lavrenti: 306–307; appeals to, 345–346, 393

Berman-Yurin, K.: 137, 164–175 passim; biography, 474

Bertynski, Wiktor: 267; biography, 474

Bielewetis, Jan: on Polish CP leaders, 119, 264; biography, 474

Blagoeva, Stella: political past, 180; report by, 245; attacks on, 245–246, 250–261 passim; biography, 474

Blum, Léon: 160; biography, 474

Bochkov, Viktor M.: 349, 350, 360, 398; biography, 475

Borowski, Noah: attacks on, 50–51; alleged Rightism, 165, 174; biography, 475

Bortnovski, Bronislaw. See Bronkovski (Bortnovski), Bronislaw

Brann, Lotta: political past, 179

Brikke, Semyon: denunciation of, 231; biography, 475